The Southerner and World Affairs

The Southerner
and
World Affairs

ALFRED O. HERO, JR.

Louisiana State University Press

Baton Rouge

1965

Library of Congress Catalog Card Number: 65–12835

Manufactured in the United States of America by
Vail-Ballou Press, Inc., Binghamton, N.Y.

Designed by William Nicoll

Published with the assistance
of a grant from the Ford Foundation.

PREFACE

As an adolescent growing up in New Orleans and nearby rural Plaquemines Parish during the late 1930's and early 1940's, I came to believe that inhabitants of my area, and of the South generally, were by and large favorable to a more active role in world affairs than our federal government was taking at the time. I learned that most of the isolationists in America were supposedly in the Midwest, Plains States, and the Rocky Mountain region rather than in the South.

My initial contacts with Southern opinion on foreign policy were with my father, relatives, high school teachers, my father's friends and associates, and other business, professional, and educated rural people. Although most of these were southern Louisianians, in some respects a unique breed of Southerners, I also met textile mill owners, lawyers, and other visitors from the Anglo-Saxon South who came to our home at Stella Plantation to hunt, fish, and enjoy the pleasures of country life. Few of these people could be considered intellectuals; they were mostly conservative-minded Southerners of privileged station who were highly critical of New Deal domestic programs. They were certainly not representative of the Southern rank and file, but theirs were the international opinions I heard and their views probably reflected those prevalent among other Southerners of education and influence.

Most of these Southerners were not particularly interested in or sophisticated about foreign policy; however, except for a sugar planter here and there, they favored lower tariffs and expanded trade. I recall

v

only negative comments concerning Senator Gerald P. Nye and the Neutrality Act. I remember the general sentiment among my father's dinner guests, after listening to H. V. Kaltenborn describe Neville Chamberlain's departure for Munich, was that Britain and France had to stand up to Hitler and Mussolini then or face war on more unfavorable terms later. Throughout this period of Axis aggressions there seemed to be the feeling that our own vital long-run interests were at stake, that we should be prepared to help the British and French, that we should even pay higher taxes if necessary, and that we should shift resources going into domestic "relief" to military and other preparedness measures. During the Allied defeats in the early part of World War II, most adults of my acquaintance appeared to think that we should be doing more to assist the European democracies, even at the risk of becoming involved in war ourselves—peacetime conscription, Lend-Lease (even to the Soviets), the arming and convoying of merchant ships, and a firmer front against Japanese advances were relatively popular ideas in these circles. Isolationists like Senator Burton K. Wheeler, Charles Lindbergh, and leaders of the Liberty League were regarded unfavorably.

Extended residence in other parts of the South as a Regular Army officer and graduate student during the late 1940's and early 1950's gave me little reason to change my impression that men and women of influence within the region were predominantly in favor of most of the Truman administration's active foreign policies—conscription, relatively expensive defense programs, maintenance of bases and troops overseas, expanded world trade, the Truman Doctrine, the Marshall Plan, Point Four, military alliance with Western Europe, active collaboration with non-Communist powers in the United Nations, and so on.

But by the late 1950's I became convinced that more and more Southerners were diverging from my own foreign-policy thinking, which was usually in agreement with the major long-term programs of the Eisenhower and, later, Kennedy administrations. Whereas I tended to support most of the foreign aid requests sent to the Congress by our Presidents, many Southern Congressmen and newspapers increasingly were suggesting that aid be greatly reduced. Whereas I favored expanded trade, they were pressing for protection of textiles and other Southern products. I was gratified to observe that my Congressman Hale Boggs, Congressman Frank E. Smith of Mississippi, Senators James W. Fulbright and John Sparkman, and some other Southern legislators continued to vote for most of the programs I thought wise, but I began to note even in New Orleans, and more so in other locales, increasing criticism by relatives, friends, and acquaintances of continued aid programs to "socialist," "leftist," and "neutralist" regimes, growing sentiment that collaboration in the U.N. was no longer likely to be in our national interest, and, outside New Orleans, expanding protectionist feelings. Colleagues working in educational programs devoted to foreign affairs and others of cosmopolitan inclinations in the South tended to agree frequently with my impressions. Finally, in preparing several monographs dealing with American public opinion on international relations, I noted certain disturbing trends in replies by Southerners as compared with those of other Americans to national surveys. Southern thinking on these issues was obviously still heterogeneous, but at a minimum an influential minority seemed to be drifting from the views I had previously assumed to prevail, at least among the educated classes, in my native section.

I, therefore, welcomed the opportunity provided by the trustees of the World Peace Foundation to direct a systematic study of the behavior of Southerners and their Congressmen toward world affairs since the mid-1930's, of significant changes that may have taken place in Southern international thinking, of the forces underlying these developments, and of potentially effective means of stimulating more widespread and responsible thought on foreign policy in the region. The results of this research pertinent to Southern Congressmen appears in Charles O. Lerche, Jr., *The Uncertain South: Its Changing Patterns of Politics in Foreign Policy* (Chicago: Quadrangle Books, 1964). *The Southerner and World Affairs* deals with their constituents back home. Part I traces trends since 1936 in Southern interest, knowledge, attention, and opinion with respect to immigration, intercultural relations, foreigners, defense, collective security, trade, colonialism, neutralism, foreign aid, and international organization. Part II considers in turn major Southern educational, social, occupational, psychological, attitudinal, religious, and ethnic groups in terms of their reactions to these international phenomena. Part III deals with probable future developments and potentially promising lines of action in the South to expand public understanding of world affairs.

Errors of fact and interpretation are those of the author alone; his observations to follow do not necessarily coincide with the views of the trustees and officers of the World Peace Foundation.

ALFRED O. HERO, JR.

ACKNOWLEDGMENTS

T his volume would not have been possible without significant contributions by many individuals of diverse callings, most of whom must
remain unnamed. A research committee—Max F. Millikan (chairman),
president of the World Peace Foundation and director of the Center
for International Studies at Massachusetts Institute of Technology;
Morris Abram, then of the firm of Heyman, Abram, and Young in
Atlanta; Holley Mack Bell, then associate editor of the Greensboro
Daily News; Rowland Egger, chairman of the Woodrow Wilson School
of Foreign Affairs at the University of Virginia; Joseph E. Johnson,
president of the Carnegie Endowment for International Peace; John
Nason, then president of the Foreign Policy Association; and Charles
Zukoski, Jr., then executive vice-president of the First National Bank
of Birmingham and chairman of the Committee on Foreign Relations
of that metropolitan community—provided preliminary encouragement, insights and hypotheses about the processes of Southern international thought and action, and suggestions for the conduct of the inquiries.

Staffs of the New York *Times,* the *Christian Science Monitor,* the
Manchester *Guardian, Foreign Affairs, The Headline Series, International Conciliation, The Economist, Harper's, Atlantic Monthly, The
Reporter, The Nation, New Republic, Time, Newsweek, U.S. News
and World Report, Life, Look,* and *Saturday Evening Post* provided
audience research data, insights about their Southern readers, and, in a

number of cases, confidential lists of subscribers in the communities where we conducted interviews. Officials of the Pulse, Inc., the A. C. Neilsen Co., CBS News, and the Research Department of NBC made available extensive data on the viewers of network television programs dealing with foreign relations. Staffs of the Foreign Policy Association; the Council on Foreign Relations; the Church Peace Union (now the Council on Religion and International Affairs); the American Assembly; the Institute for International Order; the American Foundation for Political (now Continuing) Education; the Committee for Economic Development; the Catholic Association for International Peace; the American Association for the United Nations; the International Department of the National Council of Churches; the League of Women Voters; the American Association of University Women; research and education directors of trade unions important in the South; chairmen, secretaries, and active members of Committees on Foreign Relations in the region; and personnel connected with Southern World Affairs Councils, Foreign Relations Associations, general and agricultural extensions of universities, and other organizations active in international affairs within the South posed helpful hypotheses, suggested thoughtful informants of cosmopolitan inclinations in the sample communities and elsewhere in the region, and provided suggestions relative to the interpretations of the interviews with these individuals. Louis Vexler of the American Institute of Public Opinion, Paul Sheatsley of the National Opinion Research Center, Angus Campbell, Warren E. Miller, and Stephen Withey of the Survey Research Center, Burns W. Roper of Elmer Roper and Associates, and other members of staffs of survey agencies steered the author through hundreds of polls and surveys and provided thousands of tabulations on file by geographical region, education, race, religion, occupation, and other demographic and social characteristics. Many new IBM card sortings of surveys from 1936 through 1963 were made at my request by the Roper Public Opinion Research Center at Williams College under the supervision of its director Philip K. Hastings. The Bureau of Applied Social Research at Columbia University, the Social Science Research Center at Mississippi State University, the Institute for Research in Social Science at the University of North Carolina, and other survey agencies made available and, in some instances, conducted new tabulations of studies cited below.

Approximately eleven hundred Southerners made themselves available for interviews ranging from twenty minutes to several hours in duration, frequently on two or more occasions. The author appreciated not only their frank discussions of their own thinking and that of their associates on world affairs and other controversial issues but also the many excellent meals and refreshments he consumed in their homes, clubs, and restaurants and the other gracious hospitality he experienced, including lodgings, fishing and hunting trips, and conducted tours of textile mills, cattle and timber farms, and cotton, tobacco, and sugar fields.

The author is especially indebted to the helpful suggestions on earlier versions of this manuscript as a whole or in large part by Alvin L. Bertrand, professor of sociology at Louisiana State University; Charles G. Hamilton of Booneville, Mississippi; Harold F. Kaufman, head of the Department of Sociology and Rural Life at Mississippi State University; A. William Loos, president of the Council on Religion and International Affairs; and John B. McConaughy, professor of political science at the University of South Carolina.

Many other readers have provided comments on particular chapters or sections as noted in the following paragraphs.

I am particularly indebted to Dr. Marion Pearsall of the University of Kentucky for her orientation prior to the interviews in Mountain County, her introduction to helpful informants there, her published research on Mountain County, and her constructive comments on a draft of sections of this book dealing with Mountain County, its people, and mountain societies generally.

For helpful suggestions on earlier versions of Chapter 4, the author is indebted to Solomon Barkin, then director of Research of the Textile Workers' Union of America; Percy W. Bidwell, formerly director of research of the Council on Foreign Relations; William B. Kelly, Jr., recently on the faculty of the Fletcher School of Law and Diplomacy and currently (November, 1963) with the Bureau of International Commerce of the U.S. Department of Commerce; David W. MacEachron, director of program at the Council on Foreign Relations; James G. Maddox, professor of agricultural economics at the School of Agriculture of North Carolina State College; and David J. Steinberg, chief economist of the Committee for a National Trade Policy.

Claude E. Fike, dean of the School of Arts and Sciences, University of Southern Mississippi; John E. Gonzales, professor of history, University of Southern Mississippi; and Richard I. Miller, associate director, Project on Instruction, National Education Association, were especially helpful in commenting on earlier drafts of Chapter 7.

For helpful suggestions regarding the portions of Chapter 8 dealing with trade union members in the South, I am further indebted to Mr. Solomon Barkin.

The author is particularly grateful to A. William Loos and John B. Morris, executive director of the Episcopal Society for Cultural and Racial Unity, for their helpful comments on earlier drafts of sections of Chapter 12 dealing with Southern Protestants, especially ministers.

For critical comments on earlier versions of the section in Chapter 12 dealing with Southern Roman Catholics the author is indebted to Thomas H. Clancy, S.J., Department of Political Science, Loyola University of the South at New Orleans; Dr. William T. Liu, Department of Sociology, University of Notre Dame; Maurice V. Shean, C.O., Provost, The Oratory, Rock Hill, South Carolina; and James I. Vissard, S.J., Director of the Washington, D.C., Office of the National Catholic Rural Life Conference.

The author is especially indebted for helpful comments on an earlier version of Chapter 13 to Oscar Cohen, Henry Schwarschild, and Irwin Shulman of the Anti-Defamation League; Arthur J. Levin of the Patomoc Institute; Manheim Shapiro, Philip Perlemutter, and Charles F. Whittenstein of the American Jewish Committee; Shad Polier, chairman of the Governing Council of the American Jewish Congress and native of South Carolina; Leonard S. Stein of St. Louis University and native of Greenville, Mississippi; and Rabbis Perry E. Nussbaum of Beth Israel Congregation in Jackson, Mississippi, and Joseph Asher of Temple Emanuel in Greensboro, North Carolina. A number of others provided useful suggestions on various sections of the chapter.

Harold C. Fleming of the Patomoc Institute; C. Eric Lincoln of Clark College, Atlanta University; Howard Zinn of Spelman College, Atlanta University; Benjamin Muse of Manassas, Virginia; James W. Prothro of the University of North Carolina; J. R. Larkins, consultant for the North Carolina State Board of Public Welfare; Paul M. Rilling of the Southern Regional Council; A. William Loos; J. Harvey Kerns of the Urban League of Greater New Orleans; and Charles G. Hamilton of Booneville, Mississippi, contributed valuable suggestions on earlier drafts of Chapter 14.

Particularly helpful comments on earlier versions of Chapter 16 were provided by Solomon Barkin; E. R. Bradley, professor of political science at South Georgia College; the Reverend Murray Cox of Gulfport, Mississippi; Cullen B. Gosnell, professor emeritus of political science at Emory University; A. William Loos; John B. McConaughy; Roger G. Mastrude, vice-president for Field Services of the Foreign Policy Association; Paul M. Rilling, director of Field Activities of the Southern Regional Council; Dorothy B. Robins, program executive for National Organizations of the Foreign Policy Association; and William

C. Rogers, director of the World Affairs Center at the University of Minnesota.

Dr. Robins in her position as executive associate at the national headquarters of the American Association of University Women charged with international programs and Mrs. Alexander P. Guyol, director of Public Relations of the League of Women Voters, offered particularly helpful suggestions on earlier drafts of the section on Women's Organizations in Chapter 16.

Many other sensitive Southerners and observers of Southern behavior helped through face-to-face discussions to refine interpretations; most of these will remain unmentioned. Ralph Bolton, then a graduate student in political science at the Massachusetts Institute of Technology, assisted the World Peace Foundation staff in clipping, sorting, and analyzing international content of Southern newspapers. The author is particularly grateful for the labors of Garfield Aucoin, Susan S. Bove, Anne H. Cohen, Catherine Crane, Mildred Curran, Louise De Costa, Beverly Edwards, Nancy Feinstein, Jessie R. Janjigian, Carol Ann Johnson, Helen Myrick LaFleur, Sara S. Russell, Audrey P. Woollard, and other members and former members of the staff of the World Peace Foundation who contributed the many diverse talents which were essential to the completion of this study. Finally, Dorothy C. Clair rendered invaluable assistance in editing a lengthy and involved manuscript into the published volume to follow.

Limitations of space prevented the author from including many of the data and insights provided by competent informants.

CONTENTS

Preface v
Acknowledgments ix

Introduction 3

PART III
Where To From Here?

The Southerner and World Affairs

INTRODUCTION

Southern voters sent to Congress between 1917 and 1955 a disproportionately large number of legislators who supported relatively activist policies in most spheres of world affairs of the period. Although Southern Congressmen did not invariably favor all types of international cooperation and a small minority of them voted with Northern isolationists on more questions than not, majorities of Southern members of the Senate and the House voted for most forms of collaboration with other countries proposed by our Presidents during the interwar years. Most non-Southern Congressmen, particularly those from the Midwest, Plains States, and Rocky Mountain region, opposed these proposals. Moreover, the influence of internationally activist Southerners within the Congress was augmented beyond their numbers by their typically long tenures, political talents, and skills in interpersonal relations and persuasion. More secure with the voters at home on the average than their Northern colleagues, Southerners could devote themselves to international problems and could become chairmen or other influential members of Congressional committees dealing with foreign affairs, defense, and related issues.[1]

1 Irving Howards, "The Influence of Southern Senators on American Foreign Policy" (Ph.D. dissertation, University of Wisconsin, 1955), Chap. 12 and pp. 163–64.

Southern Congressmen and International Collaboration

Before 1955

One of the major reasons for Southern secession in 1861 was the imposition of tariffs by Congressional majorities from the rest of the country. (The Confederate constitution forbade tariffs completely.) A majority of Southern legislators voted against virtually every major bill designed to raise tariffs or otherwise to raise barriers to world trade and for almost all proposed legislation encouraging expanded international commerce between 1833 and the mid-1950's.[2] On nine roll calls concerning reciprocal trade between 1934 and the late 1940's, 95 percent of Southern Congressmen voted in favor;[3] even as late as 1955 the proportion of Southerners voting for extension of this legislation was higher than that of other members of Congress.[4]

Virginian Woodrow Wilson relied considerably upon the assistance of Southerners Edward M. House, Josephus Daniels, William G. McAdoo, Carter Glass, Walter Hines Page, and John Sharp Williams. The latter, as senior Senator from Mississippi, was a major champion in the Senate of resistance to German transgressions on our neutrality prior to our entry into World War I, an active exponent of Wilson's Fourteen Points, and otherwise a defender of Wilson's internationalist proposals.[5] The campaign in the Senate for approval of the League of Nations, led by Senator Williams, was supported by a large majority of Southern senators. When President Wilson made his journey through

2 Raymond A. Bauer, Ithiel de Sola Pool, and Lewis A. Dexter, *American Business and Public Policy* (New York: Atherton Press, 1963), 14, 21, and 27–29; Alexander DeConde, "The South and Isolationism," *Journal of Southern History* XXIV (1958), 339; Marian D. Irish, "Foreign Policy and the South," *Journal of Politics*, X (1948), 307–308; and George C. Osborn, *John Sharp Williams* (Baton Rouge: Louisiana State University Press, 1943), 40–49, 110–12, 126–27, 180–85, and 379–90. A major exception was the protectionism with respect to sugar among Louisiana Senators and, especially, members of the House from the sugar sections of southern Louisiana.

3 V. O. Key, Jr., *Southern Politics in State and Nation* (New York: Alfred A. Knopf, 1949), 353.

4 "Voting Records of Present Members of the House of Representatives on Trade Legislation and Related Issues," (Washington, D.C.: The United States-Japan Trade Council, 1961), 30–35. See also Howards, "Influence of Southern Senators," 122–23 and 151–54. Roll-call votes on extension of reciprocal trade were less valid indicators of trade liberalism versus conservatism during the postwar period than previously, since this legislation had been amended to include compromises with protectionist interests.

5 Osborn, *John Sharp Williams*, vii, 3, 17–23, 196, 255–68, 287, and 342–86.

the country to win public support for the League, he and his advisors apparently felt so certain of backing by Southerners that he did not visit the South. Only the Southern Democrats stood overwhelmingly by the President in supporting a strong league and voting down the Henry Cabot Lodge reservations in the upper house.[6]

Robert "Our Bob" Reynolds of North Carolina was the only Southerner who voted with the twenty-five Northern isolationists in the Senate opposing most of President Roosevelt's vital pre-Pearl Harbor measures to limit further German, Italian, and Japanese aggressions and to support the Allies against them.[7] Southern Congressmen in both houses were more inclined than other legislators to favor liberalization of the Neutrality and Johnson acts prior to our entry into World War II.[8] The vote for Lend-Lease in March, 1941, illustrated the vital character of Southern support of the Allies—sixty senators voted for and thirty-one against, but only one Southerner, again Reynolds of North Carolina, voted against the bill. Likewise in the House, only Hugh Peterson of Georgia among Southerners voted against this legislation.[9]

Only two Southerners, Reynolds and Ellison D. "Cotton Ed" Smith of South Carolina, along with several Republicans from Tennessee and Kentucky in the House, opposed the Conscription Act of 1940 in the

6 Denna F. Fleming, *The United States and the League of Nations, 1918–1920* (New York: G. P. Putnam's Sons, 1932), 95–96, 145, 215, 260, 263–64, 284, 288, 292, 375–76, and 415; Osborn, *John Sharp Williams*, 360; DeConde, *Journal of Southern History*, XXIV, 336; Paul Seabury, "The Waning of Southern 'Internationalism'" (MS in Center of International Studies, Princeton University, 1957), 9; Dewey W. Grantham, Jr., "The Southern Senators and the League of Nations, 1918-1920," *North Carolina Historical Review*, XXVI (1949), 187–205; and *Congressional Record*, 66th Congress, 2nd Session, 4599. Senators James K. Vardaman of Mississippi and Thomas W. Hardwick of Georgia were unfavorable to Wilson's proposals for a strong League and tended to agree with the strong reservationist or isolationist Republicans and Northern Democrats of like mind. However, they were not reelected in 1918. Hoke Smith of Georgia and John K. Shields of Tennessee were the only Southerners who voted with the opponents of Wilson's version of the League on March 19, 1920.

7 Kenneth W. Colegrove, *The American Senate and World Peace* (New York: The Vanguard Press, 1944), 202–209. Reynolds was one of those twenty-six Senators who voted as isolationists on at least nine of eleven measures—revision of the Neutrality Act of 1937, the Selective Training and Service Bill, the limitation of United States armed forces to the Western Hemisphere, the two-billion-dollar loan versus Lend-Lease for the Allies, the transfer of Axis ships, the extension of Selective Service, the belligerent zone restrictions, the Armed Ship Bill, the Ship Seizure Bill, and the second Lend-Lease Bill.

8 George L. Grassmuck, *Sectional Biases in Congress on Foreign Policy* (Baltimore: Johns Hopkins University Press, 1951), 124–25, 129, and 131; and Howards, "The Influence of Southern Senators," 30–43, 62, 129, and 157.

9 Irish, *Journal of Politics*, X, 311; DeConde, *Journal of Southern History*, XXIV, 341–342; and Howards, "The Influence of Southern Senators," 51–52.

Senate. In contrast, a majority of Midwesterners voted against it.[10] Had it not been for Southern votes, many draftees would have been separated from the services in the four months before the attack on Pearl Harbor—the extension of the conscription act passed in the House by only one vote, even though representatives from twelve Southern states cast 102 votes in favor and only 6 against.[11]

Most of the isolationist Congressmen from the rest of the country had either been replaced by individuals more favorable to international commitments or had changed their own behavior before the end of World War II. However, during the war Senators John Connally of Texas, Lister Hill of Alabama, Walter George of Georgia, and Claude Pepper of Florida, along with Representative J. W. Fulbright of Arkansas, were prominent leaders in preparing Congressional and public support for the forthcoming United Nations organization.[12] Southern Senators voted without exception for ratification of the U.N. Charter in 1945.[13] Larger fractions of Southern than Northern Congressmen supported the Truman Doctrine in 1947 and the initial Marshall Plan legislation in 1948 (the Foreign Assistance Act).[14] Thirty percent of members of the House of Representatives from fourteen Southern states furnished only 16 percent of the seventy-four opposition votes to the latter bill. Throughout the duration of the European Recovery Program into the period of the Korean War, Southern legislators remained more favorable to the program than non-Southerners at roll-call time.[15] No Southern Senator voted against ratification of the North Atlantic Treaty in 1949, although twelve Northerners, including two Democrats, voted "nay";[16] 95 percent of Southern Democratic Senators as compared with 86 percent of Northern Democratic Senators voted for ratification.[17] Southerners have continued since the thirties to support

10   Irish, *Journal of Politics*, X, 312; DeConde, *Journal of Southern History*, XXIV, 341; and Ray A. Billington, "The Origins of Middle Western Isolationism," *Political Science Quarterly*, LX (1945), 63.

11   William T. Polk, *Southern Accent: From Uncle Remus to Oak Ridge* (New York: William Morrow and Co., 1953), 199.

12   Howards, "The Influence of Southern Senators," 63–71.

13   *Ibid.*, 74; and Irish, *Journal of Politics*, X, 318–31. Only Republican Senators William Langer of North Dakota and Henrik Shipstead of Minnesota voted against the Charter.

14   Howards, "The Influence of Southern Senators," 80, and 104–17.

15   These roll-call votes in the House are from Charles O. Lerche, Jr., *The Uncertain South: Its Changing Patterns of Politics in Foreign Policy* (Chicago: Quadrangle Books, 1964), 58.

16   Howards, "The Influence of Southern Senators," 86, 94, and 140. However, seven of the ten Democrats who later voted against the bill to send arms at our expense to NATO members were Southern Senators.

17   *Ibid.*, 160.

expensive defense budgets to as great or a greater degree than other legislators.[18]

The tendency of Democrats to support the proposals of Democratic Presidents and of Republicans to oppose them only partially explains these findings. There was some tapering off of Southern support for some international involvements proposed by the Harding, Coolidge, and Hoover administrations. However, Southern Senators, led by the chairman of the Foreign Relations Committee Claude Swanson of Virginia and by Joseph Robinson of Arkansas, backed President Coolidge's plan for United States membership in the Permanent Court of International Justice while most Republican Senators opposed it.[19] A majority of Southerners in both houses of Congress opposed the Fordney-McCumber Tariff of 1922 and the Hawley-Smoot Tariff of 1930—both were supported by most Republican Congressmen against the declared views of Republican Presidents. Likewise Southerners voted, more than did Republicans, for extension of reciprocal trade in 1955 under the Republican Eisenhower administration.

Moreover, with some exceptions, Southern Democratic Congressmen were typically at least somewhat more favorable to most active foreign policies than Democratic colleagues from other parts of the country. Ninety-five percent of Southern as compared with 84 percent of Northern Democrats voted for the reciprocal Trade Agreements Act through the late 1940's,[20] 98 percent of the former versus 81 percent of the latter supported the series of preparatory measures for national defense and military assistance to anti-Axis countries in the late 1930's and early 1940's;[21] 99 percent of Southern versus 73 percent of non-Southern Democrats supported ratification of the U.N. Charter, United States participation in the International Bank, and related measures without crippling amendments.[22]

Recent Trends

The shift from support of active international involvement, with the major exception of military defense and alliances, among Southern Congressmen during the late 1950's and early 1960's has been marked.[23]

18 Grassmuck, *Sectional Biases in Congress on Foreign Policy*, 41.

19 *Ibid.*, 72, 76–80, and 135; Denna F. Fleming, *The United States and the World Court* (New York: Doubleday, 1945), 41, 60, 62, 131, and 135; and Denna F. Fleming, *The Treaty Veto of the American Senate* (New York: G. P. Putnam's Sons, 1930), 187 ff.

20 Key, *Southern Politics in State and Nation*, 353–54.

21 *Ibid.*   22 *Ibid.*

23 Generalizations in this section about roll-call votes of Congressmen since 1953 were derived from tabulations by Charles O. Lerche, Jr., as part of the overall

To some extent the international issues themselves had changed since the first postwar decade, but trends toward withdrawal and insularity were apparent in several, like international trade, where our objectives at home and abroad had undergone only limited change.

Thus, Herman Talmadge attacked Senator Walter George's internationalism and supposed lack of concern for protection of local industries and advanced further isolationist arguments against the incumbent Senator prior to the latter's decision not to run in 1956.[24] The protectionist plank in the Democratic national platform of that year was largely attributable to Southern pressures; by 1958 a larger proportion of Southern than of other members of the House of Representatives voted against extension of the reciprocal Trade Agreements Act;[25] and in 1959 and succeeding years the annual meeting of Southern governors came out strongly for protection.

Whereas larger proportions of Southern than of other members of the House voted for passage of the Mutual Security Program and for the appropriation to carry it out as late as 1953, by the next year Southerners were less inclined to vote for this legislation than were House colleagues from elsewhere. Southern support for foreign aid continued to decline year by year—by 1960 seven out of ten Southerners in the House voted against the preliminary authorization for the Mutual Security Program, whereas eight out of ten non-Southerners voted for it. The South was the only region which consistently cast a majority of votes in the House against this program under both administrations from 1957 through 1962.

In the late 1950's and early 1960's Southern Congressmen were casting considerably more votes proportionally than other legislators against such measures as the Eisenhower Doctrine, contributions to international organizations, postponement of repayment of loans to Britain, United States participation in the International Atomic Energy Agency, revision of immigration laws for hardship cases, renewal of the reciprocal Trade Agreements Act, increases in United States subscriptions for the International Bank and the International Monetary Fund, the Foreign Investment Incentive Act, and establishment of the Inter-American Development Bank and the International Development Association. In a number of cases Congressmen who voted against these

---

study supported by the World Peace Foundation. For detailed documentation and interpretation of Southern congressional votes, 1953–1962, see Lerche, *The Uncertain South.*

24 Atlanta *Constitution*, January–May, 1956.
25 "Voting Record of the House on Trade Legislation," 32–36; and Seabury, "The Waning of Southern 'Internationalism,' " 23–24.

international commitments had replaced Southern supporters of the Marshall Plan, the Truman Doctrine, and reciprocal trade. However, a considerable fraction of the neo-isolationist votes in the early 1960's came from legislators who had voted for these internationalist programs in the late 1940's and early 1950's. By 1962 an influential minority of Southern Congressmen were still supporting the international programs advocated by the President in nonmilitary as well as defense spheres, but they were much fewer than a decade before.

A Study of the Varied Souths

Southerners' Attitudes

The views of residents of a Senator's state or a House member's district are only one of a number of factors influencing the Congressman's vote. To cite two examples: Arkansas elected to the Senate during the same periods William Fulbright and John McClellan, whose voting records on a number of international issues have differed considerably; and Congressman Frank E. Smith's liberal internationalist behavior in Washington prior to his defeat in 1962 did not represent predominant thinking in his Mississippi Delta district.

A legislator's personal background—including his childhood; his own preferences in world affairs; his level of knowledge and interest in foreign relations; the proportion of his very limited time and energies he allocates to this field; the international views of his advisors, friends, and particularly influential constituents; the degree of security of his seat; expectations and pressures of other legislators from his state, region, or party; his skill, prestige, and reputation among his colleagues; compromises he makes with other Congressmen for their support on bills important to his district; his conception of his role as Congressman vis-à-vis his constituency; appeals by the President and his agents—and, perhaps, other considerations determine his influence and actual vote in committee and plenary sessions.[26] Congressmen, like most other people, tend to talk about world affairs primarily with those constituents whose views are similar to their own, to pay more attention to them than to constituents who disagree, and to underestimate the incidence of contrary thinking in their districts.[27] A recent study of roll-call

26 See, for instance, Bauer, Pool, and Dexter, *American Business and Public Policy*, Part V and 403–13; and Donald R. Matthews, *U.S. Senators and Their World* (New York: Random House, 1960), Chap. 11.
27 Matthews, *U.S. Senators and Their World*, 229; Bauer, Pool, and Dexter, *American Business and Public Policy*, 418–20; and Lewis A. Dexter, "The Representative and His District," *Human Organization*, XVI, No. 1 (1957), 2–13.

votes of Congressmen compared with the distribution of views among their electorates on foreign economic aid, aid to neutrals, military aid, sending troops abroad, and several domestic issues discovered that correlations between the two were lower on foreign policy than on such domestic questions as social welfare and race relations and even negative in some constituencies on one or another international matter.[28]

These observations apply to legislators throughout most of the country. Several factors, however, more prevalent in the South than in the North have very probably lessened even more the influence of the international views of the average Southerner on his Congressman's behavior in Washington. Smaller proportions on the average have actually participated in choosing Congressmen in the South than in the North. An increasing number of Negroes are voting in both Congressional primaries and elections, and in some urban and border South constituencies their votes are of major importance to the candidates. But on the whole, particularly in rural black-belt districts, Negroes have not participated in meaningful numbers in Democratic primaries which have been tantamount to elections. Poorly educated, economically and culturally deprived whites have also voted less than their counterparts in the North. Since ignorance, indifference, and isolationist or neo-isolationist attitudes have been most widespread among these groups which have been severely underrepresented in the choice of Congressmen,[29] the legislators selected probably have been more internationally interested, knowledgeable, and responsible than would have been the case if more of these Southerners had voted.

Moreover, although interregional differences are slowly narrowing, Southerners have on the average in the past been less interested in Congressional races,[30] less likely to know who is running and who

28   Warren E. Miller and Donald E. Stokes, "Constituency Influence in Congress," *American Political Science Review*, LVII (1963), 49; Warren E. Miller, "Policy Preferences of Congressional Candidates and Constituents" (MS in Survey Research Center, University of Michigan, Ann Arbor, 1961); and discussions with the staff of the Survey Research Center.
29   When Southerners who voted in the last presidential or congressional election or primary were compared with those who did not on surveys which asked that question and posed queries on world affairs as well, the latter were almost without exception less inclined to: (1) say they were interested in international matters mentioned, (2) venture correct information about these matters, (3) pay attention to foreign relations in mass media and voluntary organizations, (4) offer any distinct international opinions, and (5) utter internationally activist or internationalist views when they did express any.
30   American Institute of Public Opinion (AIPO) 537, 9/14/54 (1,465), and AIPO 637, 10/18/60 (2,993).

represents them in the House and Senate,[31] and less inclined to consider the international orientations of candidates in Congressional and national elections. They have been more apt to stress positions on race relations, taxation, public welfare, and other domestic issues of direct personal or local import [32] and perhaps more inclined to be attracted to a given candidate because of his personality, family connections, social background, emotional oratory and rhetoric, or other appeals unrelated to international issues.[33] Many white Southerners of humble status in constituencies with large proportions of Negroes have voted for strongly segregationist candidates even when the latter's views on economic and other domestic issues—not to mention world affairs— were opposed to the voter's personal interests. When Southern voters in large numbers have used world affairs as a major criterion for selecting among candidates, the issues have seemed to be concerned with peace or war or economically oriented like trade, tariffs, and foreign aid where direct interests in jobs, income, or taxes were patent. Once in office, Southern Congressmen have received less mail, telegrams, or other pressures from their constituents relative to their behavior toward world affairs (or other issues) than have legislators from other regions; [34] smaller proportions of Southerners than of other Americans have had opinions on most foreign issues before the Congress (see p. 57).

These factors combined with relatively secure, long tenure have permitted many Southern legislators considerable latitude on world affairs. Nevertheless, the international inclinations of constituents have had some influence on the selection and behavior of their Congressmen, and developments in the South indicate that they are likely in the long run to have more. Both mass and "elite" reactions to world problems seem worthy of serious attention.

Delineation of the Several Souths

No one geographical or cultural definition of the South is entirely satisfactory for these purposes.[35] Defining it as the eleven states which

31 AIPO Release of 4/14/42.
32 National Opinion Research Center (NORC) 292, 11/22/50 (1,258); NORC 329, 8/28/52 (1,300); NORC 133, 11/17/52 (1,291); NORC 393, 9/13/56 (1,263); Roper Poll 925, October, 1956 (3,003); and NORC 399, 11/15/56 (1,286).
33 This is a speculative hypothesis. See pp. 359–62.
34 Matthews, *U.S. Senators and Their World,* 220; and Bauer, Pool, and Dexter, *American Business and Public Policy,* 61.
35 For discussions of geographical, demographic, and social composition of the South and of the subcultures within it, see John Samuel Ezell, *The South Since 1865* (New York: Macmillan, 1963), 1–6; Rupert B. Vance, *All These People: The*

seceded in 1861, formed the Confederacy, and underwent Reconstruction is no longer nearly as valid as it was some decades ago. East Texas contained a much larger fraction of the total population of that state in 1861 than it does now, and the influx of Mexicans and Americans from all over the country into parts of the state roughly west of Galveston and Tyler has given those areas cultural patterns different from those of the Deep South. Even in the eastern counties there are few areas where Negroes are as large a fraction of the population and as pressing a concern to whites as in black-belt counties further to the east, and attitudes of the Old South have been much attenuated. Northern and Latin American émigrés now form much of the population of southern Florida, and suburbs of Washington in Virginia manifest Southern thinking to only a very limited extent. Some locales, like Oak Ridge, Tennessee, and Huntsville, Alabama, in the interior of the former Confederacy have also become primarily Northern outposts, and the region as a whole has been unequally and diversely affected by national thinking. Moreover, some of the border states which did not secede contain sections which are strongly Southern in attitude. Such areas as "Little Dixie" in Southeastern Oklahoma, parts of Missouri adjacent to Arkansas and Tennessee, "black" counties in southern Kentucky, rural Maryland and Delaware, and even parts of southern Illinois and Indiana share certain traditional Southern attitudes. The South is really a congeries of different subcultures and traditions, parts of which extend beyond the geographical confines of the former Confederacy.

The plantation areas of large, fertile individual holdings with high ratios of Negroes to whites in the population have included only a relatively small fraction of Southern territories and a decreasing proportion of the total Southern population. The earlier plantations were concentrated along the Atlantic Coast, Tidewater Virginia, eastern North Carolina, the South Carolina low country, in eastern Georgia around Savannah, and along the lower Mississippi River. Most of the Black Belt extending across central Georgia and central Alabama into west central Mississippi was settled in the forty years or so immediately prior to the Civil War. Delta lands back from the Mississippi in eastern Arkansas, western Tennessee, northeastern Louisiana and northwestern

Nation's Resources in the South (Chapel Hill: University of North Carolina Press, 1945), 266–67 and 279–317; Rupert B. Vance, *Human Geography of the South* (Chapel Hill: University of North Carolina Press, 1932), 20–350; and Howard W. Odum, *Southern Regions of the United States* (Chapel Hill: University of North Carolina Press, 1936), 5–11 and 153–63.

Mississippi were not settled until the closing of the nineteenth century.

The hill or piedmont districts have included a larger fraction of both Southern land and white population than the plantation sections. They extend from south central Virginia through the central Carolinas, north of the Black Belt in Georgia and Alabama through Birmingham into northeastern Mississippi away from the Delta, Arkansas between the Delta and the Ozarks, and central Tennessee. Whites have historically outnumbered Negroes in these areas by large margins and have until recently been small family farmers with at most three or four slaves or, later, free Negroes. Until the advent of numerous textile mills in the late 1800's and other industries for the most part later, there were few people with much education or affluence, but the middle ranks have been larger than they were in plantation sections. These sections were composed primarily of a small elite of rather prosperous whites and large majorities of poor, culturally deprived Negroes and whites with only slightly more education and income. Although certainly no equalitarians, the hill whites have not been as emotionally involved in white supremacy as those in black-belt settings and their relationships with one another have been less of a hierarchical and feudal nature. It was largely out of the hill regions that economic liberals appealing to the dispossessed came—the Populists of the 1890's and their recent successors like Huey P. Long, John Rankin, James Folsom, and Olin Johnston.

Much of the industrialization of the South has been in hill locales because of the existence of water power, underemployed white labor, and the lack of plantation elites opposed to both the economic and cultural values of industry. Although textiles have been the predominant product, lumber, pulp and paper, furniture, processed food, other soft goods, iron and steel in Birmingham and Gadsden, and, in the last decade, some products requiring a high level of technology have been manufactured on the spine from Danville, Virginia, through northeast Mississippi.

The mountain counties are as much part of the Southern heritage as the plantation belt and the Piedmont. They run from northeastern Alabama, northwestern Georgia, eastern Tennessee, western North Carolina, and western Virginia through eastern Kentucky, much of West Virginia, and parts of Pennsylvania. The Ozark Mountain culture extends from northwestern Arkansas into Oklahoma and Missouri. There are few Negroes in these counties; many ancestors of present residents either took relatively little interest in the Civil War or fought with the North (although some joined the Confederate armies as well);[36] little of the long-standing class differentiation prevalent in the plantation areas is evident; and the standard of living outside the cities is still one of the lowest in America.

Most of the white South is predominantly Anglo-Saxon and Protestant. The population is of more heterogeneous origin in the port cities of the Atlantic and Gulf coasts and to a lesser extent along the major rivers, especially the Mississippi. But southern Louisiana is still predominantly Roman Catholic. Its original settlers were French and French-Canadian and its present population is composed of the descendants of a variety of national groups. It includes both the greatest port in the region and some of the most backward, isolated rural folk in the country. The economic forces, experience, and values of this area bearing on world affairs differ significantly from those in much of the rest of the region.

The South includes additional diversities—traditional cities, distribution centers, textile towns, a few locales of high-technology manufacturing, heavy industrial towns, ports, university communities, resort areas and many combinations of these. Moreover, different educational, occupational, social, religious and ethnic groups, as well as other groupings within the same community often tend to think differently about world affairs and many other public matters. Even when the apparent international attitudes in the diverse South seem similar, there are frequently different nuances due to cultural variations and other factors.

Design of the Study

Southern Reactions to a Changing World

Where methodologically feasible, the terms South, Southern, and Southerners are used to refer to the former Confederacy minus western Texas, southern Florida, and suburban Washington as well as the border areas mentioned above. The common Southern practice of using the terms North, Northern, and Northerners to refer to the rest of the country and its inhabitants is followed. An attempt has been made to compare international behavior of Southerners as a group with that of all other Americans, or Northerners, taken together. In a number of instances, replies of Southerners to questions about world affairs are juxtaposed with those of Northeasterners, Midwesterners, residents of the Plains States, and Rocky Mountain region, and Far Westerners in turn. The thinking and action about world affairs in each of the major

36 See, for instance, John C. Campbell, *The Southern Highlander and His Homeland* (New York: Russell Sage Foundation, 1921), 96–99.

demographic and cultural groups within the South is examined, and an attempt has been made to trace differential international behavior in historical, social, cultural, and psychological factors prevalent among the particular groups within the South. Trends in opinions toward the major international issues facing America from 1936 through 1962 and toward our policies with respect to these foreign problems; degree of interest in these developments; information about them; attention to foreign affairs in mass media, voluntary organizations, and interpersonal relations; and the extent to which Southerners in various social, cultural, and ideological groups engaged in relatively dispassionate, analytical consideration of world phenomena—all have been considered.

A relatively broad definition of foreign affairs has been used, including not only collective security, international organization, world trade, colonial problems, and foreign military, technical, and economic assistance but also intercultural relations, immigration, behavior toward foreign racial and national groups, domestic subversion, and national defense. None of these issues has remained static, nor has the overall world environment of which they form parts. While the world itself and the problems it presented to the United States interests changed, our general stance shifted from one of relative insularity and inaction with respect to issues beyond our hemisphere to another of serious concern and involvement in virtually every major development throughout the world. Meanwhile, important changes were also transpiring in the South itself—industrialization, urbanization, erosion of traditional and rural values, evolution of old relationships between the races, and others. Thus, in fact, this study examines Southern as compared with Northern reactions, and the diversity of reactions in the South, toward shifting challenges presented to our foreign policies and toward those fluctuating policies themselves at a time when Southerners were undergoing new experiences and pressures at home which often influenced their thinking about our posture in the world.

The major features of some of these issues and our objectives toward them changed much more than others. Foreign aid illustrates one which changed sharply. Shortly prior to the attack on Pearl Harbor it meant primarily military equipment and related support to the opponents of the Axis, particularly to the Anglo-Saxon Southerner's British cousins. During the war it consisted primarily of helping the Allies defeat a common enemy. Then, it became emergency necessities for displaced peoples and others destituted by the war and loans to British cousins again. By 1947 it was largely military and defense support assistance to Greece and Turkey to enable them to resist Communist penetration, followed shortly by economic help to reconstruct war-torn non-Communist Europe and Japan to protect against Red take-over. When it became evident that physical Communist violence might obstruct or negate this economic reconstruction, military assistance was extended to European Allies. Technical assistance of relatively low cost to underdeveloped countries increased gradually from the beginning of Point Four in 1949. During the 1950's emphasis shifted to increasing military, political, and economic aid for these backward lands. Southerners were asked to support programs designed, *inter alia*, to transform the basic economic and social systems of societies with which they often felt little in common and which were frequently populated by colored, largely illiterate peoples and led by anticolonialist, neutralist, leftist or socialist inclined leaders who criticized the United States and, in particular, the behavior of Southern whites toward Negroes. The assumptions and attitudes which led a Southern white to support some of the earlier programs did not necessarily encourage him to favor the later ones, particularly at a time of exacerbated racial tensions at home.

National Polls, 1936–1962

One principal source of evidence was a systematic inventory of surveys by the American Institute of Public Opinion (AIPO), the National Opinion Research Center (NORC), Roper (formerly Fortune) Polls, the Survey Research Center (SRC), and diverse agencies which have examined opinion in particular Southern states, communities, or social groups, beginning with the first AIPO studies in the mid-1930's and ending with surveys of June, 1962. Attempts were made to trace trends in replies over this period in the South compared with the North and, in selected cases, the major geographical regions comprising the North.

It was impossible to employ a constant geographical definition of the South since some of those poll results were categorized by state, whereas others were not, including instead all the former Confederacy plus several border states which did not secede in the 1860's. Moreover, even where data had been categorized by state, the survey agency had often tabulated replies by geographical region including all of Texas, Oklahoma, Florida, Kentucky, and sometimes even Delaware and Maryland in the South; some agencies, on the other hand, included only the former Confederacy. Since financial limitations prevented the retabulation of all such questions of the twenty-six year period, it was necessary to use the results of many tabulations which employed varying geographical definitions of the South. The reader will also observe that Southern replies were sometimes compared with those in the Northeast, the Midwest, and the West; on other occasions with those of the Northeast, the Midwest minus the Plains States, the Rocky Mountain region, and the Far West. These differences are also due to differing practices of the several survey organizations and of the same ones over the years.

Except where otherwise indicated, intergroup differences which satisfied the 10 percent level of confidence (that is, which could have been attributable to chance alone less than one time out of ten) were accepted as statistically significant. Although many of the survey samples were modified probability rather than truly random ones, the standard formula for random samples in calculating significance was employed.[37] The size of survey samples has varied with the agency conducting the survey, the purposes of the survey, funds available, and other factors. In the footnote citations the number of cases in each national sample is indicated within parenthesis after the identification of the survey by agency, number, and date. In general, most national NORC surveys prior to 1946 included 2,400 or more cases; those between 1946 and 1957 employed samples between 1,200 and 1,400, and in several instances as few as 517. Roper surveys were typically performed on more than 3,000 cases, in some instances on over 5,000. Survey samples of SRC varied considerably, but most of its studies interviewed between 1,150 and 2,100. Most AIPO surveys utilized samples of between 2,700 and 3,800, except during the period from early 1950 to mid-1959 when more of this agency's surveys than not interviewed a considerably smaller number of adult Americans— between 1,250 and 2,200.

Depending on the survey agency's geographical definition of the South, Southerners have typically numbered 26–30 percent of the total number of interviewees in the nation. Differences in interviewee replies between Southerners and non-Southerners of three or four percentage points can normally be assumed to be significant at the 10 percent level with national samples larger than 3,000; those as large as six percentage points are significant on surveys of 1,200 Americans. Smaller differences have been acceptable as significant where percentages agreeing or disagreeing with a given opinion have been very large or small. Since Southern Negroes have usually been less informed, interested, active,

---

37   $\sigma_{diff} = \sqrt{\dfrac{P_1 (100 - P_1)}{N_1} + \dfrac{P_2 (100 - P_2)}{N_2}}$, where P_1 is the percentage of one of the two samples expressing a given view, P_2 the percentage of the other sample, and N_1 and N_2 the number of interviewees in the respective samples, and σ_{diff} the standard deviation of the difference.

and internationalist than Southern whites in most fields of world affairs, all Southerners were sometimes compared with all Northerners or with each of the several Northern regional groups, and then Southern whites were alone compared with Northern whites alone. Such differences among whites were typically significant if they were as large as five percentage points on samples of 3,000 or more, seven or eight percentage points on those of 1,200 to 1,400.

Those differences which have been much smaller but which have been in the same direction on several different surveys have been accepted as significant. In a number of instances the results of different surveys have been combined in order to achieve sufficiently large samples to permit comparisons of replies among different groups within the South, such as Negroes with whites, Catholics with Protestants, rural with urban, college educated with less educated, segregationists with desegregationists, and authoritarians with more democratically inclined, and between particular Southern groups and their Northern counterparts. In some cases the questions, the results of which have been combined, have been identically worded on the several surveys. However, in others it was necessary to combine results of questions about the same or closely related international issues which have been somewhat differently worded. Such combining of differently worded questions posed sometimes several years apart by different survey agencies employing somewhat different sampling techniques introduces some theoretical and practical reservations about the validity of the differences thus determined, but it is the author's impression that most of the differences observed though this type of summation of results of different surveys do, in fact, reflect actual differences in the populations concerned.[38]

Audience Research

Studies of readerships of a number of national periodicals bearing on world affairs, performed largely by independent audience research agencies for the publications concerned, were evaluated and in some cases retabulated. Included were the *Christian Science Monitor*, the *Atlantic*, *Harper's*, *The Reporter*, the *New Republic*, the *Nation*, *The Economist*, *The New Yorker*, *Time*, *Newsweek*, *U.S. News and World Report*, *Life*, *Look*, and the *Saturday Evening Post*. A number of publishers and distributors of paperback books were interviewed to assess

38 For a discussion of this technique and its validity, see Ithiel de Sola Pool and Robert Abelson, "The Simulmatics Project," *Public Opinion Quarterly*, XXV (1961), 167–83.

their impressions about the attributes of their Southern readers. Studies of the composition of audiences for national network television world affairs programs in 1958–59, conducted by audience research organizations for the networks and local stations or for advertisers, were also analyzed to compare the composition of Southern viewers with that of Northern ones.

The Southern Press

International news and editorial opinion in ten major Southern metropolitan daily newspapers during the period December, 1960–June, 1961, were examined. News coverage was compared with that available in the first two pages of the "News of the Week in Review" of the New York *Times* Sunday edition. Analysis of interpretative material on foreign affairs in these ten papers included both locally written editorials and syndicated columns. International interpretations were compared with views expressed on race relations, domestic economic issues, labor unions, and other sociopolitical questions. Based upon the results of the content analyses of these ten papers, similar examinations of interpretive content of world affairs and national and local issues were performed on forty-three additional Southern papers published during September, 1961. Interpretive content was then checked among these fifty-three papers during twelve brief periods between 1939 and 1956 to determine changes in editorial points of view. The daily papers read in the sample communities in which interviews were conducted were included in these content analyses. The other papers were chosen to represent the diverse Souths and each of the major Southern positions on race relations, domestic economics, social welfare, Old South versus New South, and world affairs.[39]

Interviews

During the period November, 1959–December, 1962, approximately eleven hundred interviews were conducted in a sample of Southern settings, chosen to represent as much as feasible the major subcultures. Atypically cosmopolitan minorities, influential business, professional, agricultural, and political leaders, and individuals who were particularly qualified to evaluate international opinion within one or more elements of their communities were questioned.

Subscription lists, provided by seven national and international publications which deal responsibly with foreign affairs, were the primary source of names of internationally oriented minorities who were rela-

39 See Appendix A.

tively interested, informed, and thoughtful about world affairs. To these subscription lists were added names supplied by organizations which conduct relatively serious programs on international matters—such as groups affiliated with, sponsored by, or encouraged by the Foreign Policy Association, Committees on Foreign Relations of the Council on Foreign Relations, and chapters of the League of Women Voters, the American Association of University Women, the American Association for the United Nations, and the American Heritage Association. Individuals appearing on these lists suggested others.

Members of the local power structure and individuals exerting significant influence among one or another local group, including Negroes, were chosen with the assistance of local residents who were likely to be perceptive observers of these individuals and the people influenced by them. Two general types of influence were of interest: (1) influence on Congressmen, and (2) influence on communication and attitudes within the community or important individual groups within it, insofar as the communication process was related directly or indirectly to foreign policy. The occupational roles and other characteristics of these leaders varied considerably among diverse types of Southern counties, towns, and cities.

The samples of interviewees were not, of course, representative of Southerners in general. Depending on the rigor of the standards of cosmopolitanism, between a quarter and a third of the sample could be considered cosmopolitans. Of this number, five out of six had been to college, two-thirds had graduated from college, and a third had undergone some graduate or professional training. The average level of education among those influentials who were less interested and sophisticated in foreign affairs was significantly lower, but still three fourths had experienced at least some higher education, almost a half were college graduates, and approximately a fifth had undergone some professional or graduate training. The proportions of college education were even higher among those interviewees less than roughly fifty years of age. Approximately three quarters of the sample could be considered upper, upper-middle, or at least middle-middle class, and most were much more comfortably off than the rank and file in their locales. Given the rather close association of concern, knowledge, and cosmopolitan views in world affairs with education and, to a lesser measure, socioeconomic status (see Chapters 7 and 8), it is not surprising that these interviewees were much more inclined to have opinions in international relations and to express relatively internationalist views than Southerners generally. It was necessary to rely largely on national surveys, audience research, and impressions among local observers for most of the conclusions about the rank and file.

Even among these small elites, limited resources did not permit inclusion of representative samples of each of the many different types of communities comprising the region. Nor were the interviewees in each of the professions, upper- and middle-class occupations, and other categories within the more influential segments of Southern society numerous enough to permit statistical comparisons of groups within the South. Furthermore, the interviews extended over three years, during which international events changed, in some spheres significantly. Attempts were made to determine basic assumptions and postures toward world affairs and the major experiences and social forces which produced and maintained them. Of course, data thus derived would be more suggestive and impressionistic than scientifically systematic. A list of questions [40] was used as a guide for the conversations, but an attempt was made to tailor the discussions to the background and idiosyncracies of each interviewee, to encourage him to express his views in his own language about the issues he considered important as well as about those the interviewer felt important, and to develop as close rapport with him as possible. In some cases interviews had to be terminated within twenty minutes, limiting the inquiries to the more general issues. In others, several hours were spent with the interviewee and some of the questions led into extended discussions of more detailed international aspects and of related factors in the local situation. Some interviewees had only very vague opinions or leanings on even the major long-run international problems facing our country whereas others were able to discuss at great length their sentiments about specific matters.

The sample locales, chosen to represent the major subcultures in the South, were Plantation County, Delta County, Bayou Parish, Hill County, Mountain County, and the cities of Kent, New Southtown, Antebellum Town, Charleston, and New Orleans. Since several important groups were insufficiently represented in the locales studied to allow even cautious impressionistic generalizations about their international behavior, the interviews were extended to include Jews, textile and garment manufacturers, recipients of affluent incomes from the petroleum industry, local trade union officers and business agents, influential Negroes, and segregationist leaders in a number of other communities.

Plantation County. One of the three Deep South plantation communi-

40 See Appendix B.

ties was a black-belt county where Negroes outnumbered whites by almost three to one in 1960. Its economy had been shifting from cotton to cattle and timber since the boll weevil became a major problem some four decades ago. The pace of this trend had accelerated considerably since World War II. Typical of most plantation sections, Plantation County had experienced a rapid loss of white and, especially, Negro population since 1940 and had received very few new people from elsewhere. A small number of larger landowners and business and professional people—often related by blood or marriage over several generations and mostly concentrated at the small county seat and an even smaller unincorporated hamlet—were college educated, relatively prosperous, and highly influential in setting the tone of thought and running local affairs. About two dozen people owned most of the fertile land in this county. A larger, but still quite small, fraction of the white population were owners of more modest holdings, small businessmen, and the like. The great mass of the population was composed of Negroes and a much smaller number of whites of very limited (though gradually improving) education, income, and influence. There were no known Jews, Catholics, or foreign-born inhabitants. A large proportion of college-educated sons and daughters had left for cities. Since the county was initially settled in the 1820's, its genteel class would probably be considered relatively new people by the older aristocracies of Tidewater Virginia, the Carolina low country, and southern Louisiana. There was no Episcopal church, and social distinctions between the old families and the small, more recently "arrived" middle class, although sharp by standards of most hill and mountain counties, were considerably weaker than those in more traditional, older Southern communities.[41] The autobiographical novel *To Kill a Mockingbird*,[42] written by a native of a nearby black-belt county, describes many of the personalities, attitudes, and social situations that were prevalent in Plantation County.

Delta County. The second plantation locale, in the Mississippi Delta south of Memphis, was based in 1961 on a mechanized cotton-plantation

41 The social structure and cultural values of Plantation County were studied and described in considerable detail by anthropologist Morton Rubin in his *Plantation County* (Chapel Hill: University of North Carolina Press, 1951). Some changes have taken place since his research in the late 1940's, but his general observations still seemed to apply in the early 1960's. Plantation County in 1961 was also comparable in many economic, social, and cultural respects to the black-belt county examined by Paul A. Miller *et al.*, in their *Community Health Action* (East Lansing: Michigan State College Press, 1953), 57–66.
42 Harper Lee, *To Kill a Mockingbird* (New York: J. B. Lippincott Co., 1960).

economy.[43] Tractors, mechanical cotton pickers, and other machinery coordinated by the planter or his manager had gradually displaced sharecropping. Land by Southern standards was expensive; there were relatively few small-family farmers, and most of the desirable land was part of plantations ranging between 1,000 and 37,000 acres. Some timber, cattle, poultry, rice, and other food staples were raised, but cotton-growing dominated the lives of the inhabitants, including those in the two major towns which serviced the fields. One of these, Rivertown on the Mississippi, was established before the Civil War. Not really an old society by Tidewater, low country, New Orleans, or Natchez standards, it was still Old South in comparison with parts of the Delta away from the river and was viewed as such by its old families and the newer elites to the east. Its Episcopal church was old for Mississippi; its gentry mixed socially primarily among themselves and their counterparts in other Old South sections, thought much in terms of their traditions and predecessors, and regarded with some disdain the achievement-oriented, bustling doers in Deltatown, the growing commercial center to the east. Regarded as dead by many first and second generation prosperous planters and commercial people elsewhere in Delta County, Rivertown had received very few new people and had tended, like Plantation County, to lose its more dynamic college-educated sons and daughters.[44]

Most of the leaders of those parts of the county away from the Mississippi River, including Deltatown, either came from humble beginnings or their fathers or, at most, their grandfathers had. Like most of the Delta back from the river, this area was swamp and canebreak before about 1890. Enterprising underprivileged hill folk, some poor whites from older plantation sections, and other men of great energy but of largely simple, poorly educated beginnings developed this wilderness, much in the fashion of John Faulkner's single-minded, poorly lettered Otis Towne (born Town before his upwardly mobile wife changed the name).[45]

As they made money in the first decades of the twentieth century,

43 Two anthropological studies were performed in a nearby and in many respects comparable Delta county in the 1930's. See John P. Dollard, *Caste and Class in a Southern Town* (New Haven, Conn.: Yale University Press, 1937); and Hortense Powdermaker, *After Freedom: A Cultural Study in the Deep South* (New York: Viking Press, 1939).

44 Rivertown's society has much in common with that of the community described in Allison Davis, Burleigh B. Gardner, and Mary R. Gardner, *Deep South* (Chicago: University of Chicago Press, 1940).

45 John Faulkner, *Dollar Cotton* (New York: Harcourt, Brace, and Co., 1942).

they built comfortable homes (sometimes copies of antebellum mansions), sent their families for visits—or even to reside—in Memphis (capital of the Delta), and became "respectable." Some of these men and their offspring managed to keep and even expand their property regardless of periodic collapses of the cotton market, the infestation of the boll weevil, the Great Depression, and other challenges. But many did not, and a considerable proportion of the plantation and commercial leaders of the county in 1961 was composed of newer men of prosperity like William Faulkner's Flem Snopes [46] and Tennessee Williams' Big Daddy.[47] Through their native intelligence (or cunning), agility, and energy, they worked up from "redneck" or, at most, very modest origins and took over from the complacent or ineffectual Will Varners whose vigorous fathers (or, in some cases, themselves) had developed the land. Certainly many of these vigorous men were not amoral, ruthless, and generally reprehensible, as was Flem Snopes, but they and their immediate descendants seldom have had the values and cultivation (although they may adopt some of the surface attributes) of at least a significant segment of the gentry of antebellum standing. Some of these people had become Episcopalians and Presbyterians, but most were still Baptists or Methodists, and their thinking was more akin to that of the small-town, middle-class, Southern businessman than to that of the traditionalist aristocracy. After the frontier types had developed the Delta, a few members of the older societies migrated to Deltatown from more established communities, but they composed a very small minority of the influential families in 1961.

Deltatown in 1961 serviced cotton producers and had a small state college, a branch plant of a national drug manufacturer, a ceramic tile factory, and a number of smaller enterprises. Although Rivertown had no Jews, Deltatown had approximately thirty Jewish families and contained a temple attended by Jews living twenty-five and more miles away. Deltatown also supported a small Catholic church, whereas there were no known Catholics in Plantation County. Its population included a small Negro middle class beyond the teacher group of Plantation County. Over one percent of its inhabitants in 1960 were either born outside the United States or had at least one parent born abroad. Nevertheless, Delta County had many of the attributes of the plantation tradition. It was very much a society where relatively few owned the

46 William Faulkner, *The Hamlet* (New York: Random House, 1940); *The Town* (New York: Random House, 1957); and *The Mansion* (New York: Random House, 1959).
47 Tennessee Williams, *Cat on a Hot Tin Roof* (New York: New American Library, 1955).

important properties, determined the important decisions, and set the cultural tone; the middle stratum was relatively small; and the great majority comprised lower-class Negroes and, to a lesser measure, whites of humble station. Less than one adult out of a hundred had finished college in 1960 and more than half had gone no further than the sixth grade. Negroes outnumbered whites in 1960 by five to two, were mainly plantation workers and foremen or little-skilled workers in the towns, and had scant education and low incomes.

Bayou Parish. No one parish could represent the diverse settings of predominantly Roman Catholic, rural, southern Louisiana. Those along the Mississippi River have differed from others further inland; some have become prosperous from minerals or manufactures while others have remained poor; some were still plantation economies while others had few or no plantations left in 1960; and so on. The author is rather familiar with Plaquemines Parish as a participant observer and therefore chose a different type of locale for interviewing, one which incorporated many of the dissimilar attributes of other, more nearly homogeneous parishes in the vicinity.

Bayou Parish had a mixed economy of sugar-cane growing and grinding, timber growing, cattle raising, trapping, farming along the bayou, commercial fishing and shrimping in the Gulf of Mexico, and, in recent decades, sulphur mining and oil drilling. Sugar was the most important crop and the plantation tradition was still evident in many attitudes. The Catholic majority comprised roughly 85 percent of the white church-affiliated population. Until the discovery of petroleum there were few Protestants other than Negroes, and even a considerable minority of the Negroes were Catholics. Most of the white Protestants were relative newcomers, connected directly or indirectly with the oil industry and other industrial developments of the last two decades or with the local state college.

The influx of outsiders with expanding mining and oil drilling partially accounted for the fact that Bayou Parish had increased in population whereas the two plantation counties just described had rapidly lost people in recent years. But the personal proclivities of the *indigènes,* predominantly of French and French-Canadian extraction and culture, also helped explain this phenomenon. The habitual language in the home was predominantly a French dialect and older individuals often spoke little English. Their attachment to their culture, family, and friends has been intense; French Louisiana has long exerted a strong emotional grasp on its offspring—few leave even after attending college. The culture to which they have been accustomed has been so different from that of the rest of the country that most natives have felt at home only there. New Orleans has attracted most of those who have left rural areas, but relatively few have had the education and skills essential for well-paid urban employment. As in most of the rural South the most educated and sophisticated, who also have tended to be the most knowledgeable about world affairs and the most internationally responsible, have been disproportionately numerous among those departing for the city.

Although the Cajuns have been significantly "Americanized" in recent years, they have resisted acculturation longer and more effectively than virtually any other ethnic group in this country.[48] Close family ties, *joie de vivre*, a generally uninhibited society, their own language, and other attractions have prevented them from adopting American customs. Rather, they have absorbed and acculturated diverse foreign elements over the centuries—one encounters McCarthys, Hankses, Collinses, Shutzes, Foltzes, Hymels, Morrisons, Murphys, Blochs, and other non-French named persons who assure the visitor that they are French. Other families have translated their non-French names—Weber to Webre, O'Brien to Obrion, Zweig to LaBranche, Dubs to Toups, and so on.[49]

Whites outnumbered Negroes in 1960 by seven to one. Negroes were better off and more independent than in most of the rural South, and particularly than in most other plantation sections. Tenantry has never

48   For analyses of the mores and social organization of rural French Louisiana, see Vernon J. Parenton, "Notes on the Social Organization of a French Village in South Louisiana," *Social Forces*, XVII (1938), 73–82; Roland J. Pellegrin, "A Sociological Analysis of Pointe Coupée Parish" (Master's thesis, Louisiana State University, 1949); Vernon J. Parenton and T. Lynn Smith, "Acculturation among the Louisiana French," *American Journal of Sociology*, XLIV, Issue 3 (November, 1938); Roger W. Shugg, *Origins of Class Struggle in Louisiana* (Baton Rouge: Louisiana State University Press, 1939); Hodding Carter and Anthony Ragusin, *Gulf Coast Country* (New York: Duell, Sloan, Pearce, 1951), 4 ff; Vernon J. Parenton, "The Rural French-Speaking People of Quebec and South Louisiana: A Comparative Study of Social Structure and Organization with Emphasis on the Role of the Catholic Church" (Ph.D. dissertation, Harvard University, 1948); T. Lynn Smith and Homer L. Hitt, *The People of Louisiana* (Baton Rouge: Louisiana State University Press, 1952); Alvin L. Bertrand, *The Many Louisianas* (Louisiana State University Agricultural Experiment Station, Bul. 496 [Baton Rouge, 1955]), 17 and 20–31; and Edward J. Kammer, *A Socio-Economic Survey of the Marshdwellers of Four Southeastern Louisiana Parishes* (Washington, D. C.: Catholic University of America Press, 1941).

49   Smith and Parenton, *American Journal of Sociology*, XLIV, 256–64; Parenton, "The Rural French-Speaking People," 371; Smith and Hitt, *The People of Louisiana*, 107; and Pellegrin, "A Sociological Analysis of Point Coupée Parish," 128–29.

been practiced on sugar plantations, since the plantations have always required greater capital for sugar mills and other equipment and more central operation by the planter or his overseer than have cotton and tobacco plantations.[50] Mechanization has further decreased the need for Negroes on plantations and propelled them into the city or local industries,[51] and the more racially tolerant attitudes of white south Louisianians have permitted Negroes to better themselves more than in most of the rural Protestant South (see pp. 459–60).

Thus, the difference between Negro and white incomes was decidedly less in 1960 than in either of the two counties just described. Fifteen out of a total of approximately 1,300 Negro families received in 1959 incomes in excess of $10,000. In 1960 most Negroes were plantation wage earners of low status, domestic servants, and other unskilled or semi-skilled workers, but mulattoes (classified socially as Negroes) have been "chemists" and other technical workers in sugar houses for generations. By 1960 the proportion of Negroes in professional, technical, and skilled categories was several times that in Delta and Plantation counties, and much larger fractions owned their plots of land than in the other two plantation counties.

Whites were also economically considerably better off than in Delta and Plantation counties, and wealth was considerably more broadly distributed. Oil and industrialization had been largely responsible for the median white-family income of more than $4,000 per annum in 1959. Although there were a number of prosperous planters, owners of oil land and leases, fish and shrimp packers, and others whose 1959 incomes exceeded $25,000, the proportion of whites in the middle-income brackets was much larger than in the counties so far described; those in poverty formed a considerably smaller percentage of the population.

As in much of rural southern Louisiana, education has not until the last several decades generated much interest among either Cajuns or Negroes. Formal education seemed of little utility to French-speaking small farmers, fishermen, shrimpers, or trappers who lived in the marsh or on a slender strip of land extending from the bayou to the swamp.[52] Perhaps even more than most other rural Southerners, Cajuns tended to feel that experience was the best teacher and that schools educated

50 Shugg, *Origins of Class Struggle in Louisiana*, 5 and 98; and Ulrich B. Phillips, "Plantations with Slave Labor and Free," *American Historical Review*, XXX (1925), 746.
51 See, for instance, Alvin L. Bertrand, *Agricultural Mechanization and Social Change in Rural Louisiana* (L.S.U. Agricultural Experiment Station, Bul. 458 [Baton Rouge, 1957]), 9 ff and 30.
52 Kammer, *A Socio-Economic Survey of the Marshdwellers*, 69.

children to become "Americans" (long a negative term to Creole gentry and Cajun illiterates alike) and influenced them to leave their culture and the farm, marsh, and fishing village of their ancestors. Many older people were still unable to write either French or English, and most younger adults were one generation removed from illiteracy. Even the poor white fundamentalists of northern Louisiana were, on the average, better educated than Cajuns of similar economic status,[53] and Bayou Parish white Protestants were, on the whole, considerably better educated. An extremely wide gulf has traditionally separated the planter class, of Creole Catholics whose ancestors came directly from France in the 1700's and of Episcopalians who moved as Virginia or South Carolina "gentlemen" to French Louisiana after its purchase from Napoleon, from the Cajun small farmers, trappers, or even overseers.[54] There were few schools for the Cajuns until relatively recently—planters had private tutors or sent their offspring to New Orleans to be educated. The feelings of hauteur among planter families with respect to their Cajun neighbors have had few equals in America.

However, in recent years the Catholic Church and the parish government have considerably increased educational opportunities, consolidated small schools, and enforced truancy laws fairly generally. By 1960 most white illiterates were old enough to have grown to adulthood before World War II. The majority of Negroes, however, were still nearly illiterate in 1960—the median years of schooling for Negroes twenty-five and older was 4.7 years.

Hill County. It was even more difficult to select any one hill or piedmont setting which was representative of the rather heterogeneous environments which have emerged with gradual industrialization. One of the hill counties used had only recently emerged from the poverty of small-scale agriculture. Although family farming was still a major source of livelihood in 1960, Hill County had since the war developed extensive poultry raising and processing and feed mill enterprises and had attracted branches of national meat-packing and slide fastener manufacturers. Lumber and cattle had become important sources of income

53 T. Lynn Smith, "An Analysis of Rural Social Organization among the French-Speaking People of Southern Louisiana," *Journal of Farm Economics*, XVI (1934), 680–88; and T. Lynn Smith and Louise Kemp, *The Educational Status of Louisiana's Farm Population* (Louisiana State University Agricultural Experiment Station Bull. 424 [Baton Rouge: 1947]), 5.

54 See, for instance, Pellegrin, "A Sociological Analysis of Point Coupée Parish," 24 ff.; and Paul H. Price, *Louisiana's Rural Population at Mid-Century* (Louisiana State University Agricultural Experiment Station, Bull. 514 [Baton Rouge: 1959]), 38–40.

as small farmers on relatively poor land felt unable to compete with mechanized plantations in the South and Southwest. Although the county was not so affluent as to attract many outsiders—there were no known Jews or Catholics, only one inhabitant out of a thousand was born outside the United States, and one in twenty came from outside the state in 1960—it had produced several local millionaires and a number of well-to-do citizens, primarily from poor or modest farm childhoods. The local leaders were middle-class individuals possessing few of the aristocratic values of esteemed minorities in older plantation areas and traditional cities. There was more of a continuum of social strata and considerably less emotional separation between the classes, as one would assume from the self-employed status of most of the inhabitants. Although the county seat had grown to over 5,000 people by 1960, it contained mostly Baptists and a few Methodists; neither the Episcopalians nor the Presbyterians were sufficient in number to have established churches there.[55]

Kent. Part of the second piedmont county selected was composed of rather barren hills, populated for the last two hundred years by yeoman farmers. Some continued to raise cotton and most had emerged from poverty to relative comfort within the last two decades. But another part of the county was quite fertile, and a plantation society emerged there before the American Revolution and expanded up to the Civil War. Most of the Negroes lived in this part of the county and it reflected the traditions of the Old South to a considerable extent in the early 1960's. The county seat at Kent (pseudonym) became known as the Charleston of the up-country.

Descendants of antebellum planters formed in 1960 a distinct, intermarried, upper class, separated socially and ideologically from the more recently prosperous middle class. Taking its model of living from Charleston gentry, Kent's old families emphasized planter traditions —a way of life rather than occupational success, personal wealth, or economic progress. They had successfully opposed the building of a railroad through Kent for fear of its disrupting their traditions and mores and bringing strange people to town. At the time of the interviews they were strongly opposing the middle-class inhabitants on the

55 For more detailed descriptions of the social organization of Hill County, see "Health Organization and Family Utilization Patterns in a Mississippi County, 1953–1954" (MS in Department of Sociology and Rural Life, Mississippi State University, Starkville, Mississippi, 1954); Luther Clark Swords, "Health Leadership in a Mississippi County" (Master's thesis, Mississippi State University, Starkville, Mississippi, 1955); and other unpublished material available at the Department of Sociology and Rural Life of Mississippi State University.

proposed location of a supermarket next to the antebellum home of a relative of a famous Revolutionary War general. The general's relative, a well-read and cultivated gentleman who had practiced law for thirteen years in Washington before returning to Kent so that his children could "have roots" and grow up among their relatives, friends, and traditions of the Old South, was the lawyer attempting to prevent establishment of the supermarket. The local lawyer for the supermarket chain, supported by much of the middle class, was an "upstart" raised on a hill farm. An old family in control of one of two local banks opposed attracting modern large industry to Kent even though its bank needed the business. Some of the middle class and representatives of the workers in the local textile mills wanted to follow the example of many Southern communities and raise a bond issue to construct a building to which a job-producing industry might be attracted, but much of the upper class opposed this idea and the scheme was defeated. Most of the aristocracy were not trying to preserve any affluent economic status —few had much money—but, rather, they wished to maintain the traditional environment to which they were attached.

Somnolent Kent had by 1960 lost many of its more achievement-oriented, dynamic citizens. An army general, a naval admiral, an Episcopal bishop, a director of a renowned national art museum, a big-city Presbyterian minister, and many other talented people had left their upper-class relatives for better opportunities elsewhere. Few had gone into business or manufacturing ("money grubbing"); military service, law, medicine, the clergy, and the other professions had attracted most of them, as has been the case of the Southern gentry generally. The successful industries and businesses of Kent were owned, controlled, and managed by ambitious, go-getting, new people. One such person, who came from Florida, rejuvenated a bankrupt movie house and used profits therefrom to develop a prosperous construction business and other thriving enterprises in the county. Another, raised on a nearby modest cotton farm, studied engineering at a state college, joined a fabric concern in Philadelphia, convinced his superiors they should open a branch in his home county ("where I belong"), and developed it into one of the most efficient in the industry. Three brothers came from "nowhere" with little education or cultivation and became well-to-do in local textile and carpet mills.[56]

56 These observations are derived from Ralph C. Patrick, Jr., "A Cultural Approach to Social Stratification" (Ph.D. dissertation, Harvard University, 1953); unpublished interviews with Ralph C. Patrick, Jr.; and discussions in the community by the author.

As in many traditional Southern towns which have acquired low-technology industries, workers and foremen in the textile mills of Kent lived in a separate part of the community and had only impersonal contacts with the upper- and middle-class townspeople. A study of local millworkers in the late 1940's, followed by another in the late 1950's, discovered that most of them (or most of their parents) came from small, underprivileged, often failing, farms and that a considerable fraction were still commuting from farms. Like much of the Southern working class outside southern Louisiana, they were almost 100 percent Anglo-Saxon. One worker imported a foreign war bride, but "scandalous" habits like keeping beer in the refrigerator generated such social ostracism and pressures that the couple departed for a city. At the time of the second study, the majority of the children of Kent millworkers of the late 1940's were in Kent mills; only a minority of them had completed high school; and the paternalism and social and economic pressures of the owners had succeeded in keeping unions out of the mills. The townspeople continued to regard millworkers as shiftless, uncouth "lintheads." The mill child could hardly rise beyond the mill unless he left town, the more ambitious did.[57]

The local Negro population, approximately a third of the total of Kent, had profited only indirectly from the advent of the New South in the environs. Isolated from both the mill village and the downtown residents, they were concentrated in one part of Kent.[58] The mills, like many others of the Piedmont, had been initiated partly to give jobs to poor whites so that they would not be obliged to compete with and work alongside Negroes; consequently, the few Negroes employed there in 1960 were in the more menial jobs. Exclusion of Negroes from the better paying and more skilled jobs seemed to have the support of virtually all the millworkers and of their bosses. As was the case among whites, the younger, ambitious, better-educated Negroes were inclined to migrate to more progressive communities, while the older college-trained Negroes who had returned tended to criticize the traditionalist fixation on the past and lack of interest in "progress" of the local white upper class.

New Southtown. Only twenty miles from Kent, this community was

57 John Kenneth Morland, *Millways of Kent* (Chapel Hill: University of North Carolina Press, 1958); John Kenneth Morland, "Stability and Change among Mill-Village Families" (Paper presented at the annual meeting of the American Sociological Association, Chicago, 1959); and conversations with John Kenneth Morland.
58 See Hylan Lewis, *Blackways of Kent* (Chapel Hill: University of North Carolina Press, 1955).

in another world from the latter in 1960. Yet, it also contained textile workers of Anglo-Saxon hill stock and manifested a high degree of religious fundamentalism, a low educational level, and a lower class which showed docility before its betters. A textile village near the turn of the century, the community's mills still constituted the largest employer—some 11,000 of the total population of 30,000 in 1960 were members of mill families. Mills had in recent years been bought out by national chains, a phenomenon increasingly evident throughout the Piedmont. Two local mills within national corporations had been organized by trade unions, but local union leaders felt much less secure than most of their Northern counterparts, since a union had recently been "broken" in a third mill. Managers of textile mills were Southerners of rural and small-town origins like their workers, but most of the younger executives had been to engineering school.

Thus, New Southtown had many of the attributes of hundreds of other Piedmont textile communities, but it was also a prototype of the newest New South of diversified, scientifically based industry. It provided an example of the impact of high-technology upon a formerly labor-intensive Southern community and, hopefully, of the future South. Textile interests could no longer control the community or its politics to the degree they have in places where there have been no other strong economic interests and job alternatives. A national manufacturer of synthetic fibers and a subsidiary of a British firm producing hardboard and other products through technology and scientific research had recently brought to New Southtown highly trained managers and technicians (primarily of non-Southern backgrounds), higher wages for reliable, enterprising skilled workers than those in textile mills, strong trade unions, and rationalized management-labor relations rather than the plantation-like paternalism of many indigenous Southern plants. Although many local inhabitants were initially cool to these highly trained outsiders, they lived next door, joined the local service, business, and country clubs, and shortly became more or less accepted by all but a small social elite.

But the Old South gentry of Kent, Rivertown, Bayou Parish, and Plantation County had few counterparts in this small city of the twentieth century. Few of the influential people there were much interested in the past and most regarded nearby Kent as an anachronism. New Southtown had a small Jewish population of merchants and almost one out of five inhabitants in 1960 had been born outside of the state. Only a quarter of the population was Negro, and Negroes had developed a small, rather vigorous professional class of ministers, two physicians, a dentist, and teachers. A local church-supported Negro junior college furnished somewhat of an intellectual base for a comparatively cosmopolitan small Negro elite.[59]

Antebellum Town. New Southtown constituted an example of one major type of Southern industrial community—a new town developed in the twentieth century largely from yeoman farmers and other hill people, first as a textile village, later as a diversified manufacturing community. Kent was another—low-technology, paternalistic, soft goods factories built on the outskirts of an old town. A third type was the one-mill village, or town, where most of the community has been controlled by the owner if no longer owned directly by him. Antebellum Town represented still another prototype, perhaps in somewhat extreme form—a traditionalist Old South setting which had acquired diversified branches of several capital-intensive national and international corporations in a rather short period of time.

Antebellum Town, comprising in 1960 some 25,000 people, dated as a Mississippi River port from the early eighteenth century, long before Rivertown or even Kent. At the time of the secession it was the largest town in its state and was the place of abode, commercial and social center, and river port of planters whose holdings prospered on both sides of the Mississippi. Although many of the more able and enterprising descendants of the plantation and commercial elite had moved to larger cities, Antebellum Town still contained in 1960 a small, old family minority of wide prestige. By the 1920's, however, its economy was in serious difficulties. But by the 1960's it was more prosperous than ever because of the discovery of oil nearby; the production of rubber goods, quality papers, wall board and other building materials (all controlled by Northern corporations); and some fifty other smaller manufacturing establishments. Most of the managerial and technical personnel for the national plants had served in the Northern States, Latin America, Western Europe, or other far places and were rotated through the town for several years, then leaving for other parts of the country or world. Although Old South thinking still exerted strong influences on local people, the well-educated technical and managerial personnel with these enterprises were too important to everyone's standard of living to be ignored. They had therefore been integrated into the town's business and civic organizations, churches, and country clubs; their children attended the most esteemed dancing school and

59 For another variant of the Piedmont town and the values and behavior of the diverse groups within it, see Solon T. Kimball and Marion Pearsall, *The Talladega Story* (University, Ala.: University of Alabama Press, 1954).

even some parties in antebellum mansions. In this community of rather strong (for the South) trade unions, a few better-educated Negroes had succeeded in gaining skilled positions which they would have never obtained in rural settings or most textile, garment, and other low-technology industries.

Charleston. Even Charleston had not preserved unadulterated the values and way of life of the agrarian aristocratic South, although many of the living descendants of its early plantation owners and commercial and professional leaders may wish it had done so. In 1960 it was no longer quite the "museum to the antebellum mind" that it was once considered. The economic impact of the naval yard had been considerable in an otherwise rather static economy; many Charlestonians worked there and its personnel from elsewhere circulated locally and influenced Charleston thinking. Although the port was no longer a major one, except for the naval yard, it had brought outsiders to Charleston. At least the officers mixed with some of the local inhabitants, and even foreigners sometimes decided to stay. In 1960 Charleston contained considerably more foreign-born inhabitants—1.4 per cent—than the Southern average and more than twice that number were offspring of one or more foreign-born parents. These percentages approximately doubled if Negroes were not included. Even though Charleston itself had received little industry, North Charleston had experienced significantly more, and the social wall between the two Charlestons, at least below the old family stratum, was not so high as to isolate the former completely from the thinking in the latter. The slow growth of the Charleston economy had entailed the departure of a number of its better-educated youngsters, but the port and the other activities of the city had attracted more non-South Carolinians than many Charlestonians realized—one out of five of its citizenry in 1960 was born outside the state. Moreover, some of the outsiders exerted significant influence in the society. Most Episcopal ministers, for instance, were not born in the low country, and the majority of them thought differently from most of their parishioners on a number of public issues, including race relations and world affairs. The Catholic bishop until 1962 was an Irish-American Northerner with views that differed sharply from local attitudes on public matters, again including race and international relations. Specialists had been brought to Charleston, even by the city government. Old family Charlestonians had married Bostonians, New Yorkers, and other Northerners and some of these outsiders had settled in Charleston and intermingled with their in-laws and their friends.

Finally, although the two local newspapers were owned and managed by members of local old families and their editorials presented Southern traditionalist views in as pure form as any media in the region, serious national newspapers, magazines, and books communicated alternative interpretations to a minority of the better-educated residents, some of whom influenced other people's thinking.

Nevertheless, Charlestonians, particularly much of the genteel, influential group, were in the early 1960's as uncompromising with mid-twentieth-century progressive ideas as any group in the region—a sample of its leaders and cosmopolitans were interviewed. Founded in 1670, Charleston was a prosperous, multiethnic, heterogeneous comunity and by 1790 the fourth largest city in the country.[60] During its pre–Civil War history it received diverse immigrants, as did New Orleans and Northern ports—English, Protestant French, Dutch, Scotch-Irish, Irish Catholic, German, Swiss, Portuguese, Welsh, and Jewish.[61] A cultivated minority developed among the upper class of owners of surrounding indigo and rice plantations, successful commission merchants, businessmen, and professional people as early as the late 1700's.[62] The descendants of this group continued for generations to regard even the elite of places like Kent as upstart rustics or prosperous hillbillies.[63]

The prestigious class of 1960 contained the descendants of this antebellum elite. They seemed to wield more influence in Charleston than in any other major Southern community as large, in part because the slow rate of economic development had not produced many newly prosperous individuals who could challenge their influence. Whatever may have been their diverse ethnic origins, except for the Jews, they had become quite a homogeneous group in outlook and behavior in 1960. Their consciousness of the past, resistance to change and to compromise with industrialism and modernism, elitist views of mass participation in public affairs, and strong class consciousness were remarkable in the light of national, and even Southern, developments during the

60 For instance, Charles Reznikoff and Uriah Z. Engelman, *The Jews of Charleston* (Philadelphia: The Jewish Publications Society of America, 1950), 73.

61 *Ibid.*, 18–21, 79–90; Harnett T. Kane, *Gone Are the Days* (New York: E. P. Dutton and Co., 1960), 87; and Barnett A. Elzas, *The Jews of South Carolina* (Philadelphia: J. B. Lippincott Co., 1905), 166.

62 Rollin G. Osterweis, *Romanticism and Nationalism in the Old South* (New Haven: Yale University Press, 1949), 112; Frederick P. Bowes, *The Culture of Early Charleston* (Chapel Hill: University of North Carolina Press, 1942), 115–30; Clement Eaton, *The Growth of Southern Civilization* (New York: Harper and Bros., 1961), 1, 5, and 7–8; and Carl Bridenbaugh, *Myths and Realities: Societies of the Colonial South* (Baton Rouge: Louisiana State University Press, 1952), 59–60, 65–73, 76–84, 90–100, and 112–18.

63 Eaton, *The Growth of Southern Civilization*, 9.

last several decades. Finally, even Negroes of Charleston manifested many of these traditions, especially a small upper class conscious of its forebears who were frequently free men of color rather than slaves in antebellum times.

The Crescent City. New Orleans, Richmond, Savannah, Mobile, Greenville (Mississippi), and other old cities contained in the early sixties small, traditional minorities of genteel ancestry like Charleston's, but these groups had intermarried much more with newer prosperous and educated people. Few of them were quite as backward looking and uncompromising with modern thought as their Charlestonian counterparts, and their local influence had been much more attenuated by emerging leaders from less elevated strata. Interviews of both cosmopolitans and more typical leadership groups were conducted in New Orleans. This rather unique Southern community will be discussed in some detail in Chapter 12 below.

Mountain County. No one county could represent the diverse mountain region—the spectrum from urban, industrial Chattanooga to the most isolated, rural, illiterate society in a highland hollow. One of the more primitive, underprivileged counties—where mountain values and their international correlates might be apparent in purer form—was purposely chosen for interviewing. (The selected county was examined in considerable detail for the Berea College Southern Appalachian Studies.) [64] Urban places and more highly developed rural sections in the mountains probably varied considerably in 1959–62 from the findings in the sample county relative to international behavior.

Mountain County manifested, probably in rather extreme form, most of the social, cultural, demographical, and psychological aspects prevalent in the rural and hamlet settings of the Appalachians. Although the average inhabitant had been influenced more by outside modern ideas in the last two decades than perhaps in the century preceding, these people compared with the rural Cajuns in the degree to which they had preserved the attitudes and customs of their ancestors. Virtually everyone's ancestors were English, Welsh, or Scotch; there were no known Jews, no known Catholics, no Negroes. As throughout much of the

64 Thomas R. Ford (ed.), *The Southern Appalachian Region* (Lexington: University of Kentucky Press, 1962); Marion Pearsall, "Healthways in a Mountain County," *Mountain Life and Work*, XXXVI, No. 4 (1960); and "Some Behavioral Factors in the Control of Tuberculosis in a Rural County," *American Review of Respiratory Diseases*, 85 (1962), 200–10. See also her anthropological study of a similar mountain culture, Marion Pearsall, *Little Smoky Ridge* (University, Ala.: University of Alabama Press, 1959).

mountain region, several entrepreneurs had arrived in past decades from outside the mountains. They developed and profited from mineral and forest resources, but left when the resources were exhausted, with ghost towns and unemployed remaining in their wake. Only a few had settled there and helped to raise the cultural standards. The other major group of outsiders who had come into the county, and into the rural mountains generally, were religious missionaries, some of whom had broader objectives than religious conversion alone.

The acute lack of economic and cultural opportunity in the county had resulted in drastic out-migration—the population decreased by a third in the decade before 1960. Most of this migration had been to cities outside the mountains. The local rate of unemployment and underemployment was among the highest and their average income among the lowest in America. As for many years in the past, in the summer of 1961, almost half the population was receiving free commodities, primarily from the federal government, and widespread malnutrition would have resulted but for distribution of free food. The schools, such as they were, were supported primarily by state and national funds. The few small, hand-operated, un-unionized truck coal mines, farms on marginal acres, and "moonshine" establishments had not been enough to maintain the economy at even a subsistence level, nor was there much hope for new industry, given the paucity of natural resources, the unskilled manpower, and other considerations. Almost two thirds of the population twenty-five years of age and older in 1960 had not finished grade school, and most of the relatively few who went to college failed to graduate because of poor secondary schools and generally deficient cultural preparation and motivation. Many teachers themselves did not have a college degree. Interpersonal extra-legal violence was still rather widespread. By all criteria Mountain County people were among the most underprivileged in America.

Nevertheless, this county had given majorities since 1865 to Republican congressional candidates. Staunch Republicans in the line awaiting federal commodities complained that federal assistance to poor people like themselves should be greatly increased (often by cutting foreign aid) and that taxes on businesses and prosperous individuals should be raised; they advanced other views indicating their lack of understanding of the current philosophy and leadership of most of the Republican party. Not only did they vote by tradition for Republicans but their congressional choices were on the right of the Republicans in the Congress on most issues, including foreign affairs.

Religious observances were with few exceptions very fundamentalist, other worldly, and guided by untrained ministers of small, informal congregations unaffiliated with the Southern Baptist Convention or any other major denomination. Snake handling was still practiced in some groups. Few felt they could control or influence their environments or plan their future—God and fate alone would govern. Even the members of the two missionary Northern Presbyterian churches, the most prestigious denomination, were heavily influenced by literalist, emotional religious inclinations.

However, in at least some respects the residents seemed closer to national experience and attitudes than most of the non-mountain South. The lack of a slave tradition and the absence of Negroes had permitted a relative indifference to racism and politicians who would appeal to it, even though most mountain folk did not care much for Negroes (or other strangers) and those who had migrated to industrial towns often returned with racial prejudices. Moreover, the feudal, class-conscious traditions of the Deep, particularly plantation, South were nonexistent. Few mountain people seemed to trace their ancestors very far. Since they had had no contact with the plantation ethic and had been poor and largely illiterate for centuries, they did not look back nostalgically at a supposed age of glory, aristocracy, and chivalry prior to 1865. Some of their forebears did fight with the Confederacy, but more were either relatively indifferent to slavery or had sided with the Union; consequently little of the sectional resentment over the defeat of 1865 prevalent in the Deep South was apparent. Because there never was much wealth, mountaineers had been more equalitarian than even most Northerners. There was no local gentry by inheritance; owners of local mines and other enterprises often worked beside their employees; children of the most prosperous (or least poverty stricken) and best educated socialized with those of the poorest and least educated; sons of physicians and other professional men might not go to college and might work for more enterprising sons of "holler" (hollow) folk with relatively little resentment; and hardly anyone was very far above or below most others in social standing and prestige.

Thus, most of the generalizations about trends in the South as a whole or among whites in the South compared with the rest of the country, each of the major geographical regions in the North, or Northern whites have been derived from statistical results of national surveys. Since several different polling agencies have typically arrived at similar results over a period of time, the author feels relatively secure that comments based on such evidence are valid.

However, most of the observations about individual Southern groups compared with one another and with their counterparts outside the South have been derived from much less reliable evidence. The most reliable are those derived from either rather large differences within a single survey, particularly those wherein the Southern sample numbered 650 or more (that is where the national sample exceeded approximately 2,500), or statistically significant differences in the combined replies to several surveys posing the same or quite similar questions. But some influential Southern groups, like lawyers, small-town businessmen, and Jews, have been so small that even the combining of replies to a number of polls did not include a large enough sample for statistical treatment. In such cases the generalizations have necessarily been rather impressionistic, based on survey samples of as few as thirty individuals or on conversations with similarly small numbers of individuals in these categories. The samples, as has been noted, may not have been representative of all Southerners of similar description. Speculations have been ventured about the factors which have led to the apparent international behavior of individuals in such groups, based largely on the impressions from the interviews, often corroborated by the impressions of apparently thoughtful participant observers. Such impressionistic observations should be considered as working hypotheses pending systematic empirical studies of large comparative samples; most would probably be proven valid, in general, by such research, undoubtedly with amendments, reservations, ramifications, and changes in degree and tone.

PART I

Comparative Regional Trends in International Thought 1936–62

CHAPTER I

SOME GENERAL DEVELOPMENTS

AND

RELATIONSHIPS

Southerners as a group, like other Americans, became gradually more sophisticated about world affairs during the period 1936–62. By the latter date they were considerably more inclined than previously to be interested in this field, to have opinions about most of the important international issues facing their country, and to pay attention to international content in mass media, voluntary organizations, and informal conversations. They were more willing to see their country committed to long-term, costly, and active policies than in the late 1930's, although they disagreed among themselves and with Northerners about the relative emphasis to be given various international objectives and means of achieving them. Differences between the South and the rest of the country with respect to knowledge, interest, and exposure in world affairs decreased during this period, as they did in more basic economic, educational, cultural, social, attitudinal, and political spheres as well.

Critical Thought, Knowledge, and Interest

Nevertheless, significant differences continued in the early sixties between Southerners as a group and other Americans taken together. Southerners as a group were still less inclined in 1962 to think analytically, critically, or dispassionately about foreign affairs, to consider alternative interpretations of international developments, to be informed about foreign issues, to indicate interest in that field, and to venture

43

international opinions, particularly on more specialized problems, than all other Americans taken together. Elimination of Negroes from consideration on surveys usually narrowed these interregional differences considerably, but some unfortunate divergencies from national averages on the part of the white South were still sufficiently large to warrant concern.

Paucity of Sophisticated Cosmopolitans

The South of the early sixties was particularly underrepresented among the upper levels of knowledge, critical analysis, abstract thought, specialization, and general sophistication in world affairs. Staffs of national agencies interested in organizing serious discussions of international phenomena and otherwise stimulating dispassionate thought and consideration of alternative interpretations have experienced major frustrations in finding such individuals everywhere, but most with national experience feel the task has been least difficult in the Northeast, then the Far West, third the Midwest, fourth the Plains States and Rocky Mountain region, and typically most trying in the South. As Part II will demonstrate, such thoughtful individuals have tended more in the South than in the country generally to be concentrated in a relatively few segments of society.

Survey after survey has documented these impressions. The more specific or less generally known the information about foreign societies, international issues or organizations, and personalities engaged in diplomatic concerns, the smaller the proportion of Southerners among the total number of interviewees in the national sample venturing the correct information. When queried about their opinions on international problems or American foreign policies, Southerners have usually been significantly more inclined than other Americans taken as a group to say they have no opinion, they do not know, they are undecided or something equivalent. Interregional differences have been smallest, sometimes nonexistent, on very general questions which have demanded little knowledge or specialized attention or have been closely linked to such personal interests as the likelihood of peace or war, the need for peacetime conscription, advisability of higher taxes for foreign aid or national defense, or whether we should admit more or certain kinds of immigrants. But even on such general questions as whether we should take a more active or less active part in world affairs, Southerners have been less inclined to venture views and more apt to say they have no opinion, or the like, than other regional groups. Comparable results have been evident in surveys dealing with stated interest in international matters of varying levels of public prominence or complexity, and Southerners have been less inclined than other citizens to discuss world affairs either informally among themselves or, especially, within voluntary organizations.[1]

Exposure to International Information and Analysis

Studies of audiences for analysis, discussion, information, and interpretation of world developments in mass media lead to similar conclusions. The more specialized, analytical, critical, or abstract the content of the national medium, the smaller the proportion of Southerners in the total readership or audience. Only about one percent of the non-Southern adult population in 1956–59 read regularly or frequently about world issues in the better analytical, relatively profound, semi-popular periodicals, such as the New York *Times* (Sunday edition), *Christian Science Monitor*, *Harper's*, *Atlantic*, *New Republic*, *Current History*, *The Headline Series*, and *Foreign Affairs*, but the percentage in the South was approximately two fifths that figure.[2] In the late 1930's the Southern proportion was about a quarter of the Northern one. Residents of the Deep South—Arkansas, Mississippi, Alabama, Georgia, Louisiana, and South Carolina—were in the late fifties about one-quarter as likely to read such fare in *Harper's* or the *Atlantic* as New Englanders and one-half as inclined to do so as Midwesterners.[3] The more liberal or radical the point of view of the critical periodical, the less the proportion of Southerners among the total readership—interregional differences have been even greater for *The Reporter* and, particularly, the *Nation*.[4]

On a lower level of abstraction, analysis, and general sophistication, Southerners who read international coverage in the news magazines— *Time*, *Newsweek*, and *U.S. News and World Report*—constituted a larger fraction of the total national readership in the late 1950's than

1 Survey Research Center (SRC) study of June–August, 1946 (1,177); NORC 148, 2/20/47 (1,239); and NORC 303, 6/29/51 (1,300).

2 SRC survey of March–April, 1957 (1,919); Harpers-Atlantic Sales, Inc., "Audience Characteristics: *Harper's Magazine* and the *Atlantic*," July, 1958; the *New Yorker* Magazine, Inc., "*The New Yorker*: Character of Readers," 1957; unpublished data provided by Gilbert Harrison, publisher of *The New Republic;* and Alfred O. Hero, Jr., *Mass Media and World Affairs* (Boston: World Peace Foundation, 1959), 59–62.

3 Harpers-Atlantic Sales, Inc., "Audience Characteristics"; and Hero, *Mass Media and World Affairs*, 60.

4 Elmo Roper and Associates, "Some People are More Equal than Others" (A Study of Readers of the *Reporter*), 1956; an unpublished survey of readers of the *Nation*, 1953, furnished by the publisher, George C. Kirstein; and Hero, *Mass Media and World Affairs*, 60.

was the case for the rather high-brow publications mentioned above. Southerners were approximately three-fifths as inclined as other American adults to consume such international material in newsmagazines.[5] Again, the more conservative the newsmagazine, particularly on the race question, the larger the fraction of Southerners in the national readership (see pp. 425–27). An average issue of *Time*, a *bête noire* for many segregationists (see p. 426), was read in 1958 by 11 percent of adult Westerners, 8 percent of Northeasterners, 8 percent of Midwesterners, but only 4 percent of Southerners.[6] The figure for *Time* was even lower in the Deep South (Florida excepted). On the other hand, the proportion of readers of *U.S. News and World Report* approximated the national average of circulation per unit of population of that periodical in 1961.[7] Magazines composed of more pictures and less printed material on foreign affairs, such as *Life*, *Look*, and the *Saturday Evening Post* (to a lesser extent) reached still larger numbers of Southerners with international information and interpretation; the proportion of adults among readers of a given issue was closer in 1957–60 to the national average than was the case for the combination of *Time*, *Newsweek*, and *U.S. News and World Report*.[8]

Local newspapers, radio in earlier years, and television in the last decade or so have brought international events to the attention of much larger numbers of Southerners than the total of all national periodicals, books, and other publications (most of whose readers also follow world affairs in newspapers and electronic media). Southerners approach national averages more closely with respect to readership of foreign affairs in the local press than in magazines and sophisticated national newspapers. Nevertheless, Southerners were at least somewhat less inclined than other Americans to read a daily paper as late as 1957.[9] They have lagged behind the rest of the country more with respect to

5 Hero, *Mass Media and World Affairs*, 69–70; Research Company of America, "A Nationwide Survey of *Newsweek* Subscriber Families," 1957; Dun and Bradstreet, Inc., "A Sample Census of *Time* Subscriber Families," 1955; study performed for *Look* by Alfred Politz Research, Inc., comparing *Time*, *Look*, *Life*, and *Saturday Evening Post* readers; SRC survey of March–April, 1957 (1,919); Alfred Politz Research, Inc., "The Audiences of Nine Magazines," 1958; NORC poll of 1956; and *U.S. News and World Report*, "Subscriber Study," 1958.

6 Politz Research, "The Audiences of Nine Magazines."

7 From circulation figures furnished by the publisher.

8 Hero, *Mass Media and World Affairs*, 76–77; Alfred Politz Research, Inc., "The Readers of *The Saturday Evening Post*," 1957; retabulations of data on readership of *Saturday Evening Post* articles dealing with world affairs in the files of the *Saturday Evening Post*; and Politz Research "The Audiences of Nine Magazines."

9 Harry Estill Moore, "Mass Communications in the South," *Social Forces*, XXIX (1951), 365–76; and Survey Research Center, "The Public Impact of Science in the Mass Media" (Mimeographed report, 1958), 10.

reading available foreign news in whatever papers they did read,[10] particularly, to reading editorials and columnists in the international field [11] and to keeping up with foreign matters in more than one paper.[12] They have relied somewhat less than Northerners on newspapers and more on television and radio for information and opinion on foreign policy matters,[13] and a smaller fraction of them than of inhabitants of the rest of the country combined have wanted an increase in foreign content in their papers at the expense of local coverage, sports, comics, or other material.[14]

Television has been more responsible for expansion of contacts of the Southern masses with the world than any other impersonal medium, and perhaps than all other mass media combined. Network and local newscasts dealing in part with international events have reached millions of Southerners who only infrequently read about these developments. Television programs on international matters have also engaged the attention of most of the audiences for similar material in print. Interregional differences still persisted in 1958–60 for most network newscasts, but they were smaller still than those for readership of world news in the local press and for some programs differences disappeared entirely.[15] Due to their lesser exposure to printed matter on world affairs, Southerners have been more dependent on television than other Americans, on the average, for international information and ideas.[16]

Whatever little exposure to analytical and interpretive approaches to world affairs has taken place among the Southern rank and file has been predominantly through television. Some news network telecasts have included interpretation of sorts, but the networks and local Southern

10 SRC surveys of June–August, 1946 (1,177), and March–April, 1957 (1,919).

11 Wilbur Schramm, "The Nature of News," in Schramm (ed.), *Mass Communications* (Urbana: University of Illinois Press, 1949), 297. Schramm found in the late 1940's that only 23 percent of Southern women read editorials and/or columnists regularly or frequently and that most of them lived in suburbs or cities. In New England, 35 percent of the women read editorials, and in the Middle Atlantic states, 26 percent. The figures for men of these three regions were 38 percent, 52 percent, and 52 percent, respectively. These figures are, of course, optimistic for reading of editorials on international affairs, since only a minority of editorials in most Southern (and probably Northern) papers are devoted to this field and more Americans have been found to read editorials on local than on international events and problems. These differences have probably decreased since, but they were large enough to indicate that some differences undoubtedly still persist.

12 SRC, "The Public Impact of Science in the Mass Media," 20.

13 NORC 393, 9/13/56 (1,263).

14 NORC 235, 7/10/45 (2,572); AIPO 511, 1/29/53 (1,599); and SRC survey of March–April, 1957 (1,919).

15 From data provided by Pulse, Inc., and the audience research departments of NBC and CBS for the period 1958–60.

16 NORC 393, 9/13/56 (1,263); and SRC survey of March–April, 1957 (1,919).

stations have telecasted increasing numbers of critical examinations of international phenomena during peak viewing hours in the evening after supper. Moreover, most of these programs have presented considerably more liberal or internationalist views on world phenomena than most of the Southern newspaper editorials and other local sources in recent years. Programs like "Meet the Press" and the "President's Press Conference" have brought masses of Southerners, including Negroes, into relatively personal rapport with national and international figures discussing foreign relations. They have also supplemented and ramified the thinking of the better-read Southern minority.

However, attracting audiences as they have disproportionately from among the better educated and more internationally interested and informed, the programs with the more penetrating examinations of international questions like "CBS Reports," "NBC News Special," "The Face of Red China," "Behind the News," "The Open Mind," "The World of Ideas," and "Outlook" in the period 1958–60 reached on the average smaller fractions of Southerners than of Northerners. As in other media, such programs employing abstract ideas, concepts, and critical approaches attracted significantly smaller proportions of Southerners than of Americans generally. Typically about two-thirds the Northern percentage viewed these programs in the South, but they involved the attention of many everywhere who were unlikely to read comparable fare.[17]

Quality interpretive telecasts would have reached many more millions in the South had they been carried by more local stations when offered by national networks. Lack of stringent analyses of world affairs on FM radio and educational television stations in the region has also entailed unfortunate results. Audience studies in the South and elsewhere have indicated that attention to critical international discussions on noncommercial television has been disproportionately concentrated among the better educated, more intellectually alert, and generally cosmopolitan minority.[18] These programs have tended, however, to

17 From data provided by Pulse, CBS, and NBC.
18 Wilbur Schramm, Jack Lyle, and Ithiel de Sola Pool, *The People Look at Educational Television* (Palo Alto: Stanford University Press, 1963); "'Great Decisions' Telephone Survey Conducted in Greater Boston" (Mimeographed report at Survey and Research Service, Cambridge, Mass., 1959); Station Reports, A. C. Nielsen Co., to WGBH Channel 2 TV (Boston) 1958 and 1960; Wilbur Schramm, "The Audience for Educational Television in the San Francisco Area," in Ryland W. Crary (ed.), *The Audience for Educational Television* (Ann Arbor: Educational TV and Radio Center, 1957); Richard I. Evans, "An Analysis of Some Demographic and Psychological Characteristics of an Educational Television Audience," in Crary (ed.) *ibid.*; Kent Geiger and Robert Sokol, "Educational TV in

broaden the sensitivity and understanding of this relatively interested, better-read minority, and some more nearly typical Southerners have tuned in at least now and then in the relatively few areas where serious discussions of foreign relations have been available.

Interrelationships of Analysis, Knowledge, and Interest

The small minority of Southerners, like other Americans, who have approached the major international challenges to their country in relatively rational, dispassionate, and critical ways and who have made atypical attempts to compare their ideas with general facts and interpretations available in the best local paper, some television programs, and perhaps a national news magazine if not a more analytical national periodical have almost invariably been among the best informed 5 percent or so of American adults. They have also been, obviously, among the most interested of the citizenry in foreign affairs and in public questions generally.

However, the reverse has not necessarily been the case either in the South or outside. The relatively informed and interested have been several times more numerous than those manifesting a relatively analytical stance toward world developments. Some have been particularly interested in and knowledgeable on matters of some direct economic interest to them, like imports from abroad, but their views were often far from dispassionate, critical evaluations of alternative interpretations and lines of public action. Of the 10 percent or so who have been most interested and have possessed the most information about foreign relations, more than not seemed relatively rigidly attached to their particular views in this field; much of what they have known has been selectively gathered, perceived, and remembered to reinforce their thinking rather than to help them evaluate their ideas and, possibly, modify them. Whether or not more interested and informed Southerners have been more inclined to fit this description than Northerners of similar levels of interest and knowledge is difficult to determine—perhaps this has been the state of affairs everywhere.

Furthermore, each of these—analysis, knowledge, and interest—has tended to be a rather general factor. A dispassionate weighing of facts

---

Boston" (MS at Boston University, 1958); J. Stacy Adams, "An Exploratory Study of Viewers and Non-Viewers of Educational Television," in Crary (ed.) *The Audience for Educational Television*; Robert Sokol, "The Popularity of Educational Television in a Suburban Community," Report to the President of the National Television and Radio Center, 1959, pp. 45–47; and B. H. Westley, *Attitudes Toward Educational Television* (University of Wisconsin TV Laboratory, Bulletin 10, [Madison, 1958]), 153–55.

and points of view in international affairs seems typically part of an overall posture toward most social and public issues and apparently toward oneself and one's environment generally. Thus, Southerners with such attitudes have tended to read not only the international discussions in such periodicals as *Harper's, Atlantic*, the New York *Times* (Sunday edition), and *The Reporter* but also the discussions in these and other sources on domestic problems, the arts, and education, and to listen to serious music as well as to manifest other sophisticated tastes and ideas.[19] Even the more thoughtful have had their dogmatic *idées fixes* on some international (and other) issues, their rather unbalanced emotional biases, but by and large they tended to be rather analytical about most of the issues facing their country abroad.

Knowledge and interest have been less general factors; as previously observed, some have been interested and informed in only a few fields of world affairs. However, Southerners (and other Americans) who have been familiar with virtually any one issue of world affairs have been much more likely than those unfamiliar with it to be knowledgeable about others, even though the content may have varied widely. For instance, those who have provided correct answers to survey questions about foreign aid have been relatively informed about international trade, international organization, defense alliances, intercultural exchange, and so on. They have also for the most part been familiar with most important domestic issues.

The author had only rather limited direct measures of interest, but few have been informed about a subject if they have not been relatively interested. Therefore the same generalizations seem to apply to interest —with some exceptions, Southerners who have been relatively interested and alert in any major sphere of foreign policy have, for the most part, tended to be among the more concerned and attentive in most others as well.[20]

Some Attitude Patterns

Information, Interest, and Opinions

Some of the best informed and most sophisticated ultraconservatives on world affairs lived in the South in 1962—individuals who read and

---

19 From a retabulation of replies to a survey of readers of *Harper's* and the *Atlantic*, 1958, on file at Harpers-Atlantic Sales, Inc.; and a retabulation of leisure activities of readers of critical magazines among Southern residents in a sample of 10,000 college graduates studied by the Bureau of Applied Social Research in 1947.
20 See, for instance, NORC 162, 3/23/48 (1,300).

usually agreed with international views in such publications as the *National Review*, the Charleston *News and Courier*, and the less conservative *U.S. News and World Report*. The proportion of Southerners relatively well informed about an issue (and interested in it) who favored relatively conservative or relatively liberal or internationalist policies toward it has fluctuated over the years, depending on the overall world climate at the time and the details of the issue. These ratios of Southerners favoring relatively conservative to relatively liberal lines of action have also varied from one issue to another during the same periods.

But on most issues during most periods since 1936 Southerners favoring internationally cooperative, relatively liberal, or internationalist policy on a given problem have been disproportionately among the better informed about that, and usually other, international phenomena. Repeatedly, Southerners who have said they were relatively interested in world affairs or in some aspect of it on which they were queried, or who replied correctly to tests of information, have been more inclined, usually by relatively large margins, than those who said they are uninterested or relatively little interested or who have been unable to provide correct information, to feel we should take a rather active part in most spheres of international relations.

Thus, in the late 1940's and early 1950's Southerners who were informed about the Truman Doctrine, Marshall Plan, or NATO Pact were considerably more inclined to approve of these commitments and their expense than those who were less informed.[21] In the mid-fifties Southerners who could describe the purposes of UNESCO had more favorable impressions of its work than those who could not.[22] Southerners who had heard or read anything of United States arms-control proposals in the late 1950's were more inclined to favor them, once explained, than those who had not.[23] Throughout the postwar period, those who knew what a tariff is, could describe the reciprocal trade program, or otherwise manifested some knowledge about international trade were more inclined than those who were uninformed on these topics to favor more liberal trade policies.[24] Congressman Otto Passman of Monroe, Louisiana, in 1959–62 was an arch opponent of foreign

21 For instance, AIPO 392, 3/12/47 (2,884); NORC 149, 4/3/47 (1,307); NORC 154, 12/4/47 (1,293); AIPO 404, 9/10/47 (3,057); AIPO 406, 10/22/47 (2,932); AIPO 436, 1/20/49 (3,213); and NORC 166, 6/1/49 (1,300).
22 NORC 374, 8/4/55 (1,262).
23 NORC 351, 1/21/54 (1,300); and NORC 398, 10/25/56 (1,295).
24 AIPO 417, 4/21/48 (3,165); NORC 332, 10/15/52 (1,291); AIPO 526, 1/26/54 (1,493); and AIPO 540, 11/30/54 (1,473).

aid despite the fact that he was informed in great detail about it, and there were and are other Southerners like him. But most Southerners who have opposed economic assistance to underdeveloped recipients or advocated sharp reduction have been less informed about the countries receiving it, about the program itself, and about foreign affairs generally than have most of those who favored these programs at more or less the orders of magnitude requested by Presidents Eisenhower and Kennedy. The degree of correlation between knowledge and relatively liberal or internationalist opinion varied in the early 1960's with the issue, but statistically significant relationships existed for the major questions—economic and technical assistance; alliance with Western Europe, Latin America, Nationalist China, and Japan; intercultural programs; immigration policy; world trade; and international organization. Similar relationships between information and liberal opinions were apparent in the rest of America as well.

Moreover, level of knowledge and, to a lesser extent, interest in world affairs have been positively associated with degree of consistency among the individual's opinions. Relatively logical, systematic interconnection of views has been far from inevitable among the more interested and better informed, but the nearly rational adjustment of one's opinion on one issue to those one holds on others has been more prevalent among them than among less knowledgeable colleagues. As will be observed later, views on some international issues have been more closely related to one's thinking on some other international questions than others, and many better informed Southerners have harbored attitudes about some issues of foreign relations relatively inconsistent with their thinking on most others. In general, the less informed and interested the Southerner (or other citizen) has been in world developments the more were his opinions apt to be vague, diffuse, little differentiated, and relatively contradictory of one another. Since the proportion of better informed has been smaller in the South than elsewhere, it seems probable that inconsistency of international opinions has been more prevalent there than in the rest of the country taken as a unit.

Internationalism, Isolationism, and Neo-Isolationism

Given that the better informed have been more inclined to favor active international cooperation in most spheres than the less informed, it is not surprising to find that Southerners who have held relatively liberal, internationally cooperative, or activist opinions in several fields of world affairs have been likely to harbor more or less liberal or activist views in most other international spheres as well. Those who have felt we should withdraw from international commitments in some major spheres of international relations have been more inclined than others to favor reduction of involvements in other foreign matters. These are statistical statements with many exceptions, depending on the issues under consideration, the international climate at the moment, and the group or individual in question in the South. Moreover, intercorrelations have been higher among some international opinions and lower among others, again depending on the specific perceived attributes of the international matters in question at the moment.

Thus, Southerners who have told survey interviewers that they thought the United States should take an active part in world affairs or who have considered themselves internationalists have been much more inclined than those who suggested that we take a less active part or who accepted the label "isolationist" to feel in the prewar era that we should have joined the League of Nations, that tariffs and other obstacles to trade should be reduced, that restrictions on sending aid to the enemies of the Axis should be liberalized, that defeat of the Allies would pose a vital threat to the United States, that Lend-Lease and peacetime conscription were good ideas, and that most of President Roosevelt's other suggestions for international involvement should be implemented.

Likewise, during the period 1947–52 Southerners, as well as other Americans, who favored the Truman Doctrine were much more likely than those who did not to support the Marshall Plan and economic aid to Japan, reduction of import restrictions, maintenance of troops and bases overseas, active collaboration in the U.N. and other international bodies, and most other major programs of international involvement advocated by the Truman Administration. Those who favored the Marshall Plan in 1949–52 also were very likely to favor ratification of the NATO Pact and, to a lesser extent, arms aid to Western Europe. Southerners who favored any one of these programs were more inclined than those who opposed them to approve of technical assistance suggested by President Truman in Point Four of his 1949 inaugural address. As in the earlier period, correlations were far from perfect, but they were all in the expected directions. Degree of association among attitudes on diverse issues varied with the issue at the time and how the questions were worded. Some attitudes, such as support of the Marshall Plan, were more predictive of favorableness to most other international involvements suggested by the President than were others, such as advocacy of expanded trade. Thinking on immigration was only rather weakly connected with attitudes on foreign aid, trade, and world organization, although Southerners who were willing to admit more European refugees in the period 1947–56 were somewhat more inclined than those opposed to admittance to favor these other involvements.

By the late 1950's and the early 1960's associations among opinions on different international questions had changed in some respects, but it was still possible to speak in terms of some Southerners being more internationalist than others, with the understanding that some international attitudes were more closely associated with one another than others and that many individuals diverged from such patterns or syndromes of attitudes.

In recent years those Southerners who have favored continuation of capital assistance to underdeveloped countries at approximately the orders of magnitude requested of the Congress by Presidents Eisenhower and Kennedy have been very likely to support most other general international commitments proposed by their President. As has been true for virtually all issues, intercorrelations have varied with how the interviewer's question was phrased; but the vast majority of Southerners who agreed with the President's proposed economic aid programs against threatened cuts by the Congress have also favored technical assistance, intercultural exchanges (even with the Soviet bloc), and active programs of collective security with Western Europe, especially through NATO. Supporters of economic assistance among the interviewees also felt that independence for most remaining colonial dependencies, including the Portuguese ones in Africa, is virtually inevitable, and they were for the most part critical of Portuguese policies which assumed the opposite. Liberal trade views were not so predictive, but the great majority among the interviewees who favored capital assistance to underdeveloped countries at roughly current levels felt we should expand trade, even if some of the increased imports would compete with American products. The sending of arms aid to less-developed countries, with the exception of those like Viet Nam under direct attack, was less popular. Some who favored economic assistance felt our military assistance should be seriously reconsidered with a view to reducing it substantially; however, few would eliminate it entirely. Almost no Southerners who supported foreign capital aid in 1959–62 would withdraw from the U.N., and few would reduce the emphasis we gave that organization during this period, although some would modify our policies there. Finally, with relatively few exceptions, pro-aiders felt we could admit more immigrants than was currently the practice, at least if we screened them for talent, training, democratic values, and other desirable characteristics. Few would restrict desirable immigrants to Europeans alone. Insofar as any one international opinion was predictive of internationally cooperative thinking in other foreign-policy fields, favorable views on foreign economic assistance have been in recent years the most valid.

On the other hand, support of technical or military assistance, especially the former, has not been nearly as conclusive an indicator of favor for most other programs advanced by our Presidents. Many who favored technical aid in 1959–62 were critical of more expensive capital aid, at least at its magnitude in recent years. Nor was opinion on technical assistance as good a predictor of views on international trade, although opponents of technical assistance tended more than those who were favorable to stress protection of American plants and jobs. Protectionists for the most part would reduce foreign economic aid, and the more adamant of them would cut technical assistance as well. On the other hand, many Southerners who favored expanded trade, including imports, during this period felt we were "giving away too much" abroad, that our foreign economic relations should be put on more of a "business-like" basis, or the like (see pp. 176, 464). Southerners generally favorable to active United States collaboration in the U.N. with but few exceptions favored relatively vigorous policies in support of NATO (excluding a minuscule handful of Southerners with pacifist inclinations, see pp. 90–91), intercultural exchanges, and technical assistance. However, views on the U.N. were not very closely related with thinking on world trade.

Some Southern supporters of large national defense budgets accepted "Fortress America" thinking—they would withdraw from many of our foreign commitments and concentrate on defense of the Western Hemisphere and enforcement of the Monroe Doctrine. Backers of NATO as a major instrument of our foreign policy with few exceptions supported whatever major requests the President made for our own armed forces and, in a number of cases, even the larger defense budgets advocated by some Southern Congressmen against the smaller military programs suggested by the executive. Although most Southerners favorable to foreign aid supported close collaboration with other NATO members, many who were favorable to NATO would have reduced aid to backward lands. The relationship between support of NATO and opinion on trade was generally weak—most liberals on trade also favored a strong NATO, even if expensive to our treasury and manpower, but many protectionists favored a strong NATO as well.

In speaking of internationalist thinking over a period of time in the South, it must be borne in mind that policy orientations which would have been considered internationalist in the late 1930's were much more cautious about involvements abroad than those which would be thought internationalist in 1962. The Southern minority who proposed military alliance in 1936 with Britain and France such that attack against one would constitute attack against all were rather extreme internationalists in comparison with the vast majority of other Americans, even other Southerners. On the other hand, the Southerner who opposed this idea in 1962 was usually among the most isolationist minority in the country. To be considered internationalist in the 1960's required support of much wider, more profound, international commitments in many more spheres of world affairs than to be so considered prior to the Nazi attack on Poland.

Those Southerners who agreed in 1957–62 with the general philosophy of isolationists of the interwar period like Charles Lindbergh and Senators Burton K. Wheeler, Robert Reynolds, and William Borah had become a small minority of 8–15 percent. These isolationists would withdraw from the U.N., NATO, and other multilateral commitments, with the possible exception of those in the Western Hemisphere. A larger number (see p. 111) have been inclined to agree with some version of neo-isolationism: in purer form an emphasis on our own armed forces and perhaps those of Canada and on enforcement of the Monroe Doctrine coupled with withdrawal from commitments in Asia, Africa, and even Europe. A still larger number would stress defense of the Americas and alliance with Western Europe and de-emphasize collaboration with Asia and Africa.

Between these two groups—those who could be termed more or less internationalist and the other extreme which could be called relatively isolationist or neo-isolationist in terms of the issues of the late fifties and early sixties—was a continuum of Southerners who accepted to some extent some of the ideas from both groups, typically in attenuated or ramified forms and in various combinations. Intercorrelations of international opinions were strongest near the two extremes and relatively weak between. As noted previously, inconsistent, even rather mutually exclusive views were not infrequent, particularly among the majority of Southerners who were relatively little interested and poorly informed about world developments. Many of them had clear opinions, more or less intensively held, on only a few issues and had only rather diffuse inclinations on most. For instance, they might manifest relatively favorable general images of the U.N. and NATO, but have virtually no sentiments one way or the other about international trade.

The tendency of Americans with scant information and little interest to venture no opinions on survey queries in many fields of foreign affairs and the larger proportion of such individuals in the South than in the rest of the country pose difficult problems for those who would assess Southern international opinion. On the very general issues, such as whether or not we should stay in the U.N. or spend more money on defense, the problem tends to disappear since the proportion of "no opinions" on surveys has typically been small—less than a fifth of Southern adults. But on basic issues in international trade, aid to particular African or Asian countries, channeling of more aid through international agencies, and the like, as much as half the Southern adult population in recent years often ventured no opinions. The proportion who failed to express any attitudes decreased when Negroes were eliminated from the statistics, but Southern whites were still at least somewhat, and often a good deal, more inclined to say they had no views than were Northern whites in 1962. Sometimes the proportion of Southerners who were favorable to a given policy was smaller than that of Northerners; but likewise the proportion of Southerners who were unfavorable to the same policy might be smaller since larger fractions of Southerners than Northerners said they did not know, had no opinion, or the equivalent.

Thus, interpretation of the "no opinions" in the South is an important but frequently difficult matter. Since isolationist and neo-isolationist views have been much more prevalent among the poorly informed and relatively indifferent than among the more knowledgeable and interested, the inclination is to assume that Southerners (and other citizens) who offered no views or said they did not know have been more inclined than those with opinions to disapprove of most international commitments. Efforts to extract opinions from more indifferent and less informed interviewees on such issues as foreign aid, intercultural exchange, mutual security, and cooperation in the U.N. supported this observation—they were more inclined to feel these programs should be curtailed than were the interviewees who volunteered views under less social pressure. On the other hand, many Southerners (and perhaps other Americans) who have been among the most intently interested in trade restrictions have tended to be protectionists in recent years —they have feared being hurt economically by imports. The interviewees who offered no views on trade were inclined to be rather permissive on this issue—they would neither be upset nor particularly pleased by liberalization of tariffs, quotas, or other barriers.

A constant procedure was not followed in stating the results of surveys; sometimes the percentages of all Southerners who have agreed with a given policy were indicated, and, on other occasions, depending on the issue and other considerations, the percentages of those who offered opinions were noted. In other instances, percentages of Southerners who failed to offer any opinion were presented as an indication of lack of interest, ignorance, or apathy.

CHAPTER 2

IMMIGRATION,
INTERCULTURAL EXCHANGE,
AND FOREIGNERS

Southerners have long been less ethnically heterogeneous (except for the Negro) and less willing to associate with foreign people in this country than other Americans. Proportionately fewer Southerners than Northerners speak or understand any foreign language; they have seemed more than Northerners to feel that people of varied national, cultural, and religious backgrounds do not normally get along well together; and they have for the most part been proud of their role as the most "American" part of the nation. Suspicion of "furriners" and their ideas and ways has been widespread in the region for generations.

A Homogeneous Culture

Paucity of Foreign Elements

The South received few of the many immigrants who came to the United States after the Civil War; for instance, at the time of the 1910 census, only 2 percent of Southerners compared with 20 percent of Northerners had been born abroad. Historically, there were only a relative handful of better paying industrial jobs to attract immigrants, and few wished to compete with slaves and, later, with lower-class Negro and poor-white labor in agricultural pursuits in a region of high underemployment and unemployment where the standard of living was far below the national average. Moreover, a society with few cities and a white population tightly knit by blood, British origins, and rather homogeneous mores, among whom kinship and traditional social ties tended to define interpersonal relations and even occupational success, did not provide a receptive atmosphere for foreigners who spoke languages other than English. Furthermore, most of the relatively few inhabitants of foreign origins have been concentrated in a handful of port cities like New Orleans and, recently, in technologically advanced inland centers like Oak Ridge and Huntsville. Few ethnically diverse Northerners migrated South until about a generation ago, and most of them have likewise settled in a few cities, college towns, and advanced industrial locales.

Thus, in 1960, 5.4 percent of Americans generally had been born abroad and another 13.6 percent had at least one foreign-born parent. The minuscule, or nonexistent, proportions of foreign born and offspring of foreign born in the several rural, semirural, and small-town sample communities was mentioned earlier. But even metropolitan New Orleans, the Southern center which has in the past encompassed the widest diversity of ethnic groups, has received relatively few foreigners for several generations—only 2.1 percent of its population in 1960 was born abroad and 6 percent had a foreign-born parent, percentages well below the national average and several times smaller than was the case in most port cities or industrial centers of the North.

In at least one respect the absence of new Americans from the South worked for more balanced international behavior among Southern Congressmen than among a number of legislators from multiethnic Northern communities. Many of the latter were either themselves first or second generation Americans or were obliged to cater to identifications of immigrants with the "old country" and to their prejudices for or against various foreign nations important to our international interests. Thus, the Anglophobia of Irish-Americans tended to limit if not distort their Congressmen's behavior toward Britain. The presence of many voters of German extraction in the midwest probably was partly responsible for opposition among many midwestern Congressmen to intervention on the side of Britain and France against the Axis during the several years before our entry into World War II.[1] Southern Congressmen were not obliged to placate such biases and there were few ethnic influences and attachments to counter those of the predominantly Anglo-Saxon South favorable to the British and their cause.

1 Samuel Lubell, *Revolt of the Moderates* (New York: Harper and Bros., 1956), 80–83.

Lack of Experience with Foreign Habits and Ideas

But lack of associates bearing imprints of foreign cultures has meant much less contact among Southerners than among other Americans with heterogeneous thought and action. Although major tensions have been evident between different ethnic groups in Northern communities, urban Northerners of even low station have lived and worked next to people of diverse national backgrounds. Even in many Northern farming sections one or more ethnic minorities have lived side by side with old stock Americans. Northerners in close proximity to immigrants tended to develop gradually some understanding of, sensitivity to, and empathy with variegated customs, values, and attitudes. They learned a few foreign expressions and took into their families sons-in-law and daughters-in-law of different foreign origins. Successive generations introduced and integrated into Northern society a variety of ways of thought and action.

Most Southerners have experienced little of this intercultural contact. Although white Southerners have absorbed some of the hedonism and other attributes of local Negroes, by and large Negroes shed their African past and adopted the language, otherworldly religion, and much of the outward behavior of Southern whites. With the exception of former servicemen, many Southerners outside the few cities and southern Louisiana have never known anyone whose native language was not English. Many in Mountain, Plantation, and Hill counties have known virtually no Northerners, Catholics, Jews, or other native-born Americans of ethnic heritage other than Anglo-Saxon Southern white and Southern Negro. Many union locals are virtually composed exclusively of Southern-born Protestants whose ancestors have been Southern born for many generations.

This absence of intercultural experience is probably responsible to a considerable extent for the rather homogeneous thinking encountered on world affairs and some other public matters, particularly in rural and small-town locales with virtually no inhabitants of ancestry other than English, Scotch, and Scotch-Irish. The author has no comparable data on Northern rural and small-community settings, but experiences with world affairs programs in New England environments (few of which are any longer as solidly Anglo-Saxon as the Southern ones examined) create the strong impression that international opinions are significantly more diverse in the latter. Factors other than ethnic heterogeneity—such as higher education, longer proximity to dynamic urban centers, and absence of a race problem to stifle analysis and discussion [2]—help to account for this observation, but less contact with diverse cultural groups in the Southern communities is certainly one important source.

Southern communities which are more diverse culturally contain more variety of international opinion than those having less diversity, other factors being more or less equivalent. For instance, views regarded as strange in homogeneous Mountain, Plantation, and Hill counties seemed less odd to more ethnically heterogeneous inhabitants of Bayou Parish, also primarily rural and of low average education. The author could detect little nativistic dislike of foreigners in the latter, but such ethnocentricity was readily apparent in the former almost exclusively Anglo-Saxon settings.

In effect, the positive relationship between diversity of origins of population and heterogeneity of views on world questions means that larger, more complex cities encompass on the average wider diversity of opinion than smaller ones, port towns more than communities of equivalent population further inland, and urban places more than rural ones. Thus, ethnically diverse New Orleans contains a greater variety and subtlety of international orientations than more homogeneous Birmingham. New Orleanians of a given social role are more apt to have relatively close personal contacts with acquaintances and others whose thinking diverges from their own, and their thinking tends to be less dogmatic, more open to alternative interpretations, and more tolerant of ideological diversity than is the case for inhabitants of more ethnically homogeneous cities.[3] Likewise, inhabitants of small towns and even rural sections containing more varied national, ethnic, and religious groups along the Atlantic and Gulf Coasts and the shores of the lower Mississippi River seem considerably less rigid (and think of themselves as less so) in their opinions about public matters, including foreign affairs, and more aware of divergent thinking than is typically the case further inland.

Opposition to Immigration

Congressmen and New Americans

Southern Anglo-Saxons in the majority have wanted to preserve their homogeneous culture against further immigration. A major exception to the greater support for active international policies by Southern as

2   See Chapters 7, 9, and 11 within.
3   This observation is, of course, not due to ethnic composition alone. See pp. 61–67.

compared with Northern Congressmen prior to the mid-1950's was their more widespread opposition to admission of foreigners into this country.[4] Many Southern Congressmen have apparently felt that criticism of the South, particularly of its relations between the races, and "radicalism" in general in the North have been due in considerable measure to immigrant elements other than Anglo-Saxons. Senator Oscar W. Underwood, supporter of free trade, United States membership in the League of Nations, and most other internationalist propositions before the Congress, denounced "the Slav, the Iberic, and the Mongolian" who would change this country into a "South American civilization." [5] Senator Frank Gary of South Carolina commented that he would rather that "our uncultivated lands . . . forever lie fallow, and our water power go unharnessed to the sea, than that we should be overrun by a lot of aliens from Southern Europe." [6] During World War I the preponderant majority of Southern Democrats voted, as a means of reducing immigration, to override Woodrow Wilson's veto of a bill to institute rigorous educational tests.[7] Senator Benjamin "Pitchfork Ben" Tillman of South Carolina spoke of "the riff-raff of Europe . . . festering New York and other Eastern cities . . . committing all manner of crime . . . and debauching and debasing the ballot." [8] In 1921 only three Southern Congressmen voted against strongly restrictive immigration legislation.[9] A disproportionately large number of Southerners in the House of Representatives in 1937 voted (on two roll calls) to deport specified aliens who had entered this country illegally.[10] In 1941 a majority of Southerners voted against a bill which would have allowed a Jewish alien who had entered the United States illegally to remain rather than being sent back to a hostile country.[11] A large majority of Southern members of the House voted in 1945 against an amendment to the Nationality Act of 1940 to permit Americans who had acquired foreign citizenship through naturalization of their parents to return to the United States and become United States citizens outside the quota

4   Grassmuck, *Sectional Biases in Congress on Foreign Policy*, 16.
5   Paul Seabury, "The Waning of Southern Internationalism," 5.
6   Rowland T. Berthoff, "Southern Attitudes toward Immigration, 1865–1914," *Journal of Southern History*, XVII (1951), 352.
7   Seabury, "The Waning of Southern Internationalism," 6; and Francis B. Simkins, *Pitchfork Ben Tillman* (Baton Rouge: Louisiana State University Press, 1944), 517.
8   Simkins, *Pitchfork Ben Tillman*, 518.
9   Julius Turner, *Party and Constituency: Pressures on Congress* (Baltimore: Johns Hopkins University Press, 1951), 138.
10   Key, *Southern Politics in State and Nation*, 373.
11   *Ibid.*, 374–75.

system.[12] Whereas 73 percent of non-Southern members of the House voted for the Refugee Act of 1953, only 9 percent of Southerners did; 106 of the latter opposed this bill while only 11 supported it.[13]

Mass Nativism

No surveys of thinking on immigration before 1943 have come to the author's attention, but those since that date indicate that the majority of Southerners expressing views have opposed most of the major proposals in the last twenty years for relatively minor increases in the number of foreign immigrants allowed to enter this country. Incidentally, large minorities, and in some case majorities, of the residents in the Northeast, Midwest, Plains States, Rocky Mountain region, and Far West have held the same view. However, Southerners have been consistently more inclined than other regional groups to oppose immigration (with the major exception of British immigrants), regardless of the way in which the question was posed, the nationality or talents of the immigrants, and whether or not Negroes were included in the Southern sample.

Thus, at the height of World War II in 1943 when Nationalist China was an ally of the United States, only 30 percent of Southerners compared with 43 percent of other Americans (even 37 percent of Far Westerners, supposedly afflicted with widespread anti-Chinese prejudices) agreed that our laws should be changed to permit between 105 and 125 Chinese to immigrate to this country. A small majority of Southerners, but only a minority of Northerners, replying were opposed to this very minor liberalization of Chinese exclusion.[14] In September, 1944, Southerners more than other citizens felt we should stop Germans, Japanese, Mexicans, Chinese, Swedes, and Russians from immigrating here after the war.[15] In August, 1946, only 21 percent in the South as compared with 28 percent of the rest of the country were willing to let some of the "800,000 homeless people in Europe" come to this country.[16] During the next six years when the issue was salient, replys to similar questions regarding displaced persons from Europe indicated consistently greater Southern than Northern opposition to letting many of them settle in this country; at no time did a Southern majority—white or colored—react in the affirmative.[17]

12 *Ibid.*, 375.   13 Lerche, *The Uncertain South*, 103.
14 AIPO 305, 10/26/43 (3,000); see also AIPO 301, 8/24/43 (3,002).
15 NORC 228, September, 1944 (2,549).
16 NORC 243, 8/21/46 (1,286).
17 AIPO 377, 8/28/46 (3,163); AIPO 395, 4/23/47 (3,142); NORC 157, 4/22/48 (1,280); AIPO 444, 6/30/49 (2,826); NORC 323, 4/22/52 (1,250); NORC 327, 6/30/52 (1,285); and NORC 333, 11/17/52 (1,291).

Even with the increasing tensions of the cold war due to the invasion of South Korea, the formation of NATO, and other events, majorities of Southerners continued to oppose allowing Continental Europeans to come here. Asked in late 1952 whether they approved the then current proposal to admit 300,000 European immigrants over the forthcoming three years, 71 percent of Southerners, 59 percent of Northeasterners, 66 percent of Midwesterners, and 54 percent of Westerners disapproved; only 21 percent in the South compared with 38 percent in the Northeast, 28 percent in the Midwest, and 40 percent in the West approved.[18] Queried at the same time about the proposal to permit people who had escaped from East European Communist countries to enter this country and become citizens, 38 percent of Southerners, compared with 58 percent of Northeasterners, 56 percent of Midwesterners, and 52 percent of Westerners, approved; the respective percentages disapproving were 51, 38, 38, and 39.[19] It might be supposed that most Southerners would have been willing to admit a significant number of refugees from Hungary shortly after the suppression of their revolution by the Soviet army in late 1956. But such was not the case; a month after the entry of Soviet tanks into Budapest, only 39 percent of Southerners, compared with 58 percent of Northeasterners, 57 percent of Midwesterners, and 63 percent of Westerners, supported President Eisenhower's proposal that the laws of the country be changed to make it easier for these refugees to enter our frontiers. Only in the South did more oppose than approve this suggestion.[20] During the two years following the Hungarian revolution, the size of the minority in the South who favored the admission of more of its refugees declined; by September, 1957, a majority of Southerners, significantly more than among other regional groups, opposed the idea of the law being changed to permit those who had come here earlier to stay.[21]

But most of these foreigners, if admitted, would settle in Northern cities rather than in the South. They would not compete directly with Southerners for their jobs or appear physically in many communities of the South, judging from the past habits of immigrants in America. Supposedly traditional Southern hospitality apparently did not extend to East European refugees; only 18 percent of Southerners, compared with 28 percent of other citizens in 1948, favored their state's taking "10,000 of these refugees." [22] In late 1956, only 38 percent of South-

18 NORC 333, 11/17/52 (1,291).   19 *Ibid.*
20 AIPO 575, 11/20/56 (1,502).
21 NORC 401, 12/28/56 (1,232); AIPO 589, 9/17/57 (1,530); and AIPO 602, 7/28/58 (1,621).
22 AIPO 410, 12/30/47 (3,002).

erners (30 percent of Deep Southerners), compared with 56 percent of Northeasterners, 49 percent of Midwesterners, and 60 percent of Westerners, said they would be willing to have one or more Hungarian refugees stay in their home a few months.[23]

As has been the case in the rest of the country, Southerners in small towns and rural sections, especially on farms, have been more opposed than urban Southerners to liberalization of immigration regardless of how the questions were posed. The tendency of segregationists to link racial unrest with foreign-born agitators is evident in the fact that white supremacist thinking and opposition to immigration have tended to go together.[24] Moreover, although Negroes have tended to be more conservative than whites on most aspects of world affairs not directly connected with race relations and Africa, the ratio of Negroes approving to those disapproving of immigration proposals has been as large or slightly larger than among white Southerners.[25] American Jews generally, and judging from interviews in 1959–62, very probably Jews in the South as well, have been more favorable than most Americans to expanded immigration, including the entry of non-Jews. Catholics in the South have been somewhat more favorable, but differences between them and Protestants have been small.[26] The less educated the Southerner has been and the lower his social, occupational, and economic status, the more inclined has he been to oppose increased immigration.

Other generalizations about the international thinking of both those Southerners who opposed and those who favored these limited increases in immigration can be made. Most of the Southern minority who favored admission of ten thousand European displaced persons to their states in early 1948 also supported the Marshall Plan, although a considerable fraction who felt the latter was a good idea were against this proposed immigration. Most Southern opponents of the European Recovery Program were also opponents of liberalization of immigration

23 AIPO 575, 11/20/56 (1,502).   24 AIPO 589, 9/17/57 (1,530).

25 As concerning most questions about public affairs, Southern Negroes have been much more inclined than Southern whites to say they do not know, are undecided, or have no opinion. The hypothesis drawn from this study is that opposition to immigration has probably increased somewhat among whites as racial tension has increased since the last questions regarding immigration were posed in 1957, while views on this subject among Negroes either have remained about the same or have become more favorable.

26 Samples have been too small for statistical significance of differences at the 10 percent level between groups within the South. However, differences in most cases were in the directions stated, and the combining of similar questions on NORC 243, 8/21/46 (1,286); NORC 333, 11/17/52 (1,291); AIPO 377, 8/28/46 (3,163); AIPO 395, 4/23/47 (3,142); and AIPO 444, 6/30/49 (2,826), did produce a difference statistically significant at less than the 10 percent level.

for European refugees.[27] By the early 1950's the Southern minority who approved of the proposed admission of 300,000 European refugees into this country over a three-year period was significantly more inclined than those who disapproved to feel we could count on Britain, France, and Germany, and even India, to cooperate with us in world affairs, to be critical of French handling of her colonies and overseas dependencies, and to be favorable to foreign aid. But there was little connection between expectation of another world war and making sacrifices for more defense on the one hand and sentiments about European immigration on the other.[28] Southerners who opposed President Eisenhower's request to Congress in 1953 that 200,000 East Europeans be admitted were more prone to approve of the provisions of the proposed Bricker Amendment than those who felt such a change in the immigration rules would be desirable. On the other hand, a considerable minority of those opposed to this migration were also critical of the Bricker idea.[29] Most of the Southern minority who favored the eventuality of some European immigrants living near them opposed recognition of Communist China in 1955, but most of the few Southerners who approved of the latter were among those who were relatively liberal on immigration.[30] By early 1957, the minority of Southerners who supported the admission of more Hungarian refugees than were being allowed to enter at the time were more apt than those who felt we were admitting too many to feel that foreign aid to underdeveloped countries was in the national interest, but many Southerners who were more conservative than this on admission of refugees were still basically favorable to foreign aid at that time.[31] Virtually all Southerners who wished the laws amended so that most of those Hungarian refugees who were in the country nine months later could remain here permanently approved of the U.N. and United States membership therein; the minority of Southerners who opposed the U.N. usually wanted to deport most of these refugees.[32] As one would surmise, the most important single argument given by Southerners and Northerners alike against these limited admissions to our country was that they would include too many spies, Communists, "radicals," "agitators," and the like. Relatively few Southerners in late 1956 mentioned unemployment as their principal concern.[33]

Thus, Southerners who supported these rather minor proposed liber-

---

27 AIPO 410, 12/30/47 (3,000).   28 NORC 323, 4/22/52 (1,250).
29 AIPO 518, 7/23/53 (1,532).   30 AIPO 547, May, 1955 (1,503).
31 NORC 401, 12/28/56 (1,232).   32 AIPO 586, 9/17/57 (1,530).
33 AIPO 575, 11/20/56 (1,502).

alizations of immigration restrictions were for the most part among those more inclined to favor international collaboration and involvement in a number of spheres; however, many Southerners who went along with the major policies of our Presidents in defense, collective security, trade, aid to Western Europe, and international organization opposed admission of additional immigrants, even from Continental Europe.

As one would suppose from these statistical findings, those relatively liberal on immigration were more likely than those opposed to these migrations to have read books other than the Bible recently,[34] to like classical music,[35] and to consider themselves "liberals" rather than "conservatives" in politics.[36]

International Exchange of Persons and Intercultural Collaboration

Southerners have, on the whole, been more willing to go along with active programs in intercultural relations sponsored by our federal government than with expanded immigration. However, nativism, ethnic homogeneity, fear of espionage and subversion, fiscal conservatism about governmental expenditures on foreign programs other than defense and alliances, and perhaps several other factors have resulted in significantly less enthusiasm among Southerners than among other Americans for exchanges of persons and other intercultural cooperation.

For example, only 29 percent of Southerners compared with 35 percent of Northeasterners, 37 percent of Midwesterners, and 33 percent of Westerners in late 1946 approved of the proposal to bring Germans and Japanese who were not Nazis or fascists to this country "to see how democracy works here." Sixty percent of Southerners opposed the idea of bringing either Germans, or (especially) Japanese, or (often) both to this country—a significantly larger percentage than in the country generally.[37]

In the fall of 1951, 59 percent of Senator Fulbright's fellow Southerners, compared with 68 percent of other Americans, approved of "our government bringing people from other countries to study here or to observe our way of life . . . [and] . . . sending a number of Americans abroad to study and to tell about America"; 22 percent of the former, compared with 19 percent of the latter, disapproved.[38] In June,

34 *Ibid.*
35 AIPO 589, 9/17/57 (1,530).
36 AIPO 547, May, 1955 (1,503).
37 NORC 146, 11/15/46 (1,300).
38 NORC 313, 10/21/51 (1,237).

1956, 55 percent of Southerners, compared with 60 percent of other citizens, thought it a "good idea" that "U.S. school teachers who so desire be sent at government expense to various nations in the summer to study and write about these nations"; 33 percent of the former compared with 31 percent of the latter considered it a "bad idea." However, on the same survey Southerners were more opposed when the question was asked whether our government should also finance comparable foreign teachers to come, study, and write here. The difference between the South and the North was somewhat wider than for sending American teachers abroad: 43 percent of Southerners favored and 45 percent opposed financing the visit of foreign teachers here, compared with 50 percent in favor and 43 percent opposed in the North.[39]

Moreover, as was apparently true concerning other aspects of exchanges of persons, opposition to bringing foreign teachers here rose and approval declined as desegregation pressures mounted in the South; meanwhile, opposition seemed to decline and approval to increase somewhat in the North during the same period. For instance, in the summer of 1960 only 37 percent of Southerners believed it was a good idea to bring foreign teachers here "at our expense in order to get a better understanding of our country," whereas 51 percent felt it a poor one. On the other hand, in the Northeast 56 percent favored this idea, while 37 percent opposed it; in the Midwest the respective figures were 55 percent and 37 percent, and in the West 60 percent and 33 percent. Differences between the Deep South and the rest of the country were even larger, as seems typically the case in international exchanges of persons and intercultural relations. The border states and upper South have been more favorable to these programs than the Deep South. As in 1956, Southerners were more favorable to sending Americans abroad than to bringing foreigners here, whereas the reverse was true in the North.[40]

Southerners have likewise been less favorable to intercultural projects wherein Americans would be obliged to collaborate in intimate face-to-face relations with foreigners on an equal status basis. For instance, asked in May, 1949, and again in January, 1950, if the United States should take the lead in establishing a University of the World with specially qualified students of all nations permitted to attend free, only

---

39 AIPO 566, 6/13/56 (2,078). When "no opinions" were eliminated, differences between the South and the North were significant at the 10 percent level.

40 AIPO 630, June, 1960 (3,248). Since this sample included 3,248 cases, differences between the South and the rest of the country were significant at less than the 5 percent level. However, differences between the Deep South and the upper South and border states combined were not quite significant at the 10 percent level.

48 percent of Southerners as compared with 61 percent of Northerners replied in the affirmative, while 37 percent of the former versus 22 percent of the latter were opposed.[41]

Introduction of the Communist issue into international exchange and other intercultural collaboration widened the disparity between North and South, particularly as tensions with the Communist countries became more serious in the late 1940's and early 1950's. Thus, in the spring of 1948, 63 percent of Southerners, compared with 77 percent of Northeasterners, 71 percent of Midwesterners, and 78 percent of Westerners, favored allowing American reporters to go to Communist lands and report "the facts as they see them." [42] But even prior to the Berlin blockade, Southerners, and to a lesser extent other Americans, were considerably less prone to permit Communists to come here to report: 45 percent of Southerners, compared with 61 percent of Northeasterners, 54 percent of Midwesterners, and 52 percent of Westerners, were favorable to this idea; and 47, 35, 41, and 48 percent, respectively, were opposed to it.[43]

Several years after the death of Stalin, our national leaders and mass media began to speak more frequently than before of international exchanges with the Soviet bloc. The proportions of Southerners favoring such exchanges seemed to increase as tensions relaxed and decrease as they become sharper, as has been true in the case of some other dealings with the Communists. They also varied according to the type of persons to be exchanged. In general, Southerners were more inclined to accept the idea of exchanges of farmers, musicians, athletes, and others

41 From combined replies to AIPO 442, 5/19/49 (2,751), and AIPO 452, 1/26/50 (2,899). The questions on the proposed University of the World were somewhat differently worded, but Southerners were more inclined than other regional groups to oppose this idea on both surveys. Southern college graduates were more unfavorable to this idea than Northerners who had gone no further than grade school. Percentages by education for the replies to the two surveys combined were as follows:

	Good Idea	Opposed	No Opinion
South			
College	58	32	10
High School	48	36	16
Grade School	42	39	21
North			
College	80	11	9
High School	61	21	18
Grade School	52	28	20

42 NORC 157, 4/22/48 (1,280).
43 Figures from combining NORC 157, 4/22/48 (1,280), and NORC 159, 6/29/48 (1,301). Differences between the South and the North were significant at the 10 percent level.

whose occupations seemed rather unrelated to national defense and the balance of power; they were most likely to oppose visits to this country of teachers, university educators, and especially scientists, who apparently seemed more likely to be spies. However, regardless of the type of exchange proposed and of how questions were posed, Southerners were invariably more apt than residents of other regions to disapprove. Interregional differences were typically relatively large, wider than for exchanges with non-Communist countries. Whereas Northerners were more likely to emphasize the desirability of Soviet visits to this country so that Communists might learn of our way of life, Southerners were more apt to support American visits to the U.S.S.R. for the purpose of learning about that country than they were to favor Soviet visits here. In most cases a majority of Southerners offering opinions opposed exchanges, while at least a small majority of Northerners favored them. Even when those with no views were included in the statistics, in more cases than not a majority of Southerners were opposed and a majority of other regional groups taken together in favor.

Thus, when asked in March, 1955, whether it would be a good idea to exchange athletes with Russia, 43 percent of Southerners, compared with 67 percent of Northeasterners, 63 percent of Midwesterners, and 65 percent of Westerners, agreed that this was a "good idea"; 44 percent of Southerners, 25 percent of Northeasterners, 28 percent of Midwesterners, and 26 percent of Westerners thought it a "bad idea"; and the rest offered no opinions.[44] Shortly after, only 34 percent of all Southerners replied in the affirmative and 53 percent in the negative when asked, "If Russia agrees to take hundreds of U.S. tourists, should we agree to let as many Russians tour this country?" Those in the Northeast, Midwest, and West favoring the idea were respectively 47, 47, and 50 percent; and opposed, 40, 42, and 36 percent.[45] When a similar question was raised two years later in 1957, all regional groups had become significantly more favorable to exchanges of teachers: 61 percent of Northeasterners, 53 percent of Midwesterners, and 60 percent of Westerners approved of the idea, while 30 percent, 31 percent, and 26 percent, respectively, were still opposed. However, Southerners were still less favorable than other citizens—42 percent supported the idea and 43 percent were against it.[46] In March, 1955, only 39 percent

44 AIPO 545, March, 1955 (1,630). See also NORC 372, 6/23/55 (1,263) ("musicians and athletes"); NORC 376, 9/29/55 (1,250) ("musicians and athletes"); NORC 386, 4/20/56 (1,224) ("musicians and athletes"); AIPO 575, 11/20/56 (1,502) ("athletes"); NORC 402, 3/18/57 (536) ("musicians and athletes"); and NORC 404, 4/26/57 (1,279) ("musicians and athletes").
45 AIPO 548, 6/1/55 (1,462).   46 AIPO 584, 6/4/57 (1,484).

of Southerners, compared with 58 percent of Northeasterners, 62 percent of Midwesterners, and 64 percent of Westerners, approved a proposal whereby a group of Russian farmers would come to this country "to learn the methods used by our farmers." Fifty percent of Southerners, 35 percent of Northeasterners, 31 percent of Midwesterners, and 29 percent of Westerners were opposed.[47] Asked in June, 1957, whether our leaders should accept the Soviet offer to exchange "educators," 37 percent of Southerners were favorable, 53 percent unfavorable. The figures for the Northeast were 61 versus 30 percent, for the Midwest 53 versus 39 percent, and for the West 60 versus 33 percent.[48] In June, 1955, and April, 1956, surveys were taken dealing with possible exchanges of scientists; Americans generally were more opposed to this idea than to most other proposed Soviet-United States exchanges, but Southerners were even more strongly against it. Replying Southerners opposed the suggested exchange two to one.[49]

Southerners who have favored intercultural and interpersonal exchanges across national borders and particularly between the United States and the Communist countries have been disproportionately concentrated among those who went to college or, at least, finished high school; among professional, managerial, and other white collar occupational groups; among city as opposed to country and small-town people; and in the upper South and border states rather than in South Carolina, Georgia, Alabama, Mississippi, and Arkansas taken together. Negroes have tended to lower the Southern averages of those who approved of such exchanges and, to a lesser degree, of those who disapproved of them, since they have been significantly less inclined to venture any opinions. Of those offering views, the proportion of Negroes approving has typically been at least somewhat less than among Southern whites.[50]

Support of international exchanges, especially with the Soviet bloc, was also significantly more prevalent among the Southern white minority who condemned Governor Orval Faubus of Arkansas shortly after the school integration crisis in Little Rock in 1957 than among those who endorsed the governor.[51] In fact, the less conservative they have

47 AIPO 545, March, 1955 (1,630). See also NORC 372, 6/23/55 (1,263); NORC 374, 8/4/55 (1,262); NORC 376, 9/29/55 (1,250).
48 AIPO 584, 6/4/57 (1,484).
49 Results of combining similar questions in NORC 372, 6/23/55 (1,263), and NORC 386, 4/20/56 (1,224).
50 Samples in individual questionnaires contained too few Southern Negroes to permit statistical comparisons where differences were relatively small. This generalization resulted from combining Negroes who replied to AIPO 545, March, 1955 (1,630); AIPO 548, 6/1/55 (1,462); and AIPO 584, 6/4/57 (1,484).
51 AIPO 591, 11/5/57 (1,508).

been on the segregation question in recent years, the more likely have Southern whites been to feel that exchanges with the Russians would probably do more good than harm to our world interests.[52] Southerners favoring exchanges, particularly with our enemies, have usually agreed on most aspects of foreign policy with those Southerners who supported admission of displaced persons, Hungarian refugees, a few Chinese, and other selected immigrants. In fact, these two groups of Southerners have very often been composed of the same persons, depending on the type of exchange and the country with which the exchange was to take place.[53]

The distinctly lower enthusiasm for exchanges with the Communists in the South has been intimately related to divergences between Southern and non-Southern perception of the nature of the Communist problem and what our government should do about it. (This phenomenon is discussed in the next chapter.) Thus, being on the average more apt than Northerners to stress armed defense than diplomatic, cultural, and economic means of moderating the Communist threat to our security, Southerners have been more likely to fear that Communist visitors would engage in espionage and subversion here. It is not surprising that those Southerners who have opposed United States-Soviet exchanges have been more inclined than those who approved to feel that war with the Soviet bloc is relatively likely,[54] that we should not agree to international inspection to achieve arms-control agreements with the Communists,[55] that trade with them should be reduced or at least not expanded,[56] that diplomatic relations with Communist states should be discontinued,[57] and that military aid is more important than capital assistance.[58] And the less the Southerner has known about world affairs, the more inclined has he been either to have no opinion or to disapprove of exchanges with the Soviet Union and other Communist countries.[59]

Feelings toward Foreign Peoples

The point has often been made that Southern "internationalism" in the past has been to a considerable degree due to feelings of affinity with British cousins with whom Southern Anglo-Saxons felt cultural

52 NORC 386, 4/20/56 (1,224).
53 AIPO 575, 11/20/56 (1,502), and NORC 404, 4/26/57 (1,279).
54 NORC 404, 4/26/57 (1,279), and AIPO 630, 6/28/60 (3,248).
55 NORC 376, 9/29/55 (1,250).   56 AIPO 584, 6/4/57 (1,484).
57 AIPO 575, 11/20/56 (1,502).   58 NORC 313, 10/2/51 (1,237).
59 AIPO 584, 6/4/57 (1,484). Based on comparison of those who favored permitting more Soviet tourists to come to the United States and also exchanging of "educators" versus those who opposed both with interviewees who could identify Nehru and Adenauer versus those who could identify neither.

ties and carried on much of their trade in cotton and tobacco. Their support of an active foreign policy implied solidarity with Britain.

Sentiments toward the British have fluctuated in the South, as throughout the country, with the behavior of the British leaders and government, the state of relations between the two governments, the nature of the world environment at the moment, and perhaps other changing conditions. It is difficult to separate reactions to a foreign people from reactions to their leaders and the latter's policies at home and abroad. However, at any given time Southerners have been at least as favorable to the British and their policies as other regional groups have been, and, in a number of cases, they have been more so.

Thus, when asked in 1936 which European country they liked best, 61 percent in the South compared with a like percentage in the Northeast, 56 percent in the Midwest, 52 percent in the Plains States, 54 percent in the Rocky Mountain region, and 52 percent in the Far West chose England from among the alternatives offered.[60] Sixty-seven percent in the South, compared with 64 percent in the Northeast, 61 percent in the Midwest, and 60 percent in the West, favored bringing English women and children to stay in this country until the end of the war during the Nazi bombings of Britain in 1940.[61] As we mentioned earlier, British immigration has been an exception to the generalization that Southerners have been more opposed to expanded migrations to America from abroad; in 1944 a majority of Southerners (a slightly larger percentage than in the North) felt that we should not stop English people from "coming to the United States to live after the war." [62] A number of surveys since the war have found that Southerners as compared with other Americans taken together were as apt or, more often than not, somewhat more apt to say they liked England and the English better than any other foreign country or people,[63] that the English have the same general ideas as we on most world problems,[64] that we can count on them to cooperate with us abroad,[65] and

60 AIPO 61, 12/14/36 (2,813).
61 Combined replies to AIPO 202, 7/16/40 (3,226), and AIPO 204, 7/31/40 (3,079).
62 NORC 228, September, 1944 (2,549).
63 NORC 169, 9/16/49 (1,300); AIPO 483, 12/7/51 (1,317); AIPO 512, 2/20/53 (1,548); AIPO 521, 10/7/53 (1,488); AIPO 535, 8/31/54 (1,581); AIPO 538, 10/13/54 (1,530); and AIPO 637, 10/18/60 (2,993).
64 NORC 149, 4/3/47 (1,307); NORC 341–2, 6/30/53 (1,291); and NORC 382, 1/26/56 (1,238).
65 NORC 133, 8/31/45 (1,259); NORC 139, 2/2/46 (1,263); NORC 141, 3/20/46 (1,293); NORC 145, 10/2/46 (1,308); NORC 159, 6/29/48 (1,301); NORC 298, 1/30/51 (1,236); NORC 315, 12/18/51 (1,237); NORC 366, 1/21/55 (1,209); NORC 382, 1/26/56 (1,238); NORC 399, 11/15/56 (1,286); AIPO 576, 12/12/56 (1,539); and NORC 404, 4/26/57 (1,257).

that we should work closely with them.[66] The relative Anglophilia of the region is highlighted by the finding that its residents even manifested a slightly more favorable impression in the late 1940's of the Labor government than did the rest of the country taken together.[67] Moreover, these figures included Negroes—when Southern whites alone were compared with Northern whites, they were more often than not clearly more pro-British than were other Americans taken together. Finally, since even Southern whites have been less likely than Americans generally to express any opinion on the British and their country, the proportion which has been pro-British of those actually venturing sentiments has normally been even larger still than the national average.

Furthermore, the proportion of Southerners, white or colored, who have voiced negative sentiments on these queries about the British and their country has been on the whole smaller than outside the South. The scarcity of Irish, German, and perhaps other ethnic groups critical of England at least partially explains this relative paucity of Anglophobia in the region.

One should not assume that the majority of the white Southern rank and file has actually identified with the English and their problems, as has been true of many American Jews with respect to Israel. It was observed that even on general questions about Britain, its people, and its ideas Southern whites have been more inclined than Northern whites to offer no opinions at all or to indicate neutral or indifferent feelings toward the land of their ancestors. English, Welsh, and Scottish nurses with a frontier missionary medical unit in the Southern Appalachians reported that the indigenous peoples—among the purest Anglo-Saxons in America—seemed to have little idea of their own ethnic origins. But even the lowliest Southern white does not react to British names and speech on the television with the negative image he may ascribe to those of other cultures. Moreover, the educated strata in the South have been favorably disposed to the British; historically many of them seemed to have fancied themselves as descendants of the British gentry (for the most part erroneously) who supposedly lived and thought much as they did.[68] Some educated traditionalists continue to note the sympathies of the British elite for the Confederacy.

Although Southerners of neither race have empathized with Continental Europeans to the degree they have with the English, survey re-

---

66   NORC 149, 4/3/47 (1,307); NORC 333, 11/17/52 (1,291); NORC 337, 2/11/53 (1,291); NORC 359, 6/30/54 (1,217); and NORC 382, 1/26/56 (1,238).
67   NORC 149, 4/3/47 (1,307), and NORC 169, 9/16/49 (1,300). Differences were not statistically significant at the 10 percent level.
68   See, for instance, Eaton, *The Growth of Southern Civilization*, 2–3.

sults from 1949 through 1960 indicate that they have been for the most part as favorable to France and the French as have other Americans. Depending on the wording of the question, the recent behavior of the French government and leaders, and the general international atmosphere at the time, usually no more than one Southerner out of six during the postwar period (as late as October 1960) has had an unfavorable impression of the French people and only about one out of four has felt that we could not count on France and the French to cooperate with us in at least a general way in world affairs.[69] In the author's experience, even many Southerners who have doubted that the French would be effective soldiers in a military showdown with the Communists have seemed to take a relatively favorable attitude toward the French people. The anti-Catholicism still lingering among many Southern Protestants seems to have had only very limited impact on sentiments about the French. Elimination of Southern Catholics from survey data results in only statistically insignificant reduction of responses favorable to France. Apparently fundamentalists and other Southerners critical of the Roman Catholic Church have not thought of the French in terms of any Catholic affiliations.

Southerners have been more unfavorably disposed toward citizens of Communist countries than have Northerners. For instance, 45 percent of Southerners as compared with 30 percent of Northerners said they had negative impressions of the Russian people, and 46 percent of the former as compared with 37 percent of the latter indicated adverse feelings toward the people of Communist China.[70] But uncomplimentary attitudes toward peoples of Communist countries have been disproportionately concentrated among Southerners who have felt that war with their governments is very likely and that we should take a firmer line toward their leaders.

No national surveys of attitudes towards citizens of Africa and Asia other than the Communist Chinese have come to the author's attention. Although most Southerners have not applied traditional stereotypes about Negroes to non-Negroid people of color, the cultural values and mores of Asians and North Africans have been much stranger to

69 AIPO 437, 2/9/49 (3,160); AIPO 471, 2/2/51 (1,404); NORC 303, 6/29/51 (1,300); NORC 315, 12/18/51 (1,237); NORC 323, 4/22/52 (1,250); NORC 337, 2/11/53 (1,291); AIPO 512, 2/20/53 (1,548); NORC 341-2, 6/30/53 (1,291); NORC 355, 4/22/54 (1,207); AIPO 535, 8/3/54 (1,581); AIPO 537, 9/14/54 (1,465); NORC 364, 10/23/54 (518); NORC 366, 1/21/55 (1,209); NORC 370, 3/11/55 (1,225); NORC 382, 1/26/56 (1,238); NORC 390, 6/26/56 (1,275); NORC 399, 11/15/56 (1,286); AIPO 576, 12/12/56 (1,539); and AIPO 637, 10/18/60 (2,993).
70 NORC 370, 3/11/55 (1,225). See also NORC 300, 3/20/51 (1,300).

Southerners than have those of most Europeans; they have been different to most Northerners also, but the Northerners' experiences with more cultural variety have seemed to render their relationships with non-Westerners easier and less unnatural. Furthermore, as will be observed shortly, Southerners who have expressed views have tended to be more critical on the average than Northerners of the neutralist, often leftish, behavior of the leaders in a number of these lands. Lacking systematic evidence, one surmises that Southerners on the whole have felt less empathy with and perhaps more irritation at Indians, Pakistani, Egyptians, and other Asians and North Africans than have Northerners. White segregationists have undoubtedly applied many of the unfavorable stereotypes they have assigned to local Negroes to Africans as well. (Southern white reactions toward Africans south of the Sahara are discussed in Chapters 5 and 11.)

CHAPTER 3

NATIONAL DEFENSE

AND

COLLECTIVE SECURITY

T he military tradition has been more deeply rooted in the South than in any other region, with the experience of all classes rendering military values and service both natural and relatively attractive. The frontier environment provided the backdrop for hunting, horseback riding, and developing an ability to defend oneself. Slavery required posses and patrols for enforcement, and the presence of large numbers of freedmen after 1865 and the attendant fears of attacks on whites kept alive the felt need for competence with arms.[1] The lack of occupational alternatives in a rural society of underemployment also led many Southerners to enter military careers.

Nowhere else in the United States has the romantic tradition of chivalry and the gallant, hot-blooded cavalier—independent, quick to resent supposed offenses to his touchy sense of honor, and eager to display his military prowess—been so influential as among the Southern privileged classes.[2] The antebellum gentleman tended to adopt Edward Waverly, the lords and ladies of *Ivanhoe*, and Sir Walter Scott's ethic of an elite as his models. These were often reinforced by other romantic and chivalric works of Byron, Bulwer-Lytton, Schiller, Herder,

1 Eaton, *The Growth of Southern Civilization*, 80; and Henry Savage, Jr., *Seeds of Time: The Background of Southern Thinking* (New York: Henry Holt and Co., 1959), 98.
2 R. M. Weaver, "Southern Chivalry and Total War," *Sewanee Review*, LIX (1945), 267–78; and John Hope Franklin, *The Militant South* (Cambridge: Harvard University Press, 1956) viii, x, 1–13, 34–36, and 45, and Chaps. 4 and 10.

Carlyle, Michelet, De Lamartine, or their Southern counterparts such as Mirabeau B. Lamar, William Gilmore Simms, Henry Timrod, and by contents of such periodicals as *Southron* and *De Bow's Review*.[3] Their traditions were carried into the twentieth century by such authors as Thomas Nelson Page.

Thus, the code duello accounted for the early demise, often on slight provocation, of many gentlemen, while their social inferiors maimed and eliminated one another by less genteel violence.[4] Planters' sons grew up in the habit of command, and the masses learned early to admire the martial leadership of their betters in a hierarchical society. Private military academies began developing in the early nineteenth century and proliferated with the years; state-supported military colleges sprang up throughout the region, based to a considerable extent on the model of the Virginia Military Institute (the "West Point of the South"), which was established in 1839.[5] Because the planters' capital was tied up in land, sugar mills, and slaves, their sons often competed with one another for appointments to the U.S. Military Academy or attended the less costly Southern military institutions rather than the more expensive private colleges of the North and of Western Europe.[6] Hence, Robert E. Lee went to West Point partly because his aristocratic widow mother would have found it difficult to pay the expenses of another institution,[7] and other offspring of "land poor" gentry did likewise. Even today, Southern whites of all social levels have learned from childhood to revere the region's military heroes, and nowhere

3 Franklin, *The Militant South*, Chap. 10; William E. Dodd, "Social Philosophy of the Old South," *American Journal of Sociology*, XXIII (1918), 743; Osterweis, *Romanticism and Nationalism in the Old South*, 5-7, 21, 34, 38-39, 41-43, 49, 56, 65, 80-81, 105, 115-16, and 273; Eaton, *The Growth of Southern Civilization*, 318-19; Grace W. Landrum, "Sir Walter Scott and His Literary Rivals in the Old South," *American Literature*, II (1930), 256-76; Savage, *Seeds of Time*, 104; Ezell, *The South Since 1865*, 18; and George Fitzhugh, *Sociology for the South* (Richmond: Adolphus Morris, 1854), especially Chap. 5. Parenthetically, William Faulkner's upstart antebellum planter, Thomas Sutpen, named his horse Rob Roy.

4 Weaver, *Sewanee Review*, LIX, 269; Hodding Carter, *The Angry Scar* (Garden City: Doubleday, 1959), 199; Polk, *Southern Accent*, 151-53; Franklin, *The Militant South*, 18 ff.; Benjamin B. Kendrick and Alex M. Arnett, *The South Looks at Its Past* (Chapel Hill: University of North Carolina Press, 1935), 29-31; C. Vann Woodward, *Origins of the New South*, 1877-1913 (Baton Rouge: Louisiana State University Press, 1951), 158-60; Savage, *Seeds of Time*, 106; and Albert A. Fossier, *New Orleans: the Glamour Period, 1800-1840* (New Orleans, Pelican Publishing Co., 1957), Chap. 35.

5 Franklin, *The Militant South*, 146-70.

6 *Ibid.*, 138-45.

7 Douglas Southall Freeman, *R. E. Lee* (4 vols.; New York: Charles Scribner's Sons, 1934), I, 37-38.

else in the country have military titles, uniforms, and parades received so much favorable attention.[8]

Continuing Popularity of the Military

Industrialization and urbanization of the South have gradually attenuated the relative attractions of a military career. In addition to enlistment in the armed forces, industrial jobs now provide a source of employment for surplus agricultural labor. The army, the clergy, the law, and plantation management are no longer the only alternatives for the educated classes. Moreover, the life of military officers has changed: no longer do they spend much of their time in the great out-of-doors on horseback; the hunt breakfast, the steeplechase, and the horse show have departed from military life. The specialized technical tasks within the modern military service seem less enticing to the Southern gentlemen than the army life of the past.

Personal Values and Military Life

Nevertheless, Southern traditions and history have their effects today; white Southerners as a group continue to regard military careers in a more favorable light than Northerners. Southern values, though generation by generation approaching national norms, still encourage the martial spirit to a greater degree than do those in the urban North. A heritage of nationalism, the traditions of the land, a less optimistic (or a more realistic, depending on one's point of view) attitude toward human nature,[9] an experience with a more hierarchical status society, a greater prevalence of authoritarian personality traits,[10] a relative paucity of pacifistic and anti-military thinking [11]—these and other factors more evident in the South than in most of the North continue to encourage acceptance, even enthusiasm, for military life.

Extralegal violence and bellicosity in the writings of William Faulkner, Robert Penn Warren, Tennessee Williams, Flannery O'Connor, and other serious Southern writers are not coincidental, though their works tend to exaggerate the incidence in the present South. But the region has continued to have in the postwar period the highest rates of interpersonal violence, as indicated by homicides, assaults, and other crimes.[12] Negroes have been more inclined toward violence than South-

8 Franklin, *The Militant South*, 9, 177–88, and 190–92.
9 See pp. 342–51.   10 See pp. 351–55.   11 See pp. 90–91.
12 Wilbur J. Cash, *The Mind of the South* (Garden City: Doubleday, 1956), 55–59; Austin L. Porterfield and Robert H. Talbert, "Crime in Southern Cities," in Rupert B. Vance and Nicholas J. Demerath (eds.), *The Urban South* (Chapel

ern whites, but, even when Negroes were eliminated from consideration, some differences unfavorable to the region seemed to remain.
Skill with fists and more deadly weapons is highly regarded, and a
pistol, rifle, or shotgun is often part of the rural male attire. A national
survey in 1959, for instance, discovered that 53 percent of Southerners
thought it should be legal for private citizens to have loaded weapons
in their homes, compared with 35 percent of Northeasterners, 33 percent of Midwesterners, and 42 percent of Westerners. Sixty-seven
percent of Southerners had guns at home, whereas only 31 percent of
Northeasterners, 53 percent of Midwesterners, and 47 percent of Westerners did.[13]

Moreover, the more cautious, conservative Southern view of international relations,[14] the wider prevalence in the South of the feeling that
peoples of different religions, languages, and cultures are rather unlikely
to get along,[15] the greater incidence in the South of the idea that self-
interest almost alone governs international relations, and the generally
less optimistic tone of Southern assumptions about life and society[16]
have encouraged a belief that wars are more or less probable in the
future. The proportion of Americans who have believed that world
war, or more limited international violence, is likely has varied with
the state of world affairs at the moment, but Southerners at any given
time have been more prone to predict war. The differences between
opinions in the South and other regions on the likelihood of international violence have not been as large in recent years as before World
War II, but, significant differences in the expected direction were evident as late as 1961 (see pp. 105–107). Southerners more than others
have believed that diplomacy may fail to avoid armed conflict, that
strong military power makes attack on America less probable, and that
armed might is the only real guarantee of our national security.

Therefore, Southerners during most of the period since 1937 have
been more favorable than inhabitants of other regions to peacetime
conscription,[17] the possibility of Universal Military Training,[18] larger

---

Hill: University of North Carolina Press, 1954), 180–200; Polk, *Southern Accent,*
139–65; Savage, *Seeds of Time,* 222, 264; and H. C. Brearley, "The Pattern of Violence," in W. T. Couch (ed.), *Culture in the South* (Chapel Hill: University of
North Carolina Press, 1934), 678–92.
13   AIPO 616, 7/21/59 (1,539). Replies to the latter question were closely associated with those to another on the same survey, "Do you, or does your husband or
wife, go hunting?" As one would surmise, Southerners were much more inclined
than other regional groups to reply in the affirmative to this query.
14   See pp. 349–51, 365–81.   15 See pp. 347–51.   16 See pp. 342–47.
17   AIPO 67, 2/1/37 (2,970); AIPO 68, 2/8/37 (2,916); AIPO 133, September,
1938 (3,400); AIPO 140, 12/2/38 (3,102); AIPO 151, 3/8/39 (3,154); AIPO 156,

defense budgets for better military preparedness,[19] expanded military

5/2/39 (3,110); AIPO 194, 5/14/40 (3,151); AIPO Release of June 30, 1940; AIPO 198, 6/11/40 (3,090); AIPO 206, 8/9/40 (3,110); AIPO Release of August 10, 1940; AIPO 207, 8/22/40 (3,107); AIPO 216, 10/19/40 (3,165); AIPO 226, 12/16/40 (3,013); AIPO 242, 7/22/41 (2,899); AIPO Release of March 27, 1942; AIPO Release of May 2, 1942; AIPO 285, 12/2/42 (2,844); AIPO 305, 10/26/43 (3,000); AIPO 310, 1/18/44 (3,120); AIPO Releases of September 29, 1944, November 29, 1944, and December 17, 1944; AIPO 339, 1/17/45 (3,063); NORC 234, April, 1945 (2,494); AIPO Release of May 2, 1945; AIPO 350, 6/27/45 (3,086); AIPO 354, 8/22/45 (3,107); AIPO 358, 10/17/45 (3,139); NORC 239, November, 1945 (2,540); AIPO 359, 10/31/45 (3,135); AIPO 360, 11/21/45 (3,086); AIPO 399, 6/18/47 (3,088); AIPO Release of January 18, 1948; NORC 156, 3/25/48 (1,289); AIPO Release of March 4, 1949; AIPO 415, 3/18/48 (3,129); AIPO 451, 1/6/50 (1,506); AIPO Release of February 11, 1950; AIPO 463, 10/6/50 (1,501); AIPO 466, 10/20/50 (2,988); AIPO 468, 12/1/50 (1,500); AIPO 471, 2/2/51 (1,404); AIPO 473, 3/24/51 (2,102); AIPO 483, 12/7/51 (1,317); AIPO Release of January 11, 1952; and AIPO 487, 2/26/52 (2,003). There has been some erosion of the large Southern majority favorable to the draft since about 1954, perhaps due in part to integration of our armed forces during the Korean War and to general resentment among Southern segregationists toward the national government as a result of pressures for desegregation in the South. See AIPO 536, 8/24/54 (1,562); AIPO 557, 12/6/55 (1,434); and AIPO 571, 9/13/56 (2,159).

18 AIPO 409, 12/10/47 (2,907); AIPO Release of April 9, 1948; AIPO 436, 1/20/49 (3,213); AIPO 510, 1/9/53 (1,558); and AIPO Release of February 15, 1953.

19 AIPO Release of 11/12/39; AIPO 173, 10/10/39 (3,180); AIPO 183, 1/30/40 (3,179); AIPO 195, 5/16/40 (3,139); AIPO 226, 12/16/40 (3,013); AIPO 270, 6/9/42 (2,930); NORC 146, 11/15/46 (1,300); AIPO 391, 2/26/47 (2,639); AIPO 412, 2/4/48 (3,185); NORC 163, 1/26/49 (1,261); AIPO 449, 10/28/49 (2,904); AIPO 451, 1/6/50 (1,506); AIPO 453, 2/24/50 (1,450); NORC 391, 10/18/50 (1,305); AIPO 468, 12/1/50 (1,500); NORC 295, 12/28/50 (1,258); NORC 298, 1/30/51 (1,236); NORC 300, 3/20/51 (1,300); NORC 302, 4/8/51 (1,300); NORC 312, 8/27/51 (1,237); NORC 314, 11/22/51 (1,237); NORC 315, 12/18/51 (1,237); NORC 323, 4/22/52 (1,250); NORC 325, 5/28/52 (1,265); NORC 327, 6/30/52 (1,285); NORC 329, 8/28/52 (1,300); AIPO 508, 11/12/52 (3,004); NORC 333, 11/17/52 (1,291); NORC 337, 2/11/53 (1,291); NORC 341–2, 6/30/53 (1,291); AIPO 517, 7/2/53 (1,545); AIPO 519, 8/13/53 (1,613); AIPO 553, 9/13/55 (1,452); NORC 378, 10/6/55 (527); AIPO 579, 2/26/57 (1,531); AIPO 582, 4/23/57 (1,626); AIPO 583, 5/15/57 (1,570); AIPO 593, 12/31/57 (1,522); and AIPO 625, 2/29/60 (2,985). For example, in early 1940, 85 percent of Southerners as compared with 82 percent of Northeasterners, 79 percent of Midwesterners, 75 percent of residents of the Plains States, and 77 percent of Westerners approved of President Roosevelt's proposed increase of 28 percent in federal spending for national defense. AIPO 183, 1/30/40 (3,179). In late spring of that year, 93 per cent of Southerners, 90 percent of Northeasterners, 83 percent of Midwesterners (including residents of the Plains States), and 86 percent of Westerners approved of the idea of increasing spending on our armed forces during the next year by 50 percent. AIPO 195, 5/16/40 (3,139). Asked in 1950 whether the money "we are now spending on the Army, Navy, and Air Force is too much, too little, or about right," 11 percent in the South as compared with 16 percent in the North said "too much." AIPO 453, 2/24/50 (1,450). In the summer of 1953, 20 percent of Southerners versus 18 percent of Northeasterners, 16 percent of Midwesterners, and 16 percent of Westerners agreed that the "defense budget has been cut so much that the nation's safety is threatened." AIPO 517, 7/2/53 (1,545). In early 1957 only 7 percent in the South felt our defense

forces on land, sea, and air (both before and after World War II),[20] and the preparation of detailed plans in peacetime for total mobilization.[21] National defense and military preparedness have been perceived by virtually all classes, at least of whites, as one of the few valid reasons for increasing our national debt and even raising taxes.[22] Although local

budget should be decreased, 24 percent that it should be increased, and 59 percent that it should be kept the same; respective figures for the other regions were 11 percent, 22 percent, and 61 percent. AIPO 579, 2/26/57 (1,531). However, by early 1960 Southern replies to a similar question were not significantly different from the Northern average—in the South 20 percent felt we were spending "too little," 18 percent "too much," and 44 percent "about the right amount"; the Northern figures were 21 percent, 18 percent, and 45 percent, respectively. AIPO 625, 2/29/60 (2,985).

20 In September, 1938, 71 percent of those in the South, 68 percent in the Northeast, 63 percent in the Midwest, 56 percent in the Plains States, and 66 percent in the West felt that the size of our army should be "further increased." Seventy-five percent in the South, 74 percent in the Northeast, 68 percent in the Midwest, 58 percent in the Plains States, and 72 percent in the West believed that the size of the navy should be "further increased." AIPO 133, September, 1938 (3,400).

A year later, after the invasion of Poland, and again after the war in early 1948, the public was asked if the United States should increase the size of its army, navy, and air force. Regional percentages favoring increases were as follows (AIPO 171, 9/22/39 [3,064], and AIPO 412, 2/4/48 [3,185]):

	Army		Navy		Air Force	
	9/22/39	2/4/48	9/22/39	2/4/48	9/22/39	2/4/48
South	92	67	92	67	96	81
Northeast	89	61	93	63	94	75
Midwest	84	61	88	63	89	73
Plains States	79	57	79	59	84	72
West	84	61	85	65	91	79

In late 1949, 66 percent of Southerners as compared with 62 percent of Northeasterners, 63 percent of Midwesterners (including those in the Plains States), and 62 percent of Westerners approved of "increasing the number of our atomic bombs"; 88 percent of Southerners versus 85 percent of Northeasterners, 84 percent of Midwesterners, and 86 percent of Westerners approved of "strengthening our own armed forces in other ways" as well to meet "the Russian problem." NORC 170, 10/12/49 (1,300).

21 AIPO 455, 5/2/50 (2,850). Fifty-one percent of Southerners favored development of a plan for total mobilization whereby each citizen would be assigned specific functions and duties in case of national emergency; only 29 percent opposed this suggestion. Outside the South, 44 percent favored it whereas 46 percent opposed it.

22 When asked in the fall of 1938 whether they would "be willing to pay more taxes for a larger Army?" 60 percent of Southerners, 52 percent of Northeasterners, 51 percent of Midwesterners, 46 percent of residents of the Plains States, and 59 percent of Westerners replied in the affirmative. AIPO 133, September, 1938 (3,400). Shortly after the defeat of Poland, 75 percent of Southerners favored higher taxes for larger ground, air, or naval forces (all except 4 percent of these for expansion of all three), compared with 68 percent of Northeasterners, 65 percent of Midwesterners, 60 percent of those in the Plains States, and

conservative influentials among the interviewees were frequently inclined to feel we should cut national budgets for domestic welfare and foreign aid and to discount requests by specialists on foreign policy for funds for economic assistance and other nonmilitary international expenditures, they were much more apt to accept recommendations by military specialists for larger funds. At least small, and sometimes rather large, differences in these directions have been apparent in surveys for Southern adults as compared with Northern adults in general; when whites alone have been considered, the proportions in the South who ventured no views on these matters decreased and the percentages favorable to more active and financially expensive defense postures rose.

Favorable Interest in the Military

This favorable interest in the military was demonstrated in the fifty-three Southern newspapers sampled for this study. They most nearly

---

67 percent of Westerners. AIPO 173, 10/10/39 (3,180). In early 1940, 64 percent of Southerners, compared with 47 percent of Northeasterners, 47 percent of Midwesterners, 58 percent of those in the Plains States, and 47 percent of Westerners, agreed that federal income taxes should be raised by "10 percent to pay the cost of a bigger army and navy." AIPO 182, 1/19/40 (3,199); see also AIPO 195, 5/16/40 (3,138). In mid-1942, 69 percent of Southerners in contrast to 54 percent of Northeasterners, 56 percent of Midwesterners, 62 percent of those in the Plains States, and 56 percent of Westerners agreed that the federal government should put on a national sales tax on "everything people buy . . . to help pay the cost of the war." AIPO 270, 6/9/42 (2,930).

In early 1948, 62 percent in the South as compared with 55 percent in the Northeast, 55 percent in the Midwest, 50 percent in the Plains States, and 58 percent in the West were willing to pay higher taxes to support a larger army; 64, 55, 55, 49, and 58 percent, respectively, were willing to do so for a larger navy; and 71, 63, 63, 61, and 67 percent, respectively, for a larger air force. AIPO 412, 2/4/48 (3,185).

Informed in January, 1950, (AIPO 451, 1/6/50 [1,506]) that fiscal 1950 would probably be a deficit year for the federal government and asked if there was "anything the federal government spends money on now which . . . should be reduced," only one percent of Southerners as compared with 4 percent of other Americans mentioned military spending.

Asked in 1953, "Do you think too much of the taxes you pay is being spent for defense—or is too little being spent for defense?" 15 percent in the South as compared with 21 percent in the Northeast, 20 percent in the Midwest (including the Plains States), and 22 percent in the West replied "too much"; 41, 44, 48, and 44 percent, respectively, answered "about right"; 31 percent in the South versus 18, 24, and 19 percent, respectively, in the other regions responded "too little"; and the remainder had no opinion, did not know, or were undecided. AIPO 519, 8/13/53 (1,613), and AIPO Release of 9/16/53.

In early 1958, only 21 percent of Southerners in contrast to 29 percent of Northeasterners, 28 percent of Midwesterners (including residents of the Plains States), and 28 percent of Westerners said they would be unwilling to have their income taxes raised "to build up our military strength here and abroad." AIPO 593, 12/31/57 (1,522).

approached the coverage of world affairs available in the "News of the Week in Review" of the New York *Times* (Sunday edition) in the fields of national defense and military events abroad. These newspapers, according to the sample, uniformly supported public sacrifices for strong armed forces, both conventional and thermonuclear.

Moreover, voluntary enlistment has been most popular in the South and Alabama Congressman Luther Patrick's statement prior to Pearl Harbor that "they had to start selective service to keep our Southern boys from filling up the army" [23] had some validity. Thus, a national survey in 1955 determined that Southerners were still significantly more inclined than other Americans to accord prestige and general approval to career officers in the armed forces and, to a lesser extent, to enlisted men as well. For instance, 32 percent of Southern adults as compared with 19 percent of Northeasterners, 25 percent of Midwesterners, and 21 percent of Westerners placed military officers in the most esteemed category among alternative careers. The percentages for non-commissioned careers were 19 for the South, 9 for the Northeast, 13 for the Midwest, and 11 for the West. Approximately two-thirds of Southern adults said they would be pleased if their sons (if they had any) chose a military career, compared with two fifths of all Northern adults taken together. Comparable percentages in the two parts of the country said they would be pleased if their daughters married career officers.

Southerners were more likely to manifest positive images of military life and of men in uniform than were other citizens. Differences between North and South were wider among older people and narrower among younger. But even among adolescent boys aged sixteen to twenty years interregional differences were still wide: 27 percent in the South placed military officers among the most esteemed occupational category, compared with 13 percent in the Northeast, 14 percent in the Midwest, and 15 percent in the West.[24]

It is understandable from these findings that ROTC training is still more popular in the South, that military preparatory schools and colleges continue to attract sons of those able to bear the expense, and that many offspring of "established" families still tend to consider officer-

23   John Temple Graves, III, "The Fighting South," *Virginia Quarterly Review,* XVIII (1942), 61. See Savage, *Seeds of Time,* 242, for similar Southern responsiveness to the call to arms in World War I.

24   Public Opinion Surveys, Inc., "Attitudes of Adult Civilians toward the Military Service as a Career" (2,004), and "Attitudes of 16- to 20-Year-Old Males toward the Military Service as a Career" (1,031) (Princeton, N.J., 1955); and unpublished data of these two studies provided by Public Opinion Surveys, Inc. All differences were significant at 10 percent or better levels.

ship in the Regular Army as one of the more honorable and interesting of careers. It is still common to encounter Southerners of such origins, often in straitened economic circumstances, who feel that business and manufacturing are less desirable and useful ways of making a living than service as a commissioned officer. Nearly every Southerner of traditionally esteemed social connections points with some pride to military officers among his ancestors and, often, among his living relatives, in-laws, and friends as well.

Availability of appointments to West Point has extended considerably below the privileged strata in the South in recent decades, and the fraction of well-born among Southern cadets has decreased considerably. Nevertheless, a study of general officers in 1950 discovered that although only approximately 12 percent of professional and managerial men in the country were Southern, 34 percent of the generals in the army, 31 percent of the admirals in the navy, and 25 percent of the generals in the air force were Southerners. As one would have surmised, the air force, being the most technical and the least traditional of the services, was relatively least attractive to Southerners. Most senior officers were by the 1950's from middle-middle and lower-middle class or, in some cases, even more humble origins, but the majority of generals in the army who did come from socially esteemed families were Southerners. The few ranking officers of comparable genteel backgrounds from the Northeast were mainly in the navy.[25] If generals from areas of Southern tradition in Maryland, Delaware, Illinois, Missouri, and elsewhere outside the former Confederacy and others possessing one or more Southern-born parents were included in the Southern category, Southern proportions would have risen to perhaps half the generals in the army at the time of this study.[26] Even among West Point cadets of the World War II period, the author recalls numerous Southerners from prominent families in counties, towns, and even cities.

Influence of Military Ideas

These generally more favorable attitudes toward military life and people have provided a more receptive climate in the South for international views common among the military. Moreover, military individuals have been more evident and the rapport between them and the civilian population has seemed more intimate and frequent than

25 Morris Janowitz, *The Professional Soldier* (New York: The Free Press, 1960), 86–99, 107, 109–10, and 176.
26 *Ibid.*, 88.

outside the South. A disproportionately large number of military posts have been located in the former Confederacy. Officers of proper family connections (and some who were not) have been entertained in genteel homes and have married the daughters of old families. Senior officers stationed in the region and others who have visited nearby installations have spoken frequently before chambers of commerce, Rotary clubs, and other groups and presented their views on military and related international questions both formally and informally throughout the South. Their public utterances have often appeared in prominent positions in local papers. After retirement many military people have established residences in the South to be near military medical facilities and friends on and around posts, to take advantage of the lower costs of living, warm climate, or Negro servants, and to be near their birthplace and relatives or those of their wives. The social standing of many active and retired officers and their families and the groups with which they associate are immediately apparent from the society pages and the coverage of local meetings in most Southern newspapers.

Furthermore, the lack of anti-military ideology in Southern society has enhanced the relative influence of the thinking of uniformed personnel. Even comparatively liberal Southerners have continued to send their sons to military preparatory schools and to be proud of their performance in ROTC programs or at the service academies. The less conservative of the fifty-three newspapers sampled uniformly criticized General Edwin Walker and his supporters and endorsed the memorandum on civil control of the military by Senator Fulbright in 1961, but none of the newspapers—and none of the interviewees—agreed with the view of some on the left in the North to the effect that the United States has been as much to blame for the cold war as the Communist bloc. In the South there has seemed to exist relatively little of the suspicion of the "military mind" (whatever that might be) that one may note among many Northern liberals. Thus, Southerners have been less apt than other Americans to feel that military leaders "have too much to say in deciding our policy with other nations" or the like.[27]

Considering the influence of military officers and retired officers in the South, it seems useful to devote brief attention to some of their international views, especially those which they have appeared to convey to people about them. Only twenty-three officers appeared in the

27 NORC 137, 12/12/45 (1,300); NORC 155, 2/25/48 (1,271); NORC 162, 11/23/48 (1,300); and NORC 303, 6/29/51 (1,300). When the two surveys in 1948 were combined, only 9 percent in the South as compared with 16 percent in the rest of the country believed that military men had "too much" to say in our foreign policy.

formal sample for this study, but the author has developed certain impressions of them based on almost a decade of service as a Regular Army officer and numerous informal contacts with them both in and outside the South. Many officers have been apolitical; that is, they have devoted relatively little thought to political, including international political, affairs, except insofar as they were related to the military sphere. Very few could be considered isolationists in 1959–62. Some officers, especially in the air force, might be categorized as mild neo-isolationists or "Fortress America" types, for they emphasized military, naval, and air defense of the Western Hemisphere. However, these constituted apparently only a small fraction even in the air force.

However, arch-conservative groups, such as Discussions Unlimited in New Orleans and the Charleston Alert, included a number of retired officers and their wives among their leaders and active participants in 1960–61. Some of these individuals seemed to agree with many of the tenets of the military interventionist, the "let's be firmer with the Communists," anti-foreign-aid groups; others apparently agreed with some of their emphases and disagreed to some extent with others or supported such organizations even though their own thinking was less extreme, although more or less in the same direction. However, a considerable minority, and in some communities perhaps a majority, of retired officers and older officers still on active duty seemed to approve of a number of the ideas advanced by such groups, at least in moderated form. They tended to feel that since 1945 we should have followed a firmer policy with the Communist states and that we had been too infatuated with "abstract do-goodism" and "idealist mentality," even under the Eisenhower administration, too much out of line with international realities and our own world interests. We had paid too much attention to the "naïve judgements" of new nations and acted as though their criticisms were both sensible to and binding on us. These men emphasized strategic security as the most crucial aspect of our foreign policy. They doubted that the U.S.S.R. and Communist China would agree in the probable future to arms control with acceptable inspection and felt that further negotiations would probably be fruitless. Many of them appeared to stress the need for more clear-cut victories for our policies abroad rather than the ambiguous "solutions" of the recent past. They doubted that the Communist bloc would really fight if its "bluff were called" in the form of a threat of major war. Many of these former regular officers were impatient with diplomatic means; they feared that "leftists" and unrealistic "visionary idealists" in the State Department and elsewhere had permitted the Communists unnecessary successes in

the cold war. This group believed that our allies were lacking in courage and that perhaps we ought to "go it alone" if they held back. They
were often unconvinced that we should agree to limited war, and most
of them concurred with General Douglas MacArthur that we should
have attacked Manchuria and China upon Chinese entry into Korea in
late 1950. They were critical of further "surrenders of our sovereignty"
to the U.N. and to the apparent United States policy of turning its
policies over to the U.N. and other international agencies. They would
limit foreign assistance to military aid for "reliable" allies. They had
relatively little faith in capital assistance, especially for leftist-leaning
"neutrals" in the underdeveloped world. These resources could be
better used for more adequate national defense.

The, at least a significant minority of retired military officers and
older men on active duty seemed to feel little identification with many
of the nonmilitary emphases of our recent foreign policies. Their opinions tended to be harsher and more favorable to military intervention
abroad—especially in times of heightened tensions—than the thinking
of diplomatic personnel and than our recent policies. They were likely
to emphasize military force in international relations to a greater degree
and diplomatic, economic, and intercultural means to a significantly
lesser extent than have most of our civilian leaders in the executive
departments charged with foreign policy. A considerable proportion
seemed rather preoccupied with the "Communist menace" as almost the
only important problem of American foreign policy.[28]

These impressions seem supported by the findings of a systematic
study of public attitudes of senior officers in the Pentagon in the early
1950's,[29] many of whom had retired to the South by 1960. The preponderant majority identified themselves as conservatives and only one
out of twenty termed himself a "liberal," a much smaller fraction of
self-identified "liberals" than the average of all American adults or of
Southern adults (see pp. 369–70). The conservatives among these officers tended to agree with many of the ideas on world affairs advanced
by General MacArthur, under whom many of them had served in the
Far East and for whom most had much respect. The relative liberals on
foreign affairs and on public issues generally were for the most part
younger and veterans of General Eisenhower's command or that of
his successors in Europe, a finding which coincides, with some exceptions, with our impressions about officers retired to the South.

28 For similar impressions, see Daniel Bell, "The Dispossessed—1962," in Bell
(ed.), *The Radical Right* (Garden City: Doubleday, 1963), 29–30.
29 Janowitz, *The Professional Soldier*, 236–39, 275–315, and 346.

General MacArthur's views on foreign policy, and those similar in tone, seemed to have a number of adherents among younger officers as well. However, those younger officers with whom the author has been familiar both in the South and elsewhere have been, on the whole, less inclined to consider foreign policy in primarily military terms than these older men. Their more recent education at the U.S. Military Academy, in civilian colleges and graduate schools, and at advanced educational institutions in both our own and foreign armed forces and their exposure to practical international collaboration in international headquarters and armed forces have broadened the views of many of them. Only a limited minority would consider themselves "liberals" on foreign policy or domestic affairs, although the fraction very probably exceeded one in twenty in 1962. However, they have not stayed as long in any one community, their associations in the locality have tended to be less frequent (except for bachelors dating local girls), and their influences on local thinking have probably been less intensive than those of senior retired officers.

Anti-military Opinions

Pacifism, the view that it is better to be "Red than dead," support of unilateral disarmament,[30] and other anti-military opinions have been limited to a minuscule minority in the South—a minority significantly smaller than in the rest of the country. Like other forms of abstract idealistic utopianism,[31] such ideology is difficult to find in most Southern rural and small-town settings. What little pacifism exists seems concentrated among the few Quakers in the North Carolina piedmont, a few other piedmont and mountain sections, and in several cities. Since many of the more radical Quakers migrated out of the South during the increasingly tense period prior to 1861, those remaining in 1959–62 seemed on the whole more conservative about military policy than their more pacifist colleagues in the North. The Methodist pacifist of the North seems to have almost no counterpart in the South—even Southern Methodist ministers virtually uniformly support military defense expenditures and conscription. The Roman Catholic pacifist, an insignificant intellectual group in the North, seems virtually absent in the South. Pacifism in the South has long been viewed as intimately linked with abolitionism and integrationism—the worst of the Yankee "isms" (William Lloyd Garrison was originally a pacifist). Pacifist groups like the Fellowship for Reconciliation have come under attack for racial liberalism, general "leftism," and their international ideology

30 See pp. 116–19.   31 See pp. 362–64.

of unilateral disarmament and passive resistance. Pacifists appear to be considered by most Southerners as unpatriotic defeatists who either lack the courage to defend their country, are too naïve and idealistic to understand the facts of life, or promote wittingly or unwittingly the objectives of the Communists. The Southern interpersonal ethic that "nobody should be able to insult a Southerner and get away with it" has apparently been projected to the international level; surveys indicate that inhabitants of the region, both Negro and white, have been significantly more favorable to sending conscientious objectors to jail [32] and less likely to voice pacifist criticisms of large arms budgets,[33] nuclear testing,[34] and military action abroad [35] than Northerners. No traces of pacifism, even in letters to the editor, could be located in even the most liberal of the fifty-three newspapers sampled during the month of September, 1961.

Resistance to the Axis

Thus, a combination of factors—sentimental identification with the British, paucity of German-, Japanese-, Italian-, and Irish-Americans emotionally anti-British or pro-Axis; patriotic military traditions; lack of pacifists; a long history of cotton trade with Britain; a generally more conservative evaluation of individual and international phenomena than in the North; [36] and others—resulted in more widespread support in the South than elsewhere for assistance to the enemies of the Nazis, Italian Fascists, and Japanese militarists.

Whereas majorities of residents of other regions felt prior to the fall of France that it was a mistake for us to have entered World War I, only a minority of Southerners agreed; Southerners throughout the period 1937–41 were significantly more inclined than even Northeasterners to believe we were right to have joined the Allies against the Central Powers in 1917.[37]

32 AIPO 225, 1/14/41 (3,026), and AIPO 387, 12/31/46 (2,933).
33 See pp. 116–17.   34 See p. 117.
35 See pp. 108–14.   36 See pp. 343–50, 365–81.
37 AIPO poll, 6/1/37 (2,970); AIPO 174, 10/18/39 (3,141); AIPO 224, 11/19/40 (3,128); AIPO Releases of December 15, 1940, and January 10, 1941; and AIPO 234, 4/8/41 (2,986). In October, 1939, for instance, 48 percent of Southerners, 58 percent of Northeasterners, 64 percent of Midwesterners, 70 percent of those in the Plains States, and 69 percent of Westerners felt it was a mistake for us to have entered World War I. By January, 1941, 24 percent of Southerners, 27 percent of Northeasterners, 43 percent of Midwesterners, 45 percent of those in the Plains States, and 42 percent of Westerners thought it was a mistake; 55 percent of Southerners, 44 percent of Northeasterners, 35 percent of Midwesterners, 42 percent of those in the Plains States, and 38 percent of Westerners felt it was not a mistake.

The view among some Northern liberals that racially conservative Southerners have harbored "fascist" inclinations is not documented by empirical data. The reverse was certainly the case during the period 1937–45, when fascism was perceived as the principal threat to our way of life. Only 22 percent of Southerners, compared with 61 percent of Northeasterners, 47 percent of Midwesterners, and 41 percent of Westerners, said they approved in 1938 of what Father Charles E. Coughlin had to say on the radio.[38] None of the fifty-three Southern newspapers expressed opinions favorable to fascism or the Axis; during the periods for which they were examined, all of them were expressing views hostile to those Americans who did.

Among American regional groups, Southerners were invariably the strongest opponents of appeasement of the Axis. They were the least inclined to agree that the Versailles Treaty had been "too severe," [39] that former German colonies should be returned to Hitler,[40] that Germany's territorial demands in Europe were justified,[41] that Britain and France should have given in at Munich rather than going to war for the defense of Czechoslovakia,[42] and that peace should have been made with Germany in February, 1940, by letting the Nazis keep their territorial gains in Europe.[43] Regardless of their prevailing free trade tradition,[44] South-

38 Since support of Father Coughlin was significantly more prevalent among Catholic than non-Catholic Americans, removal of Catholics (few of whom resided in the South in the late 1930's) from the sample reduced differences between the South and other regions, but even when non-Catholics alone were compared, those in the South were least inclined to agree with Father Coughlin. AIPO 118, 4/6/38 (3,178). Similar interregional differences appeared on a differently worded question about Father Coughlin eight months later. AIPO 141, 12/16/38 (2,999).

39 In mid-1937, for instance, 47 percent in the South as compared with 46 percent in the Northeast, 45 percent in the Midwest, 34 percent in the Plains States, 35 percent in the Rocky Mountain region, and 27 percent in the Far West felt that the peace treaty after World War I had been "too easy"; 20 percent in the South versus 28, 35, 34, 24, and 40 percent, respectively, that it had been "too severe"; and 33 percent in the South as compared with 26, 20, 32, 41, and 33 percent respectively that it had been "about right" ("no opinions" omitted). AIPO 88, 6/21/37 (2,960).

40 AIPO Release of 11/14/37; AIPO 134, 10/1/38 (3,050); and AIPO 145, 1/20/39 (3,147). At the time of the 1939 survey, for instance, 12 percent of Southerners as compared with 19 percent of Northeasterners, 21 percent of Midwesterners, 21 percent of those in the Plains States, and 13 percent of Westerners felt that the colonies taken from Germany after World War I should be given back to her. In 1937, 22 percent of Southerners in contrast to 25 percent of Northeasterners, 24 percent of Midwesterners, 26 percent of residents of the Plains States, and 24 percent of Westerners agreed.

41 AIPO 134, 10/1/38 (3,050), and AIPO Release of 9/1/39.

42 AIPO 134, 10/1/38 (3,050).

43 AIPO 185, 2/20/40 (3,120). Eleven percent of Southerners, 18 percent of Northeasterners, 20 percent of Midwesterners, 20 percent of those in the Plains

erners, along with Northeasterners, were the most in favor among regional groups of boycotting German goods in late 1938.[45] Even as early as February, 1938, a majority of those white Southerners venturing opinions, but only minorities of other regional groups (regardless of whether non-whites were included or excluded), favored an Anglo-American "agreement to use their armies and navies together to maintain world peace." [46] By the fall of 1938, 60 percent of Southerners, compared with 48 percent of Northeasterners, 52 percent of Midwesterners, 45 percent of the Plains States residents, and 42 percent of Westerners, thought the United States would be obliged to fight Germany again in their lifetimes.[47]

Once the war began in Europe, Southerners were more apt than other regional groups to feel that the course of events overseas was vital to our national interests. Support for Britain against the Axis rose throughout the country with successive reverses suffered by the Allies. But, invariably, Southerners at any particular time agreed more than other Americans that Germany and Italy would start a war against the United States sooner or later if the Allies should be defeated,[48] that very important American interests were being defended by them against the Axis,[49] that the war in Europe was not just another struggle between

---

States, and 13 percent of Westerners favored letting Germany keep Czechoslovakia and Poland if peace could thus be achieved with Germany.

44   See pp. 139–45.

45   AIPO Release of December 18, 1938. Sixty-seven percent of Southerners, 67 percent of Northeasterners, 54 percent of Midwesterners, and 55 percent of Westerners favored such a boycott at that time.

46   AIPO 112, 2/14/38 (2,837).

47   AIPO 134, 10/1/38 (3,050). See also AIPO 115, 3/15/38 (2,902), and AIPO 136, 10/15/38 (3,070), for comparable results of posing similar questions before and after this date.

48   When asked in early 1939, "If Germany and Italy defeat England and France in a war, do you think Germany and Italy would then start a war against the U.S.?" 71 percent of Southerners as compared with 59 percent of Northeasterners, 58 percent of Midwesterners, 62 percent of residents of the Plains States, 63 percent of inhabitants of the Rocky Mountain region, and 62 percent of Far Westerners replied in the affirmative. AIPO 147, 2/2/39 (3,169). When a similar question was posed in May, 1941, 81 percent of Southerners, compared with 61 percent of Northeasterners, 59 percent of Midwesterners, 56 percent of those in the Plains States, and 62 percent of Westerners, replied, "Yes"; 13 percent of Southerners, 30 percent of Northeasterners, 32 percent of Midwesterners, 34 percent of residents in the Plains States, and 31 percent of Westerners answered, "No." AIPO 236, 5/6/41 (3,155). For the intervening period, see AIPO 169, 9/11/39 (3,072), and AIPO 207, 8/22/40 (3,107).

49   When asked at the end of 1940, "Do you think our country's safety depends on England winning this war?" 80 percent in the South, 71 percent in the Northeast, 63 percent in the Midwest, 62 percent in the Plains States, and 66 percent in the West replied, "Yes"; 17 percent, 24 percent, 30 percent, 30 percent, and

nations for power and prestige but, rather, was one of democracy against the spread of dictatorship,[50] that the interviewee would be seriously affected personally should Britain be defeated,[51] and that our country's future depended on a British victory.[52]

Throughout the late thirties, Southerners were far more inclined than other regional groups to feel that there would be another major war in Europe [53] and that this country could not or should not stay out of such a war—a majority of Southerners thought so even prior to the Anschluss in 1937.[54] Before the fall of Poland two-thirds of the South believed the United States would be obliged to enter the war against the Axis before it was over; [55] by April, 1941, almost nine out of ten Southerners thought so.[56] Similarly, Southerners were more inclined than other Americans to think that the United States would have to go to war against Japan in the near future—63 percent of them as

31 percent, respectively, answered, "no." AIPO 226, 12/16/40 (3,013). Southerners were also significantly more inclined than other regional groups to reply "yes" and less inclined to reply "no" to a similar query posed during the Nazi invasion of Poland. AIPO 171, 9/22/39 (3,064).

50   In the fall of 1939, for instance, 34 percent in the South as compared with 47 percent in the Northeast, 46 percent in the Midwest, 48 percent in the Plains States, and 45 percent in the West felt that "the present European war is just another struggle for power and prestige"; 53 percent in the South as compared with 41, 41, 39, and 43 percent, respectively, replied that it was "a struggle of democracy against the spread of dictatorship." AIPO 171, 9/22/39 (3,064).

51   AIPO 212, 9/26/40 (2,996). Seventy-nine percent of Southerners felt they would be personally affected "if the U.S. does not go into the war and Germany defeats England"; 10 percent felt they would not. The respective percentages for the North were 61 percent and 27 percent.

52   For example, in the late spring of 1941, when asked, "Do you think our country's future depends on Britain winning this war?" 70 percent in the South, 56 percent in the Northeast, 52 percent in the Midwest, 52 percent in the Plains States, 56 percent in the Rocky Mountain region, and 48 percent in the Far West replied in the affirmative; 21 percent in the South and 35, 38, 38, 33, and 41 percent, respectively, in the other regions answered in the negative; and the rest were undecided, did not know, or ventured no opinion. AIPO 237, 5/20/41 (3,089).

53   In the summer of 1937, 79 percent of Southerners, 72 percent of Northeasterners, 69 percent of Midwesterners, 69 percent of residents of the Plains States, and 75 percent of Westerners thought there would be another world war in the Old World. AIPO 91, 7/12/37 (2,917). By September, 1938, 63 percent of Southerners, 53 percent of Northeasterners, 53 percent of Midwesterners (residents of the Plains States included), and 49 percent of Westerners predicted such a war between Germany, France, and Britain within the next twelve months. AIPO 132, September, 1938 (3,063); see also AIPO 144, 1/10/39 (3,063), and AIPO 152, 3/21/39 (3,168).

54   AIPO 91, 7/12/37 (2,917). See also AIPO 61, 12/14/35 (2,813).

55   AIPO 171, 9/22/39 (3,064).

56   AIPO 234, 4/8/41 (2,986). For comparative replies by region over the period 1939–41, see also AIPO Releases of 8/20/39, 10/25/39, 4/27/41, and 5/30/41; and AIPO 144, 1/10/39 (3,063); AIPO 171, 9/22/39 (3,064); AIPO 193, 5/3/40 (3,183); AIPO 194, 5/14/40 (3,151); and AIPO 219, 10/24/40 (3,237).

compared with 53 percent of Northeasterners, 51 percent of Midwesterners, 48 percent of Plains States residents, and 50 percent of Westerners believed in this possibility several weeks before the attack on Pearl Harbor.[57]

During the pre-Pearl Harbor period on every poll question dealing with United States intervention on the side of the Allies, Southerners were willing to go further, to take greater risks of United States involvement in the war, and to make more sacrifices for the opponents of the Axis than were residents of any other region, including the Northeast. Twenty-four percent of Southerners versus 23 percent of Northeasterners, 18 percent of Midwesterners, 16 percent of Plains States residents, and 18 percent of Westerners favored revising the Neutrality Act in early 1939 to permit arms shipments to the Spanish Loyalists.[58] A majority of Southerners—53 percent—at that time favored changing these neutrality laws to give more aid to China but none to Japan; only 43 percent of Northeasterners, 32 percent of Midwesterners, 30 percent of Plains States residents, and 46 percent of Westerners agreed.[59] Six months prior to the invasion of Poland, 62 percent of Southerners, compared with 57 percent of Northeasterners, 52 percent of Midwesterners, 57 percent of Plains States residents, and 53 percent of Westerners, thought the neutrality laws should be changed to sell war materials to Britain and France in case of war.[60] By August, 1939, just prior to the opening of hostilities in Europe, 60 percent of Southerners, 50 percent of Northeasterners, 45 percent of Midwesterners, 49 percent of Plains States residents, and 51 percent of Westerners favored liberalization of the Neutrality Act to permit sale of war materials to the Allies.[61] By July, 1939, 73 percent of Southerners versus 58 percent of other citizens felt we should sell airplanes and other war materials to Britain and France but not to the Axis.[62] Forty-five percent of inhabitants in the South as compared with 26 percent in the Northeast, 30 percent in the Midwest, 20 percent in the Plains States, and 33 percent in the West in the late spring of 1939 favored amending the Johnson Act (to prevent any country which had ceased paying interest on its debts for the previous world war from borrowing more here) in order that "England and France could borrow money from our government." [63] The majority of the rest of the country believed that Congress was right in defeating a bill in the summer

---

57 AIPO 254, 11/25/41 (3,035).   58 AIPO 143, 1/7/39 (3,063).
59 AIPO 144, 1/10/39 (3,063).   60 AIPO 153, 3/30/39 (3,238).
61 AIPO 167, 8/17/39 (3,163).   62 AIPO 163, July, 1939 (3,146).
63 AIPO Release of 5/14/39. See also AIPO 155, 4/19/39 (3,124); and AIPO 157, 5/10/39 (3,074).

of 1939 which would have permitted sale of war materials to Britain and France in case of war; only in the South did a majority feel that Congress was wrong.[64]

Once the war had actually begun, the majority of Southerners in favor of revising or eliminating the Neutrality and Johnson acts mounted considerably higher, remaining consistently larger than in other regions. As it became apparent that Poland would be crushed between German and Soviet armies, 68 percent of the South—71 percent of Southern whites—approved of the idea of changing the neutrality law to permit the Allies to buy military supplies in America; [65] by the end of September and early October the figure for Southern whites had risen to 84 percent.[66] With the advent of the "phony war" between the fall of Poland and the invasion of Denmark and Norway the next spring, the majority in the South favoring revision of the Neutrality Act to permit "cash and carry" by the Allies decreased somewhat, but at no time below two thirds, and the percentage was always significantly higher than in any other region of the country.[67] By the end of May, 1940, as the fall of France appeared very probable, a majority of Southerners—53 percent—favored changing or eliminating the Johnson Act so that Britain and France could borrow money from our government to purchase military materiel in this country; only 32 percent in the Northeast, 30 percent in the Midwest, 32 percent in the Plains States, and 35 percent in the West agreed.[68]

After the fall of the Low Countries and France and the beginning of the massive air attacks on Britain, a majority of Southerners—53 percent—compared with only 38 percent of Northeasterners, 37 percent of Midwesterners, 33 percent of Plains States residents, 41 percent of inhabitants of the Rocky Mountain region, and 41 percent of Far Westerners, felt that the neutrality laws should be changed to permit

64   AIPO 166, 8/8/39 (3,117); and AIPO 167, 8/17/39 (3,163). The combined replies of these two surveys indicated that 52 percent of Southerners, 41 percent of Northeasterners, 37 percent of Midwesterners, 33 percent of residents of the Plains States, and 48 percent of Westerners felt Congress was wrong.

65   Combined results of AIPO 169, 9/11/39 (3,072), and AIPO 170, 9/19/39 (3,149).

66   AIPO 171, 9/22/39 (3,064); AIPO 172, 10/3/39 (3,139); and AIPO 173, 10/10/39 (3,180).

67   AIPO 174, 10/18/39 (3,141); AIPO Release of 11/3/39; and AIPO 175, 10/24/39 (3,139).

68   AIPO 197, 5/29/40 (3,163). Fifty-three percent of Southerners, more than in any other region, had said in February, 1940, that they would favor such amendment or elimination of the Johnson Act "if it looked as though England and France would lose the war unless we loaned them money to buy war supplies here." AIPO 184, 2/6/40 (3,175).

even the sending of war materials to Britain in American ships.[69] By January, the Southern percentage had risen to 58,[70] by late October, 1941, to 73.[71] In late 1940, 69 percent of Southerners (73 percent of whites) favored changing the Johnson Act to permit Britain to borrow money from our federal government to pursue its war effort against the Axis; only 57 percent of those in the Northeast, 49 percent in the Midwest, 49 percent in the Plains States, and 57 percent in the West agreed.[72] By January, 1941, 91 percent of the South as compared with 60 percent of the Northeast, 48 percent of the Midwest (including the Plains States), and 49 percent of the West were of this view.[73]

Throughout the pre-Pearl Harbor period Southerners were much more inclined than other sectional groups, including the Northeasterners, to agree that we should take whatever actions seemed necessary to help Britain and France, and later Britain alone, to defeat the Axis, even if such actions increased the risk of our getting into the war. The differences were usually striking—for instance, immediately after the fall of Poland, 47 percent of Southerners (51 percent of Southern whites) agreed with this view, compared with 30 percent of Northeasterners, 25 percent of Midwesterners, 26 percent of residents in the Plains States, and 28 percent of Westerners.[74] Whenever those persons included in national samples were asked whether we should be doing more to assist the Allies, Southerners invariably replied in larger proportions than other regional groups in the affirmative.[75] By early spring of 1941, 59 percent of Southerners (62 percent of Southern whites) favored sending war materials to Britain in armed American ships with American crews and under the guns of United States naval convoys; of like mind were only 41 percent of those in the Northeast, 35 percent in the Midwest, 33 percent in the Plains States, and 42 percent in the West.[76] By

69 AIPO 215, 10/9/40 (3,135).
70 AIPO Release of 1/17/41. At that time 42 percent in the Northeast, 38 percent in the Midwest, 38 percent in the Plains States, and 45 percent in the West agreed.
71 AIPO 251, 10/22/41 (3,064).
72 AIPO 215, 10/9/40 (3,135), and AIPO Release of 12/20/40.
73 AIPO 228, 1/9/41 (3,033).
74 AIPO 172, 10/3/39 (3,139). See also AIPO 147, 2/2/39 (3,169); AIPO 152, 3/21/39 (3,168); AIPO 196, 5/25/40 (3,198); AIPO Release of 9/22/40; AIPO 224, 11/19/40 (3,128); AIPO 227, 12/31/40 (3,107); AIPO 226, 12/16/40 (3,103); AIPO Releases of 12/29/40 and 1/10/41; AIPO 229, 1/22/41 (3,124); AIPO 236, 8/6/41 (3,155); AIPO 238, 5/29/41 (3,152); AIPO 248, 9/17/41 (3,059); and AIPO 250, 10/7/41 (3,059).
75 AIPO 200, 7/3/40 (3,135) and AIPO 248, 9/17/41 (3,059).
76 AIPO Release of 4/23/41. See also AIPO 227, 12/31/40 (3,107); AIPO Release of 5/21/41; and AIPO polls 237, 5/20/41 (3,089); 238, 5/29/41 (3,152); 239, 6/7/41

September, 1941, 80 percent of Southerners, but only 62 percent of Northeasterners, 55 percent of Midwesterners, 57 percent of Plains States residents, and 61 percent of Westerners, felt we should arm our merchant ships and shoot Axis submarines and other warships on sight.[77] Southerners were significantly more apt than other sectional groups to agree that we should let Americans volunteer for military service in Allied armies.[78] The "swap" of United States overage destroyers for British bases was probably the turning point in United States intervention on the side of Britain; 68 percent of Southerners, but only 56 percent of Northeasterners, 51 percent of Midwesterners, 49 percent of Plains States residents, and 61 percent of Westerners favored this idea in August, 1940.[79]

Interregional differences in favor of intervention to aid Western Europe were typically wider than differences with respect to assisting other enemies of the Axis. However, after the Panay bombing in 1937, 23 percent of those in the South, compared with 19 percent in the Northeast, 12 percent in the Midwest, 8 percent in the Plains States, 11 percent in the Rocky Mountain region, and 10 percent in the Pacific Coast area, "would like to see the U.S. send more warships to China." Fifty-four percent of the South versus 51 percent, 71 percent, 70 percent, 58 percent, and 64 percent respectively of the other regions felt we should "withdraw those there now." [80] In early 1938, 45 percent of Southerners as compared with 38 percent of Northeasterners, 30 percent of Midwesterners, 31 percent of Plains States residents, 43 percent in the Rocky Mountain region, and 29 percent on the Pacific Coast thought the United States "should allow shipment of arms and ammunition from this country to China." [81] Thus, Southerners were more inclined to favor intervention in the Far East than even residents of our West Coast, traditionally the area supposedly most interested in developments in East Asia.

(3,078); 240, 5/24/41 (3,063); 241, 7/9/41 (2,990); 243, 7/29/41 (3,048); 244, 8/5/41 (2,973); 246, 8/26/41 (3,022); 247, 9/9/41 (3,059); 249, 10/13/41 (2,949); and 251, 10/22/41 (3,064).

77 AIPO 248, 9/17/41 (3,059). See also AIPO 247, 9/9/41 (3,059); AIPO Release of 10/5/41; AIPO 251, 10/22/41 (3,064); and AIPO 254, 11/25/41 (3,035). Southerners were the most favorable of regional groups to shooting on sight on all these surveys.

78 AIPO 197, 5/29/40 (3,163).

79 Twenty percent in the South were opposed, compared with 38 percent in the Northeast, 39 percent in the Midwest, 42 percent in the Plains States, and 26 percent in the West. AIPO 206, 8/9/40 (3,117). See also AIPO 232, 3/7/41 (3,044), and AIPO 234, 4/8/41 (2,986).

80 The remainder of those with opinions felt we should keep about as much naval power there as at the time. AIPO 106, 12/13/37 (2,859).

81 AIPO 111, 2/3/38 (2,908). See also AIPO 125, 6/9/38 (3,240).

Entry of the Soviet Union into the war introduced conflicting sentiments throughout the country. During the Soviet attack on Finland after the partition of Poland, 71 percent of Southerners were in favor of the United States government lending money to Finland to purchase war supplies in this country, while only 65 percent in the Northeast, 61 percent in the Midwest, 65 percent in the Plains States, and 55 percent in the West agreed.[82] In February, 1940, 80 percent of Southerners compared with 73 percent of Northeasterners, 74 percent of Midwesterners, 70 percent of the Plains States residents, and 69 percent of Westerners approved of letting Finland "raise money for her war against Russia by selling bonds to Americans." [83] By mid-March, 80 percent of Southerners, compared with 73 percent, 73 percent, 70 percent, and 69 percent respectively, approved of both loans by our government to Finland, "even if chances of repayment are slender" (as advocated by Senator Pat Harrison of Mississippi), and "letting Finland raise money for her war against Russia by selling bonds to Americans." [84]

Nevertheless, when asked in late 1938 whether they would prefer that Germany or Russia win in case of war between them, 89 percent of Southerners replying said, "Russia," compared with 85 percent of Northeasterners, 85 percent of Midwesterners, 80 percent of Plains States dwellers, and 84 percent of Westerners.[85] Besides other Soviet acts, the Soviet signing of the nonaggression pact with Nazi Germany and her attacks on Poland and Finland reduced the size of the national majority in America favorable to the Soviets in case of war with the Axis. Nevertheless, shortly after the Nazi attack on the U.S.S.R. in June, 1941, 86 percent of Southerners as compared with 68 percent of Northeasterners, 72 percent of Midwesterners, 70 percent of Plains States residents and 72 percent of Westerners said they wanted the Russians to win; only 2 percent of Southerners, less than in any other region, replied that they wanted the Germans to win.[86] The same survey revealed that only in the South did a majority not oppose supplying Russia with arms, airplanes, and other materials "on the same basis as Britain." [87]

Although only a minority of Southerners wished to declare war on the Axis or send United States troops and warships to aid the Allies

82   AIPO 180, 12/22/39 (3,085). See also AIPO 182, 1/19/40 (3,199).
83   AIPO 184, 2/6/40 (3,175).   84   AIPO Release of 3/10/40.
85   AIPO 138, 11/14/38 (3,117).   86   AIPO 240, 6/24/41 (3,063).
87   *Ibid.* Forty-one percent of Southerners as compared with 34 percent of Northerners favored this proposed extension of Lend-Lease to the Soviets on the same basis as to Britain; 47 percent of the former versus 56 percent of the latter disapproved.

before December 7, 1941, the proportion was always larger than that within any other region. Even shortly before the beginning of active hostilities in Europe, 24 percent of Southerners, compared with 14 percent of Northeasterners, 18 percent of Midwesterners, 14 percent of Plains States dwellers, and 17 percent of Westerners, felt the United States should "send our army and navy abroad to fight Germany." [88] A 57 percent majority of the South as compared with 48 percent of the Northeast, 43 percent of the Midwest, 40 percent of the Plains States, and 52 percent of the West felt a few days before the Nazi invasion of Poland that we should enter the war if there should be one and that it appeared Britain and France would be defeated if we did not.[89] Several weeks before the attack on Pearl Harbor, 38 percent of the South in contrast to 27 percent of the non-South advocated that the Congress declare war on Germany.[90]

Shortly after Hitler's invasion of Czechoslovakia in the spring of 1939, a majority of Southerners (56 percent) thought that every able-bodied young man should be made to serve in the army or navy for at least a year. The figure for the North was only 37 percent—41 percent in the Northeast, 38 percent in the Midwest, 34 percent in the Plains States, and 35 percent in the West.[91] The Southern percentage mounted to the eighties with the fall of France.[92] Two thirds of Southern opinion agreed with most Congressmen from the region in the summer of 1941 that the draft should be extended beyond the year shortly to expire to keep Americans in uniform, whereas only 48 percent of non-Southerners agreed.[93] Shortly after Pearl Harbor, three quarters of the South—more than in other regions—favored drafting women for war-time jobs,[94] a remarkable majority considering the

88   AIPO 168, 8/30/39 (3,114).
89   *Ibid.* For changes in this attitude between the attack on Poland and the Japanese attack on Pearl Harbor, see AIPO Release of 10/22/39; AIPO 183, 1/30/40 (3,179); and AIPO 237, 5/20/41 (3,089).
90   AIPO 251, 10/22/41 (3,064). For the evolution of Southern and Northern thinking about sending our armed forces to fight the Axis and declaring war on Germany, Italy, and/or Japan, see the following: AIPO 171, 9/22/39 (3,064); AIPO 195, 5/16/40 (3,139); AIPO 199, 6/25/40 (3,101); AIPO 201, 7/11/40 (3,174); AIPO Release of October 12, 1940; AIPO 212, 9/26/40 (2,996); AIPO 227, 12/31/40 (3,107); AIPO 231, 2/27/41 (3,025); AIPO Release of 5/16/41; AIPO 233, 3/19/41 (3,121); AIPO 237, 5/20/41 (3,089); AIPO 238, 5/29/41 (3,152); AIPO 243, 7/29/41 (3,048); AIPO 244, 8/5/41 (2,973); AIPO 246, 8/26/41 (3,022); and AIPO 251, 10/22/41 (3,064).
91   AIPO 156, 5/2/39 (3,110).
92   AIPO 198, 6/11/40 (3,090); AIPO 206, 8/9/40 (3,117); AIPO 207, 8/22/40 (3,107); and AIPO 216, 10/19/40 (3,165).
93   AIPO 242, 7/22/41 (2,899).
94   AIPO Release of March 27, 1942.

emphasis on "Southern womanhood" and femininity among both sexes in that region. In the summer of 1940, 90 percent of Southerners, compared with 83 percent of Northeasterners, 82 percent of Midwesterners, 87 percent of Plains States residents, and 86 percent of Westerners, approved of calling the National Guard to active duty.[95] Eighty-two percent of those in the South versus 71 percent in the Northeast, 69 percent in the Midwest, 58 percent in the Plains States, and 73 percent in the West thought, in the fall of 1941, that high school boys should be given military training in their communities.[96]

It was noted previously that Southerners, though more conservative fiscally on the average than Northerners, were more willing to pay higher taxes for defense and to increase our budgets for stronger military forces.[97] Although Southerners as a whole had benefited disproportionately more than other Americans from the domestic New Deal due to their more depressed economic status, they were the most inclined of regional groups in early 1940 to say that federal relief should be reduced sharply and the money thus released put into national defense and aid to the Allies.[98] Seventy-six percent of Southerners said in late 1940 that they would personally be willing to spend five hours each week without pay in defense work—the non Southern figures were 65 percent in the Northeast, 63 percent in the Midwest, 58 percent in the Plains States, and 73 percent in the West.[99] Throughout the period between the fall of France and the attack on Pearl Harbor, increasing majorities of Southerners venturing views, invariably larger than in any other major region, felt that the then current rate of war production was too low, that greater resources should be allocated to national defense, that assistance to the British was too little, and that our own armed forces should be increased at a faster rate.[100]

95 AIPO 204, 7/31/40 (3,079).   96 AIPO 249, 10/13/41 (2,949).
97 See notes 19, 20, and 22 for this chapter.
98 AIPO 181, 1/10/40 (3,134), and AIPO 183, 1/30/40 (3,179).
99 AIPO 227, 12/31/40 (3,107). See also AIPO 226, 12/16/40 (3,013).
100 AIPO 200, 7/3/40 (3,135); AIPO 204, 7/31/40 (3,079); AIPO 208, 9/3/40 (3,200); AIPO 226, 12/16/40 (3,013); AIPO 232, 3/7/41 (3,044); AIPO 236, 5/6/41 (3,155); AIPO 238, 5/28/41 (3,152); and AIPO 248, 9/17/41 (3,059). For example, at the time of the AIPO survey of July 3, 1940, 27 percent of Southerners as compared with 34 percent of Northeasterners, 28 percent of Midwesterners, 37 percent of residents of the Plains States, and 33 percent of Westerners said that they were satisfied with our rate of defense production, whereas 43 percent of Southerners in contrast to 41, 41, 33, and 39 percent, respectively, said they were dissatisfied. By the time of the AIPO survey of March 7, 1941, only 21 percent of Southerners versus 30, 30, 35, and 29 percent, respectively, felt satisfied; 63 percent of Southerners as compared with 50, 57, 47, and 55 percent, respectively, in the other regions were dissatisfied.

In the fall of 1941, majorities of residents of other regions opposed sending draftees to fight outside the Western Hemisphere or "this country's possessions," but three out of five Southerners thought that Congress should change the laws so that the U.S. Army could send draftees to "any part of the world." [101] Sixty-six percent in the South approved of the United States taking over the defense of Iceland; only 9 percent disapproved. Comparable approvals and disapprovals in other regions were 64 and 16 percent in the Northeast, 57 and 20 percent in the Midwest, 56 and 21 percent in the Plains States, and 62 and 15 percent in the West.[102] The South was more opposed than other regions to proposed changes in our Constitution which would require a majority vote in a national plebiscite before United States soldiers could be sent overseas or war could be declared; as late as mid-1941, 49 percent in the Northeast, 56 percent in the Midwest, 57 percent in the Plains States, and 48 percent in the West thought this proposition a good idea, but only 31 percent in the South agreed.[103] Southern reactions to isolationism were further indicated by surveys of attitudes toward isolationist or defeatist leaders and their proposals—only 28 percent of the South as compared with 52 percent of the rest of America agreed in August, 1940, with Charles Lindbergh's view that the United States should try to have friendly trade and diplomatic relations with the Nazis if they won the war in Europe; [104] 22 percent of the South, compared with 32 percent of the North, thought that Britain should try to work out a "peace" with Germany rather than continuing to fight in the spring of 1941; [105] and 9 percent of the former in contrast to 17 percent of the latter said in the fall of 1941 that they would vote for a "Keep-Out-Of-War" party led by such figures as Senator Burton K. Wheeler, Senator Gerald P. Nye, and Lindbergh.[106] They had no major supporters among Southern Senators other than Senator

101 AIPO 250, 10/7/41 (3,059). Fifty-nine percent in the South as compared with 39 percent in the Northeast, 42 percent in the Midwest, 39 percent in the Plains States, and 42 percent in the West felt that our laws should be changed to permit sending draftees anywhere in the world; 36 percent in the South versus 56, 53, 55, and 52 percent, respectively, opposed this suggestion. See also AIPO 241, 7/9/41 (2,990); AIPO 243, 7/29/41 (3,048); and AIPO 254, 11/25/41 (3,035).
102 AIPO 241, 7/9/41 (2,990).
103 AIPO 238, 5/29/41 (3,152). See also unnumbered AIPO survey of 11/17/36 (2,873); AIPO 98, 9/7/37 (2,960); AIPO 132, September, 1939 (3,063); AIPO 151, 3/8/39 (3,154); AIPO 168, 8/30/39 (3,114); AIPO 181, 1/10/40 (3,134); AIPO Release of 1/28/40; AIPO 196, 5/23/40 (3,198); and AIPO 226, 12/16/40 (3,013); for earlier replies to this and similar questions.
104 AIPO 206, 8/9/40 (3,117).
105 AIPO 234, 4/8/41 (2,986). See also AIPO 239, 6/7/41 (3,078).
106 AIPO Release of 9/11/41.

Bob Reynolds of North Carolina, and their few adherents among Southern voters were primarily some former Northerners and immigrants from Germany and Italy.[107]

These findings are particularly interesting in that the other great agricultural areas, the Midwest and the Plains States, were the most isolationist sections of the country on most of these questions. The most isolationist groups outside the South were farmers, rural people, the poorly educated, and those in the less complex occupations. But the South was by far the most rural and agricultural region and had the smallest percentages of educated individuals and persons in the more complicated occupations. Furthermore, Southern Negroes lowered the Southern averages favoring intervention and mutual security against the Axis—with but minor exceptions, they were less favorable to active support of the Allies than Southern whites and more inclined to feel that we should avoid international commitments and risks which might entail war or lesser personal sacrifices. Moreover, when Southerners who replied on surveys that they had voted in the immediately preceding Congressional primary or election were compared with those who said they had not, the former were noticeably more inclined to favor active assistance to the enemies of the Axis and related foreign involvements. Differences between the South and the rest of the country in replies to such questions as those discussed above increased sharply from the figures cited (percentage differences sometimes even doubling) when only voters were compared, or when whites of comparable education were compared. These findings help considerably to explain the much more widespread support for activist, anti-Axis policies by Southern than by Northern Congressmen; most of the Southern isolationists did not vote whereas most of the Northern ones did.

The Postwar Communist Challenge

The Narrowing of Regional Differences

After the attack on Pearl Harbor, most Americans who had previously opposed foreign "entanglements" quickly accepted the idea that we should take a more active part in world affairs after the war. Most of the relatively few isolationists in the South and of the much larger number in the North had come to this conclusion by early 1943; at that time 80 percent of Southerners, compared with a like proportion of residents in the Northeast, 75 percent in the Midwest (including the

107 Wayne S. Cole, "America First and the South, 1940–1941," *Journal of Southern History*, XXII (1956), 36–38.

Plains States), and 77 percent in the West, said we should take an active part in world affairs. Only 11 percent in the South, 12 percent in the Northeast, 14 percent in the Midwest, and 12 percent in the West replied that we should either "stay out" or "mind [our] own business and keep out of foreign affairs."[108] The proportions favoring more active involvement remained around three quarters of the adult population with only minor variations among the regions throughout the war and declined only relatively little even after V-J Day.[109] The size of the majority favoring active involvement rose and fell with frustrations and other developments on the world scene, but throughout the postwar period between one half and four fifths of the national adult population either rejected isolationist alternatives or said they favored an active international stance. Interregional differences, when "no opinions" were eliminated, remained small, typically not statistically significant at the 10 percent level of confidence.[110]

As in other regions, postwar isolationist sentiments in the South were concentrated primarily among the lower occupational, social, and economic groups, the poorly educated, farmers, Negroes, and older people. Erosion of prewar insularism was particularly conspicuous among the minority of the Southern educated classes who were isolationists prior to Pearl Harbor. Judging from the isolationists among the interviewees in 1959–62, most had been of that persuasion all their adult lives, during the interwar years as well if they were old enough.

Southerners' Perceptions of the Communist Menace

One source of the remaining differences between the South and the rest of the country in views about security policy has been the greater incidence in the South of pessimism or, at least, greater caution about

108   AIPO 288, 1/27/43 (3,095).
109   AIPO Release of June 20, 1943; AIPO 317, 4/26/44 (2,996); Roper survey of May, 1945 (3,584); AIPO 357, 10/3/45 (3,097); and AIPO 366, 2/27/46 (3,122). Seventy-two percent of Americans in March, 1946, felt it would be "best for the future of this country if we take an active part in world affairs"; only 22 percent felt we should "stay out." AIPO Release of 3/27/46.
110   NORC 143, 6/21/46 (1,307); NORC 145, 10/2/46 (1,308); NORC 151, 6/24/47 (1,273); AIPO 403, 8/27/47 (2,999); NORC 156, 3/25/48 (1,289); NORC 159, 6/29/48 (1,301); NORC 165, 4/19/49 (1,300); NORC 169, 9/16/49 (1,300); NORC 170, 10/12/49 (1,300); NORC 273, 1/18/50 (1,284); AIPO 455, 5/2/50 (2,850); NORC 282, 6/14/50 (1,276); AIPO 467, 11/10/50 (1,367); NORC 295, 12/28/50 (1,258); AIPO 469, 12/30/50 (1,389); NORC 337, 2/11/53 (1,291); AIPO 518, 7/23/53 (1,532); AIPO 519, 8/13/53 (1,613); NORC 348, 9/24/53 (526); NORC 355, 4/22/54 (1,207); AIPO 534, 7/14/54 (1,549); and NORC 370, 3/11/55 (1,225). Questions have not been identically worded, but this generalization applied to the varied queries 1945–55.

the probable behavior of the Communist bloc. The more prevalent rugged agrarian individualism (see p. 374), laissez-faire economic ethic (see pp. 373–77), and general conservatism (see pp. 365–81) in the South than in the North have tended to render its citizens even more hostile to Communism than most Northerners.

Even during the war, Southerners seemed somewhat less optimistic than non-Southerners about the possibility of western collaboration with the Soviets in the postwar era. In the latter part of World War II, somewhat larger proportions of Southerners than others felt there would probably be another war in the next twenty-five years or less.[111] Despite the enthusiasm immediately following ratification of the U.N. Charter and the defeat of Germany, approximately one third of adult Southerners in contrast to slightly over one fifth of Northerners believed there would be another world war within the next twenty-five years.[112] Although more Southerners than not at the end of August, 1945, thought that the development of the A-bomb rendered future wars "less likely," 15 percent of those in the South as compared with 9 percent in the Northeast, 9 percent in the Midwest (including the Plains States), and 10 percent in the West felt it made war "more likely."[113] With increasing disagreements with the Soviets over such issues as the Balkans, Iran, and control of nuclear weapons, the percentage of Southerners who expected another world war within twenty-five years rose to 74 by August, 1946, compared with 62 of residents in the Northeast, 64 in the Midwest, 67 in the Plains States, 57 in the Rocky Mountain region, and 69 in the West.[114] By midsummer of 1947, several months after President Truman proposed assistance to Greece and Turkey and shortly after Secretary of State George C. Marshall's Harvard University speech advocating the plan bearing his name, 78 percent of inhabitants in the South versus 67 percent in the Northeast, 71 percent in the Midwest (including the Plains States), and 65 percent in the West predicted another world war in ten years or less.[115] The proportions who have expected world war within a given period in the South and in the country generally have oscillated throughout the

111 AIPO 309, 1/4/44 (3,028); AIPO 341, 2/20/45 (3,057); NORC 233, March, 1945 (2,500); AIPO 344, 4/5/45 (3,134); AIPO 350, 6/27/45 (3,086); and NORC 235, July, 1945 (2,572). Summation of replies to similar questions revealed differences significant at the 10 percent level.
112 NORC 235, July, 1945 (2,572).   113 NORC 133, 8/31/45 (1,259).
114 AIPO 375, 7/24/46 (3,124). For data indicating rapid increase in incidence of prediction of another war in twenty-five years during the intervening period, see NORC 237, September, 1945 (1,270); AIPO 358, 10/17/45 (3,139); and AIPO 366, 2/27/46 (3,122).
115 AIPO 400, 7/2/47 (3,000).

postwar years, depending on perceived Communist threats and other factors, but usually at any specific moment larger percentages of Southerners than of other regional groups have expected World War III in which the Communist powers and the West, particularly the United States, would be the main protagonists.[116] Majorities in the South of both races have been expecting such a war in their lifetimes or within the next twenty-five (sometimes even the next five) years for much of the period since 1947. For example, in late June, 1960, shortly after Premier Khrushchev insulted President Eisenhower in Paris and torpedoed the summit conference there and also following a period of rather accentuated tension over Berlin and the U-2 incident, 70 percent of those in the South versus 56 percent of the rest of the country believed that there was "bound to be" a major war with the Communists "sooner or later." [117] Less than a month later, 57 percent of Southerners,

116   AIPO 400, 7/2/47 (3,000); NORC 152, 10/10/47 (1,290); NORC 155, 2/25/48 (1,271); NORC 288, 9/20/50 (1,254); AIPO 412, 2/4/48 (3,185); AIPO 415, 3/18/48 (3,129); AIPO 416, 4/7/48 (3,169); NORC 158, 6/2/48 (1,295); AIPO 422, 7/28/48 (3,142); NORC 163, 1/26/49 (1,261); NORC 164, 3/3/49 (1,300); NORC 165, 4/19/49 (1,300); NORC 166, 6/1/49 (1,300); NORC 167, 6/30/49 (1,284); AIPO 444, 6/30/49 (2,826); NORC 168, 8/11/49 (1,300); NORC 169, 9/16/49 (1,300); NORC 170, 10/12/49 (1,300); NORC 171, 11/11/49 (1,300); NORC 273, 1/18/50 (1,284); NORC 276, 3/1/50 (1,300); NORC 280, 4/17/50 (1,274); AIPO 455, 5/2/50 (2,850); NORC 282, 6/14/50 (1,270); NORC 287, 7/24/50 (1,302); NORC 291, 10/18/50 (1,305); NORC 292, 11/22/50 (1,258); NORC 295, 12/28/50 (1,258); AIPO 469, 12/30/50 (1,389); NORC 298, 1/30/51 (1,236); NORC 300, 3/20/51 (1,300); AIPO 472, 3/24/51 (1,500); NORC 302, 4/18/51 (1,300); NORC 303, 6/29/51 (1,300); NORC 307, 5/24/51 (1,282); AIPO 475, 5/17/51 (2,070); AIPO 477, 7/6/51 (2,013); NORC 312, 8/27/51 (1,237); NORC 313, 10/2/51 (1,237); NORC 314, 11/22/51 (1,237); NORC 315, 12/18/51 (1,237); NORC 320, 3/19/51 (1,260); NORC 323, 4/22/52 (1,250); NORC 325, 5/28/52 (1,265); NORC 327, 6/30/52 (1,285); NORC 332, 10/15/52 (1,291); NORC 333, 11/17/52 (1,291); NORC 334, 12/29/52 (1,291); NORC 337, 2/11/52 (1,291); NORC 339, 4/1/52 (1,291); NORC 341-2, 6/30/53 (1,291); NORC 347, 8/21/53 (526); AIPO 521, 10/7/53 (1,488); NORC 349, 11/25/53 (1,300); AIPO 527, 2/23/54 (1,511); AIPO Release of April 10, 1954; NORC 355, 4/22/54 (1,207); AIPO 529, 4/6/54 (1,482); NORC 363, 9/10/54 (1,198); AIPO 538, 10/13/54 (1,530); NORC 365, 11/26/54 (1,201); AIPO 541, 12/29/54 (1,446); NORC 366, 1/21/55 (1,209); AIPO 544, 3/1/55 (1,395); AIPO 548, 6/1/55 (1,462); NORC 372, 6/23/55 (1,263); NORC 374, 8/4/55 (1,262); NORC 378, 10/6/55 (527); AIPO 555, 10/25/55 (1,577); AIPO 556, 11/15/55 (1,545); NORC 379, 11/23/55 (1,276); AIPO 558, 1/4/56 (1,385); NORC 382, 1/26/56 (1,238); NORC 385, 4/20/56 (1,224); AIPO 566, 6/13/56 (2,078); AIPO 568, 8/1/56 (2,173); NORC 393, 9/13/56 (1,263); NORC 398, 10/25/56 (1,295); NORC 399, 11/15/56 (1,286); AIPO 575, 11/20/56 (1,502); NORC 401, 12/28/56 (1,232); AIPO 581, 4/4/57 (1,654); AIPO 582, 4/23/57 (1,626); NORC 404, 4/26/57 (1,279); AIPO 598, 4/14/58 (1,396); AIPO 614, 5/27/59 (1,537); AIPO 617, 8/18/59 (2,982); AIPO 620, 10/14/59 (2,750); AIPO 628, 6/24/60 (3,033); AIPO 631, 7/14/60 (2,900); AIPO 639, 12/6/60 (2,846); AIPO 642, 3/8/61 (3,511); and AIPO 650, 9/16/61 (3,476).
117   AIPO 628, 6/24/60 (3,033).

compared with 41 percent of Northeasterners, 48 percent of Midwesterners (including residents in the Plains States), and 38 percent of
Westerners, felt we were "likely to get into another world war in the
next five years"; only 26 percent of Southerners as compared with 44
percent of Northeasterners, 40 percent of Midwesterners, and 42 percent of Westerners were contrary-minded.[118] However, by the spring
of 1961, two months after the change in federal administrations, the
percentages of persons thinking that war would be likely in the next
five years fell to 46 percent in the South, 25 percent in the Northeast,
30 percent in the Midwest, and 25 percent in the West.[119]

Related to these observations is the finding that Southerners have
been at least somewhat, and at times considerably, less optimistic than
other regional groups about the feasibility of cooperating with the
Communist powers on any long-term basis to preserve a just peace. As
in the case of prediction of another world war, this time with the Communists, the proportions in the South and outside who have felt United
States-Soviet collaboration feasible or likely have varied with the international climate at the time, but virtually without exception smaller
minorities of Southerners than of other Americans have thought that
we will ever be able to trust the Russians to "meet us half way,"[120] that
we can expect them to "cooperate" with us in international affairs[121]
and to change their aggressive behavior and attempt to make "real
peace" with the non-Communist world.[122] Southerners more than other

118 AIPO 631, 7/14/60 (2,900).   119 AIPO 642, 3/8/61 (3,511).
120 NORC 151, 6/24/47 (1,273), and NORC 152, 10/10/47 (1,290). For instance,
at the time of the first of these two surveys, 18 percent in the South as compared
with 30 percent in the Northeast, 26 percent in the Midwest (including the Plains
States), and 28 percent in the West felt we could count on Russia to "meet us half
way"; 68 percent in the South versus 58, 62, and 59 percent, respectively, believed
we could not; and the rest said they did not know, were undecided, or had no
opinion.
121 AIPO Release of 4/30/43; NORC 133, 8/31/45 (1,259); AIPO 358, 10/17/45
(3,139); NORC 139, 2/2/46 (1,263); AIPO 366, 2/27/46 (3,122); NORC 141,
3/20/46 (1,293); AIPO 368, 3/27/46 (3,225); AIPO 369, 4/10/46 (3,152); NORC
142, 5/17/46 (1,292); AIPO 376, 8/14/46 (3,005); NORC 145, 10/2/46 (1,308);
AIPO 386, 12/11/46 (3,029); and AIPO 442, 5/19/49 (2,751).
122 NORC 160, 7/30/48 (1,300); NORC 315, 12/18/51 (1,237); NORC 291,
10/18/50 (305); NORC 295, 12/28/50 (1,258); NORC 333, 11/17/52 (1,291); NORC
339, 4/1/53 (1,291); NORC 341-2, 6/30/53 (1,291); NORC 372, 6/23/55 (1,263);
NORC 374, 8/4/55 (1,212); NORC 376, 9/29/55 (1,250); NORC 379, 11/23/55
(1,276); NORC 390, 6/26/56 (1,275); and AIPO 639, 12/6/60 (2,846). As with most
questions related to United States-U.S.S.R. relations, the minority relatively optimistic about cooperation with the Soviet Union rose at least somewhat after the
Korean War. For instance, at the time of the survey of November 17, 1952, 22
percent of Southerners as compared with 26 percent of Northeasterners, 30 percent of Midwesterners (residents of the Plains States included), and 28 percent

citizens have thought that the Soviets would attack parts of the world not yet under their control if they believed that the West could not or would not employ the military force necessary to defend the victim [123] and, consequently, that it was unlikely that the free world could reach a peaceful settlement of differences with the Communist bloc.[124]

Emphasis on Military Means against the Communists

The size of the minority of Southerners who have advocated "preventive" war or policies to that effect has also varied with the general state of our relations with the Communist powers. Only 3.5 percent of Southerners, not significantly more than in other regions, thought we should "declare war on Russia now" in the fall of 1946.[125] As disagreements with the U.S.S.R. became sharper, however, those advocating war against that country grew in numbers in all regions, but

---

of Westerners felt that Russia might change its aggressive behavior and make "real peace"; 67 percent of Southerners in contrast to 64, 62, and 63 percent, respectively, believed that Russia would not do so. But by the time of the survey of November 23, 1955, 26 percent of Southerners versus 31, 31, and 32 percent, respectively, were of the opinion that Russia would try to make "real peace" with the United States; 62 percent of Southerners versus 60, 59, and 58 percent, respectively, believed she would not. (The remainder of these two samples either offered no opinion or replied that they did not know or were undecided.) In July, 1963, 18 percent of Southerners, compared with 23 percent of Northeasterners, 27 percent of Midwesterners, and 26 percent of Westerners, agreed that one of the likely results of the disagreements between Communist China and the U.S.S.R. would be that "one or both of them might become less actively hostile to us." Roper 148, July, 1963 (3007).
123 AIPO 371, 5/15/46 (3,089); AIPO 375, 7/24/46 (3,124); AIPO 411, 1/21/48 (3,161); AIPO 419, 5/26/48 (1,500); AIPO 442, 5/19/49 (2,751); AIPO 450, 11/29/49 (1,500); AIPO 466, 10/20/50 (2,988); AIPO 467, 11/10/50 (1,367); and AIPO 517, 7/2/53 (1,545). During the time the Soviets were increasing their harassments of the West in Berlin, an AIPO survey (January 21, 1948) asked, "Do you think Russia would start a war to get something she wanted, such as more territory or resources, or would she fight only if she were attacked?" In reply, 87 percent of Southerners in contrast to 73 percent of Northeasterners, 73 percent of Midwesterners (including inhabitants of the Plains States), and 77 percent of Westerners felt that Russia would start such a war; only 6 percent of Southerners as contrasted with 13, 14, and 17 percent, respectively, were of the view that Russia would fight only if she were attacked, and the remainder ventured no opinion, were undecided, or said they did not know.
124 AIPO 472, 3/2/51 (1,500); AIPO 622, 12/8/59 (2,550); AIPO 639, 12/6/60 (2,846); and AIPO Release of 1/1/61. At the time of the December 6, 1960, survey, for example, 43 percent in the South versus 51 percent in the Northeast, 50 percent in the Midwest (including the Plains States), and 58 percent in the West thought it possible for us to reach a peaceful settlement of differences with the Soviets.
125 AIPO 378, 9/11/46 (3,432).

somewhat more rapidly in the South than in the country as a whole. Since the beginning of the Korean War, the proportion of Southerners supporting this idea has typically exceeded the Northern average by one fifth to almost a half.[126] Southerners and other Americans advocating war with Russia were most numerous in January, 1951, shortly after the Chinese Communists entered the war in Korea; at that time, 27 percent of Southerners, 19 percent of Northeasterners, 23 percent of Midwesterners (including residents of the Plains States), and 19 percent of Westerners thought we should go to war with Russia, whereas 59 percent, 71 percent, 66 percent, and 72 percent, respectively, felt we should not.[127] However, by early 1955 only 12 percent of Southerners as compared with 9 percent of other Americans advocated preventive war or declaration of war against the U.S.S.R.; [128] by July, 1963, only 4 percent of Southerners, compared with 2 percent of residents of each of the other three major geographical regions, agreed that we should "plan to fight a preventive war with the Communist nations just as soon as our military leaders think we can win, and get the whole thing over with." [129]

The small minority of Southerners who still advocated preventive war among the interviewees, as well as those included in other studies of Southern opinion,[130] seemed to hold the view in most cases that Communists could only be stopped by military might, that they would attack us when we were weakest and they were strongest, that they were "winning the cold war," that their strategic capabilities were increasing relative to ours, that war with them was virtually unavoidable in the future, and that we should therefore take a firmer line toward the Russians and Chinese than hitherto. This minority appeared to reason that our opponents would probably not actually resort to war if they thought we really meant to defend our interests even at the risk of World War III, but if they did, the sooner the better from the point of view of the United States. Some cited our experiences with the Axis, pointing out that we might have had less of a war, or none at all, had we been willing to risk it earlier.

On the other hand, frustrations in Korea, the development of missiles

126 AIPO 458, 7/7/50 (1,426); AIPO 460, 8/18/50 (1,541); AIPO 469, 12/30/50 (1,389); NORC 314, 11/22/51 (1,237); NORC 320, 3/19/52 (1,260); NORC 327, 6/30/52 (1,285); NORC 332, 10/15/52 (1,291); AIPO 536, 8/24/54 (1,562); NORC 363, 9/10/54 (1,198); and NORC 366, 1/21/55 (1,209).
127 AIPO 469, 12/30/50 (1,389).   128 NORC 366, 1/21/55 (1,209).
129 Roper 148, July, 1963 (3,007).
130 NORC 320, 3/19/52 (1,260); NORC 366, 1/21/55 (1,209); Roper 148, July, 1963 (3,007).

with nuclear warheads, and other technological advances in the last decade seem to have rendered "Fortress America" policies attractive to a significant minority of Southerners as alternatives to active nonmilitary programs beyond the Western Hemisphere. Shortly after the entry of Communist China into the Korean War over one third of Southerners thought that the "United States should keep all her troops over here and defend only North and South America" rather than sending "more troops to Europe to be ready to help fight communism there." [131] Almost as large a fraction believed we should "rely mainly on our own armed forces, and stay out of world affairs as much as we can." [132] However, by late 1954 the proportion of Southerners agreeing with such views had fallen below one out of four and this proportion remained approximately constant into the early 1960's.[133] Nevertheless, in early 1958, 34 percent of Southerners, compared with 31 percent of Northeasterners, 29 percent of Midwesterners, and 29 percent of Westerners, felt that "the best hope of solving our problems with Russia" would be to "rely completely on building up our military strength and to keep it strong enough to handle the Russians as long as we need to." When "no opinions" were eliminated, 38 percent of Southerners expressing views, compared with 33 percent in the Northeast, 32 percent in the Midwest, and 30 percent in the West, chose this alternative over either trying "to negotiate some kind of settlement with Russia, while keeping up on our military strength at the same time" or "concentrating on trying to end the arms race by seeking disarmament agreements with Russia." [134]

Most of the interviewees, and those of other studies,[135] who agreed

131   AIPO 469, 12/30/50 (1,389).
132   NORC 300, 3/20/51 (1,300). See also NORC 303, 6/29/51 (1,300); AIPO 489, 3/25/52 (2,058); and AIPO 506, 10/7/52 (3,098).
133   NORC 363, 9/10/54 (1,198); NORC 399, 11/15/56 (1,286); and Roper 148, July, 1963 (3,007). At the time of the latter survey, for example, when asked, "With which of these four ways of handling the Cold War situation do you come closest to agreeing," 20 percent of Southerners, compared with 18 percent of Northeasterners, 15 percent of Midwesterners, and 12 percent of Westerners, agreed with the "Fortress America" idea that we should "rely completely on building up our own military strength and keep it so strong that no one will dare attack this country—whatever may happen in the rest of the world." At that time 4 percent of Southerners preferred preventive war, 64 percent would "keep up our own military strength but at the same time do everything possible to build up our alliances and strengthen other countries so as to prevent the further spread of Communism," 4 percent felt we should "stop relying on military strength and start right now working out some agreement with the Communist nations—even if this means giving in to them on some important things," and 9 percent ventured no opinions.
134   Roper 963, January, 1958 (1,500).
135   Roper 963, January, 1958 (1,500), and Roper 148, July, 1963 (3,007).

with such "Fortress America" policy alternatives also either accepted generally isolationist or neo-isolationist ideas, were willing to run much greater risks of world war with the Communists, or both. Those who were not isolationists or neo-isolationists tended to feel we should "draw a line" around the areas vital to our interests, inform the Reds that we were doing so, and "let them have it" if they crossed it. The latter group also expressed the opinion that we should try to convince our allies, at least in Europe, of the desirability of such a policy, but should adopt it even though many of them might object. Frequently associated with this point of view was the feeling that West Germany should be our principal ally in Europe, if we stayed there at all. Also, we should concentrate our resources on the armed forces of the United States and Canada, enforce the Monroe Doctrine in Latin America by arms when required, and tell the Western Europeans that they must bear more of the load of their own defense. These Southerners would emphasize our air forces, missiles, and missile submarines in the national budgets and would dispense with large ground forces in Europe and Asia. If our allies wanted to purchase weapons, we would sell them, but not give them away.

The roughly one quarter to slightly over a third of Southerners in 1954–62 who agreed with these ideas in various, often rather inconsistent, forms and modifications included most of those who had always been among the Southern isolationist or neo-isolationist minority. Although the more clear-cut expressions of these opinions occurred among a better-informed minority of this group, most supporters of these ideas were rather ignorant of world developments, relatively poorly educated, and in the less sophisticated occupations and social strata. Whites among them in recent years have usually been strong segregationists and conservatives in most spheres other than domestic economics.

To these could be added other Southerners who have apparently accepted less extreme versions of these tenets: they supported adoption of "firmer," or harsher, policies toward our foreign opponents than those followed by the recent administrations, and they felt we should be as "tough" and determined toward the Communist powers as they seemed to be toward the West. These Southerners had ideological allies outside the South, but Southerners have been at least somewhat more willing to risk the possibility that limited wars will turn into more general ones than have Northerners taken together. The feeling has been rather widespread in the South that, should we be attacked, we should fight to "lick" our assailants.

Thus, 69 percent of white Southerners as compared with 55 percent of white Northerners took the position shortly after the dismissal of General MacArthur that President Truman was wrong to "fire" him, whereas 17 percent of the former compared with 36 percent of the latter felt the President was right.[136] Similar differences between the regions appeared in more polls than not later in 1951.[137] Some of these Southerners disagreed with the General's proposed extension of hostilities to Manchuria, and possibly to China itself, but felt that the handling of the dismissal was ungentlemanly or the like. However, a number of more sophisticated Southerners who agreed with General MacArthur's ideas about destroying the enemy in its home bases supported the dismissal because they believed in civil control of the military and viewed the General's behavior as insubordinate and as a threat to constitutional government.[138]

Southerners' greater willingness to expand the Korean limited war in order to defeat our opponents was apparent in several surveys of the period. Southern whites (and Southerners in general) who offered opinions were somewhat more apt than Northerners to say we should either withdraw from Korea or advance beyond the 38th Parallel until we had freed all of North Korea from the Communists.[139] Of those in the South responding to queries during the Korean War, slightly larger majorities than in other regions favored bombing Communist bases in Manchuria or even in China proper.[140] In November, 1951, 53 percent of those Southerners venturing opinions, compared with 46 percent of other Americans offering views, endorsed using atomic bombs on military targets in Korea, most of them without further qualification.[141]

136   NORC 302, 4/18/51 (1,300).
137   AIPO 475, 5/17/51 (2,070); NORC 303, 6/29/51 (1,300); NORC 307, 7/24/51 (1,282); NORC 312, 8/27/51 (1,237); NORC 313, 10/2/51 (1,237); NORC 314, 11/22/51 (1,237); and NORC 315, 12/18/51 (1,237). Southern Negroes who ventured opinions were less inclined than Southern whites to support General Mac-Arthur and his ideas against President Truman, but small differences in the expected direction were evident even when Negroes were included in the Southern sample.
138   From the interviews for this study; NORC 303, 6/29/51 (1,300); and NORC 313, 10/2/51 (1,237).
139   From combining replies to AIPO 461, 9/15/50 (1,400); NORC 298, 1/30/51 (1,236); NORC 300, 3/20/51 (1,300); AIPO 473, 3/24/51 (1,202); NORC 302, 4/18/51 (1,300); NORC 307, 5/24/51 (1,282); AIPO 476, 6/14/51 (1,997); NORC 314, 11/22/51 (1,237); NORC 315, 12/18/51 (1,237); NORC 320, 3/19/52 (1,260); NORC 323, 4/22/52 (1,250); NORC 329, 8/28/52 (1,300); NORC 333, 11/17/52 (1,291); and NORC 334, 12/29/52 (1,291).
140   NORC 302, 4/18/51 (1,300); NORC 307, 5/24/51 (1,282); NORC 312, 8/27/51 (1,237); NORC 313, 10/2/51 (1,237); NORC 320, 3/19/52 (1,260); NORC 327, 6/30/52 (1,285); NORC 329, 8/28/52 (1,300); and AIPO 513, 3/26/53 (1,590).
141   AIPO 482, 11/9/51 (2,021). See also AIPO 460, 8/18/50 (1,541).

Forty-three percent of Southern whites advancing views in contrast to 39 percent of Northern whites thought in mid-1952 that we should try to force the Communists to sign a truce in Korea by staging sea and air attacks against China itself.[142]

Asked in April, 1954, if they would approve or disapprove of our using H-bombs against cities in China should the Chinese Communists make "an all-out attack on Indo-China," 48 percent of Southern whites (45 percent of all Southerners) as compared with 28 percent of Northern whites (29 percent of all Northerners) approved; 42 percent of Southern whites (45 percent of all Southerners) as compared with 65 percent of Northern whites (65 percent of all Northerners) disapproved.[143] Another survey agency, asking a slightly differently worded question on the same issue shortly afterwards, found that 42 percent of Southerners as opposed to 31 percent of Northeasterners, 31 percent of Midwesterners (including those in the Plains States), and 30 percent of Westerners would use H-bombs against Chinese cities in case of war with Peking in Indo-China; 39 percent of Southerners in contrast to 51 percent of Northeasterners, 51 percent of Midwesterners, and 54 percent of Westerners felt we should not.[144] At the same time, 68 percent of Southerners, compared with 62 percent of Northeasterners, 59 percent of Midwesterners (including the residents of the Plains States), and 60 percent of Westerners, thought we should use atomic artillery shells in Indo-China if we became involved militarily there; 18 percent of Southerners and 24 percent, 26 percent, 31 percent of those in the other regions, respectively, said we should not.[145]

During the period of accentuated tensions over Communist Chinese behavior toward Quemoy and Matsu in January, 1955, 36 percent of Southern whites (and of all Southerners) as compared with 28 percent of Northern whites (29 percent of all Northerners) favored using hydrogen bombs against cities in China if the Chinese Communists made

142 NORC 325, 5/28/52 (1,265). See also AIPO 473, 3/24/51 (2,102).
143 NORC 355, 4/22/54 (1,207). Cross tabulations with other questions on this survey indicated that many of the Negroes who disapproved of this proposition were isolationists in that they would reduce foreign aid, terminate our commitments in Western Europe, and the like.
144 AIPO 531, 5/19/54 (1,418). See also AIPO 530, 4/30/54 (1,415), and AIPO 532, 6/10/54 (1,435). When replies to these three surveys were combined, 40 percent of Southerners in contrast to 30 percent of Northeasterners, 28 percent of Midwesterners (including residents of the Plains States), and 30 percent of Westerners replied that the United States should use H-bombs on Chinese cities; 40 percent of Southerners in contrast to 53, 55, and 57 percent, respectively, said the United States should not; and the remainder were undecided, did not know, or offered no opinion.
145 AIPO 531, 5/19/54 (1,418).

"an all-out attack on Formosa"; 49 percent of Southern whites (48 percent of all Southerners) versus 59 percent of Northern whites (58 percent of all Northerners) disapproved of this idea.[146] Two months later, as the Communists shelled Nationalist installations on these islands, as the United States fleet became more overtly active, and as the situation became more tense, a different surveying agency determined that 62 percent of the residents in the South, 49 percent in the Northeast, 53 percent in the Midwest (Plains States included), and 58 percent in the West felt that we should use atomic weapons against the Chinese Communists in case of war; only 23 percent in the South versus 42 percent in the Northeast, 35 percent in the Midwest, and 34 percent in the West thought we should not. On the same survey, 47 percent of the South compared with 41 percent, 43 percent, and 47 percent of the other three regions, respectively, would use H-bombs against China proper in this event; only 35 percent of the South in contrast to 50 percent, 43 percent, and 45 percent, respectively, opposed the employment of this ultimate weapon.[147]

In the spring of 1954, 61 percent of Southern whites felt it would be a good idea to warn Russia that, if Communist armies attacked any other country, we would immediately employ hydrogen bombs against Soviet cities.[148] Twenty-nine percent of white Southerners as compared with 24 percent of white Northerners believed that we should issue this warning even if our allies were unwilling to join us.[149]

Nor is there much doubt that most Southerners favoring use of nuclear weapons, particularly H-bombs, under such circumstances realized that escalation of any of these Asian struggles into a major war would probably result in explosions of hydrogen weapons by the Soviets over the United States; in fact, the majority thinking so in the mid-fifties was larger in the South than in any other major geographical section of the country.[150] Thus, whereas 47 percent of Southerners in late 1961 felt that a nationwide shelter program would not be a waste of time

146   NORC 366, 1/21/55 (1,209).
147   AIPO 544, 3/1/55 (1,395). See also AIPO 537, 9/14/54 (1,465), and AIPO Release of 4/3/55. Similar interregional differences were evident on a somewhat differently worded question posed during the more recent exacerbation of tension in the Formosa Strait in the fall of 1958. AIPO 604, 9/8/58 (1,522).
148   NORC 355, 4/22/54 (1,207).   149   *Ibid.*
150   AIPO 529, 4/4/54 (1,482), and AIPO 566, 6/13/56 (2,078). At the time of the latter survey, 67 percent in the South, 59 percent in the Northeast, 62 percent in the Midwest (including the Plains States), and 62 percent in the West felt that H-bombs would be likely to explode over the United States in case of another world war; 12, 19, 19, and 21 percent, respectively, thought not; and the rest were undecided, did not know, or ventured no opinion.

and money, 23 percent that it would, and 30 percent were undecided, the figures for the other major geographical regions were 36 percent, 44 percent, and 20 percent.[151] Those among the interviewees supporting allocation of considerable federal resources to shelter construction tended to believe that such a program would convince the Communists of our determination to defend the non-Communist world and, consequently, lessen the likelihood of Communist aggressions and the probability of World War III. If our enemies persisted in their aggressive behavior, shelters would strengthen our determination, and that of our allies, to fight and reduce our casualties in the event of thermonuclear war.

Arms Control

As with other aspects of United States relations with the Communist world, the proportion of Southerners, and of other regional groups, venturing a given view about limitation or reduction of armaments and military forces has varied with the overall international situation. However, at any particular time, Southerners have tended to be at least somewhat less optimistic than other Americans about achieving acceptable agreements with our opponents with respect to either conventional or thermonuclear arms, more cautious in the terms they would be willing to accept, and less inclined to offer further compromises to the Communist powers to achieve major reductions or controls of weapons or manpower.

In the first place, related to their view that the Russians and other Communists do not really want to come to any reasonable accommodation with the free world, Southerners have been less apt than Northerners to think that the Soviets and their friends actually want arms control—in late 1961, for example, only 5 percent of Southerners as compared with 9 percent of other Americans thought Premier Khrushchev "sincerely" wants disarmament." [152] Thus, smaller fractions of Southerners than non-Southerners have believed that the Soviets, and particularly the Communist Chinese, would actually agree to an equitable system with sufficient inspection and enforcement provisions to be acceptable to us.[153] Secondly, Southerners have been more inclined than other citizens to feel that the Communists would "cheat," that the system of inspection and other safeguards would probably not in fact be adequate to assure compliance by our opponents, or that any satisfactory agreement would be effectively implemented.[154] In late 1955,

---

151 AIPO 652, 11/15/61 (2,765).   152 *Ibid.*   153 *Ibid.*
154 NORC 376, 9/29/55 (1,250), and NORC 382, 1/26/56 (1,238).

for instance, when the Eisenhower "open skies" proposal was being discussed, only 10 percent of Southerners in contrast to 21 percent of other Americans felt that we could probably count on Russia to live up to whatever agreements might result from arms-control negotiations; 83 percent of the former as compared with 71 percent of the latter believed we could not.[155]

It is understandable that Southerners have been on the whole more cautious than other regional groups about reducing or limiting our forces under most of the disarmament proposals advanced by the West since World War II.[156] They have been less inclined than other citizens to agree with such sentiments as "we should stop relying on military strength and start right now working out some agreement with the Russians, even if we have to give in to them on some important things." [157] In early 1958, for instance, when asked which of three alternatives offered the "best hope of solving our problems with the Russians," only 8 percent of Southerners versus 16 percent of Northeasterners, 17 percent of Midwesterners, and 13 percent of Westerners chose to "concentrate on trying to end the arms race by seeking disarmament agreements with Russia" over relying "completely on building up our military strength" or trying "to negotiate some kind of settlement with Russia while keeping up our military strength at the same time." [158]

Although more Southerners have replied in the affirmative than in the negative to such queries as "Do you think we should agree to limit the size of our armed forces, if other countries agree to limit the size of theirs?" the proportion agreeing has been smaller in the South than in the North and the proportion disagreeing larger.[159] Southerners

155 Combined results of NORC 376, 9/29/55 (1,250), and NORC 379, 11/23/55 (1,276).
156 AIPO 367, 3/13/46 (3,249); AIPO 373, 6/12/46 (3,071); NORC 146, 11/15/46 (1,300); NORC 147, 12/11/46 (1,289); AIPO 417, 4/21/48 (3,165); NORC 314, 11/22/51 (1,237); NORC 325, 5/28/52 (1,265); AIPO 514, 4/7/53 (1,520); AIPO 550, 7/12/55 (1,397); NORC 376, 9/29/55 (1,268); NORC 382, 1/26/56 (1,238); NORC 390, 6/26/56 (1,275); NORC 404, 4/26/57 (1,279); AIPO 585, 6/25/57 (1,521); and AIPO 596, 3/4/58 (1,610).
157 Roper 737, August, 1953 (3,502).
158 Roper 963, January, 1958 (1,500).
159 In late spring of 1952, for instance, 54 percent of white Southerners (51 percent of all Southerners) and 62 percent of white Northerners (63 percent of all Northerners) felt that the United States should agree to limit the size of its armed forces if other countries agreed to do likewise; 28 percent of white Southerners (30 percent of all Southerners) and 21 percent of white Northerners (21 percent of all Northerners) believed that the United States should not; 11, 9, 13, and 12 percent, respectively, said their reply would depend on the guarantees involved; and the rest were undecided, did not know, or offered no opinion. See NORC

more than others were wary about accepting an uninspected moratorium on nuclear bomb and warhead testing in the late 1950's, largely for fear that the Soviets would prepare secretly while the United States abided by such an agreement. In November, 1956, for instance, only 36 percent of Southerners (and a like percentage of Southern whites) as compared with 45 percent of Northerners agreed with the view "that the U.S. should take the lead in offering to stop any further hydrogen bomb tests, assuming Russia and England will do the same," whereas 54 percent of Southerners (56 percent of Southern whites) as compared with 51 percent of Northerners disapproved of this idea.[160] The proportion of Southerners favoring actual disarmament—that is destruction of weapons and sharp reduction of military personnel—without rigorous inspection and means of enforcement, and, particularly, unilateral disarmament, has been insignificant, even smaller than outside the South where those accepting such views have been more vociferous than numerous.[161] Thus, Southerners have taken an even more negative attitude than other Americans toward proposals to destroy United States atomic and hydrogen warheads, to cease manufacturing them, and to turn their production or control over to international agencies.[162] Likewise, Southerners have been less inclined to favor sharing of our atomic secrets with other countries, particularly Communist ones, even for so-called peaceful uses.[163]

325, 5/28/52 (1,265). In early 1956, 62 percent of white Southerners (61 percent of all Southerners) and 63 percent of both white and all Northerners were willing for us to agree to limit the size of our forces if other countries did too; 31, 32, 30, and 29 percent, respectively, thought we should not; and the remainder did not know, offered no opinion, or were undecided. See NORC 382, 1/26/56 (1,238). When asked in the spring of 1957, "How would you feel about the idea of signing an agreement with Russia and other countries in which all would promise to reduce their armed forces—would you approve or disapprove?" 42 percent of both white and all Southerners and 47 percent of both white and all Northerners approved; 55, 54, 49, and 49 percent, respectively, disapproved; and the remainder expressed no opinion, did not know, or were undecided. See NORC 404, 4/26/57 (1,279).

160 NORC 399, 11/15/56 (1,286). See also NORC 366, 1/21/55 (1,209); NORC 370, 3/11/55 (1,225); NORC 398, 10/25/56 (1,295); AIPO 582, 4/23/57 (1,626); AIPO 585, 6/25/57 (1,521); and AIPO 598, 4/14/58 (1,396).

161 NORC 170, 10/12/49 (1,300), and Roper 737, August, 1953 (3,502).

162 AIPO 369, 4/10/46 (3,152); NORC 143, 6/21/46 (1,307); AIPO 384, 11/14/46 (3,203); NORC 146, 11/15/46 (1,300); NORC 148, 2/20/47 (1,239); NORC 151, 5/24/47 (1,273); NORC 152, 10/10/47 (1,290); NORC 158, 6/2/48 (1,295); NORC 170, 10/12/49 (1,300); and NORC 366, 1/21/55 (1,209).

163 AIPO 357, 10/3/45 (3,097); AIPO 368, 3/12/46 (3,225); AIPO 379, 9/25/46 (2,966); NORC 353, 3/9/54 (535); and AIPO 552, 8/23/55 (1,500). For example, when the 1955 survey asked, "In order that all countries, including Russia, could work together in the development of atomic energy for peaceful uses, do you

On the other hand, the idea of international inspection—such as "a group of inspectors from the U.N. going into any country, including the United States, to see if it actually was keeping down the size of its armed forces"—has been viewed with less favor in the South than outside. In early 1956, for example, 58 percent of Southern whites in contrast to 48 percent of Northern whites opposed this idea whereas 38 percent of the former as compared with 46 percent of the latter favored it.[164] Nor have Western proposals involving only aerial surveillance, like President Eisenhower's "open skies" proposal, fared any better with Southern opinion; in 1955–56 a significantly larger majority of Southerners (about three fifths of those venturing views) than of other regional groups opposed this idea whereby United States aircraft could photograph Soviet bases and defense plants in return for similar privileges over our territory for the Soviets.[165] In the fall of 1960, only 36 percent of Southerners, compared with 48 percent of Northeasterners, 50 percent of Midwesterners (residents of the Plains States included), and 50 percent of Westerners, were willing for the United States to disarm to the same extent as the Russians if the latter agreed "to disarm under careful inspection." [166] Southern nationalism, nativism, and fear of espionage have been the basic reasons for their opposition to foreign inspectors under the U.N. or other international control

---

think the United States should or should not share atomic secrets with all countries?" 21 percent in the South in contrast to 31 percent in the Northeast, 38 percent in the Midwest (including the Plains States), and 39 percent in the West replied in the affirmative; 68 percent in the South and 59, 55, and 52 percent, respectively, in the other regions replied in the negative; and 11, 10, 7, and 9 percent, respectively, were undecided, did not know, or offered no opinion.

164 NORC 382, 1/26/56 (1,238).

165 AIPO 551, 8/2/55 (1,502); NORC 374, 8/4/55 (1,262); NORC 376, 9/29/55 (1,250); NORC 382, 1/26/56 (1,238); and NORC 390, 6/26/56 (1,275). The first of these five surveys, for example, found that 32 percent in the South in contrast to 39 percent in the Northeast, 36 percent in the Midwest (including the Plains States), and 42 percent in the West approved of the open skies proposal and its associated proposition by President Eisenhower that the United States and the Soviet Union exchange information on defense plants and military bases; 49 percent in the South in contrast to 47, 47, and 42 percent, respectively, disapproved; and 19, 14, 17, and 16 percent, respectively, offered no opinion, did not know, or were undecided. The last of these surveys asked: "President Eisenhower has offered to let Russian planes take photographs of our military bases in the United States, if the Russians let Americans take similar photographs in Russia. In general, do you approve or disapprove of this idea?" In reply, 35 percent of white (34 percent of all) Southerners and 40 percent of both white and all Northerners approved; 62, 62, 56, and 56 percent, respectively, disapproved; and 3, 4, 4, and 4 percent, respectively, ventured no opinion, were undecided, or said they did not know.

166 AIPO 635, 9/7/60 (2,950).

examining our defenses—Southerners who have been opposed to expanded immigration and intercultural exchanges have typically also disapproved of such inspection, especially on the ground.[167]

Furthermore, larger majorities of Southerners than of other regional groups have disagreed with suggestions that we promise not to use nuclear weapons first in any future war.[168] (It was noted earlier that they have been more willing than other citizens to employ such weapons in case of conventional attacks in Asia.[169]) In January, 1955, 52 percent of Southerners in contrast to 37 percent of other Americans felt that the United States should use H-bombs against Soviet cities if their armies should attack one of our West European allies; 37 percent of the former as contrasted to 51 percent of the latter said we should not.[170]

Negotiating with Communist States

In line with the more prevalent sentiments in the South than outside that a very firm policy and willingness to fight will be most likely to limit further predatory Communist behavior, that "appeasement" or other compromises with Communists are unlikely to be in our national interest, and that Soviet and other Communist foreigners in our country engage in important espionage and other activities contrary to our well being, a larger minority of Southerners than of Northerners have advocated termination of diplomatic relations with the U.S.S.R. Almost two out of five of those Southerners venturing replies in late 1952 advised breaking off diplomatic relations, whereas less than one third of other Americans agreed.[171] The Southern proportion has been smaller since the end of the Korean War, about one out of three expressing opinions, but among regional groups at any given time Southerners have been most inclined to approve and least to disapprove of such a rupture.[172]

167 NORC 376, 9/29/55 (2,950), and NORC 404, 4/26/57 (1,279).
168 NORC 158, 6/2/48 (1,295); AIPO 444, 6/30/49 (2,826); NORC 170, 10/12/49 (1,300); NORC 273, 1/18/50 (1,284); AIPO 479, 1/12/51 (1,500); NORC 355, 4/22/54 (1,207); and NORC 366, 1/21/55 (1,209).
169 See pp. 112–14.   170 NORC 366, 1/21/55 (1,209).
171 NORC 332, 10/15/52 (1,291).
172 NORC 363, 9/10/54 (1,198); AIPO 540, 11/30/54 (1,473); NORC 401, 12/28/56 (1,232); NORC 404, 4/26/57 (1,279) and AIPO 682, 12/10/63 (1,330). When the survey of November 30, 1954, asked, "Do you think it would be a good idea or a poor one for the United States to break off diplomatic relations with Russia at this time?" 26 percent of Southerners, 19 percent of Northeasterners, 20 percent of Midwesterners (including residents of the Plains States), and 19 percent of Westerners replied that it would be a good idea; 50, 69, 71, and 68 percent, respectively, thought that it would be a poor idea; and 24, 12, 9, and 13 percent, re-

Related to this observation is the finding that Southerners have typically been at least somewhat more apt than other Americans to think that we should reorganize the U.N., excluding the Soviets and other Communist countries.[173] By the spring of 1948, more Southerners than not felt that peace would be more likely and that the U.N. would be a stronger, more useful international agency if Russia were not a member.[174] The majority of Southerners with opinions on the subject who believed that it was hopeless to try to work with the Communists in the U.N. and who favored a U.N. without them increased with the invasion of Korea in June, 1950, and particularly with the entry of the Communist Chinese into that war in December of the same year.[175] However, by the beginning of 1953 more Southerners than not once again thought it was better to have Russia in than out of the international organization,[176] and they continued, through the last survey on

---

spectively, said they did not know, were undecided, or had no opinion. The NORC survey of December 28, 1956, inquired, "Do you think we should continue to exchange ambassadors with Russia, or would it be better to break off diplomatic relations with Russia?" In reply, 66 percent of Southern whites (67 percent of all Southerners), and 76 percent of both white and all Northerners (77 percent of Northeasterners, 75 percent of Midwesterners—including the residents of the Plains States—and 76 percent of Westerners) replied in the affirmative. Twenty-five, 26, 17, 18, 16, 19, and 18 percent, respectively, answered that it would be better to break off diplomatic relations; and the remainder ventured no opinion, said they did not know, or were undecided. The following spring, 71 percent of white Southerners (70 percent of all Southerners) and 80 percent of white Northerners (79 percent of all Northerners) replied in the affirmative to this same question; 22, 23, 16, and 17 percent, respectively, believed we should break off diplomatic relations; and the remainder offered no opinion, were undecided, or said they did not know. The breakdown by regions for Northern percentages in reply to this question was 81 percent of Northeasterners, 77 percent of Midwesterners (including inhabitants of the Plains States), and 79 percent of Westerners replying in the affirmative, whereas 16, 18, and 18 percent, respectively, replied in the negative. When asked in December, 1963, "Do you think the United States should or should not continue diplomatic relations with Russia?" 65 percent in the South in contrast to 78 percent in the Northeast, 77 percent in the Midwest (including the Plains States), and 69 percent in the West felt that we should continue diplomatic relations, whereas 21, 13, 14, and 21 percent, respectively, felt that we should not, and 14, 9, 9, and 10 percent offered no opinion, said they did not know, or were undecided.

173   NORC 141, 3/20/46 (1,293); NORC 143, 6/21/46 (1,307); AIPO 395, 4/23/47 (3,142); NORC 157, 4/22/48 (1,280); NORC 162, 11/23/48 (1,300); AIPO 448, 9/23/49 (2,919); AIPO 455, 5/2/50 (2,850); NORC 282, 6/14/50 (1,276); AIPO 458, 7/7/50 (1,426); NORC 288, 9/20/50 (1,259); NORC 314, 11/22/51 (1,237); NORC 334, 12/29/52 (1,291); NORC 363, 9/10/54 (1,198); NORC 370, 3/11/55 (1,225); AIPO 545, 3/22/55 (1,630); and NORC 399, 11/15/56 (1,286).

174   NORC 157, 4/22/48 (1,280); NORC 162, 11/23/48 (1,300); AIPO 448, 9/23/49 (2,919); and AIPO 455, 5/2/50 (2,850).

175   NORC 282, 6/14/50 (1,276); AIPO 458, 7/7/50 (1,426); NORC 288, 9/20/50 (1,254); and NORC 314, 11/22/51 (1,237).

176   NORC 334, 12/29/52 (1,291).

this matter in late 1956,[177] to favor U.S.S.R. membership. However, the proportion who preferred a U.N. without the Soviets to those who preferred a U.N. with them continued to be larger in the South than in the country generally. In March, 1955, for instance, 35 percent of Southerners felt the U.N. would be better able to keep the peace if Russia and other Communist countries were no longer members; 4 percent thought departure of these regimes from the U.N. would make little difference; and 37 percent agreed with the majority of those Americans in other regions venturing opinions who believed the U.N. would be less able to keep the peace if these countries were not members. Only in the South did more citizens than not feel departure of the Communists from the organization would either improve its effectiveness or make no difference; 47 percent in the Northeast, 49 percent in the Midwest (the Plains States included), and 46 percent in the West felt a U.N. without the Communists would be less able to keep the peace in contrast to only 37 percent in the South of this opinion.[178] Shortly after the Hungarian and Suez crises of late 1956, 63 percent of Southerners versus 70 percent of Northerners thought it would be better if Russia remained in the U.N.; 28 percent of the former and 22 percent of the latter believed it would be better if she did not.[179]

The size of the minority of Southerners, as of others, favorable to recognition of Communist China, her entry into the U.N., or both has also fluctuated with tensions between the Communist bloc and the West in general, and between Communist China and ourselves in particular. During the months following the retreat of the Nationalists to Formosa but prior to the attack on South Korea, as many as 27 percent of Northerners and 23 percent of Southerners favored one or both of these ideas.[180] With the entry of Communist China into the Korean War, these figures dropped to less than 10 percent of the South and only slightly more for the rest of the country.[181] Never, after June, 1950, did more than 18 percent of Southerners favor Chinese Communist membership; the Northerners favoring this idea were typically three to eight percentage points more numerous.[182] For example, during

177 NORC 363, 9/10/54 (1,198); NORC 370, 3/11/55 (1,225); AIPO 545, 3/22/55 (1,630); and NORC 399, 11/15/56 (1,286).
178 AIPO 545, 3/22/55 (1,630).   179 NORC 399, 11/15/56 (1,286).
180 AIPO 443, 6/9/49 (2,765); AIPO 449, 10/28/49 (2,904); NORC 273, 1/18/50 (1,284); and AIPO 455, 5/2/50 (2,850).
181 AIPO 456, 6/2/50 (1,450); AIPO 516, 5/28/53 (1,549); and AIPO 519, 8/13/53 (1,613).
182 *Ibid.*; and NORC 349, 11/25/53 (1,300); NORC 353, 3/9/54 (535); NORC 355, 4/22/54 (1,207); AIPO 534, 7/14/54 (1,549); NORC 365, 11/26/54 (1,201); AIPO 552, 8/23/55 (1,500); NORC 393, 9/13/56 (1,263); AIPO 603, 5/18/58 (1,563); and AIPO 642, 3/8/61 (3,511).

the stepped-up threats by the Peking regime against the offshore islands of Quemoy and Matsu in August of 1955, only 11 percent of Southerners as compared with 20 percent of Northeasterners, 19 percent of Midwesterners (residents of the Plains States included), and 18 percent of Westerners thought the Communist regime should be admitted as a member of the U.N.; 77 percent of Southerners as compared with 67 percent of Northeasterners, 72 percent of Midwesterners, and 69 percent of Westerners felt she should not.[183] In March, 1961, 10 percent of Southerners in contrast to 24 percent of Northeasterners, 17 percent of Midwesterners, and 25 percent of Westerners thought that the Peking government should become a member of the U.N.[184] A smaller minority in the South than in other regions replied affirmatively to such questions as, "Suppose other members of the U.N. decide to give the Chinese Communists a seat on the Security Council—do you think the U.S. should agree to this, or not?"[185] Although most Southerners would not withdraw from the U.N. if a majority of other members voted to admit Communist China, between a fifth and slightly over a third of those offering opinions during the post–Korean War period would have us do so—larger fractions than elsewhere during the same periods.[186] When asked in February, 1961, for instance, whether the United States should "go along or not" if "a majority of members of the U.N. decide to admit Communist China to the U.N.," 36 percent of Southerners versus 30 percent of Northerners offering views replied in the negative.[187] In December, 1963, 35 percent of Southerners venturing opinions as compared with 34 percent of Northeasterners, 19 percent of Midwesterners, and 29 percent of Westerners felt that the United States "should withdraw from the United Nations" if "Communist China were elected a member" of that body.[188]

Likewise, somewhat larger proportions of Southerners than of other regional groups have disapproved of the idea of attempting to bring Communist China into discussions of Far Eastern problems, including those of the offshore islands and Formosa.[189] Thus, in February, 1954,

---

183 AIPO 552, 8/23/55 (1,500).   184 AIPO 642, 3/8/61 (3,511).
185 In May, 1953, 17 percent of Southerners as compared with 26 percent of Northeasterners, 24 percent of Midwesterners, and 23 percent of Westerners replied affirmatively to this query. See AIPO 516, 5/28/53 (1,549); also see AIPO 456, 6/2/50 (1,450) and AIPO 567, 7/10/56 (2,105).
186 AIPO 478, 8/1/51 (2,200); NORC 353, 3/9/54 (535); AIPO 534, 7/14/54 (1,549); AIPO 547, 5/10/55 (1,503); NORC 393, 9/13/56 (1,263); AIPO 577, 11/15/ 57 (1,496); and AIPO 682, 12/10/63 (1,330).
187 AIPO 641, 2/8/61 (2,873).   188 AIPO 682, 12/10/63 (1,330).
189 AIPO 527, 2/23/54 (1,511); NORC 353, 3/9/54 (535); NORC 363, 9/10/54 (1,198); AIPO 546, 4/12/55 (1,536); NORC 371, 4/29/55 (1,226); NORC 372, 6/23/55 (1,263); and NORC 374, 8/4/55 (1,262).

when posed the question, "When the U.S. and other nations sit down to discuss peace in Asia, would it be better to ask Communist China to take part in the meeting or better to leave them out?" 66 percent of Southerners versus 61 percent of Northeasterners, 60 percent of Midwesterners, and 54 percent of Westerners advocated leaving the Communist Chinese out and only 20 percent of Southerners as compared with 28 percent of Northeasterners, 24 percent of Midwesterners, and 25 percent of Westerners would ask them to join such discussions.[190] Asked in February, 1961, whether the United States should "take steps to improve our relations with Communist China," 47 percent of Southerners as compared with 51 percent of Northeasterners, 57 percent of Midwesterners, and 56 percent of Westerners answered in the affirmative.[191] At the same time, only 44 percent of Southerners favored offering surplus American food to famine-racked China whereas 57 percent of Northeasterners, 57 percent of Midwesterners, and 50 percent of Westerners did.[192]

The minority who favored breaking diplomatic relations with the Soviet Union and withdrawing from the U.N. if Communist China were admitted to membership was regarded as a rather extreme group by most college-educated Southerners among the interviewees. But many more Southerners with opinions on world affairs seemed to feel in 1959–62 that our policies vis-à-vis our enemies have been too altruistic, based too much on unrealistic idealism, and have indicated too great a willingness to compromise with the Communists who offer little in return. Only a very limited minority among the interviewees seemed persuaded that we should try to encourage a "mellowing" process in Communist societies through policies more lenient or "flexible" than those of the Eisenhower and Kennedy administrations of the period. The Reds would not reduce their hostility because of any such compromises, and would only use them for further intrigues. "Appease-

190 AIPO 527, 2/23/54 (1,511).
191 AIPO 641, 2/8/61 (2,873).
192 *Ibid.* Anti-American behavior of Communist China since early 1961 apparently has resulted in lowered support in the South as well as the North for sending food there. An SRC survey of May–June, 1964 (1,501), posed the query: "Now the President of the United States might decide that it was in our best interests to take certain new actions with regard to Communist China. For each thing I mention, would you tell me how you would feel about it if the President suggested that action . . . Suppose the President suggested selling things like wheat to Communist China?" Among 72 percent of the national sample who knew that a Communist government controls most of mainland China, 34 percent in the South were in favor as compared with 48 percent in the Northeast, 46 percent in the Midwest (including the Plains States), and 42 percent in the West; 55 percent in the South were opposed, compared with 40 percent, 45 percent, and 48 percent, respectively; and the remainder voiced no opinion, were undecided, or said they did not know.

ment," as in the case of Hitler and Mussolini, would likely result in further demands, pressures, and aggressions.

Hence, Southerners have been at least somewhat more apt than other citizens to say that we should not be more willing to compromise with Russia or China than the policy of our government at the time, rather we should, perhaps, be less willing,[193] that our policies should be "firmer" or "tougher," [194] that we should discontinue negotiations until our opponents seemed willing to negotiate reasonably, that we have gone too far or far enough in our efforts to settle our differences,[195] and that it is more important to stop further Communist expansion than to keep out of war.[196] A larger minority of Southerners than other Americans—of the order of two out of five of those offering opinions—favored breaking off truce talks in Korea after several months of frustration at Panmunjom.[197] Furthermore, larger minorities of Southerners than of Northerners venturing views since the death of Stalin in 1953 have been opposed to summit conferences and other meetings between heads of state of the U.S.S.R. and the United States (with or without Britain and France). Many Southerners felt these conferences to be useless, Soviet propaganda forums, and potentially negotiations wherein we come out on the short end of the bargain or which are otherwise likely to be detrimental to our national interests.[198] In early 1961, for example,

193   NORC 163, 1/26/49 (1,261); NORC 166, 6/1/49 (1,300); NORC 276, 3/1/50 (1,300); NORC 323, 4/22/52 (1,250); NORC 340, 5/14/53 (1,291); NORC 347, 8/21/53 (526); NORC 349, 11/25/53 (1,300); NORC 386, 4/26/56 (1,224); and Roper 148, July, 1963 (3,007).
194   Significant at the 10 percent level as a result of combining similar questions on AIPO 379, 9/25/46 (2,966); AIPO 396, 5/7/47 (3,137); AIPO 422, 7/28/48 (3,142); NORC 162, 11/23/48 (1,300); AIPO 436, 1/20/49 (3,213); and NORC 386, 4/20/56 (1,224).
195   A result of combining similar questions in NORC 303, 6/29/51 (1,300); AIPO 513, 3/26/53 (1,590); and NORC 398, 10/25/56 (1,295).
196   Significant at the 10 percent level after combining similar questions in NORC 133, 8/31/45 (1,259); NORC 141, 3/20/46 (1,293); NORC 145, 10/2/46 (1,307); NORC 149, 4/3/47 (1,307); NORC 154, 12/4/47 (1,293); AIPO 458, 7/7/50 (1,426); and NORC 357, 5/18/54 (517).
197   Significant at the 10 percent level when similar questions in the following were combined: NORC 313, 10/2/51 (1,237); NORC 314, 11/22/51 (1,237); NORC 317, 2/5/52 (1,260); NORC 320, 3/19/52 (1,260); NORC 321, 3/12/52 (521); NORC 327, 6/30/52 (1,285); and NORC 329, 8/28/52 (1,300).
198   NORC 363, 9/10/54 (1,198); NORC 371, 4/29/55 (1,226); NORC 372, 6/23/55 (1,263); NORC 374, 8/4/55 (1,262); AIPO 552, 8/23/55 (1,500); AIPO 563, 4/17/56 (2,009); NORC 386, 4/20/56 (1,224); NORC 393, 9/13/56 (1,263); NORC 401, 2/28/56 (1,232); AIPO 594, 1/22/58 (1,550); and AIPO 602, 7/28/58 (1,621). For example, when the NORC survey of April 29, 1955, posed the question, "If these statesmen (the Big Four) get together personally, do you think they will be able to reach agreement on any big problems of the world?" 19 percent of white Southerners (22 percent of all Southerners) and 25 percent of white Northerners,

56 percent of Northerners as compared with 49 percent of Southerners (among those offering views) favored a meeting between President Kennedy and Premier Khrushchev, and 34 percent of the former versus 40 percent of the latter opposed the idea.[199]

Thus, by the early 1960's Southerners seemed more inclined than other Americans to agree with General Charles de Gaulle (when they knew of his stand) about not negotiating with the Communists over Berlin and other issues until there was some sign that our opponents would be likely to be more reasonable than in the past and to offer truly acceptable proposals. In the late summer of 1961 only 4 percent of Southerners, mostly Negroes and poorly educated whites who were general isolationists, felt we should not keep our troops in Berlin if remaining there might run the risk of war.[200] Later in 1961, Southerners were somewhat more likely than other Americans to think that we should try to fight our way into Berlin if the Communists closed all roads and railroads and did not permit our planes to enter the city—only 13 percent of the former as compared with 20 percent of the latter thought we should not attempt to force our way into Berlin under such circumstances.[201] Large majorities of Southerners and their newspapers seemed to feel that President Kennedy was wise to call for

---

(26 percent of all Northerners) replied in the affirmative; 64, 60, 57, and 56 percent, respectively, in the negative; and the rest were undecided, said they did not know, or ventured no opinion. A year later, 42 percent of Southerners, 54 percent of Northeasterners, 50 percent of Midwesterners (including residents of the Plains States), and 62 percent of Westerners responded in the affirmative when queried whether Bulganin and Khrushchev, who were then in Britain, "should be invited to come to the United States to talk to Eisenhower and Dulles." The percentages replying in the negative were 34, 30, 32, and 24, respectively; 24, 16, 18 and 14 percent, respectively ventured no opinion, said they did not know, or were undecided. (AIPO 563, 4/17/56.) When asked in early 1957, whether they thought it was a "good or bad idea for President Eisenhower to invite Russia's top leaders to visit America," 50 percent of white Southerners (51 percent of all Southerners) and 59 percent of white Northerners (60 percent of all Northerners) felt that it would be a good idea; 44, 43, 34, and 34 percent, respectively, thought that it would be a bad idea; and 6, 6, 7, and 6 percent, respectively, offered no opinion, said they did not know, or were undecided. (NORC 401, 12/28/56.) When the AIPO survey of July 28, 1958, asked, "If Khrushchev comes to a meeting at the United Nations in New York City, do you think President Eisenhower should invite him to the White House?" 42 percent of white Southerners (39 percent of all Southerners) and 49 percent of white Northerners (50 percent of all Northerners) answered in the affirmative; 38, 36, 36, and 36 percent, respectively, replied in the negative; and 20, 25, 15, and 15 percent, respectfully, offered no opinion, said they did not know, or were undecided.
199 AIPO 640, 1/10/61 (2,649).   200 AIPO 648, 7/25/61 (1,462).
201 AIPO 650, 9/19/61 (3,476). Differences in the same direction were evident in replies to similar questions on AIPO 649, 8/22/61 (3,165), and AIPO 651, 10/17/61 (3,753).

a military buildup to convince the Communists that we "meant business" in Berlin in 1961 and early 1962.

Judging from the interviewees, the author concluded that many Southerners influential in their locales were inclined to believe we should stand just as firmly against Communist threats and call their "bluffs" elsewhere as well. We should stop "pussyfooting" and "backtracking" before Communist bluster. "It is better to die on our feet than live on our knees," and once our friends and enemies understand this to be our international posture they will know what to expect from us and behave accordingly. Although many Southerners who felt this way would reduce foreign spending on economic development of Africa and Asia and other nonmilitary programs both at home and abroad, few of them, or even few of Southern liberals who favored expanded economic aid, would oppose increased military expenditures if requested by the Defense Department and supported by the President.

Collective Security after 1945

Since the war Southern whites and Southern voters have been as or more willing than other Americans to send our armed forces abroad to counter Communist aggressions—in Indo-China, Lebanon, Berlin, the Formosa Strait, Latin America, and so on—either in collaboration with our allies or unilaterally.[202] They have in equal or larger majorities as compared with Northerners thought that we should agree in advance to help defend countries attacked, provided they undertook similar military commitments commensurate with their resources,[203] and that the Communists would be most likely to desist from aggression if we and our allies presented a strong military front.[204] Although, as will be noted later, Southerners as a group have been less inclined than Northerners to favor continuation of foreign economic aid in the amounts which were extended in recent years to underdeveloped, particularly neutralist and "leftist," countries (see pp. 211–14), they have been as apt as any other regional group to approve of sending military supplies

202 NORC 151, 6/24/47 (1,273); NORC 312, 8/27/51 (1,237); NORC 315, 12/18/51 (1,237); NORC 327, 6/30/52 (1,285); NORC 332, 10/15/52 (1,291); NORC 347, 8/21/53 (526); NORC 349, 11/25/53 (1,300); NORC 351, 1/21/54 (1,300); NORC 355, 4/22/54 (1,207); NORC 378, 10/6/55 (527); AIPO 640, 1/10/61 (2,649); AIPO 648, 7/25/61 (3,159); AIPO 649, 8/22/61 (3,165); AIPO 650, 9/19/61 (3,476); and AIPO 651, 10/17/61 (3,753).
203 NORC 171, 11/11/49 (1,300); NORC 288, 9/20/50 (1,254); and NORC 295, 12/28/50 (1,258).
204 NORC 292, 11/22/50 (1,258).

and advisors at our expense to the more "dependable" allies who are economically unable to manufacture or pay for them.[205]

The minority who would withdraw from our more important world-wide military commitments has been confined primarily to those who have been isolationists in virtually all spheres of international activity and concentrated, as in other parts of the country, among the less informed, less interested, little educated, and underprivileged strata. Considering the fact that there have been disproportionately large numbers of citizens in these lower strata in the South, it is notable that the region has been for the most part at least as willing as the rest of the country to make sacrifices in order to continue and even expand our military presence and alliances abroad. When Southerners have been compared with Northerners of comparable education, income, or knowledge about world affairs, they have usually been somewhat and, in some instances, considerably more likely to support the sacrifices necessary to continue active military participation beyond our shores.

Western Europe

As in the past, white Southerners, more than other Americans taken together, have tended in the postwar era to emphasize the importance of international commitments in Western Europe over those in other parts of the Eastern Hemisphere.

Southerners' greater hostility toward the Germans of the pre-Pearl Harbor period persisted for a considerable period thereafter. During the war Southerners were more inclined than inhabitants of other regions to support the doctrine of unconditional surrender [206] and the view that long-term occupation and control and otherwise stringent peace terms should be carried out in Germany.[207] Both during and after World War II, larger majorities of Southerners than of other regional groups rejected the suggestion that our entry into that war

205 NORC 160, 7/30/48 (1,300); NORC 163, 1/26/49 (1,261); NORC 164, 3/3/49 (1,300); NORC 165, 4/19/49 (1,300); NORC 166, 6/1/49 (1,300); NORC 167, 6/30/49 (1,284); NORC 168, 8/11/49 (1,300); NORC 169, 9/16/49 (1,300); NORC 170, 10/12/49 (1,300); SRC survey of November-December, 1949 (606); NORC 273, 1/18/50 (1,284); NORC 276, 3/1/50 (1,300); NORC 282, 6/14/50 (1,276); NORC 287, 7/24/50 (1,302); NORC 291, 10/18/50 (1,305); NORC 292, 11/22/50 (1,258); NORC 295, 12/28/50 (1,258); NORC 298, 1/30/51 (1,236); NORC 300, 3/20/51 (1,300); NORC 307, 5/24/51 (1,282); NORC 313, 10/2/51 (1,237); NORC 314, 11/22/51 (1,237); NORC 329, 8/28/52 (1,300); AIPO 506, 10/7/52 (3,098); NORC 334, 12/29/52 (1,291); NORC 340, 5/14/53 (1,291); NORC 348, 9/24/53 (526); NORC 351, 1/21/54 (1,300); NORC 386, 4/20/56 (1,224); and AIPO 577, 1/15/57 (1,496).
206 AIPO 285, 12/2/42 (2,844).   207 AIPO 344, 4/5/45 (3,134).

was a mistake.[208] In line with their tendency to view human nature as perverse and difficult to change (see pp. 345–47), Southerners were significantly more likely shortly after the war to believe that Germans would "always want to go to war to make themselves as powerful as possible," [209] that they could not be "reeducated" to a "peaceful way of life," [210] and that they could not be trusted to govern themselves in a democratic way.[211] In the late summer of 1949, for instance, majorities in every major region except the South thought that "Germany, on the whole, has been punished enough for its part in World War II." [212] Although the proportion of Americans throughout the country who manifested negative sentiments toward the Germans decreased during the first decade after V-E Day, Southerners at any given time were at least somewhat more inclined to feel unfriendly toward them than were other regional groups.[213]

However, as the cold war became more intense with the coup in Czechoslovakia and especially with invasion of South Korea by the Communists, Southern pragmatism combined with the feeling that we should make use of as many anti-Communist allies as possible brought proportionately somewhat more Southerners than Northerners to the view that the Germans and their government, after the Canadians and

208 AIPO 311, 2/1/44 (3,009); AIPO 369, 4/10/46 (3,152); and AIPO 404, 9/10/47 (3,057). At the time of the 1947 survey, for instance, 72 percent in the South felt our participation in World War II was not a mistake as compared with 67 percent in the Northeast, 61 percent in the Midwest, 66 percent in the Plains States, and 70 percent in the West. (See above, p. 91, for comparable interregional differences during the late thirties and early forties in attitudes toward our participation in World War I.)
209 Forty percent of Southerners as compared with 30 percent of Northeasterners, 25 percent of Midwesterners (including residents of the Plains States), and 24 percent of Westerners were of this view in the spring of 1946. NORC 241, May, 1946 (2,589).
210 In late 1946, 60 percent of Southerners, compared with 67 percent of Northeasterners, 76 percent of Midwesterners (residents of the Plains States included), and 71 percent of Westerners felt it would be possible "to reeducate the Germans to a peaceful way of life." NORC 146, 11/15/46 (1,300).
211 AIPO 444, 6/30/49 (2,826).
212 Fifty-one percent in the Northeast, 53 percent in the Midwest, 61 percent in the Plains States, 56 percent in the West, but only 42 percent in the South believed that Germany had been punished enough; 36 percent in the South as compared with 33, 29, 22, and 26 percent, respectively, of the other regions felt she had not. AIPO 445, 7/21/49 (3,103).
213 AIPO 387, 12/31/46 (2,933); AIPO release of 4/3/53; and NORC 370, 3/11/55 (1,225). At the time of the 1953 survey, for example, 45 percent of Southerners as compared with 53 percent of Northeasterners, 53 percent of Midwesterners, and 60 percent of Westerners said they felt friendly toward the German people. In 1955, 16 percent of Southerners in contrast to 11 percent of other Americans said they had an unfavorable impression of the Germans.

British, were among the more reliable and potentially effective of our allies.[214] By 1951 the South came to believe as much as other regions that the Germans, together with the Canadians and British, could be relied upon more than most others to cooperate with us; by the mid-1950's Southerners were somewhat more inclined than other Americans taken together to think so.[215] Several weeks after the Chinese Communist entry into the Korean War in December, 1950, only 23 percent of Southerners, contrasted to 31 percent of Northeasterners, 32 percent of Midwesterners, and 38 percent of Westerners, opposed the idea of letting Germany rearm; 58 percent of Southerners as compared with 57 percent of Northeasterners, 52 percent of Midwesterners, and 58 percent of Westerners approved of this suggestion.[216] By August, 1954, for instance, only 28 percent of Southerners versus 43 percent of Northeasterners, 37 percent of Midwesterners, and 35 percent of Westerners felt that there would be "much danger" of Germany "again becoming a threat to world peace" if she were rearmed; 50 percent of Southerners as compared with 44 percent, 48 percent, and 53 percent, respectively, of the other regions thought there would not be "much danger" in such an eventuality.[217]

On the other hand, Southerners have been somewhat less inclined than non-Southerners to believe that the Italians would put up a "real fight" in case of attack by the Soviet bloc or that we could "count on Italy to cooperate with us" in world affairs.[218] A number of the interviewees observed that the Italians failed to perform well militarily in World War I and World War II and that they would probably not offer serious resistance to an attack by the U.S.S.R. or its East European satellites.

Even as late as August, 1943, Southerners were markedly more favorable to the idea of a "permanent" alliance with Britain whereby each nation would agree to come immediately to the other's defense if the

214   NORC 303, 6/29/51 (1,300).
215   NORC 315, 12/18/51 (1,237); NORC 323, 4/22/52 (1,250); NORC 337, 2/11/53 (1,291); NORC 364, 10/23/54 (518); NORC 366, 1/21/55 (1,209); NORC 382, 1/26/56 (1,238); NORC 390, 6/26/56 (1,275); NORC 399, 11/15/56 (1,286); and AIPO 576, 12/12/56 (1,539).
216   NORC 285, 12/28/50 (1,258). See also NORC 287, 7/24/50 (1,302).
217   AIPO 535, 8/31/54 (1,581).
218   AIPO 471, 2/2/51 (1,404); AIPO 521, 10/7/53 (1,488); and NORC 355, 4/22/54 (1,207). At the time of the 1954 survey, for example, 33 percent of Southerners (35 percent of Southern whites) as compared with 47 percent of Northerners (48 percent of Northern whites) thought we could count on Italy to cooperate with us in international affairs; 26 percent of Southerners (25 percent of Southern whites) versus 25 percent of Northerners (25 percent of Northern whites) felt we could not.

other were attacked after the war; 71 percent of the South approved of this proposition in contrast to 59 percent of the Northeast, 57 percent of the Midwest, 59 percent of the Plains States, and 58 percent of the West.[219] After the war such rather large differences have not been often apparent, but during the initial postwar years Southerners, particularly Southern whites and those who voted in the immediately previous presidential or congressional election (or primary), remained somewhat more inclined than other Americans taken together to approve of the idea of a military alliance with Western Europe.[220] Small differences in the expected direction were apparent on more surveys than not on similar queries during the 1950's.[221] Throughout the postwar period Southerners, particularly when Negroes or nonvoters were eliminated from samples, have been at least as, and sometimes more, inclined than other Americans to feel that we should work "closely" with Western Europe,[222] that we should go to the aid of Europe with our armed forces if it were attacked by the Communist powers,[223] that we should maintain major military forces and bases in that part of the world,[224] that we should station as many or more of our military personnel in Europe than were there at the time and should not reduce the number there,[225] and the like. Virtually without exception, majori-

219 AIPO 300, 8/18/43 (3,065). See also AIPO 303, 9/28/43 (3,072).
220 AIPO 367, 3/13/46 (3,249); AIPO 408, 11/26/47 (2,968); AIPO 417, 4/21/48 (3,165); AIPO 432, 11/1/48 (3,000); NORC 162, 11/23/48 (1,300); AIPO 436, 1/20/49 (3,213); NORC 164, 3/3/49 (1,300); NORC 165, 4/19/49 (1,300); NORC 166, 6/1/49 (1,300); NORC 169, 9/16/49 (1,300).
221 NORC 276, 3/1/50 (1,300); AIPO 455, 5/2/50 (2,850); NORC 312, 8/27/51 (1,237); NORC 341–342, 6/30/53 (1,291); NORC 357, 5/18/54 (517); NORC 378, 10/6/55 (527); NORC 399, 11/15/56 (1,286); and AIPO 592, 11/23/57 (1,542).
222 NORC 282, 4/14/50 (1,274); NORC 313, 10/2/51 (1,237); and NORC 364, 10/23/54 (518).
223 In October, 1948, 49 percent of white Southerners as compared with 46 percent of white Northerners thought we should promise to "go to war on their side if these (England, France, and other countries of western Europe) are attacked"; 39 percent of the former versus 44 percent of the latter felt we should not. However, since Southern Negroes were much more inclined than whites of either section to think we should make no such promises, their inclusion in the sample reduced the Southern to the Northern average on this question. See NORC 161, 10/13/48 (1,300). Approximately a year later, 47 percent of Southerners (48 percent of Southern whites) as compared with 41 percent of Northerners approved of "the United States using its armed forces to help stop any attack on a country of Western Europe"; 34 percent of Southerners (35 percent of Southern whites) versus 42 percent of Northerners disapproved. See NORC 169, 9/16/49 (1,300).
224 NORC 137, 12/12/45 (1,300); NORC 142, 5/17/46 (1,292); and NORC 169, 9/16/49 (1,300).
225 NORC 288, 9/20/50 (1,254); NORC 295, 12/28/50 (1,258); NORC 298, 1/30/51 (1,236); NORC 300, 3/20/51 (1,300); NORC 302, 4/18/51 (1,300); NORC 307, 5/24/51 (1,282); NORC 315, 12/18/51 (1,237); NORC 349, 11/25/53 (1,300); NORC 363, 9/10/54 (1,198); and NORC 399, 11/15/56 (1,286).

ties of Southerners replying approved of such opinions when they were presented to them in surveys, and seldom were these majorities smaller than outside the South, especially when "no opinion" replies were eliminated.

It is not surprising, therefore, that the defense pact among West European countries in 1948 was a bit more favorably received among Southerners than non-Southerners who had heard of it.[226] In late 1948, only 14 percent of Southerners as compared with 22 percent of Northeasterners, 22 percent of Midwesterners, 17 percent of residents in the Plains States, and 17 percent of Westerners opposed the spending of some two billion dollars in the coming year to help these countries rearm.[227] Southerners, particularly whites, were in at least as large majorities as white Northerners favorable to negotiation and ratification of the NATO pact and, since 1949, to its active support by our country.[228] The proportions of Southerners (and other Americans) favoring our sending military supplies to our European allies at our expense have decreased considerably since we attempted to rearm an economically weak Europe in the late 1940's and early 1950's, but during the period 1948–56 the fraction of Southerners approving this program was as large or larger than among non-Southerners.[229] Southerners have been

226 NORC 156, 3/25/48 (1,289); NORC 157, 4/22/48 (1,280); NORC 161, 10/13/48 (1,300); AIPO 432, 2/9/49 (3,160); NORC 169, 9/16/49 (1,300); and AIPO release of September, 1949.
227 AIPO 432, 11/1/48 (3,000). See also NORC 157, 4/22/48 (1,280).
228 NORC 165, 4/19/49 (1,300); NORC 166, 6/1/49 (1,300); NORC 169, 9/16/49 (1,300); AIPO 438, 3/4/49 (3,090); AIPO 440, 4/7/49 (2,719); AIPO 443, 6/9/49 (2,765); NORC 167, 6/30/49 (1,284); AIPO release of 7/8/49; NORC 276, 3/1/50 (1,300); AIPO 455, 5/2/50 (2,850); NORC 287, 7/24/50 (1,302); NORC 295, 12/28/50 (1,258); NORC 312, 8/27/51 (1,237); NORC 341-2, 6/30/53 (1,291); NORC 357, 5/18/54 (517); NORC 378, 10/6/55 (527); NORC 379, 11/23/55 (1,276); NORC 386, 4/20/56 (1,224); NORC 399, 11/15/56 (1,286); and AIPO 592, 11/23/57 (1,542).
229 NORC 161, 10/13/48 (1,300); NORC 292, 11/22/50 (1,258); NORC 314, 11/22/51 (1,237); and NORC 399, 11/15/56 (1,286). Replies in percentages were as follows to the question, "Do you approve or disapprove of sending military supplies to the countries of Western Europe in order to strengthen them against any future attack?"

	All Southerners	Southern Whites	All Northerners	Northern Whites
		Approve		
1948	54	58	54	54
1950	74	72	71	71
1951	63	66	65	65
1956	67	69	64	65
		Disapprove		
1948	36	33	39	40
1950	19	21	23	23

as satisfied, or more satisfied, with the performance of our European allies than have other regional groups: in mid-1952, for example, 39 percent of Southerners, compared with 37 percent of Northeasterners, 34 percent of Midwesterners (Plains States residents included), and 28 percent of Westerners, said that they were "in general satisfied with the way England, France, and our other European allies are cooperating with us in the struggle against world Communism"; only 39 percent in the South as compared with 50 percent in the Northeast, 53 percent in the Midwest, and 60 percent in the West were "dissatisfied." [230]

By 1959 most of the locally influential interviewees had come to feel that we probably could not trust many of our supposed allies in Southeast Asia, the Far East, and the Middle East to fight effectively in case of actual Communist military action. But proposals that we work more through NATO and our other West European arrangements and less through the U.N. with its often critical Communist-neutralist majorities, symbols like "Atlantic partnership," and other suggestions for more emphasis on European and less on Asian and African objectives, opin-

	All Southerners	Southern Whites	All Northerners	Northern Whites
		Disapprove		
1951	29	26	29	29
1956	27	26	31	30
		No opinion		
1948	10	9	7	6
1950	7	7	6	6
1951	8	8	6	6
1956	6	5	5	5

Differently worded questions during the first year of the Atlantic Pact resulted in rather diverse replies, but Southerners were without exception at least as favorable to sending military supplies to Western Europe as other regional groups, and typically more so. For instance, when asked in the summer of 1949, "Do you think the United States should or should not send arms and war materials to the North Atlantic nations which have joined us in the Atlantic Pact?" 37 percent in the South, 33 percent in the Northeast, 32 percent in the Midwest (including the Plains States), and 35 percent in the West felt that the United States should; 9, 21, 18, and 23 percent, respectively, that it should not; and 54, 46, 50, and 42 percent, respectively, said they had never heard of the Atlantic Pact, did not know, were undecided, or had no opinion. See AIPO 445, 7/21/49 (3,103). When asked a month later, "Do you approve or disapprove of President Truman's plan to send war materials and money to countries who want to build up their military defense as a protection against Russia?" 57 percent in the South approved, compared with 46 percent in the Northeast, 45 percent in the Midwest, 41 percent in the Plains States, and 40 percent in the West; 27, 40, 42, 44, and 46 percent, respectively, disapproved; and 16, 14, 13, 15, and 14 percent respectively ventured no opinion, said they did not know, or were undecided. See AIPO 446, 8/12/49 (3,272).
230   NORC 327, 6/30/52 (1,285). See also replies to the same or similar questions on NORC 307, 5/24/51 (1,282); NORC 313, 10/2/51 (1,237); NORC 320, 3/19/52 (1,260); NORC 348, 9/24/53 (526); NORC 353, 3/9/54 (535); NORC 363, 9/10/54 (1,198); NORC 364, 10/23/54 (518), and NORC 372, 6/23/55 (1,263).

ion, and pressures seemed to have received rather broad support among those who had heard of such propositions. These sentiments frequently extended to the feeling that we should accord the colonial powers of Western Europe more support than we had up to then in their controversies with their underdeveloped, often colored, dependencies. The Western Europeans were considered our real allies, because of common traditions, values, general outlook, interests, and race.

The Western Hemisphere

Southerners, like most other Americans, have typically placed even greater stress on defense of Canada and Latin America against attack or penetration by hostile extra-American powers than on security arrangements with Western Europe. Nowhere in the United States has the Monroe Doctrine been more widely accepted as a cornerstone of our foreign policy than among literate Southerners. Thus, during the Nazi-Soviet invasion of Poland, 81 percent of Southerners, 74 percent of Northeasterners, 66 percent of Midwesterners, 66 percent of those in the Plains States, and 77 percent of Westerners said that we should fight to keep any European power out of Cuba or any other area within fifteen hundred miles of the Panama Canal.[231] In the same survey, 77 percent of Southerners, compared with 75 percent of Northeasterners, 70 percent of Midwesterners, 74 percent of those in the Plains States, and 71 percent of Westerners, felt that our army and navy should aid Canada if she were invaded by any European power; 67 percent of Southerners as compared with 56 percent, 52 percent, 44 percent, and 53 percent, respectively, of the other regional groups thought that the United States should use its armed forces to prevent any European invasion of any South American country. In the summer of 1940, 94 percent of Southerners in contrast to 87 percent of Northeasterners, 84 percent of Midwesterners, 87 percent of residents in the Plains States, and 88 percent of Westerners advocated that we take possession of English, French, and Dutch dependencies in the Caribbean should Germany defeat Britain.[232] Through the four years immediately prior to our entry into the war, Southerners were more apt on a variety of questions than inhabitants of other regions to feel that we should use all the means at our disposal, including military, to keep any Axis influence out of this hemisphere.[233]

Differences between the South as a whole and the other regions since World War II have been neither as large nor as consistent. When Ne-

231 AIPO 171, 9/22/39 (3,064).   232 AIPO Release of 7/21/40.
233 AIPO 112, 2/14/38 (2,837); AIPO 140, 12/2/38 (3,102); and AIPO 196, 5/30/40 (3,198).

groes have been included in the sample, the South has either not differed or differed only very slightly from the national average on questions relative to United States commitments in Latin America and the prevention of foreign influence hostile to our interests in the Western Hemisphere. However, since Negroes have tended to be less inclined than whites in the South to support active American involvements south of the border, their elimination from the Southern sample usually revealed that Southern whites were somewhat more favorable to such policies than were Northern whites—although interregional differences between whites were seldom large.

Thus, in the spring of 1947, 57 percent of Southerners (and of Southern whites) as compared with 52 percent of Northerners (51 percent of Northern whites) agreed that we should send arms to South American countries "to strengthen military defenses in our part of the world"; 26 percent of Southerners (and of Southern whites) versus 35 percent of Northerners (and of Northern whites) disagreed.[234] In the fall of 1949, 53 percent of Southern whites (48 percent of all Southerners) as compared with 48 percent of Northerners (and of white Northerners) said they would approve of the United States using its armed forces to help stop any attack on a country in South America.[235] In April, 1956, 87 percent of Southern whites (and of all Northerners) approved of our "defense agreements with South and Central America [whereby] the United States and these countries have promised to defend each other against any attack"; 6 percent of Southern whites (7 percent of all Southerners) versus 7 percent of Northerners (whether or not non-whites were included) disapproved.[236]

White Southerners who had heard of the action of our government toward the leftist regime in Guatemala in 1954 were somewhat more inclined than Northerners who had also heard of it to approve,[237] but Southerners have probably been a bit more apt to favor vigorous United States behavior to assure the existence of friendly leadership in Latin America generally. The feeling was rather widespread among the locally influential interviewees that we should have done more in the early 1960's to topple the Castro regime.[238] They felt that, if we "cleaned up" Cuba, we would have much less difficulty with the rest of Latin America. We should not have tolerated seizure of United States

234 NORC 149, 4/3/47 (1,307). Similar small differences in the same direction were apparent a year later among replies to a somewhat differently worded query; see NORC 155, 2/25/48 (1,271).
235 NORC 169, 9/16/49 (1,300). See also NORC 165, 4/19/49 (1,300).
236 NORC 386, 4/20/56 (1,224).   237 NORC 359, 6/30/54 (1,217).
238 See also AIPO 643, 4/26/61 (2,974).

private and public property without fair compensation, mistreatment of our citizens, and Fidel Castro's example to other Latin demagogues. Before most trade with Cuba was curtailed by the federal government and before the abortive invasion at the Bay of Pigs in April, 1961, the conservative newspapers in the sample and many of the interviewees advocated embargo of Cuba and complete support, if required, of internal revolution with our military assistance. Few of the interviewees, other than among the better read, more cosmopolitan minority, would have been critical of open support of the Cuban invasion of April, 1961, by U.S. Air Force units and even by our ground troops, and most would not have objected to naval blockade and even outright military invasion by United States forces in 1962. Interviewees commented that it is not the Southern (or the American) way to take insults from "tin Caesars" and that we should do something more drastic about this one on our doorstep.

The Defense of Asia

As in the case of Germany and the Germans, Southerners were more likely than other regional groups to feel in the early years after V-J Day that the Japanese were fundamentally warlike [239] and that any effective effort at changing their undemocratic habits of mind would necessarily be unfruitful or, at least, very long term.[240] Likewise, Southerners were more apt to approve of strong punishment, including military occupation of Japan for many years.[241] As the Nationalist Chinese were gradually forced from the mainland and the cold war intensified in Asia, particularly after the invasion of South Korea in June, 1950, Southerners like other Americans came to accept Japan as our principal ally in the Far East.[242] However, up through 1960 Japan was never considered to be as important or as trustworthy a partner as Britain, Canada, Germany, or France by most Americans, and particularly by most Southerners.[243] In mid-1960, for instance, when asked, "Do you think Japan is or is not a dependable ally (friend) of the United States?" only 25 percent of Southerners, compared with 28 percent of Northeasterners, 33 percent of Midwesterners (residents of the Plains States

239 In May, 1946, 41 percent of Southerners, 29 percent of Northeasterners, 33 percent of Midwesterners, and 36 percent of Westerners agreed that the Japanese "will always want to go to war to make themselves as powerful as possible." NORC 241, May, 1946 (2,589).
240 AIPO 445, 7/21/49 (3,103).
241 AIPO 356, 9/19/45 (3,075), and AIPO 445, 7/2/49 (3,103).
242 NORC 295, 12/28/50 (1,258).
243 NORC 315, 12/18/51 (1,237); NORC 355, 4/22/54 (1,207); NORC 382, 1/26/56 (1,238); NORC 401, 12/28/56 (1,232); and AIPO 632, 7/28/60 (3,150).

included), and 45 percent of Westerners, replied in the affirmative while 59 percent, 57 percent, 54 percent, and 43 percent, respectively, answered in the negative.[244] Southern whites have felt somewhat less friendly toward the Japanese than other Americans,[245] although the differences between Northern and Southern whites have not been as great as for Africa south of the Sahara. Better informed Southerners among the interviewees were often worried that anti-American leftists had great influence in Japan.

The prevalence in the South of attitudes favoring "tougher" policies toward Communist China and opposing its entry into the U.N. and its diplomatic recognition by the United States has frequently been paired with rather favorable views of Chiang Kai-shek and his Nationalists on Formosa, at least among those Southerners who had heard of him.[246] The more widespread Southern tendency to think that conservative foreign regimes are more pro-American and more reliable allies than governments to the left of center (see pp. 192–96) has tended to foster relatively favorable feelings toward the leaders on Taiwan and to encourage the view that we should accord Chiang greater support than has sometimes been the case since his retreat from the mainland. Chiang's Methodist religion also stimulated some favorable comment among the better informed interviewees and in the Southern press. In 1961, Chiang had a relatively favorable press in a majority of newspapers in the sample, and a particularly favorable one among the more generally conservative third or so of them. Hence, in April, 1948, 57 percent of Southerners as compared with 57 percent of Northeasterners, 51 percent of Midwesterners, 55 percent of those in the Plains States, and 52 percent of Westerners approved of our "giving the Chiang Kai-shek (Nationalist) government more military supplies, goods, and money"; only

244 AIPO 632, 7/28/60 (3,150).
245 AIPO 439, 3/17/49 (2,193); NORC 300, 3/20/51 (1,300); AIPO 511, 11/29/53 (1,599); and NORC 370, 3/11/55 (1,225). At the time of the 1953 survey, for instance, 50 percent of Southerners said they felt friendly toward the Japanese people, 17 percent unfriendly; the respective percentages for the Northeast were 56 and 15, the Midwest (Plains States included) 54 and 14, and the West 64 and 13.
246 NORC 162, 11/23/48 (1,300), and NORC 371, 4/29/55 (1,226). The earlier survey revealed that Southern whites were both somewhat less enthusiastic about Nehru and more enthusiastic about Chiang than Northern whites (or Northerners generally). Thus, 57 percent of white Southerners had a favorable impression of Chiang, 15 percent an unfavorable one, and 28 percent ventured no opinion, whereas the respective figures for the white Northerners were 55, 22, and 23 percent. On the other hand, only 28 percent of white Southerners at that time had a favorable impression of Nehru, 19 percent had an unfavorable one, and 53 percent were undecided, whereas the respective white Northern figures were 37, 16, and 47 percent.

26 percent of Southerners in contrast to 31 percent of Northeasterners, 35 percent of Midwesterners, 32 percent of those in the Plains States, and 33 percent of Westerners disapproved.[247] A somewhat larger minority of white Southerners than of white Northerners expressing opinions has typically favored our assisting the Nationalists to retake China proper,[248] and support of the idea of encouraging them to withdraw from Quemoy and Matsu has been somewhat less evident in the white South.[249]

These observations applied to a lesser extent to Syngman Rhee and South Korean defense prior to his displacement from power.[250]

Southerners have been more willing than other Americans to intervene militarily with more conventional forces as well as with nuclear weapons in Southeast Asia against Communist aggression. In April, 1954, for example, 68 percent of Southerners as compared with 56 percent of other citizens felt we should send our air force into the fighting in Indo-China if it looked as though the Communists might take over the whole country, while 22 percent of the former versus 35 percent of the latter felt we should not; 42 percent of Southerners as compared with 39 percent of non-Southerners would send in our ground troops, while 36 percent and 46 percent, respectively, would not.[251] In mid-1964 Southerners were significantly less inclined than other Americans to favor compromise with Communist China in order to achieve a solution in Vietnam. A series of questions about alternative lines of United States policy in Southeast Asia were asked the public, among them, "How about trying to make some compromise agreement with Communist China on this—like making all Viet Nam neutral?" Only 36 percent in the South as compared with 47 percent in the Northeast, 51 percent in the Midwest (including the Plains States), and 50 percent in the West approved of this possibility; 34, 25, 25, and 34 percent, respectively, disapproved; and the rest offered no opinions, said they did not know, or were undecided.[252] Southerners, like other Americans, have placed much less faith in SEATO as an instrument of collective security than in NATO or even the OAS.[253] In fact, they have been somewhat less

247 AIPO Release of 4/28/48.
248 NORC 302, 4/18/51 (1,300); NORC 307, 5/24/51 (1,282); NORC 312, 8/27/51 (1,237); NORC 320, 3/19/52 (1,260); and NORC 363, 9/10/54 (1,198).
249 NORC 371, 4/29/55 (1,226).   250 NORC 341-2, 6/30/53 (1,291).
251 NORC 355, 4/22/54 (1,207). As usual, inclusion of Negroes decreased somewhat the proportion of Southerners favorable to intervention, both in the air and on the ground.
252 SRC survey of May–June, 1964 (1,501).
253 NORC 359, 6/30/54 (1,217); NORC 363, 9/10/54 (1,198); NORC 365, 11/26/54 (1,201); and NORC 386, 4/20/56 (1,224).

enthusiastic about SEATO than the rest of America taken together.[254]

Southern attitudes about defense of the Middle East have been approximately the same as those of other regions except for the expected finding that larger fractions of Southerners have been uninformed and have ventured no opinions. Of those whites replying, similar proportions in the white South and outside have felt that what happens in the Middle East is important to our national interests.[255]

Some Political Implications

As prior to World War II, Southern voters since the war have been significantly more favorable to expensive military forces, both conventional and nuclear, and to vigorous United States involvement in strategic alliances abroad than non-voters in the region. As before, Southern voters have been more inclined toward these policies than Northern voters, the differences being considerably larger than most of the figures cited above would suggest. Larger fractions of the more isolationist Southern minority than earlier have been voting in recent years—poorly educated whites, underprivileged Negroes, and so on—but still larger proportions of their Northern ideological allies were voting, choosing Congressmen, and influencing their behavior in Washington, even as late as 1960.

254 *Ibid.* When asked in the spring of 1956, "Under the SEATO treaty the United States and these [Southeast Asian countries named previously] countries have promised to defend each other against any attack. Do you approve or disapprove of this arrangement?" 74 percent of all Southerners, 76 percent of Southern whites, and 81 percent of both all and white Northerners approved; 11, 11, and 7 percent, respectively, disapproved; and 15, 13, and 12 percent, respectively, had no opinion, were undecided, or said they did not know. See NORC 386, 4/20/56 (1,224).
255 NORC 317, 2/5/52 (1,260), and NORC 329, 8/28/52 (1,300).

CHAPTER 4

INTERNATIONAL COMMERCE

AND

RELATED ISSUES

Until relatively recently the South was more closely tied to the world economy than was the industrialized North. Southerners produced raw materials and the coarser types of manufactured goods which were sold to the factories of Europe and Japan as well as to those of the North; about half of Southern cotton and rice and between one third and two fifths of its tobacco were exported during the interwar period.[1] (A chart of world prices for these commodities would have described the economic cycles of most of the South.) Besides exporting their own products, Southerners wanted to purchase their farm equipment and consumer articles in the often cheaper markets abroad rather than in the North, and the Western Europeans and Japanese had to sell their products in the United States in order to obtain dollars to pay for the Southern cotton, tobacco, and rice.

The Evolution of Southern Views on World Trade

Tradition of Freer Trade

As a consequence of these factors, it is not surprising that a decade and more ago most Southern leaders regarded tariffs as unfortunate. Even the small minority of Southern Congressmen who voted with the Northern isolationists against United States entry into the League of

1 Irish, *Journal of Politics*, X, 307.

Nations and the Permanent Court of International Justice and against the major preparedness measures immediately prior to World War II —men like James K. Vardaman, Coleman L. Blease, and Robert Reynolds—were among the opposition to most protectionist proposals. It was not that the Southern rank and file were particularly interested in or informed about international economics and world trade—as in most fields of world affairs, they were and still (to a lesser extent) remain significantly less likely than inhabitants of other regions to say they are interested in this field and to be able to define tariffs, quotas, the reciprocal trade program, the General Agreement on Tariffs and Trade (GATT), or the like.[2] Depending on the wording of the question, more than half the Southern public have said they are little interested or uninterested in these matters and have been unable to provide even the most basic information when trade issues are being debated in the Congress and the press. Also, Southerners have been considerably more apt than other regional groups to reply "no opinion," "don't know," "undecided," or the like to requests for their views on trade questions.[3]

However, those Southerners who actually held opinions on trade, or who offered views after being informed about the reciprocal trade program, quotas, tariffs, and so on, were typically more inclined than Northerners taken together to approve of trade expansion and the reduction of barriers to foreign imports. Larger fractions of Southerners than of other Americans who ventured views prior to the mid-1950's

2 For example, in the late summer of 1946, 34 percent of Southerners as compared with 40 percent of Northeasterners, 41 percent of Midwesterners, 41 percent of residents of the Plains States, and 40 percent of Westerners said they took a "good deal" of interest in "our trade with other countries"; the rest commented that they took little or no interest. See NORC 243, 8/21/46 (1,286). Sixty percent of Southerners (54 percent of Southern whites) did not know at that time what a tariff was, compared with 43 percent of Northeasterners, 50 percent of Midwesterners, 48 percent of residents of the Plains states, and 40 percent of Westerners. When asked in September, 1953, whether they had heard of any discussion or arguments recently about tariffs, 72 percent of Southerners versus 65 percent of Northerners replied in the negative. See AIPO 520, 9/10/53 (1,535). In December, 1961, at the height of national discussion of the proposed Trade Expansion Act, 56 percent of Southerners as compared with 49 percent of Northerners admitted that they had not heard anything about this proposal or about any recent discussions of tariffs and trade. See AIPO 653, 12/5/61 (2,990); also see AIPO 408, 11/26/47 (2,968); NORC 156, 3/25/48 (1,289); NORC 332, 10/15/52 (1,291); AIPO 512, 2/20/53 (1,548); NORC 340, 5/14/53 (1,291); and NORC 371, 4/29/55 (1,226).

3 Differences between the South and the other regions were smaller when Negroes were omitted from samples, but some differences toward lower interest and knowledge of trade were evident even when Southern whites were compared with Northerners of the same race.

favored increased rather than decreased imports,[4] lower tariffs rather than higher ones,[5] extension or liberalization of the reciprocal Trade

4 AIPO 309, 1/4/44 (3,028); NORC 135, 10/17/45 (1,460); NORC 243, 8/21/46 (1,286); AIPO 384, 11/14/46 (3,203); AIPO 444, 6/30/49 (2,826); NORC 171, 11/11/49 (1,300); NORC 313, 10/2/51 (1,237); NORC 325, 5/28/52 (1,265); NORC 332, 10/15/52 (1,291); NORC 334, 12/29/52 (1,291); AIPO 513, 3/26/53 (1,590); and NORC 351, 1/21/54 (1,300).

5 AIPO Release of 9/25/38; NORC 243, 8/21/46 (1,286); AIPO 389, 1/29/47 (2,985); AIPO 404, 9/10/47 (3,057); AIPO 408, 11/26/47 (2,968); NORC 156, 3/25/48 (1,289); NORC 171, 11/11/49 (1,300); NORC 298, 11/30/51 (1,236); NORC 333, 11/17/52 (1,291); NORC 334, 12/29/52 (1,291); AIPO 512, 2/20/53 (1,548); AIPO 516, 5/28/53 (1,549); AIPO 520, 9/10/53 (1,535); AIPO 526, 1/26/54 (1,493); AIPO 535, 8/31/54 (1,581); and NORC 371, 4/29/55 (1,226). Replies were as follows to the question, "Do you think it would be a good thing for the United States, or a bad thing, if we reduced our tariffs on goods we buy from other countries?"

	South	Northeast	Midwest	West
		Good thing		
May 21, 1946	38	33	33	36
Jan. 30, 1951	30	26	28	28
Nov. 17, 1952	32	30	39	31
		Bad thing		
May 21, 1946	25	39	38	36
Jan. 30, 1951	35	47	44	43
Nov. 17, 1952	40	50	44	41
		No opinion		
May 21, 1946	37	28	29	28
Jan. 30, 1951	35	27	28	28
Nov. 17, 1952	28	20	17	28

Replies varied with the wording of the question. For instance, at the time of the NORC survey of March 25, 1948, when asked, "Do you think you personally would be better off if the tariffs on most things coming into this country were high or low?" 17 percent in the South as compared with 23 percent in the Northeast, 21 percent in the Midwest (including the Plains States), and 30 percent in the West replied "high tariffs." Forty-one percent in the South as compared with 38, 37, and 33 percent, respectively, answered "low tariffs"; and 42, 39, 42, and 37 percent, respectively, offered no opinion, said they did not know, or were undecided. When a NORC survey of November 17, 1952, asked, "If we reduced our tariffs and let more foreign goods into the United States, do you think it would help you personally in any way, or not?" 23 percent in the South in contrast to 21 percent in the Northeast, 21 percent in the Midwest (including the Plains States), and 22 percent in the West replied in the affirmative; 61, 69, 71, and 68 percent, respectively, answered in the negative; and 16, 10, 8, and 10 percent, respectively, offered no opinion, said they did not know, or were undecided. In reply to an AIPO survey of February 20, 1953, inquiring whether "the United States should do away with tariffs," 4 percent of Southern whites (3 percent of all Southerners) and 7 percent of Northern whites (6 percent of all Northerners) felt the United States should; 1, 1, 2, and 2 percent, respectively, said their reaction depended on the conditions relevant to the abolition of tariffs; 45, 42, 56, and 56 percent, respectively, responded that the United States should not eliminate tariffs; and 50, 54, 35, and 36 percent, respectively, were undecided, ventured no opinion, or answered that they did not know. When this same survey asked, "Would you favor or oppose lower-

Agreements Act rather than its termination,[6] and, in 1947–48, United States entry into the General Agreement on Tariffs and Trade [7] and

---

ing tariffs?" 16 percent of Southern whites (15 percent of all Southerners) and 19 percent of Northern whites (18 percent of all Northerners) favored lowering tariffs; 15, 14, 26, and 26 percent, respectively, opposed this suggestion; and 69, 71, 55, and 56 percent, respectively, were undecided, said they did not know, or offered no opinion.

Replies were as follows to the AIPO surveys which asked, "By and large do you favor higher tariffs or lower tariffs, than we have at present (now)?"

	South	Northeast	Midwest	West
		Higher		
May 28, 1953	9	15	14	16
Sept. 10, 1953	8	15	14	18
Jan. 26, 1954	7	12	10	21
Aug. 3, 1954	25	30	26	25
		Lower		
May 28, 1953	35	28	29	28
Sept. 10, 1953	29	30	30	23
Jan. 26, 1954	34	32	26	26
Aug. 3, 1954	51	50	43	53
		Same		
May 28, 1953	14	23	22	21
Sept. 10, 1953	15	17	18	17
Jan. 26, 1954	21	19	25	19
Aug. 3, 1954	16	12	21	16
		No opinion		
May 28, 1953	42	34	35	35
Sept. 10, 1953	48	39	38	42
Jan. 26, 1954	38	37	39	34
Aug. 3, 1954	8	8	10	5

6   AIPO 181, 1/11/40 (3,134); NORC 334, 12/29/52 (1,291); AIPO 516, 5/28/53 (1,549); and NORC 371, 4/29/55 (1,226). In the 1940 survey, a majority of Southerners had never heard of the reciprocal trade program, but 57 percent of those who had, felt that Congress should "give Secretary Hull the power to make more such treaties" compared with 50 percent outside the South. In 1953, 73 percent of Southerners either had not heard of the reciprocal Trade Agreements Act or had no opinion about its continuation, compared with 67 percent outside the South; however, those who did have views were four to one in favor of its extension, both in the South and in the North. The 1952 survey posed the question, "As you know, the United States collects a tariff, or tax, on many goods coming here from foreign countries. Do you think the United States should reduce its tariffs on goods that other countries want to sell here, providing they reduce their tariffs on goods we want to sell to them?" Seventy-one percent outside the South as compared with the same figure in the South replied in the affirmative, but only 11 percent of Southerners in contrast to 17 percent of Northerners replied in the negative. However, when the same question was posed in 1955, there was no difference among those Southerners and those Northerners who expressed opinions; 67 percent in the North and 66 percent in the South replied in the affirmative, 22 percent in both regions in the negative.

7   When an AIPO survey posed the question, "Twenty-two foreign nations have agreed, starting next year, to allow certain United States products to come into their countries at low tariff rates and we, in return, have agreed to let certain of

ratification of the proposed International Trade Organization.[8] Although differences between the South and the other regions in replies to queries about trade narrowed in the early 1950's, consistently more Southerners favored lower tariffs, liberalized quotas, and expanded imports than approved of higher tariffs, more restricted quotas, and reduced imports.

Differences between the South and the other major regions in attitudes toward trade were seldom as sharp as differences in roll-call votes of their Congressmen, even in the prewar period. The possession of any views at all on trade issues was, and remains, even more concentrated among the better educated and more elevated social strata in the South than has been the case for opinions on most other aspects of international affairs. As has been true of more liberal, or internationalist, thinking on world affairs generally, support of expanded trade has been most evident among the well educated in the South as well as in the rest of the country. But the South has comprised the largest proportion of poorly educated people, and educated, higher-status Southerners were considerably more favorable to freer trade than Northerners of similar standing and education. Moreover, Southerners voting in the general or primary election immediately prior to the survey—more inclined to be among the relatively privileged than in the North—were also significantly more favorable than either Northern voters or Southern nonvoters. Southern newspapers, controlled and edited by the more privileged and educated classes, with few exceptions opposed the Fordney-McCumber Tariff in 1922 and the Hawley-Smoot Tariff in 1930, favored the reciprocal Trade Agreements Act and its successive extensions with minimum protectionist amendments throughout the period from 1934 until the early 1950's, and approved of the establishment of and United States participation in the GATT.

One should not assume, however, that this support for expanded trade in the South was typically part of any general liberal ideology, such as the reasoning that increased commerce would encourage democratic objectives or promote other long-term political purposes of our country abroad. Trade liberals were not necessarily liberal on other public questions—self-interest, tradition, and other factors could ren-

---

their products come into this country at lower tariff rates. Do you favor or oppose this?" 60 percent in the South in contrast to 64 percent in the Northeast, 60 percent in the Midwest (Plains States included), and 68 percent in the West favored this agreement; 7 percent in the South versus 11, 16, and 13 percent, respectively, opposed it; and 33, 25, 24, and 19 percent, respectively, ventured no opinion, said they did not know, or were undecided. See AIPO 408, 11/26/47 (2,968).

8 NORC 161, 10/13/48 (1,300).

der one a free trader and, at the same time, conservative indeed on the New Deal, governmental fiscal policy, our relations with Communist and neutralist countries, and other domestic and foreign problems.

Some linkages between trade liberalism and support of active international commitments in other spheres were evident in the surveys of the twenty years following 1935. In early 1940, for example, Southerners who favored the reciprocal trade program were more inclined than those who did not, or who had never heard of it, to say they had given some thought to "what should be done to maintain world peace after the present European war is over," to oppose the proposed amendment of our Constitution to require a national vote before Congress could draft men for war overseas, and to favor lending money to Finland for war materials to fight the U.S.S.R. and paying higher taxes for military defense and aid to the opponents of the Axis.[9] During the initial postwar decade, Southerners who favored lower over higher tariffs, extension or liberalization of reciprocal trade legislation, United States adherence to the GATT, or other measures designed to expand world commerce were more inclined than those who opposed these ideas to think that the U.N. should remain in the United States,[10] the U.N. had been useful,[11] the U.N. had justified its existence,[12] we could take in more immigrants than in the recent past,[13] the Marshall Plan [14] and technical and economic assistance to Asian countries were worthwhile programs,[15] the Korean War was worth fighting,[16] and our entry into World War II was not a mistake.[17]

However, these intercorrelations were on the whole relatively small, smaller than those among opinions on most other problems of foreign policy. Support of the Marshall Plan or economic aid to Asia was a much better predictor of approval of the U.N., expanded immigration, intercultural exchange, and the like than was espousal of freer trade. Association between trade liberalism and general internationalism was small indeed on some questions; for instance, in March, 1948, and October, 1952, Southern supporters of lower tariffs were only slightly more inclined than advocates of higher ones to feel that we should "take an active part in world affairs." [18] Since support of both freer trade and

---

  9 AIPO 181, 1/11/40 (3,134).   10 AIPO 384, 11/14/46 (3,203).
11 NORC 332, 10/15/52 (1,291).   12 AIPO 512, 2/20/53 (1,548).
13 AIPO 444, 6/30/49 (2,826), and NORC 371, 4/29/55 (1,226).
14 AIPO 404, 9/10/47 (3,057); NORC 156, 3/25/48 (1,289); AIPO 444, 6/30/49 (2,826); and NORC 298, 1/30/51 (1,236).
15 NORC 334, 12/29/52 (1,291).   16 NORC 332, 10/15/52 (1,291).
17 AIPO 404, 9/10/47 (3,057).
18 NORC 156, 3/25/48 (1,289), and NORC 332, 10/15/52 (1,291).

active international cooperation in other fields was more prevalent among the better educated, as it still was in 1962, it is probable that interconnections between attitudes on world trade and most other international issues remained less among the more educated and influential elements than among the Southern public generally.

Thus, the majority of free-trade cotton and tobacco planters and members of the New Orleans Cotton Exchange as well as protectionist sugar planters approved of rather active United States involvement abroad, harbored relatively conservative, cautious views of human nature, and desired conservative, domestic economic programs. Correlation in the late 1930's between approval of the reciprocal trade agreements program and support of New Deal measures was virtually nil; in fact, less educated and more economically deprived Southerners were the more favorable to domestic welfare measures, the more ignorant about international trade, and the more inclined to accept protectionist arguments. Southern newspapers which championed expanded trade—such as the Charleston *News and Courier*, the Jackson *Clarion-Ledger*, and the Natchez *Democrat*—included most of the more generally conservative in the region concerning domestic questions. Many economically conservative members of the elite thought of free trade as part of the general philosophy of rugged individualism and free enterprise without interference by the government. Trade seemed to be considered primarily a matter of business rather than of foreign policy. Traditionalists, including the Vanderbilt Agrarians or Fugitives, tended to view tariffs as Northern persecution of their region.

Traditional Protectionists

Nevertheless, there were some protectionists in the South even prior to World War I, and Southerners were as much or more inclined to demand protection as other Americans when their particular products were in danger of foreign competition at home. For instance, Southerners in 1944 were somewhat less inclined than Northerners to think that we should let foreign countries export farm products to this country which they could produce less expensively than we could and that our farmers should switch to other products which they could grow more cheaply than most foreign farmers.[19]

Sugar producers and grinders of southern Louisiana have been protectionists of long-standing because of their believed inability to compete with Cuban, Dominican, and other foreign sugars due to a less favorable climate, higher costs of labor, and other disadvantageous dif-

19 AIPO 309, 1/4/44 (3,028).

ferentials in this country.[20] Many were damaged severely by imports in the first decade of the twentieth century when wages for field hands went up to around a dollar a day. Planters and associated individuals frequently voted for Republican congressional and presidential candidates when the rest of the plantation South was solidly Democratic, largely because of the protectionism of the Republicans. Sugar men's anxieties were moderated by a quota system, but Congressmen from their districts frequently voted with Northern protectionists on trade legislation, apparently in return for the latter's support in limiting sugar imports.[21]

Coal-mining interests in the mountain South were often favorable to restraints on imports, and the tendency of these districts more than others in the South to elect Republican Congressmen frequently resulted in protectionist votes in Washington for their constituencies. Even during Grover Cleveland's second administration, Congressmen from coal and iron districts of Alabama helped to devitalize the Wilson tariff bill. And Congressman Tate of Georgia, in arguing for protection of his marble quarries, commented, "I'm a free-trader in general, but this is my marble." [22] Moreover, some of the relatively few Southern manufacturers have long pressed for restrictions on competing imports. As European cotton mills entered world trade even before World War I and Japanese textiles were able to enter this country in significant quantities, Southern mill owners expressed increasing doubts about the virtues of low tariffs and expanded imports.[23]

But these rather limited minorities did not alone account for the considerably more numerous minority of Southerners who favored more restrictions on imports and the like. Surveys indicated that most of this minority was composed of people of comparatively low education and humble social, economic, and occupational status; most Southerners who had not completed high school and were among the economically and culturally less privileged had little or no information and few opinions about these issues, but those who did express views were much more inclined to favor protection than were more educated and influential Southerners.

This combination of widespread apathy and ignorance about world

20 Shugg, *Origins of Class Struggle in Louisiana*, 14, 151–52, and 157.
21 Howard R. Smith and John Fraser Hart, "The American Tariff Map," *Geographical Review*, XLV (1955), 327–46.
22 Kendrick and Arnett, *The South Looks at Its Past*, 111.
23 Cash, *The Mind of the South*, 257; Dewey W. Grantham, Jr., *Hoke Smith and the Politics of the New South* (Baton Rouge: Louisiana State University Press, 1958), 248; Kendrick and Arnett, *The South Looks at Its Past*, 111–12; and Simkins, *Pitchfork Ben Tillman*, 387.

trade among the masses, articulate protectionism among a minority of the elite who feared foreign competition with their economic interests, at least latent protectionist leanings among a considerable fraction of the humbler classes which were more numerous in the South than in the North, and lack of intellectual identification of liberal trade with a generally dynamic foreign policy in noneconomic spheres even among Southerners of low-tariff inclinations—all help to explain the shift of a number of Southern Congressmen toward protectionism during the later 1950's. However, as late as the early 1950's, the great majority of Southern Congressmen apparently experienced little home pressure for protection, and they were usually able to find strong countervailing forces in their constituencies to neutralize those protectionists who attempted to change their votes on trade legislation.[24]

Recent Trends

Results of national surveys indicate that interest and information in world trade gradually increased during the postwar period, as they did in most fields of foreign relations; however, by the early 1960's only a relatively small minority of Americans had more than a vague knowledge of the issues of international commerce.[25] Attitudes toward tariffs, quotas, and other barriers oscillated during the 1950's; the proportion who had no views declined during brief periods of general public discussion of reciprocal trade, the proposed Trade Expansion Act, and other trade matters while the proportion who favored higher tariffs (or other restrictions) and that who preferred lower ones both increased. As one would surmise, the energizing of the less interested, less informed, and "don't knows," most of whom were the same individuals, usually resulted in greater increases in the fraction who wanted higher tariffs than in that who favored lower ones.

When the public was asked during the 1950's and early 1960's whether they "by and large" favored higher, lower, or about the same level of tariffs as was current at that time, the largest fraction favoring lower tariffs (50 percent) occurred in August, 1954, having risen to that level from the 25 to 31 percent approving during the period since World War II. However, by March, 1962, during the discussions over the proposed Trade Expansion Act, the figure had fallen to 29 percent, approximately the same level as during the late 1940's and early 1950's. Those Americans favoring higher tariffs rose from around 13 percent

24 From interviews with Congressmen, businessmen, and other influentials in 1953–54 for the study of attitudes toward international trade and tariffs by Ithiel de Sola Pool, Raymond A. Bauer, and Lewis A. Dexter. The author is grateful for permission to use this material and for insights provided by Lewis A. Dexter.
25 Bauer, Pool, and Dexter, *American Business and Public Policy*, 82–83.

in the early 1950's to 30 and 31 percent, respectively, in 1959 and 1961. In the height of the controversy over the trade expansion bill in 1962, however, only 14 percent favored higher tariffs.[26] In the late summer of 1960, 50 percent of American adults favored a "decrease" in the "amount of Japanese goods that come into this country"; 30 percent would hold Japanese imports to the then current level; and only 10 percent would permit any increase.[27]

Thus, there had been a decline since the summer of 1954 in the proportion of Americans favorable to freer trade while the fraction desiring higher tariffs in 1962 was about the same as in 1953. The minority favoring lower tariffs had not declined any further since the early 1950's, despite the facts that our barriers to imports were on the average considerably lower in 1962 than a decade earlier, and especially than during the 1930's, and that the previously war-wrecked economies of Western Europe and Japan had developed through the Marshall Plan, other economic and technical assistance, and their own efforts into major exporting areas by the early 1960's.

In general, these national trends were apparent in the South through the 1950's more or less as in other regions. There was some decline in Southern support for liberalized trade after the early 1950's, but this shift in opinion was not nearly as sharp as that in roll-call votes of Southern Congressmen during the same period.[28] In fact, as late as 1959 Southerners were still significantly more inclined to favor lower tariffs and less apt to approve of higher ones than were other regional groups.[29] In mid-1960 Southerners were slightly more inclined than

26 Replies to the question, "By and large, do you favor higher tariffs or lower tariffs than we have at present?" are given in percentages below:

	Higher	Lower	Same	No opinion
AIPO 516, 5/28/53 (1,549)	13	31	19	37
AIPO 520, 9/10/53 (1,535)	13	29	17	41
AIPO 526, 1/26/54 (1,493)	13	29	21	37
AIPO 535, 8/31/54 (1,581)	27	50	16	7
AIPO 614, 5/27/59 (1,537)	30	40	18	12
AIPO 653, 12/5/61 (2,990)	31	40	14	15
AIPO 656, 3/6/62 (3,486)	14	29	18	39

27 AIPO 632, 7/28/60 (3,150).
28 See p. 8; and "Voting Records of the House on Trade Legislation," 30–35.
29 When an AIPO survey queried, "By and large, do you favor higher tariffs or lower tariffs than we have at present?" 18 percent in the South in contrast to 41 percent in the Northeast, 28 percent in the Midwest (including the Plains States), and 26 percent in the West favored higher ones; 54 percent in the South as compared with 37, 37, and 37 percent, respectively, favored lower ones; 15, 13, 21, and 26 percent, respectively, preferred to keep tariffs about as they were at the time; and 16, 12, 11, and 15 percent, respectively, said they did not know, had no opinion, or were undecided. AIPO 614, 5/27/59 (1,537).

other regional inhabitants to approve of some increase in Japanese imports and less inclined to favor a decrease [30]—a rather remarkable finding since Japanese imports had for several years been a primary target of propaganda and political pressure by Southern textile manufacturers, the largest manufacturing interest in the region.

However, by 1961 Southerners had changed from the regional group most favorable to freer trade in the early 1950's to one somewhat less favorable than the non-South taken together—at least on the questions posed in 1961 and 1962. For instance, when the public was asked in March, 1962, whether or not it was "important for this country to increase the amount of goods we buy from and sell to other countries," 58 percent of the South replied that it was important as compared with 67 percent of the non-South; 19 percent of the former versus 17 percent of the latter said it was "not important," and 23 percent versus 15 percent, respectively, expressed no opinion.[31]

But this kind of abstract question usually results in an overestimate of the support for specific policy changes necessary to effectuate expanded trade and an underestimate of the potency of practical protectionist sentiments. On no survey during the late 1950's and early 1960's did a majority of Southerners, or even of Southerners who had opinions, favor lower tariffs or other reductions of trade barriers. The combination of those Southerners who would raise duties and other obstacles to trade and of those who would maintain them at the then current levels outnumbered those who would reduce such barriers. In late 1961, for instance, 34 percent of Southerners favored lower tariffs, 29 percent higher ones, and 11 percent the *status quo*, whereas 26 percent ventured no views; the respective Northern figures were 42 percent, 31 percent, 15 percent, and 12 percent.[32] In March, 1962, 32 percent of Northerners approved of the general idea of reducing tariffs in contrast to only 21 percent of Southerners (23 percent of white Southerners); 18 percent of Northerners as compared with 17 percent of Southerners (16 percent of white Southerners) would maintain them as they were; 14 percent of Northerners versus 15 percent of Southern-

30 AIPO 632, 7/28/60 (3,150) asked, "Would you like to see the United States increase or decrease the amount of Japanese goods that come into this country?" In reply, 12 percent in the South as compared with 8 percent in the Northeast, 10 percent in the Midwest (including the Plains States), and 7 percent in the West said they would like to see Japanese imports increased; 46 percent in the South as compared with 56, 51, and 50 percent, respectively, favored a decrease; 26, 24, 28, and 28 percent, respectively, wanted to maintain the level of Japanese imports at the then current level; and 16, 12, 11, and 15 percent, respectively, said they did not know, had no opinion, or were undecided.
31 AIPO 656, 3/6/62 (3,486).   32 AIPO 653, 12/5/61 (2,990).

ers (16 percent of white Southerners) would raise them; and 36 percent of Northerners compared with 48 percent of Southerners (45
percent of white Southerners) expressed no opinions.[33]

Moreover, judging from the interviews, many who said they wanted
obstacles to trade or imports to remain at their then current levels
either were little interested or informed in trade matters or actually
harbored protectionist sentiments. A number of them felt relatively
able to deal with the foreign imports at the levels of 1959–61 and
believed it was probably politically unrealistic to try to get the federal
authorities to reduce them. But they feared increased foreign competition in the future and sought protection therefrom. Furthermore, a
number of protectionists, besides those in the textile industry, commented that they favored expanded world trade, but without increased
imports in their particular field; some even said they approved of gradual reduction in some tariffs, provided that other nations reciprocated,
but that their own industry should have stricter quotas for its own
protection.[34]

Protectionist thinking seemed somewhat more closely linked with
opposition to international commitments in other fields in the late 1950's
and early 1960's than earlier. The number of Southerners who would
reduce significantly or terminate economic assistance to underdeveloped countries was considerably larger than that of protectionists who
advocated higher tariffs, stricter quotas, termination of reciprocal
trade,[35] and the like. Therefore, some who would significantly curtail
economic aid favored freer trade. This attitude was apparent in editorials urging cutting of aid in such free-trade papers as the New Orleans
Times Picayune, the Montgomery (Alabama) *Advertiser*, and the
(Little Rock) *Arkansas Democrat* in 1961, and in the rather conservative views on economic assistance of a majority of the predominantly
free-trade interviewees connected with cotton and tobacco raising,
exporting and importing, shipping, and other occupations benefiting
from world commerce. However, the vast majority of active protectionists favored reduction or even elimination of economic assistance
in 1959–62; they agreed with the Southern protectionists in the Congress who voted with few exceptions for sharp reduction if not virtual
elimination of economic aid.

33   AIPO 656, 3/6/62 (3,486).
34   For similar observations based on a national sample of manufacturers, bankers,
and other businessmen, see Bauer, Pool, and Dexter, *American Business and Public
Policy*, 202–10.
35   Prior to introduction of the proposed Trade Expansion Act into public discussion in 1961.

It is also true that most who would withdraw from the U.N. and NATO, that is, general isolationists, were also inclined to favor reduction of imports or, at least, curtailment of their further expansion. There was also a negative relationship between knowledge about international developments and protectionist leanings.[36] But most of the protectionists among the sample of, on the whole, better educated, more influential Southerners did not consider themselves isolationists and tended to regard that term as a negative one; few of them would withdraw from our European alliance, our strategic commitments in Latin America, or even the U.N., even though they often expressed criticisms of our particular policies toward these involvements. Moreover, a significant minority of the free traders in the black belt counties and in the Delta were very critical of our policies in the U.N. (some would have us withdraw therefrom), of foreign capital aid, and of our "unrealistic" policies toward Africa and the other unaligned, underdeveloped countries. Although protectionism had probably become somewhat more closely related to neo-isolationist, if not isolationist, thinking than previously, the relationship was still a relatively loose one, particularly if such factors as education and social status were held constant in comparing Southern protectionists with free traders in terms of their attitudes toward other aspects of foreign policy.

Southern Protectionists

The most important factors in the growing concern about imports among the Southern public and, especially, in the marked shift of the region's Congressmen toward restriction of imports have been the movement of economically vulnerable industries into the South during the last two decades, the growth of foreign competition for these and for others which were already located in the area, and the reduction in the proportion of Southerners employed in cotton production and other export-oriented enterprises.

With some exceptions, American manufacturers who have been successful in foreign commerce in recent years have been those employing complex technology, advanced scientific ideas, high rates of product and manufacturing innovation, skilled manpower, and relatively large amounts of capital per employee. Although a number of plants approaching this description have moved into the South in the postwar period, the South was the only major region in 1960 in which individu-

36 AIPO 614, 5/27/59 (1,537).

als producing nondurables outnumbered those manufacturing durable goods. Thus, a larger proportion of its industry than of that of the country as a whole was still composed in 1962 of enterprises whose capital was relatively small compared with its labor content, whose workers—given the comparatively depressed level of mass education in earlier decades—were necessarily little skilled and poorly paid, whose rates of scientific change were low, and whose sales were particularly vulnerable to cyclical shifts in both the domestic and the world economy.

A related factor in the South has been the relative lack of alternative employment for workers in many of these plants. The region has long been one of chronic underemployment; mill operators and other users of little-skilled female labor spoke in the early sixties of ten or more applications for each job opening. Much Southern manufacturing in the early 1960's took place in formerly rural areas and small towns where few alternative industrial or other jobs existed, and most of the remaining industry was on the outskirts of small cities where other employment was limited.

Many workers either came from agricultural backgrounds or followed their parents into older enterprises. In 1962 a considerable number still commuted from farms (see pp. 319–20). Farm women who had never before received such wages, albeit low by national standards, were determined to continue their jobs in textile and garment plants and others of a similar character. Their men often maintained the family farm, or rotated with the wife at the mill while farming part time. Such families were likely to be traditionalist and reluctant to move from their ancestral areas ("How would they move the cemetery?"). Even if they did move, their relatively low level of education and skill would not permit them to hold many alternative industrial jobs, and it would be rather difficult for them to be trained for more complicated tasks. If the local mill, garment factory, coal mine, or shrimp cannery closed or discharged them, there were usually few other enterprises nearby likely to hire them. Industries apt to migrate to such a community, given the limited talents of its manpower, were likely to be equally vulnerable to imports from cheap-labor areas like Hong Kong, Japan, and India. There was little to entice high wage, scientific industries; and, if they were to come, they would probably bring most of their highly trained labor with them. It is scant wonder that most of these relatively simple folk seemed in 1959–62 little impressed by proposed federal programs to retrain them or to move them elsewhere in case of damage to their livelihoods by imports.

Textile Leaders and Their Influence[37]

The most consistently protectionist press and legislators since 1955 have been located in settings where textiles have accounted for a large proportion of local jobs. Every member of the House from districts where textile mills were the largest employer voted against extension of the reciprocal Trade Agreements Act in 1958; all members of both Houses from South Carolina, the state where textiles employed the largest fraction of manufactured workers, voted against extension at that time.[38] By 1960 textiles were by far the largest manufacturing employers in the region, and this industry helped to account for over half of the Southern protectionists in the Congress in the late 1950's. It is not surprising that it constituted a rather extreme example of the factors normally associated with protectionism which were just mentioned.

Producers of cotton goods have found themselves increasingly

37 Interviews of textile and garment manufacturers and employees upon which this and the following section are based were held in 1959–61. This was prior to the considerable efforts of the Kennedy administration in late 1961 and 1962 to placate the textile industry by depreciation allowances; conclusion of a five-year, nineteen-nation agreement whereby European countries would permit entry of more Japanese textiles and the United States received the right to impose quotas to protect domestic producers; an increase in tariffs on carpets and further restriction of cotton imports from Hong Kong; and the promise of consideration of an 8.5 cent tariff per pound of cotton content on imported textiles to make up the difference between the world price of cotton and the domestic price to American manufacturers. These developments and, especially, the advent of a Southern President in late 1963 as well as the enactment into law of legislation in the spring of 1964 permitting cotton goods manufacturers to purchase cotton at approximately the world price at which it is sold abroad, probably dissipated significantly the bitterness against the federal executive which appeared in the interviews of textile executives.

38 Votes on the 1958 extension are from "Voting Records of the House on Trade Legislation." Employees by industry in Southern congressional districts were determined from reports on the 1960 census. See also Howard R. Smith and John Fraser Hart, "Georgia's Representatives and the Tariff," *Georgia Business*, XV (September, 1955).

The fact that a number of Congressmen (though far from all) from textile districts voted for the Trade Expansion Act of 1962 (New York *Times*, June 29, 1962, and Bauer, Pool, and Dexter, *American Business and Public Policy*, 360) may indicate the beginning of a gradual shift away from protectionism. However, this remains to be seen. The federal executive was apparently successful in "appeasing" or "buying off" many Southern manufacturers of cotton goods just prior to and during public debate on this legislation. Moreover, this legislation was so worded that it was not expected to result in much increase in textile imports. Furthermore, the proposed Trade Expansion Act was viewed both in and out of Congress primarily as a vehicle for closer economic relations with Western Europe—the area of the world which had long been the principal emphasis of articulate and influential Southerners (see pp. 127–33).

squeezed economically by the ever-growing competition from man-made, synthetic fibers for a relatively slowly expanding textile market at home. A number of Southern manufacturers have shifted to synthetics or to goods made partly of them and partly of cotton and have modernized their equipment to compete with the most advanced technology both in the United States and abroad. Such men among the twenty-eight textile-manufacturer interviewees seemed to feel more secure vis-à-vis both domestic and foreign competition than those operators who had not so transformed their plants. But most of the relatively cheap, low quality goods produced in America in the early 1960's were manufactured in the South, largely due to the unskilled nature of much of Southern labor and the relatively low capital investment in many Southern mills, particularly the rather small, still independent ones. Low-cost textiles and apparel have been the types of products in these industries most vulnerable to competition with the inexpensive Japanese, Hong Kong, and other Asian imports. Quality goods in which styling for the American market is important have, on the whole, held their own against foreign competition, but relatively few producers of these were apparently located in the South at the time of the author's study.

Textile mill owners and executives commented in 1959–61 that imports from Japan began in "large" volume around 1955,[39] after reductions in textile tariffs through GATT negotiations in that year. Japan agreed to voluntary quotas in 1957, but imports continued to increase thereafter from Europe as well as from Hong Kong, India, Korea, Pakistan, Formosa, and other low-wage, largely underdeveloped countries. The executives and owners noted that imports of apparel had further reduced the markets for textiles.[40] Although textile imports had secured only approximately 7 percent of the United States market by 1960, foreign textiles had acquired considerably larger percentages of certain fields within the industry—even relatively limited imports of inexpensive goods often had a serious effect on prices. Furthermore, our textile exports had decreased considerably during the same period.[41]

---

39 It was no coincidence that 1955 was also the year in which Congressmen from Southern textile districts first began to experience massive, stimulated letter-writing campaigns, in which mill workers were energized to write by the thousands, and other forceful pressures from mill owners and employees against extension of the reciprocal Trade Agreements Act. Many of these Southern legislators had never received much mail on any subject from home before. A number of them voted against extension for the first time that year (Bauer, Pool, and Dexter, *American Business and Public Policy*, 60–62, 65, and 361).

40 At the time of these interviews apparel imports were approximately 2 percent of domestic consumption.

41 As late as 1955, cotton textile exports of the United States were twelve times

Executives and owners pointed to the decreasing numbers of Americans employed in the industry, the static postwar prices of textiles, and the stagnation in the industry's rate of growth. They observed that, although the industry contained a few chains of considerable size, more than most manufacturing it still was comprised of a rather large number of small chains or even individual operators with relatively slender capital, sharply competing with one another for dwindling markets and lacking the resources of larger enterprises which could open plants abroad to limit the impact of these factors.

Textile producers were concerned about the current level of imports, but they seemed especially to fear continued increases which might drive them out of business. Furthermore, earlier imports had been of poorer quality than domestic goods, but gradually improved standards of foreign manufacturers by 1960 had resulted in competition in more discriminating markets. Producers commented that it was virtually impossible, regardless of the efficiency of American mills, to compete with capable Asian mills which could buy cotton 8.5 cents per pound cheaper than could American plants and hire labor at a small fraction of the wages prevalent here. In their house organs, speeches, local mass media, and conversations with the author, textile leaders cited examples of mills which had closed due to imports, although, in fact, a number of these closings may have resulted from poor management, failure to modernize equipment or to shift into synthetics and out of lines where demand had fallen, or a combination of factors of which imports were only one.

The more sophisticated mill leaders went on to say that they were not isolationists and that they realized that some imports were essential to our foreign policy objectives. However, as late as the summer of 1961 they complained that their particular industry seemed selected to bear more than its just share of the brunt of imports from abroad and had apparently been regarded as expendable by the Eisenhower and, later, the Kennedy administrations. They stated that textile delegations to the federal executive seldom appeared to receive a sympathetic hearing, and some added that this seeming disregard for the feelings and valid interests of Southerners on the part of the executive appeared to be evident in other spheres, such as the race issue. Some commented that they could compete with Japanese and other foreign manufacturers if they could purchase cotton at the world price, but they hesitated to suggest that the government subsidize the difference between the price paid the planter and the domestic sales price. Many

---

imports—6 percent and 0.5 percent, respectively, of our domestic production (Bauer, Pool, and Dexter, *American Business and Public Policy*, 61).

noted that the minimum wage law was a major source of their difficulties in competing internationally. Most also believed that quotas should be frozen, if not reduced, for each country exporting to the United States and that specific quotas should be imposed on each type of product. (They had little faith in so-called voluntary limitations by the Japanese and other foreign competitors.) Tariffs were mentioned only infrequently as a desired "solution" during the interviews in 1959–62, and most textile people were opposed to proposals that the government assist them to shift to other products and to retrain and relocate their employees for other kinds of work.

The preponderant majority of the twenty-eight textile men were also opposed to continuation of the reciprocal trade agreements program; they tended to complain that the program was no longer really reciprocal in 1959–61, in that our barriers to trade were already lower than those of most other countries and we gave important concessions for relatively minor ones in return. They were also critical of United States concessions in the GATT and cautious about our active participation in the Organization for Economic Cooperation and Development (OECD) and other international agencies whose objectives included multilateral economic bargaining and, particularly, negotiation of quotas and tariffs. They would prefer that these matters be left in the hands of the Congress as prior to 1934, because they felt Congressmen were more sensitive than the federal executive to their interests.

The sentiments of these men on international trade integrated with their typically general conservative outlook to influence their thinking on foreign aid. Most of them opposed economic aid—even as loans at low interest—or advocated its sharp reduction. They also tended to feel that whatever materials and equipment were involved should be purchased in this country. Thirteen of the twenty-eight opposed expanded technical assistance if it were to include advice to actual and would-be textile manufacturers abroad. They complained that foreign aid and technical assistance had encouraged the development of efficient, modern, highly competitive textile mills. Most commented that they had not opposed the Marshall Plan and economic and technical aid to Japan; one even had gone abroad on these programs as a textile expert. However, they felt that United States know-how and capital rebuilt these foreign industries with advanced American machinery which many United States manufacturers could not afford. One of the first industries which underdeveloped countries seemed to construct with our aid was textiles. Not only did the domestic industry lose its foreign markets to these people, but the American government had also refused to protect domestic producers from the flood of resultant cheap imports. The executives observed that these aid programs, if they continued, would generate still more competition from India, Pakistan, and other underdeveloped lands. With some exceptions, the textile manufacturers, and especially the smaller ones, tended to oppose foreign aid of most types other than foodstuffs, medicines, and other such charitable goods for depressed and unfortunate peoples. Most of these textile producers did not seem much more inclined to encourage private United States investments in these lands either. They tended to view movement of private capital to foreign countries as "exporting American jobs" and increasing foreign competition for their markets both at home and abroad.

The international thinking of the textile manufacturers was more heterogeneous on issues not connected so closely with their economic interests. However, most of them seemed to manifest relatively little interest in long-run national and international issues beyond those which impinged on their businesses. Few had much contact with foreigners or with internationally sophisticated members of esteemed large financial, manufacturing, and legal institutions outside the South. Only a few discussed world affairs with people who were really informed about such matters. The preponderant majority did not appear to feel that they should be expected to have responsible, realistic opinions about foreign affairs as leaders in their communities. Only a small minority would be considered reasonably informed about foreign policy—even regarding the basic realities of world trade which determine federal policies to which they objected—in comparison with the leaders of large national and international corporations. They tended to be even less knowledgeable about the complex strategic, economic, and political factors which underlie our trade policies and made little reference to such considerations in discussing imports. Most of these men were profound conservatives about virtually everything—fiscal policy, trade unions, welfare programs, social change, and human beings generally. Some were racists, but perhaps the majority were too busy with their businesses to be emotionally involved in race relations; however, a number of textile manufacturers in the South seemed willing in recent years to employ racial prejudices, or allow them to be used, to activate their workers against trade unions and to generate support for ultraconservative politicians who manipulated racism as a mass appeal.

U.S. News and World Report was a major source of ideas for most of these men, and several cited with approval other conservative (or reactionary) publications like *Human Events* and political figures like Senator Barry Goldwater. The failure of most of them to consider trade in relation to our international political objectives seemed in part due to their tendency to view our security in primarily military terms. Most were not nearly so concerned about "waste" in the military as in foreign aid programs. They tended to approve of military intervention abroad, particularly in Latin America, and even against the desires of our major allies. A continuing theme in their replies was the view that the rest of the world, including the neutralists, would respect us if we pursued our national interests with directness and integrity and "stood up" to our international enemies and critics. They felt that our government paid too much attention to irresponsible "so-called" world opinion in neutralist, anti-colonial, and leftist backward countries. A minority believed that our NATO allies would not really fight, but most regarded that alliance as important to the United States and thought we should support our European allies against "distorted" criticisms from these backward lands.

The exceptions to these observations seemed for the most part among the most sophisticated, best educated, and urban-raised textile executives and proprietors, frequently associated with the larger, more complex, and more research-oriented firms. For example, the late J. Spencer Love, chairman of Burlington Industries, though outspokenly critical of trade unions, was relatively well read and informed on world affairs and espoused many of the international views prevalent among responsible conservatives associated with the Committee for Economic Development, of which he was a trustee. His observations on race, domestic economics, and such fields of foreign affairs as economic aid, technical assistance, the Congo, Angola, and the U.N. were comparable to those expressed by responsibly conservative and liberal business and banking leaders of New York, Boston, or Philadelphia. Although he was cautious about textile imports, just prior to his death in early 1962, he expressed public approval of the proposed Trade Expansion Act as being "in the national interest." [42] His cosmopolitan background, however, was highly atypical of that of most Southern textile owners and executives, particularly in the smaller firms; he was descendant of a prominent Southern family, son of a Harvard professor, graduate of Harvard College, and so on. Moreover, his firm, different from most Southern textile operations, was the largest in the industry, permitting it to manufacture in several foreign countries, conduct extensive research,

42 *Trade Talk* (Washington, D.C.: Committee for a National Trade Policy), January 5, 1962.

manufacture in many diversified fields, and otherwise minimize the unfavorable impacts of both domestic and foreign competition.

Another thoughtful cosmopolitan of responsibly conservative views was a member of a Jewish family [43] which operated a smaller, but still considerable, group of mills. He too was relatively liberal on race issues, had attended a nationally esteemed college, and associated with other liberal, internationally-oriented Republicans in New York and other large Northeastern centers.

A few such cosmopolitans have been associated with small independent mills. But major aspects of their background seemed to have been atypical of leaders of most small textile firms. One owner of a mill with about two hundred employees favored expanded world trade and noted, "If I can't make a living producing textiles, then I'll do something else." However, he had been raised in Switzerland and rejected many prevailing local attitudes, including those about the Negro. Young, well-educated, members of second and later generations among mill owners are often, though far from always, less conservative and more internationally sophisticated. But, thoughtful, well-educated sons have tended to enter the professions—an ultraconservative local vice-president of a national textile chain commented that his son, student at one of the best Southern law schools, felt that he was a "reactionary." However, the author has known several members of the recently deceased or retired generation of mill owners whose sons and sons-in-law, running the family mills in the early sixties, were distinctly more opposed to foreign aid and generally more conservative about world affairs than they were.

Furthermore, most Southern textile owners and senior officials in the South have seemed to exert considerably more influence than the average Northern manufacturer on both their Congressmen and local public opinion. The atmosphere of the mill town has been one of paternalism patterned after the plantation. Since there had often been little or no town before the construction of the mill, the owner frequently built and owned the houses inhabited by his workers and the company commissary they patronized, ran the local public enterprises such as the fire and police departments, controlled the school and its teachers, organized local recreation, and strongly influenced the choice of ministers and others brought to town. In recent years a number of owners have sold houses to their workers and otherwise reduced their direct control of mill towns. But in 1960, a considerable proportion of mill communities still fitted the traditional description. Kannapolis, an unincorporated

43 See Chapter 13.

city of over 30,000 in the North Carolina piedmont, controlled by Cannon Mills, was the most populous and perhaps one of the purer examples.

Moreover, even when the mill operator has not been the proprietor of most of the town, his influence has often been formidable, particularly where there have been no other major sources of income. Mill owners have frequently controlled the local newspaper, radio station, and other mass media, or exerted considerable influence upon them. Although some editors privately expressed more internationalist views, most typically advanced arch-protectionist arguments, and usually anti-foreign aid ones as well, in mill-town papers. Furthermore, less than 10 percent of mill workers in 1961 were organized; agrarian individualism, unfamiliarity with voluntary organizations and group collaboration generally, low literacy, emotional dependence on employers, fear of management reprisals, and other factors prevalent in the South had seriously limited unionization.[44] Trade unions had succeeded primarily in a few of the larger cities and among some of the branches of the national chains where pressure could be exerted by the union through a Northern unit of the firm. Workers thus had not been exposed for the most part to this major alternative source of interpretations of public issues, including world affairs. Given the homogeneous, provincial, and rural background or several generations of mill experience of the majority of workers, their otherworldly, fundamentalist, and emotional religion, and their low exposure to outside influences, they have often known little of the world beyond mill and family. Generations in the hierarchical, paternalistic social system had prepared these unsophisticated products of poor farms or (to a lesser extent) plantation tenant plots for relative docility and acceptance of the thinking and personalized leadership of the owners.[45]

Thus, in the mill communities visited, those workers who had opinions on international trade usually expressed views rather similar to those of their bosses, typically with more glaring inaccuracies of fact.

44 For discussions of the difficulties of organizing Southern textile workers, see Solomon Barkin, "Organization of the Unorganized," in *Proceedings of the Ninth Annual Meeting of the Industrial Relations Research Association* (Madison: Industrial Relations Research Association, 1957), 232–37; Solomon Barkin, "The Personality Profile of Southern Textile Workers," *Labor Law Journal*, XI, No. 6 (June, 1960), 457–72; F. R. Marshall, "Impediments to Labor Organization in the South," *South Atlantic Quarterly*, LVII (1958), 409–18; and Marshall, "The Textile Workers and the South," *Carolina Israelite* (July–August, 1959), 6–13.

45 For pertinent mores and values of mill workers vis-à-vis their employers, see *ibid.*; Morland, *Millways of Kent*, especially 42–48; Vance, *All These People*, 286–87; Liston Pope, *Millhands and Preachers* (New Haven: Yale University Press, 1942), 68 ff; and Solomon Barkin, "Southern Views of Unions," *Labor Today* (Fall, 1962), 31–36.

However, their protectionism seemed on the whole less intense, perhaps since their economic interest was not so completely tied to the local mill as that of the owners, especially where some alternative jobs were available. Nevertheless, their opposition to imports was often generalized; for instance, one leader among mill workers in Kent noted that he and his friends refused to purchase foreign-made products of any kind—toys, clothing, or a second-hand Volkswagen car—even though these items were often less expensive than American-made counterparts and the resources of these families were meager.

Mill proprietors have been, on the whole, less successful in communicating their views on world issues not directly associated with local jobs, such as foreign aid to underdeveloped countries. Most mill workers seemed to have little interest in such matters. In the few mills where workers had been unionized, the unions appeared to have reduced or at least tempered opposition to economic assistance abroad. But textile union representatives themselves have sometimes been hesitant in recent years about foreign imports, if not actually opposed to them, and those who have been more liberal on trade reported intense pressure against their views from officers and members in their locals. In small communities which were unorganized and where there were few alternative sources of information, employees tended to feel that aid money should be spent in the United States. Former mill worker Senator Olin Johnston's opposition to foreign aid seemed fairly representative of the vague sentiments of most mill workers.

From the author's limited observations, primarily in New Southtown and Kent, most merchants, public utility officials, lawyers, and other influential people in communities where mills have been the major source of income likewise tended to voice, typically with less vehemence, emotional identification, and detail, the protectionist views of the mill leadership. Their organizations, like chambers of commerce and Rotary Clubs, had presented speakers who urged such opinions. Some of the better educated ministers spoke more moderately and criticized the extreme protectionism of the mill leadership in private conversations with interviewers from the outside, but they had been rather hesitant to express such thoughts publicly due to the contrary thinking of many of their influential church members and the local overall atmosphere.[46] Only a few socially secure, courageous, cosmopolitan local citizens, if any, had spoken out in recent years against

46 Expressions critical of protection were more frequent in larger, more economically heterogeneous New Southtown than in smaller, less diversified Kent. One of the few public critics of economic isolationism in Kent was the pastor of the local Roman Catholic mission, a New Yorker by birth with considerable graduate training in the social sciences and broad intellectual interests.

the prevailing protectionist ideology, and the number who had publicly expressed themselves in favor of foreign aid and other programs opposed by the textile leadership had been only somewhat larger.

The Apparel Industry

Clothing manufacturers and their workers in 1959–61 were not only much smaller in number and less influential on Southern Congressional votes regarding trade, but also, on the whole, less adamant in their protectionism than textile people. Some clothing plants were located in the same areas in the Piedmont as textile mills, and owners of these seemed more intensely protectionist than others, perhaps due in part to their social contacts and the general ideological climate about them as well as to economic interest.

Moreover, the backgrounds and experiences of many clothing manufacturers often differed significantly from those of most textile mill operators and managers. Whereas most of the latter came from Southern farms or small towns, many of the former had operated plants in the urban Northeast, and most had been born there or in Europe. The Northern apparel industry has been composed largely of foreign-born Jews and other immigrants. A considerable fraction of the earlier Southern apparel manufacturers, largely of urban background, have been Southern-born Jews, such as the Haspels in New Orleans. Perhaps as many as half of those who have moved from the North have been Jewish. The managers of Southern plants in national firms were often Southern at the time of our investigations, but the political influence of the company was exerted primarily by their national headquarters. The smaller, independent operators, however, usually had moved from the North in search of inexpensive, unorganized, and docile labor and low taxes, bringing with them at most one or two foremen or skilled workers. Many Southern communities, searching for jobs for people left unemployed by the mechanization of agriculture and the movement of cotton planting to the Southwest, offered long tax holidays and even raised bond issues to build plants for these manufacturers.

On the average, clothing producers seemed at least somewhat more sophisticated and less provincial in their views than typical textile producers of similar size. Furthermore, many clothing manufacturers did not feel in 1960 and 1961 the magnitude of competition from abroad of which most textile manufacturers complained. In 1961 imports were less than 2 percent of United States consumption. Imports of inexpensive suits and ties from Hong Kong, shirts from Japan, and other apparel from low-wage countries had increased over the previous decade, but in 1961 they still represented smaller fractions of the domestic markets than was true for most textiles. Several of the clothing manufacturers interviewed noted that they were not particularly concerned about the current level of imports, although they would become anxious about any major increases in their own lines. Others, in products where imports had been heavier, advanced protectionist views comparable to those prevalent in the textile industry.

Thus, more heterogeneous thinking on trade applied to clothing than to textile manufacturers, and a significantly larger proportion were relatively unworried about imports. Many Northern-born operators, especially Jews, had wider knowledge and understanding of world affairs than their Southern textile brethren, and on the whole their conservatism was more moderate and complex. Some were relatively thoughtful cosmopolitans, particularly in larger cities like New Orleans. Even when *émigré* Jewish manufacturers were opposed to expanded trade, they tended to favor foreign economic assistance to underdeveloped societies, an active policy in the U.N., and other international collaboration in nonmilitary as well as defense fields to a greater extent than textile producers. Moreover, their protectionism was often rather apologetic.

The differences between clothing and textile manufacturers should not be exaggerated. Domestic competition has been intense and the margin of profit small among this large number of predominantly small, independent manufacturers; added foreign competition has been feared by many. In 1959–61 they, like the small textile producers, carried on little research, and had little diversification, capital, or intention of investing abroad. Those apparel manufacturers who left the North for cheap labor, low taxes, right-to-work laws, and other Southern "advantages" were probably on the average among the less internationally oriented, liberal, educated, and intellectually inclined of Northerners in the business. They were perhaps also more apt to accept rugged free enterprise ideology. Even in the North, apparel manufacturers have tended to be among the less cultivated and intellectually sophisticated of manufacturers. Some who expressed nationally responsible, even liberal, international views to the author were apparently regarded by local cosmopolitans and trade unions as antilabor, anti-public welfare, and anti-expanded trade in practice, and seemed even willing to copy their Southern-born associates in using racism to defeat unions and manipulate their workers. Small Jewish operators often enjoyed social standing in Southern towns they never imagined on Seventh Avenue, and a large fraction of them seemed quick to adopt the local conservative attitudes, at least for public consumption.

In 1959–61 some clothing producers were as influential in their communities as were their textile counterparts, but this was not true of the group as a whole. Clothing plants were more apt to be located in or near cities than were textile mills and to be outside the Piedmont. Infrequently were they the only industry in town, and, as more recent arrivals, they less often controlled local housing, town services, mass media, and organizations. Although unionization, as in textile mills, has been confined primarily to larger firms with Northern units, International Ladies Garment Workers and, especially, Amalgamated Clothing Workers local representatives tended at the time of our visit to be more vigorously internationalist than seemed the case among textile union representatives, although there were major exceptions. Many, perhaps most, business agents and organizers of the garment and clothing unions were themselves ideologically identified with liberal trade, even though a majority of their local members, including elected officers, were often protectionists. The public positions of their national headquarters, with some wavering in the early 1960's, had been favorable to expanded trade. Too few rank-and-file clothing workers were interviewed for this study to permit definitive conclusions about their international attitudes. However, approximately a dozen discussions with such individuals and a like number with elected local union officers and local union professionals provided the firm impression that perhaps most union members and an even larger proportion of unorganized workers harbored protectionist sentiments, insofar as they had opinions on trade. The fractions with opinions who opposed foreign aid were probably smaller, but still large, although union publications favored international economic assistance. In general, the less intensely economically isolationist plant owners and managers and the greater independence of apparel workers had apparently resulted in at least somewhat less adamant hostility to trade and aid than among textile workers.

Sugar

Southern Louisiana still accounted in 1961 for approximately three fourths of the cane sugar produced in the continental United States. Articulate sugar producers continued not only to demand relatively tight quotas on foreign imports and a price of 2 cents per pound above the international market in 1961, but also to press for still further restrictions on imports to permit them to expand production. Most of the fifteen interviewees, ten of them in Bayou Parish, felt that American producers should be permitted to supply the American market and that they and domestic beet producers were capable of doing so.

As has been the case with much of Southern agriculture, sugar plantations by 1960 had been combined into the hands of a relatively few producers, since the smaller independent farmers had largely sold out. Large holdings were often run by local managers for landlords living in New Orleans or elsewhere. Some were part of sizeable corporations. Other holdings, often of several thousand acres, were operated by the owners themselves. The vast majority of these fifteen producers and managers, and of other interviewees who had considerable capital invested in sugar production, appeared sympathetic to protectionist ideology, although a minority of them supported the idea of tariff reduction and quota liberalization in manufactured goods. Those sugar interests who seemed willing to envisage increased imports from the Caribbean were either involved in refineries which processed raw sugar from abroad or had other major sources of income which would remain unaffected.

Thus, even discovery of oil on their properties had unpredictable effects on their international thinking. In more cases than not, oil income tended to enhance their protectionist leanings, although restriction of petroleum imports was usually not as prominent in their thinking as sugar quotas. But in a minority of instances wealth from oil royalties and rentals seemed to reduce their concern about sugar markets (and hence imports); two of the fifteen indicated that they raised sugar largely due to family tradition and their attachment to that way of life. One of these noted that he would quit raising sugar if it were no longer profitable and turn to cattle raising as a combination hobby and source of income. The other smilingly observed that he would spend more time with the duck blind, the bird dogs, and the fishing boat. Although neither could be termed a free trader, they did not seem particularly concerned about sugar quotas.

Relatively few planters actually living on their lands seemed well informed or especially interested in the broad issues of foreign policy, other than those close to home such as sugar imports and developments in Cuba. Judging from the small sample, it appeared that most involved in sugar production probably felt we should have sent the Marines into Cuba or taken other forceful action as soon as Castro began seizing United States private and public property without compensation. Over half of the fifteen interviewed opposed the "tractors for freedom" proposal then in the headlines (summer of 1961). Many influential landowners had friends and relatives economically interested in Cuban sugar; several mills had employed skilled people who were formerly with Cuban sugar enterprises. Sugar men tended to identify with their counterparts who had been expropriated and otherwise persecuted in Cuba.

The conservatism of these sugar men was typically profound. Several of the better informed and more thoughtful read the *National Review*, the international content of which described fairly well their views on foreign aid, military intervention in the Western Hemisphere, and other world issues. *U.S. News and World Report* seemed the typical fare of the majority of them and David Lawrence was one of their more popular columnists. Most appeared to regard Senator Allen J. Ellender as a good representative of their views on foreign policy and other matters. However, none gave as a reason for their opposition to economic assistance to underdeveloped countries any fear of encouraging competitive sugar production, as was the case with many textile manufacturers. The majority supported technical assistance and were not antagonistic to "businesslike" loans through the International Bank, private banks, or even the federal government.

The handful of individuals among sugar interests whose views on international matters would correspond more or less with those of liberal Republicans in the Northeast or of the Kennedy administration were primarily descendants of prosperous planters and did not actually manage the production of sugar—although part of their income may still have come from that source and perhaps from oil under the cane fields as well.

Most field hands and other low-skilled labor, living and working on plantations and in mills, have been poorly educated Negroes. Only a small fraction of them have voted and most seemed to have only vague opinions on international relations other than the general prospects of war or peace. Catholic whites of primarily French-Canadian ancestry tended to hold the more technical jobs and to occupy the more desirable and skilled positions in the sugar mills. Some enterprising Negroes occupied the more highly skilled positions in the mills, although they did not supervise whites. Efforts to unionize the field workers had failed, but several of the larger mills and refineries had been organized. Union leaders tended to favor international collaboration and to be relatively liberal by local standards on world affairs, domestic economics, and even race relations.

Most of the rank-and-file whites seemed to devote little attention to foreign affairs and to hold few opinions on the subject; they appeared to feel little opposition to expanded world trade, provided that sugar was protected. In contrast to the textile areas, few comments were expressed against local purchases of foreign products other than sugar, and among a few landowners, oil. Although protectionism had not been expanded to apply to foreign goods in general, most of the rank and file engaged in sugar production seemed to agree with Senator Ellender on foreign aid: that it was probably not worth the money, that it was unlikely to accomplish much in the way of "making friends," and that these resources could be better used in this country. The author's conversations in Bayou Parish antedated Senator Ellender's reported statement while in Africa in late 1962 to the effect that he had seen virtually no African leaders and peoples capable of governing themselves effectively; but the discussions in the sugar country indicated that he probably reflected the views on Africa of most of the white people who had opinions on these issues. Although relatively little of the active internationalism in the national trade union resolutions and in their publications seemed to have reached the members in Bayou Parish's organized mills and refineries, some did seem to have come to the attention of at least a more alert minority, albeit in rather diluted and sometimes distorted form.

Oil and Gas

Discovery of oil and gas and development of the petroleum industry in Texas, Louisiana, Mississippi, and small parts of several other states have also contributed to protectionist sentiments. Some landowners had heard that foreign oil imports had prevented the oil companies who were leasing their properties from drilling and from paying royalties as well as rents for leases. Others who had few wells thought the oil company might drill more if it were not for imports, or that they would extract more oil from their wells. However, many property owners receiving oil income did not seem much affected by these ideas, and some hardly thought of them. A number apparently preferred relatively slow extraction of oil to minimize income taxes and to spread their income over several generations.

The oil industry itself in the South has been a mixed picture. Much of the drilling, refining, and manufacturing of petrochemicals in the region was performed in 1962 by large international oil companies, like Standard Oil of New Jersey, Standard Oil of California, Socony Mobile, and Texaco. The leadership of these companies has for the most part favored economic internationalism, including relatively liberal trade. The author's five interviews with local managers associated with these corporations and impressions of local observers indicated that few managerial and technical personnel of these corporations were either publicly or privately protectionist; however, almost none seemed to make much of an effort locally to generate public support for expanded trade, including liberalized imports.[47] Support of freer trade did not necessarily imply approval of other relatively internationalist or multilateralist foreign policies, as among liberal traders generally, but the tendency indicated by these limited sources is that most managerial and technical personnel with international oil enterprises at least went along with the generally responsible international conservatism of the editorials of the *Wall Street Journal* and some with even less conservative international policies.

Eleven interviews of relatively small, independent drillers and observations by local informants lead to the impression that they, on the other hand, were typically protectionists—favoring much curtailed crude oil import quotas—and strong conservatives and arch-free enterprisers as well. The self-made wildcatters and independent producers tended to be of less cultivated tastes and general backgrounds than their more restrained and better-read colleagues with the larger international companies. Like a considerable proportion of Southern textile manufacturers, many independents came from rather limited rural origins, underwent fundamentalist religious upbringing, and either did not go to college or emphasized technical training—all factors negatively correlated with thoughtful attention to world affairs and nationally responsible thinking on foreign policy (see p. 305).

These elements in Shreveport were probably reasonably representative of like groups in Dallas, Tulsa, Houston, and elsewhere. Although there were certainly exceptions who favored most of the basic policies of the Eisenhower and Kennedy administrations abroad, including expanded economic aid to underdeveloped countries and even to Yugoslavia, the author's limited evidence tended to indicate that oil independents were not only protectionists but also by and large opponents of foreign economic assistance to such countries. A number were critical of our behavior in the U.N., particularly with respect to colonial issues; and a significant minority were clearly neo-isolationists of "Fortress America" inclinations. Those who would agree with most of the general thinking of educated Northeastern liberal Republicans like Christian Herter and John McCloy, or with their Democratic counterparts, seemed for the most part of the second or later generation of

47 One mentioned that his international company purchased crude oil from a protectionist independent and implied that silence on the trade issue by his organization was desirable to minimize friction.

prosperity and of broader, more liberal college backgrounds, as was the case among textile producers and to a considerable extent among Southern businessmen in general (see p. 308).

The influence of these independent oil and gas producers in their communities depended on their relative economic importance and the existence of countervailing forces, such as more sophisticated manufacturers and professional classes, cosmopolitan minorities from older, more socially secure, and more generally cultivated groups, one or more colleges with intellectually vigorous faculties, and a cosmopolitan press. Shreveport seemed to be a community where such moderating influences were relatively few and weak (though not entirely absent), and much of the international thinking of the independents appeared to have widespread following among lawyers, real estate agents, businessmen, and others in the professional, managerial, and propertied classes. The tone among much of the influential strata in Shreveport was described with apparent accuracy by a cosmopolitan member of a local prosperous family when he noted that officers at the local air base were by and large more "liberal" on world affairs, including trade and aid, than most of the local middle and upper class who ventured views on these matters. Opposition to oil imports tended to be less intense and based on less information than among producers whose incomes were directly tied to oil and gas, but the general direction of attitudes on world affairs of most associates of the independents seemed similar.

Greater diversity of opinion on trade and other international questions has been apparent in more heterogeneous cities like Dallas where a stimulating, internationally oriented university faculty has provided a place for thoughtful analysis of public affairs, where a considerable fraction of the educated classes have moved in from urban environments throughout the country, and where some leaders of large retail establishments, manufacturers interested in foreign sales, and other cosmopolitans have expressed their views. However, Dallas oil independents have to a considerable extent tended to agree with ultraconservative, neo-isolationist thinking on world affairs, including trade and foreign aid, and to exert significant influence on local thought. Dallas, like Shreveport and some other Southern centers of oil and gas independents, has experienced rapid economic growth; few of the genteel traditions of moderation and cultivation of parts of the Old South; an economic leadership including a large proportion of men with rural and small-town backgrounds who had had economically and culturally deprived, religiously fundamentalist childhoods; and a working and lower-middle class of similar origins—a combination likely to result in

ultraconservatism and one form of unilateralism or neo-isolationism or
another (see pp. 136–40). Moreover, many of the former Northerners
attracted to such locales were probably of comparable latent if not overt
orientation before they came, and they seemed to take on the coloration of the oil and gas leaders rather quickly.

Seafoods

In recent years the shrimp and fish packing industry along the Gulf
Coast has become more concerned about competing imports, particularly from Japan. In Bayou Parish where shrimping and fishing were
major industries in 1961, the fears of the men in these enterprises supplemented those of sugar planters and holders of oil leases. The combination tended to produce strong protectionist feelings; sometimes all
three economic interests impinged on the same family. Most influential
individuals were affected in Bayou Parish—indirectly at least—by one
or more of these enterprises. Shrimp processors on the Mississippi Gulf
Coast have combined with tung oil producers, hardboard manufacturers, and other protectionist interests in Representative W. M. Colmer's district to support his protectionist behavior in the Congress,
even though his constituency has also included shipyards, a port, and
other economic enterprises dependent on world trade.

Coal

Mining interests in Mountain County in 1961 were perhaps more
adamantly protectionist than coal interests generally: the local unemployment and underemployment levels were especially high and the
competitive position of mining was particularly weak due to the
smallness of the mines, the mediocre quality of the coal, the antiquated
and otherwise substandard equipment, and the marginal state of mining
operations in general. Moreover, alternative sources of potential income
were minimal. It is understandable that their Congressman had voted
consistently protectionist on every important trade bill since 1955 and
that most of the interviewees in Mountain County expressing opinions
were of similar persuasion.

However, interviews with several union representatives, mine operators, and more articulate miners in a nearby area of more competitive, larger scale mining lead to the impression that their counterparts
throughout the coal sections of the Appalachians were often among
the more uncompromising opponents in the region of expanded trade
in the early 1960's. Their principal fear was of importation of more
foreign residual oil as an alternative fuel and, to a lesser extent, of foreign coal, but influential mining employers and union leaders seemed

willing to "cooperate" with other industries desiring protection in return for their support in limiting fuel imports. Their Congressmen for the most part—like Cleveland Bailey of West Virginia, William C. Wampler of Virginia, and Eugene Siler of Kentucky—had voted almost consistently with the protectionists.

Other Protectionists

Sawmills have been an important source of income in the hills for several generations. The typical sawmill had been a small operation surrounded by a temporary lumber camp for its largely unskilled workers from unsuccessful hill farms and poor plantation tenant plots; the sawmill moved on after cutting the timber nearby. Some of these small mills were still in operation in 1959–62. But much of Southern timberland had come under the control of corporations of considerable size, some of which complained of imports of lumber, woodpulp, or paper from Canada, Central America, and elsewhere. According to the observations of informants in their locales and their own public utterances, plywood and hardboard manufacturers seemed particularly anxious about supposedly competing Japanese and other low-cost products.

The large-scale production of organic chemicals is relatively new to the South, but it has increased in importance and has become the main source of income in some communities. Its leaders have been among the more protectionist within the chemical industry, and some of their local personnel have let it be known through their own efforts and those of local mass media that their headquarters supported a strengthened Tariff Commission, increased congressional control of trade policy, the end of most-favored-nation agreements, and restrictive quotas. Some of the shoe industry in the South has likewise indicated serious reservations about expanded imports. To these were added the anti-liberal trade influences of miscellaneous industries based on relatively low-skilled labor and limited capital, such as some furniture manufacturers and even handicrafts in the mountains. Although workers and operators of these enterprises were not usually influential enough alone to determine the votes on trade of their senators, or even of their representatives in the House, they often combined with other protectionist interests to exert considerable pressure, especially where few articulate freer-trade groups were in evidence.

Southerners Favoring Expanded Trade

From a systematic analysis of the Southern economy, one would probably conclude that gradual lowering of restrictions to world trade would benefit more Southerners than it would harm, both in the short and, especially, in the long run. The degree to which the South would benefit from expanded trade would, of course, depend upon the particular fields in which exports on the one hand and imports on the other increased.

However, Southern protectionists in 1959–62 were more inclined than liberal traders to hold their views intensely, to articulate their protectionist ideology both to their Congressmen and to the public, to spend time, energy, and money to convert their fellows to their way of thinking on trade, and to organize with like-minded groups both locally and nationally to translate their opposition to imports into action. Their interest in limiting foreign competition in the home market was much more direct than that of the Southern consumer whose purchases included perhaps only one of the articles concerned, or even of the producer who exported a fraction of his goods and whose concern with imports was confined primarily to their indirect effects in permitting foreigners to purchase his products. Moreover, even the Southerner who exports might wish to avoid irritating protectionist associates and, especially, protectionist domestic customers for his products.[48]

Thus, the volume and vehemence of protectionist propaganda circulating in many areas of the South in recent years have often been far out of proportion to the size of the local minorities who were damaged by imports, while freer traders have often been almost silent in constituencies where the benefits from expanded commerce greatly outweighed the risks for the local economy. A reader of editorials within the sample of fifty-three newspapers in 1961 would have been apt to overestimate the proportion of the Southern economy likely to be damaged by and to underestimate that likely to profit from liberalized trade. It is difficult to assess the impact of these communications and other efforts of protectionist interests on the thinking of Southerners with no direct interest in protection; but the gradually changing posture of Southern opinion compared with that of the rest of America toward world trade noted previously indicated that protectionist thought had extended considerably beyond owners and employees in vulnerable enterprises and the local professional, commercial, and service personnel intimately dependent on them for their own incomes.

Conversations with Southerners indicated that adherence to protectionist ideology has been proportional to degree of direct economic

48 For comparable observations on a national sample of businessmen, see Bauer, Pool, and Dexter, *American Business and Public Policy*, 202–15; and 279.

interest in supposedly vulnerable enterprises. However, most Southern consumers have little inkling of the amount of duty on the products they buy or of the degree to which duties may be responsible for the prices they pay for domestically manufactured articles; neither their schools, their mass media, nor their political leaders seemed to have explained even the most basic facts of international trade to them. Even Southerners who produced goods which were exported frequently hardly realized their products were sold abroad and depended on foreign sales here to maintain their markets. Others who knew that some of their produce went overseas underestimated the proportion which did; they sold to a middleman who might have sold part of it to an exporter in a distant port or to a manufacturer who processed it or combined it with other goods, sold it to still another middleman, and so on. The propaganda of the protectionists, direct contact with protectionists, and other communications favorable to import restrictions had often influenced these Southerners.

Thus, a cotton farmer's wife and daughter in Kent County commuted to work at a textile mill in New Southtown, and the farmer gradually adopted the protectionist views which they brought home. A tobacco trader's brother-in-law in the Carolinas who was an assistant manager of a synthetic organic chemical plant had a similar effect on the tobacco man. A prosperous raiser and processor of poultry in Hill County shipped much of his produce to New Orleans wholesalers who sent some of it (the producer hesitated to guess how much) to Germany. But, because he had friends in a nearby wood products factory and he himself received some income from timber on his land holdings, he expressed some protectionist sentiments. In the Delta a large planter whose attitudes had some protectionist overtones noted that he had been told by domestic textile manufacturers that over half his cotton was purchased by them. He had received literature from textile producers to this effect, had heard them at meetings within organizations in which he was active, and knew some of them as hunting and fishing companions, but none of these men really understood much about world commerce or seemed to perceive the inconsistency of wanting to export while simultaneously accepting protectionist arguments from domestic industries. Many others had also apparently modified and attenuated their former trade liberalism with reservations, exceptions, second thoughts, and the like. If their parents were relatively well educated, they had probably been free traders.

Nevertheless, major economic groups in the South still favored expanded trade over restrictions to international commerce in 1959–62.

Agriculture

It was observed previously that some farmers—sugar producers, tung oil growers, some timber raisers, and mountaineers who farmed and supplemented their incomes from coal mines—were opposed at the time of the conversations for this study to trade expansion unless it excluded their products. These were, however, a minority of Southern farmers.

A study in 1956 comprising extensive interviews in several Georgia counties determined that a large majority of successful farmers there —mostly cotton and poultry farmers—favored lower trade barriers, while most local manufacturers, especially textile producers, were of the opposite view.[49] Combined replies to surveys in 1959–62 indicated that Southern farm people were less inclined than Southern factory and related workers to venture any opinions on international trade issues, but that the ratio of Southern farmers approving of lower tariffs to those favoring higher ones was larger than among the factory group.[50]

Nevertheless, protectionist influences from without, such as the examples cited, had taken the former zeal out of even many cotton growers' traditional opposition to trade restrictions. Simultaneously, cotton raising, like other agricultural interests, composed a sharply decreased proportion of the Southern economy; those interested in this commodity in the early 1960's constituted only a fraction of their former number. In some areas, such as Plantation County, cotton had been largely replaced by timber or livestock raising, dairying, and other enterprises unconnected with exporting. Even in the few locales which still produced much cotton, such as Delta County, fewer people were involved than previously in cotton because of growing mechanization. The expansion of protectionist enterprises had reduced to some extent, and frequently to a large extent, the relative influence of cotton producers on both Southern Congressmen and public opinion. As each former cotton farmer moved to the textile plant or other protectionist industry, it was usually not long before he abandoned the tradition of freer trade in favor of the opposite position.

Federal subsidies resulting in higher cotton prices for the farmer than those offered by the international market and federal participation

49 From mimeographed reports of the League of Women Voters of Georgia which made this survey, provided by Mrs. Charles Benson of Athens, then President of the League of Women Voters of Georgia and Chairman of its International Relations Committee.

50 AIPO 614, 5/27/59 (1,537); AIPO 653, 12/5/61 (2,990); and AIPO 656, 3/6/62 (3,486).

in the determination of acreage have further weakened the producers' concern for expanded world trade. Formerly the planter, ginner, and middle man in cotton, without any price protection, were more directly dependent on world markets. A reduction of sales by British mills to Indians, for instance, curtailed the demand for Southern cotton, entailing a drop in international cotton prices. Southern cotton interests were, therefore, relatively sensitive to international developments— cotton linked them intimately to the world economy.

But by the 1960's cotton producers had become a protected economic group with considerable interest in minimizing some imports. Planters among the interviewees sometimes mentioned with irritation the small quota of specialized cotton entering this country from abroad. Moreover, although some 45 percent of United States cotton was exported in the early sixties, the federal government protected American producers from foreign competition in this country through tight quotas coupled with a subsidy of 8.5 cents per pound above the international price and made possible foreign exports through a like subsidy whereby the government defrayed the difference in prices paid the domestic producer and those at which the cotton was actually sold to foreign textile mills.

Articulate, well-informed, and influential men among the twenty-seven cotton producers and factors in the Delta and elsewhere complained that they believed in free trade as a general principle but that "socialistic" federal legislation which had artificially raised wages and other costs above those of their foreign competitors made it very difficult for them to compete. They observed that United States foreign aid and technical assistance programs were continuing to stimulate development of further efficient production abroad so that even large mechanized cotton planters in this country experienced difficulties in competing. Hence, the federal government was paying a subsidy over the world price to domestic producers in order to keep our exports at the same level as some years past.

These cotton producers and agents objected to limiting our acreage, and they felt that our voluntary limitation (in effect) of our exports was regarded cynically by foreign producers and their governments. As the federal government forced our producers to reduce their production, foreigners expanded theirs and won most of the expanding markets. The producers tended to feel that the more efficient American planters could increase considerably their share of the world market if federal restrictions were reduced or, preferably, removed entirely and the economic laws of supply and demand were allowed to operate more freely. Vexed by these impressions, influential cotton men maintained that they were favorable to Cordell Hull's reciprocal trade program in former decades but that lack of experience on the part of our negotiators, unrealistic international political considerations, or internationalist altruism among Washington "idealists" had resulted, in recent years, in major concessions by the United States in return for relatively minor ones.

Nonetheless, the presence of considerable cotton production in a congressional district usually moderated the protectionist influence of local industries which feared imports. Where there have been no major protectionist industries or the factory work force has been a relatively minor segment of the population compared with the numbers in cotton production, the local Congressman has typically been relatively favorable to most liberal trade proposals before the House of Representatives. Overall there was still considerable sentiment in 1962—albeit reduced in the past decade or so—for expanded trade among literate cotton producers, merchants and professional people in towns servicing cotton areas, and Southerners of planter traditions who no longer raised that crop themselves. Thus, former Congressman Frank E. Smith of the Mississippi Delta was until his defeat in 1962 a strong free trader with little apparent criticism from his electorate. Representative Otto Passman of the Louisiana Delta voted with the trade liberals until 1962 when he opposed the proposed Trade Expansion Act. Likewise, Representative Frank W. Boykin of the Alabama Black Belt and Mobile voted consistently with the liberals on trade matters until the trade expansion bill which he opposed after his defeat for renomination in the statewide Democratic primary. On the other hand, Congressmen from cotton districts which also contained textile plants or other strongly protectionist interests have tended in recent years to vote against liberalized trade.

As in the case of other Southerners who tend to be liberals on trade, one cannot assume that cotton interests are liberal in other aspects of world affairs. Their economic ideology, judging from the small sample, is that of free enterprise, of which free trade forms a part. Over half of the twenty-seven cotton men interviewed would either eliminate or sharply reduce foreign economic assistance, except in the form of private investment and relatively "businesslike" loans to foreign entrepreneurs and, in limited cases, foreign governments as well. Those who had heard of the International Bank had a generally favorable image of its activities and its president at the time, Georgian Eugene Black, but they were by and large critical of "soft" loans at low rates of interest where the debtor "controls the printing presses for paper money." On the other hand, they reacted favorably to a strong and relatively expensive defense establishment. NATO and close collaboration with Britain and Western Europe in world affairs were regarded by virtually all twenty-seven as important to our international security and general interests. Only five, all arch-segregationists, would have us withdraw from the U.N. or curtail seriously our collaboration there, although more than half were critical of some of our policies within that organization, such as some of Adlai Stevenson's "anti-colonial" pronouncements and votes and our support of "leftish" delegates against Moise Tshombe in Katanga.

The author's impressions of the international behavior of tobacco interests have been based on the limited evidence provided by reading a number of their publications, interviewing eight producers and middle men, and talking with various other individuals in positions to observe tobacco people. From the imperfect data gathered, it appeared that smaller growers of tobacco have known relatively little of the problems of international trade, but whatever opinions they have voiced have tended to be rather liberal. The larger producers and manufacturers of cigarettes and pipe tobacco have generally been free traders and have been sensitive to suggestions that the Common Market or other areas to which they export may increase trade restrictions on their products or that the policies of our government may reduce the ability of foreigners to purchase here. They seemed to be more articulate supporters of freer trade than their counterparts in cotton production. More than cotton producers, tobacco people were still able to compete effectively in world markets at the time of the interviews—approximately one quarter of American tobacco was sold abroad in the early 1960's. Nor were the American customers of tobacco growers protectionists, as were those of most cotton growers. Where tobacco has remained a major source of income in districts including protectionist interests, leaders in the former industry seem to have provided a significant countervailing force to the latter's influence on their Congressman.

This limited evidence seemed to indicate that tobacco people also tended in the early 1960's to be less conservative regarding capital assistance to underdeveloped countries. Furthermore, most tobacco growing in 1959–62 took place outside the Deep South where the forces of insularity have been most intense, particularly since the 1954 Supreme Court decision on desegregation; most cotton production in the South, however, has remained in the Deep South. Attitudes about Africa and other international questions which have been associated with white-supremacist thinking (see pp. 397–404) should have been less prevalent among tobacco interests; this was apparently the case.

Capital-Intensive, Scientific Industries

Although none of the twenty-seven interviewees among local executives, managers, and technicians with plants in New Southtown, Antebellum Town, and elsewhere, which made considerable use of scientific research, had high rates of product and manufacturing innovation, and employed highly skilled labor, felt it was politically or economically realistic to reduce trade restrictions drastically over a short period, none would increase trade restrictions. They observed that their companies sold abroad, had subsidiaries there, or both.

Like many engineers and other technical and managerial men with industry, these individuals were often relatively conservative on domestic economics by national standards. But they were on the average considerably more sophisticated about world affairs and less provincial in their attitudes and were more inclined to agree on foreign policy with internationalist Republicans like Nelson Rockefeller or Christian Herter, or, in much fewer cases, internationalist Democrats like President Kennedy, than most other Southern manufacturing and commercial people interviewed, and, in particular, those small-scale entrepreneurs whose labor was little skilled and whose capital investment per worker was small. Most read international news in both a daily paper and a newsmagazine. Six of the twenty-seven regularly read international content in critical publications, such as the New York *Times* (Sunday edition), *Atlantic*, and, in one case, the British *Economist*. Only eight of the twenty-seven would have reduced considerably our foreign economic aid program. The complaint was rather widespread, however, that we should be more discriminating in the projects we aided and that we should reduce waste. None advised reduction in our intercultural activities, including exchanges with the Communists. Only one would appreciably reduce our technical assistance to and training of able foreigners here. Although most hoped Communist China would not be admitted to the U.N., only two would have us withdraw if she obtained membership.

Some of the sources of their international thinking (which was on the whole more alert than that of most Southern businessmen) were readily apparent. Of the twenty-seven, less than half were Southerners by birth and upbringing; three were foreign-born and half of the rest had served either abroad or in other regions of the United States before coming to these Southern plants. Almost two fifths had been to graduate school, and all except one had at least a bachelor's degree. Since all of their firms had branches outside the South and most had foreign subsidiaries as well, these men assumed that they would move elsewhere in the country and probably abroad, either with their present firms or others. In contrast, most of the textile, saw mill, and other executives of low-technology plants were born, raised, and educated in the South [51] and expected to remain there.

These highly trained men and their families also seemed as a group to have exerted subtle, if not direct, influence on local international thinking. They usually lived for several years among Southerners of similar income and status and, after a relatively brief period, have participated in PTA's, service organizations, country clubs, and other local activities with local individuals. Some of their ideas have been accepted by a number of the local middle class.

The advent of these complex industries also had some direct impact on working-class society in these communities. In New Southtown, for example, many of the most alert, educated, and dependable workers in the several textile mills had moved to semi-skilled jobs at higher pay and in more pleasant environments with the two newly built scientific industries, one a British firm and the other with important British connections. In both New Southtown and Antebellum Town strong trade unions either arrived with the new plants or followed shortly. Most union leaders in these plants in both communities were of internationalist persuasion, concerning trade, foreign aid, the U.N., intercultural exchange, collective security, and other international questions. Although most of their locals were probably more conservative than they about world affairs, these corporations with thousands of stockholders had helped to upset the whole paternalistic management-worker relationship in the local textile mills, introducing more rational, "un-Southern" relations between employer and employee and reducing the influence of protectionist and generally arch-conservative employers on their workers. Trade union agents and the managerial and technical personnel did manage to transmit some of their ideas about world affairs to these men and their families, and through them to the general community.

Nevertheless, one should be cautious in estimating the influence of these enterprises on local attitudes. The observations mentioned previously about the relative impacts of liberal traders and protectionists seemed highlighted among this group. Whereas their managerial and technical personnel were only temporary residents and therefore tended

51 Apparel plants excepted.

to have relatively limited rapport with the general community, the more internationally conservative and economically isolationist local textile and other small to medium sized labor-intensive manufacturers, retailers, bankers, and other businessmen have typically lived in these communities for many years, often most of their lives. The latter have known "everybody," worked within the power structure, and exerted intimate, often potent, influence on their Congressman and on local thinking about trade, aid, and other issues.

The local manager for a national corporation, on the other hand, has been a "hired man" whose bosses in New York, Boston, or Chicago do the thinking and make the decisions on international economic affairs. Sophistication in such fields and ability to communicate to Congressmen and the public about them have not normally been among the criteria whereby superintendents and technicians have been hired. Often they have not known if their headquarters had any position on trade questions. When they have understood the views of their superiors, they have not typically conceived it to be their job to transmit these ideas to the local community and few of them have been encouraged to do so. Furthermore, perhaps because large national corporations like International Paper, Standard Oil of New Jersey, and International Business Machines have felt "visible" politically and have wished to carry on their local operations with minimal friction and to develop smooth relations with the local community and politicians, both their central and local managements seemed cautious about public expressions of views different from local norms on subjects of little direct pertinence to their local operations. Even when foreign trade has been profitable or potentially so and when the national leadership has been active in the Committee for Economic Development, the Council on Foreign Relations, the International Chamber of Commerce, or other liberal trade and generally internationally sophisticated groups in New York, Southern subsidiaries seemed rather silent on the same questions, particularly where influential local groups had been identified with opposing views. Active support of expanded trade by such technologically sophisticated, export-oriented enterprises in constituencies where they provide well-paying jobs and contribute to the general well-being could probably countervail considerably the relative influence of articulate economic isolationists.

Furthermore, these industries, though increasing, were still relatively few and concentrated in a limited number of areas of the South in 1962. Many Congressional constituencies had none. These enterprises have required highly trained managements and technical personnel and skilled workers—all of which have been in short supply in much of the South. Educated personnel from "outside" have desired to be near other talented research installations and individuals, generally advanced cultural facilities, and good schools for their children. These men in New Southtown complained about the lack of such advantages in the community. Consequently, in 1962 such industries were disproportionately located in the Piedmont of North Carolina with its research triangle of Duke, North Carolina, and North Carolina State universities, paucity of plantation traditions, relative indifference to segregation, emphases on education, and longer experience with industrialization; in or near modern cities like Huntsville, Atlanta, Baton Rouge, New Orleans, and Orlando; and in the few other locales where these charactistics were most evident.

Moreover, reliable observers indicated that local conservative planters, tradespeople, and cheap-labor manufacturers have frequently been unenthusiastic, even opposed, to entry into their communities of such industries with their strong trade unions, high wages, extensive benefits, rather pleasant working conditions, and tendency to upset traditional Southern labor-management relations. Some industries of this type have experienced great difficulties in Deep Southern, tightly controlled towns in securing exemptions from local taxation, inexpensive land and facilities, and other advantages which smaller, more indigenous enterprises have received.

Ports

Protectionist interests have developed influence to some extent even in Southern ports. The dependence of Charleston on the economy of a hinterland whose principal income has been provided by textiles coupled with the relatively low activity of its port—except for the naval base—helps to account for much of the recent protectionism of its press and other mass media, of influential members of its elite, and of its Congressman. Antagonism toward the federal government for its desegregation policies together with a preoccupation with the traditions of the low country have further encouraged economic insularity (see pp. 34–36, 405). Congressmen from Mobile, Tampa, Biloxi, and Gulfport, all engaged to a significant extent in international trade, voted against the trade expansion bill of 1962, whereas they or their predecessors had supported the reciprocal Trade Agreements Act and liberal trade generally ten years before and more. In each of these constituencies important protectionist interests—tung oil, textile, and garment manufacturers, shrimp canners, hardboard and plywood producers, lumber and wood products processors, organic chemicals producers and others—have become increasingly important since World War II. They seemed to have exerted disproportionate influence on their Congressmen.

But Congressmen from Norfolk, Newport News, Portsmouth, Wilmington, Savannah, Jacksonville, Baton Rouge, and New Orleans have voted with only minor exceptions for more liberal trade and against more restrictive legislation in foreign trade, including the trade expansion bill of 1962. As shall be noted later (see pp. 462–63) in the case of New Orleans, individuals connected with ports or engaged in careers related to them have with few exceptions been favorable to freer trade.[52] Although their economic interest in international commerce has not made more than a limited minority of them particularly sensitive or thoughtful with respect to world affairs in general, including economic development in Asia, Africa, and Latin America, contacts through trade have tended to broaden the thinking of a considerable fraction of local citizens on other foreign issues as well. Although the author has no statistical evidence on the matter, there seems to be little doubt from limited interviews and other observations that the proportion of neo-isolationists in Southern ports has remained considerably smaller than the regional average and than in most inland cities which have enjoyed neither trade connections nor sophisticated industry to introduce a more international attitude into local thinking about foreign policy.

52 Interviews by the League of Women Voters in a number of locales in Georgia in 1956 determined that support for freer trade was more prevalent in Savannah than in the several inland communities surveyed. (From unpublished reports by the League of Women Voters of Georgia.)

CHAPTER 5

COLONIALISM, NEUTRALISM,
AND
FOREIGN AID

American foreign policy until quite recently was concerned primarily with relatively developed countries—Europe, the Soviet Union, and Japan. The less developed regions were either dependencies of Western Europe or controlled by conservative landed-classes. The United States dealt with these lands either through their European masters or small indigenous elite groups. But between 1947 and 1962 most of these dependencies became independent. The mass appeals of leftist, nationalistic ideologies had toppled many conservative regimes and were threatening others by 1962. These developments and their implications for United States policy have affected public attitudes about our role in world affairs throughout the country, but in no other region to the degree evident in the South.

Southerners Observe Decolonization

The South's Colonial Tradition

The South has historically had much in common with the underdeveloped colonial dependencies of Western Europe—it has been primarily agrarian, exchanging agricultural goods and extractive products for finished goods; its few industries have been owned or controlled to a considerable extent by residents of the economically developed North; wealth, influence, and education have been concentrated among a small number of inhabitants. As has been the case in recent years in much of the underdeveloped colonial world, articulate Southerners have long complained that their region had been treated like a colonial dependency and "conquered province" by the North, especially by the "imperialist" financial and industrial interests of the Northeast. The literature, the press, and the leaders of the South have attacked the "distant tyranny of money," the supposed manipulation of local subsidiaries by New York capital and management for the benefit of the North and to the detriment of the South, the enchaining of the region as a source of cheap raw materials for Northern "monopolies" through debts, differential freight and interest rates, protective tariffs, and other inequities.[1]

Results of several surveys of the late thirties and early forties indicated that these ideas were fairly widely accepted among the Southern masses.[2] But Southern suspicion of supposed attempts by Northern cul-

1 Benjamin B. Kendrick, "The Colonial Status of the South," *Journal of Southern History*, VIII (1942), 21–22; William H. Nicholls, *Southern Tradition and Regional Progress* (Chapel Hill: University of North Carolina Press, 1960), 31; Donald Davidson, *Still Rebels, Still Yankees* (Baton Rouge, Louisiana State University Press, 1957), 205; Woodward, *Origins of the New South*, 186 and Chapter 11; Savage, *Seeds of Time*, 232–34; Vance, *Human Geography of the South*, 278 and 467–76; Eaton, *The Growth of Southern Civilization*, Chapter 9; Odum, *Southern Regions of the United States*, 353; and Wilma Dykeman and James Stokely, *Seeds of Southern Change* (Chicago: University of Chicago Press, 1962), 203–204.

2 Thus, although Southerners have been more inclined than other regional groups to oppose "socialism" and federal intervention in their society (see pp. 370–71), they have been more suspicious of "big" business and finance, located primarily outside their own section of the country, and more willing to see "the interests" controlled by the federal authorities. For instance, in 1937 a national survey asked, "Which presents the greater danger to America: (1) too much power lodged in Washington officials, or (2) too much power lodged with business and industrial leaders?" In reply, 37 percent in the South, 60 percent in New England, 52 percent in the North Atlantic seaboard region, 51 percent in the Midwest, 44 percent in the Plains States, 42 percent in the Rocky Mountain region, and 47 percent in the Far West (after "no opinions" had been omitted) replied that too much power in Washington was the greater danger; 63, 40, 48, 49, 56, 58, and 53 percent, respectively, answered that too much power in the hands of business and industrial leaders was the greater menace. See AIPO 73, 3/10/37 (2,959).

In the summer of 1938 in replying to the query, "Do you think the federal government should buy, own, and operate the railroads?" 43 percent in the South in contrast to 29 percent in New England, 36 percent in the North Atlantic region, 26 percent in the Midwest, 26 percent in the Plains States, 32 percent in the Rocky Mountain region, and 31 percent in the Far West (when "no opinions" were omitted) replied in the affirmative. See AIPO 127, 7/2/38 (3,104).

When asked in October, 1940, "During the next four years, do you think there should be more regulation or less regulation of business by the federal government than at present?" 31 percent in the South as compared with 25 percent in New England, 31 percent in the North Atlantic region, 22 percent in the Midwest, 26 percent in the Plains States, 24 percent in the Rocky Mountain region, and 24 percent in the

tural and social "imperialism" to make the South over into the "Yankee" image has apparently been even more intense.[3] Pressures for desegregation have recently aggravated these Southern feelings of "colonial exploitation" and "oppression" (see pp. 393–96). Some conservatives comment to the effect that the doctrine of self-determination and independence, adopted by our government for backward foreign peoples, should also be applied to the South.

A Background of Colonialist Sympathies

Given the underdeveloped nature of the Southern economy and the sensitivities of Southerners to the "colonialism" of the North, one might have assumed that more widespread sympathy for and identification with anticolonial movements in agrarian Asia and Africa would have been present in the South than in the rest of the United States. Perhaps such would have been the case had it not been for the presence of the Negro and his complex influences on Southern thought. In fact, the reverse has been true among Southern whites. The white South, more than other parts of the country, has long supported the doctrine of the white man's burden—his responsibility to civilize and govern backward and "childish" colored races. Southerners backed the expansionism, or imperialism, of the McKinley regime and had for years prior to 1898 accepted the view that this was a white man's world and that he should govern the inferior races for their own good.[4]

National surveys from the mid-1930's until the initial prominence of African nationalist demands for independence in the mid-1950's indicate that white Southerners (and often all Southerners) continued to be at least somewhat more hesitant than other regional groups about decolonization and to side with the metropolitans against anticolonial leaders in their dependencies. For example, when a national survey asked in 1937 whether the Philippines should be granted independence in the

---

Far West (after "no opinions" were eliminated) favored more regulation; 31, 17, 19, 23, 32, 20, and 19 percent, respectively, favored the same amount of regulation; and 38, 58, 50, 55, 42, 56, and 57 percent respectively, less regulation. See AIPO 219, 10/24/40 (3,237).

In June, 1941, when asked, "Do you think that business should be regulated to a greater extent by the federal government?" 60 percent in the South versus 49 percent in New England, 50 percent in the North Atlantic region, 49 percent in the Midwest, 42 percent in the Plains States, and 52 percent in the West replied in the affirmative; "no opinions" were omitted. See AIPO 238, 5/29/41 (3,152).

3 Nicholls, *Southern Tradition and Regional Progress*, 143–44; and James McBride Dabbs, *The Southern Heritage* (New York: Alfred Knopf, 1959), 174.

4 Carter, *The Angry Scar*, 385, and Franklin, *The Militant South*, Chapter 6.

near future, only 39 percent of Southerners offering opinions replied in the affirmative, compared with 47 percent of Northeasterners, 47 percent of Midwesterners, 45 percent of residents in the Plains States, 45 percent of inhabitants of the Rocky Mountain region, and 46 percent of Far Westerners.[5] In mid-1944, 75 percent of Southerners versus 71 percent of Northeasterners, 64 percent of Midwesterners (residents of the Plains States included), and 72 percent of Westerners felt that the United States should keep all the conquered Japanese islands between Hawaii and the Philippines; 12 percent, 16 percent, 20 percent, and 19 percent, respectively, replied in the negative.[6] Shortly after V-J Day, 40 percent in the South in contrast to 57 percent in the Northeast, 54 percent in the Midwest (Plains States included), and 56 percent in the West would have turned Hong Kong over to Nationalist China, whereas 30 percent, 25 percent, 26 percent, and 26 percent, respectively, would have returned it to Britain.[7] At the same time, 24 percent of Southerners as opposed to 20 percent of Northeasterners, 22 percent of Midwesterners, and 19 percent of Westerners would have returned the former Italian colonies to Italy; 13 percent versus 20 percent, 16 percent, and 30 percent, respectively, would have granted them independence; and 9 percent versus 20 percent, 16 percent, and 15 percent, respectively, would have placed them under U.N. supervision.[8]

As tensions between West European colonial powers and indigenous nationalist movements grew after the war, white Southerners (and usually Southerners in general) continued to be significantly more inclined than their non-Southern counterparts to support the former rather than the latter. Thus, in early 1949, among those who had read or heard about the then current conflict between the Dutch and the Indonesians, 16 percent of Southern whites as compared with 10 percent of Northern whites said they sympathized with the Dutch, 31 percent of the former as compared with 46 percent of the latter sympathized with the Indonesians, and the rest either sided with neither or had no opinions.[9] During the late 1940's and early 1950's somewhat larger majorities of Southern whites than others thought that the British, and even the French, had treated the people in their dependencies fairly rather than unfairly.[10] In mid-1956, the fraction of Southern whites who supported the Algerian Moslems rather than the French

5 AIPO 97, 8/23/37 (2,955).   6 AIPO 317, 4/26/44 (2,996).
7 NORC 133, 8/31/45 (1,259).   8 *Ibid.*
9 NORC 163, 1/26/49 (1,261).
10 NORC 149, 4/3/47 (1,307); NORC 323, 4/22/52 (1,250); and NORC 337, 2/11/53 (1,291).

and the *colons* was significantly smaller than in the rest of the country. However, most Southern whites, like most Northerners, said that they did not favor either or that they were indifferent.[11] Later in the same year, 54 percent of the white North in contrast to 41 percent of the white South disapproved of British and French action against Egypt in the Suez. Seventeen percent of the latter as compared with 12 percent of the former approved.[12] Finally, when a sample was asked by a national survey in the fall of 1957 whether it would approve or disapprove of the U.N.'s conducting elections in any country where the leaders or the population expressed a desire for a plebiscite on independence, 52 percent of all Southerners, compared with 63 percent of Northeasterners, 61 percent of Midwesterners (including inhabitants of the Plains States), and 70 percent of Westerners, replied in the affirmative.[13]

Increasing Uneasiness about Independence Movements

These differences, although in the expected direction even when not statistically significant at the 10 percent level of confidence, were of limited magnitude. No comparable survey results for the period since 1957 are available, and, therefore, observations about Southern thinking on decolonization and related issues in the last few years are based on less systematic evidence, particularly on interviews between 1959 and 1962 and analysis of newspaper content in 1961. Unfortunately, no equivalent evidence on Northern thinking during this later period is available. The author feels reasonably secure that his impressions are valid, but more systematic study would be required before definite conclusions could be made.

Southerners with views on these matters seemed by the early 1960's to have become distinctly more cautious about the desirability of rapid independence for remaining colonial areas. They observed that most of the new countries and peoples demanding independence prior to about 1957 were more advanced economically, educationally, socially, and politically than most of the new black African states which would achieve their independence in the late 1950's and early 1960's. Moreover, these Asian and North African peoples of the earlier period were not Negroid. (It was noted previously that most Southern whites do not apply their negative assumptions and attitudes about Negroes to other non-Caucasians.) The Indians, Burmese, Egyptians, and others were not as vociferously critical of race relations in the South as these South-

11   NORC 390, 6/26/56 (1,275).   12   AIPO 574, 11/7/56 (1,505).
13   AIPO 589, 5/17/57 (1,530).

erners perceived the new black African leaders to be; nor were white Southerners as sensitive to criticism of their mores before 1957 as they would be under increasing pressure for desegregation in the later 1950's and 1960's (see pp. 393–96). Moreover, increasing frustration of a sizeable minority of Southerners with the apparent failures of some of our postwar policies and the supposedly expanding influence of the Communist bloc into Southeast Asia, Cuba, and other areas seemed to have resulted in a growing hostility to neutralism in the form evident in many newly independent countries.

With very few exceptions those among the interviewees who firmly supported the racial policies and actions of the government of the Union of South Africa, agreed with the public utterances of white leaders in the Rhodesias, and approved of the activities of the OAS in Algeria were racists.[14] But many attitudes present in exaggerated form among ultrasegregationists were found in a more moderate, attenuated form among white Southerners who preferred segregation and were sorry to see the relations between the races change, but who felt that gradual integration was likely and were willing to live with it however grudgingly. Only a minority even among the interviewees, who were chiefly better educated and economically prosperous Southerners, possessed much information about developments in the new states or the territories still under colonial control which were seeking independence in 1959–62. But many whites besides those who viewed Negroes as innately inferior were uncomfortable about independence for these supposedly unsophisticated societies and had reservations and anxieties about the advisability of United States support of their independence.

By the early 1960's most Southern whites with views on these issues seemed to hold the opinion that independence had been all but inevitable for the new countries and would probably come rather quickly for the remaining colonial dependencies. But many of them wondered if our government could not have assisted the metropolitans in delaying somewhat the apparently overly rapid and uncontrolled independence of these supposedly unprepared peoples and in gradually readying them for responsible government. Even some rather well-informed people—readers of such periodicals as the New York *Times* (Sunday edition) and *Harpers*—were of the opinion that neither the masses nor the leaders of most African countries were really capable of responsible self-government, and the comment to this effect by Senator Ellender

14 See pp. 402–403, for a detailed discussion of attitudes prevalent among white supremacists regarding the independence of African territories.

in late 1962 was viewed as probably correct by an even larger fraction of the less sophisticated upper and upper-middle class interviewees who were contacted afterwards. Rather well-informed Louisianians who were less conservative than most in the privileged classes informed the author that they were gratified that the Senator had had the courage to say what they and most of their associates felt to be true.

Many rather thoughtful and influential Southerners among the interviewees agreed with a number of their newspapers that we should not have been surprised by such events as disorder in the Congo and lesser excesses in other new states. They tended to feel that Northern liberals had been overly optimistic ("as they usually are") about the likelihood of establishment of orderly, stable regimes in these primitive lands. They expressed the opinion that the oratory of too many of our national leaders concerned with foreign affairs had been rosy and unrealistic, overselling anticolonialism—colonial regimes were not unmixed blessings, but they had done much for these lands, leading them from barbarism to their current state of limited stability, prosperity, and civilization.

Stories of revolt, rape, and murder of whites in Africa by blacks have complemented the traditional fears among many Southern whites in heavily Negro areas of similar behavior by local Negroes. They empathized with white victims in Africa as few Northerners would. Even rather well-read and relatively thoughtful whites in plantation settings expressed the concern that these excesses in Africa might provide frightful examples for unsophisticated Southern Negroes.

Readers in Delta and Plantation counties and in Kent of such responsible publications as the *Christian Science Monitor*, the New York *Times* (Sunday edition), and *Atlantic* commented that independence for most of these half-savage tribes or illiterate masses is likely to result in a return to the Dark Ages whereby much of the civilized behavior introduced from Europe will be submerged or annihilated. Some of these readers went on to say that termination of imperfect, yet civilized, efficient colonial administrations of Britain, France, Belgium, and Portugal will probably usher in demagoguery and repression of freedom of thought and expression rather than democracy, peace, and progress, at least in the short run. These interviewees believed that if the Africans were to take over in the Union of South Africa or Southern Rhodesia, they would reverse the accomplishments of the Europeans over decades. Perhaps these undisciplined societies will gradually overcome their native naïveté and violence, but the process will probably take several generations.

Furthermore, among the Southern consultants many besides bitter-end segregationists accorded considerable credence and justice to the arguments of *colons* in these countries. Although they criticized the firing on the Bantus at Sharpeville, the extremes of the OAS, and other excesses of whites against Africans, many observed that they could understand why these *colons* felt as they did and that these disputes have been far from one-sided—all the right with the blacks and all the wrong with the whites. They believed that *colons* were entitled to the fruits of their labors and those of their ancestors who left Europe to work in these primitive lands, for they had cut their farms and businesses out of the wilderness, as the ancestors of many Southerners did. The Africans had nothing before the *colons* arrived and would have less than they now do if these whites had remained in Europe. Nor did these Southerners feel that the Africans were likely to profit by taking these enterprises from the whites: the Africans' lack of sophistication and training would probably allow the jungle to reclaim these accomplishments. Many relatively informed Southerners had little faith in guarantees from African leaders for the property and civil rights of whites and felt the latter to be realistic in their fears. They were inclined to agree that the European homelands for which these former Europeans carved out empires were ungrateful and irresponsible in abandoning them to "savages": *colons* are entitled to protection by their European compatriots against the injustices and violence of childish and emotional natives.

Likewise, many college-educated white interviewees who considered that the massacre at Sharpeville and other excesses committed by whites in Africa were more harsh than necessary believed that our government had encouraged African unrest by "gratuitous" statements such as "Africa for the Africans" and by open support of immoderate demands made by African politicians in the U.N. and elsewhere. They regarded as unfortunate the interference and criticism by our leaders of European governments and of whites in Africa. Sensitive to Northern "meddling" in the South, they felt they understood the irritation of colonial governments at similar "impertinence" by Americans with respect to problems which they knew first hand—the people in the region understand the circumstances much better than Northern liberal "busybodies" both in and out of government.

Furthermore, many white Southerners who thought that desegregation of the South is probably inevitable—though perhaps unfortunate—tended to agree to a measure with more intransigent racists that the leaders of newly independent colored countries (including Asians as well as Africans) have been guilty of unwarranted meddling in this country, particularly in the South. Our diplomats and private visitors to their countries abide by their local customs, but they flagrantly violate ours and stage dramatic incidents for the sensational press here and in their own lands. An American visitor to Ghana, Guinea, and other former colonial territories who criticized restrictions on free speech and assembly and the jailing of the political opposition would be ejected, although his statements would be more justified than ignorant or exaggerated comments on our society, particularly the South, by African visitors here. A number of Southern interviewees felt that American Negroes enjoy a standard of living and a freedom that few Africans know and that the tasks of developing and running these African lands should be difficult enough for their political leaders without devoting their energies to ill-considered remarks about the United States—which has kept so many of them afloat financially.

The Southern interviewees fell along a continuum from a limited minority who sided more or less with the government of the Union of South Africa and felt Portugal in Angola and Tshombe in Katanga deserved virtually complete support to others who agreed with the general policies of the federal executive on these matters—including Secretary Herter's criticism of the South African government after Sharpeville. Some overtones of the sorts noted above were evident among over half of those white interviewees who ventured opinions on these questions and also appeared, at one time or another in 1961, in approximately three out of five of the fifty-three newspapers surveyed.

Estimates of the prevalence of these sentiments in the white South generally in 1962 are necessarily speculative. Most white Southerners probably had only relatively diffuse leanings rather than distinct views on these questions, as on most other international problems. Undoubtedly their opinions have varied with attitudes toward the Southern Negro and desegregation in the South—the more conservative the Southerner has been on integration, the more inclined have his views been to reflect these themes. As reflected in the interviews, these ideas have undoubtedly been more prevalent in the Deep South than in the border states and in other sections where there are relatively few Negroes. Clear-cut views on these issues, as on most other international matters, have certainly been most prevalent within the upper educational levels. Thinking more favorable to independence of the remaining colonial territories and more critical of *colons* has likewise been most widespread among the better educated.

Neutralism

Nonalignment of Underdeveloped Lands

The personal interviews and the analysis of Southern newspapers indicated that many white Southerners, probably in some sections a majority of those with views on the matter, also felt in the early 1960's that newly independent states, and underdeveloped countries generally, would be likely to develop leftist regimes—at worst pro-Communist and at best socialist and neutralist—which would criticize the United States more than they did the Communist bloc. Many, and in some communities most, of the white interviewees who offered opinions feared that formal agreements and mutual guarantees prior to independence would probably be rather worthless later—the newly independent regimes would shortly violate them and unilaterally change them to their own advantage. These Southerners felt that either the few relatively responsible and moderate leaders in these countries at the time of independence would be replaced in time by anti-Western individuals who would bring Communist influences into their countries or else the initial leaders would shift in this direction themselves.

As one would surmise from the previous discussion of Southern assumptions about the nature of the Communist menace and the most effective means to meet it, white Southerners (and often all Southerners taken together) have on the whole been at least somewhat less sympathetic to neutralism in the underdeveloped world than have other regional groups. Thus, although there has been relatively little racial prejudice in the white South against non-Negroid colored foreigners, more white Southerners than not and larger proportions of them than of other white Americans have thought that we cannot count on India to cooperate with us; [15] that it is relatively unimportant for us to attempt to cooperate closely with that nation; [16] that countries such as India have a duty to join the "countries on our side" in order to stop

[15] NORC 298, 1/30/51 (1,236); NORC 323, 4/22/52 (1,250); NORC 341–2, 6/30/ 53 (1,291); NORC 355, 4/22/54 (1,207); NORC 366, 1/21/55 (1,209); NORC 382, 1/26/56 (1,238); NORC 390, 6/26/56 (1,275); NORC 399, 11/15/56 (1,286); NORC 401, 12/28/56 (1,232); and NORC 404, 4/26/57 (1,279). The percentages of Southerners and other Americans who thought we could probably count on India varied, depending on recent behavior of the Indian government and other factors, but during the period 1951–57 more Southerners felt we could not count on India than felt we could.

[16] NORC 313, 10/2/51 (1,237), and NORC 382, 1/26/56 (1,238). In October, 1951, 24 percent of white Southerners as compared with 16 percent of white Northerners felt it was not important for us to cooperate with India.

the spread of communism; and that refusing to take sides is not justified.[17] Southern whites have tended more than white Northerners to
manifest unfavorable impressions of Nehru and other neutralists [18] and
to think that we should not compromise further with "countries like
India, Egypt, and Burma" in order to "win their friendship." [19] In the
summer of 1955, 61 percent of Northern whites as compared with 49
percent of Southern whites felt it was a "good thing" that some countries remained neutral and did not join in alliance "with our side or
with Russia"; 25 percent of the former as compared with 30 percent
of the latter thought it was a "bad thing." [20]

The more widespread inclination in the South to view international
relations in primarily defense and alliance terms and to feel that con-
flicts between the West and the Communists cannot be reconciled short
of compromising our security helps to explain these findings. But if
these were the only or the primary reasons for Southern dislike of
neutralism in former colonial areas, white Southerners would be similarly critical of the continental European neutrals—Austria, Switzerland, Sweden, and Finland.

The interviews, however, lead to the impression that such is very
probably not the case. Furthermore, the acceptance of neutralism in
European countries appears due only in part to traditional Southern
identification with Europeans and indifference to, or even racial or ethnic prejudice against, Asian and African societies. Many of the more
literate Southerners among the interviewees felt that they could understand and sympathize with the neutral postures of these small European lands: tradition, historical experience, or a precarious position on

17 In reply to NORC 390, 6/26/56 (1,275), 57 percent of Southern whites (56
percent of all Southerners) and 49 percent of Northern whites (48 percent of all
Northerners) felt that neutralist regimes, such as that in India, have a duty to join
our side; 29, 34, 38, and 39 percent, respectively, that their neutrality is justified;
and 14, 13, 13, and 13 percent, respectively, were undecided, did not know, or expressed no opinion.
18 NORC 371, 4/29/55 (1,266), revealed that 28 percent of Southern whites (30
percent of all Southerners) and 37 percent of Northern whites (38 percent of all
Northerners) had a favorable impression of Nehru; 19, 17, 16, and 16 percent, respectively, an unfavorable one; and 53, 53, 47, and 46 percent, respectively, had no
view, were undecided, or said they did not know.
19 In early 1956, 34 percent of Southern whites (37 percent of all Southerners)
and 41 percent of Northern whites (42 percent of all Northerners) said that the
United States should try harder to win the friendship of "countries like India,
Egypt, and Burma," which had not sided with the United States in its struggle with
the Communist powers; 58, 55, 51, and 50 percent, respectively, thought we were
already doing enough; and 8, 8, 8, and 8 percent, respectively, ventured no opinion, were undecided, or said they did not know.
20 NORC 372, 6/23/55 (1,263).

the border between East and West renders their neutralism reasonable and responsible. Moreover, their governments have for the most part been truly neutral, even though their ideological and cultural identifications are primarily with the West. Nor, according to the interviewees, do the European neutrals feel compelled to "pontificate," offer "gratuitous, sanctimonious advice," or advance "unrealistic" and "irresponsible" criticisms on Western policies which are more rational than their own and which, in final analysis, are the real defense of their countries against Communist take-over.

The neutralism of many Asian and African leaders, on the other hand, was perceived by many of those with views on the matter as "phony." Their countries would be absorbed into the Communist bloc but for the military power of the Western world, particularly the United States. These Southerners expressed the opinion that neutralism is realistic for them only because they are protected, at least indirectly, by the West. (They act as though the West was as or even more guilty than the Chinese and the Russians in the cold war.) In fact, more anti-Western and pro-Communist than neutral, they are largely opportunists who want to be on the winning side and in the interim extort as much economic aid as possible from both sides. Furthermore, they are silent about blatant Communist transgressions but vociferous in their moralistic and often emotionally biased criticisms of Western defensive reactions against Communist intrigues. Pressing for peace at any price, they are apparently really afraid of the Communists but assume that they need do nothing to secure the friendship and assistance of the West; they have no responsible orientation toward international issues of worldwide significance except in terms of their own short-run selfish interests; most of their moralizing about Western behavior is hypocritical, especially in light of their own predatory behavior against their neighbors regardless of world opinion, as in Goa and New Guinea. Many of the Southern interviewees felt that it was difficult to understand how any non-Communist government which looks realistically at Communist as compared with American international behavior can believe that the Communists are not aggressive, that they are not a danger to world security and to the independence of small nations, and that their totalitarian systems are no worse than the democratic regimes of most of the West.

Criticisms of Our Policies Toward Nationalistic Neutralists

Southerners who tended in the early 1960's to agree with the above sentiments would like to modify the recent behavior of our government and national leaders toward these regimes. They felt we accorded too much importance to the criticisms of men like Sukarno, Kwame Nkrumah, Sekou Touré, and other neutralist "demagogues," whose hostile comments are not based on balanced evaluation of the facts but are reflections of unrealistic racial biases, irrationalities, feelings of supposed slights, and efforts to divert attention from the poverty, disorder, and injustices of their own countries and regimes. We act as though such so-called world opinion was justified and was a major determinant of our policies.

A number felt that perhaps we should take a note from the Russian experience: "world opinion" has never stopped Communist aggressions. Communists paid cynical lip service to non-Communist opinion, but have never let it deter them from actions in their own self-interest, such as in Hungary, South Korea, Vietnam, and Finland. These interviewees observed that neutralist leaders have not criticized the Communists for these aggressions—they have more respect for power and the will to use it than for the altruism and "do-goodism" of the United States. The more attention we pay to their pompous, self-righteous entreaties, the more critical they will become. Only the more extreme racists would have our government ignore justified criticisms abroad, but many literate Southerners would prefer that we take whatever international action we deem sensible and just, even when some of these dictators and "two-bit" demagogues might use it for political "mileage" at home against the United States. These same Southerners tend to believe that "Yankees" and liberals generally put too much emphasis on "being loved" and that the neutralists know how to take advantage of this weakness. Britain was never so interested in winning the affection of other peoples; Russia is even less so, and we should seek international respect rather than some unattainable "wishy-washy" friendliness. Vigorous defense against Communist incursions, according to these interviewees, is more likely to gain such respect.

Southerners of these views tended to feel that we should stand by those of our demands which are essential to our security and publicly inform the world why we refuse to compromise further. If the neutralists do not understand such carefully explained reasons, then either they do not want to understand or they have no responsible interest in this issue of worldwide significance. Those expressing these opinions applied the same principle to relations with Communist states in general. For example, only a minority of the Southern interviewees have favored invading Cuba since the Bay of Pigs fiasco (as of 1962), but most seemed to think that there may come a time when United States intervention will become necessary and that we should try to convince the other Latin American regimes of the wisdom of our decision. If they refuse to agree, probably for reasons of domestic politics, then we should assume the responsibilities of a world power and act accordingly. Many of these interviewees felt that most of the regimes in Latin America would privately applaud such decisiveness, which would win for us some respect among Latins who are disdainful of indecision and cowardly acceptance of insults.

Furthermore, many of the informants favored our paying more attention to the interests and advice of our real allies in Europe, Australia, New Zealand, and other developed, primarily white countries rather than compromise our cooperation with them in hopeless attempts to win the friendship and collaboration of the anticolonialists, neutralists, and emotional nationalists of Africa and Asia. Most of the Southerners were of the opinion that we will not secure the active support of the latter anyway as they have no true respect for the values of the West and no real commitments except to their own petty imperialisms, local power struggles, and the maximum extraction of financial aid from West and East alike. Virtually none are as reliable allies as those we have in Western Europe, and even if they did support the West their actual power would be almost negligible in any showdown with China or Russia.

Economic Development

These attitudes of many Southerners concerning newly independent countries and the neutralist and "leftist" orientations of many of them, as well as the Southern emphasis on military defense and, to a lesser measure, military alliance with Western Europe and other proclivities at least somewhat more prevalent in the South than in the North have tended to influence their positions on foreign aid to these lands and to underdeveloped societies generally. Attitudes of large numbers of Southerners toward economic assistance have changed significantly with the shift of United States aid from Western Europe and Japan to these countries.

Earlier Thinking on Foreign Aid

Our first major aid program was composed primarily of war materials for the enemies of the Axis. As noted previously, Southerners, by wide margins, constituted the regional group most favorable to Lend-Lease before our formal entry into the war (see pp. 95–96).

These differences between the South and the rest of America decreased considerably after the attack on Pearl Harbor. During most of the war and the immediate postwar period Southerners were about as inclined or slightly more inclined (white Southerners more often than not were more inclined) than Northerners to approve of continuation after the war of sacrifices in order to feed, clothe, house, and otherwise help war-torn peoples "get back on their feet." [21] In May, 1946, 43 percent of white Southerners (41 percent of all Southerners) in contrast to 35 percent of Northern whites (36 percent of all Northerners) approved of the proposed loan of several billions to Britain; 40 percent of Southern whites (42 percent of all Southerners) as compared with 55 percent of Northern whites (54 percent of all Northerners) disapproved of this suggestion.[22] Again in 1949, Southerners, particularly whites, were more apt to favor another large loan to Britain than were other Americans taken together.[23] Differences were typically greater when only those Southern whites who ventured opinions or voted in the previous national or congressional election or primary were compared with Northerners who also had views or voted.

The Southern public was never so solidly favorable to the Truman Doctrine or the Marshall Plan as the roll-call votes of their representatives in Washington would suggest, nor was Southern public opinion as different from Northern thinking on these matters as the large differences in voting behavior of their Congressmen would lead one to surmise. However, some differences toward slightly greater support in the South, or somewhat lesser opposition, for these programs were evident—differences which usually widened when Negroes, non-voters, and, especially, both were eliminated from survey statistics.

Thus, a month after President Truman's proposed assistance to

21 NORC 201, February, 1942 (2,537); NORC 205, July, 1942 (2,582); NORC 210, January, 1943 (2,466); NORC 216, September, 1943 (2,448); AIPO 307, 11/23/43 (2,980); AIPO 244, 4/5/45 (2,973); NORC survey of 3/45 (2,499); AIPO 354, 8/22/45 (3,107); AIPO 356, 9/19/45 (3,075); and NORC 135, 10/17/45 (1,260). For example, when asked in late 1943, "For a year or two after the war, should people in the United States continue to put up with shortages of butter, sugar, meat, and other rationed food products in order to give food to people who need it in Europe?" 67 percent in the South in contrast to 63 percent in the Northeast, 62 percent in the Midwest, 65 percent in the Plains States, and 63 percent in the West replied in the affirmative; 19, 22, 22, 21, and 22 percent, respectively, replied in the negative; and the rest ventured no opinion, did not know, or were undecided. See AIPO 307, 11/23/43 (2,689).
22 NORC 142, 5/17/46 (1,292). See also AIPO 355, 9/6/45 (3,084); NORC 135, 10/17/45 (1,260); NORC 137, 12/12/45 (1,300); NORC 139, 2/2/46 (1,263); AIPO 366, 2/27/46 (3,122); AIPO 367, 3/13/46 (3,249); NORC 141, 3/20/46 (1,293); AIPO 370, 4/24/46 (3,224); and AIPO 372, 5/29/46 (3,118).
23 AIPO 446, 8/12/49 (3,272).

Greece and Turkey was made public, 52 percent of Southern whites (51 percent of all Southerners) versus 51 percent of Northern whites (and of all Northerners) said they would like to see their Congressman vote for the suggested aid to Greece; 29 percent of Southern whites (26 percent of all Southerners) as compared with 38 percent of Northern whites (39 percent of all Northerners) wanted their Congressman to vote against it. Forty-five percent of Southern whites (44 percent of all Southerners) versus 39 percent of Northern whites (38 percent of all Northerners) preferred that their Congressman vote for the suggested aid to Turkey; 33 percent of Southern whites (31 percent of all Southerners) in contrast to 47 percent of Northern whites (and of all Northerners) wanted their legislator to vote against such assistance.[24] Several months later, 58 percent of those in the South, 55 percent in the Northeast, 53 percent in the Midwest (Plains States included), and 56 percent in the West approved of "our government's policy of sending aid to Greece."[25]

Interregional differences, although more often than not in the expected direction, were small, normally statistically insignificant, with regard to the Marshall Plan, and even these disappeared during the last year or so of the European Recovery Program as both Southern and Northern opinion tended to come to the view that this program had gone on long enough. In early 1948, for instance, 57 percent of Southerners (59 percent of Southern whites), compared with 61 percent of Northeasterners, 50 percent of Midwesterners, 56 percent of residents of the Plains States, and 58 percent of Westerners, expressed favorable opinions about the Marshall Plan, whereas 14 percent of Southerners (13 percent of Southern whites) and 16 percent, 25 percent, 18 percent, and 16 percent, respectively, of the other regions ventured unfavorable impressions of it.[26] When asked in early 1951 whether they approved or disapproved of "continuing to send economic aid to western Europe under the Marshall Plan," 59 percent of Southerners (62 percent of Southern whites) as compared with 63 percent of Northeasterners, 54 percent of Midwesterners (including residents of the Plains States), and 59 percent of Westerners approved whereas 23 percent of Southerners (22 percent of Southern whites) versus 32 percent, 36 percent, and 31 percent, respectively, of the other regions disapproved.[27] As elsewhere

24   AIPO 394, 4/9/47 (3,044).
25   NORC 151, 6/24/47 (1,273). See also AIPO 392, 3/12/47 (2,884); NORC 149, 4/3/47 (1,307); NORC 154, 12/4/47 (1,293); NORC 163, 1/26/49 (1,261); and NORC 164, 3/3/49 (1,300).
26   AIPO release of 3/3/48 and AIPO 411, 1/21/48 (3,161).
27   NORC 295, 12/28/50 (1,258). For other comparative regional replies to

in America, opposition to these expenditures was concentrated among those who knew little or nothing of the European Recovery Program, or of world affairs in general, typically the poorly educated and otherwise underprivileged. Since the South contained disproportionately large numbers of such citizens, better educated Southerners were usually significantly more inclined to support the Marshall Plan and Truman Doctrine than their counterparts of roughly equivalent educational backgrounds in the North.

Most of the Southern press was controlled and edited by such better educated people; consequently, even the more conservative Southern newspapers typically supported most of our aid programs prior to the mid-1950's. For instance, the Jackson *Clarion-Ledger* championed extension of Lend-Lease directly to the U.S.S.R. and to Turkey through Britain, general expansion of aid to enemies of the Axis, and increased taxes if necessary.[28] Among the most conservative quartile of the sample of papers on domestic economics, four out of five favored the loans to Britain in 1946 and 1947. The *Clarion-Ledger* and the (Little Rock) *Arkansas Democrat* backed a loan to Mexico to encourage "economic development" in 1947;[29] the Columbia (South Carolina) *State* approved of a loan of $100,000,000 to Israel in early 1949;[30] and the Charleston *News and Courier* and Montgomery *Advertiser* favored UNRRA and other assistance to needy peoples, including the Germans.[31] Of the fifty-three papers in the sample, only one did not support aid to Greece and Turkey within two weeks after President Truman proposed it on March 12, 1947. Few Southern papers, including those in Mississippi, seemed to have made much mention of Dean

---

queries on the European Recovery Program from shortly after the Secretary of State's speech at Harvard University to the termination of this program, see AIPO 400, 7/2/47 (3,000); AIPO 401, 7/23/47 (3,024); AIPO 402, 8/6/47 (3,000); AIPO 403, 8/27/47 (2,999); AIPO 404, 9/10/47 (3,057); AIPO 405, 10/1/47 (2,832); NORC 152, 10/10/47 (1,290); AIPO 406, 10/22/47 (2,932); AIPO 407, 11/5/47 (2,981); NORC 154, 12/4/47 (1,293); AIPO 410, 12/30/47 (3,000); AIPO 411, 1/21/48 (3,161); NORC 155, 2/25/48 (1,289); NORC 156, 3/25/48 (1,289); NORC 159, 6/29/48 (1,301); AIPO 432, 11/1/48 (3,000); NORC 162, 11/23/48 (1,300); NORC 163, 1/26/49 (1,261); NORC 164, 3/3/49 (1,300); AIPO 439, 3/17/49 (2,193); NORC 165, 4/19/49 (1,300); NORC 166, 6/1/49 (1,300); NORC 167, 6/30/49 (1,284); NORC 168, 8/11/49 (1,300); NORC 169, 9/16/49 (1,300); NORC 170, 10/12/49 (1,300); NORC 273, 1/18/50 (1,284); AIPO 452, 1/26/50 (2,899); NORC 276, 3/1/50 (1,300); AIPO 454, 3/24/50 (1,458); NORC 280, 4/17/50 (1,274); NORC 287, 7/24/50 (1,302); NORC 292, 11/22/50 (1,258); NORC 298, 1/30/51 (1,236); AIPO 477, 7/6/51 (2,013); AIPO 478, 8/1/51 (2,200); NORC 313, 10/2/51 (1,237); NORC 315, 12/18/51 (1,237); and NORC 327, 6/30/52 (1,285).
28 November 2–12, 1941.
29 Jackson *Clarion-Ledger*, May 18, 1947.
30 January 21, 1949.   31 March–May, 1947.

Acheson's speech of May 8, before the Delta Council in which he launched the "trial balloon" for the forthcoming Marshall Plan (an address apparently well received in Cleveland, Mississippi, by the audience of cotton planters, ginners, factors, and others dependent on that crop), but all except four of the fifty-three papers supported the general idea of the European Recovery Program as it was discussed and passed in Congress in the ensuing months. Criticism of the administration of the plan and of supposed lack of vigor of European self-help appeared from time to time in the press in the late 1940's, but even in 1951 only a small minority of Southern papers felt that the appropriations should be terminated.

Majority support for and the rather limited opposition to these programs in the white South are partly explained by their emphasis on Western Europe (with the exception of Turkey). There was less support for economic aid for Japan and Nationalist China than for Europe throughout the country, but the gap was usually wider in the South than outside. Thus, during the period when white Southerners venturing opinions were as, or somewhat more, favorable to the Truman Doctrine and the European Recovery Program than were other regional groups, they were typically somewhat less favorable to economic aid for Nationalist China before her defeat on the continent,[32] to Japan,[33] to Korea,[34] and to "friendly Asian countries to help develop them economically." [35] In April, 1953, Southerners were somewhat less willing than other regional groups for the United States to shift its economic aid from Western Europe to Asian allies,[36] and by the end of 1957 Southerners taken together were significantly less apt to favor raising taxes "to meet Soviet economic competition and promises of economic aid to countries in Asia and Africa." [37]

Another factor encouraging Southern approval of postwar aid was the economically developed, modern nature of these societies which had been ravaged by war. They had educated populations, skilled work-

32 NORC 135, 10/17/45 (1,260); AIPO 384, 11/14/46 (3,203); and AIPO 391, 3/26/47 (2,639).

33 AIPO 439, 3/17/49 (2,193), and NORC 365, 11/26/54 (1,201).

34 AIPO 477, 7/6/51 (2,013). In reply to the question, "The United Nations have had to destroy many Korean cities in the fighting there. Would you favor or oppose the United States helping to rebuild South Korean cities?" 41 percent of all Southerners (42 percent of white Southerners) and 54 percent of all Northerners (54 percent of white Northerners) favored such aid; 48, 47, 38, and 38 percent, respectively, opposed it; and 11, 11, 8, and 8 percent, respectively, ventured no opinion, were undecided, or said they did not know.

35 NORC 169, 9/16/49 (1,300); NORC 287, 7/24/50 (1,302); NORC 302, 4/18/51 (1,300); and NORC 303, 6/29/51 (1,300).

36 AIPO 514, 4/17/53 (1,520).   37 AIPO 593, 12/31/57 (1,522).

ers, talented technicians and managers, and efficient administrative institutions. The objective was to put these people back to work, not to transform the basic values and social structures of semifeudal agricultural or tribal societies, as would be the case with underdeveloped countries in the late 1950's and early 1960's. A number of newspapers in cotton-producing areas of the period noted at least in passing that a prosperous Japan and, particularly, Europe would probably again be good customers for Southern cotton, although few of the interviewees who said they had supported aid to Europe and Japan in the late 1940's mentioned this likelihood.

Moreover, the Truman Doctrine, the Marshall Plan, and similar economic aid to Japan were popularized in much of the Southern press largely as measures designed to thwart Communist penetration rather than as means of stimulating social change. As one would surmise from the tendency more widespread in the South than in the North to perceive world affairs as primarily a struggle with the Soviet bloc and to feel that our disagreements with communism are probably irreconcilable, white Southerners favorable to the European Recovery Program were somewhat more inclined than Northern supporters of this program to mention to survey interviewers defeat of Communist subversion or the like as the major objective for the project.

However, interregional differences in this regard were small and other evidence indicates that the anti-Communist tone of these publicized programs was only one of a number of reasons for Southern support. For instance, Southern whites were somewhat more favorable than Northern whites toward the loan to Britain in 1946—before the cold war had become intense and before much emphasis on anticommunism appeared in official propaganda. Furthermore, Southerners, like most other Americans, were more apt to emphasize economic aid for civilian reconstruction in Europe than assistance in the form of military equipment, except for a brief period during the Korean War. Although the proportion of Southerners who have felt that military supplies were more important than economic aid in preventing the spread of communism has typically been larger than in the rest of the country, more Southerners than not thought during most of the initial postwar decade (and were still of this opinion in 1962) that economic assistance was the more important of the two or that both were equally important.[38]

38 In October, 1949, for example, 63 percent of all Americans approved of sending economic aid to Western Europe under the Marshall Plan as compared with 50 percent who approved of sending military supplies to the same countries; 26

Another major reason for Southern approval of the Truman Doctrine, the Marshall Plan, and economic aid to Japan and Nationalist China was the fact that the recipient countries were either formally allied with the United States or pursued policies overtly opposed to the U.S.S.R. and world communism. In 1949 Western Europe, with several exceptions, joined the NATO pact. Japan was first controlled by United States occupation forces and then became a formal ally in 1951, and the Chinese Nationalist regime has been an ally of this country since World War II. These recipients of capital assistance did not attempt to remain uncommitted in the struggle between the West and communism, and their political leaders did not voice anti-Western, leftist-leaning, nationalistic views for public consumption. National surveys from the late 1940's into the late 1950's repeatedly showed that white Southerners were as favorable as the rest of the country toward sending economic aid or "making loans" to "countries that have agreed to stand with us against Communist aggression," "our allies," or "friendly countries"—between 71 and 87 percent of Southerners (75 percent and 89 percent of white Southerners) approved of such aid throughout this period.[39]

---

percent disapproved of economic aid, 40 percent of military supplies. Sixty-three percent of Southerners approved of the Marshall Plan and only 21 percent disapproved, but 54 percent in the South favored sending military supplies whereas 30 percent disapproved. See NORC 170, 10/12/49 (1,400).

In late summer of 1952, Southerners were slightly more inclined to feel that military aid was more important than economic aid, whereas Northerners were more apt to place greater importance on economic aid. NORC 329, 8/28/52 (1,300) revealed that 39 percent of all Southerners (42 percent of white Southerners) felt that economic aid was the more important, whereas 41 percent of all Southerners (40 percent of white Southerners) felt military aid was; the rest were undecided, did not know, or ventured no opinion. On the other hand, 48 percent of all Northerners (and of white Northerners) viewed economic aid as the more important, whereas 35 percent of all Northerners (34 percent of white Northerners) emphasized military rather than economic aid and the remainder were undecided, offered no opinion, or did not know.

But by the spring of 1957, 70 percent of all Southerners (72 percent of white Southerners) regarded economic aid as the more important; 18 percent of all Southerners (17 percent of white Southerners) felt military aid was the more important; and the rest were undecided or offered no opinion. At the same time, 74 percent of both all and white Northerners viewed economic aid as the more important; 15 percent of both so viewed military aid; and the rest were undecided. See NORC 404, 4/26/57 (1,279).

See also NORC 291, 10/18/50 (1,305); NORC 302, 4/18/51 (1,300); NORC 303, 6/29/51 (1,300); NORC 313, 10/2/51 (1,237); NORC 314, 11/22/51 (1,237); NORC 321, 3/12/52 (1,260); NORC 363, 9/10/54 (1,198); NORC 379, 11/23/55 (1,276); and NORC 390, 6/26/56 (1,275).

39 NORC 167, 6/30/49 (1,284); NORC 321, 3/12/52 (521); NORC 323, 4/22/52 (1,250); NORC 329, 8/28/52 (1,300); NORC 340, 5/14/53 (1,291); NORC 351,

However, Southerners have been significantly less favorable than Northerners to assistance, particularly capital assistance, to neutralists during the postwar era. The proportions endorsing economic assistance to "countries like India, which have not joined us as allies against the Communists," for instance, have been much smaller throughout the United States than those approving of similar aid to allies; the proportion supporting aid to allies but not to neutralists has been largest in the South. During the period 1947–57, more Southerners consistently opposed than favored economic aid to neutralists whereas somewhat more Northerners than not usually favored it. As neutralist regimes increased in number and became more vociferous in their denunciations of the West and more open in their affiliations with the Soviets and some of their policies, Southerners seemed to grow more critical of capital assistance to them and the gap between Southern and Northern thinking on aid to neutralists apparently widened. By early 1957 only 37 percent of Southerners (and of Southern whites) in contrast to 58 percent of Northerners favored continuation of economic aid to India and other countries which "have not joined us as allies against the Communists," and 54 percent of Southerners (57 percent of Southern whites) as compared with 37 percent of Northerners opposed such assistance.[40]

Southern skepticism about aiding neutralists was not limited to expensive capital aid, although it was most widespread for that type of costly assistance. When Southerners were asked in early 1955 whether "the United States should withdraw aid to nations who refuse to cooperate with us," 74 percent felt we should and only 15 percent that we should not.[41] Southerners have been more inclined than not to approve of emergency relief and charity for unfortunates in underdeveloped neutralist countries, but even on such questions they have been less apt to favor assistance than Northerners. For example, in late March, 1951, during a period when the Indian government was pursuing a rather vocally neutralist policy toward the war in Korea, 48 percent of Southerners (and of Southern whites) versus 55 percent of Northerners replied in the affirmative when asked whether or not our govern-

---

1/21/54 (1,300); NORC 355, 4/22/54 (1,207); NORC 366, 1/21/55 (1,209); NORC 378, 10/6/55 (527); NORC 382, 1/26/56 (1,238); NORC 386, 4/20/56 (1,224); NORC 393, 9/3/56 (1,263); NORC 399, 11/15/56 (1,286); and NORC 404, 4/26/57 (1,279).

40 NORC 401, 12/28/56 (1,232). For the period 1947–57, see NORC 148, 2/20/47 (1,239); AIPO 473, 3/24/51 (2,101); NORC 302, 4/18/51 (1,300); AIPO 541, 12/29/54 (1,446); NORC 366, 1/21/55 (1,209); NORC 382, 1/26/56 (1,238); NORC 386, 4/20/56 (1,224); NORC 390, 6/26/56 (1,275); NORC 393, 9/13/56 (1,263); NORC 399, 11/15/56 (1,286); and NORC 404, 4/26/57 (1,279).

41 AIPO 541, 12/29/54 (1,446).

ment should give grain to India because of the recent crop shortages there. Thirty-four percent of Southerners (35 percent of Southern whites) as compared with 29 percent of Northerners answered in the negative.[42]

These hesitations about aiding neutralists have been associated, as one might assume, with the more prevalent feeling in the South than outside that conflict, including war, with the Communist powers is relatively probable, that our differences with them are relatively unlikely to be resolved, that the non-European neutralists are duty bound to support the West against the Communist bloc, that alignment against the latter is the only morally justifiable position, and the like. Surveys have indicated that Americans who stress military and strategic considerations in our foreign policy and who advocate United States military intervention in Latin America and elsewhere abroad tend to believe that we should not aid neutralists and that we should apply more pressure on the foreign policies and internal politics of aid-receiving countries than we have exerted in the past.[43] Furthermore, although the less educated have been least apt to favor aid of any sort, they have been particularly unenthusiastic about aid, especially expensive capital assistance, to neutralists, and the South, as previously observed, has continued to have the largest fraction of ill-educated in the nation.

Southerners in 1959–62 who had approved of Lend-Lease, early postwar loans to Britain, the Truman Doctrine, and the Marshall Plan but were opposed to aid in the 1960's mentioned several additional reasons for their earlier support: Lend-Lease had been viewed as an exceptional wartime program; the European Recovery Program and other aid during the earlier part of the postwar period were publicized as temporary or emergency in nature, for relatively well-defined, concise, limited objectives, and as an expense which would end within several years. Aid to underdeveloped countries, on the other hand, seems to be permanent, and by the late 1950's and the initial years of the 1960's some of its supporters were advocating its increase year after year; its purposes are vague, probably more theoretical than pragmatic. Many felt that we had overdone this "dole." Moreover, earlier aid was used more intelligently and efficiently, with a minimum of corruption or absorption by politicians, wealthy classes, and hangers-on. Many Southerners in 1959–62, including a number of the better educated, had images of major waste, stupidity, and frustration in our aid programs of the late fifties and sixties, whereas they thought that these negative factors

42 AIPO 473, 3/24/51 (2,102).
43 SRC survey of November–December, 1949 (606).

were minimal in Lend-Lease, postwar loans to Britain, and the European Recovery Program. Also, there was more enthusiasm and optimism shortly after the war throughout the country for efforts to build a peaceful world order than there would be later, following the many disillusionments abroad with the Communists, the neutralists, and the underdeveloped countries. Furthermore, Southerners, particularly whites, had much respect for Virginia Military Institute graduate George C. Marshall,[44] and therefore for the program bearing his name. Loans to Britain and other aid programs prior to 1947 occurred during the tenure of James Byrnes, a prominent son of South Carolina, as Secretary of State. Finally, the domestic race situation was much less tense, and less patently related to the societies aided, than it later became (see pp. 419–30).

Point Four and Beyond

The shift of our technical and economic assistance from primarily war-damaged, developed societies to underdeveloped, often formerly colonial and neutralist, ones has been gradual, starting with enunciation of the Point Four program in the 1949 inaugural address of President Truman. Initially, aid was limited to relatively inexpensive technical assistance, international exchanges of persons, and training of prospective leaders, specialists, and students. Military assistance to allies in the underdeveloped world was another important emphasis in the early 1950's, while capital aid for economic development of backward lands expanded considerably during the Eisenhower and the Kennedy administrations.

There seems to be little doubt that support for foreign aid in general decreased and opposition increased throughout the country, including the South, during the period from the Marshall Plan to the concentration of most types of assistance on underdeveloped countries. Because the same questions have not been posed by surveys over this period and because replies have varied from equivalent groups when questions have been worded differently and posed more or less around the same time, the author has no completely comparable systematic evidence. But the overall trend seems apparent when one observes that only 13 percent of Americans in late 1948 said they were "dissatisfied with the Marshall Plan for European recovery" [45] and only 14 percent felt that

44 According to a study of ten thousand college graduates by the Bureau of Applied Social Research in 1947, Southern college-educated men and women were significantly more inclined than those of the rest of the country taken together to harbor favorable impressions of Secretary of State Marshall.
45 NORC 162, 11/23/48 (1,300).

Congress should not continue this program,[46] whereas 30 percent in early 1963 replied that they were "in general . . . against" foreign aid.[47]

At the time of the latter survey 58 percent of the country—60 percent of those in the Northeast, 58 percent in the Midwest (including the Plains States), 59 percent in the West, and 55 percent in the South —said that they were "in general . . . for" foreign aid.[48] However, a considerable fraction of Southerners and other Americans who favored at least some foreign aid "in principle" in the late 1950's and early 1960's would have virtually eliminated some major assistance programs and severely reduced others; there was little agreement in the South or outside among this favorable 58 percent on which particular parts of our foreign assistance programs should be continued, which should be curtailed, and which, if any, should be expanded or modified. Only 6 percent in the South and 10 percent in the other regions could provide even a rough approximation of the order of magnitude of foreign aid during the then current year or of the percentage of our national budget or gross national product involved therein. Fifty-one percent of Southerners and 48 percent of other Americans much overestimated the amount and the proportion of our national budget or income in foreign aid—calculating up to even half of the nation's yearly outlay.[49] It was apparent both from surveys and the interviews that many who continued to approve of foreign aid in recent years did so reluctantly, for lack of any idea of how we might terminate it.

Moreover, those who have opposed international assistance since the mid-1950's have, for the most part, identified considerably more intensely with their opinions than have those in favor.[50] Most Southerners (and perhaps other citizens) who did favor aid in 1959–62 seemed to attach relatively little importance to these programs; they very probably felt more lukewarm toward aid in the early sixties than toward Lend-Lease and the European Recovery Program.[51]

Relatively inexpensive technical assistance has been considerably more widely accepted as a desirable policy than more costly aid programs for underdeveloped lands. Virtually all of the sample of Southern newspapers expressing opinions, and the great majority of Southerners who had heard of Point Four in 1949 and the early 1950's, were favorably

46   AIPO release of 11/28/48.   47   AIPO 667, January, 1963 (4,383).
48   *Ibid.*   49   *Ibid.*
50   V. O. Key, Jr., *Public Opinion and American Democracy* (New York: Alfred A. Knopf, 1963), 213–14.
51   *Ibid.*, 214–15; and Angus Campbell, Philip E. Converse, Warren E. Miller, and Donald E. Stokes, *The American Voter* (New York: John Wiley, 1960), 176.

disposed toward such technical aid to underdeveloped societies. A larger fraction of Southerners than of other citizens have been unfamiliar with this program, and the less they have known about it the more likely they have been to oppose it when its provisions were brought to their attention.[52] As with most continuing activities of our government abroad, the proportion of Southerners (and of other Americans) who have heard of our technical assistance efforts has increased gradually since their inception. Between 65 and 83 percent of Southerners venturing opinions from 1949 through 1956 felt that we should help these countries to develop and approved of the general magnitude of the sums appropriated by Congress for technical aid.[53]

However, the majority of Southerners who have supported technical assistance has typically been a somewhat smaller fraction of the total Southern population, and of those expressing opinions, than in the rest of the country. Conversely, the minority who have thought that we should not spend this money on these programs has been a somewhat larger fraction of the Southern population, and of those venturing views, than outside the South. Southern Negroes, particularly, have been less inclined to favor technical assistance and more apt to feel the money should be spent in this country than have Northerners, and even than Northern Negroes. Nevertheless, white Southerners have on more surveys than not been at least slightly less enthusiastic about technical assistance than Northerners.[54]

Southerners who have believed that federal resources should not be expended on these relatively inexpensive programs designed to communicate American methods and know-how to underdeveloped countries have been for the most part among the generally isolationist minority—those who disapproved of the Truman Doctrine and the

---

52   NORC 280, 4/17/50 (1,274), and NORC 371, 4/29/55 (1,226).

53   NORC 163, 1/26/49 (1,261); NORC 164, 3/3/49 (1,300); NORC 171, 11/11/49 (1,300); NORC 280, 4/17/50 (1,274); NORC 292, 11/22/50 (1,258); NORC 317, 2/5/52 (1,260); NORC 329, 8/28/52 (1,300); NORC 370, 3/11/55 (1,225); NORC 371, 4/29/55 (1,226); and NORC 386, 4/20/56 (1,224).

54   *Ibid.* Differences on most surveys between the South and other regions have often been too small to be statistically significant. A year after President Truman's inaugural address in 1949, 67 percent of Southern whites felt that "it is a good policy for the United States to try to help backward countries to raise their standard of living," whereas 27 percent thought this was not "any concern of our government"; the respective figures among Northern whites were 75 percent and 21 percent. See NORC 280, 4/17/50 (1,274). By mid-1956, 83 percent of Southern whites and 80 percent of all Southerners replied in the affirmative; 11 percent of the former and 12 percent of the latter answered in the negative. Eighty-seven percent of Northerners felt that this was a concern of our government and a "good policy," whereas 10 percent said it was not. See NORC 386, 4/20/56 (1,224).

Marshall Plan,[55] who felt the U.N. was either of no use or only slightly useful to our interests,[56] and who believed that we have been too active in world affairs generally.[57] Few Southerners (or Northerners) who approved of the Marshall Plan or of active participation by our country in world affairs have disapproved of technical assistance expenditures. By the late 1950's opposition to technical assistance efforts had also become disproportionately prevalent among white Southerners who believed Negroes were innately inferior to whites and who were strongly against integration.[58] Most who thought ill of Point Four assistance and training of foreigners from underdeveloped lands at our expense have been among the little-informed, poorly educated, and economically deprived segments of Southern society, especially non-voting Negroes and poor whites.

According to the interviews between 1959 and 1962, technical assistance by Americans in underdeveloped countries and training of nationals of these lands in the United States have remained considerably more popular, or more tolerated, in the South than capital aid for developmental purposes and military aid have. Nevertheless, some disillusionment with technical help was evident among a considerable minority of the sample of rather well-educated, influential Southerners. A number mentioned that too many Asian, Latin American, and African students and trainees in the United States seemed to become leftist leaders of anti-American movements on returning home. Some apparently have helped to steer their countries into collaboration with the U.S.S.R. or even Communist China. Others have criticized American ways while enjoying our hospitality here. Pragmatic Southerners fearful of "leftist abstractions and theories" and the like sometimes mentioned that too many foreigners in our colleges were studying the social sciences and humanities rather than practical fields like engineering, medicine, public health, and commerce which would be more useful in developing their countries.

Southern attitudes about the Peace Corps have paralleled those regarding technical assistance, although the two programs have been separately administered. Sixty-one percent of Southern adults, only five percentage points less than the Northern average, said in early 1961 that they would like their son, if they had one who was qualified, to participate in the Peace Corps then being discussed.[59] A considerable minority among the Southern sample in 1961, including some who felt

55 NORC 292, 11/22/50 (1,258).   56 NORC 370, 3/11/55 (1,225).
57 NORC 292, 11/22/50 (1,258).   58 NORC 386, 4/20/56 (1,224).
59 AIPO 640, 1/10/61 (2,649).

the Peace Corps was "worth a try as an experiment," were anxious about the aptness of youngsters to make unfortunate mistakes because of their immaturity; this minority believed that more experienced specialists would probably be of greater value to underdeveloped countries. A smaller fraction seemed to agree with the more conservative Southern newspapers of the time that "egghead draft dodgers," "utopian do-gooders with rosy views of life and mankind," "equalitarian mongrelizers," "pacifist fools," "radicals," "Ivy League theorists," "liberal one-world brotherhooders," and other "unsavory" sorts might comprise too high a percentage of the participants. They felt such youngsters were unlikely to have any real understanding of their own country, of backward societies, or of human beings generally; that they would give false impressions of this country abroad; and that their contacts with Africans, Asians, and Latin Americans would be apt to arouse antipathy rather than understanding. However, these reservations were prevalent in 1961 and early 1962 among only a limited minority of the interviewees, and apparently of Southerners generally

It has already been noted that Southerners have been more hesitant than other Americans about sending food to underdeveloped Communist and even neutralist countries. However, relatively few persons in the Southern sample other than the more economically (and culturally) underprivileged disapproved of disposal of agricultural surpluses in underdeveloped countries, either as gifts of charity after disasters or in exchange for local currencies under Public Law 480. The most widespread opposition was evident among Mountain County residents who were themselves receiving government relief, usually including foodstuffs. Many conservative, tax-conscious individuals were critical of domestic agricultural policies which resulted in surpluses and encouraged "rocking-chair farming." However, only a minority—largely in the lowest economic brackets among both Negroes and whites—felt this surplus should be distributed exclusively in this country. Even cotton interests and textile manufacturers who feared stimulation of foreign competition by capital and technical assistance, with but few exceptions, considered it preferable to feed undernourished foreigners rather than to let surpluses accumulate in warehouses at increasing storage expense. Many of the interviewees, however, added that we should do more to assure that recipients abroad know the source of these commodities, that food does not rot on foreign docks, and that corrupt politicians and bureaucrats do not use it to their own selfish advantage.

Likewise, relatively little active opposition was indicated to "businesslike" loans by the International Bank for Reconstruction and Development, private American banks, or private institutions and individuals to governments of underdeveloped countries or to private enterprises within them. The textile men who were mentioned previously as opponents of even foreign investment by American corporations were a small minority of the Southerners interviewed. Most, and undoubtedly much larger majorities of Southerners in general, had little information about the International Bank and its activities, but the image of this institution among the minority (largely within the upper and middle classes) who had some knowledge of it was generally favorable. Much of the hostility toward "Wall Street bankers" and the financial institutions of the North formerly fanned by neo-populists and demagogues generally has faded in recent years. Many conservative members of the elite in the sample who opposed capital assistance to governments of underdeveloped societies by our government felt that there would be sufficient private capital available both from abroad and within these countries without "giveaways" by Washington if these states pursued responsible fiscal and political policies. They also thought that if these countries really wanted economic growth, they should change their anti-American behavior, stop confiscating foreign enterprises, and set up climates which would attract private capital, as we did before World War I.

But whereas Southern support for technical assistance, the Peace Corps, distribution of surplus food in low per-capita income societies, "hard" loans by the International Bank or private banks, and investment by American private enterprise abroad seemed to have either remained stable or increased during the later fifties and the early sixties, frustration, disillusionment, criticism, and opposition with regard to supposedly expensive capital aid apparently increased significantly.

No surveys which singled out economic from other types of aid and posed similar queries over the decade ending in 1962 were available. However, as late as 1956–57 larger proportions of both Southerners and other Americans approved of the then current annual aid budgets of around four billion dollars than would reduce these expenditures. Thus in early 1956, 53 percent of Southerners (54 percent of white Southerners), compared with 56 percent of Northeasterners, 61 percent of Midwesterners (including residents of the Plains States) and 57 percent of Westerners, agreed that Congress should appropriate about four billion dollars, as in recent years, for the forthcoming fiscal year "to help prevent other countries going Communist." [60] A year later

60   AIPO 558, 1/4/56 (1,385).

the respective regional figures were 55 percent for the South, 60 percent for the Northeast, 59 percent for the Midwest, and 56 percent for the West.[61] In the spring of 1957, 52 percent of Southerners (54 percent of Southern whites) felt that the four billion dollars requested by President Eisenhower was "about the right amount of foreign aid" for the forthcoming fiscal year; one percent felt it was "not enough"; and 38 percent thought that it was "too much." Respective figures for the rest of the country were 55 percent, 3 percent, and 34 percent.[62] About the same time, Southerners were only a bit more inclined than other regional groups to suggest that the federal budget be reduced by cutting foreign aid.[63]

But by the spring of 1958, 50 percent of Southerners as compared with 42 percent of other Americans felt that Congress should appropriate less aid money than President Eisenhower requested for fiscal year 1959, that the somewhat less than four billion dollars he asked Congress for was "too much." [64] The author has located no completely comparable survey results for the period since 1958, but replies to two questions, one early that year and another almost three years later, tend to indicate significant decline in support of economic aid at magnitudes current at the time—approximately four billion dollars per annum. Thus, asked in January, 1958, whether we should "expand our program of aid and loans to Asian and African countries," "keep it about at the present level," or "cut it back," 11 percent of Southerners as compared with 21 percent of non-Southerners recommended expanding it, 39 percent of the former in contrast to 44 percent of the latter advised keeping it at approximately the "present level," and 24 percent versus 21 percent, respectively, advocated cutting it.[65] By late 1960 only 45 percent of Southerners (47 percent of Southern whites), compared with 64 percent of Northeasterners, 52 percent of Midwesterners (including residents of the Plains States), and 48 percent of Westerners, agreed that "the United States should give economic help to the poorer countries of the world even if those countries can't pay for it," [66] a minority of whom would certainly have advocated reduction in the prevailing order of magnitude of such economic assistance. Moreover the impression obtained from the Southern interviews and newspaper editorials is that Southern support for foreign economic assistance budgets requested by

61 AIPO 576, 12/12/56 (1,539).
62 Combined replies to NORC 402, 3/18/57 (536), and NORC 404, 4/26/57 (1,279).
63 AIPO 582, 4/23/57 (1,626).   64 AIPO 596, 3/4/58 (1,610).
65 Roper 963, January, 1958 (1,500).
66 SRC 440, September–November, 1960 (1,954).

President Eisenhower and then by President Kennedy probably declined still further. For instance, by 1961 more than half the newspapers in the sample advanced the view that capital assistance, or foreign aid in general, should be considerably reduced or even terminated, although most of these same papers had approved of the Marshall Plan and the Truman Doctrine.

By the time of conversations in the South for this study, opposition seemed particularly strong against outright grants to underdeveloped countries. Southerners interviewed were considerably less inclined to disapprove of loans, even at uneconomically low interest. Giving money away abroad was viewed by many as leading to contempt for the United States, to the feeling that Americans are "suckers"; peoples in backward countries neither understand nor appreciate the "something for nothing" philosophy of the "sentimental humanitarians." The same group tended to feel that loans on a business-like basis would save these peoples' self-respect, and they would be more likely to use loans more intelligently than "doles."

Nevertheless, opposition to "soft" loans, repayable in local currencies, and even to "harder" ones at low interest rates was widespread. Better-informed opponents felt that "soft" loans were "gimmicks" which camouflaged actual grants; that new regimes in unstable, underdeveloped countries would probably refuse to honor debts contracted by predecessors of more conservative political hue or would otherwise fail to pay; and that the few who would pay could easily give us inflated currency worth only a small fraction of the original loan. Furthermore, availability of "unbusiness-like" or "political" loans depresses the market for truly intelligent, economic ones and encourages sloppy economic and administrative practices in these backward lands.

As previous discussions have indicated, the shift of capital assistance to underdeveloped neutralist, including African, societies coupled with increasing anti-Western nationalistic, and often pro-socialist and generally leftist, pronouncements among aided countries has been a principal, and probably the primary, source of declining support for this type of relatively expensive intergovernmental aid. Opponents of aid to such countries among the informants tended to consider it absurd to assist people who are so irrational, unstable, and unbalanced in their judgments of the West as compared with their judgments of the Communists. They felt that we should not aid governments which seize American properties without fair compensation. Our aid seems to have encouraged anti-Americanism—poor people seldom appreciate what is given to them but, rather, feel resentful and envious of the giver. Furthermore, they continued, we cannot buy friends and real allies (our efforts to do so make us ridiculous in the eyes of the cynical leaders of these countries). The more money we put into Cuba, the more Castro was able to label us "imperialists." People like Castro respect firmness and vigor, not "do-goodism" and "bribes" to stay out of Communist hands. These opponents expressed the opinion that we are being played for "sugar daddies" by these opportunists, who threaten to commit suicide by going to the Soviets for help, and who, in any case, will be worth nothing to us when we need them. The more they receive, the more they want. The Soviets do much promising but deliver little —perhaps we ought to call the bluff of the Nassers and Nkrumahs and let them go to the Russians.

Southerners have been still less enthusiastic about aid to Communist Poland and Yugoslavia, labeling it a "strengthening [of] our self-declared enemies." For instance, even a few months after comparatively liberal and independent stirrings in Poland in late 1956, 52 percent of Southerners (51 percent of Southern whites) as compared with 47 percent of Northerners opposed sending economic aid to "Communist countries like Poland which have rebelled against Russian control"; 41 percent of Southerners (42 percent of Southern whites) as compared with 49 percent of Northerners approved.[67] A smaller minority of Southerners than of other Americans replying approved of aid, including foodstuffs, to Yugoslavia even during the initial years after Tito's break with Stalin in 1948.[68] At the end of 1950, during a period when the war of words between Belgrade and Moscow was relatively intense, 38 percent of Southerners, compared with 43 percent of other Americans,[69] felt the United States should continue aid to Yugoslavia. But by April, 1962, when tensions between these two Communist regimes had apparently abated considerably, only 17 percent of Southerners in contrast to 29 percent of those from other regions favored continuing aid to Tito's government.[70] Of those expressing opinions in 1962, more than two out of three Southerners wanted both economic and military aid to Yugoslavia terminated. It is the author's impression that the remaining 48 percent in the South who said they had no opinion on the matter would be disproportionately numbered among the opposed if they were pressed on the matter.

Opponents of aid to underdeveloped neutralist countries on surveys

---

67 NORC 404, 4/26/57 (1,279); see also NORC 399, 11/15/56 (1,286), and NORC 402, 3/18/57 (536). A slight majority in the South approved of aid to Poland in the fall of 1956 immediately after publicity on Polish disagreements with the U.S.S.R., but the fraction who were favorable declined thereafter (as it did elsewhere in the country).
68 AIPO 422, 7/28/48 (3,142), and AIPO 463, 10/6/50 (1,501).
69 AIPO 468, 12/1/50 (1,500).   70 AIPO 657, 4/4/62 (3,753).

and among the Southern interviewees were also, with only limited exceptions, against aid to Yugoslavia and Poland.[71] On the other hand, a considerable number who favored aid to India, Latin America, and even Africa opposed assistance to those Communist governments. Those who disapproved of aid to the latter, typically, also disapproved of expanding trade with the Soviet bloc, but a small fraction of opponents of aid to Yugoslavia and Poland would limit our economic relationships to profitable trade. Those Southerners who have been against both trade with and aid for Poland and Yugoslavia have also been for the most part unfavorable to intercultural exchanges with them, have tended to feel that our tensions with the Communists are incapable of resolution through diplomatic means, and have feared that war with the Reds is relatively likely.[72]

Southerners, like most other Americans, have thought that most United States capital assistance should be allocated and administered directly by our government rather than through the U.N. or other international agencies. Even before the entry of large numbers of new, largely underdeveloped members into the U.N., beginning in 1955, and before the ensuing attenuation of pro-Western majorities in the General Assembly, a somewhat larger majority of Southerners than of other Americans venturing views felt the United States should not turn over much, if any, of its assistance for Greece and Turkey or, later, for underdeveloped countries to administration by the world body.[73] For instance, when those citizens who thought "it is a good policy for the United States to try to help backward countries to raise their standards of living" were asked in April, 1950, whether this money should be handled entirely by our own government or some spent through the U.N., 53 percent in the South (52 percent in the white South) versus 43 percent in the North preferred that all aid be handled bilaterally; 39 percent in the South (40 percent in the white South) as opposed to 50 percent in the North would channel some through the international body.[74] Five years later, in 1955, 57 percent in the South (and in the white South) would handle all aid bilaterally and 23 percent would route some through the U.N.; the respective Northern figures were 52 and 27 percent.[75]

The expanded influence of the neutralists, including the Africans, in the U.N. and the resulting diminution of United States influence

71   NORC 399, 11/15/56 (1,286).   72   NORC 404, 4/26/57 (1,279).
73   AIPO 394, 4/9/47 (3,044); NORC 280, 4/17/50 (1,274); and NORC 370, 3/11/55 (1,225). This generalization also applied when Negroes were eliminated from samples.
74   NORC 280, 4/17/50 (1,274).   75   NORC 370, 3/11/55 (1,225).

there as well as the increasing criticisms of that organization in the Southern press and other local mass media have undoubtedly reduced support for channeling economic aid, other than inexpensive technical assistance, through the U.N. Many of the Southerners interviewed for this study, including a considerable fraction of those who supported the general idea of economic aid, felt that it would be subject to "log-rolling" and other undesirable influences, that the Communists would distort its use and perhaps get some themselves, and that there would be even less identification than now of the American source of the assistance in the minds of the recipient peoples. On the other hand, the preponderant majority of those who had heard of Paul Hoffman, the U.N. Special Fund, or other technical assistance programs of the U.N. or its specialized agencies was rather favorable toward these activities and believed that the United States should help to support them financially if other industrialized nations also did so.

Southerners in favor of proposals to put economic aid on a long-term rather than a year-to-year basis have been a minority, and a smaller one than in the North.[76] Most Southerners among the interviewees seemed to trust the judgment of Congress more than that of the "bureaucrats" in the State Department or other executive agencies in the foreign aid field on aid expenditures. They felt that "waste" and support of unworthy projects would increase if allocations and appropriations were not made annually by both houses of Congress. A few thought that our promise to finance individual projects over a period of several years might reduce the overall cost of aid by cutting lost

76 NORC 382, 1/26/56 (1,238), asked the question, "In the past, our economic aid to other countries has been granted for only one year at a time. Some projects, like large dams, require five to ten years to complete. Do you think that in some cases like these the U.S. should agree to contribute for a period of years—or should we refuse to commit ourselves beyond a year at a time, when it comes to economic aid to other countries?" In reply, 20 percent of Southerners (22 percent of Southern whites) as compared with 28 percent of Northerners thought we should agree to furnish aid for a period of years; 67 percent of the former versus 64 percent of the latter would commit ourselves for only one year at a time.

However, linking the idea of long-term commitments to the wishes of President Eisenhower resulted in more favorable replies. Shortly afterwards, NORC 386, 4/20/56 (1,224), asked, "President Eisenhower has asked Congress for authority to put a small portion of our economic aid on a long term basis—that is, our government would have the authority, which it does not have now, to commit itself to help a few countries build such things as highways and dams that would take five or ten years to complete. Do you think this is a good idea, or a bad idea?" Forty-four percent of Southerners (43 percent of white Southerners) versus 52 percent of Northerners replied that it was a "good idea" and 38 percent of Southerners as compared with 31 percent of Northerners that it was a "bad" one. See also NORC 404, 4/26/57 (1,279).

motion and confusion, but most Southerners of conservative economic persuasion feared that such power in the hands of the executive would have the opposite effect.

Supporters and Opponents of Capital Assistance to Underdeveloped Lands

By the early 1960's, those Southerners among the interviewees who approved of capital assistance to underdeveloped neutralist countries, particularly in Africa, and of aid programs for Yugoslavia and Poland were with few exceptions general internationalists: they believed that we live in an increasingly interdependent world; that military policy is only one aspect of foreign policy (one designed primarily to prevent armed aggression while we use the time thus gained to encourage development of backward lands and relaxation of totalitarian controls in the Communist bloc); that expansion of world trade is important to our national political and economic interests; that we must strive to make the U.N. an effective instrument for international order and progress; and so on. With few exceptions they believed that decolonization is inevitable and that we should attempt through aid and other means to facilitate independence with a minimum of disorder and antagonism to the West and to the democratic process.

The interviews indicated that support of expanded aid under the Kennedy administration was very probably most prevalent among the college-educated (particularly the offspring of the college-educated and relatively prosperous), the economically comfortable, and members of the liberal professions—teachers, educated clergymen, lawyers, social workers, and perhaps a few others. Advocates of aid at the levels requested by the President were located primarily in cities and college towns, but they were present in small numbers among the socially secure, educated strata in the rural areas and in small towns as well. They were more evident in complex, scientific industries than in low-wage, protectionist ones, but there were a few, usually well-educated and rather young, in even low-technology enterprises. Religious Southerners who advocated large aid budgets tended to have some interest in the social implications of the gospel, even if they were not particularly enthusiastic about the liberal ideas typically associated with the social gospel among many Northern clergymen; few were strong fundamentalists. Jews were more apt to endorse vigorous aid programs than other ethnic groups, and Negroes were the least likely to do so. Most supporters of these programs were relatively liberal or moderate about social change and segregation in the South. Finally, foreign-aid supporters were disproportionately numerous among Southerners who read critical national publications dealing with world affairs and otherwise exposed themselves to national thinking on international problems.

However, many thoughtful Southerners among the informants who believed that foreign aid is in general desirable were uneasy about certain aspects of it, particularly under the Kennedy administration. Some feared that enthusiasts in and out of the government might be laying foundations for future public reactions against aid by overoptimism and exaggerated expectations. Some Southern liberals felt that "overselling" of the U.N. in its early years as an instrument capable of preserving peace had been partly responsible for some recent disillusionments with that organization and that Northern liberals might be repeating this unfortunate history by grandiose and utopian claims for aid. They also felt that our leaders should point out to the public more than they have that the countries receiving our aid differ greatly among themselves in their economies, social organization, values, and politics; that many of them are, or will probably become, unstable, turbulent societies with rather demagogic leadership; that our ability to influence them through aid (or other means) is relatively small and, at best, long term in nature; that the processes of development we are trying to encourage are complex; that we still do not know a great deal about how best to influence change in our national interest, although through experimentation over the last decade or so we know more now than previously. These informed Southerners thought that our national leaders, starting with the President, should be preparing the people for years, perhaps decades, of foreign aid to counter the sentiment that short-run projects, such as the Marshall Plan, should have solved our problems with backward societies. Our leaders ought to be educating Americans to expect frustrations and failures as the price of the necessary experimentation and of succeeding to some degree in a reasonable proportion of these aided countries. They should inform the voters that aid is a means of increasing somewhat the probability that some recipients will develop in a significantly more orderly, moderate, democratic fashion, in line with our long-run interests.

Furthermore, relatively well-informed Southerners who believed in aid also mentioned that our government has to share much of the blame for the skepticism, even cynicism, of some of the public who have never been told that much of our aid is not and has not been for development purposes, but rather is for bolstering imperfect, often rather ineffective and irritating, regimes because the alternative groups which might otherwise take power are more anti-American, pro-Communist, or irresponsible. These same Southerners felt that voters should be informed that some of our aid projects are consequently somewhat like bribes to rather undeserving, narrow regimes and that much of our assistance has been in military supplies and budget-balancing subsidies in order to prevent the bankruptcy of governments which would otherwise collapse due to military expenditures or lack of national resources.

Moreover, many relatively sophisticated Southerners who supported the general idea of aid took the position that we should be more careful and realistic in selecting the countries and projects to be assisted and the Americans to administer these efforts. Suggestions that we concentrate our aid more, limit it to fewer, more deserving countries and endeavors, and organize it more tightly and efficiently have been well received among thoughtful Southerners. They believed that many claims of waste, stupidity, mediocrity, and corruption in the aid programs in underdeveloped countries have probably been justified and that the foreign governments and individuals involved were often obviously poor risks at the time we extended aid. Although we should be cautious about encouraging extremists and social revolution in underdeveloped countries, we should demand more effective guarantees that the aid will really improve the lot of the masses. Moreover, they believed that we should be less willing to turn the other cheek when American property is seized without adequate payment and when these governments enact legislation designed to discourage foreign investment while demanding more intergovernmental aid. There was little support (even among sophisticated Southerners) in 1959–1962 for aid "without strings."

In addition, a considerable number of the Southern proponents of the general idea of aid felt that other developed societies were not bearing their just share of the expense. They believed our government should more vigorously urge those countries which were aided by the Marshall Plan to shoulder more of the burden. Unfortunately, only a handful seemed to know that Britain and France in recent years had expended as large or larger proportions of their national incomes and governmental budgets on nonmilitary foreign aid, mostly to their former dependencies, than had the United States.

On the other hand, Southerners who wanted economic assistance to underdeveloped countries to be seriously reduced or eliminated included virtually all isolationists and neo-isolationists of various nuances; most who emphasized unilateral rather than multilateral actions in foreign affairs; many who were apathetic about foreign policy; and most of those who believed we should concentrate our resources in the foreign relations field on military strength (both conventional and thermonuclear), shift our emphasis more toward alliance with Western Europe, Canada, Australia, and New Zealand, and take a generally less conciliatory position toward Communists, neutralists, underdeveloped "leftists," and others whose interests were apparently opposed to those of the West.

Statistically these Southerners were disproportionately numerous among the less educated, the lower-middle and particularly the lower social orders, the rural population, religious fundamentalists, white supremacists, individuals with authoritarian personality inclinations, and white residents of sections with large proportions of Negroes. Although some relatively well-educated and better-informed people would greatly reduce economic aid to underdeveloped countries, the less Southerners knew of world affairs, the more they were apt to be of this persuasion. Both underprivileged Negroes and whites seemed especially likely to think that this money should be spent at home.

The opponents of aid among the prosperous, on the other hand, were against spending this money at all; they wanted instead to reduce our national debt, alleviate our international balance of payments, and cut taxes. They often mentioned that we were probably playing into Communist hands by spending ourselves into bankruptcy. Our "leftist" domestic programs seemed ill-conceived and costly enough, but now the liberals want to expand them to backward countries at our expense. Administration of extensive aid programs was viewed by a number of its well-to-do opponents as one more excuse for "big government bureaucracy," which tends to be expensive and to meddle in one's private affairs. Charity without end saps human initiative and self-assurance and creates ne'er-do-wells waiting for handouts. Rather than encouraging socialism abroad, our government should be stimulating private investment. According to local observers, many Southern opponents of foreign aid in 1959–62 who had become prosperous fairly recently were considerably less opposed to aid abroad when they were less affluent and paid lower taxes.

In the late 1950's and early 1960's lack of information about foreign aid was a major correlate of opposition. According to national surveys and the interviews, most who would severely curtail our economic assistance had only vague, confused, or false images about the program itself. They tended for the most part to overestimate considerably the order of magnitude of this aid,[77] and, especially, of outright grants, to think of cash rather than goods purchased in the United States being

77 See especially AIPO 667, January, 1963 (4,383).

sent abroad, and to lump together military aid, defense support, agricultural surplus disposal, capital assistance, bankers' loans, "soft" loans, long-term loans at low interest, and "giveaways." They frequently exaggerated the proportion of our aid which has been economic rather than military, or grants rather than loans. Nor did more than a handful of those who would drastically reduce aid think in terms of different levels of development and readiness to use aid of such disparate societies as India and the Congo. And most Southern newspapers and organizations which opposed aid in 1961 seemed little more discriminating or factual.

Therefore, the emotional reaction against foreign aid typically attacked the concept in general rather than singling out some aspects for criticism and others for support. However, conversations with influential local individuals who opposed "give-aways" abroad indicated that a number of them in fact did not disapprove under certain conditions of: technical assistance (if we send able people abroad); military supplies and advice to our more reliable allies who are "really trying to help themselves"; commercial loans at normal interest rates by the International Bank, the Export-Import Bank, and private financial institutions; activities of the U.N. Special Fund (once they were described to them); training of worthy foreigners at American institutions; feeding underfed non-Communist peoples with our agricultural surpluses; and even some long-term loans by our government for particularly promising projects, such as schools and hospitals, in better-run countries. But in order to elicit these rather favorable reactions one was obliged to question the individual on each specific program in turn.

A related factor was that most opponents of economic assistance, as well as some of its supporters, thought of it primarily in terms of emergency charity for starving, homeless, sick, or otherwise unfortunate individuals—an international community chest—rather than as capital assistance. The concept of our national interest in the basic economic development of backward economies had not made much impression among more than a small minority of the Southerners interviewed. In some respects, this image of feeding the hungry and caring for the sick generated support which would be lacking for such "un-Southern" ideas as "progress" through organized planning and development, or "socialist utopias" (see pp. 362–65).

Nevertheless, lack of understanding of our objective of long-range economic development abroad has been a major reason for lack of support of foreign aid. Surveys have determined that Southerners, like other Americans who have thought of aid primarily as charity or "relief," have been significantly more apt than those who have mentioned economic, social, and political development as objectives to believe that aid has gone on too long, to favor large reductions or elimination of aid, to oppose guaranteeing funds for more than one year, and to feel that "charity begins at home." [78] The number of traditionalists who opposed industrial development and urbanization on principle in the early sixties was only a small minority; by this time most white Southerners wanted industrialization of the South, albeit often, if possible, without changing appreciably the social and racial system. The task of convincing some of them that industrialization is also desirable abroad should not be impossible.

Other trends of thought which appeared to be at least somewhat more prevalent in the South than elsewhere seemed to reinforce lack of support for capital assistance. Many of our informants wondered if we would really succeed in raising the living standards of these backward societies, considering all the obstacles indigenous to them. Northern liberals seemed to these Southerners to have overly idealistic, unrealistic images of the true nature of backward peoples and their leaders and of the possibilities of "reforming" them through economic means (or any other way). Some relatively sophisticated Southerners felt that our programs would help unsettle social systems which have functioned for hundreds of years with minimal violence and chaos and as a consequence produce immoderation, disorder, dissension, and release of mass passions to the advantage of anti-American demagogues like Castro, Nasser, and Lumumba. Nor did these same Southerners think we could expect to change very much the attitudes and actions of landed classes in Latin America and Asia—perhaps their grandchildren would be more open to modern thinking. Meanwhile foreign leaders from landed classes are more likely to be anti-Communist and amenable to American interests. Furthermore, the view that prosperous, economically developed peoples are more apt to function in our national interest than less developed ones was considered by a number of Southerners, some relatively well informed, others not, as being open to serious question; living standards, they felt, have little bearing on the appeals of communism, fascism, or other types of extremism hostile to our national interests. For instance, National Socialist Germany, imperialist Japan, and Soviet Russia have been industrialized menaces to world peace, and Communist China will undoubtedly become a worse threat than before when she becomes industrialized. In addition, revolutionary, pro-

78 SRC surveys of November–December, 1949 (606); NORC 166, 6/1/49 (1,300); and AIPO 455, 4/28/50 (2,830).

Communist Cuba has been more prosperous than stable, anti-Communist Paraguay. Nor has the Communist appeal in Italy declined with expanded economic development; instead, most Italian Communists are among the industrial workers rather than the agrarians. They also felt that if we succeed in industrializing Africa and Asia, we may well strengthen peoples with whom we have little in common so that they become more dangerous opponents; or at least we may be helping to industrialize peoples to attack one another with more lethal weapons than they possessed as peasants or jungle tribes. Thus, urbanization and economic "progress" may entail worldwide disorder and rebound to the benefit of the Communists.

Finally, a number believed that we should channel more of our assistance through private agencies which have dedicated staffs and considerable experience in these countries. Many who were active advocates of foreign religious missions were not particularly favorable to assistance through the federal government. Evangelical Protestants have long supported missionaries in Africa, Latin America, and Asia, and they seemed frequently to feel that these ministers, teachers, and other church-connected groups have done more good for less money than have federal programs. Some thought primarily in terms of converting heathens and caring for the sick, famished, and otherwise unfortunate, that is, of aid as charity, as mentioned previously.

CHAPTER 6

THE
UNITED NATIONS SYSTEM

S outhern newspapers and opinion surveys of the 1930's indicate
that the Southern public, like its political leaders, was more favorable
to the League of Nations, the World Court, and international organization generally than other regional groups, including Northeasterners.
With but few exceptions the Southern press favored American support
of efforts within the League of Nations to obstruct Japanese aggression in Manchuria in the early thirties.[1] In 1937, 44 percent of Southerners felt that we should join the League, compared with 33 percent
of Northeasterners, 31 percent of Midwesterners (including residents
of the Plains States), and 27 percent of Westerners.[2] In almost every
annual report from 1924 to 1936, the Social Service Commission of
the Southern Baptists—by far the most numerous religious group in
the South (see p. 439)—urged the United States to join the Permanent
Court of International Justice, and finally carried its appeal directly
to the members of the Senate Foreign Relations Committee.[3]

With entry of the United States into the war, the country as a whole
quickly became more favorable than ever before to active United States

1 Denna F. Fleming, *The United States and World Organization, 1920–1933*
(New York: Columbia University Press, 1938), 467–74.
2 AIPO 101, 10/18/37 (2,932); See also AIPO 106, 12/13/37 (2,859); AIPO 133,
9/23/38 (3,400); AIPO 237, 5/20/41 (3,089); and AIPO 243, 7/29/41 (3,048).
3 John Lee Eighmy, "The Social Conscience of Southern Baptists from 1900 to
the Present as Reflected in their Organized Life" (Ph.D. dissertation, University
of Missouri, 1959), 61.

participation in whatever international organization might be feasible after the defeat of the Axis. The differences between the South and the rest of the country narrowed greatly; in July, 1942, 78 percent of Southerners as compared with 71 percent of Northeasterners, 74 percent of Midwesterners (residents of the Plains States included), and 74 percent of Westerners felt we should participate in such an international body after the war.[4] By early 1944, even this small Southern lead had disappeared, and has not reappeared.[5]

The First Decade

As in most fields of world affairs, the Southern public has from the beginning been less informed than the rest of the country on most aspects of the U.N. and its activities.[6] The gradual narrowing of the gap between average levels of education in the South versus the non-South since the war has helped to reduce this lag in knowledge, but the proportions of "no opinions," "don't knows," and "undecideds" on surveys in 1959–62 showed that significantly larger fractions of Southerners than others were still uninformed about the basic structure, functions, and activities of the U.N. and its specialized agencies and that interregional differences were larger when Southerners and Northerners were questioned for more specific or detailed knowledge on this organization.

Popular support of active American participation in the U.N. has been more prevalent among the better educated and informed throughout the United States, including the South. Given the generally lower level of education and knowledge of world affairs in the South, one might assume that Southerners were on the average less favorable to the U.N. than other Americans. Southerners were more critical of the U.N. in some spheres, which will be mentioned shortly; however, on most aspects of the organization there was no significant difference between the regions. When differences in surveys were larger than those likely to be due to chance alone, they were only slightly so, and they normally disappeared when Negroes or non-voters were eliminated from national samples or when Southerners and Northerners of

---

4 AIPO Release of 7/5/42.

5 NORC 223, February, 1944 (1,006); AIPO 320, 6/7/44 (2,924); NORC 230, November, 1944 (2,030); NORC 231, December 1944 (2,471); NORC 233, March, 1945 (2,500); and NORC 234, April, 1945 (2,495).

6 E.g., NORC 235, July, 1945 (2,572); NORC 139, 2/2/46 (1,263); NORC 143, 6/21/46 (1,307); NORC 241, May, 1946 (2,589); NORC 151, 6/24/47 (1,273); NORC 154, 12/4/47 (1,293); and NORC 300, 3/20/51 (1,300).

comparable levels of education were compared with respect to their thinking on the U.N.

Ratification and Membership

Only approximately 10 percent of Southerners in the spring and summer of 1945 opposed ratification of the U.N. Charter by the Senate and United States membership in the new international organization. This figure was three percentage points above the average of the other regions, but this difference disappeared when Negroes or non-voters were omitted from consideration.[7]

All fifty-three papers in the sample favored ratification and membership. Racially and economically conservative papers which were to become strongly critical of the U.N. in the late 1950's and early 1960's pressed for favorable United States action and continued to support active participation over most of the next decade. Thus, the Augusta (Georgia) *Chronicle* (April 27, 1945 and January 31, 1949) saw the new organization as "our only hope for keeping the peace." The Jackson *Clarion-Ledger* commented on April 26, 1945, "The majority of Mississippians, we think . . . want the U.S. to participate fully in the creation and functioning of the world organization," and, later on August 31, 1946, "The machinery for handling international differences has been established in the U.N." The Charleston *News and Courier* said on June 30, 1945, "The U.S. Senate should ratify . . . without delay. . . . No one can say with certainty that the charter will forever keep the peace . . . but the charter is a great step toward peace." On January 1, 1949, this same paper observed, "The U.N. still exists and while it lives there is hope for peace." The Columbia (South Carolina) *State* noted on June 26, 1945, "A great step toward world peace has been taken . . . the League of Nations was sabotaged in our country . . . how ineffective it was . . . due largely . . . to the failure of the U.S. Senate to confirm Woodrow Wilson's ideas . . . we must have learned a lesson . . . now for ratification and actual enforcement." The Little Rock *Arkansas Democrat* (June 24, 1945) blasted "the little group of wilful men" in the Senate who rejected the league and the World Court and concluded similarly that "narrow-minded" men should not be allowed to duplicate this failure. The Montgomery *Advertiser* opined (June 26, 1945), "Imperfect though the U.N. Charter may be, it is a long step forward toward a civilized world," and, two years later on June 17, 1947, "There is a chance yet that a real working U.N. can

7 Combined replies to similar questions in NORC 233, March, 1945 (2,500); AIPO 350, 6/27/45 (3,086); and NORC 235, July, 1945 (2,572).

be put together from the seeming wreckage. We must keep working for that slim chance."

Similar views were expressed in the editorials of the other traditionalist and conservative papers which were to become profoundly critical of the U.N. and our participation in it by the late 1950's—the Charleston *Evening News*, the Columbia (South Carolina) *Record*, the Meridian (Mississippi) *Star*, the Greenville (South Carolina) *News*, the Montgomery *Alabama Journal*, the Beaufort (South Carolina) *Gazette*, the Shreveport (Louisiana) *Journal*, and the Savannah *Morning News*, and others. Some papers voiced certain reservations—particularly that an effective U.N. would depend on continuing agreement among the permanent members of the Security Council (or the Great Powers) and their active support of the organization as a means of enforcing the peace—and few viewed it as an agency which could achieve a utopian world of peace-loving peoples, a be-all and end-all of human institutions. However, all viewed participation as desirable, as did the vast majority of Southern voters and political leaders.

The South and Stronger International Organization

Southerners from the beginning of its organization have viewed the U.N. primarily, and more often than not exclusively, as an instrument for preventing war. The proportion of those offering views which has mentioned preservation of peace as the major function of the U.N. has varied from survey to survey—between 55 and 80 percent—but only one fifth or less of Southerners questioned has mentioned any one other general objective or function of that organization, such as technical and economic assistance. Inhabitants of other geographical and cultural regions also have tended in the majority to perceive the U.N. largely as an organization to preserve peace,[8] but Southerners have been at least somewhat more inclined to mention this purpose exclusively.

Although it could be argued that Southerners have been more apt to be nationalistic, or even chauvinistic, than other regional groups, they were at least as willing as other Americans during the first postwar decade to limit American sovereignty to the extents proposed by our Presidents, Secretaries of State, and other national leaders in order to strengthen the peace-keeping powers of the U.N.

Since Southerners generally are less abstract and utopian than other Americans (see pp. 362–65), it is not surprising that somewhat smaller proportions of them than of other Americans were enthusiastic about

8 William A. Scott and Stephen B. Withey, *The United States and the United Nations* (New York: Manhattan Publishing Co., 1958), Chapter 3.

drastic surrenders of sovereignty, such as transforming the U.N. into a world government or creating such a supranational regime outside the U.N.[9] For instance, in March, 1951, 28 percent of Southerners (30 percent of Southern whites), compared with 33 percent of Northeasterners, 38 percent of Midwesterners (including inhabitants of the Plains States), and 40 percent of Westerners, said they favored the "idea of world government," whereas 31 percent of Southerners (and of Southern whites), 28 percent of Northeasterners, 25 percent of Midwesterners, and 24 percent of Westerners opposed this idea. Thus, only in the South did a majority replying feel negatively about world government as an idea in 1951.[10] But when informed in a general way about the meaning of world government, 45 percent of Southerners (47 percent of Southern whites) versus 50 percent of Northeasterners, 48 percent of Midwesterners (including residents of the Plains States), and 52 percent of Westerners agreed that the U.N. should be "strengthened to make it a world government with power to control the armed forces of all nations, including those of the U.S."; 38 percent of Southerners (and white Southerners), 34 percent of Northeasterners, 37 percent of Midwesterners, and 35 percent of Westerners were opposed.[11] By 1955, 33 percent of Southerners (35 percent of Southern whites) in contrast to 41 percent of Northerners approved of this proposal; 40 percent of Southerners (42 percent of Southern whites) versus 42 percent of Northerners disapproved.[12] As these figures indicate, interregional differences, although sometimes significant statistically and more often than not in the expected direction when not significant, were limited. The traditionalist Montgomery *Advertiser* and Savannah *Morning News* apparently reflected a considerable segment of Southern opinion in 1947 when the former on May 16 approved of further surrender of American sovereignty to a world government, and the latter commented on June 19, that "the veto vitiates the whole U.N. as a real peace organization" and (on June 12) "if the nations of the world really desire universal peace they would be wise to stop kidding themselves and . . . establish a world government."

Although Southerners were less inclined than Northerners to feel that the U.N. could transform the nature of world politics and sharply

9 AIPO 373, 6/12/46 (3,071); AIPO 375, 7/24/46 (3,124); AIPO release of 8/18/46; NORC 146, 11/15/46 (1,300); NORC 157, 4/22/48 (1,280); NORC 166, 6/1/49 (1,300); NORC 167, 6/30/49 (1,289); NORC 171, 11/11/49 (1,300); AIPO 455, 5/2/50 (2,850); NORC 291, 10/18/50 (1,305); AIPO 473, 3/24/51 (2,102); Roper 737, August, 1953 (3,502); and AIPO 545, 3/22/55 (1,630).
10 AIPO 473, 3/24/51 (2,102).
11 *Ibid.* 12 AIPO 545, 3/22/55 (1,630).

reduce the need for United States armed power in the postwar world, they were at least as likely to approve of active United States participation and multilateral cooperation in that organization. For example, in late 1946, 74 percent of Southerners (76 percent of Southern whites), compared with 72 percent of Northeasterners, 68 percent of Midwesterners, 65 percent of residents of the Plain States, 64 percent of inhabitants of the Rocky Mountain region, and 76 percent of Far Westerners, felt the permanent U.N. headquarters should stay in the United States rather than move elsewhere; only 5 percent of the South in contrast to 10 percent, 9 percent, 7 percent, 7 percent, and 6 percent, respectively, would have it moved.[13] When some U.N. officials proposed moving the headquarters to Europe in 1948 because of lack of funds for building in this country, 68 percent of Southerners, 57 percent of Northeasterners, 63 percent of Midwesterners, 66 percent of residents of the Plains States, and 56 percent of Westerners felt this would be a "bad thing" and only 6 percent of Southerners versus 15 percent, 10 percent, 8 percent, and 9 percent, respectively, felt it would be a "good thing." [14] The minority of Southern whites who felt we should withdraw from the U.N. if the Soviets continued to block the will of the majority in 1947 was only 13 percent as compared with 70 percent who felt we should remain even under such frustrations; this was only a slightly larger (and not statistically significant) proportion for withdrawal than in the rest of the country.[15] The figure rose several percentage points in the South after the Chinese invasion of Korea, but it did so elsewhere in the United States as well. The figure for those who would withdraw from the U.N. returned by mid-1952 to between 6 and 11 percent in the South, on the average only slightly above the North, and remained at this level through the end of the first postwar decade.[16]

Moreover, when asked in early 1953, before the end of the Korean War, whether the U.N. was "in any way dangerous to our own country's interests," only 17 percent of Southerners replied affirmatively, not significantly more than in the North.[17] When queried a year later whether the U.N. had made it any "harder for us to do the things we've

13   AIPO 384, 11/14/46 (3,203).
14   AIPO 421, 7/1/48 (3,117). See also NORC 334, 12/29/52 (1,291).
15   AIPO 402, 8/6/47 (3,000), and AIPO 403, 8/27/47 (2,999) combined.
16   NORC 298, 1/30/51 (1,236); AIPO 470, 1/12/51 (1,489); AIPO 475, 5/17/51 (2,070); AIPO 482, 11/9/51 (2,021); NORC 325, 5/28/52 (1,265); NORC 337, 2/11/53 (1,291); NORC 341-2, 6/30/53 (1,291); NORC 349, 11/25/53 (1,300); NORC 364, 10/23/54 (518); NORC 374, 8/4/55 (1,262); NORC 386, 4/20/56 (1,224); and NORC 399, 11/15/56 (1,286).
17   NORC 337, 2/11/53 (1,291).

wanted to do in the world," Southern whites were about as likely as Northerners of the same race to feel that the U.N. had made it easier rather than harder.[18]

During the period from the end of the war into 1956, clear majorities of Southerners approved of the idea of setting up international police forces on either a permanent or an *ad hoc* basis.[19] Thus, in April, 1948, 57 percent of Southerners as compared with 50 percent of Northeasterners, 46 percent of Midwesterners (inhabitants of the Plains States included), and 50 percent of Westerners approved of the idea of sending United States troops to Palestine as part of a U.N. force.[20] In May, 1951, 53 percent of white Southerners (50 percent of all Southerners) versus 57 percent of white Northerners (and of all Northerners) favored giving "the U.N. the power to call out American troops, along with those of other countries, to help stop an aggressor"; 33 percent of white Southerners (and of all Southerners) versus 34 percent of white (and all) Northerners were opposed. Of those who favored this suggestion, 43 percent of Southerners as compared with 37 percent of Northerners agreed that in such a case our armed forces should move into action right away in support of the U.N. decision without awaiting approval by the Congress; 51 percent of the former versus 60 percent of the latter would not permit such action until Congress had approved.[21] In November, 1956, 62 percent of Southerners in contrast to 77 percent of Northeasterners, 68 percent of Midwesterners (including residents of the Plains States), and 74 percent of Westerners favored "the U.N. forming an international police force, made up of volunteer soldiers from small nations with a reserve force made up of soldiers from the big powers, to be used when needed"; 11 percent of Southerners as compared with 7 percent, 12 percent, and 9 percent, respectively, disapproved.[22] About the same time, 62 percent of Southerners versus 77 percent of Northeasterners, 67 percent of Midwesterners (including residents of the Plains States), and 73 percent of Westerners approved of the "U.N.'s plan to set up a police force to patrol the borders between Israel and Egypt"; and 43 percent, 43 percent, 43 percent, and 59 percent, respectively, approved of having United States forces take part in such an eventuality.[23]

18 NORC 355, 4/22/54 (1,207).
19 NORC 155, 2/25/48 (1,271); NORC 157, 4/22/48 (1,280); NORC 158, 6/2/48 (1,295); NORC 162, 11/23/48 (1,300); AIPO 462, 9/29/50 (1,500); NORC 307, 5/24/51 (1,282); AIPO 517, 7/2/53 (1,545); AIPO 574 11/7/56 (1,505); and AIPO release of 11/18/56.
20 NORC 157, 4/22/48 (1,280).   21 NORC 307, 5/24/51 (1,282).
22 AIPO release of 11/18/56.   23 AIPO 574, 11/7/56 (1,505).

Southerners, particularly white Southerners and Southern voters, were also as likely and in some cases slightly more likely than other Americans to feel that the U. N. should be strengthened,[24] that it was not "too powerful in world affairs," [25] that it should be given more "power," [26] that it was "useful," [27] that it had "justified its existence," [28] and that it was important for us to make the U.N. a success and that we should strive to do so.[29] Southerners were also about as or, in the case of whites especially, a bit more inclined than Northerners to say they were satisfied with the progress the U.N. had made "so far," [30] that it

24 AIPO 412, 2/4/48 (3,185). Sixty-three percent of the South as compared with 64 percent of the Northeast, 64 percent of the Midwest, and 58 percent of the West approved of the idea of a "world convention of the United Nations . . . to amend the U.N. Charter to make it a stronger organization"; 14 percent of the South versus 12, 13, and 17 percent, respectively, disapproved.

25 NORC 348, 9/24/53 (526).

26 NORC 171, 11/11/49 (1,300).

27 NORC 303, 6/29/51 (1,300); NORC 332, 10/15/52 (1,291); NORC 370, 3/11/55 (1,225); NORC 386, 4/20/56 (1,224); NORC 398, 10/25/56 (1,295); NORC 399, 11/15/56 (1,286), and NORC 402, 3/18/57 (536). Replies to this question, except for the first year or so of the Korean War, have been remarkably stable. As the following table indicates, even the failure of the U.N. to take effective action toward Soviet suppression of the uprising in Hungary and the controversial behavior of the U.N. toward the Suez crisis in the fall of 1956 had no appreciable effect on public perception of the organization as useful to our national interests.

	All Southerners	White Southerners	All Northerners	White Northerners
	U.N. is very useful			
April 20, 1956	48	43	40	39
Nov. 15, 1956	48	41	42	42
	Only moderately useful			
April 20, 1956	39	43	52	53
Nov. 15, 1956	41	49	52	51
	No use at all			
April 20, 1956	4	4	4	3
Nov. 15, 1956	4	4	3	3
	No opinion			
April 20, 1956	9	10	4	5
Nov. 15, 1956	7	6	3	4

28 AIPO 512, 2/20/53 (1,548), and AIPO 545, 3/22/55 (1,630).

29 NORC 157, 4/22/48 (1,280); NORC 164, 3/3/49 (1,300); NORC 314, 11/22/51 (1,237); and AIPO 575, 11/20/56 (1,502).

30 NORC 143, 6/21/46 (1,307); NORC 243, 8/21/46 (1,286); AIPO 384, 11/14/46 (3,203); AIPO 386, 12/11/46 (3,029); NORC 154, 12/4/47 (1,293); NORC 155, 2/25/48 (1,271); AIPO 417, 4/21/48 (3,165); NORC 160, 7/30/48 (1,300); AIPO 435, 1/5/49 (3,112); NORC 164, 3/3/49 (1,300); NORC 165, 4/19/49 (1,300); NORC 167, 6/30/49 (1,284); NORC 171, 11/11/49 (1,300); NORC 307, 5/24/51 (1,282); NORC 314, 11/22/51 (1,237); NORC 325, 5/28/52 (1,262); NORC 341-2, 6/30/53 (1,291); NORC 347, 8/21/53 (526); NORC 337, 2/11/53 (1,291); NORC 351, 1/21/54 (1,300); NORC 374, 8/4/55 (1,262); NORC 386, 4/20/56 (1,226); and

was important and its importance was not decreasing,[31] that they "approved" of the U.N.,[32] and that the organization had done a "good" or a "fair job in trying to solve the problems it has had to face." [33] Like

---

NORC 399, 11/15/56 (1,286). The growth of satisfaction with the U.N. over the decade since its initial meetings in 1946 and the decline in the proportion of citizens who voiced no opinion, said they did not know, or expressed other indications of apathy toward the world organization are apparent in the following table:

	Satisfied with U.N. Progress		Dissatisfied		No opinion	
	8/21/46	1/5/49	8/21/46	1/5/49	8/21/46	1/5/49
Southern whites	39	32	40	42	21	26
All Southerners	38	32	40	42	22	26
Northeasterners	29	27	53	47	18	26
Midwesterners	33	28	49	47	18	25
Westerners	37	28	51	50	12	22
	4/20/56	11/15/56	4/20/46	11/15/56	4/20/56	11/15/56
Southern whites	73	75	15	16	13	9
All Southerners	75	74	13	15	12	11
Northern whites	73	70	17	23	10	7
All Northerners	73	71	17	22	10	7

31   AIPO 468, 12/1/50 (1,500); AIPO 475, 5/17/51 (2,070); AIPO 519, 8/13/53 (1,613); and AIPO 575, 11/20/56 (1,502). At the time of the 1953 survey, for instance, 34 percent in the South as compared with 37 percent in the Northeast, 39 percent in the Midwest (including the Plains States), and 34 percent in the West thought the U.N. was increasing in importance; 22 percent in the South as compared with 21, 16, and 14 percent, respectively, thought that its importance remained about the same as previously; and 28 percent in the South compared with 29, 33, and 44 percent, respectively, felt that it was decreasing in importance. In 1956, 85 percent in the South versus 85 percent in the Northeast, 83 percent in the Midwest (including the Plains States), and 89 percent in the West felt the U.N. was "very important."

32   In the summer of 1954, 78 percent of Southerners, 73 percent of Northeasterners, 77 percent of Midwesterners (including residents of the Plains States), and 80 percent of Westerners said they approved of the U.N.; 9, 13, 11, and 10 percent, respectively, said they disapproved; and 13, 14, 12, and 10 percent, respectively, expressed no opinion, said they did not know, or were undecided. See AIPO 534, 7/14/54 (1,549). About a year later, 78 percent of Southerners, 79 percent of Northeasterners, 77 percent of Midwesterners (including residents of the Plains States), and 74 percent of Westerners approved of the U.N.; 6, 8, 9, and 8 percent, respectively, disapproved; and 16, 13, 14, and 18 percent, respectively, ventured no opinion, were undecided, or said they did not know. See AIPO 548, 6/1/55 (1,462).

33   NORC 241, May 19, 1946 (2,589); AIPO 468, 12/1/50 (1,500); AIPO 475, 5/17/51 (2,070); AIPO 519, 8/13/53 (1,613); AIPO 524, 12/9/53 (1,483); AIPO 534, 7/11/54 (1,549); and AIPO 554, 10/4/55 (1,500). The first table below indicates the stability of public opinion, when offered in surveys of 1946 and 1953 the alternatives of "good," "fair," and "poor" job. The second table demonstrates the much larger proportions of inhabitants of all regions who will say the U.N. had done a good job when "fair job" is not offered in the question as an alternative and the only other choices presented are "poor job" and "don't know, no opinion, or undecided."

other Americans, Southerners became much more dissatisfied with the
U.N. with Communist China's entry into the Korean War: many felt
that other members of the U.N. were not doing their just share of the
fighting in Korea, and a significant minority believed pressures from
the U.N. prevented us from following General MacArthur's advice and
carrying the war to Manchuria and the Chinese mainland. However, a
similar change in attitude took place in the North, and the proportions
of Southerners (and white Southerners) among those advancing opinions shifted approximately as did those of residents of other regions.[34]

Early Southern Deviations from National Thinking

It was previously observed that Southerners were more inclined than
other regional groups to favor reorganizing the U.N. without the
U.S.S.R. and other Communist states, to oppose entry of Communist
China as a member of the U.N., to disapprove of channeling American
foreign aid through that world organization, and to reject the idea of

	Southerners	Northeasterners	Midwesterners	Westerners
		Good job		
May, 1946	30	23	25	23
Aug. 13, 1953	29	36	26	31
		Fair job		
May, 1946	39	46	45	52
Aug. 13, 1953	39	31	40	32
		Poor job		
May, 1946	10	22	20	20
Aug. 13, 1953	12	10	12	11
		No opinion		
May, 1946	21	9	10	5
Aug. 13, 1953	20	23	22	26

	Good job		Poor job		No opinion	
	12/9/53	7/14/54	12/9/53	7/14/54	12/9/53	7/14/54
Southerners	53	58	33	26	14	16
Northeasterners	58	57	27	26	15	17
Midwesterners	53	63	31	23	16	14
Westerners	58	57	29	29	13	14

34 This increase in dissatisfaction was markedly evident when the question, "In
general, are you satisfied or dissatisfied with the way the U.N. has handled the
Korean problem?" was posed shortly before and shortly after the entry of the
Chinese Communists into the Korean War in 1950. See NORC 288, 9/20/50 (1,254),
and NORC 295, 12/28/50 (1,258); replies in percentages follow:

	Dissatisfied		Satisfied		No opinion	
	9/20/50	12/28/50	9/20/50	12/28/50	9/20/50	12/28/50
South	21	41	61	32	18	27
Northeast	24	53	62	33	12	14
Midwest	25	53	60	32	15	15
West	25	58	61	30	14	12

converting the organization into a world government (or other utopian schemes relative to the U.N.).

As one would suppose from earlier discussions, Southerners were typically at least somewhat less inclined than Northerners to believe that the U.N. would succeed in preventing future wars between major powers,[35] that it could do anything to "bring about more agreement between the U.S. and Russia," [36] or that it would "succeed in spite of disagreements." [37] However, even these differences, though in the expected directions, involved only from 2 to 8 percentage points, and they could be attributed to the generally more cautious Southern view of human beings and international relations rather than to opposition to the U.N.

It has already been noted that Southerners were less apt to have heard about the activities of the specialized agencies than were other citizens and somewhat less inclined to venture opinions about them if they had. However, when local mass media, politicians, and other popular sources tied a specialized agency or activity of the U.N. to liberalism on race, "human rights," "civil rights," or the like, white Southerners developed views more antagonistic to the agency or program than those manifested by most Northerners. The Human Rights Commission and Eleanor Roosevelt's membership thereon, plus Article 55 of the U.N. Charter stating "universal respect for, and observance of, human rights and fundamental freedoms for all without distinction as to race . . . ," and the supposedly "race-mixing" activities of UNESCO received negative criticism from time to time by some more racially sensitive papers and politicians even in the late 1940's.

Nevertheless, these tendencies were of quite limited magnitude, since racial equalitarianism was not a central theme of the U.N. during the initial postwar period. By August, 1955, for example, only 19 percent of Southerners as compared with 34 percent of Northerners had ever

35 NORC 235, July, 1945 (2,572); NORC 143, 6/21/48 (1,307); NORC 152, 10/10/47 (1,290); NORC 157, 4/22/48 (1,280); NORC 165, 4/19/49 (1,300); and NORC 307, 5/24/52 (1,282). In November, 1947, for example, 18 percent in the South as compared with 23 percent in the Northeast, 23 percent in the Midwest, and 26 percent in the West felt the U.N. had a "good" chance to "prevent wars between big nations."

36 SRC survey of October, 1948 (605).

37 NORC 141, 3/20/46 (1,293); NORC 143, 6/21/46 (1,307); and NORC 370, 3/11/55 (1,225). At the time of the last of these surveys, for instance, 60 percent of Southern whites (60 percent of all Southerners) and 65 percent of Northern whites (65 percent of all Northerners) felt that the U.N. would succeed in spite of disagreements; 23, 22, 20, and 20 percent, respectively, thought it would fail; and 17, 18, 15, and 15 percent, respectively, had no opinion, were undecided, or said they did not know.

heard of UNESCO, and only one Southerner out of twelve in contrast to one out of seven other citizens could give even a rough or vague description of its role, objectives, or functions. The small sample of fifty-eight white Southerners who had heard of this specialized agency were approximately two fifths more likely than Northerners who had heard of it to manifest unfavorable impressions. However, when informed that our government contributes money to UNESCO which, among other functions, attempts to improve education around the world, only 16 percent of white (14 percent of all) Southerners versus 11 percent of Northerners disapproved of our participation and the expense entailed; 79 percent of white (80 percent of all) Southerners approved as compared with 84 percent of Northerners.[38]

Early Southern Opposition

The proportions of Southerners who ventured a given response about the U.N. increased and decreased throughout the first postwar decade, as they would later, depending on the international climate and developments in the world body at the time. In general, Southerners, like other Americans, were most favorable to the U.N. when tensions were apparently relatively low, and most critical of the U.N. when patently serious crises and frustrations faced American policy abroad. Thus, some Southerners who felt the U.N. justified its existence during the first year or so after the war became less certain that it did so during the Berlin Blockade of 1948–49. The fraction who disapproved of the U.N., considered that it had not justified its existence, approved of reforming the organization without the Soviet bloc, and advocated that the United States withdraw from membership was highest during the retreats of U.N. forces in Korea in late 1950 and 1951. It declined as the struggle in Korea stalemated, and declined further with the end of open hostilities in Korea.

The widest shifts in reactions to the U.N. during the first decade (and later) seemed to have taken place primarily among the more unsophisticated, the poorly informed, and the little interested, who were, in turn, concentrated among the underprivileged and poorly educated. Since their views of the U.N. and its activities were typically composed of rather amorphous emotional leanings instead of any critical reactions to the facts, their rather sentimental attachment to the organization as a way to preserve peace could be quickly shaken by defeat of a primarily American force nominally under U.N. control in Korea or by pressures by U.N. members for limitation of the hos-

38 NORC 374, 8/4/55 (1,262).

tilities there to conventional warfare in South Korea proper. Comparable shifts in support of the U.N. took place among similarly poorly informed, poorly educated, unsophisticated Americans in other regions, but, as repeatedly noted, the South included considerably more than its proportionate share of such citizens.

The small fraction who felt that the United States should withdraw from the U.N., that the U.N. had not justified its existence, and that the organization was dangerous to United States interests, or some combination of these negative views—not more than 18 percent even in 1951 shortly after General MacArthur's dismissal—usually disapproved of most major spheres of U.N. operations. They would, for example, have reorganized the U.N. without the U.S.S.R. and its satellites; they opposed United States troops under U.N. command and U.N. control of atomic energy; they disapproved of United States participation in technical assistance through the U.N.; they believed that the U.N. made implementation of our international objectives more difficult; they felt that it was unimportant for us to try to make the U.N. a success; and they feared that the U.N. had "too much power."

Moreover, these Southerners, like other Americans opposed to the U.N. in the initial postwar years, tended to be unenthusiastic about multilateral international involvements generally. Thus, most felt that the Truman Doctrine and the Marshall Plan were not worth the money, that war with the Communists was virtually inevitable or highly likely, and that the United States should rely primarily on its own armed might. A large fraction felt we "should go to war and get the whole thing over with." They would have terminated negotiations with the U.S.S.R. for arms control and similar efforts through frustrating deliberations to relax tensions; they felt the Korean War was "not worth fighting"; they emphasized unilateral intervention abroad; and they stressed military rather than diplomatic and economic means of protecting our national interests. Few Southern opponents of the U.N. would have shifted more of our policies from the U.N. to NATO, as a number among the interviewees advocated in the late 1950's and early 1960's, or favored arming some of our European, Latin American, and Asian allies instead of strengthening the U.N.

Furthermore, opposition to the U.N. in its more extreme form was apparently more limited to the less educated and less privileged in the South than was to be the case in the early 1960's. As noted, increased hostility occurred mainly in less sophisticated strata in times of accentuated international tensions. Although small minorities of the privileged were always opposed to active United States collaboration in the

U.N., most of the negative criticism among the more educated seemed
to take place from about 1957 on, starting with the influx of so many
underdeveloped, neutralist, especially black African, members. During
the earlier period, correlations of opposition to the U.N. with conservative thinking among the educated classes on trade unions, wages and
hours laws, taxation and government spending, and even race relations
were low. For example, most conservative upper-class whites believed
that we should try to strengthen the U.N. even if it cost more money
and entailed more American military personnel under U.N. control.
Attitudes toward the U.N. and views on domestic issues, particularly
race relations, were to become more closely interconnected in later
years.

Later Southern Opposition

By 1961 most newspapers in the Southern sample of fifty-three had
become more cautious than they had been in the 1940's about the
value of the U.N. to our national interests and its effectiveness in keeping the peace. Whereas all of them had welcomed United States entry
into the U.N. in 1945 and had been relatively enthusiastic about the
organization at least until the Korean invasion, almost a quarter were
recommending in 1961 that the United States withdraw from the U.N.
either immediately or if and when Communist China were seated or if
some other event contrary to our policies should transpire. Several of
the papers which in the late 1940's had advocated more effective international law, a stronger International Court of Justice, and even world
government were by 1961 editorializing about our sovereignty being
endangered by the World Court, the Human Rights Commission,
UNESCO, or a General Assembly supposedly controlled by Communists, neutralists, and the colored nationalists (especially Africans).
Several papers which were suggesting in 1961 that the U.N. be moved
outside the United States had advocated its location here in 1945–48.
Approximately two fifths of the newspapers were recommending in
1961 that one policy or another which was supposedly being distorted or
frustrated in the U.N. be carried out either unilaterally or through
our allies, particularly in Western Europe.

Likewise, a number of conservative Southern organizations or chapters of national groups took increasingly critical positions toward the
U.N. and American participation in that international body. There
were some indications of anti-U.N. sentiment in patriotic organizations
and several veterans' groups in the late 1940's and early 1950's, particularly during the Korean War, but hostility became more extreme,

widespread, and vociferous during the late 1950's. (This trend among Citizens Councils and other segregationist groups will be discussed in Chapter II.) Similarly, patriotic, "historical," and "genealogical" bodies like the Paul Revere Ladies' Society, the Daughters of the Patriots, the Daughters and Sons of the American Revolution, the Sons of 1812, and the American Legion became more and more vehicles for communication of the ideas that the U.N. is dangerous to our sovereignty, that it is influenced too much by Communists, socialists, and neutralists, and that we should withdraw from it and expel it from this country.

Southern thinking was undoubtedly influenced by such views expressed by these sources, particularly the editorial writers and syndicated columnists in the papers. But the proportion of Southerners who agreed in the period 1957–62 with strongly negative views of the U.N. was, in most spheres, considerably smaller than the proportion of newspapers expressing such attitudes. Although Southerners in this period tended somewhat more than in the past to diverge from the thinking of the Northern majority on these issues, one would overestimate considerably differences between Southern and Northern opinion from reading Southern newspaper editorials. A considerable number of Southerners who had views on international organization (as on other world questions) exposed themselves to alternative, more pro-U.N. attitudes expressed by national television programs, magazines, and other less conservative sources of ideas; such interpretations from outside their communities (and usually from outside the region) tended to moderate the impact of interpretations prevalent in the local press.

Thus, the number of white Southerners who thought that the U.N. should be moved out of the United States to some other country had risen to only 13 percent by late 1960,[39] and some of these were relatively favorable to United States participation whether it moved or not. Although a smaller Southern than Northern majority in 1956 and 1962 would have us continue to belong to the U.N., the Southern supporters of our U.N. membership rose from 74 percent in May, 1951 (during Communist Chinese assaults in Korea), to 83 percent in 1956 and to 85 percent in 1962, whereas Northern supporters mounted from 75 percent to 90 percent and then to 91 percent. During the same period Southerners favorable to United States withdrawal from the world body fell from 13 percent in 1951 to 8 percent in 1956 and 9 percent in 1962, whereas Northerners of like views decreased from 13 percent to 6 percent and 5 percent.[40] Whereas Southerners, particularly whites,

39 AIPO 637, 10/18/60 (2,993).
40 Figures are from AIPO 475, 5/17/51 (2,070); combined replies to NORC 386, 4/20/56 (1,224), and NORC 399, 11/15/56 (1,286); and AIPO 654, 1/9/62 (3,421).

were about as inclined as Northerners to "approve" of the U.N. and somewhat less apt to "disapprove" of it in 1954–55, they were somewhat more likely to disapprove than Northeasterners and Midwesterners (including residents of the Plains States), but slightly less inclined to do so than Westerners in late 1957. By the latter date, only 72 percent of Southerners as compared with 82 percent of Northeasterners, 77 percent of Midwesterners, and 75 percent of Westerners approved of the organization, while 8 percent, 5 percent, 6 percent, and 10 percent, respectively, disapproved. The ratio of Southerners who approved to those who disapproved had become somewhat smaller than the Northern average, but was still nine to one.[41] Surveys in 1956, 1960, and 1962 indicated that whereas Southerners had been at least as likely as Northerners in earlier years to feel the U.N. had done a "good job" rather than a "poor job" in facing its problems, by the late fifties and early sixties they had become significantly less inclined to feel it had done a "good job" and somewhat more apt to feel it had done a "poor" one. But compared with the earlier period, Northerners had become more inclined to feel the U.N. had done a good job rather than a poor one, whereas Southerners reacted to this question about as they had in the past, or only slightly more favorably than before.[42]

Similarly, 77 percent of Southerners (79 percent of Southern whites) versus 86 percent of Northerners believed in late 1960 that it was "very important" for us to "try to make the U.N. a success"—a statistically significant, though relatively small, difference;[43] but the percentage

41 AIPO 589, 9/17/57 (1,530).
42 For replies to this question before 1955, see p. 23. Replies in percentages to AIPO 575, 11/20/56 (1,502); AIPO 637, 10/18/60 (2,993); and AIPO 654, 1/9/62 (3,421) were as follows:

	South	White South	North	Northeast	Midwest	West
			Good job			
1956	48	49	53	50	52	56
1960	42	45	61	—	—	—
1962	45	47	52	—	—	—
			Fair job			
1956	24	25	27	25	28	30
1960	26	28	22	—	—	—
1962	27	26	27	—	—	—
			Poor job			
1956	13	13	9	11	9	7
1960	14	13	7	—	—	—
1962	12	12	10	—	—	—
			No opinion			
1956	15	13	11	14	11	7
1960	18	14	10	—	—	—
1962	16	15	11	—	—	—

43 AIPO 637, 10/18/60 (2,993).

throughout the country of those who agreed with this view had increased from 77 to 83 percent since 1952. It was observed earlier (see p. 187) that a larger minority of Southern whites than of Northern whites or Northerners generally sided with the British and French in the Suez invasion of late 1956, an attitude reflected in regional views in March, 1957, on whether the influence of the U.N. had increased or decreased as a result of "actions it has taken recently." Differences were statistically significant—only 34 percent of Southerners as compared with 45 percent of Northeasterners, 44 percent of Midwesterners (including residents of the Plains States), and 44 percent of Westerners felt the influence of the U.N. had increased as a result of the Suez actions. But only 22 percent in the South thought that U.N. action in the Suez affair had decreased U.N. influence.[44]

There was in the early sixties considerable criticism among conservative Southern newspapers and politicians about the U.N. operation in the Congo and the supposedly pro-Lumumba and anti-Tshombe policies of the world body there. As a result partly thereof, Southerners were significantly less inclined than other regional groups in the summer of 1960 to think it would be a good idea to develop a U.N. emergency force strong enough to deal with "brush-fire" wars. However, 67 percent in the South supported this idea and only 12 percent opposed it. Opposition grew and approval declined somewhat over the next six months with the various frustrations of the U.N. operation in the formerly Belgian Congo, but 64 percent of Southerners approved while only 17 percent disapproved of this proposition in January, 1961.[45]

The proportion of Southerners agreeing with such ideas as "we should start now working toward transforming the United Nations into a real world government of *all* nations of the world, in which every nation would in effect become a state, somewhat like the different states of this country," fell sharply during the second decade after World War II; only 8 percent of Southerners agreed with that suggestion in July, 1963. However, support for such politically unrealistic

44 AIPO 580, 3/13/57 (1,624).
45 AIPO 631, 7/14/60 (2,800) and AIPO 640, 1/10/61 (2,649) posed the question, "A proposal has been made to build up the U.N. emergency force to a size great enough to deal with 'brush fire' or small wars throughout the world. Does this sound like a good idea or a poor idea to you?" Results in percentages were as follows:

	Good idea		Poor idea		No opinion	
	7/14/60	1/10/61	7/14/60	1/10/61	7/14/60	1/10/61
South	67	64	12	17	21	19
Northeast	72	65	12	16	16	19
Midwest	76	68	10	17	14	15
West	74	66	12	20	14	14

lines of action fell almost as precipitously in other parts of the country as well; only 11 percent of those in the Northeast, 13 percent in the Midwest (including the Plains States), and 14 percent in the West were of this persuasion by mid-summer of 1963. Moreover, at that time 34 percent of Southerners as compared with 41 percent of Northeasterners, 40 percent of Midwesterners (including residents of the Plains States), and 41 percent of Westerners felt that "we should immediately get behind strengthening the United Nations and do everything necessary to give it more power and authority than it has—enough to actually keep even a strong nation from starting a war." Only 8 percent of Southerners versus 5 percent of those in the other major regions in July, 1963, were of the view that "we shouldn't get tied up in any more alliances or joint commitments with other countries and we should aim at getting out of as many as we can as soon as we can," including presumably the U.N.[46]

Thus, on most aspects of the U.N. to which Southerners and Northerners had reacted more or less similarly in the first decade, somewhat greater divergence from national norms on the part of the South seemed apparent by the late fifties and early sixties. However, in absolute terms Southerners were more favorable by then to active participation in the U.N. and to a realistically strengthened organization than during the Korean War.

The most marked increases in Southern opposition have been in the areas of U.N. affairs in which Southern whites had long diverged significantly from the Northerners. It has already been mentioned (p. 122) that only 10 percent of Southerners in contrast to 24 percent of Northeasterners, 17 percent of Midwesterners (including residents of the Plains States), and 25 percent of Westerners in 1961 felt the Peking government should be permitted to become a member of the U.N. and that approximately a third of the South would withdraw from the U.N. or otherwise "not go along" with Chinese Communist entry should it take place. By early 1957, only 35 percent of those in the South as compared with 49 percent in the Northeast, 43 percent in the Midwest (Plains States included), and 38 percent in the West thought the U.N. stood a "good chance of keeping the peace in the world"; 28 percent of the South versus 32 percent, 31 percent, and 32 percent, respectively, considered it had a "fair chance"; and 24 percent in the South versus 16 percent, 20 percent, and 23 percent, respectively, a "poor" one.[47] Likewise, according to the interviews in 1959–62, the entry of many new African states into the U.N., their demands for racial equality and independence in Africa and throughout the world,

46 Roper 148, July, 1963 (3,007). 47 AIPO 577, 1/15/57 (1,496).

and their behavior in New York and elsewhere in the United States undoubtedly augmented Southern hesitations about the organization, especially in fields related to race relations.

Thus, compared with foreign aid, the U.N. as a general symbol has fared rather well in the South. Whereas the former has been losing supporters during the decade prior to 1963, Southern approval of the U.N. has remained steady or even increased in most respects. Although criticism of the U.N. has increased considerably in the more conservative newspapers, and some politicians of similar mind have adopted the U.N. as one of their major whipping boys, the number of newspapers and political figures who recommended withdrawal in 1961 was only a fraction of those who would considerably decrease foreign economic assistance.

The relatively limited minority of Southerners who would withdraw from the U.N. or sharply reduce our collaboration there was in the early sixties, as earlier, isolationist or neo-isolationist in most fields of world affairs; this group would adopt an international posture of "Fortress America," use "big-stick" policies in the Caribbean, including military intervention, and reduce our activities outside the Western Hemisphere primarily to unilateral military intervention or, at most, to cooperation with a few European, South African, Australian, and, of course, Canadian allies. Virtually all anti-U.N. Southerners in 1959–62 were also opposed to foreign aid at its then current magnitude; but many who would remain in the U.N. would still greatly reduce, or eliminate, capital assistance to underdeveloped lands, particularly to "socialist," neutralist, and Communist regimes. However, the monetary cost for participation in the U.N. was only a small fraction of the expense of foreign aid.

It is apparent from the interviews that relatively few Southerners who were opposed to the U.N. in the earlier period, except perhaps during the worst reverses in the early part of the Korean War, changed their views much—those still alive were equally or more critical than in the late 1940's. They were more convinced than ever that we should withdraw. The decrease in the fraction of Southerners who would pull the United States out of the U.N. and push the U.N. out of the United States was primarily attributable to the death of many older Southerners holding this view and the emergence of many younger, better-educated, more informed citizens who were adolescents or children in the earlier period. The incidence of anti-U.N. views among the young —who on the whole were more educated and more knowledgeable in the early sixties—was considerably less than among their elders.

However, although active opposition to United States participation in the U.N. in 1962 was a small minority in the South, so was really active support. Thus, the enthusiastic opponents of the U.N. could operate in many Deep Southern locales in relative vacuums. And many white Southerners who felt we should continue to belong to the organization were not enthusiastic about its future or optimistic about its long-run utility for our national objectives abroad.

As previously, disproportionately large numbers of Southerners were still indifferent to the U.N., replied "don't know" to questions about it, and really cared little one way or another about its future effectiveness. Many Southern conservatives tended in the early sixties to feel that the organization was controlled or, at least, much influenced by a coalition of enemies of the United States and, particularly, of the Southern way of life—the Communists, "leftists," neutralists, "barefoot republics," and colored peoples. The U.N. was viewed as no longer likely to take unbiased stands on cold war issues and matters in which the newly independent, backward, often colored, peoples had selfish interests. The U.N. Charter would be interpreted against the West but would not be applied to Communist or neutralist transgressions, as in Goa and New Guinea. A large minority of Southerners among the interviewees would downgrade the U.N.'s role in United States foreign policy because of these developments.

Racially conservative whites feared infringements on American sovereignty by the General Assembly, the International Court of Justice with its several Communist and otherwise anti-American judges, or other U.N. bodies. A major source of their anxiety was indicated by conservative Southern newspaper editorials: "If and when South Africa's hide is nailed to the U.N. barn door, African extremists can use the same pressure tactics against Mississippi and other Southern states . . . Dixie's turn might come later," [48] and "We predict that in less than ten years Communist bloc and neutralist countries will demand that U.N. investigators be sent into Alabama to probe alleged violations of 'human rights.' " [49] The older apprehensions about UNESCO and the Human Rights Commission had become exacerbated.

To these irritations were added the feeling that the United States bears too much of the expense of the international organization, that we pick up the bill when the Soviets and others fail to pay. Many Southerners in the sample felt in 1961–62 that the proposed U.N. bond issue was only camouflage for further American donations since the loan would probably never be repaid in full. As our influence

48 Jackson (Miss.) *Clarion-Ledger,* November 3, 1961.
49 Charleston (S.C.) *News and Courier,* June 8, 1961.

seemed to wane, our share of the expenses increased. Fundamentalists feared that the organization is a godless, atheistic one, and, since these people were usually also racially conservative in the Deep South, they tended to reflect other critical views as well. A number of the sample of Southerners also were apprehensive that the U.N. was a hotbed of spies and subversives within our frontiers.

Many of these anxieties were shared by the same individuals, and only a small minority of Southerners thought that we should go so far as to withdraw from the U.N. in the near future. But the fact that more than one out of three Southerners believed in the early sixties that we should withdraw if Communist China should become a member indicated the relatively feeble support for active use of the U.N. under trying circumstances among a considerable minority of Southerners.

PART II

The Diverse Souths

CHAPTER 7

EDUCATIONAL FACTORS

No one demographic, social, historical, or psychological factor alone explains the behavior of Southerners, or other Americans, toward foreign affairs. Southerners in different walks of life, of divergent backgrounds, and living in diverse settings have been influenced to varying extents and in complex combinations by many phenomena, some of them reinforcing, others countervailing, and still others ramifying one another. In dealing with social and demographic groups and aspects of Southern society which bear some relation to international thought and action, one should bear in mind that separation of these factors is for the purposes of analysis only.

Formal Education and International Thought

Throughout America the most important single demographic correlate of responsible international thinking has been amount, subject matter, and quality of formal education. The South has been no exception.

On literally thousands of survey questions since 1936 Southerners and other Americans who had more years of schooling have been significantly more inclined than those with less to be interested and have opinions in world affairs, to consider that field in their choice of congressional and presidential candidates, to know something about foreign developments, to consider alternative interpretations of these issues, to read about them and pay attention to them on radio and, later, on television, and in voluntary organizations, to discuss them informally with associates, and to harbor relatively cosmopolitan views on what this country should do about these issues. Illiterates have been at the bottom of all these continua, grade-school graduates somewhat higher, high-school graduates above those who had only a smattering of high school, college-trained people still farther up the continua, and those with professional or graduate training (depending on the field) the most thoughtful and cosmopolitan of all. The proportion of Southerners (and Northerners) advancing a given opinion of an international phenomenon has varied with changes in the phenomenon itself, the overall international climate at the moment, developments within the South and the United States in general, and perhaps other factors, but at any given moment these relationships with education have been apparent.

The Crucial Role of College

The sharpest differences on most aspects of world affairs have been between those who went to college and those who did not. Moreover, among college graduates international orientations have varied according to college attended, course of study, and level of performance. People whose parents also went to college or were of the more sophisticated social strata have been more likely to fit the criteria of interest, thoughtfulness, and responsibility in world affairs than those from less-educated or privileged homes. Those who majored in the humanities and social sciences have been more apt to be realistic internationalists than others who majored in technology, premedicine, commerce, and other technical fields unassociated with world affairs. Those who received technical graduate or professional education have tended more in this direction if they had broad undergraduate educations rather than technical ones. Those who majored in the purer sciences have on the whole been more interested, informed, and thoughtful about foreign policy than those who focused on the applied sciences. People who made high grades have been on the average more sophisticated about world affairs than those whose grades were average or, particularly, poor.[1]

1 From retabulations of results of a study of 10,000 college graduates by the Bureau of Applied Social Research of Columbia University in the late 1940's; hereinafter cited as Bureau of Applied Social Research survey. These generalizations about Southerners who had graduated from college were apparent in varying degrees with respect to the following aspects of international behavior: (1) incidence of reading about world issues in newspapers, magazines, and books, of listening to international material on the radio, and of discussion of similar matters with "friends"; (2) favorable images of internationally thoughtful public figures identified with multilateral cooperation; (3) tendencies to differentiate between the ide-

Southerners, like other Americans, who graduated from such stimulating institutions as Swarthmore, the University of Chicago, Bryn Mawr, Oberlin, Amherst, Barnard, or Harvard, have been on the average more cosmopolitan and internationally liberal in their thinking than those whose experience was at less vigorously intellectual institutions. Alumni of such intellectually rigorous Southern colleges as Duke, the University of North Carolina, Randolph Macon, Vanderbilt, and Davidson have on the average known more about world affairs and have been more internationally inclined than Southerners who went to institutions of lesser quality, although the former have not been quite so apt to fit this description as graduates of the most nationally renowned universities and colleges. In general, the gap in international behavior between the latter and graduates of the best Southern institutions has been less than that between products of the best Southern colleges and those of the least effective Southern schools.[2] There have been, of course, large overlaps in international sophistication among graduates of different types of institutions—the interviewers encountered graduates of Yale, Princeton, Harvard, the University of Berlin, and so on who were neither much interested, well-informed, nor particularly cosmopolitan, and some men and women from relatively unknown and very limited Southern colleges who were among the most thoughtful in foreign affairs.

These differences in international attitudes between graduates of diverse institutions have not been, of course, due entirely, or even perhaps primarily, to differences in their educational experiences in college. Particularly in recent years, the most invigorating institutions, especially those of national esteem, have attracted, accepted, and graduated primarily the more thoughtful and intellectually oriented Southerners—those who were most apt to be or become reflective cosmopolitans. Undoubtedly the stimulating educational experience of latently internationally thoughtful Southerners in the best national universities and colleges and, to a probably somewhat lesser extent, in the most able Southern institutions, encouraged their development to-

ologies and practices of communism, socialism, and fascism; (4) emphasis on the external rather than the internal Communist danger as the principal one; (5) support of gradual lowering of barriers to international trade; (6) approval of expanded selective immigration of talented foreigners; (7) support of a strengthened U.N.; (8) approval of United States assistance to help foreign societies to raise their standards of living; (9) rejection of the view that "foreigners have peculiar and annoying habits"; and (10) acceptance of the idea that "we now have enough scientific and technical knowledge to substantially eliminate poverty, disease, and ignorance in the world, if we would only apply our knowledge."

2 *Ibid.*

ward international sophistication. However, most cosmopolitan Southern graduates from such institutions among the informants seemed to
feel that they were inclined in this direction before they matriculated,
that formal and informal intellectual experiences in college helped make
them aware of what they already were, lessened some of their intellectual confusion, and helped them organize their disconnected impressions and thoughts. Quality of educational experience has been an
important factor in the development of the small thoughtful minority,
but it was typically one of a number of relevant variables.

These generalizations have applied to Southern adults who have left
college, in many cases several decades ago. The best Southern colleges
have improved their scholarly standards considerably in recent years
and many of the more typical ones have also exerted themselves to
approach rising national norms. What of the international behavior of
college students in the South in the late fifties and early sixties?

Apparently there were still some statistical differences between college students in the South and in the North with respect to cosmopolitanism. A recent study of students in a representative sample of American institutions of higher learning determined that those in white
Southern colleges were less informed about a variety of international
topics than the national average. Southern white college students were
about as well (or poorly) informed about world affairs as students in
the Plains States, slightly less informed than those in the Midwest, and
significantly less than those on the West Coast and, particularly, in the
Northeast.[3] Moreover, this research did not include any students at
Negro colleges of which the great majority are in the South; had it
done so, the Southern average would with little doubt have been lower
as compared with Northern figures (see p. 518). As among college
graduates, there was great variation in knowledge about world affairs
among students in the South and even among those at individual Southern colleges; however, the sample was not large enough to permit
statistical comparison of students at different Southern institutions.

The author knows of no comparable national study of international
opinion among college students. However, three recent investigations
have attempted to compare public interests and attitudes at several
Southern and Northern institutions of roughly equivalent academic reputation. One discovered that students at the University of North Carolina, one of the better Southern institutions, were more conventional,
conformist, and conservative on a gamut of values and public issues than

3 Percy W. Bidwell, *Undergraduate Education in World Affairs* (New York:
King's Crown Press, 1962), 152.

those at Haverford, Wesleyan (Connecticut), Harvard, and several other well-known Northern colleges.[4] Another came to similar conclusions about Louisiana State University students as compared with those at the University of Maryland and Washburne University in Topeka.[5] A third study determined that undergraduates at the University of Georgia were considerably less "worldminded" than a comparable sample in the Northeast—the criterion was "a frame of reference or value orientation favoring a world view of the problems of humanity, with mankind, rather than nationals of a particular country as the primary reference group." The measurements were support for expanded immigration, belief that there would not be another world war in the next five or twenty-five years, and favorable attitudes toward the placing of United States atomic raw materials and plants under international control if the Soviets and other nations did likewise, liberalized world trade, a strengthened U.N., arms limitations in both the nuclear and conventional fields under international supervision, and a U.N. police force.[6]

The latter research also discovered differences in "worldmindedness" among University of Georgia students which the author's investigations tend to indicate probably applied in the late fifties and sixties in many other Southern institutions of higher learning. The more mature and advanced were more "worldminded" on these issues than the less matured and advanced; the more racially moderate than the strongly white supremacist; those who made better grades than those of lower academic standing; seniors than freshmen; those who had come from the North or had resided for some time there than those who had lived all their lives in the South and among the latter those who had lived in Southern states outside of Georgia than those who had always resided in their native state; students from urban than those from agricultural backgrounds; those whose fathers were college educated and, particu-

4 Philip E. Jacob, *Changing Values in College* (New York: Harper Bros., 1957), 106–10.

5 Eugene L. Gaier and Bernard M. Bass, "Regional Differences in Interrelations among Authoritarianism, Acquiescence, and Ethnocentrism," *Journal of Social Psychology*, XLIX (1959), 47–51. Differences between Louisiana State University and Washburne students were significant at the one percent level of confidence.

6 Karl C. Garrison, "Worldminded Attitudes of College Students in a Southern University," *Journal of Social Psychology*, LIV (1961), 147–53; Karl G. Garrison, "A Comparative Study of the Attitudes of College Students toward Certain Domestic and World Problems," *Journal of Social Psychology*, XXXIV (1951), 47–54; and D. L. Sampson and H. P. Smith, "A Scale of Measure Worldmindedness Attitudes," *Journal of Social Psychology*, XLV, (1957), 99–106. See also James G. Kelly, Jean E. Ferson, and Wayne H. Holtzman, "The Measurement of Attitudes toward the Negro in the South," *Journal of Social Psychology*, XLVIII (1958), 305–17.

larly, in the professions than those whose parents were less well educated and in more humble or less sophisticated occupations; Jews,
Catholics, and students with no religious preferences than Protestants
taken together; among the Protestants, Presbyterians, Episcopalians, and
Methodists than Baptists and, particularly, members of fundamentalist
sects; and girls somewhat more than boys.[7]

Education and International Analysis, Knowledge, Interest, Action, and Opinion

Amount and kind of education have been most closely associated
with critical, responsible, and dispassionate habits of mind toward foreign policy. Throughout the country, including the South, people who
have thought in this manner—no more than one percent of our national
adult population, depending on the rigor of criteria—have been predominantly college educated.[8] For instance, of the Americans in the late
1950's who read analytical material on world affairs in such publications as *Atlantic, Harper's, The Reporter, The New Republic, The
Economist, The Guardian,* and the New York *Times* (Sunday edition),
approximately 85 percent had attended college, 70 percent had received
a degree, and almost half had attended a graduate or professional
school.[9]

Southerners who have paid frequent attention to such periodicals
have been somewhat more concentrated among the college-educated
minority than have Americans outside the South—about 11 percent of
Southerners as compared with 15 percent of Northerners who thought
in the late fifties on the level of abstraction and sophistication about
world affairs mentioned above, judging from audience research, did
not attend college. The few who did not go to college tended to be
"genteel" older ladies who went to finishing school or members of
either sex, largely from "old families" or the upper-middle class, whose
parents were in such straitened circumstances as to be unable to send
them to college. However, the general cultural level and taste of these
few people have coincided closely with those of the minority of college
graduates who have been cosmopolitans. Furthermore, the proportion
of college graduates who have approached this description of thoughtful attention to international relations in the South has been still smaller

---

7 Garrison, *Journal of Social Psychology,* LIV, 147–53; and Garrison, *Journal
of Social Psychology,* XXXIV, 47–54.
8 Alfred O. Hero, Jr.; *Americans in World Affairs* (Boston: World Peace
Foundation, 1959), 6, and 22–23.
9 Hero, *Mass Media and World Affairs,* 54.

than among college graduates in the North—about one out of ten in the North as opposed to one out of fifteen in the South in recent years.[10]

Thus, reinforcing educational factors have helped to account for the relative rarity of critical thought about world affairs in the South—smaller fractions of those residing in the South than of Americans elsewhere went to college at all, and, of those who graduated, disproportionately fewer attended the more stimulating institutions in this country, made excellent grades there, and went into careers where continuing interest in world affairs was encouraged.

It was observed previously that Southerners having fair amounts of information about international matters outnumbered by several times those manifesting a relatively analytical posture toward foreign affairs. Possession of information has not been nearly so limited as critical thought on foreign policy to a small, largely college-educated, minority. However, knowledge about foreign affairs has been more closely associated with higher education than has interest in and, especially, most attitudes on foreign policy. In general, the more detailed or comprehensive the information, the more limited has it been to college-exposed Southerners. As in the case of critical thought about world affairs, possession of more detailed information has been somewhat more limited to the college-educated in the South than in other regions, although the proportion of high-school trained Southerners among the better informed in recent years has been considerably larger than among the analytically inclined.

Interest in foreign relations, although less closely associated with college exposure than having information in that field, has been most prevalent among the better educated, especially the college educated. The more specific or abstract the issue on which interest has been solicited on surveys, the more has concern been limited to the relatively well educated. This generalization may be observed in replies to poll queries asking respondents about their degree of interest in various international questions; in the proportions that have said they were uninterested, did not know, or had "no opinion" when asked about their views; and in the percentages that have exposed themselves to programs of voluntary organizations and mass media on foreign relations. For instance, the less the education, the more directly must an issue have related to the individual's immediate experience, interests, and locale to have evoked any opinion.

10 *Ibid.*, 54–55; and audience research data on *Harper's, Atlantic, Christian Science Monitor*, and within the Bureau of Applied Social Research survey.

In 1947 a significantly smaller proportion of Southern than Northern college graduates followed international events in weekly news magazines,[11] and more recent audience studies in the late 1950's and early 1960's of *Time, Newsweek*, and *U.S. News and World Report* indicate that, while readerships have increased throughout the country, Southerners who have been to college were still somewhat less inclined than Northerners of college backgrounds to expose themselves frequently or regularly to these periodicals. However, differences between the regions among the college educated have been smaller for these than for more analytical publications like *Harper's*. Moreover, the Southern readership of international material in the three major weekly newsmagazines not only has been approximately ten times more numerous than that of more critical periodicals, but also has included a much larger proportion of citizens who had no more than a high-school education. Considerably more Southerners read pictorial magazines like *Look* and *Life* (despite their racial liberalism) and international material in such popular media as the *Saturday Evening Post;* there were several times more readers of these popular publications who had not finished high school than of the weekly newsmagazines. Although the people in the South who had not attended college were less inclined to read the international content of *Life, Look,* and the *Saturday Evening Post* than those in the North, differences were smaller than for *Time* and *Newsweek.*

International news in local papers has reached even further down the Southern educational spectrum—37 percent of college-educated Southerners in the late 1950's read all or most of the foreign news in a daily paper more often than not, but so did 18 percent with some high-school training and 9 percent with only a grade-school education. The proportion of Northern college people who read international coverage in daily papers was only slightly larger, and only 15 percent of those Northerners who attended only grade school read most of such material in a daily paper.[12] In the late 1940's Southern college graduates were approximately three quarters as likely as Northern college graduates to read regularly or frequently editorials, syndicated columns, and other interpretations of international (and national) affairs in a daily newspaper.[13]

Finally, depending on the program, thoughtful national television pro-

11 Bureau of Applied Social Research survey.
12 NORC 393, 9/13/56 (1,263). See also SRC survey of March–April, 1957 (1,919). Both samples were too small for statistical significance, but differences were in the expected directions.
13 Bureau of Applied Social Research survey.

ductions on foreign relations during peak viewing hours reached during the late 1950's larger proportions still of less-educated Southerners. Typical grade-school educated Southerners were approximately a quarter as inclined as were college-educated Southerners to view critical international programs, depending on the topics, levels of abstraction, techniques of presentation, and other considerations. Southerners with some high school education were about half as inclined to do so. The fraction of less educated in the North technically able to receive such telecasts who actually paid attention to any one of them was normally only a third or so larger than in the South.[14]

As observed in Part I, international attitudes have also been related to education, but on most issues the degree of linkage has been considerably less than for analytical thought and information, and somewhat less than for interest. The significantly greater prevalence of citizens in the South as compared with other regions who have informed survey interviewers that they had no opinions has been due more to the larger fraction of Southerners in the lower educational groups than to any other factor. College-educated Southerners have been about as apt as their Northern educational counterparts to venture views on most problems of world affairs, but the differences between the regions have widened as one moved down the educational spectrum.

The better educated have been much more likely than the less educated to see the implications of world developments. However, correlations between education and international opinions have varied with the foreign-policy issue. In general, the smaller the proportion of Southerners who have agreed with a relatively liberal internationalist, multilateralist, or active policy or program, the more concentrated has it been among the better educated. Thus, support of foreign capital assistance for underdeveloped neutralists at levels requested by the President in recent years has been much more widespread among the college educated than among Southerners who did not complete high school. On the other hand, when the great majority in the South have approved of a policy, such as continued active United States participation in the U.N. and in NATO in the late 1950's and early 1960's, the minorities opposed have been disproportionately numerous among the poorly educated, but differences among educational groups have been much smaller. Finally, support of military expenditures and most other aspects of national defense has been so general in the South that differences between the educational groups have been very limited.

14 From Pulse, CBS, and NBC studies of 1958–60; NORC 393, 9/13/56 (1,263); and AIPO 575, 11/20/56 (1,502).

Thus, whenever surveys in recent years have discovered Southerners as a group to be more opposed to active international collaboration or to be more isolationist or indifferent than Northerners, regional differences have declined sharply when only college-educated Southerners were compared with college-educated Northerners.

The less educated throughout the country have been least inclined to think of ways to influence policy toward world problems and least apt to write to Congressmen or otherwise to try to influence them.[15] But Southerners of limited education, still a considerably larger proportion of the South than of the North in the early 1960's, have been even less apt than Northerners of deprived educational backgrounds to think in terms of influencing the behavior of their federal authorities toward foreign problems. The tendencies to feel that these matters should be left to the privileged classes, not to vote in congressional and presidential elections (or primaries tantamount to elections), or to base their votes almost exclusively on personalities and domestic issues seemed in 1962 still rather widespread among many Southerners of little schooling.

These generalizations have applied since the first national opinion surveys in the mid-1930's. In fact, critical interest, knowledge, and especially an analytical, reality-testing posture with respect to world affairs were more limited to the better-educated strata in the South a generation ago than now. The gaps in these regards between the college educated and the less educationally privileged have narrowed over the past generation—the proportion of Southerners without the benefit of high-school diplomas who had some interest in the U.N., knew something of what transpired there, and favored United States cooperation there was considerably higher in 1958–62 than was the case for Southerners of similar education with respect to the League of Nations in the 1930's. Furthermore this proportion has differed less in recent years in its thinking about the U.N. as compared with college-educated Southerners than did similar educational groups during the era of the League. Active United States involvement in world affairs, wider experience, more cosmopolitan content of Southern elementary and secondary education, the growth of television and other means of popular communication of world phenomena, and other factors have had significant effects on even the lower two thirds of the Southern educational spectrum. And, of course, the spectrum itself has shifted significantly

15 SRC of November–December, 1949 (606), and AIPO 446, 8/12/49 (3,272). The latter survey determined that 40 percent of college, 22 percent of high-school, and 12 percent of grade-school educated Northerners had ever written or wired their Congressman or Senator. The respective Southern figures were 37, 15, and 5 percent.

toward more education: those who had been to college by 1962 were a much larger, and those who did not finish high school a much smaller, fraction of the population than in prewar times. It is not surprising that Southerners as a group were much better informed, more interested, and more thoughtful about foreign affairs in the early sixties than they were two decades and more ago, and that they more nearly approached the Northern averages in these regards.

Better-educated Southerners in the thirties were also more apt to support active United States involvement in world affairs than less educated residents of the region, as was true in the sixties. The same was true in the most isolationist section, the Midwest and Plains States region, and in the country generally. But Southerners as a group were so much more favorable to liberalization of the Neutrality and Johnson Acts, exchange of destroyers for bases with Britain, Lend-Lease, freer trade, and so on (immigration excepted) than Northerners that Southerners who had not completed high school were as or more apt than college-trained Northerners to approve of these commitments. The whole spectrum of Southern attitudes on most issues was more favorable to international collaboration with respect to the issues of the day than was that of Northern opinion, and particularly than that of Midwestern and Plains States attitudes. By the 1960's, as the problems abroad changed, Southerners of given education were about as favorable as Northerners of equivalent education on some questions, more favorable on others, and less favorable on still others.

The Southern Educational Heritage and World Affairs

Definitive conclusions about the impact of Southern education on the foreign-policy orientations of Southerners must await systematic research on relevant educational experience both currently and when the several generations of today's adult Southerners were in school. The author is able to advance here only rather speculative observations from historical discussions of Southern education and from his own experiences and conversations in the region.

Southern Leadership and Public Education

The concentration of interest, knowledge, and, particularly, critical thinking about foreign affairs among a small, relatively privileged stratum who had the benefit of atypically high education for the region has been due in large measure to the limited availability of easily accessible free schools and some of the qualities of whatever public education was offered in much of the rural South.

Until recent decades, much of the Southern elite, especially outside the few cities and college towns, was not particularly interested in mass education. The children of planters and other privileged groups had long been educated by private tutors, in private rural and small-town academies, or in the private schools in nearby cities like New Orleans, Charleston, Savannah, Richmond, Natchez, or Mobile.[16] Because these rural landowners and their urban commercial and professional-class allies owned most of the taxable property, taxes for the public schools would fall primarily on them. Consequently, most were not enthusiastic about public education, and as their influence in local and state governments after Reconstruction was vastly out of proportion to their numbers,[17] the development of mass education was hampered. By the turn of the century Negroes were barred from the polls and political influence, and many poor whites and small, white farmers of the hills and mountains whose children would use the public schools, if they existed, were either too illiterate and apathetic to vote or were disfranchised by the poll tax or other means.

The situation at the college level was significantly different. The sons of some of the more affluent went to Princeton, Yale, Harvard, and other Northeastern colleges or even to universities in England, or those from Southern Louisiana, to France.[18] But only a limited minority of the planter, commercial, and professional elite could afford to send their offspring out of the South for an education; and many feared the "strange" ideas their children might learn in New Haven, Cambridge (Massachusetts or England), Oxford, or Paris. Therefore, the prosperous few tended to favor allocation of considerable resources to Southern public colleges, which antedated lower public schools in much of the region.[19] State colleges began in the South with the establishment of the University of Georgia in 1785,[20] and antebellum Southern taxpayers spent more per capita on higher public education than did other Americans.[21] By 1860 the South contained half the colleges and college

16 Bridenbaugh, *Myths and Realities,* 75 and 101–102; Bowes, *The Culture of Early Charleston,* Chapter 3, pp. 34–53; Eaton, *The Growth of Southern Civilization,* 114–20; Savage, *Seeds of Time,* 102–103; Fossier, *New Orleans: The Glamour Period,* 237; and Ezell, *The South Since 1865,* 241.
17 E. g., Shugg, *Origins of Class Struggle in Louisiana,* 68–69 and 74–75.
18 Shugg, *Origins of Class Struggle in Louisiana,* 69–70.
19 H. Clarence Nixon, "Colleges and Universities," in Couch (ed.), *Culture in the South,* 229; and Nicholls, *Southern Tradition and Regional Progress,* 106–107.
20 Ezell, *The South Since 1865,* 258.
21 Kendrick and Arnett, *The South Looks at Its Past,* 67–68.

students in America, but only a quarter of the white population.[22] However, since most youngsters could not prepare for college unless their parents could pay for private primary and secondary education, the Southern privileged classes were supporting both private and public institutions populated principally by their own children.[23]

But interest in cheap government and low taxes was not the only source of opposition, or at least indifference, to public education among the privileged classes. They had long tended to feel that education was an individual rather than a governmental responsibility and that only a small fraction of the population could absorb "real" education.[24] One could not teach culture to innately inferior whites or Negroes. The masses could at best be fed predigested fare; should the schools descend to this level of mediocrity, they would be inferior indeed. The belief that the majority could learn Latin and Greek, ancient history, and philosophy was patently absurd, and more practical subjects were not education at all.[25] The idea of education for the masses was supposedly imported by carpetbaggers, Yankee "reformers," and other "crackpots" from the North.[26] The idea that the leadership of the South should have assumed the social responsibility of raising the education and general level of culture of the masses, or that the "herd" could be improved even if one tried, did not take root to much extent in the Southern planter class or their commercial allies in smaller towns.[27]

Moreover, the "wool hats" and Negroes were regarded by the privileged Southerner as happy in their ignorance and would presumably

22 Carter, *The Angry Scar*, 176; Clement Eaton, *Freedom of Thought in the Old South* (Durham: Duke University Press, 1940), 67–73; and Savage, *Seeds of Time*, 103.

23 Ronald F. Howell, "Education for the Uncommon Man," in Louis D. Rubin, Jr., and James J. Kilpatrick (eds.), *The Lasting South: Fourteen Southerners Look at Their Home* (Chicago: Henry Regnery, 1957), 145 and 148–49.

24 Nicholls, *Southern Tradition and Regional Progress*, 104; and Franklin, *The Militant South*, 129 ff.

25 Some of the Vanderbilt Fugitives or Agrarians and their followers reflected the views of the more sophisticated Southern elitists. See especially John Gould Fletcher, "Education, Past and Present," in Twelve Southerners, *I'll Take My Stand: The South and the Agrarian Tradition* (New York: Harper Bros., 1930), 80–121; Howell, "Education for the Common Man," in *The Lasting South*, 145–62; and Edd Winfield Parks, *Segments of Southern Thought* (Athens: University of Georgia Press, 1938), 39, 236, and 281–85. See also the editorials of the Charleston *News and Courier* and the columns of John Temple Graves during the period 1959–61.

26 Nicholls, *Southern Tradition and Regional Progress*, 106–107; Cash, *The Mind of the South*, 88–89; C. Vann Woodward, *Origins of the New South, 1877–1913*, 61–64; and Ezell, *The South Since 1865*, 242.

27 Nicholls, *Southern Tradition and Regional Progress*, 49; and Cash, *The Mind of the South*, 89.

have no use for education, considering their callings. Most poor whites seemed to accept the verdict of their "betters" with a frontier scorn for formal "schoolin'." Since they were hard pressed for help in the fields and saw little instrumental value in education in a static agrarian society, their children often went to work picking cotton and tobacco, cutting sugar cane, hunting, fishing, and working around the house and farm at any early age.[28]

These attitudes unfavorable to mass education were compounded for Negroes in that antebellum Southern states had laws prohibiting the teaching of Negroes to read or write,[29] for fear education would spoil them for rural labor and generate discontent among them. Later, the expense of maintaining two school systems, one for whites and another for Negroes, in an economically underdeveloped society was a contributing factor to this negative attitude, but many (though a decreasing proportion of) Southerners opposed Negro nonvocational education as a matter of principle until the threat of integration pressed them to develop better evidence for their arguments for "separate but equal" schools.

Gradual Change of Secondary and Primary Education

These attitudes unfavorable to the development of effective primary and secondary education and the dearth of public schools outside the cities resulting from them have been changing, particularly in the last two or three decades, but as late as the 1920's when many adult Southerners of 1962 were youngsters public high schools were frequently relatively inaccessible in many poorer rural counties and parishes of the region.[30] Rural elementary schools were often one room or otherwise rather limited establishments taught frequently by rather poorly professionally trained teachers from the local area. The elementary schools which were operating in rural settings typically had funds for less than six months per annum for white children, and much less for Negroes.[31] Even when this rather limited education was available,

28 Ezell, *The South Since 1865*, 247.
29 Nicholls, *Southern Tradition and Regional Progress*, 48; Shugg, *Origins of Class Struggle in Louisiana*, 207; and Woodward, *Origins of the New South*, 93 ff. These laws were, however, frequently violated, particularly for household servants and free men of color.
30 E.g., Ezell, *The South Since 1865*, 255.
31 Kendrick and Arnett, *The South Looks at Its Past*, 100–101, 129–31; and 176–77; Carter, *The Angry Scar*, 188–91; Edgar W. Knight, "Recent Progress and Problems of Education," in Couch (ed.) *Culture in the South*, 211 ff; and Albert D. Kirwan, *Revolt of the Rednecks: Mississippi Politics: 1876–1925* (Lexington: University of Kentucky Press, 1951), 137.

many underprivileged parents of both races continued to keep their children out of school for extended periods to help on the farm, as had their ancestors. The few cities provided significantly better educational opportunities, approaching those of the North and including free education through high school,[32] but the vast majority of adult Southerners of 1962 were raised in the country and small towns.

Many Southern state and local governments have made major efforts to improve their primary and secondary education in the last several decades; most Southern governments in the early 1960's were spending larger fractions of their total budgets and even of per capita incomes on education than the non-Southern average.[33] However, due to lower individual incomes, higher ratios of children to adults, and considerable out-migration of educated, prosperous adults, Southern expenditures per student were still significantly below those of most Northern locales in 1962.[34]

Aristocratic notions about the uneducableness of the majority have been much diluted recently, but Southerners of planter and other traditionalist backgrounds in black-belt and Old South locales like Charleston and Antebellum Town continued to express in the early sixties attentuated versions of some of the ideas of their grandparents. A number of these genteel folk educated in the humanities had observed "democratic" education and found it seriously wanting. According to some of them, the new public school system spread factual knowledge more and more thinly as it touched greater numbers of the rank and file; it crowded out excellent private academies; and the classics were hardly taught any more. Implementation of the notion that everybody should be exposed to education has reduced us to our lowest common denominator because of the loss of quality in our schools with the wholesale entry of the "common man." These Southerners felt that public education might well be limited to grade school for typical offspring of the masses because they pay few taxes, most are incapable of absorbing more, and secondary education for many of them is a waste of money. This group tended to feel that even Negroes have gotten the idea that they should be trained as lawyers, social scientists, historians, and other intellectuals; few of them can ever do more than memorizing facts or the oversimplified ideas of others. What the Negro race needs is more trained practical nurses, home economists and agri-

---

32 Vance, *All These People*, 437–39; and Fossier, *New Orleans: The Glamour Period, 1800–1840*, 232–37.
33 Ezell, *The South Since 1865*, 425 and 472.
34 New York *Times*, June 23, 1963.

cultural specialists, and skilled artisans. These traditionalists felt that
we have too many "overeducated," newly middle-class pseudo-intel-
lectuals already—Negro and white.[35]

These views were openly expressed by only a limited minority of
privileged Southerners among the interviewees—more often than not
middle-aged and older. Many influential Southerners, joined by Northern migrants to the South, rejected these ideas about mass education,
and the Southern majority seemed to want more and better education
for their children.

Basic, of course, to the impact of the school on the international
thinking of the child is the international interest and sophistication and
general intellectual quality of the teacher. No empirical study of the
pertinent thinking and performance of Southern teachers employing
a large enough and well enough drawn sample for regional and intra-
regional generalizations has come to the author's attention. A study
of ten thousand college graduates in the late 1940's determined that
Southern teachers among this sample were somewhat less inclined than
their Northern counterparts to expose themselves to international discussions in critical magazines and books, to favor expanded immigration, and to reject the view that "foreigners have peculiar and annoying
habits;" [36] however, the sample of Southern teachers was too small for
statistical significance. A study in the early sixties determined that primary and secondary school teachers enrolled in summer courses at the
University of Georgia were significantly less "worldminded" on a
number of international issues than teachers attending comparable
courses at Portland State College in Oregon, although the Georgia
teachers were more "worldminded" than undergraduate students at the
Georgia institution.[37] The significantly lower salaries for teachers in
most of the South as compared with the North [38] have tended to discourage migration of the more professional teachers into the region

35 See also Nicholls, *Southern Tradition and Regional Progress,* 111, 114, and
125–26; and Fletcher, "Education, Past and Present," in *I'll Take My Stand,* 114–15
and 118–20.
36 Bureau of Applied Social Research study.
37 Karl C. Garrison, "A Comparison of Worldminded Attitudes of Georgia and
Oregon School Teachers," *Journal of Teacher Education,* XIV (1963) 151–53. Criteria and measurements were those employed in the study of international attitudes
of University of Georgia undergraduates cited earlier (p. 251).
38 Of the sixteen states in the United States where average annual teachers' salaries
were less than $5,000 in 1962, ten were in the South (including Kentucky and West
Virginia); only Florida and Louisiana in the region were not in this lowest income
category—average annual salaries were $5,450 and $5,100, respectively, still significantly below the Northern average (New York *Times,* June 23, 1963).

and to encourage many of the most able ones to move out. Thus, more than in other regions, Southern teachers have tended to come from nearby, to be anchored in their particular community through marriage and other ties, and, from the author's impression, probably to be less inclined to focus their full-time energies on improving their professional competence as teachers.

However, the two studies mentioned immediately above and the interviews in the sample communities indicated a wide range of international interest, knowledge, and sophistication among Southern secondary and primary teachers. It was apparent that the quality of exposure of students to world affairs varied widely throughout the region. At one end of the continuum of excellence were a small number of schools, primarily in college communities and the larger cities, where the principal and teachers were intellectually alert cosmopolitans and the students were carefully selected from among the most talented and highly motivated of the public school population. At the other end was a considerable number of rural and small-town schools where the old patterns seemed to continue.

There were in 1959–62 still many school districts where the superintendent either was a low-quality, parochial politician or was regarded as a "hired man" who should reflect the interests and views of the local community, especially its conservative power structure. Teachers in such situations seemed, with notable exceptions, to be of indifferent ability, or, if competent, subject to political and social pressures which tended to inhibit their effectiveness as generators of critical thought. In some rural and small-town schools, such as in Mountain County, a considerable number had not themselves finished college. Most were local housewives and only part-time teachers tied to their husbands' jobs in the same communities. Typical social-studies teachers who instructed in fields related to world affairs grew up in the local area, frequently on farms or in hamlets, attended normal schools or teachers' colleges, and had encountered at best only second- or third-hand ideas about the role of the United States in the world. In some instances, as in Mountain County, teachers who were interested and experienced in other academic subjects were assigned the chore of teaching social studies because of the lack of individuals qualified and interested in that field. In Kent the traditionalist who taught "Problems of American Democracy" and other social studies was a racial paternalist, states' righter, and rather unenlightened critic of foreign aid and "retreats" before foreign threats and "so-called world opinion." A similar type taught social studies in Plantation County. Those social-studies teachers who disagreed with prevailing thought in heavily Negro areas of plantation or Old South traditions tended to feel that increasing racial tension since the mid-1950's had inhibited their open discussion of Africa, colonial questions, foreign aid, and other international problems (see pp. 427–30).

Some secondary school administrators and teachers in even the more unfavorable environments had developed their own international interpretations considerably at variance with local norms and had exposed their students to ideas regarded as highly questionable among most influential taxpayers. Although for the most part intellectually isolated from thought among able university scholars and teachers, these atypically analytical and intellectually curious educators read some of the better semipopular periodicals like *Harper's* and integrated some of the opinions they saw there with their own. For instance, the teacher of social studies in Hill County was an admirer of Chester Bowles and a reader of *Time, Newsweek,* and other rather internationalist material in the school library. Her superintendent of schools was a national Democrat who had supported President Truman against the Dixiecrats in 1948 and candidates Stevenson and Kennedy against the states' righters and Republicans in the three following national elections. His views on most international issues were more conservative than those of Northern liberals like Senators Hubert Humphrey and Joseph Clark, but cosmopolitan nevertheless. And social-studies teachers in the cities seemed, in the majority, favorable to active international collaboration, even if it should entail considerable expense.

Southern Higher Education

Even as late as 1961, only 29 percent of Southerners of college age as compared with 43 percent of Northerners in the same age brackets were actually in college, and the interregional differences were much larger when most Southern voters of 1962 were in their late teens.[39] Although more youngsters of less privileged backgrounds than in the past were going to college in the South, full scholarships have been relatively few and a smaller proportion of Southern than other parents have been able or have seen fit to pay even the relatively low tuitions of Southern state institutions regardless of the fact that college educations have tended to cost less than in the North.[40] Reinforcing these

39 New York *Times,* November 19, 1961. The Southern percentage would be considerably less divergent from the national one if Negroes were excluded from the statistic.
40 *Ibid.* The average income of Southern parents is, of course, lower than that of of Northern parents. However, a higher percentage of Southern students were still in public colleges rather than private ones in the sixties.

considerations has been the fact that on the average there has been less emphasis among the Southern as compared with the Northern rank and file on sending their children to college.[41]

Moreover, the type of migration out of and into the South has apparently tended on the whole to result in a less cosmopolitan college-educated population than would otherwise be the case. A number of internationally thoughtful Southern college graduates have remained in the region, and some Northerners of similar orientation have migrated there in such roles as college teachers, researchers, newspapermen, and technical and managerial personnel with the relatively few scientifically based industries. But on the average the most intellectually talented and internationally knowledgeable and liberal Southerners have tended to go to the University of Chicago, Harvard, Swarthmore, and other outstanding Northern schools, particularly if their parents could afford it or they could win large enough scholarships. The author has no systematic empirical data on the subject, but professors in some of those institutions observed that the most intellectually curious and internationally sophisticated of these students have been relatively likely to remain in the North, whereas the more provincially minded and those with prosperous family businesses, law firms, medical practices, and so on have been more inclined to return. Out-migration among equally cosmopolitan graduates of Southern colleges appeared considerably less—at least immediately after college. But as they have distinguished themselves and national opportunities became evident, a significant fraction of them have left the region as well. On the other hand, the Northerners who have moved South seemed not to have been for the most part the most intellectually alert and internationally able minority among their graduating classes up North. There have been outstanding exceptions to these generalizations, but the overall nature of the migration seems apparent enough.

The traditions and atmosphere of many—though certainly far from all—Southern white[42] colleges have also been relevant to the quality of thought on world problems and other public questions offered to their students. As Southern society became increasingly defensive against outside critics during the several decades prior to the secession,

41 The South has long been the most rural part of the country (see pp. 317-21) and rural Americans generally have been less inclined to expect or encourage their offspring to go to college. See Seymour Martin Lipset and Reinhard Bendix, *Social Mobility in Industrial Society* (Berkeley: University of California Press, 1959), 219–20; and Howard W. Beers, "Rural-Urban Differences: Some Evidence from Public Opinion Polls," *Rural Sociology*, XVIII (1953), 8–10.

42 The discussion to follow applies primarily to white colleges. In most instances these generalizations apply in a considerable measure to Negro institutions as well; however, Negro education is considered in Chapter 14.

professors and students interested in critical discussion of public questions departed for the North or remained silent, and polemicists for slavery and other aspects of the "Southern way of life" dominated the campuses and the communications media generally.[43]

Many Southern colleges were obliged to close their doors due to lack of money and students able to pay tuition after the Civil War. Others were greatly weakened and just managed to avoid bankruptcy. For over a generation few went to college. Termination of Reconstruction ushered in dominance by an ultraconservative elite of planters and commercial leaders of the New South who were not known for much attachment to academic freedom or hesitancy to intervene against professors critical of the economic, political, or racial *status quo*. Although there was considerable emphasis on the classics and other fields of interest to the Southern leisure class, the tone of many Southern campuses became that of a romanticized treatment of the past rather than a dynamic, analytical posture toward the social, economic, and public problems of the present and future. The exceptions were primarily at institutions located outside the Deep South, and, particularly, away from sections of plantation traditions.[44]

"Progress" in the 1880's brought into being institutes and departments of universities focused on textile engineering and other applied sciences, and Southern technical schools have continued to develop toward the standards of the better national institutions.[45] But the social sciences and other studies oriented toward critical examination of public questions remained weak in all except a handful of the best Southern colleges,[46] partially accounting for the relative unpopularity of the social sciences among graduates of Southern institutions of higher learning.[47]

By the early sixties more resources than ever were going into higher education in the South; national foundations were helping to develop a number of significant institutions; expenditures per student had in-

43   See, for instance, Eaton, *Freedom of Thought in the Old South;* Eaton, *The Growth of Southern Civilization,* 97 and 298–317; and pp. 383–84.
44   Nicholls, *Southern Tradition and Regional Progress,* 134–35; Carter, *The Angry Scar,* 177 ff; Cash, *The Mind of the South,* 322–28; James McBride Dabbs, *The Southern Heritage* (New York: Alfred Knopf, 1958), 170–79; Rubin and Kilpatrick, *The Lasting South,* 142–45 and 148–49; and Thomas D. Clark, *The Emerging South* (New York: Oxford University Press, 1961), 161.
45   E.g., Clark, *The Emerging South,* 114.
46   Nicholls, *Southern Tradition and Regional Progress,* 151.
47   The Bureau of Applied Social Research study found that graduates of Southern colleges still residing in the region were significantly less likely than Northern college graduates to feel that "the government should promote and subsidize research in the social sciences" and that "the findings of psychologists are helpful in fitting workers to jobs."

creased faster than in the North (from a much lower base); [48] and the quality of instruction in subjects related to foreign policy had improved greatly, as it had outside the South. Some improvement had been evident in all major categories of institutions of higher learning; in fact, the range between the best and the worst had probably widened since the pre-Pearl Harbor period. The quality of thought and instruction at Duke, for instance, with major research and teaching programs in world affairs, was vastly different from that at isolated, economically weak colleges in 1962. Moreover, most graduates attended Southern colleges when they were much weaker in international affairs and other social sciences, both in absolute terms and in comparison with the North.[49]

Nevertheless, residues of historical factors mentioned above continued to plague many Deep Southern institutions. The South has had no monopoly on undue pressures against academic freedom, but thoughtful local observers noted that exacerbation of the race issue since 1954 had resulted in increasing pressures against articulate, critically minded, professors by influential conservative alumni, trustees, state legislators, and taxpayers. Cosmopolitan professors were denounced by Citizens Councils and other racially conservative groups and individuals as "pinko," "red," "brainwashed," "commies," and the like.[50] Although a number of college presidents, trustees, and influential alumni have defended and striven to keep the faculty members so attacked, they too have feared loss of state or private funds and other difficulties which might reduce the effectiveness of their educational institutions. Actual pressures and anxieties about potential difficulties have been most evident with respect to liberal thinking on race relations and, to a lesser measure, domestic economics and state and local politics, but they have tended to inhibit serious analysis of some international questions as well. Expression of views out of harmony with those locally prevalent on such issues as United States policy toward Africa has been regarded by faculty members at some Deep Southern institutions as "touchy," and some teachers have hesitated to argue openly for freer trade in locales dominated economically by strong protectionists.

48 New York *Times,* November 19, 1961.
49 For discussions of the intellectual atmosphere on Southern campuses when the middle-aged college graduates of the early sixties were students, see H. Clarence Nixon, "Colleges and Universities," *Culture in the South,* 229–44; and Howard Odum, *Southern Regions of the United States,* 503–23.
50 James W. Silver, *Mississippi: The Closed Society* (New York: Harcourt, Brace, and World, 1964); and Benjamin Muse, *Ten Years of Prelude: The Story of Integration Since the Supreme Court's 1954 Decision* (New York: The Viking Press, 1964), especially pp. 168–70.

Although a number of cosmopolitan professors have remained in even those institutions which have been under the more persistent pressures of this sort, these difficulties together with increasing opportunities outside the South have resulted in the departure of a considerable fraction of more internationally sophisticated and intellectually vigorous faculty members. Even when there has been little or no pressure against expression of multilateralist ideas in world affairs and pay has been roughly equivalent to that at Northern institutions (as it usually has not [51]), able Northern specialists on international relations and related subjects have frequently been hesitant to accept positions at most Deep Southern schools due in large measure to rumors of restriction of academic freedom and anxiety over the potential impacts of the racial controversy on their children. Likewise, capable Southern graduate students at Northern and foreign graduate schools have been reluctant to return to Deep Southern colleges to teach and their counterparts at Southern graduate schools have sought Northern jobs for similar reasons.[52]

Thus, the social sciences and other courses of study relevant to international relations were still relatively weak in the early sixties at most Deep Southern institutions, and only a handful of graduate schools in the region could be considered advanced in these fields.[53] Only at a very few colleges did students undergo the intensive intellectual stimulation, the exposure to a wide variety of controversial ideas, or the rigorous training in social and public analysis available to a considerable minority in non-Southern institutions. Southern students at only a few colleges have had continuing contact with creative professors doing original research on major aspects of America's role in world affairs. Many of the smaller, less affluent colleges offered relatively few courses in foreign affairs, and much of what has been available has had rather low priority or was taught by rather uninspiring teachers.[54] Student groups concerned with international issues, such as international relations clubs, have been really active on only a few campuses, and these were typically the results of diligent efforts of a professor; liberal and,

51 Peggy Heim, "Academic Compensation in the South: Its Present and Future," *Southern Economic Journal*, XXIX (1963), 345–49.
52 Nicholls, *Southern Tradition and Regional Progress*, 146–51; Harry S. Ashmore, *An Epitaph for Dixie* (New York: W. W. Norton, 1958), 155–58; and Wilma Dykeman and James Stokely, *Neither Black Nor White* (New York: Rinehart, 1957), 191.
53 Nicholls, *Southern Tradition and Regional Progress*, 151–52.
54 For statistical support of these impressionistic observations, see Fred Cole, *International Relations in Institutions of Higher Learning in the South* (Washington, D.C.: American Council on Education, 1958).

especially, radical groups have been virtually nonexistent at most institutions.

It is therefore understandable that some Southern faculties in the
early 1960's included some of the country's most conservative political
scientists, historians, economists, and other specialists in the social
sciences and humanities. In some institutions the men and women who
stressed military and other forms of power as the principal source of
international developments and as the proper emphasis of our foreign
policy, who felt we had made too many compromises with our international opponents, and who would have us adopt a "tougher" posture
toward leftist, anticolonialist, and strongly nationalistic regimes in the
underdeveloped world had reportedly been promoted faster than more
liberal faculty members, given larger resources for research, and accorded disproportionate attention by conservative newspapers, state
legislators, and various voluntary groups. Since most of these conservatives on foreign policy were also relatively traditional on the race problem, they were often popular as speakers before such conservative
audiences as Cold-War Seminars, Alerts, and service and patriotic
groups and they frequently took a rather active part in nonacademic
community life.

Nevertheless, critical thought and liberal thinking about world affairs, as well as other issues, and tolerance of views divergent from
local norms had developed over the years at a number of Southern
colleges in spite of accentuated racial tension.[55] In some colleges it
was difficult to find teachers in fields related to foreign affairs or the
social sciences generally whose thinking on foreign relations was to
the right of the policies of the Kennedy administration. Some internationalists continued to teach students and compare ideas with a few
cosmopolitan colleagues at even some of the more conservative state
and private institutions in Mississippi and other Deep Southern locales
where racial tension was high and the tradition of academic freedom
to comment vigorously on controversial issues feeble. These faculty
members were obliged to be subtle and cautious in their criticisms of
prevailing local thinking in order to retain their positions. Sociologists
continued to teach and perform research in noncontroversial, pragmatic fields not directly related to perception of foreign policy, such
as investigation of local attitudes toward public health, economic de-

55 The following observations are based primarily on interviews for this study.
For discussions of the dilemmas of the analytically critical faculty member of public institutions in the Deep South, see Iredell Jenkins, "Segregation and the Professor," *AAUP Bulletin*, XLIII (1957), 10–18; Muse, *Ten Years of Prelude*, 168–69;
and Nicholls, *Southern Tradition and Regional Progress*, 150–52.

velopment, new agricultural knowledge, and church participation. Any broadening of horizons and development of critical facilities in even these fields probably have indirectly influenced thought patterns on other, more controversial problems. Others who taught in fields like political science, international economics, and modern history, where foreign affairs was part of the content, have frequently realized the unfortunate impacts of racial tension on critical discussion, attempted to separate the race issue from international questions, and continued to expose their students to information and alternative ideas which tended to contradict or moderate thinking prevalent in their conservative homes or in the cultural climate generally, with the hope that a few students would develop critical postures toward world affairs and many more would carry from college some wider acquaintance with the world and with thinking beyond the local scene. Many of those professors seemed to feel that they must compromise on some abstract principles not directly pertinent to their objectives of educating youngsters and limit their nonconformity to issues and circumstances where it would be apt to be effective.

Colleges and the General Community

As no systematic evaluation of the actual and potential impacts of Southern institutions of higher learning on thinking about foreign affairs in nearby locales beyond their own student bodies is available, the author can advance here only a few impressions derived from limited interviews, observations, comments by participant observers, and the sparse amount of published material bearing on this problem.

An increasing number of thoughtful programs in world affairs for adults have been conducted by Southern colleges and universities in recent years—programs which might serve as points of departure for further experimentation by the same and other institutions. Although general extension agencies of state universities and land-grant colleges could provide one of the primary vehicles for this purpose, only a handful of these units throughout the United States have developed really imaginative programs or executed them with much sensitivity or dynamism thus far.[56] Most of the shortcomings of general extension in the South are probably apparent in other regions as well, judging from complaints of perceptive foundation officials and specialists in world affairs communication with national organizations concerned with adult education in this field.

56 Some of the more promising programs in world affairs which have been conducted both in and out of the South and which might be employed as prototypes elsewhere in the region are discussed in Chapter 16.

Only a very few Southern colleges, such as the University of North Carolina and, more recently, Florida State University, have developed much of a tradition of inspired, rigorous communication of knowledge about world affairs and the social sciences and public questions generally into their communities, states, and region. There has been little money for general extension activities in public affairs and the social sciences pertinent to them, in contradistinction to agricultural extension which has been relatively strong in the region. With some exceptions, trustees, influential state legislators, and college administrators have not assigned much priority or funds to developing vigorous liberal arts programs of a nonvocational nature for adults. Moreover, the task itself has been difficult in settings where the average level of education and cultural and intellectual curiosity has been relatively low, apathy about world affairs widespread, and poorly educated electorates and strongly conservative elites suspicious of social scientists, "ivory towers," and dispassionate examination of controversial public issues. Furthermore, the teaching loads of professors in relevant fields have tended to be heavier in the South than in the country generally, leaving them less time and energy for either research or programs for adults. Prestige at the best Southern institutions, as at their Northern counterparts, has been accorded to able teachers of students and, increasingly, to researchers, not to effective adult educators. Administrators speak of the difficulties of providing the faculty to handle growing numbers of students —the pressures of more youngsters clamoring for college educations do not bode well for the allocation of considerably greater funds and more able personnel to liberal adult education. Thus, general extensions and the like were already in the early sixties experiencing growing demands that they become financially self-supporting, although this requirement has not been applied to the education of regular students.

Given these factors, it is not surprising that few of the general extension staffs and practitioners of other university agencies devoted to nonvocational adult education were regarded as especially exciting individuals by either talented professors of international affairs, able administrators, or thoughtful potential audiences in their vicinities. Most of them seemed to limit their efforts more or less to offering formal courses designed for undergraduates to those adults who might be interested. No service centers had developed—like the World Affairs Center at the University of Minnesota which furnishes advice on subject matter, speakers and other experts, and educational techniques to both private and public groups in the state, agencies which may be interested in designing their own international-affairs activities to reach their particular audiences. Extension instructors in fields related to foreign policy, poorly paid for the most part, were apparently rather frequently of indifferent competence, both in the subject matter and in teaching ability. In many cases participants tended to be adults who did not finish college and teachers striving for additional credits which would be rewarded by their respective school systems. Many able Southerners who have completed college and have been potentially interested in insightful programs on world affairs have not been interested in credits, and they have been sufficiently matured emotionally and intellectually that they might not have cared to devote their energies to formal academic courses designed for youngsters. Many have preferred more informal discussion, coupled with prior reading of serious material. "Canned" programs have frequently been regarded as overly rigid and not especially interesting, particularly among busy college graduates of some influence in their communities and of at least latent concern about world developments. Even if funds were more readily available, the organizing of vehicles to involve the varied potentially concerned groups in the South would demand originality, sophistication in foreign relations, insightful perception of the forces and effective individuals operating in the locality, and abilities to gain the respect of and work with diverse citizens apparent among only a very few of the personnel of university adult education agencies.

Moreover, professors who have been anxious about expressing controversial ideas on public issues in classes including offspring of leading state legislators, members of state sovereignty commissions and Citizens Councils,[57] arch-conservative contributors to college coffers, and so on have been apt to be even more hesitant about doing so publicly before the general community. For instance, a professor in the humanities at a major state institution in the Deep South was attacked by conservatives in the state legislature for criticizing that body for making itself "the laughing stock of the world" by its debates and proposed actions relative to segregation in the early sixties. The right of a professor at a state institution to disagree publicly with and to criticize the state legislators was questioned. The board of trustees, dependent for funds and other support from the legislature, was encouraged to "root out" such individuals with "un-American" (and "un-Southern") ideas. The professor shortly resigned. It is not surprising that internationally

57 One internationally thoughtful professor who had undergone various extra-university pressures in the past at a Deep Southern public institution reported that the son of the isolationist-segregationist leader of the legislature tape recorded in class the professor's lectures and comments insofar as they might be at variance with views of his father (and of himself).

sophisticated professors at many Deep Southern institutions have tended to "cultivate their own gardens" and remain relatively silent on the public controversies among the local nonacademic population.

Yet the presence of a college, even a relatively weak and conservative one, in a Southern community typically has been associated with a wider tolerance of diverse ideas and a moderation of dogmatic attitudes in the general community. Some of the faculty who know something of world affairs have mixed at least now and then with business and professional people. They have participated in churches, lodges, and other organizations, and their ideas have had some impact beyond the campus. There has been a great difference between the effects of Duke, Vanderbilt, the University of North Carolina, and other vigorous institutions and those of some small state or denominational colleges, but even at the latter there have usually been a few cosmopolitans who have set some critical standards and influenced some, largely better-educated, citizens toward international responsibility.

CHAPTER 8

SOCIAL CLASS
AND OCCUPATION
IN THE OLD SOUTH
AND THE NEW

Some General Observations

T he Importance of Social Class and Occupation
as Compared with Education

Neither occupation, nor social standing, nor income has been as crucial for interest, understanding, and thoughtful attitudes with respect to
world affairs as quantity, subject matter, and quality of formal education. Most social and occupational differences have themselves been
intimately connected with education.

Thus, Southerners in the liberal professions—teachers, the clergy of
the major denominations, and to a lesser extent, lawyers—have been
more apt in recent years to be thoughtful, relatively informed and interested, better read, and more internationalist or cosmopolitan than
have businessmen. But Southerners in these walks of life usually received
more education, often graduate training. They were more likely to have
received liberal rather than technical undergraduate training and have
tended to associate with others in their professional group who received
similarly broadening educations. Lawyers as a group have more nearly
approached international criteria than physicians, but the former's educational experience was typically less narrowly technical. The few
physicians whose undergraduate education was in the liberal arts have

seemed more thoughtful, better informed and read, and more liberal on foreign policy than those who were in premedicine, as has been the case outside the South as well.[1]

Southerners whose parents and grandparents were among the more esteemed, influential, or socially or economically secure in their locales have been more inclined to be thoughtful cosmopolitans, or at least not dogmatic, arch-conservative, or know-nothing neo-isolationists, than others of similar occupation and income who sprang from more lowly station. But the former were also more likely to have attended the better colleges in the South if not outside, and to have taken some nonvocational, general courses, and their parents were apt to have been well educated as well. Differences in international thinking have been wider between the Southern lower classes—especially those members from deprived rural backgrounds, as most of them were even in 1962—and the more economically and occupationally privileged classes than between comparable strata outside the South, but differences in education with which interest and liberal opinion in world affairs have been closely associated have been wider also. Furthermore, realistic discussion of world developments not only has been more limited to the educated few in the South than in other regions, but has also been concentrated more among the small minority with relatively secure social standing in the South.

Economic affluence has had less bearing on social standing in the South than elsewhere, including New England. Descendants of the antebellum elite were still usually viewed in 1962 with some deference in Southern settings of plantation and associated traditions, and for that matter in many of the "newer" parts of the South as well, regardless of their often small incomes. "Newer," wealthier families have tended to be looked down upon by the less affluent gentry in traditional sections of the South, and many average Southerners, including Negroes, have seemed to accept the judgment of the latter to a degree.

Nevertheless, cosmopolitan Southerners in the late fifties and early sixties were disproportionately numerous among the relatively financially comfortable,[2] as well as among the more socially esteemed. Pros-

1 The Bureau of Applied Social Research study. The sample of Southern physicians was too small for comparisons among those of different educational experience, but this difference was statistically significant for the national sample.

2 Likewise, Charles O. Lerche, Jr., discovered a high positive correlation between per capita income in congressional districts and tendencies of Southern members of the House of Representatives to vote for important multilateral programs on roll calls in the late 1950's and early 1960's. (See, Lerche, *The Uncertain South*, 201–205).

perity frequently has encouraged economic conservatism, including opposition to expenditures for capital assistance abroad, negative attitudes toward foreign regimes advancing partly socialist policies or slogans, and opposition to imports of products related to one's economic interests. But interest in and attention to foreign policy have been more likely when the family has had the funds to purchase books, magazines, and newspapers, to participate in voluntary organizations, and to spare the leisure from activities directly related to financial solvency. Among the prosperous the better educated have been more inclined to have these habits (and thus to know a good deal about world affairs) than have the less educated of similar income; in the late fifties and early sixties those affluent Southern whites who favored such liberal foreign economic policies as capital assistance to socialistically inclined neutralist regimes were for the most part college educated. Moreover, when education has been held constant on surveys, differences in information and opinion about world issues have decreased considerably between income groups. Likewise, the college educated with lower incomes have been on the average better informed and more cosmopolitan than more affluent Southerners who did not finish high school.

The Southern Underprivileged

The South has been narrowing the economic and occupational differentials between itself and the North, especially during the last two decades or so. Although important pockets of low per-capita income persisted in a number of rural areas, much of the grinding poverty prevalent in the region before World War II had been sharply reduced by the 1960's.

Nevertheless, the region still unfortunately included in 1960 disproportionately large numbers of citizens in the lower reaches of income and occupational skill, as was the case in education as well. The rural sections, such as Mountain, Plantation, and Hill counties, have been for the most part much further below national norms than urban locales, but with the exception of a few Southern communities which have had strong universities or scientifically based industries and highly trained labor forces, the majority of Southern cities still contained larger proportions in lower educational, economic, and occupational categories than most Northern ones. Morever, the middle and higher income groups in Southern urban areas on the average were composed more than in the North of small business and tradespeople—an occupational category among the middle class throughout the nation in which the more parochial, ill informed, uninterested, and conservative about world affairs have been quite prevalent (see pp. 303–306). Conversely, the prosperous groups were less apt than in the North to be in those callings where international sophistication has been more apparent—teachers in the social sciences, natural sciences, and humanities, research workers, psychiatrists, formally trained clergy, and technical personnel with graduate training. Elimination of Negroes from these statistics—except in the mountains where they were very few—would reduce considerably the disparity between the South and North, but some interregional differences between whites alone would still remain.

Moreover, when replies to similar questions on several surveys were combined to provide a large enough sample, it was discovered that the group which did not complete high school, worked in unskilled, semiskilled, or poor farm roles, and received annual family incomes below $3,000 was on most foreign issues at least somewhat and on some questions considerably more indifferent, less well informed, and less apt to read about international developments than roughly comparable economic, social, and occupational groups in the rest of the country. The majority of those Southerners in the lower half or so of the regional socioeconomic spectrum have been rather unfamiliar with most problems except the most general ones facing this country since 1945, have failed to mention foreign policy as a major determinant of their votes for Congressmen and the President (when they voted) except possibly during the Korean War, and have offered no opinions to many survey questions dealing with world trade, intercultural exchange, international organization, and other continuing issues facing the United States abroad. When they did venture views they tended more often than not to think that we should either spend at least part of our foreign aid at home or not at all, that we should withdraw from some of our more demanding nonmilitary international commitments, that our allies, particularly non-Western European ones, were untrustworthy, and so on.

Some exceptional individuals have interested themselves to a significant extent in international affairs, but they were more likely to be in the lower-middle class than in the working or lower class, to be in skilled or supervisory positions rather than in unskilled or semiskilled ones, and to live in the cities and, much less frequently, the towns rather than in the rural sections. They have been either vigorous, atypically broad in thought and action, or, more likely, foreign or Northern-born or otherwise different in crucial respects from most Southerners of their calling.

For instance, an immigrant from Italy, who operated a small corner grocery in a working-class district of New Orleans and who had not completed high school, read the *New Republic*, the New York *Times* (Sunday edition), *The Reporter*, and even *Foreign Affairs*, as well as books dealing with world affairs and other public issues. His views were vigorously internationalist, favorable to expanded economic assistance to India and other "deserving" underdeveloped countries, including Poland (depending on the details), and to exertion of further pressure on Portugal to prevent an "explosion" in Angola, and so on. Another example was a Jewish clerk in a New Orleans dry goods store serving a predominantly working class clientele—he read the *Christian Science Monitor* and expressed international views favorable to most foreign actions of President Kennedy (except for the Bay of Pigs affair). A third was a foreign-born Jewish shopkeeper serving Negroes and lower-class whites in Charleston; a fourth was a Roman Catholic, raised in New York, who had come South as a foreman with a clothing plant when it moved to a Carolina city.

Several times this number, but still a very small minority in the supervisory and skilled if not lower-middle class, kept up in the early sixties with international coverage in news magazines. For example, the head loom mechanic of one of the mills in Kent, raised on a poor farm and with limited education, read *Time* and approved of its attitudes on international problems. He also read the Charlotte (North Carolina) *Observer* and agreed with most of its editorials, although most of the white population of Kent who read newspapers subscribed to more conservative ones of Columbia or Charleston, South Carolina. But most of the mill people did not read newspapers, and certainly not their editorials on foreign affairs. However, this head loom mechanic had been the elected mayor of Kent, was a dynamic leader among the mill workers, was the brother of a former state senator from the local district, and was generally outstanding in the mill community.

One group in the South which has apparently had some impact on the thinking of some of the Southern underprivileged and which has itself, with some exceptions, been relatively favorable toward multilateral international involvements has been the local representatives of trade unions in the few places where there has been unionization. Some representatives of national unions were Northerners; others were of Southern origins. But with few exceptions at the time of the interviews they all approved of foreign economic assistance and most other active international programs of the Eisenhower and, later, the Kennedy administrations. Probably most local union leaders in the coal industry and a large minority in apparel and, particularly, textile fields have been protectionists in recent years (see pp. 161, 164, 170), but this opposition, or at least caution, about imports seldom seemed to carry over into other international fields, as it frequently did among owners of textile mills. Many of these representatives were not particularly well informed about world affairs, nor very interested, and it was not a field that many of them talked much about with their members. But they were on the whole better read and informed than most of their members, including the officers of their locals.

The local elected officers, on the other hand, were almost exclusively of Southern origins. Although they tended to manifest some of the thinking of their national headquarters—largely favorable to multilateralism—they were also typically influenced to a major degree by more conservative international attitudes among their members. Some of their international thinking diverged considerably from that of union leaders in New York, and even from that of local business agents. Racism was not uncommon among shop stewards in racially tense Deep Southern locales, and support of white supremacy was often associated with very conservative international views, as it was among white Southerners generally (see Chapter 11).

The international behavior of rank-and-file union members was more difficult to estimate because of the lack of a large, systematically selected sample. The generalizations advanced previously about unionized textile, garment, and coal-mine workers seemed applicable with some modifications to Southern union members generally. Although a number, especially of Deep Southern rural origins, have continued, despite the urging of union leaders, to vote for racists who have also frequently been economic conservatives and opponents of a number of multilateral commitments before the Congress, the proportion of union members who have voted for less conservative candidates has, from various reports, been larger than among workers who were unorganized. Workers who have helped elect less conservative Congressmen have usually voted for their liberal domestic economic programs rather than for their ideas on foreign aid, intercultural exchange, the U.N., and the like, but with the exception of Senator Olin Johnston and a few others these workers have typically in fact assisted in the election of individuals who voted for multilateral commitments in these fields once in Congress. In reducing to at least some extent the "boss's" control and paternalistic influence over his employees, unions have usually also provided ideas alternative to those he advanced—one of several major reasons why many Southern employers have opposed unionization.

Unions which have been highly insecure vis-à-vis local management and government—as have most of those in the South—have tended to focus their programs and educational activities on matters more immediately pragmatic than world affairs, but gradually at least some of the rank and file have apparently learned from the union periodical, the business agent, and sessions with regional or national union officials that the national leadership favored foreign economic assistance, intercultural exchange, active multilateral collaboration in the U.N. and other international bodies, and so on. The impact on workers' thinking has normally been limited, but some of them have become considerably more inclined toward these international orientations over a period of time than most nonunionized workers, and a larger fraction have been influenced to some degree. Although samples of individual surveys have been too small for statistical significance, the combining of similar questions on different polls and conversations with union members in the sample communities indicate that they have probably been somewhat better informed and less conservative about foreign policy than unorganized workers, although the differences did not appear on the whole to be large. Unionized Southern workers should, of course, have been less poorly informed and neo-isolationist than unorganized workers even if the unions had exerted no effect whatsoever on their thinking. This should be true because most of the least skilled and little educated, particularly in small enterprises in smaller towns, have been unorganized whereas the unionized workers in the region have been disproportionately concentrated in larger cities, among the bigger, more efficient plants in national chains, and within the higher wage, more technological industries—business environments with the more alert, skilled, educated, and broad-minded employees.[3]

The Southern Gentry

So much of the literature of the South has dealt with the descendants of the antebellum elite, they have maintained such prestige and exercised so much influence on the values of other Southerners, and there has been so much controversy about their contributions to thought in their region that examination in some detail of their international behavior and influence seems warranted.

The Aristocracy

Since virtually everyone in the South was poor after Appomattox, Southerners have been able to claim genteel forebears when their real

3 For supporting observations, see Solomon Barkin, *The Decline of the Labor Movement* (Santa Barbara: Center for the Study of Democratic Institutions, 1961), 15, 17, and 30.

ancestry was much less elevated. Some with little real claim to ante-bellum aristocratic antedecents have so integrated the myths of the plantation into their mental furniture as to believe they are in fact of esteemed lineage and to act as though they were. But plantations comprised only a relatively small part of Southern geography and included an even smaller fraction of the white population. About a quarter of Southern white families had any slaves in 1860, and of those most had between one and four. Only 3 percent had as many as twenty, some eight thousand had fifty or more, and less than three thousand—roughly one out of five hundred white families—as many as a hundred.[4] Half the total income in the South from cotton was received by slightly over a thousand out of the 667,000 families who raised the crop.[5] Thus, only a very small minority of the approximately eight million whites in the slave states of 1860 had the affluence, slaves, and leisure to have been considered aristocrats by the criteria of the day.

But certainly by 1861 only a minority among even this small group of prosperous planters plus perhaps a roughly equivalent number of well-off business and professional people—maybe a total of several thousand families—had held their wealth long enough and had developed the habits required to satisfy the criteria of the gentry of Tidewater Virginia, the Carolina low country, the lower Mississippi Valley, and the few remaining sections where plantations had been in the family for two or more generations and sons had been educated as "gentlemen."[6]

The majority of even larger planters at the time of the secession were *nouveaux riches*, rough-and-ready frontiersmen from "nowhere" with very limited educations, few social graces or intellectual interests, and a strong desire for land, slaves, and money. Thus, Nathan Bedford Forrest, later famous as a leader of Confederate cavalry and the Ku-Klux Klan, left school at an early age to become prosperous as a slave trader and planter. William Faulkner's fictional Thomas Sutpen, a poor, semiliterate mountaineer who succeeded in amassing thousands of acres and building a great mansion, was probably an exaggerated version of

---

4 Ulrich B. Phillips, *Life and Labor in the Old South* (Boston: Little, Brown, and Co., 1951), 239; Virginius Dabney, *Below the Potomac* (New York and London: Appleton-Century Co., 1942), 3; Eaton, *Freedom of Thought in the Old South*, 35–36; Kendrick and Arnett, *The South Looks at Its Past*, 42; Eaton, *The Growth of Southern Civilization*, 98; Savage, *Seeds of Time*, 87; A. J. N. Den Hollander, "The Tradition of 'Poor Whites,'" in Couch (ed.), *Culture in the South*, 404; Lillian Smith, *Killers of the Dream* (New York: W. W. Norton, 1961), 168; Ezell, *The South Since 1865*, 8; and, for Louisiana, Shugg, *Origins of Class Struggle in Louisiana*, 31–33, 77, and 97.

5 Savage, *Seeds of Time*, 87.   6 *Ibid.*, 109–10.

many who became planters in the developing Black Belt.[7] Even the second generation, the offspring of these ambitious, vigorous, often buccaneering pioneers, like Faulkner's Henry Sutpen, were probably for the most part regarded as rather naive rustics unacquainted with ideas beyond those of their neighbors in the nearby country and market towns by sophisticated people in New Orleans (as was the younger Sutpen), Charleston, and other older Southern societies. A few sons of the gentry of older regions migrated to fertile acres in the interior of the Deep South, but they were a small fraction of the planters there and most of them probably did not maintain whatever interest in literature, culture, and other aristocratic tastes they may have known on the coast.[8]

If one omits the parvenus regarded as "cotton snobs" in Charleston and other Old South communities, perhaps as many as one out of several hundred white Southerners in 1962 was actually descended from one or more landed gentlemen or ladies or comparable professional and commercial leaders of the Old South—and usually from many more of a "lesser breed" as well.

Moreover, most surviving antebellum planters who owned several dozen or more slaves and the somewhat less esteemed class of prosperous business and professional people were ruined financially by the war—as were Faulkner's ruthless upstart Sutpens and chivalric (but still relatively "new") Sartorises alike. Their slaves were freed without compensation, their homes burned and agricultural capital destroyed, the values of their land vastly depreciated, and their markets disrupted. Among the minority who succeeded in saving some of their property, high taxes under carpetbagger-Negro governments, oscillations of the cotton, tobacco, rice, and sugar markets, the boll weevil, incompetence or lack of competitive abilities (and of sharp dealing proclivities) vis-à-vis aggressive "new" men from the hills and other lowly origins and other misfortunes resulted in mortgage foreclosures and transfers

7   William Faulkner, *Absalom, Absalom!* (New York: Random House, 1936), 9 ff.
8   For discussions of the incidence and qualities of antebellum black-belt planters, see Cash, *The Mind of the South*, 201 ff; Rudolf Heberle, "The Changing of Social Stratification in the South," *Social Forces*, XXXVIII (1959), 42–44; Eaton, *Freedom of Thought in the Old South*, 53–58; Eaton, *The Growth of Southern Civilization*, 15, 21–24, and 35–40; Savage, *Seeds of Time*, 71–72, 196, and 110–13; Kendrick and Arnett, *The South Looks at Its Past*, 22; Phillips, *Life and Labor in the Old South*, 109–11 and 251–83; Woodward, *Origins of the New South, 1877–1913*, 7, 14, 18, and 20; Vance, *Human Geography of the South*, 187; C. Vann Woodward, *Reunion and Reaction* (Garden City: Doubleday, 1956), 56; and Shugg, *Origins of Class Struggle in Louisiana*, 31–33.

of holdings of a large fraction to successive generations of Flem Snopeses and others of like character. Some of these former planters or their progeny were able to deal effectively with such competition— probably in some cases by adopting the values and practices of the strivers from below for material success (like Faulkner's Jason Compson) and by collaborating with Northern capitalists, but most of the agrarian gentry, looking upon trade and industry as beneath their dignity, lost out.[9]

Hence, by the 1960's the antebellum families for the most part had lived on limited finances for most of the past century and had lost most of their political influence—though not their social esteem. As in Plantation and Delta counties and Bayou Parish, the active planters of 1962 included only a small minority of descendants of the comparable antebellum class; most were, rather, descendants of poor whites, yeoman farmers, overseers, "scalawags," and even "carpetbaggers." Economic power throughout most of the South in the sixties resided with first, second, and at most third generation wealth.

Southerners who were assumed to be of antebellum genteel ancestry were still considerably admired, even by the more prosperous of newer vintage, in Old South locales where there had been little new industry, where the economy had remained relatively static, and where by 1960 there was relatively little new wealth to challenge these old families. But in other locales with Old South roots, such as New Orleans, where successive waves of enterprising new people had achieved prosperity and influence, the antebellum gentry had intermarried into these new groups after they had achieved two or three generations of postbellum wealth and position. Even when the grandsons and granddaughters of the new elite of 1880 to 1910 had not married spouses with claims to antebellum gentility, they were often accepted as old families. Finally, in parts of the New South where there were no plantation traditions, as in the mountains and most of the Piedmont, even immediate offspring of self-made industrialists, merchants, speculators, and other prosperous men tended by 1960 to be regarded as "older money," although few of the aristocracy of antebellum origins would consider them social equals.

Each of these groups, from the few descendants of the families who

9 For discussions of the fate of the antebellum elite during the postwar period, see Nicholls, *Southern Tradition and Regional Progress*, 23, 34, and 51; Heberle, *Social Forces*, XXXVIII (1959), 44; Woodward, *Origins of the New South*, 152–54 and 179; Hodding Carter, *The Lower Mississippi* (New York: Farrar and Rinehart, 1942), 393–94; Shugg, *Origins of Class Struggle in Louisiana*, 191–95, 248–49, and 276; and Ezell, *The South Since 1865*, 219–22.

had owned many thousand acres and a hundred or more slaves for two or more generations by 1861 through grandchildren of new postbellum businessmen, bankers, manufacturers, and professional people, included in 1959–62 disproportionately large numbers of the small minority of thoughtful cosmopolitans in the South. Since inherited privilege is a heterogeneous category, it seems wise to discuss first the small minority of Southerners who have internalized the traditions of the Old South planter class even if their claims to the aristocracy of the period were tenuous and to consider next the progeny of the wealthy and middle classes of later origin, dating from the industrialization of the Piedmont which began in earnest in the 1880's, although in reality these groups have merged considerably in some sections and are gradually doing so in others.

The Cosmopolitans

Southerners of genteel tradition have provided political leaders like Oscar W. Underwood, John Sharp Williams, and Woodrow Wilson who pressed for active participation in international affairs when most of the rest of the country was isolationist. The plantation gentry have been and continued in the early sixties to be for the most part favorable to freer international trade (with the exception of sugar planters) and collective security with Britain and Western Europe. Many of them apparently agreed in 1919 with Woodrow Wilson that we should join the League of Nations, and they backed with some exceptions United States entry into the U.N., the Truman Doctrine, and the Marshall Plan of the early postwar years. These views did not necessarily imply serious reading or profound knowledge about the issues, but a minority of this socially secure class—like Senator Williams of Mississippi [10] and, to a lesser extent, Senator Underwood of Alabama [11]—was well read and knowledgeable.

A disproportionately large number of this social group were still among the small, thoughtful cosmopolitan minority in the South in the early 1960's. At least a few of the progeny of Old South tradition have remained relatively well-read multilateralists. Their presence in rural counties of older plantation tradition and their absence from many hill counties and almost all rural mountain counties account to a considerable extent for the existence of some relatively critical cosmopoli-

10 Osborn, *John Sharp Williams;* the cosmopolitan interests, thinking, and reading habits of Williams are apparent throughout this volume. The following are suggestive: vii, 15–16, 19–21, 235–53, 357, 446, 460, and 463.
11 Robert W. Woolley, "Underwood of Alabama, Democracy's Chieftain," *American Review of Reviews,* XLIV (1911), 296–99.

tans in plantation sections, of significantly fewer in most rural hill settings, and of the extremely few in the rural mountains (except for tourist and retirement areas). Moreover, the antebellum gentry has exported to cities and university communities many of their most talented, cosmopolitan sons and daughters.

Thus, in Plantation County there were in 1960 fifteen known regular or frequent readers of one or more national publications of the quality of the *Christian Science Monitor, Christianity and Crisis,* and the *Saturday Review.* Nine of these fifteen paid more than glancing attention to the international articles in such periodicals. Six were primarily interested in literary, dramatic, cultural, and other content not directly related to world affairs, and five of the nine who read foreign material were at least as interested in content on art, education, literature, and other nonpolitical phenomena. All fifteen were white (although the majority of the county population was Negro) and members of the planter, banker, and professional group. Only three, all from middle-class backgrounds—the Presbyterian minister who read and tended to agree with much in the *New Republic*, the Methodist minister who read *Christianity and Crisis* and *Newsweek*, and a former teacher with a master's degree from Teachers College, Columbia University, now a banker were not members of local old families of plantation traditions. About half of planter, commercial, and professional-class families which did not receive any of these more analytical periodicals subscribed to a newsmagazine; the less conservative took *Newsweek*, or even *Time*, and the more conservative *U.S. News and World Report.* The number of recipients of these was five times that of critical publications, and they included a much higher proportion of individuals in the self-made, middle-class group.

The majority of old family readers of *Time* and *Newsweek* were more conservative about a number of aspects of foreign policy than the typical interpretations therein, as were eight of the fifteen readers of critical periodicals. The international views of the more conservative who read this international fare ranged from those of Senator Richard Russell to those of Senator Harry Byrd, or even Senator Strom Thurmond, as did the thinking of most of their peers whose exposure to world affairs included neither critical nor newsmagazines, but was limited largely to daily papers and television.

But one of these gentlemen of genteel cotton-plantation tradition was a professor of European history who commuted from a nearby college to his inherited home and acres each weekend and holiday. He had been a religious agnostic and a socialist, and in late 1960 was still somewhat to the left of John F. Kennedy's public utterances on foreign policy—he favored recognition of Communist China, expanded aid to underdeveloped countries, sharply lower restrictions on world trade, much increased intercultural exchange with Communist countries, United States encouragement of more liberal, often socialist, leaders against "reactionary" members of the elite in underdeveloped societies, and so on.

Another was a middle-aged lady, a descendant of several of the more esteemed antebellum planters of that part of the Black Belt, who had published with a university press a book on plantation life and thought, using her family as examples, and who had formerly taught in the local high school. Among her favorite periodicals were the *Atlantic* and the New York *Times* (Sunday edition). Her general thinking about world affairs approximated fairly closely the views typically appearing in these publications, as has that of most readers of such periodicals in the North.[12] She felt that Senator Fulbright would make an excellent Secretary of State if the Democrats were to win in the following November. She would expand aid to underdeveloped countries, including anticolonialist, neutralist ones, and believed that the Marshall Plan saved Europe from communism. She also felt that demand for more nearly equalitarian race relations is part of a worldwide movement, and

12 Critical publications of liberal or internationalist orientations in world affairs have attracted as readers primarily Americans whose views on foreign relations have more or less coincided with those prevalent within these periodicals. Only a minority of their readers have been more conservative on world problems than most of the contents; very few have been neo-isolationists or arch-conservatives. Thus, among college graduates who read parts of two out of three issues of either *Harper's* or the *Atlantic*, 78 percent of those venturing opinions even as early as 1947 felt that over the coming decade the United States should try to make the standard of living abroad rise more rapidly than here; 82 percent believed that we had enough scientific and technical knowledge substantially to eliminate poverty, disease, and ignorance in the world "if we would only apply our knowledge"; 89 percent agreed that lowering American tariffs would not lower our standard of living; 91 percent stated that the U.N. should have the right to make conclusions which would bind members, including the United States, to a course of action; and 89 percent thought that contemporary painters, designers, playwrights, and musicians were engaged in work as important as their own. Eighty-nine percent disagreed with the view that allowing increased immigration would lower our standard of culture, and 88 percent took issue with the suggestion that foreigners usually have peculiar and annoying habits. (Bureau of Applied Social Research study.) In 1939 only one percent of readers of *The Nation* said that they usually disagreed with the points of view expressed; 58 percent said that they agreed generally with them; 17 percent felt somewhat to the left; 10 percent said they were somewhat to the left about half the time and somewhat to the right the other half (when they did not agree with the opinions expressed); and only 15 percent felt that their view was normally somewhat to the right of the magazine's. (From an unpublished study of readers of *The Nation* made available by the publisher.)

she would permit the better-educated local Negroes to vote—a very radical view in Plantation County. Although she thought that apartheid is a "suicidal" policy of the white South Africans, she feared drastic change in local as in international affairs, especially where the majority is as unsophisticated as in Plantation County.

A third was a scintillating older lady, a descendant of a re-nowned pre-Confederacy plantation family, who could still read some Latin and Greek, read serious fiction, drama, poetry, and periodicals ranging from the *Sewanee Review* and the *Virginia Quarterly Review* to the New York *Times* (Sunday edition). As in many similar families her two well-educated lawyer sons had departed for a large Southern city. Highly critical of the lack of thought among most of even her genteel peers, she was profoundly disturbed that the "age of mass man" would entail mediocrity, conspicuous consumption and immoderate demagoguery everywhere, but particularly in backward countries. Perhaps the Europeans had blundered in withdrawing too quickly from colonial societies, but on the other hand too few metropolitans had really exerted themselves to educate the more promising of future local leaders. Our policies abroad as here should try to promote excel-lence—we should employ stricter standards in choosing promising foreigners to be educated here and assist foreign political regimes which really "clean house" and attempt to face their problems intelli-gently. However, she was pessimistic about achievement of competence and integrity through mass democracy anywhere. "I am not a demo-crat; the herd has never respected ability and honor in any field; and as it destroyed Socrates, it will destroy the sensitive, the intelligent, and the excellent everywhere."

On the other hand, the largest landholder in Plantation County, a descendant of a carpetbagger, was a prominent leader of ultra-white supremacists, arch-conservatives, and advocates of "Fortress America" in the Black Belt. He labeled himself an "isolationist," and his views fitted that description.

With relatively minor modifications, comparably genteel people predominated among the more internationally responsible conservatives and semiliberals who held responsible views on world affairs in Kent. One of the five best-read inhabitants was an antebellum traditionalist, paternalist segregationist, and lawyer who lived in his ancestral home which was built in the late 1700's. He felt that we should recognize and trade with Communist China, permit it to enter the U.N., and "bring Chiang Kai-shek down to reality" concerning return to the mainland where few want him—all very "eccentric" ideas in Kent. He cited ideas drawn from James B. Reston of the New York *Times*, Walter Lippmann, and other leading columnists and analysts of foreign policy. A *grande dame* of Kent, descendant of many generations of physicians, lawyers, and planters, was a vociferous reader of semipopular and even more critical literature, as were many of her ancestors. She felt that foreign affairs would probably require more of the resources of our country than currently and that Senator Fulbright's views were more realistic than those of most Southern legislators. Others of more or less internationalist opinion and considerable knowledge were the Episcopal minister of First Family of Virginia origins and a retired Foreign Service officer and Consul General in North Africa, likewise of planter background and married into a local old family. All of the thoughtful internationalists who kept up with foreign developments in serious analytical periodicals were blue bloods or nearly so, except for an internationalist Roman Catholic missionary priest raised in New York and trained at graduate school in sociology; a middle-class merchant's son who had absorbed many of the manners and much of the ethic of the upper class, operated the town's historical and art museum, and wrote articles on Kent and environs for a nearby paper; the principal of the high school (of middle-class background); and an alert, well-educated, young Negro minister who commuted to his church in Kent from New Southtown where he taught at a Negro junior college.

The interviewer found no one in Rivertown who favored foreign aid, a stronger U.N., and arms-control inspection in the United States by international teams other than the young Episcopal minister whose mother and wife were raised on plantations and who lived in Deltatown near the larger of his two churches. But all five readers of *Harper's*, *Atlantic*, the New York *Times* (Sunday edition), and similar publications were of genteel tradition. In parts of Delta County which had been developed in the last seventy years from forest and swamp, individuals of such tradition together with Jews and teachers at the local state college made up all except a tiny proportion of the readership and, particularly, of the less conservative readers of these periodicals and of books dealing with international relations.

Three of the seven such readers in Hill County were individuals of some plantation background, one of them in straitened economic circumstances. These three had migrated to Hill County, as it became more prosperous, from Natchez and other Old South locales. A thoughtful retired Baptist minister with atypical interest (for Baptists of his age) in the social implications of the gospel, a Canadian-born physician, the high-school social-studies teacher, and the superintendent of schools completed the list of thoughtful cosmopolitans reading serious literature. None of the newly well-to-do in poultry processing, feed mills, meat-packing, and other developing enterprises read more internationally multilateralist or analytical material than *U.S. News and World Report*, and the views of its editor David Lawrence approximated those of most of these people on foreign policy. Much of the remaining newly prosperous group were still further to the right in foreign affairs, especially on foreign aid.

The arch-conservatives among the old families of traditionalist Charleston outnumbered the well-read internationalists of liberal or responsibly conservative—by Northeastern standards—persuasion by several times, but the few thoughtful cosmopolitans who fitted the latter description were primarily from this group, along with Jews, "immigrant" Northerners, clergymen, and university teachers. A number of the cosmopolitan clergy and some teachers also came from Old South origins.

Some Sources of Their Cosmopolitanism

No systematic research on the processes whereby cosmopolitan interests, analytical habits of mind, and nationally responsible thought about world affairs have developed among a small minority of Southerners has been located. Nor have there been controlled empirical investigations of personality development and ideology among a sufficiently large, representative sample of Southerners of genteel tradition to warrant definitive generalizations about their thinking and its origins.

However, the author's interviews in the South and other experience there indicate that certain kinds of backgrounds tend to appear repeatedly among Southern cosmopolitans. These favorable phenomena have not been limited to Southerners of old family origins, but have been more prevalent among this socially secure class than among most other Southern groups.

Perhaps more important than any other consideration has been the emotional security, the sense of being at the top of the Southern social spectrum and not having to strive for social acceptance. Cosmopolitanism and dispassionate thinking about world affairs have been correlated throughout America with secure social status; Americans whose parents were of more elevated standing have tended everywhere to be more thoughtful, informed, and internationally sophisticated than others of comparable education, income, and occupation whose parents were of the lower or lower-middle classes.[13] The insecurities and anxieties about

13 E.g., Bureau of Applied Social Research study.

social acceptance by "older" money and about losing one's recently
attained prosperity which have been relatively likely among those who
have moved up rapidly from the lower social orders have been frequently associated with various irrational fears: preoccupations with
one's own economic, psychological, and social problems; rather dogmatic, oversimplified thinking on controversial public questions (including foreign policy); indifference or hostility to views different
from one's own and those of one's particular circle or the group to
which one aspires; and either apathy or highly conservative, neo-isolationist, strongly nationalistic thinking on foreign policy.[14]

But upper-class Southerners have been perhaps as or more secure
until recently than any group in America. Although most had little of
the money characteristic of much of the Northeastern aristocracy,
money meant little for social acceptance—anyone who was prosperous
in the early postbellum period was suspected of either failing to invest
in Confederate bonds or "scalawagging" with "Yankee" carpetbaggers.
In a society where antebellum pedigree counted more than in any
other part of the New World, they had the right ancestors. There were
relatively few "new" people in the South due to paucity of industrialization and prosperity, and one paid little attention to parvenus except
to disdain their conspicuous consumption, immoderation, middle-class
morality, and lack of refinement. One was born an aristocrat and stayed
one regardless of poverty, lowly occupation, eccentricity, or such
forms of degeneracy as alcoholism. Only by marriage into the aristoc-

14 Survey Research Center, *Interest, Information, and Attitudes in the Field of
World Affairs* (Ann Arbor: University of Michigan, 1949) 4; T. W. Adorno, *et al.,*
The Authoritarian Personality (New York: Harper Bros., 1950); Herbert Mc-
Closky, "Conservatism and Personality," unpublished paper delivered before the
annual meeting of the American Political Science Association, 1957; Patricia O'Connor, "Ethnocentrism, Intolerance of Ambiguity, and Ambiguity and Abstract Reasoning Ability," *Journal of Abnormal and Social Psychology*, XLVII (1952), 526–
30; Maurice L. Farber, "The Anal Character and Political Aggression," *Journal of
Abnormal and Social Psychology*, LI (1955), 486–89; Harry Grace, "Hostility,
Communication, and International Tension," *Journal of Social Psychology*, XXXIV
(1951), 31–40; Seymour Martin Lipset, "The Radical Right: A Problem for American Democracy," *British Journal of Sociology*, VI (1955), 196 ff; Daniel J. Levin-
son, "Authoritarian Personality and Foreign Policy," *Conflict Resolution*, I (1957),
37–38; William J. MacKinnon and Richard Centers, "Authoritarianism and Internationalism," *Public Opinion Quarterly*, XX (Winter 1956–57), 621–30; Richard
Hofstadter, "The Pseudo-Conservative Revolt—1955," in *The Radical Right*, 70–79;
David Riesman and Nathan Glazer, "The Intellectuals and the Discontented Classes
—1955," in *The Radical Right*, 90–95; Joseph Greenblum and Leonard I. Pearlin,
"Vertical Mobility and Prejudice," in Reinhard Bendix and Seymour Martin Lipset
(eds.), *Class, Status, and Power* (Glencoe: The Free Press, 1953), 480–91; and
Bruno Bettelheim and Morris Janowitz, "Ethnic Tolerance: A Function of Per-
sonal and Social Control," *American Journal of Sociology*, IV (1949), 137–45.

racy could the descendants of the *nouveaux riches* become acceptable among the gentry.

This self-assurance among the traditional upper class rendered far too many of them overly proud, snobbish, arrogant, and oblivious to alternative thinking of others from outside their circle. But their sense of having arrived in an hierarchical society which seemed indestructible regardless of individual economic or occupational success has also been associated, as in the Northeast,[15] with an emphasis on perfecting oneself and cultivating one's intellectual interests, on leading the "good life," and on developing one's intrinsic merits rather than on achieving utilitarian competence related to industrial "progress" or achievement likely to impress "doers." [16]

One result of this emphasis was the attraction of this class into occupations where there was enough financial reward to permit one to live according to traditions but without the economic competition of business and manufacturing. The upper class went into planting, law, medicine, teaching, journalism, the officers corps of the Regular Army, the clergy, architecture, and similar professions. Most of these have been

15 For empirical studies of the values of the Northeastern upper class, see E. Digby Baltzell, *Philadelphia Gentlemen* (Glencoe: Free Press, 1958); Charles McArthur, "The Effects of Need Achievement on the Content of TAT Stories: A Re-Examination," *Journal of Abnormal and Social Psychology*, XLVIII (1953), 532–36; Charles McArthur, "Personality Differences Between Middle and Upper Classes," *Journal of Abnormal and Social Psychology*, L (1955), 247–54; Charles McArthur, "Upper-Class Intelligence as the Critical Case for a Theory of 'Middle-Class Bias,'" *Journal of Counseling Psychology*, IV (1957), 23–28; Charles McArthur, "Long-Term Validity of the Strong Interest Test in Two Subcultures," *Journal of Applied Psychology*, XXXVIII (1954), 346–53; Charles McArthur, "Personalities of Public and Private School Boys," *Harvard Educational Review*, XXIV (1954), 256–62; Charles McArthur, "The Validation of Expressed Interests as Compared with Inventoried Interests: A Fourteen-Year Follow-Up," *Journal of Applied Psychology*, XXXIX (1955), 184–89; Florence R. Kluckhohn, "Dominant and Substitutive Profiles of Cultural Orientations: The Significance for the Analysis of Social Stratification," *Social Forces*, XXVIII (1950), 376–93; and Patricia Smith, "The Problems of Occupational Adjustment for the Upper-Class Boston Man," (Master's thesis, Radcliffe College, 1950). For impressionistic and literary insights, see C. Morley, *Kitty Foyle* (New York: The New American Library, 1944); James P. Marquand, *The Late George Apley* (Boston: Little, Brown, and Co., 1937); and James P. Marquand, "A Confession of an Educated Man," *Harvard Alumni Bulletin*, LV (1953), 755.

16 For example, Morton Rubin, *Plantation County*, 51; Parks, *Segments of Southern Thought*, 15 ff; Louis D. Rubin, Jr., "An Image of the South," in *The Lasting South*, 6; Twelve Southerners, *I'll Take My Stand* and other works of the Vanderbilt Agrarians; Ralph C. Patrick, Jr., *A Cultural Approach to Social Stratification* (Ph.D. dissertation, Harvard University, 1953); William Alexander Percy, *Lanterns on the Levee* (New York: Alfred A. Knopf, 1944); John Dollard, *Caste and Class in a Southern Town*, 80–83; and Viola Goode Liddell, *With a Southern Accent* (Norman: University of Oklahoma Press, 1948).

occupations in which, throughout the country as well as in the South, contact with world affairs and critical thought about it have been more likely. Furthermore, until the industrialization of the South, particularly after World War II, these occupations and the incomes which established families received from other sources were quite likely to have been linked directly or indirectly with international economic affairs —cotton, tobacco, rice, and professions tied thereto.

The fraction of the gentry who have actually employed their leisure to broaden their understanding of world challenges facing this country has been small, but a significant minority have used their security and free time in part to think critically about the present, usually along with the past. This minority of the upper class have felt that there need be no inconsistency between the best traditions of the Old South— unhurried politeness, sensitivity to people, attachment to nature, a feel- ing for historical experience, and a cautious view of complex human nature and its foibles—and realistic thinking on the public questions of the present and the future.

In some old families of the South there have been for several genera- tions individuals whose thinking was not restricted by local mores and who read serious material on national and foreign problems, often along with good novels, poetry, and other intellectually stimulating material. Some secure families have brought up their children to think that learn- ing and books were important and that they should use their advantages and prestige to broaden their own talents and apply them to service to society. In other families there have existed at least one or two well- read, thoughtful individuals—if not a mother or father, then a grand- parent, an aunt, or at least a cousin once removed or by marriage. And even in the few cases where no relative fitted this description, there often existed a warm relationship with an intellectually alert teacher, minister, lawyer, or woman of Old South background who did fit into this pattern and whose thinking was known to diverge from prevailing arch-conservative, semifeudal norms.[17] Intimate early contact with such thoughtful elders and with good reading material was mentioned again and again by the cosmopolitan interviewees as a major probable source of their intellectual development.

17 The author recalls a number of examples from his childhood and later con- tacts among such families of the Deep South, and interviewers encountered many more during investigations for this research. See also, for example, Katherine Du- pré Lumpkin, *The Making of a Southerner* (New York: Alfred A. Knopf, 1947); Smith, *Killers of the Dream*, 31–32; Dykeman and Stokely, *Seeds of Southern Change*, 5–9; and the relationships between Harper Lee and her father in her partly autobiographical *To Kill A Mockingbird*.

Finally, there has been the exposure of this class to college educations for several generations, rather unique in the South. Some of them and some of their parents, grandparents, and more distant ancestors attended Harvard, Yale, and other renowned national and foreign universities, and the others went for the most part to the better Southern institutions. The incidence of cosmopolitan inclinations among Southerners of two or more generations of college education has been, as we have seen (p. 248), relatively high, though not so high as in the Northeast.

The Majority of the Gentry

Judging from the limited evidence and considerable experience with the counterparts of the Southern upper class in the Northeast, the author does not feel that the overall breadth of perspective, sophistication, sense of responsibility, and realism of the Southern gentry compares favorably with the Northeastern. This does not imply that more than a minority of Cabots, Lowells, Biddles, Adams, Roosevelts, Schuylers, or members of other Northern aristocratic families have been particularly interested, thoughtful, and responsible in their international thinking. A number of them, too, have been playboys, overly concerned with genealogies and local histories, class conscious, and antagonistic to change. But the fraction which has used its traditions and security as a point of departure for concern with world problems and for action toward facing them has seemed much larger than in the South in recent years.

Regardless of traditions to the contrary, there were only a relatively few much-used libraries of high quality in the homes of the predecessors of the gentry of 1962; real interest in comprehending the ideas in the classics and in realistic, serious literature generally among this group has been greatly overestimated by many of their descendants.[18] Much of the reading among the Southern privileged classes, as noted previously (pp. 78–79), was rather romantic, sentimental fare.

The male progeny of these Southerners have continued to be largely outdoorsmen, interested in horses and dogs and such rural pastimes as hunting and fishing. Reading of serious books or of periodicals like *Harper's* and the New York *Times* (Sunday edition) was evident among only a rather limited minority of them in the communities examined.

18 Parks, *Segments of Southern Thought*, 21; Eaton, *Freedom of Thought in the Old South*, 53 ff; Eaton, *The Growth of Southern Civilization*, 15 and 124; Carter, *The Lower Mississippi*, 205–18; Kendrick and Arnett, *The South Looks At Its Past*, 26–28; Cash, *The Mind of the South*, 105; Savage, *Seeds of Time*, 104; Nicholls, *Southern Tradition and Regional Progress*, 37; and Bridenbaugh, *Myths and Realities*, 103–105, and 191.

The proportion of serious readers among the women was higher, but most upper-class Southern ladies have concerned themselves more with antiques, china painting and embroidering, the ways of the past, their homes, churches, children, and servants, and entertaining their husband's and their own families and friends. And much of whatever reading beyond Southern subject matter has taken place has been focused on the arts, poetry, novels, and other relatively uncontroversial content with little direct applicability to social and public questions of the present. Southern upper-class reading in the social sciences and other disciplines which analyze public questions has been particularly sparse.[19]

Insofar as the sample of individuals of genteel origins in the South was representative, one can estimate that no more than one out of ten of them in 1959–62 read about foreign affairs in any periodical of the critical quality of the *Atlantic, Christian Science Monitor,* the New York *Times* (Sunday edition), or *The Reporter.* Only a minority of that group exposed themselves to discussions of world problems in as many as two of these periodicals or in more specialized publications such as *Foreign Affairs, The Headline Series,* and semipopular books in the field. The author's impressions in New England, and, to a lesser extent, elsewhere in the Northeast, lead to the tentative conclusion that the comparable Northeastern class includes proportionally two or more times as many relatively serious readers in world affairs. The fraction in the Northeast who have participated in organized, high quality discussions of foreign policy sponsored by universities and other educational institutions, World Affairs Councils, Committees on Foreign Relations, Friends Service Committee branches, Leagues of Women Voters, and the like has been smaller than the proportions who read on comparable levels of abstraction. As in the South, most who have taken part in such discussions have been among the readers, but most readers have not participated in such organized discussions. However, certainly upper-class participation in such organized thoughtful deliberations in the Northeast has been several times more prevalent than among the Southern gentry.

Even upper-class Southern cosmopolitans who have read and taken part in discussions at such levels of complexity and sophistication have frequently been regarded as rather "odd" and have only been tolerated by their peers. Discussions of foreign policy in upper-class circles of Boston or Philadelphia were more sophisticated, abstract, systematic, rigorous, realistic and in a more meaningful context than most conversations on similar topics among comparable groups in Charleston,

19 See, for instance, Smith, *Killers of the Dream,* 208–10.

Mobile, Antebellum Town, and even New Orleans in 1959–62. Likewise, the general quality of discussion of international issues in genteel groups in Plantation County, Bayou Parish, Kent, and Rivertown was distinctly lower than among comparable social strata in rural and small-town settings of the author's acquaintance in Vermont, Maine, New Hampshire, and Massachusetts. Many of the assumptions, assumed facts, and ideas advanced by more typical upper-class Southerners would be rejected as distorted by chance conversations with their social counterparts along the Northeastern seaboard. Furthermore, probably most of the upper class of New England would regard the thinking on foreign affairs of typical Southern gentry as very conservative if not reactionary.

These gaps between Southern and Northeastern old families have been partly due to the fact that the Southerners have had much less money to spend on serious periodicals, books, and foreign travel. Nor have Southerners of upper-class standing attended the broadening preparatory schools frequented by their Northeastern equivalents, and only a small fraction of the Southerners have gone to the outstanding Northeastern colleges. Moreover, the Southern upper class has been predominantly rural, isolated from the stimulation of the large, multi-ethnic cities of the Northeast where one could meet a wide diversity of national, religious, and ideological groups rather than being limited to provincial, class-bound environments and discussions. With notable exceptions, there have been few opportunities for serious discussions of foreign affairs with people who knew a great deal about that field. Southern cosmopolitans outside a very few centers have been obliged to develop their understanding of international phenomena either from governmental service in Washington or abroad or virtually entirely from reading because of lack of contacts with experts face-to-face in their rural and small-town settings.

Furthermore, these deficiencies of intellectually stimulating opportunities have been reinforced by cultural factors more prevalent among the Southern gentry. The Northeastern aristocracy traces its sources to commercial and manufacturing wealth rather than to a tradition of landed feudalism. The Northern patrician has been less inclined to be influenced by ideals of romantic chivalry, or the glamorous, gallant daredevil personified in dramatic form by Faulkner's Bayard Sartoris. Serious thought about public questions is highly unlikely to develop in individuals of such leanings. The Northern upper class has on the whole made considerably more of an effort to understand and to come to terms with industrialism, a fluid, less rigidly stratified social system, mass democracy, vigorous central government, and other developments where modern experience and ideas have been much more compelling. Even most Boston Brahmins can hardly imagine the intense awareness of the past long dead and the preoccupation with matters of family, ancestry, and local history particularly among older women of the Southern patriciate. The sense of complacency that everything has already been accomplished by one's ancestors and the feeling that one need not achieve much in this generation are gradually disappearing from among younger privileged Southerners, but these emotional sentiments seemed significantly more prevalent than among Northeasterners of equivalent social esteem. It would probably be difficult to find many privileged Northeasterners who would agree with the comment of one cultivated Southern gentleman to the effect that the important values in life had already been determined and therefore one needed to devote little attention to ephemeral matters like troubles in the Congo.

Arch-conservatives do exist among the aristocracy of the Northeast; but most of them have been identified politically and ideologically with the moderate, internationalist wing of the Republican party and the remainder with even more internationalist liberal Democrats. Successive generations of money and family traditions have made most of them rather conservative on domestic economics, but liberal on most other issues, domestic or foreign. Few have been as suspicious and opposed to gradual change or "progress" as many of their Southern counterparts among the interviewees seemed to be. As among other Southerners, fear of agitating the racial *status quo* has been partly responsible among the Southern gentry for the inhibition of critical discussion of public issues, in world affairs as in other fields. The Northern intellectual aristocracy has long been accused of "radicalism" by its Southern peers. Many of its members have been suspected of supporting the abolitionist cause and modern equalitarian movements. Elite Northern universities have been viewed as centers of anti-Southernism. The defeat of 1865 and fear of "meddling" by the North in the Southern social system have developed a Southern upper class much of whose intellectual energies have focused on defense of their region from "outside" criticism. This proclivity seems to have been further augmented by recently increased pressures to change Southern race relations (see Chapter 11).

Thus, most of the Northern upper class have supported the general lines of foreign policy of their two peers who were Secretaries of State under President Eisenhower—John Foster Dulles and Christian Herter. Although critical of some of the specific actions of the Kennedy administration, most also seemed to agree with its general international objectives and orientations, as well as with those of President Johnson. During the 1964 presidential campaign, lifetime Republicans of privileged ancestry and elite education in the Northeast were typically, at least privately and sometimes publicly, critical of the "irresponsible" and "reactionary" statements of Senator Barry Goldwater and Representative William Miller concerning arms control, relations with the Soviet Union and Communist governments in Eastern Europe, United States policy in Vietnam, barriers to world trade, foreign aid, and other issues of foreign policy. Even when they tended to agree with some of the ideas of the Republican presidential and vice-presidential candidates on domestic economic and welfare issues, as a number of them did, their thinking about world affairs diverged so greatly from that of the national candidates of their party that many decided to vote for President Johnson. Henry Cabot Lodge, Jr., represented much of the thinking of his social peers in the Northeast on foreign affairs.

But the basic social and political attitudes prevalent among perhaps most of the Southern gentry of the early sixties showed through in the international thinking of a large proportion of even the better informed of the interviewees. On most issues of foreign affairs other than international trade, defense, and collective security with Western Europe, even those interviewees of the Southern upper class who read such material as *Harper's* and the New York *Times* were on the average more conservative than most readers of the same publications in the North (see p. 286).

The international views of these better-informed Southerners of esteemed pedigree were far from homogeneous—as already noted, a number of them were cosmopolitan internationalists. But somewhat over half of the better-read interviewees of this station were inclined to distrust mass participation in the political process either here or abroad, but particularly in underdeveloped countries. They felt we should support the whites in Africa and in European *métropoles* more than we had in their disputes with the "natives" or that we should remain silent on colonial questions and leave these problems to the colonial powers who, being on the ground, know how to handle them. They feared that the U.N. may decline as a useful instrument of policy for the United States on account of the combined votes of the Communists and underdeveloped, colored neutralists. They felt we should have been firmer and made fewer compromises with either the Soviet bloc or such leaders as Nasser, Nkrumah, and Sukarno in the underdeveloped world. Some even advanced the historic Southern aristocratic idea that showers, toilets, screens, and other material things and economic development generally have little to do with "the good life." They expressed the opinions that we are helping to create "Yankee" (and New South) styled parvenus in these agrarian societies and that these backward, emotional regimes are of relatively little value to our international interests anyway. They would have us enforce the Monroe Doctrine as was done before the promulgation of the good-neighbor policy. Lack of firmness encourages leftists and demagogues and Soviet penetration into Latin America and other underdeveloped lands. The feeling seemed common that too many "brash, middle-class, liberal doctrinaires" have influenced our foreign policy in recent years.

Most of the Southern upper class of 1959–62 was not so well informed as this segment of the interviewees. The majority of this esteemed group in Plantation County, Kent, Charleston, and Bayou Parish was more conservative than these readers of magazines and books on foreign relations and than the Eisenhower administration's policies on foreign aid, colonial issues, and negotiations with the Soviet bloc, and even further to the right of the policies of the Kennedy administration in 1961–62.

Their Influence on Southern International Thought

Some genteel cosmopolitans have been active in Leagues of Women Voters, forums, church organizations, and other groups attempting to stimulate thought about foreign policy in the South. Others have supported and often operated the libraries in their county seats and towns and provided the leadership for local literary societies and American Heritage and other discussion groups organized in some libraries, colleges, schools, and private homes. Some have controlled, edited, or written for newspapers and other mass media. Many of the women have taught in local rural high schools, and the thoughtful offspring of the genteel class have reinforced the cosmopolitan minorities in Southern cities where they have settled after college. Still others have spoken and encouraged the invitation of other informed internationalists to make talks before local service and professional groups only marginally interested in foreign policy. Others have introduced foreign students and other international visitors into their communities.

The interviews indicated that the cosmopolitan minority among the secure upper class—together with a number of Jews and educated professional people of the middle class—have constituted the nucleus of responsible international thinking throughout the Black Belt, in traditionalist cities, and wherever else they live. At a minimum, the very existence and local prestige of these individuals have tended to moderate somewhat the distorted international attitudes about them. Even in Charleston, where the balance has been strongly favorable to ultraconservative thinking on foreign policy, contact of ultraconservatives with a few of their social peers of more internationalistic bent has helped to prevent even more extreme ideas. The influence of "know-nothing" neo-isolationist ideology in Birmingham, Shreveport, and Jackson, Mississippi—where there have been relatively few thoughtful descendants of the Old South elite—has been more marked than in Antebellum Town, Kent, and Greenville, Mississippi. And even ultra-traditionalist upper-class Charleston manifests more moderate, intellectually responsible conservative international thought than the less well-bred (and cultivated) leadership of Jackson, Shreveport, or Monroe.

But many of even the relatively well-read gentry had not thought much in terms of communicating knowledge beyond themselves and the few others of like turn of mind. Many seemed lacking in vigor and generally ineffectual as personalities beyond their kin and a few peers. Some seemed weak, rather ambitionless, drained of energy, passive, and in various ways futile and incompetent creatures. Often disdainful of even the college-educated New South middle class, they seldom seemed to try to deal effectively with these products of modernism in any realistic way. Chekov has described some of the interviewees in his *Cherry Orchard;* Ellen Glasgow has done so in *The Sheltered Life;* and William Faulkner has portrayed them in Horace Benbow and others of his gentry who, living in the glories of their ancestral pasts, have little sense of actively grappling with surrounding developments they dislike. Whatever discussion these people have undertaken in world affairs or other issues has been largely confined to literary clubs and other groups composed of their own kind.

Aristocratic assumptions about human nature and class differences have also militated against serious efforts by many of even the better informed of this class to broaden public understanding about foreign affairs. Some implied that real understanding of world developments could not be learned through formal education alone if the youngster had not been exposed to sophisticated parents, libraries, and friends from an early age. Some of the informants advanced class-determined explanations of "true" intelligence, integrity, and the other virtues essential to comprehending life which, in turn, were felt to be necessary for understanding public questions. Only a limited minority seemed to think of the ignorance and indifference of the Southern masses as products of the social system and possibly improvable through modifications in the structure and institutions of their society.

Most would leave Leagues of Women Voters and other organizations designed to broaden public understanding to "eager beavers" of the "earnest" middle class. The idea that it is a social responsibility of the privileged to raise the level of understanding of the rest has not penetrated beyond a small minority of the upper class—evangelism ("crusading") was not favorably considered. Some were more than indifferent—they were derisive about the effects of efforts to "civilize the rednecks, be they still dirt farmers or bourgeois in Cadillacs." They disliked "world improvers," "do gooders," "mass uplifters," and "reformers of others." These efforts would fail and perhaps would energize base people who were better left dormant. Their own approach would be to try to fence in the passions of the "common man," to limit his influence, rather than to attempt the hopeless task of improving him. Many would rather restrict the ballot to the educated and sophisticated —they would prefer educated Negroes on the rolls to poor whites, but few thought that this was really feasible politically. Since they could not thus limit the ballot, they despaired of preventing further inroads against honor, quality, and dispassionate thought in world affairs and other fields of government. The best one could expect of the masses would be the election of "styleless peasants" like Eisenhower or "haberdashers" like Truman—Jefferson could never be elected President in 1960.

These condescending attitudes were less evident among younger members of this privileged class. Many of those in their thirties and younger no longer took their family trees seriously and were amused by their elders who did. Some of the younger gentry by 1962 had come to believe that some progress—perhaps not as much as the New York and Cambridge liberals expect—is perhaps possible through education, improvement of the content of mass media and activities of voluntary organizations, and other means of stimulating concern and thought about public questions. They were less familiar with Greek, Latin, and the classics than some of their elders, but they seemed more concerned on the whole with the problems of the present in the South, the nation, and the world. Some of their parents, as we have seen, were thoughtful and responsible about our role in the world of the latter half of the twentieth century and attempted in their own ways when opportunities were available to broaden somewhat the thinking of others. Considerable increase in the number of such critical individuals seems probable as the college generation matures.

The Upper and Middle Classes of the New South

The Virtually Omnipresent New South

The New South refers more to a mode of thinking than to particular communities, although it is much more prevalent in some than in others. Moreover, it is found in relatively pure form in only a very few individuals, often Northerners living in the South. The traditions of the South have exerted some impact on the thinking of virtually all Deep Southerners, including some who are in high-technology roles in growing industrial cities.[20] But increasing numbers have accepted in varying measures and combinations the primarily urban, industrial, occupational achievement and success-oriented, future-directed thinking of the economically developed North. Southerners fall along a spectrum from strongly Old Southern traditionalist to primary interest in efficiency, economic competition, and "progress."

The New South's values were strongest and most prevalent by 1962 in manufacturing, distribution, commercial, research, and professional centers like Baton Rouge, Atlanta, Charlotte, Huntsville, and Nashville. But by the early sixties the New South's ways of thought had made major inroads into even relatively isolated, little-industrialized plantation settings, as evident in relatively pure form among a handful of individuals and in various degrees of influence on the thinking and actions of many other residents, including younger men of genteel Old South heritage.

Thus, in rural Plantation County, which had virtually no industries, a dynamic man in his early forties had worked his way through the state university from a yeoman farm background, become a major in the Military Intelligence in World War II, and gradually acquired control of a small bank and extensive rural real estate which gained him considerable influence in the county. He had little interest in the past or emotional commitment to preserving the "Southern way of life"; rather he was concerned with using the most efficient accounting equipment and banking procedures in his bank and employing the scientific knowledge available from agricultural experiment stations and other research centers in his agricultural enterprises. The self-made

---

20 A personnel director and several other managerial and technical men with capital-intensive Southern branches of national corporations among the interviewees felt that native Southerners among college-educated personnel in their plants were on the average more conservative about foreign affairs, particularly foreign aid, than were Northerners in similar jobs. The sample for this study was too small to permit generalizations about differences between these two groups.

owner of the automobile agency at the county seat, the son of a farmer of limited means who did not go to college, harbored similar values. These and others of New South orientation were trying, like similar residents of many agrarian counties, to attract industries which would provide work for people displaced by mechanized agriculture and the shift of the local economy from cotton to cattle and timber. By 1960 several sons of plantation families were supporting their efforts and had themselves adopted many of their New South attitudes.

In Kent, with its strongly traditionalist aristocracy, four textile mills and a carpet plant in operation in 1960 were run by New South types, all of whom were indifferent to most antebellum traditions (other than segregation and paternalism) and energetically pursuing economic "progress." The son of a modest farmer who lived nearby had, for instance, returned with an engineering degree, a reserve major's commission from the war, and several years' experience with a fabric manufacturer in Philadelphia to open a local manufacturing branch of his Pennsylvania firm. Although demonstrating traditional attitudes on race and Northern "meddling," he was an industrial man, interested in time-motion studies, rational personnel management practices, and industrialization of Kent and environs. He had brought from the North as his chief assistant a Roman Catholic Italian-American.

Southern Businessmen

Most of the previous comments about textile manufacturers seemed to apply with some amendment to Southern businessmen generally. Many of the cultivated genteel minority have believed that most tradespeople, entrepreneurs, manufacturers, and other commercial groups in the region have been rather indifferent and insensitive to literature, the arts, culture, and foreign affairs and unacquainted with them. The sample of approximately one hundred-ninety commercial people interviewed (depending on the definition of this group) seemed to indicate that this notion has considerable validity. Only a small minority, a much smaller fraction than among the genteel group, manifested much concern, except insofar as economic self-interest was engaged, as in the case of protectionists on trade. A large fraction expressed concern about taxation for foreign aid. Most read international news in a local daily paper, viewed some newscasts on television, and approximately half read a weekly newsmagazine—*U.S. News and World Report* was more popular than *Newsweek* or *Time*. The proportion among them who read critical publications on foreign affairs like *Harper's*, the New York *Times* (Sunday edition), and the Manchester

Guardian was roughly one third of the percentage among the old family group, and that third was concentrated among a few categories within the business community.

About three fifths of the business and manufacturing group tended to agree more or less with the political utterances of such ultraconservative Southern political figures as Harry Byrd, James Eastland, Strom Thurmond, Allen J. Ellender, and Herman Talmadge. On the national level most of these interviewees regarded favorably Barry Goldwater and others in the conservative wing of the Republican party. Most of the businessmen in the sample were rather provincial and out of touch with internationally sensitive and responsible thought among leaders of complex national and international corporations and financial institutions and other national economic leaders, located with but few exceptions outside the South. It is not surprising that less than a third, employed largely in just such research-oriented, larger enterprises or numbered among the highly educated and cultivated minority of the commercial group, accepted many of the ideas of the Northeastern corporate elite on foreign policy, as reflected in the *Harvard Business Review*, publications of the Committee for Economic Development, and public utterances of such internationalist Republican figures as Christian Herter, Clifford Case, Jacob Javits, and Nelson and David Rockefeller.[21]

Most of the more conservative majority of businessmen among the informants seemed much more interested in the postures of leaders like Harry Byrd and Barry Goldwater on taxation, governmental spending, and other domestic economic questions than on world affairs, but they usually agreed with them that nonmilitary expenditures abroad should be reduced considerably. A majority of the sample of businessmen favored termination or sharp curtailment of aid to countries which are Communist or which expropriate American property without fair compensation, and somewhat over half advised withdrawing or significantly reducing economic assistance to leftist neutralists as well. About two thirds seemed to agree with most of the thinking on foreign policy typical of *U.S. News and World Report* or even more conservative publications such as *Human Events*.

These general observations seemed related to the character of much of the Southern economy and the backgrounds of many of the businessmen interviewed. Although there have been exceptions, thinking on public affairs among small businessmen whose markets have been

21 For international attitudes among the Northeastern big city bankers and corporate leaders, see Raymond A. Bauer, Ithiel de Sola Pool, and Lewis A. Dexter, *American Business and Public Policy*, especially 251–64 and 282–86.

largely local and whose technology has been relatively simple has been discovered throughout the country to differ significantly from that of corporate executives of big banks, manufacturing concerns, and other enterprises in New York and other urban centers who associate with their counterparts in London, Paris, and Frankfort on the Main; consult experts on foreign trade and finance within their own headquarters and elsewhere; read the daily New York *Times, Wall Street Journal,* and other sophisticated publications; meet with friends at the Council on Foreign Relations, the Committee for Economic Development, the International Chamber of Commerce, and like organizations; and think in terms of long-term investment both at home and abroad for diverse world markets. International thinking among these men is not homogeneous, but most of them think in much broader economic, political, and foreign-policy terms than do small entrepreneurs in relatively isolated, particularly small, communities.[22]

The latter have been much less interested, informed, sensitive, and internationally responsible in their views than the former. Out-and-out isolationists, neo-isolationists, "Fortress America" ideologues, sharp curtailers of foreign aid, opponents of intercultural exchanges with Communist countries, businessmen intolerant of foreign mores and ideas, distrusters of expanded immigration, supporters of simplistic, chauvinistic clichés about "Americanism," opponents of United States collaboration with "socialistic" foreign regimes, enthusiasts of "tough" talk vis-à-vis the Soviet bloc, advocates of ousting the U.S.S.R. from the U.N., and individuals who have feared that the internal Communist menace is a serious one have been disproportionately numerous in America generally among small local rather than large national and international commercial elements. In fact, this observation has applied in some foreign societies as well; the Croix de Feu, the Poujadist movement, and other individuals and groups advocating arch-conservative domestic and foreign policies in France since the mid-1930's have been supported within the business community primarily by small tradesmen and other provincial business people who felt economically squeezed between large French corporations and banks and big trade unions.[23]

22 This and the following paragraph are derived primarily from *ibid.,* 162, 175–78, 180, 183, 194–95, 476, and 487; John H. Bunzel, *The American Small Businessman* (New York: Alfred A. Knopf, 1962), 106, 109–20, and 215–28; Hofstadter, "The Pseudo-Conservative Revolt," in *The Radical Right,* 75–77; and Riesman and Glazer, "The Intellectuals and the Discontented Classes," in *ibid.,* 90–95.

23 See, for instance, Stanley Hoffmann, *Le Mouvement Poujade* (Paris: Colin, 1956), especially, 9–22; and François Goguel, *La Politique des Partis sous La III* *République* (Paris: Seuil, 1946), Livre IV.

The sample did not permit comparison of Southern and non-Southern businessmen, but it was apparent that these generalizations were valid in the South. The least well informed and sophisticated and least interested in world issues, those least apt to read responsible discussions of foreign policy, and those most inclined to accept arch-conservative or neo-isolationist thinking were, to a disproportionate degree, men who were raised on modest farms or in other culturally deprived rural or small-town homes by little educated parents, were brought up in one branch of Protestant fundamentalism or another, were proud of their rural, fundamentalist upbringing, did not go to college or, if they did, experienced a primarily technical or vocational education, and had become prosperous in local trade and services or in simple small-scale manufacturing in towns and smaller cities of a rather primitive cultural level.

The South seemed to include in 1959–62 disproportionately large numbers of such self-made, rugged, free enterprisers of limited backgrounds among its business and manufacturing group. Fewer of them than of Northeastern, and probably even Midwestern, businessmen appeared to have experienced complicated operations of broad national and international scope as corporate managers or technicians. As noted above (pp. 151–52), much of Southern industry in the early sixties was still composed of small enterprises based on relatively poorly educated, little skilled, rather docile labor of rural backgrounds—sawmills, turpentine producers, food processors, furniture, cotton textile and clothing manufacturers, and other labor-intensive industries related more or less closely with agriculture. Since the genteel class tended to avoid manufacturing and trade, most Southern industrial development has been by Northerners and native sons of businessmen or by rather intellectually unsophisticated but ambitious men of poor white, yeoman farm, or mountaineer backgrounds.[24] Around these manufacturers have developed contractors; operators of truck fleets, supermarkets, and automobile, farm machinery, and appliance agencies; real estate promoters; prosperous undertakers and restaurateurs; and all manner of wholesalers, retailers, and other self-employed entrepreneurs, often of similarly uncultivated parentage. Unsolicited comments by interviewees within this group indicated that many, and perhaps most, approximated Herbert Spencer's type (without knowing who he was or what he said)— staunchly *laissez faire*, strongly anti-trade union (and oftentimes anti-large corporation as well), fearful of federal intervention in the econ-

24 Cash, *The Mind of the South*, 199–202; and Nicholls, *Southern Tradition and Regional Progress*, 34–35, and 54.

omy and erosion of "states' rights," concerned about "creeping (or galloping) socialism," frustrated by "confiscatory" or "exorbitant" taxation, and worried that their property will be taken from them.

These newly prosperous, sometimes avaricious but frequently honest folk, much influenced by the Calvinist ethic of hard work, seemed numerous in the power structure and appeared to exert considerable influence on mass media, civic organizations, churches and the general atmosphere. They were especially prevalent in communities, such as Jackson in Mississippi, Shreveport and Monroe in Louisiana, and Birmingham [25] in Alabama, which have grown from virtually nothing in the last two or three generations, or even less, and where there has been relatively little older, more secure, well-educated, more-refined wealth. Congressman Otto Passman, himself a prosperous self-made businessman of Monroe from rural fundamentalist background who left school at an early age, appeared to reflect rather well the international thinking of other businessmen of like experience and livelihood in his roll-call votes against the Refugee Act of 1953, United States participation in the Inter-American Development Bank in 1959 and in the International Development Association of the next year, the Mutual Educational and Cultural Exchange Act of 1961, the creation of the U.S. Arms Control Agency in 1961, the proposed purchase of U.N. bonds by the United States in 1962, and foreign aid during much of the decade prior to 1963.[26]

In older cities men with such backgrounds and international inclinations typically seemed to have less relative influence because of the countervailing presence of business, financial, and professional leaders of more extensive education, wider culture, broader knowledge, and more moderate, nationally and internationally responsible conservative views. Although many self-made, little-educated men in trade or low-technology manufacturing in New Orleans, for instance, apparently have accepted some of these ideas, their location in a larger, more sophisticated city with more knowledgeable economic leaders of

25 Birmingham has not grown as rapidly in recent decades as a number of other Southern cities. However, it was only incorporated in 1871 and had a total population of less than four thousand in 1880. The proportion of wealth of several generations standing is much smaller there than in New Orleans or even Atlanta.

26 Voting record from Lerche, *The Uncertain South*, 1964, 299. Congressman Passman voted for the Emergency Famine Relief Act of 1953, the proposed increases in United States subscriptions to the International Monetary Fund and the International Bank for Reconstruction and Development in 1959, and the International Health and Medical Research Act of 1960—all of which would probably also have been acceptable to most Southern businessmen had they known of them. On the other hand, Congressman Passman voted against the Peace Corps Act of 1961, which most businessmen among our interviewees would have supported.

broader horizons from more elevated social origins has both limited their influence and moderated to some extent the poorly informed and more extreme thinking found among similar people in newer, less heterogeneous, less complex urban societies.

The limited interviews for this study suggested that systematic examination of a large representative sample of Southern businessmen would reveal that the proportion of nationally responsible, realistic thought on world affairs increases as each of the factors of low education, fundamentalism, rural underprivileged upbringing, parochial, small-scale, low-skill or self-employed economic enterprise, and isolated location is moderated. Although there were a number of arch-conservatives who favored major curtailment of economic assistance to unaligned regimes, further restriction of imports, United States military intervention in Cuba, generally firmer, and less compromising relations with our opponents, etc., among college-educated businessmen of humble beginnings, the few from such origins who were relatively thoughtful cosmopolitans were typically men who had been to college.

Thus, the poor farmer's son who had worked his way through the state university and by 1960 had come into possession of a bank and extensive acreage in Plantation County preferred the views expressed in *Time* to those of David Lawrence in *U.S. News and World Report;* was not particularly upset by *Time's* "pro-Negro" orientation; thought we should trade more with Communist countries, encourage exchanges of visitors with mainland China, and put more of our foreign aid on more than a one-year basis for worthy projects in "well-run" underdeveloped countries like India; and commented that Senator Barry Goldwater seemed to be "talking about a past era." In June, 1960, he believed that Henry Cabot Lodge, Jr., and William Fulbright would respectively make good Republican and Democratic Secretaries of State. The manager with a textile engineering degree, of the efficient branch of the Philadelphia fabric concern in Kent, was more conservative, but he preferred the international coverage in *Time*, which he read regularly, to that of *U.S. News and World Report*. He was distinctly less conservative than most prosperous whites of Kent, including the owners or managers of the other mills who were also of modest parentage but were older and without college experience.

As in other occupations, broader, liberal arts educations among businessmen seemed to be associated more often than not with having more information about foreign affairs and, to a lesser extent, with maintaining more favorable views toward economic assistance and other economic, diplomatic, and cultural cooperation abroad. Many formerly internationalist students who had pursued general courses in even the better colleges had probably moved to the right in world affairs as they had become integrated into the executive levels of utilities, independent petroleum companies, textile mills, and other conservative commercial circles in towns and growing cities like Jackson and Shreveport. But even when they had, they seemed on the average better informed than businessmen who did not go to college, and at least somewhat more knowledgeable than those with primarily technical educations.[27]

The international attitudes prevalent among many of the newly prosperous in the older cities seemed also to have been moderated by the urban, less-fundamentalist background of some. Another reason for the less reactionary and poorly informed views of many prosperous New Orleans residents of limited childhoods was very probably their urban and Jewish, Roman Catholic, or more sophisticated Protestant upbringing. The proportion of active businessmen of any background in New Orleans who have been interested in and thoughtful about foreign affairs and who read such material in publications like the New York *Times* (Sunday edition) has been quite small and much lower among the newly well-to-do than the more secure of several generations of economic comfort and education. But the proportion among the newly prosperous of urban non-fundamentalist upbringing who opposed the U.N., would eliminate aid to neutralists, and were neo-isolationists seemed significantly smaller in New Orleans than in Jackson, for instance.

Some families have been relatively prosperous or even affluent for three generations or more without producing any offspring whose intellectual interests have extended much beyond their businesses and whose international views have not been defined by and large by those of their economic and social peers. The one or two thoughtful cosmopolitans have frequently left the family business for law, teaching, the clergy, or some other profession. But in most families of several generations of relative prosperity, at least one and typically several readers of responsible national publications on foreign affairs (and other subjects not directly related to their occupations) have developed who have agreed with most of the general assumptions and policies supported by the Northeastern internationalist Republicans or the national Democrats. Some have stayed in business careers—even relatively "uninteresting" ones like real estate, wholesaling and retailing, and small-scale clothing and textile manufacturing—although most probably have not.

27 Such was the case throughout the country, including the South, at the time of the Bureau of Applied Social Research study.

Age also seemed a pertinent factor among business as well as other occupational groups. Even in families of several generations of education and prosperity, the younger generation appeared more inclined to read critical literature and otherwise pay some attention to serious discussions of international issues and to approve of the general lines of policy prevalent among Northeastern internationalist Republicans or even internationalist Democrats. This generalization has perhaps been less applicable to low-technology, low-skill, and purely local enterprises in smaller cities and towns, but it was true to some extent there as well. The college education and other experiences of these younger men have been on the whole broader and more "liberal" than those of their elders.

The Legal Profession

Lawyers seemed to reflect many of the international views of their clients: labor lawyers among the interviewees were Democratic multilateralists; those whose income was drawn heavily from textile manufacturers were for the most part protectionists who were also conservative about foreign aid to underdeveloped countries, and so on. An increasing number of Southern lawyers have become employees of corporations and have apparently lost much of their former independence to express their own views insofar as they might diverge from those of their employers.

Most lawyers in the sample of fifty-seven for this study ranged from conservative to very conservative on world affairs as well as on other public issues. Only a rather small minority of these Southern lawyers seemed much interested in or informed about international questions. Apparently many Southern law schools and prelaw courses had done relatively little to expand the thinking of lawyers beyond pragmatic aspects of the legal profession and the prevailing attitudes of their communities. At least half of the small-town lawyers, particularly in Deep Southern communities, agreed more or less with the general international thinking among the local business and agricultural leadership. Small-town lawyers with political aspirations, like a considerable fraction of those in office, were likely to advocate cutting considerably economic assistance requested by Presidents Eisenhower and Kennedy, to feel that aid to Poland and Yugoslavia should be discontinued or reduced, and to advise that we take less seriously criticisms from underdeveloped, anticolonialist, countries in determining and executing our foreign policy.

However, the small cosmopolitan minority throughout the South has included a much larger (though still rather small) fraction of lawyers than of businessmen and agricultural groups. Most serious organized discussions of world affairs in the South—Committees on Foreign Relations, Southern Assemblies, the Foreign Relations Association of New Orleans, Great Decisions programs, and so on—have attracted much larger proportions of lawyers than of businessmen and manufacturers. A larger minority of attorneys who have not been so interested in world affairs as these have been at least somewhat better informed and less conservative about foreign relations than the general run of their clients in the business community. They have on the average been more broadly educated than most local businessmen; although some of the older ones passed their bar examinations without systematic training, few younger lawyers have not completed law school. The Southern lawyers were normally more removed from the competition of business and more inclined to read and think beyond immediate local problems. Most who came from rural, limited backgrounds were critical of foreign aid to underdeveloped countries at the level of the early 1960's and were otherwise conservative on foreign policy, but a larger minority than among the businessmen interviewed of like origins were not.

Even in the sampled rural counties one or more lawyers were among the handful of readers of critical periodicals and an occasional book dealing in part with world affairs, and most of these were at least cautiously internationalist in the sense of liberal Northeastern Republicans or national Democrats. Thus, in Plantation County a young attorney of planter traditions read most of the foreign content of the New York *Times* (Sunday edition) with considerable care and considered himself a national Democrat on foreign policy; another read the Manchester *Guardian* and *Harper's*. The local judge in Delta County, an older man of similar heritage, was even more liberal on world affairs and about as well read—his daughter worked as a research assistant for *Time* in New York. Even in relatively isolated and economically deprived Mountain County, two lawyers, readers of *Newsweek* and *Time* respectively, as well as of the international coverage in the Louisville *Courier-Journal*, were among the best informed half a dozen in the county, and their international views coincided more or less with those of an internationalist Republican Senator from their state and internationally oriented Republicans generally.

But these rural counties, like most others, had lost many of their more vigorous, able, and intellectually alert college graduates—including lawyers—to cities and university towns. In general, the larger, the more dynamic, and the more complex the community, the greater the proportion of relatively well-informed and internationalist men among its lawyers. Six in Kent, with a 1960 population of approximately five thousand, were readers of analytical national periodicals, and four of these were either internationalist national Republicans or Democrats of similar attitude. Only one was a neo-isolationist—anti-foreign aid, protectionist, and favorable to withdrawal from the U.N. if Communist China became a member, to United States military action against Cuba (summer of 1960), and to "gunboat" diplomacy in the Western Hemisphere generally. However, he felt that a strong NATO and other collaboration with Western Europe were "essential" to our interests. Another was a former Wilsonian, paternalist segregationist, who had "soured" on the federal government (the Eisenhower administration) generally, including its diplomatic and economic policies abroad. Lawyers in the cities ranged from isolationists to strong internationalists, but internationally sophisticated attorneys tended to be with the better firms in the larger centers. Those in the larger, more outstanding firms usually came from relatively privileged childhoods and the better colleges and law schools, many from nationally famous ones in the North; a few were Goldwater or Harry Byrd ultraconservatives on foreign policy, but most seemed to agree with much of the general thinking of the internationalist Republicans of the Northeast and a smaller fraction with that of the Kennedy administration on international affairs.

Other Professional Groups

Trained social workers even in the more conservative Deep Southern towns and smaller cities visited were in most cases less conservative on foreign relations than even most other local college-educated Southerners, but only a very limited minority seemed much interested, informed, or well read in the field. The thinking of Southern journalists varied with the editorial opinions of their papers and of their senior editors and publishers; internationalist journalists typically were attracted to and employed by the more liberal, cosmopolitan papers; neo-isolationists by the most conservative ones, and so on. However, a number of those with newspapers which were either relatively indifferent to world affairs or considerably more conservative than the Eisenhower administration's policies in the underdeveloped world and vis-à-vis the U.S.S.R. were internationally thoughtful and less conservative than would be expected from the content of the papers on which they worked. Few newspapermen seemed more conservative on world issues than the papers employing them. Thus, one would undoubtedly overestimate the incidence of anti-foreign aid, protectionist, anti-U.N., and otherwise neo-isolationist Southern journalists from the proportion of newspapers advancing these views in print.

Physicians were on the whole less interested, less informed, and more conservative about foreign policy than other professional groups in their communities. Physicians have been active in significant numbers in local John Birch Society branches, Citizens Councils, and other ultra-conservative, neo-isolationist groups. Psychiatrists are underrepresented in most of the South. The author's acquaintance with several dozen of them in the sample communities and elsewhere in his Southern experience lead to the tentative conclusion that they have been as a group generally more liberal on such matters as foreign aid, flexible negotiations and compromises with Communist powers, and possible entry of Communist China into the U.N.—they seemed to be more liberal about most public questions than the rest of the medical profession taken together. Few, however, appeared to devote more than passing attention to foreign affairs, and only a minority in the author's experience were as well informed as cosmopolitans in some other professions.

Some observations on university and secondary school teachers have been advanced previously. Brief attention will be devoted later to the clergy.

Women of the Privileged Strata

Surveys indicate that Southern women as a group have on the whole been less inclined to vote, less informed about most aspects of foreign policy, less likely to read international coverage and analysis in magazines and newspapers, and less apt to pay attention to programs on foreign policy on radio and television than have Southern men. They have also been more inclined than their men to fail to offer opinions on most fields of foreign affairs. These differences between the sexes have usually been larger in the South than in the rest of the country, especially among the lower educational and social strata.[28] By and large Southern women's international attitudes have paralleled those of Southern males of their class. Those women who have ventured views have been more inclined than men to disapprove of military intervention abroad and other lines of action which might lead to war; in general,

28 Throughout the country the gap in knowledge, interest, and understanding in world affairs between women and men has been larger in the less educated and lower socio-economic strata than in the better-educated, higher ones (see, for instance, Angus Campbell *et al; The American Voter*, 485), but this divergence between the sexes has been larger in the South than outside on most international issues.

their posture toward foreign developments has been at least somewhat less bellicose and more inclined to stress negotiation and other means short of violence. Slightly larger minorities of women than men have ventured isolationist opinions favoring United States withdrawal from our major international commitments.

These observations have applied particularly to the lower-middle and lower classes; the experience of women in these strata has been largely limited to their homes, children, and church (often of one degree of fundamentalism or another). Expansion of labor-intensive, low-skill industries like textile and garment manufacturing and shrimp and crab-meat canning has resulted in increasing numbers of them working outside their homes and has undoubtedly resulted in at least somewhat broadened horizons in world affairs as in other fields. But whatever little thinking about world problems has taken place at this level of the society has been largely among men. Whatever views these women have had have usually reflected those of their men or of their employers —often protectionist and opposed to foreign aid at the order of magnitude prevailing under the Eisenhower and Kennedy administrations.

Many older women of the more traditional privileged classes still seemed at the time of the conversations for this study to feel that interest in culture, literature, music, and family and that running a pleasant home were feminine roles; women were not expected to know much of world politics. Public questions and other controversial issues were regarded by them as the affairs of husbands, brothers, and sons. They felt that ladies should remain silent and not disagree with males on these matters and that they should certainly not be aggressive intellectuals or incisive in expressing their ideas in such spheres. Few women of these persuasions seemed to have relatively liberal, multilateralist outlooks; in most cases they disclaimed having opinions or referred the interviewer to their husbands.

But these feminine attitudes among the privileged classes have been declining—younger women even in the traditional Old South settings were much less inclined to accept such roles vis-à-vis men than were their elders. The limited sample seemed to indicate that internationalist thinking was more evident among women than men within the upper-middle and upper classes of our communities. Some of them identified themselves sentimentally with international cooperation without knowing much about it, and many of their ideas were not particularly realistic. But educated women in much of the South have provided the prime movers and workers of internationally oriented groups such as Leagues of Women Voters, American Association of University

Women branches, church and library discussion groups, sessions sponsored by the Foreign Policy Association and American Heritage Foundation, and others. A number of college-educated women among the informants read serious critical publications on world affairs, whereas their husbands read and agreed with *U.S. News and World Report* and still more conservative material. Even some wives of hard-bitten ultraconservative textile manufacturers and other local businessmen have been internationalist readers of liberal church publications and such magazines as *Newsweek*. A number of these women who supported foreign aid and other expensive international collaboration noted that their husbands considered them "impractical idealists," "fuzzy-headed liberals," or the like, and husbands volunteered comments which supported this impression.

Thus, a combination of relative isolation from economic competition, more general education in the liberal arts, greater leisure, allocation of cultural and literary interests to upper- and upper-middle-class women, and closer contact with church activities in denominations with internationalist stances nationally seemed to have resulted in more well-read, relatively liberal internationalists among women than men in the privileged groups. These women have influenced the development of their children and of others through participation in various organizations; some, as teachers, have imparted their thinking to the children of others; and perhaps they have also moderated to some degree the more conservative international opinions of their husbands. However, most of them seemed hesitant to disagree publicly with their spouses' known views.

Prevalence of Vigorous Cosmopolitanism

Although relatively well-informed cosmopolitans exist among the Old South upper classes, the internationally thoughtful minority in the economically developing parts of the region has in recent years been much more numerous (though not proportionally so). The views of the internationally concerned minority among the professional groups in the cities have tended to be less elitist and less generally conservative and they have more nearly approached those of Northern cosmopolitans than have those of most of the equally informed rural and small-town gentry—though with many exceptions. Moreover, New South cosmopolitans in the developing cities have been more apt to think in terms of attempting to do something about local indifference, ignorance, and irresponsible international thinking than have members of the genteel class who have been more likely to limit their energies to developing their own understanding and comparing interpretations with a small, like-minded minority. The younger urban cosmopolitans particularly have been relatively inclined to participate in organizations and otherwise to cooperate with others in trying to modify local thought and the behavior of legislators on world problems.

CHAPTER 9

RURALISM AND URBANISM
IN INTERNATIONAL AFFAIRS

Rural values have exerted much more profound influences on international thought and action in the South than in the rest of the country. The proportion of Southerners actually living in the rural areas in 1960 was still much larger than among Northerners. Moreover, of those residing in rural sections, a larger proportion in the South than outside were in occupations directly connected with agriculture. The percentage of Southern rural people not engaged in farming with urban orientations and associations was significantly smaller than in most of the rural North.

Profound Agrarian Influences

Disproportionate Political Impact of Rural Voters

Southern congressional districts in rural sections have more often than not comprised many fewer inhabitants than have urban constituencies. At the time of the inquiries for this study, the Georgia legislature, controlled by a rural minority, still maintained a county-unit system whereby no county—regardless of population—had more than six or fewer than two votes in congressional primaries which were normally equivalent to elections. Georgia cities had been combined with two or more rural counties in such a way that the latter with a minority of the population typically could choose Congressmen against the will of the majority in the urban area.[1]

1 See, for example, Cortez A. M. Ewing and James E. Titus, "Urbanism and Southern Politics," in *The Urban South*, 236–38.

Furthermore, Negroes throughout the South have been counted for districting purposes, but they have voted mainly in the cities and hardly at all in plantation sections where they have often constituted majorities. In some plantation districts as few as twelve thousand voters have elected Congressmen whereas seventy-five thousand in some cities have been unable to do so. Moreover, the votes of many of the rural masses have often been heavily influenced through various devices by a small planter-commercial elite, especially in plantation sections. The poll tax in some states has limited voting by poor whites, and its payment by prosperous supporters of conservative congressional candidates has provided a means of buying votes. Illiteracy, economic dependence on the rural and market town leadership, and tendencies to accept the guidance of that leadership in paternalistic atmospheres have further multiplied the influence of the small elite. As will be noted in Chapter 11, manipulation of the rural white majority outside the mountains and hill sections (where there are few Negroes) by this elite through appeals to rusticity and racial prejudices in order to elect economically and politically conservative Congressmen has reduced the attention paid by poor whites to other issues, even domestic economic ones closely associated with their own standards of living.[2]

Paucity of Urban Traditions

But the impact of the Southern rural heritage has been considerably greater than even these considerations would lead one to assume. With the exception of New Orleans, the South had no real cities until after the turn of the century. Cities in the North have been the sources of intellectual discussion, ideas, and information in world affairs as in other fields. However, even in old Savannah, Charleston, and to a lesser degree New Orleans, much of the leadership until the last generation or so made their livings directly or indirectly from agriculture, and many divided their time between their urban homes and their plantations.[3] Smaller towns and cities have been for the most part economic, social, and psychological extensions of the agricultural activities about them— they provided markets and services for farmers and contained the homes of many of the more prosperous of them. Successful planters went into business and banking in these towns and townspeople bought farms.

2 For an analysis of the disproportionate influence of rural groups, particularly black-belt elites, on Southern politics, see Key, *Southern Politics in State and Nation*, especially 116 and 513 ff.

3 Bowes, *The Culture of Early Charleston*, 8–9; Reznikoff and Engelman, *The Jews of Charleston*, 75; Fossier, *New Orleans: The Glamour Period, 1800–1840*, 48; Kendrick and Arnett, *The South Looks at Its Past*, 52; and Bridenbaugh, *Myths and Realities*, 76–77.

These local areas were relatively self-sufficient without much communication between even parts of the same state: they were individual colonial economies selling cotton, sugar, tobacco, rice, turpentine, and unfinished products to the North and abroad, purchasing their farm equipment and consumer goods from outside the South, and raising much of their food locally.[4] The limited manufacturing in the region was intimately tied to agriculture and raw materials. Agriculture permeated most institutions, individual ideologies, and conversations; few people came into contact with urban ideas; and virtually none experienced the impersonality and anonymity of the great Northern metropolises.

It is small wonder that Southerners of all classes have clung to their love of the soil and traditional agrarian attitudes to a degree which is difficult for most Northerners to comprehend. The planter has been at the top of the social pyramid, for one has had to own rural acres to be considered a gentleman in much of the South. Or, as one of William Faulkner's characters said, "People don't own land. . . . It's the land that owns the people." As a youngster in the thirties attending school in New Orleans and spending his free time in the country, the author recalls such advice as that attributed to the eighteenth-century planter-statesman John Randolph, "Take care of your land and it will take care of you"; the only property which is really worth much is that which you can "feel with your toes"; "country people see the broad horizons while city folks' vision is obscured by artificial buildings." In 1937, 70 percent of Southerners thought that the man who lived on the farm was better off than the one who lived in a city;[5] 41 percent said that they preferred to live and work on a farm, 30 percent in a small town, and only 25 percent in a city.[6] Talented intellectuals of the region—John Crowe Ransom, Allen Tate, Robert Penn Warren, Donald Davidson, and others of the Nashville Fugitive or Agrarian group and their sympathizers—have defended rural modes of life and thought against industrialism and urbanism. William Faulkner, Elizabeth Spencer, Eudora Welty, Thomas Wolfe, and others who have been more moderate critics of the New South have also been emotionally attached to the land and have questioned whether the human concomitants of industrial "progress" have been on the whole desirable.

Recent Developments

These agrarian values have been attenuated by the growing urbanization of the South, the development of highways and other trans-

4 See, for instance, Odum, *Southern Regions of the United States,* 355–57.
5 AIPO 105, 11/30/37 (2,821).   6 AIPO 88, 6/21/37 (2,760).

portation systems, the advent of higher literacy and better quality education, wider newspaper circulations, the coming of radio and television, the extended experience of many Southerners in uniform and in other roles outside the region, and other such cosmopolitan influences. But one must be careful not to overestimate changes in basic attitudes in contradistinction to the surface behavior of the New Southern urbanites.

Southerners in 1955 were still considerably more inclined than other Americans to feel that farming was a more useful and attractive way of life than most urban occupations.[7] Moreover, much of the recent industrialization has been, as already observed, linked to agriculture. As noted in the case of mill villages, many other postwar factories were constructed in open fields, hamlets, small towns, and on the outskirts of urban places where management-labor relations remained similar in many respects to those prevailing on plantations. Large fractions of those who have worked in these plants have continued to live on farms and to farm part time. Thus, a recent study of industrial workers in southeast Louisiana demonstrated that three out of five living in surrounding areas reported no change in farm operations after going to work in a box factory, and most of the remaining 40 percent reported only relatively minor changes. Only one worker had stopped farming altogether, and most preferred the night shift so that they could continue their agricultural activities.[8] A survey of workers in a furniture plant in Mississippi revealed that one fourth of all workers were still farming, two thirds lived in the open country, and most of the rest had operated farms at some time in their lives.[9]

Many factory workers would rather farm, raise cattle, or pursue other rural existences if they could make a decent living. A study of workers in northern Florida noted that the basic stimulus for engaging in part-time farming was normally not income, but the emotional satisfactions and perceived advantages of farm life.[10] Even in underdevel-

7 Public Opinion Surveys, Inc., "Attitudes of Adult Civilians toward the Military Service as a Career" (Princeton, 1955), Appendices 1–4; and Public Opinion Surveys, Inc., "Attitudes of 16 to 20 Year Old Males toward the Military Service as a Career" (Princeton, 1955), Appendices 9–12.

8 Alvin L. Bertrand and Harold W. Osborne, "Rural Industrialization: A Situational Analysis," *Rural Sociology*, XXV (1960), 391; and Bertrand and Osborne, "The Impact of Industrialization on a Rural Community," *Journal of Farm Economics*, XLI (1959), 1,132.

9 Sheridan T. Maitland and George L. Wilber, *Industrialization in Chickasaw County, Mississippi: A Study of Plant Workers* (State University Agricultural Experiment Station, Bull. 566 [Starkville, Miss., 1958]), 9–10.

10 Daniel E. Alleger, *Agricultural Activities of Industrial Workers and Retirees: A Survey of Small Agricultural Holdings in an Industrial Area of Florida* (Florida Agricultural Extension Service, Bull. 582 [Gainesville, 1953]).

oped rural sections young people who have said they expect to move
to cities due to economic considerations more often than not thought
of rural living as the "good life." [11] Fiercely antiurban farm people
still tended in the early sixties to look down on factory workers who
could not be their own bosses and had to accept orders and standardiz-
ation from superiors they might neither know nor like. Many farm
boys in the textile mills of Kent, New Southtown, and elsewhere seemed
to long for the farm, to regard themselves as failures in the truly higher
calling of agriculture, and to be so regarded by former associates still
on farms. Insofar as feasible, large numbers of industrial workers have
tried to maintain their rural connections; over half the employees in the
Louisiana box works cited above said that their plant jobs had changed
little their rural leisure pastimes, and most of the others engaged in no
more than one town amusement or activity.[12]

Residents of Southern cities have been significantly more inclined
than inhabitants of small agrarian and factory towns and, particularly,
of the open country to feel that urban people lead more desirable, interesting lives than farmers and rural people [13] and that urban occupations
are more appealing than rural ones.[14] However, they have been less apt
to think so than inhabitants of non-Southern cities.[15] The proportion
of urbanites of farm backgrounds and values varied in the early 1960's;
the newer and faster growing the city, the larger the proportion of its
inhabitants who were raised on farms and in agrarian towns. Perhaps
as many as three out of four in rapidly expanding Jackson sprang from
agrarian and related origins; on the other hand probably only one out
of three or four in New Orleans came from such backgrounds. Nashville was somewhere in-between.

Even in cities composed predominantly of former country people,
urban values have somewhat eroded rural ways of mind and action. But
many of those who have become financial successes have continued to
invest in farms, timberlands, and cattle; to chat about hunting dogs,
hogs, crops, and feed; to spend their leisure fishing, hunting, and raising livestock; to dream of retiring to the country; and to regard with
some suspicion the urbanite who does not care for these pastimes.

In such cities as Jackson where most of the working class came from

11 Alvin L. Bertrand, *Older Youth in Rural Louisiana* (Louisiana State University Agricultural Experiment Station, Bull. 478 [Baton Rouge, 1953]), 47.
12 Bertrand and Osborne, *Rural Sociology*, XXV (1960), 35.
13 AIPO 88, 6/21/37 (2,760), and AIPO 105, 11/30/37 (2,821).
14 Data made available by Public Opinion Surveys, Inc., from a study of a national sample in 1955.
15 *Ibid.;* AIPO 88, 6/21/37 (2,760), and AIPO 105, 11/30/37 (2,821).

unsophisticated farm backgrounds, one gains the impression that many of them have not learned much about urban habits and attitudes or how to live in cities. Uprooted from warm, stable ties of family and friendship and other psychological supports in traditional agrarian settings, they seem frequently to be rather confused and insecure, to fall back on inapplicable mores of their rural past, and to resolve their frustrations in the city through acceptance of dogmatic emotional clichés or even violence. Most have been difficult to unionize partly because of residues of rural individualism, absence of habits of participation in organized social activities, and acceptance of paternalistic management which maintained the rural social system they had always known. Thrown into equal-status competition with Negroes for the first time, many former country lads have been open to extremist appeals by racist and otherwise irresponsible demagogues. Anxious in their new, more complex environments and limited in education, information, and the analytical qualities to understand them, they have been drawn to charismatic leaders who have offered quick, simple-minded "solutions" to delicate local, national, and international problems.

Ruralism and World Affairs

It is not surprising, therefore, that much of the thinking about world affairs in the South in recent years has been more similar to that among Northern farmers than to that of other major Northern groups. The adult sons and daughters of farmers have been significantly less inclined to hold internationalist or multilateralist opinions than offspring of urban parents, regardless of whether they have lived in the South or North or in urban, small-town, or rural environments. Thus, in 1956, adults who had grown up on farms were more apt than those who had been raised in cities to feel that this country would be better off if we "just stayed home and did not concern ourselves with the problems of other parts of the world," that the United States should not "give economic help to the poorer countries if they could not pay for it," and that we should not economically help foreign countries "if they are not as much against Communism as we are." [16]

Both Northern farmers and Southerners who have volunteered opinions have been more inclined than other Americans to feel that world war is relatively likely (see p. 106), we will probably be unable to settle our differences with the Communist bloc and other opponents short

16 SRC survey of 1956 cited in Key, *Public Opinion and American Democracy*, 114 and 308–309.

of armed conflict (see pp. 106–107), and we should be less compromising with such powers (see pp. 108–14). Both have had less respect than have Northern urbanites for pacifist, abstract, or "utopian" thinking,[17] and both have tended more than most other citizens to emphasize military preparedness as the most important—or virtually the only—means of defending our national interests (see p. 81). On the other hand, Southerners and Northern rural people have in recent years been less enthusiastic about the effectiveness of expensive programs designed to encourage economic growth in underdeveloped countries,[18] intercultural exchanges,[19] extended, but seemingly fruitless, negotiations with the Communists for arms control and other purposes (see pp. 115–26), and other nonmilitary, primarily subtle diplomatic, economic, and educational efforts to advance our national goals (see pp. 68–73, 203–204). Neither group has been as favorable as urban and rural nonfarm Northerners to "foreign" ways of thinking and living and to the apparent surrender of some national sovereignty in recent times to supranational agencies. However, until relatively recently, both Southerners and to a lesser extent rural Northerners were less opposed to liberalization of international trade than were urban Northerners (see pp. 140–43).

A Comparison of Southern and Northern Farm People

Samples have been too small to permit comparison of Southern with Northern farmers and other rural folk on individual surveys. But by combining replies to similar questions on several polls and mass media studies, it was observed that Southern country people as a group have more often than not lagged behind even Northerners in rural settings in their interest, knowledge, and exposure to foreign relations.

A study of farm operators in 1945 found that 78 percent received a daily paper in the North, whereas only 38 percent did in the South; and 89 percent of the former as compared with 55 percent of the latter received any magazines at all.[20] However, the latter figures underestimated regional differences between farm families in their attention to international subjects in print.

17   AIPO 225, 1/14/41 (3,026); AIPO 387, 12/31/46 (2,933); and pp. 90–91, 362–65.
18   AIPO 558, 1/4/56 (1,385); AIPO 576, 12/12/56 (1,539); AIPO 596, 3/4/58 (1,610); and AIPO 667, January, 1963 (4,383).
19   AIPO 566, 6/13/56 (2,078); AIPO 584, 6/4/57 (1,484); and AIPO 630, 6/28/60 (3,248).
20   Cited in Charles P. Loomis, *et al., Rural Social Systems and Adult Education* (East Lansing: Michigan State College Press, 1953), 296–97. See also SRC survey of June–August, 1946 (1,177).

Circulation figures in 1960 for a sample of a hundred predominantly rural counties in the South as compared with an equal number of rural counties in the North indicated that rural people generally were much less inclined than urbanites to read sophisticated analytical treatments of foreign affairs in periodicals like the New York *Times* (Sunday edition), *Harper's*, and *The Reporter*, but that Southern rural dwellers were only about two fifths as likely to do so as Northern ones. The more liberal, or analytical, the publication, the greater the disparity between rural and urban people throughout the country and the smaller the proportion of Southerners among rural readers. Thus, the rural South lagged behind its Northern counterparts to a lesser degree with reference to readership of *U.S. News and World Report*, to a greater degree with respect to *Time*, and to an even greater degree regarding *The Reporter*. The same generalization applied to Southern as compared with Northern urbanites, but differences were wider for Southern rural as compared with Northern rural people.

The difference between the regions has been much smaller for watching television newscasts than for reading on foreign affairs, but it was considerable in 1958–60 for half-hour or hour-long discussions of particular issues, like Cuba, the U.N., and international economic relations. Rural Southerners have been more likely than rural Northerners to derive their information on world affairs from radio and television than from reading.[21] Face-to-face programs on foreign issues have been sparse in most agricultural settings, but the existence of such programs and the presence of educational or other organizations likely to sponsor them have been lacking most in the South.

Consequently, smaller proportions of rural Southerners than rural Northerners have been able on surveys to provide information about most international issues, including foreign trade to which the Southern agrarian economy has long been tied. They have been less apt than other farm people to venture opinions on most aspects of foreign policy, except for such general areas as the probability of war or the desirability of keeping troops abroad. They have been more likely to say that they had relatively little or no interest in most world problems.

Samples have been too small—even when similar questions on several surveys have been combined—for comparison of international behavior of Southern and Northern farmers of comparable education, income, and other demographic characteristics. However, it is apparent that differences in education and, to a lesser measure, income between the

21   NORC 393, 9/13/56 (1,263); AIPO 575, 11/20/56 (1,502); and AIPO 638, 11/15/60 (3,128).

rural dwellers of the regions go far to explain the Southern lag in inter-national concern and knowledge. Half the rural farm population of Mountain County aged twenty-five and over in 1960 had not com-pleted as much as the sixth grade. The median schooling for farm peo-ple in Plantation County was a little over six years; for Delta County a bit over five years; for Hill County eight and a half years; and for Bayou Parish six years—all sharply below the average farm educations outside the South. Education of Northern farmers more nearly ap-proached that of urbanites than was the case in most of the South in 1960. The fact that education of urban Southerners has been closer to that of urban Northerners than has education of rural Southerners to rural Northerners [22] has been partly due to the concentration of little-educated Negroes in the rural South, but the generalization has also applied to hill counties where Negroes have been less prevalent and to mountain ones where there have been few Negroes. The negative effects of lower education have been reinforced by the concentration of the poorest farmers in the South [23]—per capita incomes in Southern cities have more nearly approached those in Northern cities than have incomes for Southern as compared with Northern rural settings.

Furthermore, although mechanization of Southern plantations and the shift from cotton to cattle and timber has reduced considerably the number of little-educated, lower-class workers, the disparity between the income and education of the Southern rural elite and the agrarian majority was still considerably wider in the South than in Northern farming sections in 1960. As already observed, a minority of the South-ern landed gentry in the plantation sections has paid attention to world issues and read rather thoughtful literature on the subject. A larger proportion of them and of relatively prosperous business and profes-sional people in county seats and other agrarian towns has read fairly regularly the international content of a weekly newsmagazine and a nearby daily paper. This small minority—roughly one frequent reader of international articles in analytical publications like the *Atlantic* and the New York *Times* (Sunday edition) out of a thousand inhabitants and one frequent reader of newsmagazines out of fifty—was probably

22 T. Lynn Smith and Homer L. Hitt, *The People of Louisiana* (Baton Rouge: Louisiana State University Press, 1952), 98–105; C. A. Anderson, "Social Class Differentials in the Schooling of Youth within the Regions and Community-Size Groups of the United States," *Social Forces*, XXV (1947), 434–40; and Lipset and Bendix, *Social Mobility in Industrial Society*, 219 ff.
23 Depending on one's definition of the South, the proportion of Southern rural families with incomes of less than $1,000 in 1959 was almost twice that in the rest of the country. See also Jackson V. McElveen and Kenneth L. Bachman, *Low Production Farms* (Agricultural Information Bull. 108 [Washington: U.S. Depart-ment of Agriculture, 1953]), especially Tables 11–13.

as well informed as the cosmopolitans among the leaders of Northern agricultural counties. But this group was a significantly smaller proportion of the total Southern rural population. The majority of Southern country dwellers was less informed on world developments and less inclined to venture opinions to survey interviewers than were rank-and-file adults in Northern farm sections.[24]

Plantation, Hill, and Mountain Counties

There have been, of course, important differences among Southern rural sections. In plantation counties which were prosperous before the Civil War a dozen or more persons in 1959–62 were usually relatively frequent readers of international material in critical periodicals of the quality of *Harper's*, had reasonably differentiated opinions on the major long-term issues facing this country abroad, and were relatively well informed and thoughtful on foreign relations. Their views ranged from liberal internationalist through elitist conservative neo-isolationist (in a few cases, even isolationist) and unilateralist, but approximately half of them supported the major international programs of the United States of the late 1950's and early 1960's, perhaps with some reservations. Most of these cosmopolitans in the older plantation sections which had not received much nonagricultural industry generally were of secure social standing in the area as a result of their family's being esteemed for several generations. One or more educated ministers or (in southern Louisiana) priests, high-school administrators and teachers, lawyers or their wives of less-esteemed ancestry were also normally among these internationally thoughtful individuals. If there were several Jewish families in the county, one or two Jews were likely to be among these better read and more internationally concerned people. The proportion of middle class, particularly professional, individuals among the cosmopolitans increased as the plantation economy became more mixed with industries and as the size of the county seat or market town in the county increased. Middle-class professionals were also found more often among small cosmopolitan minorities in newer plantation settings, as in much of the Delta, because of a scarcity of traditional Old South groups. Rarely were there any Negroes among these relatively sophisticated cosmopolitans in plantation settings, although occasionally a social-studies teacher or principal appeared among them.

With some exceptions, prosperous planters, plantation managers,

24 Removal of Negroes from Southern rural samples improved the Southern showing as compared with Northern rural people with respect to interest, knowledge, and exposure in world affairs. However, considerable differences remained between the sections even when whites alone were compared.

cattle raisers, timberland owners, merchants, and physicians of middle-class background read at most a newsmagazine, *U.S. News and World Report* being the most popular. But well over half of the middle class in the plantation country either gained their international information and interpretation almost exclusively from conversations with family and friends and television newscasts, or at most read about world affairs more or less frequently in a newspaper. Reading of critical literature, interest in ideas about foreign affairs (or other fields), and curiosity about foreign civilizations and problems were highly atypical of the Southern rural middle class anywhere, including the plantation sections. Their reading of magazines tended to be in *Good Housekeeping*, the *Reader's Digest*, and the like, and agricultural or other pragmatic periodicals pertinent to their occupations. However, a considerably larger proportion of them were reading newsmagazines than a decade or more before.

A few of the wives of these men were relatively liberal about world affairs: they favored aid to India, expanded international exchanges of students and adults, a strengthened U.N., and so on. Their participation in church activities and associations with liberal ministers were major sources of their divergence from the opinions prevailing among their male and most of their female peers. The preponderant majority of the men were fiscal conservatives par excellence, fearful of "socialism" in Washington, strongly opposed to trade unions, unenthusiastic about foreign aid and the entry of underdeveloped nations (particularly African ones) into the U.N., critical of compromises with communism abroad and at home, and favorable to military intervention in Latin America, starting with Cuba. They tended to feel that we had been "pussyfooting" too long with our enemies and "two-bit" neutralists. Only a few of these extreme conservatives would accept the label "isolationist," since they were hostile to "America First" and similar isolationist movements and had been favorable to diplomatic and military resistance to the Axis in the late 1930's; they would again support an active military policy against aggressors. Senators like James Eastland, Harry Byrd, Herman Talmadge, and Barry Goldwater were popular with most of the middle class in plantation locales, and views of these Senators on foreign policy seemed agreeable to most of this middle-class group.

The remaining 95 to 99 percent of the population formed a continuum from those who were illiterate and ignorant of world affairs to a minority who viewed television programs and occasionally read press coverage on the subject. *Life, Look,* and other pictorial publications including international content were read by the rural middle class, but many of them have shied away from these magazines due to their supposedly pro-Negro, "anti-Southern" views (see pp. 425–27).

In the early fifties and before, plantation counties provided a disproportionate part of the support for internationalist Congressmen who voted for Lend-Lease, the loan to Britain shortly after the war, the Truman Doctrine, the Marshall Plan, and expanded trade. But during the late 1950's and early 1960's Congressmen from such primarily rural, little industrialized, heavily Negro areas, with their low average education and income and rather static economies, provided significantly more than their share of roll-call votes by Southerners against foreign aid, admission of refugees to this country, United States participation in the Inter-American Development Bank and the International Development Association, expanded intercultural exchanges, and other types of multilateral cooperation.[25]

Because of the lack of interviews of a representative sample of the rank-and-file whites and Negroes in these counties in the early 1960's, one can only speculate on the extent to which these Congressmen represented their international views. The few interviewees below the small, white upper and upper-middle class in plantation settings tended to indicate that most whites of limited education and low income had very little information and relatively few distinct attitudes except on issues which patently affected them directly, such as war and peace, spending tax money on foreign aid, and "putting our foot down" with the Reds. The concentration of the most intense white opposition to desegregation, to Negro voting, and to other racial changes in the plantation sections seemed to result in some of the most marked opposition in the South to "niggers in the U.N.," decolonization, and foreign aid to Africa and, to a lesser degree, underdeveloped neutralist countries generally, and in other international thinking associated with white-supremacy ideology (see pp. 396–404). Preoccupation with the race issue seemed the most important single reason for the apparently marked shift of whites in these counties toward isolationism since the 1954 Supreme Court desegregation decision.

In Mountain County almost everybody living away from the small county seat, a smaller mining hamlet, and the road connecting them was illiterate or semiliterate, near the bottom of the national economic spectrum, and among the Americans most isolated from developments beyond their immediate experience. Almost no one read much of anything, including a daily paper, and only a minority had easy access to

25 Lerche, *The Uncertain South*, 188–246.

television, and few of these seemed to pay much attention to the international content thereon, except for an occasional fifteen-minute newscast. The exceptions were a handful of missionaries, frontier nurses, and other "outsiders."

A number of the younger men had served outside the moutains in the armed forces; however, relatively large numbers were rejected from the draft due to physical disabilities and illiteracy. Some had also worked for a time in cities and then returned to the mountains; but those who had come back tended to be less alert and more provincial in their thinking than those who stayed away. Moreover, their associations while away were largely with lower-class people like themselves whose views on world affairs and general values differed relatively little from their own. A fair number of those who worked in cities beyond the mountains at the time of the interviews did return home to visit their families and friends, in some cases rather often. They were perhaps one of the major contacts with the world beyond for those who remained in the mountains; but foreign affairs was certainly not a frequent topic of conversation between them.

Similar to the poorly educated of the plantation South, few of these mountaineers seemed to have clear-cut opinions on international questions not directly related to their experience and local interests. (Perhaps an expert interviewer of mountain background could extract more intense international attitudes from a majority of them.) When questions about foreign aid were expressed in language they could understand, most opposed "so much of" it and urged that the money be spent here. They even seemed to react unfavorably to sending food to underdeveloped lands—they tended to consider themselves in competition with Africans, Latin Americans, and Indians for this aid and resented American products being given away abroad. Foreign expenditures should be limited to military garrisons. Even those who had heard of foreign aid for the most part disapproved of it. Thus, when interviewers in a recent survey of mountain people asked rural adults, "What things do you think the government is now doing which it shouldn't be?" over a third of those who felt the government was engaged in programs which should be eliminated mentioned foreign aid on their own initiative, more than twice as many as mentioned any other budgetary cut.[26] Opposition to immigration and to foreigners generally seemed as widespread as hostility to foreign aid, and most rural mountaineers were either isolationists or thought of foreign policy in terms

26 Unpublished data from the Berea College study of the Appalachians, provided by the Research Director, Professor Thomas Ford of the University of Kentucky.

of national defense, military alliances, and sending "believers" (defined as members of their own fundamentalist sect) abroad to preach to the heathens.

A small middle class resided primarily in the unincorporated county seat, the mining community, and along the main road. However, with a few exceptions, most of this group was rather close in thought and often by birth to the semiliterate rural majority. Their thinking seemed comparable to that of much of the lower-middle class in the United States generally. The majority of these small merchants, undertakers, fairly prosperous farmers, small mine operators, local politicians, and the like had relatively little interest in or information about world affairs. They seldom talked or thought about foreign problems. Most read foreign news only infrequently in a daily paper and viewed television newscasts several times a week. They confined their television viewing primarily to entertainment. Even most recipients of a daily paper seemed to have rather little knowledge about foreign policy.

Having relatively little perception of the international behavior of their Senators, many of even this small middle class seemed rather unpleasantly surprised to learn that the most popular of the two had consistently supported foreign economic assistance, and vociferously so for India shortly before. Some agreed with the less well-off majority that foreign aid should be channeled to poor Americans, but more seemed to feel that it should either not be spent at all and the national debt and taxes reduced instead or that such funds should be used to encourage economic development of underdeveloped or depressed domestic areas like Mountain County. Scholarships should be awarded to worthy American youngsters rather than to foreigners. But if our government sponsored educational, technical, or economic aid, our country should get the credit for it and handle it directly rather than through any international organization. They were fundamentalists with few exceptions and most were very "anti-Communist." They strongly opposed the entry of Communist China into the U.N.; they did not think a feasible arms-control settlement would be reached and wondered why we acted as though it would be attained. A significant minority seemed to accept outright "Fortress America" thinking.

With the exception of a very few better educated, more intellectually alert individuals with upper-middle-class values, the majority of the county, including most of the middle class, seemed to be rather poorly informed on even the general foreign policy postures of their local Congressman and their two Senators. Their votes were determined primarily by traditional and local considerations. The same individuals voted for an internationalist Republican who was a graduate of an Ivy League law school as Senator and for a fundamentalist preacher of limited education who was also a Republican as their local Congressman. The latter had voted typically with the isolationists or neo-isolationists in the Congress—consistently against foreign aid since 1955, in opposition to the Refugee Act of 1953, the proposed increase in the United States subscription to the International Monetary Fund and the International Bank in 1959, United States participation in the Inter-American Development Bank in 1959, the International Health and Medical Research Act of 1960, United States participation in the International Development Association in 1960, the Alliance for Progress in 1961, and the proposed purchase of U.N. bonds by the United States in 1961.[27] Both men were popular, but not for reasons related to foreign policy. Most voters seemed more interested in elections of the county judge (who administered federal commodity distribution and other welfare benefits) and other local officials. Many did not vote, and a number who did were reported to have been "bought" through liquor, food, promises, or cash. Fundamentalist preachers were suspected, apparently on good grounds, of being paid to "throw" their congregations. Most local people voted Republican as had their ancestors with little attention to issues beyond the county.

The few relatively informed and interested mountaineers were on the average significantly less sophisticated about foreign affairs than were the most cosmopolitan dozen or so in older plantation counties. Even more than in plantation counties with little industry, the young college graduates who have been most cosmopolitan in their interests tended to move to cities. There were very few local opportunities for highly educated sons and daughters. Moreover, the aristocratic values supporting interest in "culture" seemed entirely lacking. There were no book clubs or groups which met for meals and discussions of issues beyond the local setting as there were in Old South upper-class circles. Whatever reading about foreign affairs there was took place primarily among the college educated—teachers, lawyers, the physician, the dentist, and the few ministers of less fundamentalist churches. But teaching jobs were regarded as political plums for they paid better than most other positions. Consequently, teachers—mainly wives of local people—could be dismissed for controversial expressions of opinion and their insecurity tended to limit serious concern with public issues. The task of teaching social studies—apparently regarded as of less importance than most other subjects—had been rotated from one teacher to another over the past decade, none of whom was trained or particu-

27 Lerche, *The Uncertain South*, 292 and 295.

larly interested in that field. The lawyers did not have the broad intellectual interests of more outstanding urban ones.

The only readers of analytical material were a physician and his wife of comfortable urban background, associated with the local hospital and a nursing group supported by outside philanthropy. Several of the British nurses and their American associates with this group were readers of newsmagazines and internationalist in their views, but the indigenous people associated with them almost exclusively as patients. Except for a young officer of the local bank, the thirty-nine readers of newsmagazines and regular followers of international news and editorials in the daily press had been to college and most had a bachelor's degree. The most sophisticated were two missionary Northern Presbyterian ministers, a seminary-trained Southern Baptist minister, the dentist from another state, two lawyers, and a former high-school principal who had lost his job reputedly for political reasons. The most dynamic was a young college-educated businessman and mine owner who was the son of a relatively affluent (for Mountain County) father; this young educated businessman was attempting (with little success) to attract industry to the locale. All eight except the former principal were less than forty-five years old.

Many of these better-informed people held views similar to those of their less interested and knowledgeable peers. But the citizens who did favor active nonmilitary international programs, including foreign aid, the Peace Corps, active collaboration in the U.N., and expanded world trade, were in large measure among the better informed and better read. Although their thinking was far from monolithic, it was influenced in most cases by many of the ideas prevalent among the general population: foreign capital assistance should be real loans and not gifts or "make-believe" loans never to be repaid in their true value; aid should be direct rather than through international agencies, though some multilateral technical assistance seemed acceptable; we should take a firm stand against Red intrigues and should resist "to the bitter end" entry of Communist China into the U.N.; it would be preferable to send matured, able technicians rather than youngsters (as in the Peace Corps) on technical assistance missions; we might have to raise taxes for more effective national defense; and we should be firmer with Castro and apply the Monroe Doctrine. At least two of these eight were overtly concerned that too many diplomats, liberals, and "theorists" influencing our policies had overly optimistic, "rosy" views of foreign peoples and their leaders and as a result would probably pursue grandiose schemes.

However, several beliefs found among many white Southerners in areas with numerous Negroes, and particularly in the Black Belt, were distinctly missing among inhabitants of Mountain County of all strata and attitudes. None who knew of the apartheid policy of the Union of South Africa approved. No one seemed to feel that there were many Communists in positions of national influence. No paternalism or "white man's burden" thinking with respect to Africa or other underdeveloped areas was located, and there was no observable support for continued colonial control of remaining dependencies like Angola for more than a limited period. The elitism of the plantation regions found little counterpart in Mountain County.

Hill County, like most of the Piedmont area, incorporated some of the features of both rural mountain and plantation sections plus some effects of the New South. Several individuals of more or less genteel traditions had moved into the county and three of them read such sophisticated critical material as the New York *Times* (Sunday edition), *Harper's*, and the *Virginia Quarterly Review*. The school superintendent, the social-studies teacher, a Canadian-born physician, the wife of another physician, and a thoughtful retired Baptist minister also read periodicals of this nature. Newsmagazines reached a much larger fraction there than in Mountain County, but there were fewer relatively interested, cosmopolitan people than in antebellum plantation areas. As elsewhere, newsmagazine readers with few exceptions had attended college, though some had not graduated. All readers of more analytical material held degrees.

In Hill County most college-educated farm families, teachers, clergymen, bankers, merchants, operators of poultry processing, feed, and hatchery plants, lawyers, physicians, the local weekly newspaper owner and editor, and other middle-class men or their wives, or both, viewed television newscasts and read the foreign coverage in one of several extremely conservative newspapers published in nearby cities —all critical of foreign aid, the U.N., the Peace Corps, and so on. Roughly two out of five of this middle class also read a newsmagazine or equivalent periodical. Only two Negroes, both high-school teachers, fitted this description in Hill County. At least half of the newsmagazine readers and well over half of the rest of the middle class felt that foreign aid could either be eliminated or reduced considerably; but the U.N., expanded international trade, technical assistance, and most other foreign programs of our government were less unpopular. Most of the middle class, including most newsmagazine readers but no reader of more critical periodicals, felt satisfied with Senator Eastland's international ideas, insofar as they knew about them.

As in other rural settings, the great majority had few opinions on foreign issues other than foreign aid, military service, and war and peace, and they paid rather scant attention to world events. However, the proportion of more or less prosperous farmers and workers in the several small local industries who had attended or completed high school was larger than in either the plantation or the mountain settings, and a number of these read one of the local neo-isolationist daily papers, viewed news and occasionally a public affairs program on television, and had at least somewhat more information and opinions on foreign policy than was the case in rural plantation or mountain society. Although only a minority could be termed isolationists, many were disenchanted with foreign aid and compromises with the Communist powers. Large majorities had supported in recent years congressional and gubernatorial candidates who were arch-conservatives on foreign policy as on most issues, and few seemed discontented about the thinking and behavior of their representatives in Washington toward world affairs.

The Plight of Rural and Small-Town Cosmopolitans

The most internationally concerned and sophisticated in all these rural settings tended not to return after graduation from college, but usually moved to cities. Those who did return were for the most part less interested and knowledgeable about world affairs at the time. Once home, much of the small minority who read about foreign relations in books and the better periodicals became involved in the complex web of rural and small-town demands and social relationships and gradually discontinued their reading of the New York *Times* and the like. As their reading of critical material declined, their thinking tended to evolve more and more toward that prevalent among the local middle and upper classes. Only the most intellectually vigorous handful continued to read serious treatments of foreign policy in the better national publications.

Moreover, this small, most thoughtful group have likewise been obliged to labor against potent debilitating factors. Their information and interpretations of foreign issues have necessarily been derived almost exclusively from reading supplemented by public-affairs programs on television. They have had for the most part very little if any contact since college with experts on international subjects. Only the most interested have traveled to hear lectures or to take part in conferences and other organized discussions in cities and university communities. Nor have they had many analytical associates with sharp critical facul-

ties to amend, systematize, deepen, and ramify their international thinking and eliminate distorted interpretations of whatever they learned
from mass media. These isolated cosmopolitans have frequently been
intellectually lonely, unable to find people to talk to about their interests, and fearful of being judged "odd" by their peers.

As a result, the majority of even the most internationally thoughtful
in rural and small-town environments have been more or less vaguely
so, as much or more on account of emotional, philosophical, or religious
inclinations than because of examination of the facts of international
relations. Many of their opinions have been rather naïve, undifferenti-
ated, inconsistent, based on unrealistic assumptions, and rather easily
brushed aside as "irresponsible" by much more numerous "hardheaded"
conservatives. Most have not been well enough informed, nor have their
ideas been systematically enough worked out, for them to refute effectively the many arch-conservative attitudes about them and the biased
assumptions on which they have often been based. Thus, there have
been few serious standards of sensible thought on international questions or vigorous, able defenses of the more subtle policies of our
federal government in such locales.

Lack of contact with expertise in world affairs, combined with local
pressures and involvements, has also resulted in the gradual drift of
even most of the small cosmopolitan minority toward the international
attitudes typical of these communities. They have become on the average more conservative about foreign aid, decolonization, compromise
with our international opponents, and other issues than equally well-
read and informed Southerners in the more complex cities. Contact
with others who thought differently and really knew a great deal about
these topics would probably have given many more of them the courage of their convictions against prevailing opinion.

These factors have also militated against communication of information and interpretation in world affairs by these few thoughtful individuals beyond their families, intimate friends, and the few of their peers
who have read comparable material. Less cosmopolitan associates have
felt uncomfortable around "intellectuals," so that the well read have
tended to play down their serious concerns. Most of them have come to
assume, like a number of the Old South gentry among them, that they
could not exert much influence on local thinking even if they tried.
The gaps in interest, knowledge, and views between themselves and
the vast majority have seemed too wide and the opinions of the others
too firmly anchored to be changed by them. Cosmopolitans who were
more optimistic about influencing others in their youth have often de-

spaired of success, become emotionally exhausted by a sense of futility, and frustrated because their earlier efforts to stimulate more widespread intelligent concern required more energy, resources, and sacrifices than the meager results appeared to warrant. This feeling that they could not use knowledge about foreign policy to much effect also tended to reinforce the other factors leading to shifts of their interest from international to local problems.

Consequently, some of the general views of this minute cosmopolitan group were known to some of their more conservative, less-informed associates, but most seemed to express their ideas primarily to a few interested and relatively sophisticated individuals of like mind locally and in nearby counties and cities. Some of these people among our informants were virtually recluses with their books and periodicals, offering only pleasantries except to the handful of their associates with similar concerns. Asked for suggestions of techniques likely to extend the small number of responsible thinkers about world affairs, the typical response of most rural and small-town cosmopolitans was that there probably were none. They often replied by asking the interviewer if he had any suggestions on the matter. They frequently felt ignored by outside internationalists and cosmopolitan organizations. They seemed to believe that few of these have tried to understand their frustrating situation and that such organizations were not much interested in assisting them.

The Cities

Urban-Rural Differences

Congressmen representing districts including the larger Southern cities have on the average been significantly more inclined than their colleagues from constituencies made up primarily of rural and small-town people to vote for most of the multilateral commitments before the House since 1953—foreign aid, admission of European refugees, financial and other support of international organizations, the U.N. bond issue of 1962, expanded intercultural collaboration, and so on.[28] Likewise, inhabitants of Southern cities have been more likely to approve of these measures and other international cooperation than have Southerners living in the country and in small towns. When responses to similar questions on several surveys have been combined to obtain sufficiently large samples for statistical treatment, urban Southerners

28 *Ibid.*, 144, 148–50, 193–96.

(both races taken together) have been on the whole more favorable than others to foreign economic assistance to underdeveloped and neutralist countries,[29] continued negotiations with the Soviets to alleviate disagreements and tensions,[30] admission of refugees from Communist countries,[31] exchanges of persons with the Soviet bloc,[32] and active United States collaboration in the U.N.[33] Urban Southerners have also been better informed, generally more interested, and better read in world affairs on the average than their rural and small-town fellows.

Diversity of Urban Attitudes

However, Southern cities have differed considerably among themselves in local thinking about world affairs and in the behavior of their members of the House of Representatives toward foreign policy. Although Southern congressional opponents of foreign aid and other multilateral collaboration have been elected in disproportionately large number by predominantly rural and small-town constituencies, some have represented primarily urban districts or have received majority votes over less conservative opponents from urbanites in their constituencies. Thus, among Democratic Congressmen who have opposed foreign aid at the levels requested by Presidents Eisenhower and Kennedy and a number of other international proposals of these Presidents since the mid-1950's have been Otto Passman supported by majorities in Monroe (Louisiana), Overton Brooks in Shreveport, Robert R. Casey in Houston, John Bell Williams in Jackson (Mississippi), William Arthur Winstead in Meridian (Mississippi), and L. Mendel Rivers in Charleston (South Carolina). Non-mountain Republican Congressmen in the South (like Bruce Alger of Dallas, Page Belcher from the district including Tulsa, and the somewhat less internationally conservative C. R. Jonas of Charlotte) have come primarily from urban constituencies and have on the whole been more inclined to oppose foreign aid, the U.N. bond issue, and other multilateral cooperation than have Southern Democratic Congressmen.[34] Ultra-conservative Republicans

29   NORC 393, 9/3/56 (1,263); NORC 399, 11/15/56 (1,286); NORC 401, 12/28/56 (1,232); and NORC 404, 4/26/57 (1,279).
30   NORC 401, 12/28/56 (1,232); NORC 404, 4/26/57 (1,279); and AIPO 602, 7/28/58 (1,621).
31   NORC 327, 6/30/52 (1,285); NORC 333, 11/17/52 (1,291); AIPO 575, 11/20/56 (1,502); NORC 401, 12/28/56 (1,232); and AIPO 586, 9/17/57 (1,534).
32   NORC 372, 6/23/55 (1,263); NORC 374, 8/4/55 (1,262); NORC 376, 9/29/55 (1,250); and AIPO 584, 6/4/57 (1,484).
33   AIPO 631, 7/14/60 (2,800); AIPO 637, 10/18/60 (2,993); and AIPO 640, 1/10/61 (2,649).
34   Roll-call votes for 1953–62 are from Lerche, *The Uncertain South*, 292–300.

W. D. Workman and James D. Martin, running for the Senate in South Carolina and Alabama respectively, carried majorities in Greenville and Montgomery (Hill's hometown) with platforms including anti-multilateralist, even isolationist, planks against Democratic incumbents Lister Hill and Olin Johnston, the former clearly internationalist and the latter significantly less isolationist than his Republican opponent.

At the other, internationalist or multilateralist, end of the spectrum from these Congressmen have been Representatives Hale Boggs and F. Edward Hébert, supported by majorities in New Orleans, Porter Hardy in Norfolk and Portsmouth, Joseph C. Loser in Nashville, and Frank E. Smith in Greenville, Mississippi.

Since interviews of representative samples in these diverse Southern cities are not available, one can only speculate on the distribution of international thinking within them. One cannot, of course, assume necessarily close association between local opinion and congressional behavior. The postures of candidates toward world affairs have been only one, and frequently a relatively minor one, of their sources of public appeal. However, there seemed to be somewhat higher correlation between public opinion and congressional behavior on foreign policy in urban than in largely rural Southern constituencies.[35] Thoughtful concern about foreign relations and support for broad international cooperation in 1959–62 seemed more widespread in New Orleans, Norfolk, Nashville, and Greenville, Mississippi, than in Monroe, Shreveport, Jackson, Meridian, Charleston, Tulsa, and perhaps Dallas, Houston, and Charlotte as well.

No one of several factors can alone account for differences in international thought in Southern cities. Several of those mentioned previously which have tended to encourage greater cosmopolitanism and support for multilateral cooperation are: (1) relatively high rather than low average education; (2) presence of vigorous, intellectually stimulating institutions of higher learning and active cultural organizations; (3) an upper and upper-middle class in which individuals of second or later generation prosperity and education rather than newly wealthy, self-made men of humble origins are the more influential; (4) relatively heterogeneous white ethnic composition rather than almost exclusively Anglo-Saxon white population; (5) export-oriented and high-technology economic enterprises rather than labor-intensive, non-durable goods industries; and (6) strong rather than weak or nonexistent trade unions. The favorable impacts of the prevalence of a Jewish minority, of a low ratio of Negroes to whites, of paucity of religious fundamentalism, and

35 Lerche, *The Uncertain South*, 273–74 and 280.

of internationally sophisticated newspapers and television will be considered in Chapters 13, 11, 12, and 16, respectively. The more of these
positive forces that apply and the more dynamic they are, the more
general is responsible international thought likely to be.

Related to several of these factors, and important in its own right,
has been the proportion of the urban population who were raised in
the country or in small communities closely tied to surrounding agriculture. It was observed previously that rapidly growing cities which
have emerged from small towns or even open country in the last several generations have frequently produced a power structure of business and related leaders of limited general education, modest rural
upbringing, and new wealth whose international attitudes have approximated those of Goldwater Republicans. Moreover, cities including
upper and middle classes of such orientations have also been typically
populated by a working class made up chiefly of people of similarly
limited agrarian childhoods. The impression was obtained from interviewing a score or so of newly urbanized workers and a number of
their trade union and other leaders that the combination of their simple
rustic experience, low education, fundamentalist religion, racism, and
emotional insecurity and confusion in their newly urban surroundings
have resulted in unfortunate reactions to international issues, such as
irresponsible opposition to "foreign giveaways," "niggers in the U.N.,"
and lack of understanding of the value of nonmilitary means in foreign
policy.

Even in more sophisticated cities working-class voters of simple
rural beginnings have been more inclined than their urban-born fellows
to harbor neo-isolationist if not isolationist ideologies. For instance, in
Memphis many workers of rural origins in low-skill jobs voted for Andrew "Tip" Taylor against Estes Kefauver in 1960. A considerable
fraction of even unionized workers of these backgrounds in Atlanta
garment plants have supported Herman Talmadge and others who have
appealed to "wool hat" prejudices against the urgings of union representatives. In New Orleans, trade union leaders and other observers
noted that the minority who came from the country—particularly
fundamentalist Protestant north Louisiana and Mississippi—have been
typically more conservative than locally reared workers about race,
foreign aid, the U.N., and international collaboration in general. Much
of the relatively small vote for the States' Rights or Independent Electors ticket in 1960 in New Orleans came from a combination of newly
prosperous ultraconservatives and working-class migrants from humble
farms. Although the strongly segregationist postures of Taylor, Tal-

madge, and the States' Righters were certainly a much more crucial determinant of the votes of former country folk than their pronouncements on world affairs, these candidates usually spoke out against foreign aid and other international commitments and almost invariably harbored anti-multilateralist thinking even when they did not proclaim their world views publicly (see Chapter 11).

These former country people have numbered too few in New Orleans, Atlanta (since the abolition of the county-unit system), Nashville, Norfolk, Virginia, and other relatively old cities to carry the vote. However, they have succeeded in electing Congressmen and other political representatives in a number of rapidly growing, newer cities, particularly where several other negative factors have been influential. For example, Jackson, Mississippi, composed largely of rural migrants, has also been much influenced by religious fundamentalism, ethnic homogeneity, cultural isolation, preoccupation with the presence of many Negroes, isolationist newspapers, and lack of old, cultivated wealth. Its atmosphere has had more in common with that of its rural environs than with that of such Northern cities of comparable size as Worcester, Albany, and Portland, Maine. Its population of rural origins has given large majorities to its isolationist Congressman John Bell Williams, to former Governor Ross Barnett, and to its present Governor Paul Johnson, all of similar international inclinations. Shreveport has manifested comparable social and cultural characteristics, except that it has also been a protectionist community and has had no college of the quality of Millsaps. Greenville, South Carolina, has seemed a somewhat more sophisticated community than either of these, but it too has been composed, in large measure, of migrants from the country and protectionist enterprises and has been influenced by several of the other negative forces; W. D. Workman carried Greenville in 1962 at least in part due to his articulate attacks on his opponent, incumbent Senator Olin Johnston, for the latter's support of the establishment of a United States disarmament agency and of the Trade Expansion Act. Monroe, Louisiana, has had much in common with Jackson, including large numbers of rural migrants.

In the long run, as such Southern cities as the latter ones mature, as urban-born, college-educated generations become more influential, as religious fundamentalism is attenuated, as educational institutions improve their quality and vigor, as scientific industries replace labor-intensive ones, as gradual desegregation becomes accepted, however grudgingly, by most whites, these urban places should approach New Orleans, Atlanta, Nashville, Greenville (Mississippi), Greensboro,

Huntsville, and others (where many of these processes seem already well along) in both incidence of internationally responsible thought and election of Congressmen who will support active international co-operation in economic, diplomatic, and cultural as well as military fields. But in the short run these and other fast-growing cities with little urban tradition may produce more Republican Congressmen like Bruce Alger (or at least like C. R. Jonas) and Democratic ones like John Bell Williams and Otto Passman.[36]

36 See also Lerche, *The Uncertain South*, 275–91, for a discussion of the probable evolution of international thought among the inhabitants and congressional representatives of diverse Southern cities.

CHAPTER 10

SOME PERSONALITY

AND

VALUE ASPECTS

D ifferences in international posture both within the South and between it and other regions cannot be understood in terms of demographic differences alone. Although many basic attitudes about life, society, and other fundamental questions related to international thinking in the South have changed gradually toward national norms during the period of the inquiry for this study, some interregional differences in traditions, underlying assumptions about people and institutions, and personality inclinations still seemed evident in the early 1960's.

Social scientists have only begun to study the complex relationships between international outlooks and the personality factors of which they are in part projections. Little of the sparse research on these complicated phenomena has been performed with Southerners. However, in some cases national surveys and local studies in the South have asked questions about international affairs and about more basic personality aspects on the same questionnaire, permitting comparisons of personal inclinations and international views. These findings, impressions among thoughtful Southerners, and impressionistic observations from conversations with interviewees in the region have led to a few relatively firm conclusions and a larger number of tentative ones pending further evidence about interconnections of international thinking and traditions, personality factors, and values within the region.

Pessimism Versus Reformism and Utopianism

Divergent Historical Experience of the South

Southerners have been much more concerned with traditions of the past than most other Americans. Northerners have continued to be surprised at the Southern pride in family—even when humble—and the detailed knowledge of genealogy, blood lines, and distant cousins. Southern history has not been only what Southerners learned from books—many have heard it in personalized terms from grandparents and other elders, usually as it happened to their ancestors, and the Southern past has influenced their thoughts and actions and defined major aspects of their psychological worlds. As Faulkner's Gavin Stevens observed:

Yesterday won't be over until tomorrow and tomorrow began ten thousand years ago. For every Southern boy fourteen years old, not once but whenever he wants it, there is the instant when it's still not yet two o'clock on that July afternoon in 1863, the brigades are in position . . ., the guns are laid . . . and Picket himself . . . waiting for Longstreet to give the word. . . .[1]

"The past is never dead. It's not even past." [2]

Moreover, the past of the South has been unique in North America. Whereas most Northerners have moved from one success to another, ascending "upward" with few major mishaps, Southerners have experienced tragedy, suffering, failure, frustration, and despair. The South has been the only part of the country which has been defeated militarily and humiliated through occupation by a hated enemy army. Not only did the region fail to gain its independence but it was laid waste; its economy and social system were overturned, and the "bottom rail was placed on top," at least for a time. Industrialization, stimulated by the Civil War, progressed in the North with only minor slowdowns; Northerners came to expect improved living standards generation after generation. Most Southerners, instead, were more prosperous in 1860 than they would be for several decades and, for some families, than they would ever be. Most Southerners lived decade after decade in un-American poverty and expected little material improvement. "The War" left the South with a problem the North was never to know—release from bondage of over a third of the population. While Northerners innocently could dream of human perfectability, Southern whites

1 William Faulkner, *Intruder in the Dust* (New York: Random House, 1948), 194.
2 William Faulkner, *Requiem for a Nun* (New York: Random House, 1951), 92.

were laden with guilt. Whereas Northern industrial life became more and more equalitarian, the antebellum social organization of concentrated privilege and power continued in much of the South, and most of the Deep South is still at odds with the rest of the country over further changes in a semifeudal, inequalitarian society.[3]

Disbelief in Progress

One result of these experiences and expectations has been relative paucity of innocent optimism with respect to both things and people. The mythological "golden age" of traditionalist Southerners with sufficient education to concern themselves with international affairs has been in the past; that of most Northerners has remained in the future. The Northerner grew to think that hard work and ingenuity could usually achieve success and control over his environment. But the Southerner had learned that frustration was frequently the reward for effort; like most of Faulkner's characters, good and bad alike had typically been defeated by circumstances or "fate," and suffering and futility were accepted as the natural lot of man.

Because of the determining influence of rain, sun, drought, the boll weevil, the seasons, and other unpredictable and uncontrollable features of agrarian life on their success, many Southerners were convinced that even the most able application of their energies might fail to avert bankruptcy. They rejected what they thought to be the naïve Northern notion that virtue necessarily or even typically produced success or individual advancement—it usually had no reward beyond itself. Consequently, whereas most Northerners came to expect change and to feel that they could help bring it about, most Southerners came to view with skepticism, if not disapproval, new people, new ideas, and new methods and to adapt themselves to an imperfect, apparently immutable, physical and social world as they found it. They learned to accept with stoic fatalism and resignation the misfortunes entailed in being Southern. When Henry James's Southern character, a Mississippi planter's well-read son, was asked by a Boston blue-stocking in the

3 For discussions of these theses, see Woodward, *Origins of the New South, 1877–1913*, 107–11; Louis D. Rubin, Jr., "Southern Literature: The Historical Image," in Louis D. Rubin, Jr., and Robert D. Jacobs (eds.), *South: Modern Southern Literature in Its Cultural Setting* (Garden City: Doubleday, 1961), 29–47; C. Vann Woodward, *The Burden of Southern History* (Baton Rouge: Louisiana State University Press, 1960), 16–25 and Chapters 6 and 8; Robert Penn Warren, *The Legacy of the Civil War* (New York: Random House, 1961), 53 ff; and T. Harry Williams, *Romance and Realism in Southern Politics* (Athens: University of Georgia Press, 1961), 1–16.

"city of reform," "Don't you care for human progress?" he replied, "I don't know—I never saw any." [4]

Such impressionistic generalizations of historians, creative writers, and other observers as these never, of course, applied equally to all Southerners nor to all parts of the South. Industrialization, urbanization, and the replacement of older generations emotionally close to the defeat of 1865 and Reconstruction by younger, future-oriented ones whose grandparents were born after these catastrophes have resulted in gradual attenuation of these proclivities.

Nevertheless, greater tendencies in the South toward fatalism, inertia, feelings of inability to improve or "reform" one's environment and the social and economic forces determining one's future, and disbelief (or cautious hesitation) that change would be for the better have been reflected in replies to survey questions on a variety of issues, including world affairs. The proportions of Southerners and Northerners offering pessimistic or fatalistic replies has varied with the issue and the circumstances of the moment, but at any given time Southerners have been more apt than Northerners to advance pessimistic thinking.

Thus, in 1939, when asked whether they thought "people who are successful get ahead largely because of their luck or largely because of their ability," 21 percent of those in the South, compared with 18 percent in the Northeast, 14 percent in the Midwest, 10 percent in the Plains States, and 13 percent in the West, replied, "because of their luck." [5] Asked in 1937 whether they thought there would always be as many as five million unemployed in the United States, 64 percent of Southerners replied in the affirmative as compared with 54 percent of Northeasterners, 56 percent of Midwesterners, 50 percent of residents of the Plains States, and 60 percent of Westerners. [6] A month later, only 4 percent of Southerners versus 17 percent of Northeasterners, 12 percent of Midwesterners, 13 percent of those in the Plains States, 17 percent of inhabitants in the Rocky Mountain region, and 19 percent of Far Westerners felt that poverty would ever be done away with in this country. [7] From the 1930's throughout the period of inquiry for this study, Southerners have been more inclined than other regional groups to believe that unemployment would increase rather than decrease in the future, [8] that there would be another depression in the next year

4 Henry James, *The Bostonians* (New York: Dial Press, 1945), 16.
5 AIPO 166, 8/8/39 (3,117).   6 AIPO 91, 7/12/37 (2,917).
7 AIPO 96, 8/16/37 (2,998).
8 In early 1953, 32 percent of Southerners thought there would be more people out of work in this country in the next six months than at the time of the interview; only 17 percent in the Northeast, 24 percent in the Midwest (Plains States

or so,[9] that the standard of living of most Americans or the average American would decline in the next specified lapse of time,[10] and to otherwise manifest generally more pessimistic economic outlooks.[11] When Americans were queried in 1951 and again in 1962 whether they thought "life" or "things" would be generally worse, better, or about the same in the future, only in the South did a majority of those venturing replies say "worse" or "about the same." [12] Related thinking was directly reflected in replies to a survey question about international relations posed in 1950, "Do you think the world will ever get out of the mess it's in?" Only in the South did a majority of those offering opinions say, "No." [13]

Imperfectable Human Nature

This greater tendency of Southerners to disbelieve in progress and especially in the feasibility of achieving man-made utopias in this life has been closely associated with more widespread inclinations in the

---

included), and 16 percent in the West agreed. See AIPO 511, 1/29/53 (1,599). In May of that year, 37 percent of Southerners versus 26 percent of Northeasterners, 23 percent of Midwesterners, and 29 percent of Westerners believed that unemployment would increase during the forthcoming six months. See AIPO 515, 5/7/53 (1,557). In March, 1957, 42 percent of Southerners as compared with 28 percent of Northeasterners, 28 percent of Midwesterners, and 28 percent of Westerners were of the opinion that there would be more people out of work in their communities in the next six months. See AIPO Release, 3/6/57.

9 AIPO 397, 5/21/47 (3,000), and NORC 351, 1/21/54 (1,300).

10 In early 1953, 13 percent of Southerners versus 17 percent of Northeasterners, 18 percent of Midwesterners, and 20 percent of Westerners thought wages for the average "working man" would go up in the next six months; 26 percent of the South versus 18, 15, and 18 percent, respectively, thought they would go down; and 55, 53, 59, and 55 percent, respectively, believed they would remain about the same. See AIPO 512, 2/20/53 (1,548).

11 See, for instance, results of an SRC survey in 1956, cited in Campbell, Converse, Miller, and Stokes, *The American Voter,* 397.

12 When asked in the summer of 1951, "Looking ahead about ten years from now, do you think things will be generally better, or generally worse than they are today?" 43 percent of all Southerners (42 percent of white Southerners) as compared with 41 percent of Northeasterners, 47 percent of Midwesterners (including residents of the Plains States), and 44 percent of Westerners replied "better"; 34 percent of all Southerners (40 percent of white Southerners) in contrast to 27, 31, and 27 percent, respectively, answered "worse"; 13 percent of all Southerners (9 percent of white Southerners) versus 13, 6, and 14 percent, respectively, responded "about the same"; and 10 percent of all (and of white) Southerners said they had no opinion, did not know, or were undecided, versus 19, 16, and 15 percent, respectively. See NORC 303, 6/29/51 (1,300). By July, 1962, 52 percent of Southerners as compared with 38 percent of Northerners venturing opinions replied to a somewhat differently worded question that they felt life would get worse or remain about the same. See AIPO 661, 7/24/62 (4,040).

13 AIPO 455, 5/2/50 (2,850).

South than in the North to reject optimistic assumptions of many Northern "progressives" or rationalist liberals about the nature of mankind. Acceptance by perhaps most Southerners of the Calvinist emphasis on original sin and their intimate contact with racial inequality, poverty, and violence have reinforced the impacts of Southern tradition and experiences of an agrarian people, producing the rather general view that evil and guilt are everywhere, in every human being to some extent and in considerable numbers of people to a rather large extent. Society and the life of the individual in it have been viewed as made up of continuing struggles between the forces of good, reason, honor, and integrity against deeply rooted irrationality, depravity, cruelty, and threat of ruin.

Repeated in different forms has been the tale of the poor white, hill "peckerwood" or mountaineer father who stood before his young son who was sitting on top of a corn crib, stretched out his arms, and said, "Jump, son." Then stepping aside and letting the boy fall to the floor, he commented, "Now let that learn you never to trust nobody." Or the humorous autobiographical anecdote of the Southern liberal minister, "I got to be somewhat of an agnostic as a kid—they kept saying the Lord created man in his own image, but the image I saw in my Mississippi town was so bad that I figured I didn't want any part of a Lord like that—I came back to religion later, when I realized that God really surpasseth all understanding if he could love such a bunch as these." Thus, when replies to the question, "Do you think most people can be trusted?" on six surveys between 1948 and 1957 were combined, 40 percent of Southerners as compared with 29 percent of Northeasterners, 26 percent of Midwesterners (residents of the Plains States included), and 27 percent of Westerners felt they could not; 56 percent of Southerners versus 68 percent, 71 percent, and 69 percent, respectively, thought they could be trusted.[14]

Moreover, most Southerners who harbored these cautious or pessimistic views of man even in the early 1960's seemed unconvinced that his basic nature could be much improved by social, economic, or political reforms and manipulations, or by such endeavors as education and psychiatry. Fear of disturbing the racial *status quo* apparently has combined with assumptions about the unmalleability of deeply embedded human motivations to produce derision and even hostility toward those who would attempt to make people "better" through social action. Critical epithets like "world improvers," "do-gooders," "social

14 NORC polls 156, 3/25/48 (1,289); 329, 8/28/52 (1,300); 349, 11/25/53 (1,300); 351, 1/21/54 (1,300); 365, 11/26/54 (1,201); and 404, 4/26/57 (1,279).

uplifters," "bleeding hearts," "holier-than-thou reformers," "idealist moralizers," "misguided humanitarians," and "starry-eyed visionaries" abounded during 1959–62 in conservative Southern newspapers and among individual Southerners who accepted much of the traditional Southern view of man.

"Progress" on the International Scene

Episcopalian scholar-planter-lawyer-aristocrat John Sharp Williams, trained at the universities of Virginia, Heidelberg, and Dijon, was both anticolonialist and pro-British and the leading champion of the League of Nations in the Senate at the end of World War I. But Senator Williams of Mississippi disagreed with most other Southerners of his time about the perfectibility of man and the feasibility of progress. "It is a lie to say you cannot change human nature. With God's help, you can change it upward and onward more and more . . . there is no way of securing progress . . . of going forward from savagery to barbarity and from barbarity to civilization, and from civilization to enlightenment except by changing human nature," said Williams in attacking opposition to the League before the Senate in 1919.[15] The proportion of Southerners who would agree with Senator Williams had increased considerably by 1962, although probably only a relatively limited minority, maybe one out of five or so, would have accepted his views in such optimistic form.

The alternative view of man, society, and nations was stated clearly by the sophisticated, traditional Southern gentleman and columnist John Temple Graves shortly before his death in 1961: "Human history is a chronicle of conflict between races, religions, cultures, and nations. As long as there is life, there is likely to be struggle." [16] Graves expressed to his readers disbelief in human improvement and in the feasibility of achieving "the better life" through materialistic "progress," "social engineering," or "utopian schemes." Only a minority of Southerners seemed to accept Graves's thinking in this rather exaggerated form in 1962, but that minority was probably larger than the one who agreed with Senator Williams, and many more Southerners had been considerably influenced by more moderate versions of Graves's ideology.

By piecing together correlations of pessimistic or fatalistic versus optimistic assumptions and attitudes with opinions on world issues in surveys and observing similar combinations in Southern editorials and

15 Denna F. Fleming, *The United States and the League of Nations*, 284. See also Osborn, *John Sharp Williams*, 21, 80–87, and 252.
16 Charleston *News and Courier*, November 21, 1961.

columns and among the interviewees for this study in 1959–62, some general relationships among these proclivities may be described in at least a tentative way.

Those Southerners during the prewar period who felt that "things" would improve, that unemployment and economic underprivilege would probably be alleviated, that people are successful more because of their ability than their luck, and that the world might "get out of the mess it's in," etc., were more likely than those of the opposite opinion to support active international involvement with respect to the foreign questions of the day. Differences in international orientation between these two groups were sometimes of considerable magnitude, other times small, but usually in the expected direction. The more optimistic were more inclined to support increased assistance to Britain and France against the Axis, increased military preparedness by the United States, and liberalization of the Johnson and Neutrality acts. They were also somewhat more apt than more pessimistic or fatalistic Southerners to feel that we should have joined the League of Nations, as did their ideological ally Senator Williams.

But on the whole, a pessimistic, "nonprogressive" turn of mind probably had relatively little negative impact on support of international action toward the problems of the prewar period. Both pessimism and fatalism on the one hand and isolationism on the other were concentrated disproportionately among the poorly educated and economically deprived and among Negroes in the South. Moreover, the proportion of the Southern fatalists and pessimists who did support international commitments was often as large as and sometimes larger than that among Northerners of more optimistic inclinations. Samples were too small to compare international views of Southern pessimists and optimists of equivalent education and occupation, but the impression derived from newspaper editorial pages and polls is that differences were probably small or nonexistent on most foreign problems.

In fact, traditional Southern thinking about the human race and national societies may have facilitated somewhat support of the international involvements requested by President Roosevelt. Such social assumptions probably encouraged the view that one could not negotiate successfully with Hitler, Mussolini, or the Japanese militarists, that efforts to change their behavior through compromise or "appeasement" would undoubtedly fail, and that the most likely way of preventing further aggression was a firm stand, backed by willingness to fight. Certainly support of military preparedness, including conscription, prior to the attack on Pearl Harbor was not obstructed by this view of mankind; on the contrary, such social assumptions in the South and elsewhere have been correlated with bellicosity and the belief that military power in the final analysis is the only adequate defense of our national interests against predatory foreign regimes.

These observations with some amendment seemed to apply to most of the more pressing international questions of the early postwar period as well. Polls and editorial opinion in newspapers indicated that Southerners with the more traditional regional views of man and "progress" were somewhat less willing than more optimistic Southerners to support continuation of the draft, Universal Military Training, an expensive defense establishment, and the maintenance of relatively numerous military installations and troops abroad. As before, the more pessimistic and fatalistic were more apt to be apathetic about these and other problems of world affairs and more inclined to favor inaction rather than costly sacrifices for a dynamic defense posture. But differences were probably small or nonexistent among better-educated Southerners whose views on the human race diverged; samples were too small for statistical comparisons.

Southerners who felt that most people could not be trusted or that the world would not "get out of the mess it's in" were less inclined than those who thought the reverse to support the Marshall Plan and, to a less marked degree, the Truman Doctrine and NATO.[17] Again, differences were smaller, though perhaps existent to some extent, among individuals who were better educated, in more complex occupations, and white. The limited impact of traditional Southern views of man on thinking about these issues was evident in the fact that Southerners (including Negroes) were about as inclined as other Americans to support most of these international commitments in the late 1940's and early 1950's, and certainly no more apt to oppose them.

But in the mid and late fifties as some of our international programs changed, differences in thinking on some world issues between the relative optimists and the relative pessimists did become more apparent.[18] Southerners and Southern newspapers which accepted the view that most people are both unreliable and unreformable continued (ap-

17 NORC surveys 156, 3/25/48 (1,289); 329, 8/28/52 (1,300); and 349, 11/25/53 (1,300); and AIPO 455, 5/2/50 (2,850).

18 Generalizations to follow were derived from cross tabulations of AIPO 455, 5/2/50 (2,850); NORC 349, 11/25/53 (1,300); NORC 351, 1/21/54 (1,300); NORC 365, 11/26/54 (1,201); NORC 404, 4/26/57 (1,279); and AIPO 661, 7/24/62 (4,040); as well as from editorials in the following newspapers: the Charleston *News and Courier,* the Summit (Miss.) *Sun,* the Charleston *Evening Post,* the Augusta *Chronicle,* the Shreveport *Journal,* the Richmond *News Leader,* the Columbia *Record,* the Columbia *State,* the Columbus (Miss.) *Commercial Dispatch,* the Jackson *Clarion-Ledger,* the Natchez *Democrat,* and the Mobile *Press Register;* and from interviews in 1959–62.

parently as in the past) to be at least somewhat more inclined than those who were more optimistic about the human race and the feasibility of seriously modifying the problems of this world to believe that we would continue to have wars, including perhaps a thermonuclear one; that military power would remain the principal or even exclusive arbiter of international affairs rather than altruism, justice, or other ideals; that arms-control negotiations with the Communists were unlikely to result in success; and that the best way to stop Communist aggressions and intrigues would be to show more firmness and make more apparent to our enemies our willingness to fight for our rights. Although only a minority of Southerners who harbored pessimistic views on the human race would end negotiations with the Communists, and an even smaller fraction would terminate diplomatic relations, most Southerners who would go these lengths apparently rejected the progressive thinking of John Sharp Williams concerning mankind.

Most of the minority of Southerners who were isolationists or "Fortress America" supporters during the late fifties and early sixties have been among the less optimistic about human beings and their institutions. Those who have not accepted patently isolationist ideas have tended more than relatively optimistic Southerners (and Northerners) either to pay little attention to world affairs or to favor policies of neo-isolationist hues. For instance, the relative pessimists were from available evidence more inclined than the optimists to view our national interest in terms of military collaboration and alliance with Western Europe and the white nations of the Commonwealth—the allies who seemed most likely to fight in case of a showdown with the Communists. They were more inclined than were more optimistic Southerners (or other Americans of like optimism) to feel that we should not have gone to the defense of Korea in 1950, or that we should have withdrawn, or that we should have fought for a clear military victory through bombing of Manchurian and Chinese bases if required. More frequently than less pessimistic citizens, these Southerners (and other Americans of similar orientation toward people and society) felt we should "call the Russian and Chinese bluffs" around the world.

Some of the emphases in our policies of the late fifties and after were particularly apt to run counter to the general thinking of the more pessimistically inclined. Newspaper editorials, columnists, and interviewees with these leanings were for the most part critical of proposed compromises with the Communists for arms control and of the establishment of the U.S. Disarmament Agency. With some exceptions they would either reduce considerably or eliminate economic assistance to underdeveloped, particularly neutralist and "leftist," countries. Some of these had opposed the Marshall Plan as well, but many had at least gone along with it. Their reasoning seemed to be that the latter was designed to put developed economies back on their feet after war damage. Not only were these societies white but they were also composed of people who had a good deal in common with us culturally, militarily, and otherwise. But these Southerners tended to doubt that "grandiose schemes" to "transform barefoot republics" in Africa and, to a lesser measure, in Asia, would succeed. People and societies would not change to fit our preconceived utopias, and certainly not in the short time the liberals seemed to feel was possible. Nor would economic development necessarily be in our best interests—we might well find friendly regimes replaced by more anti-Western pro-Communist ones. We have little in common with these people anyway. Most Southerners who felt that decolonization was unfortunate held these less optimistic general opinions about people and society. Finally, these Southerners were evidently more inclined than those with contrary views about life and humanity to feel that whatever aid was extended should be limited to allies.

These international opinions were primarily apparent among newspapers and better-educated Southerners of these basic inclinations toward people and life. Among the less educated who have accepted the rather fatalistic view that most people cannot be improved by "social tinkering" and that international conflict will probably be intense virtually forever, there seemed to be relatively few clear attitudes except on the most general questions. Fatalism discouraged interest in problems about which they felt they could do little.

Authoritarianism

Greater Prevalence in the South

Frequently associated with pessimistic assumptions about the nature of mankind and the difficulty of changing human beings and social institutions has been the sentiment that the world and one's domestic environment are such hazardous places that a hierarchical system and strong authority are necessary to bring order out of the natural confusion and predatory inclinations of most people. It is not surprising that these authoritarian tendencies have been discovered by national surveys to be more widespread in the South than in the rest of the country taken together.

In fact, the view that most people cannot be trusted has been closely

associated with other ideas related to authoritarian personality tendencies. Southerners have been more inclined than Northerners to offer
authoritarian replies to each of the several questions related to this personality type posed by national surveys. Thus, in 1953–54, 71 percent
of those in the South replying agreed that there are primarily two kinds
of people in the world—the weak and the strong; only 59 percent in
the Northeast, 63 percent in the Midwest (including the Plains States),
and 54 percent in the West agreed.[19] Seventy-two percent of Southerners as compared with 52 percent of Northeasterners, 54 percent of
Midwesterners (including residents of the Plains States), and 52 percent
of Westerners agreed at that time that "any good leader should be
strict with people under him in order to gain their respect"; 24 percent
of Southerners, 45 percent of Northeasterners, 40 percent of Midwesterners (including inhabitants of the Plains States), and 45 percent of
Westerners disagreed.[20] Seventy-three percent of Southerners versus
66 percent of Northeasterners, 65 percent of Midwesterners (those in
Plains States included), and 50 percent of Westerners felt in 1953 that
"the most important thing to teach children is absolute obedience to
their parents."[21] Seventy-one percent of the inhabitants of the South
in contrast to 57 percent of other Americans agreed in 1958 that "fathers
should be the top boss of the family in this country."[22] Seventy-four
percent of Southern adults as compared with 48 percent of other Americans replying said in 1954 that "school officials should have the right
to give pupils a 'licking.' "[23]

As in the rest of the country, authoritarianism in the South has been
more widespread among the less educated as opposed to the better educated, among Negroes rather than whites, among the economically
and socially insecure rather than the emotionally self-assured, among
dogmatic and emotional religious groups (especially fundamentalists)
as compared with denominations interested in the social implications
of the gospel and in less literal interpretations of the Scriptures, among
people isolated from complex cultural and social experiences rather
than those active in heterogeneous social and cultural groups, and among
older rather than younger individuals. All these variables have been, of
course, themselves intercorrelated.

The presence of those social groups most addicted to authoritarianism (other than older people) in disproportionately large numbers in

19 The average of NORC 341–2, 6/30/53 (1,291), and NORC 365, 11/26/54
(1,201).
20 *Ibid.*   21 NORC 341–2, 6/30/53 (1,291).
22 AIPO 593, 12/31/57 (1,522).   23 AIPO 538, 10/13/54 (1,550).

the South has accounted in considerable measure for the greater prevalence of authoritarian thinking there than elsewhere. There has been some debate as to whether Southerners of a given demographic and social status have been any more authoritarian than Northerners of equivalent status.[24]

The limited evidence seems to indicate that even Southerners of most specified roles have tended on the average to be somewhat more authoritarian than Northerners in comparable ones. A national study of ten thousand college graduates in the late 1940's revealed that Southerners were more inclined to accept several authoritarian attitudes than were Northerners.[25] A study of the values of college students found that even those at the University of North Carolina—one of the more "liberal" in the region—were more inclined to agree with certain ideas related to authoritarianism than students at several Northern colleges of comparable renown.[26] Another investigation concluded that students at Louisiana State University were more authoritarian and more inclined to accept traditional values and leadership than were those at Washburne University in Topeka and the University of Maryland.[27] The inclusion of more typical, less distinguished colleges, and particularly Negro ones, would probably have resulted in a still wider gap between Southern and Northern students with respect to emphasis on authority and hierarchical social organization (see p. 249).

The tentative conclusion, pending further evidence, that authoritarian orientations have been at least somewhat more prevalent in most Southern groups even when compared with equivalent Northern ones

24 Social scientists who argue that Southerners have not been more authoritarian as compared with Northerners of comparable demographic status point to methodological shortcomings of the authoritarian questions. They argue that less-educated individuals have tended to agree with ideas presented by interviewers regardless of whether they have in fact agreed, whereas better-educated people have been more inclined to disagree. They also note that better-educated authoritarians have been more apt to reject blatantly authoritarian statements, whereas poorly educated individuals of the same or less authoritarianism have not been so sophisticated as to reject them. Moreover, a study which applied the Edwards Unlabelled Fascist Attitudes Test to a sample of South Carolina legislators discovered that they scored slightly lower than did students in a Northern college. See John B. McConaughy, "The Personality Characteristics of South Carolina Legislators," *American Political Science Review*, XLIV (1950), 894–903. Definitive evidence on the relative authoritarianism of Southerners and Northerners with demographic factors controlled must await further research. However, whatever human variables have in fact been reflected in replies to these queries, those variable have been more prevalent in the South and they have been correlated with certain international attitudes.

25 Bureau of Applied Social Research study.

26 Jacob, *Changing Values in College*, 106–10.

27 Gaier and Bass, *Journal of Social Psychology*, XLIX (1959), 47–51.

is also supported by the impression that Southern society has manifested to a greater degree phenomena which have been among the sources of authoritarian personality development in America. Deprivation in childhood and striving in later life to alleviate psychic anxieties related to insecurity have been associated with authoritarian proclivities,[28] and both these factors have been prominent in Southern society. In fact, the static, educationally and economically underprivileged agrarian setting where most had a well-defined place probably provided considerably more emotional security and certainty than the relatively depersonalized, confusing Southern cities to which so many unsophisticated farm boys and girls have recently migrated. As was mentioned previously, the newly urbanized Southern working class has seemed especially open to leadership by charismatic and authoritarian figures who would appeal to their anxieties and insecurities with dogmatic, oversimplified "solutions." [29] But authoritarian ideology has also seemed relatively attractive to the small minority of urban Southerners of similar rural childhoods who have become economically successful. People who have moved up into the middle class from the lower class and who have been largely interested in social acceptance in their newly achieved financial stratum rather than in substantive achievement within their occupation have tended to be more authoritarian than individuals who were born into the middle class.[30] Thus, it is understandable that authoritarian movements like the John Birch Society and the Christian Anti-Communist Crusade in the South and elsewhere in the United States have tended to derive much of their financial support from among these newly prosperous people.[31] Furthermore, most Southerners have been raised in a hierarchical social system of superiors and inferiors

28   See, for example, Adorno, *et al.*, *The Authoritarian Personality*, 387–88; Else Frenkel-Brunswik, "Interaction of Psychological and Sociological Factors in Political Behavior," *American Political Science Review*, XLVI (1952), 44–65; Robert A. Harper, "Is Conformity a General or a Specific Behavior Trait?" *American Sociological Review*, XII (1947), 81–86; and Herbert McClosky, "Conservatism and Personality," *American Political Science Review*, LII (1958), 27–45.

29   For discussions of the appeals of authoritarianism to urban workers of deprived rural childhoods, see William Kornhauser, *The Politics of Mass Society* (Glencoe: The Free Press, 1959), 150–82; Lipset and Bendix, *Social Mobility in Industrial Society*, 70; Robin Williams, *American Society* (New York: Alfred A. Knopf, 1959), 480; Seymour Martin Lipset, "Democracy and Working Class Authoritarianism" (MS in possession of author, 1957) and Seymour Martin Lipset, *Political Man* (Garden City: Doubleday, 1960), 113–14, and 138.

30   Fred B. Silberstein and Melvin Seeman, "Social Mobility and Prejudice," *American Journal of Sociology*, LXV (1959), 258–64.

31   Seymour Martin Lipset, "The Sources of the Radical Right," in Daniel Bell (ed.), *The New American Right* (New York: Criterion Books, 1956), 178 and 192–97.

and it seems relatively natural that many of them should have integrated the assumptions of their society into their own personalities.

Moreover, many of the psychological, cultural, and social correlates of authoritarianism in America, as determined by social research, have been among those felt to be particularly prominent in the South by serious students of that region. For example, authoritarians have tended to think in terms of unfavorable stereotypes and to have adverse prejudices about ethnic and cultural groups other than their own or those to which they have aspired. They have been more likely than more equalitarian Americans to identify with prestigious groups and to judge people in terms of their social status rather than their individual characteristics. They have tended to conform to local mores and to regard unconventional people and ideas with distrust. Most authoritarians have been relatively unanalytical; they have viewed most problems in the narrow frame of reference of their own experiences and strivings rather than in more dispassionate, nationally responsible contexts. Complexities and nuances of issues have usually escaped their notice, so that they have tended to judge issues and people to be alike even when their similarities have been rather superficial. They have attempted to maintain things as they are, since the familiar, traditional, safe, and orderly *status quo* has been most comfortable and secure for them. Related to this inflexibility has been a tendency to eschew abstractions and to emphasize concrete, apparently pragmatic detail rather than overall problems. Authoritarians have been inclined to demand quick, oversimplified solutions to complicated problems and to press for action rather than reflection. They have often been rather intolerant of frustration, turning to rough, overly "masculine" aggression and even violence, and they have normally been relatively uninterested in systematic planning and work toward long-term or ambiguous goals.[32]

32 Adorno, *et al., The Authoritarian Personality*, 152–53, 360, 461, and 873; Frank Barron, "Complexity-Simplicity as a Personality Dimension," *Journal of Abnormal and Social Psychology*, XLVIII (1953), 163–72; Bruno Bettleheim and Morris Janowitz, *The Dynamics of Prejudice: A Psychological and Sociological Study* (New York: Harper and Bros., 1949), 63 and 95–98; Bettelheim and Janowitz, "Ethnic Tolerance: A Function of Social and Personal Control," *American Journal of Sociology*, LV (1949), 137–45; Donald T. Campbell and Boyd R. McCandless, "Ethnocentrism, Xenophobia, and Personality," *Human Relations*, IV (1951), 185–92; Raymond B. Cattell and L. G. Tiner, "The Varieties of Structural Rigidity," *Journal of Personality*, XVII (1949), 321–41; E. L. Cowen and G. G. Thompson, "Problem Solving Rigidity and Personality Structure," *Journal of Abnormal and Social Psychology*, XLVI (1951), 165–76; Richard I. Evans, "Personal Values as Factors in Anti-Semitism," *Journal of Abnormal and Social Psychology*, XLII (1952), 749–56; Maurice L. Farber, "The Anal Character and Political Aggression," *Journal of Abnormal and Social Psychology*, LI (1955),

Authoritarianism, Equalitarianism, and World Developments

The greater prevalence of authoritarian predelictions in the South
has helped along with other factors to account for differences in international behavior in the region as compared with the North as well as
for some of the divergences in world thinking within the region. Particularly those Southerners (and other Americans) who have agreed
with all or most of the authoritarian ideas presented to them on surveys
have thought differently about world affairs than those who have re-

486–89; Seymour Fisher, "An Over-view of Trends in Research Dealing with
Personality Rigidity," *Journal of Personality*, XVII (1949), 342–51; Else Frenkel-
Brunswik, *American Political Science Review*, LII (1958), 27–45; Frenkel-Brunswik,
"A Study of Prejudice in Children," *Human Relations*, I (1948), 295–307; Frenkel-
Brunswik and R. Nevitt Sanford, "Some Personality Factors in Anti-Semitism,"
Journal of Psychology, XX (1945), 271–91; Kurt Goldstein, "Concerning Rigidity:
A Critical Evaluation," *Psychological Review*, LIII (1946), 43–52; Harrison G.
Gough, "Studies of Social Intolerance: I. Some Psychological Correlates of
Anti-Semitism," *Journal of Social Psychology*, XXXIII (1951), 237–46; Harry
Grace, "Hostility, Communication, and International Tension," *Journal of So-
cial Psychology*, XXXIV (1951), 31–40; Eugene L. Hartley and Ruth Hartley,
Fundamentals of Social Psychology (New York: Alfred A. Knopf, 1952); Leonard
D. Goodstein, "Intellectual Rigidity and Social Attitudes," *Journal of Abnormal
and Social Psychology*, XLVIII (1953), 345–53; Irving L. Janis, "Personality Corre-
lates of Susceptibility to Persuasion," *Journal of Personality*, XXII (1954), 504–18;
J. S. Kounin, "The Meaning of Rigidity," *Psychological Review*, LV (1948), 157–66;
Paul F. Lazarsfeld, Bernard Berelson, and William McPhee, *Voting* (New York: Co-
lumbia University Press, 1954), 241; Kurt Levin, *A Dynamic Theory of Personality*
(New York: McGraw-Hill, 1935), 211; Leo Lowenthal and Norbert Guterman, "Self
Portrait of the Fascist Agitator," in Alvin W. Gouldner (ed.), *Studies in Leader-
ship* (New York: Harper Bros., 1950), 80–99; McClosky, *American Political Sci-
ence Review*, LII (1958), 7, 11, 18, and 22–24; Theodore Millon and Laurence D.
Simkins, "Suggestibility of Authoritarians and Equalitarians to Prestige Influence,"
Paper read at the August, 1957, meeting of the American Psychological Association,
New York; H. T. Moore, "Innate Factors in Radicalism and Conservatism," *Journal
of Abnormal and Social Psychology*, XX (1925), 234–44; Paul H. Mussen and Ann
B. Wyszynski, "Personality and Political Participation," *Human Relations*, V (1953),
65–82; National Opinion Research Center, *UNESCO and Public Opinion Today*,
Report 35 (University of Chicago, 1947); Patricia O'Connor, "Ethnocentrism, Intol-
erance of Ambiguity and Abstract Reasoning Ability," *Journal of Abnormal and Social Psychology*, XLVII (1952), 526–30; Suzanne Reichard, "Rorschach Study of
Prejudiced Personality," *American Journal of Orthopsychiatry*, XVIII (1948),
280–86; Milton Rokeach, "Generalized Mental Rigidity as a Factor in Ethnocentrism"
(Ph.D. dissertation, University of California, 1947); Milton Rokeach, "Generalized
Mental Rigidity as a Factor in Ethnocentrism," *Journal of Abnormal and Social Psy-
chology*, XLIII (1948), 259–77; Rokeach, "Rigidity and Ethnocentrism: A Re-
joinder," *Journal of Personality*, XVII (1949), 367–474; Rokeach, "Prejudice,
Concreteness of Thinking, and Reification of Thinking," *Journal of Abnormal and
Social Psychology*, XLVI (1951), 83–91; Alvin Scodel and Paul H. Mussen, "Social
Perceptions of Authoritarians and Non-Authoritarians," *Journal of Abnormal and
Social Psychology*, XLVIII (1953), 181–84; and Karen Horney, *Neurosis and Human
Growth* (New York: W. W. Norton, 1950).

jected all or most of these. Correlations between international and authoritarian attitudes have been far from perfect on any one question associated with authoritarianism, but the roughly 10 percent of the North and 14 percent of the South who have been most authoritarian on a number of questions have in most cases disagreed on important aspects of foreign policy with the 25 percent of the former and the 15 percent of the latter who have been least authoritarian or most equalitarian.

Given the rather close relationship between pessimistic views of human nature and social "progress" and authoritarian tendencies, it is not surprising that Southern (and other) authoritarians have been more inclined than more equalitarian individuals to agree with the international postures associated with such pessimism.[33] Most working-class, poorly educated authoritarians and many in the more privileged categories as well have been rather apathetic about world affairs. They have been more apt than more equalitarian citizens to reply that they "don't know" or have no opinions. They have been less inclined to vote in primaries and general elections and to consider international postures of the candidates in their electoral choices. Perhaps they have been too busy striving for personal security and social acceptance to concern themselves with foreign policy except during periods of dramatic or sensational events, such as the U-2 incident in 1960, or on issues which affect them directly, such as the draft and taxes for foreign expenditures.

Among individuals who have advanced opinions, authoritarians have been considerably more inclined than more democratically oriented Southerners and other Americans to feel that power alone, largely of a military nature, decides international questions;[34] that military expansionism has been with us throughout history and is unlikely to subside in the future; and that the United States should use its power to achieve its national interests as other countries have seemed to do, that is, with relatively little concern about the opposition of weak countries in the underdeveloped world or elsewhere. Southerners who have believed that it is virtually hopeless to try to negotiate with the

---

33 Except where otherwise indicated, generalizations about the international behavior of authoritarians versus nonauthoritarians have been derived from cross tabulations of NORC 156, 3/25/48 (1,289); SRC survey of November-December, 1949 (606); NORC 329, 8/28/52 (1,300); NORC 341-2, 6/30/53 (1,291); NORC 351, 1/21/54 (1,300); AIPO 538, 10/13/54 (1,530); NORC 365, 11/26/54 (1,201); NORC 404, 4/26/57 (1,279); and AIPO 593, 12/31/57 (1,522); and from John B. McConaughy, "The Politicometrics of International Aggression," (MS at University of South Carolina, 1960).
34 NORC 156, 3/25/48 (1,289).

Communist bloc [35] and that another world war, this time a nuclear one, is very probable have also been more likely than not to be relatively authoritarian.[36] Those who have favored preventive war or its equivalent against the Soviets or the Chinese Communists have been for the most part more authoritarian than most Southerners, as has been the case among those who would withdraw from the U.N. Most who have felt that we should break off diplomatic relations with the U.S.S.R.[37] and that we should not permit international inspection in the United States even if the Soviets agreed to reciprocal inspection for arms control have been concentrated among the more authoritarian. South Carolina authoritarians in 1960 were much more inclined than their more equalitarian neighbors to recommend that we discontinue negotiating with the Soviets until they apologized for Premier Khrushchev's attack on President Eisenhower at the Paris Summit Conference in May of that year.[38]

Since authoritarians have been less inclined than more democratic citizens to emphasize and sympathize with people different from themselves, particularly other ethnic, religious, and national groups, it is understandable that they have been more apt to perceive in an unfavorable light foreigners whose cultures have been strange to them. Ultra-nationalism—the view that Americans can learn little from foreigners and that our society is better than others—has been associated with this personality orientation, as have nativism, opposition to expanded immigration, and lack of support for international exchanges of persons and intercultural programs. Those who have felt that the United States should not take an active part in world affairs have tended toward the authoritarian end of the spectrum.[39] Southerners and others who have endorsed continuing our military activities, or even expanding military interventions in Latin America and elsewhere, but who have favored discontinuing or sharply curtailing the Marshall Plan [40] and later economic aid programs,[41] have been disproportionately authoritarian. Those who have opposed aid and other forms of economic and diplomatic collaboration with "countries which have not joined us as allies against the Communists" and, even more, with Yugoslavia and Poland have been particularly concentrated at the authoritarian end of the continuum and sparse at the equalitarian end.[42]

Moreover, it has been difficult for educational agencies and other

35 *Ibid.*   36 NORC 404, 4/26/57 (1,279).   37 *Ibid.*
38 McConaughy, "Politicometrics of International Aggression."
39 NORC 156, 3/25/48 (1,289).   40 *Ibid.*
41 NORC 404, 4/26/57 (1,279).   42 *Ibid.*

thoughtful groups to reach Southern (or other) authoritarians through rational appeals and factual argument, which tend to be too complex to hold their attention or satisfy their emotional needs. As a group, authoritarians have had little respect for or interest in abstract ideas, theories, or systematic analysis of international or other phenomena. Nor have they placed much stock in give-and-take discussion as a means of refining their thinking. They have wanted "practical action which will work." Having little respect for intellectuals and analytical experts on foreign policy, they have tended to maintain their rather rigid, dogmatic, and often empirically unrealistic views in spite of information and analyses to the contrary. To a greater extent than more democratically inclined Southerners they have limited their thinking to that prevalent among people like themselves, seldom comparing ideas with individuals who have thought differently.

Traditionalism, Personalism, and Critical Thought

Impact of a Romantic Past

Sensitivity to the lessons of the past and the security provided by tradition can encourage one to face with realism threatening current and future problems and can help to prevent immoderate thinking and repetition of the errors of one's predecessors. Some traditions, such as that of Jews and, to a lesser extent, that of Anglo-Saxon New England, have emphasized education, rational analysis, realism, and dispassionate thought. Nor need knowledge of the past imply such preoccupation with ways gone by and no longer applicable to the current world that the individual fails to adapt himself to change when warranted and shows little inclination to concern himself with the responsibilities of facing the present.

It was already observed that an important minority of Southerners have used their sense of history to think realistically about international issues of the postwar era. Unfortunately, however, some of the traditions of the South seem to have discouraged rather than stimulated objective thought about world developments as well as about other questions of national concern. Southern emphasis on a rather romantic sentimental ethic of chivalry has tended to limit dispassionate analysis and reality testing among the privileged classes most inclined outside the South to think seriously about public issues. Many Southerners have grown used to an exaggerated sense of honor rather than unemotional debate of points of responsible disagreement on controversial matters; to flowery, emotionally stirring oratory and rhetorical overstatement rather than logical, systematic argument; to giving vent to feelings rather than to emphasis on consistent thought; and to a hedonistic unreality largely immune to rigorous examination of facts and of responsible alternative interpretations of events.[43]

Intensive Interpersonal Relations

Moreover, most Southerners have lived in small communities which have changed slowly or hardly at all until relatively recently. Few new people had moved in with different ideas or modes of behavior. Each Southerner had known almost everybody for several miles around, and virtually everyone knew him. His father, grandfathers, and great-grandfathers had lived nearby and had been cronies of the fathers, grandfathers, and great-grandfathers of his current associates. If he was a man of education and social position—an individual who might exhibit some interest in world affairs—he was kin to many of the others of comparable standing. The local judge was not just Judge Jones; he was the third cousin once removed of Aunt Matilda, husband of one's brother-in-law's sister-in-law, and great grandson of one's grandfather's regimental commander at Shiloh. The Southerner, in close contact much of his life with a small number of individuals, has known a great deal about them, even when they have not been related to him by blood, just as his ancestors knew much about the ancestors of the same neighbors.

One result of such close social relations has been the evolution of a code of manners, politeness, and smooth interpersonal relations which has tended to make life pleasant and human contacts devoid of rudeness, especially among the privileged classes. But a concomitant has too often been the stifling of critical discussion. When a Southerner has lived with the same people all his life and has expected to associate with them for the remainder of it, when a traditional system has prescribed for him detailed rules of genteel behavior, and when his family and associates have come to expect certain attitudes and actions of him, inhibitions against his introducing controversy into his locale have tended to be formidable. Even a considerable fraction of those who have given some thought to world affairs have seemed to feel that it is ungentlemanly, unladylike, or ungracious to disagree in polite conversation with dis-

---

43 See, for example, Osterweis, *Romanticism and Nationalism in the Old South;* Cash, *The Mind of the South,* 57-65 and 238 ff; Eaton, *Freedom of Thought in the Old South,* 48-53; Woodward, *Origins of the New South,* 167-69; Eaton, *The Growth of Southern Civilization,* 316-19; and the Introduction by Harvey Wish in *Ante-Bellum: Writings of George Fitzhugh and Hinton Rowan Helper on Slavery* (New York: Capricorn Books, 1960), especially 4 ff.

torted thinking about world developments and that it is pretentious to press one's interests and views on others.

Even when the atypically cosmopolitan Southerner has been willing to embroil himself in dissension arising from his expression of attitudes contrary to local ideas, he has often shied away from doing so for fear of stirring disagreement among his extended, close-knit family of siblings, uncles, aunts, and cousins and involving the family name in controversy before the community. Many a Southern cosmopolitan has heard from childhood advice to the effect that he should "keep the peace" and that he "has no right" to divide one branch of the family from another or to blemish its reputation by identifying himself with "radicals."

Discussions have, therefore, too frequently tended to deal with matters on which most have agreed and have left aside examination of issues which might adversely affect rapport with local people. Southerners have become accustomed to finding approximately the same general assumptions and attitudes on most issues among those with whom they have had close personal relationships. If, perchance, one inadvertently discovered a sphere of disagreement with an associate, one tended henceforth to avoid that topic. Even discussions among many relatively well-read, cosmopolitan Southerners have tended to be gracious, polite, well-mannered, leisurely, and less abruptly critical than among Northerners of comparable sophistication.

Traditional interpersonal ties have also tended, along with a one-party system and other factors, to shift attention from issues to personalities. For instance, it has usually been difficult for candidates raised outside their predominantly rural and small-town constituencies to be elected to Congress, and almost impossible for former Northerners to do so in such sections. Inhabitants of the native county of a candidate have tended to vote for him even when their own private views have more nearly coincided with those of one of his opponents.[44] A recent study in South Carolina determined that issues played almost no part in the voting of the vast majority of either Negroes or whites in congressional primaries and that only about a third voted on issues more than on personalities in presidential elections.[45]

Moreover, whereas many Northerners have tended to reject, accept, or consider information or ideas qua ideas, one gains the impression that Southerners have been more concerned than other regional groups

[44] Key, *Southern Politics in State and Nation,* 304–306.
[45] From unpublished research by John B. McConaughy, University of South Carolina.

about the human source of the communication. Interpersonal influence has been a potent means of transmitting information and influencing attitudes throughout the United States,[46] but the identity and pedigree of the bearer of the ideas have seemed considerably more crucial to the successful transmission of information in the traditional South. Many Southerners must be assured that the new thought is not another of those "Yankee isms" subversive of local traditions. Southerners have tended to pay closest attention to comments by local kin and peers, but next have been likely to listen to ideas from a previously unknown member of a Southern family whose credentials and social connections have seemed "proper." A visiting descendant of the planter class from another locale can introduce relatively liberal views in a gentlemanly way into conversations in the most reactionary circles of the Black Belt and be invited back to dinner, whereas the same thinking from a Northerner would be rejected out of hand and he himself probably labeled as "leftist" or the like.

Paucity of Abstract Reasoning

Intensive interpersonal relations, concern with personal and other concrete details rather than issues, romantic rather than critical traditions, authoritarianism, uneasiness with rationalist, optimistic views of man, disbelief in utopias, experience in a frontier culture in direct contact with nature where expedient action rather than theories were effective, fear of disturbing the racial and social *status quo*, concentration of liberal education among a small elite and the tendency of the masses to leave broad national and international problems to their "betters"—these and other features of Southern experience help to account for the more widespread unfamiliarity with analytical processes and more prevalent distrust of broad theories and abstract ideas in world affairs and in most other fields in the South as compared with the North.[47]

Thus, Robert Penn Warren speaks of "the instinctive fear, on the part of black and white, that the massiveness of experience, the concreteness of life, will be violated; the fear of abstraction."[48] Virginia

---

46 Elihu Katz and Paul F. Lazarsfeld, *Personal Influence* (Glencoe: The Free Press, 1955).

47 See, for instance, Dabbs, *The Southern Heritage*, 172–74; and Polk, *Southern Accent: From Uncle Remus to Oak Ridge*, 210.

48 Robert Penn Warren, *Segregation* (New York: Random House, 1956), 15. See also Percival Skrogg in Warren's *World Enough and Time* (New York: Random House, 1950); and Adam Stanton in his *All the King's Men* (New York: Harcourt, Brace, and Co., 1946), who "has a picture of the world in his head, and when the world doesn't conform in any respect to the picture, he wants to throw the world away."

Rock notes "a rage for the concrete, a rage against the abstract." [49] James McBride Dabbs tells of his uncle's feeling that "ideals are sin." [50] Louis D. Rubin, Jr., observes that "the Southerner is . . . temperamentally opposed to the kind of necessarily abstract analysis that would permit him to work out a long-range solution." [51] Faulkner's Ratliff explains Southern as compared with Northern sentiments toward abstract ideas, grand schemes, long-term planning, and systematic thought generally in his conversation with a Southern associate about the Yankee who wanted fifty more goats for his ranch.

Northerners do things different from us. If a fellow in this country was to set up a goat-ranch, he would do it purely and simply because he had too many goats already. He would just declare his roof or his front porch or his parlor or whatever it was he couldn't keep the goats out of a goat-ranch and let it go at that. But a Northerner don't do it that way. When he does something, he does it with an organized syndicate and a book of printed rules and a gold filled diploma. . . . He don't start off with goats or a piece of land either. He starts off with a piece of paper and a pencil and measures it all down setting in the library—so many goats to so many acres and so much fence to hold them . . . he buys the land first so he can have something to build the fence on, and he builds the fence around it so nothing cant get outen it, and then he goes out to buy some things not to get outen the fence . . . then he found he had done run out of goats. He combed this country up and down . . . to find the right number of goats. . . . In spite of all he could do, he still lacked fifty goats to take care of the rest of that fence. So now it ain't a goat-ranch; it's a insolvency.[52]

Like other regional proclivities, reactions to abstractions have formed a continuum among Southerners, from the enemies of "theorists," "one worlders," and the like to a minuscule minority who have thought in systematic, abstract terms about social, political, and other intellectual problems. The latter, who also have tended to be most likely to agree with John Sharp Williams' relative optimism about the possibility of improving individuals, societies, and international institutions, have most nearly approached Northern liberal internationalists in their thinking about foreign policy.

But even most internationalists among Deep Southern interviewees who read about foreign affairs in such publications as the Manchester *Guardian* and the New York *Times* (Sunday edition) had been influenced to a noticeable extent by traditional Southern hesitancy about abstract ideas, preconceived long-term "solutions" to complex prob-

49 Virginia Rock, "Agrarianism in Southern Literature: The Period Since 1925," *Georgia Review*, XI (1957), 157.
50 Dabbs, *The Southern Heritage*, 191.
51 Rubin and Kilpatrick (eds.), *The Lasting South*, 15.
52 Faulkner, *The Hamlet*, 80–81.

lems, and rationalistic, optimistic assumptions about human nature. They tended to be wary about ideas which were not closely tied to empirical experience, in foreign affairs as in other fields. They often thought in terms of individuals they had known, expressed their ideas in anecdotes about concrete people, parables, and recollections of past events, and spoke of pragmatic, patient, *ad hoc* ways of dealing with the problems and peoples of the world as they are, of trying to make small improvements where opportunities presented themselves. More than many Northern liberal internationalists of the author's experience, theirs was a combination of realism, pragmatic idealism, and cautious hope of human progress. Southern internationalists seemed, on the average, to think real international improvement more difficult to achieve and to plan in advance than did their Northern counterparts—they expected failure perhaps as or more often than success. Many, perhaps most, of those viewed as liberals by their Southern peers have been more akin in international thinking to the responsible, well-informed internationalist conservatives of the Northeast than to the ideological liberals of Cambridge, New York, Philadelphia, and Washington.

The paucity of doctrinaire liberal internationalists in the region seemed related to another observation hypothetically applicable to many of the internationally thoughtful Southern minority. The international opinions among even the more knowledgeable interviewees—more than among most of the author's roughly comparable associates in the North —were frequently reactions to specific issues in turn, with relatively little inclination to organize them into systematic theories. Each problem was likely to be faced separately, in terms of the individuals involved and other concrete aspects. The Southern cosmopolitan's reactions to a second international matter, connected in the minds of the theoretically inclined Northerner with the first, might seem logically inconsistent with his views on the first issue. Whereas the Northern, especially Northeastern, liberal seems to tend toward liberalism on almost all foreign issues, his Southern colleague may favor for quite pragmatic reasons diplomatic recognition of Communist China, stronger conventional armed forces and certain types of military intervention abroad, greater firmness with irresponsible, neutralist or leftist regimes in underdeveloped countries, expanded economic aid to India and reduced aid to other countries, and so on.[53] Such apparent inconsistencies

53 These speculations could be tested by comparing intercorrelations in the South and outside among responses to questions on diverse international issues appearing on the same surveys. The author's hypothesis is that even among the better informed on world affairs intercorrelations would be higher outside the South.

may have been partly due to different assumptions about international relations in the South compared with the Northeast, but they were also probably related to a more prevalent tendency among Southerners to think in terms of particular cases rather than of theories supposedly applicable to broad categories of international phenomena.

The general impression received from the interviews and other experiences in the South is that the more abstract or theoretical the reasoning for a given international program, the more difficult it is likely to be to "sell" in the South as compared with the North, particularly the Northeast. Some of the rather optimistic theoretical assumptions and abstract arguments presented by foreign-policy spokesmen in and out of the administration for the "New Frontier" in 1961–62 seemed to run head on against these Southern tendencies. Most Southerners appeared particularly disinclined to comprehend, or if they did, to accept, some of the theories about transforming tribal or feudal societies through assistance programs, about risking the fall of pro-American conservative regimes in these locales for some long-term, abstract ideals and objectives about parliamentary democracy, freedom of expression, and so on. Many of the informants tended to fear that broad, impractical schemes of Northern internationalist theorists might lead to unnecessary risks and unfortunate results.[54]

Conservatism of the South

Related to these traditional, psychological, social, and other factors has been a rather general conservatism toward a variety of social and public questions. The incidence of conservative thinking in the region, as outside, has varied with the issue and the domestic and international context at the moment. Moreover, although some Southerners have been conservative about most major public questions, and others liberal about most of them, many have been more liberal, or more conservative, on some than on others, and a considerable number in the South have been even relatively conservative on some and relatively liberal on others.

Nevertheless, Southerners taken together have been more conserva-

54 At this writing (January, 1965) it appears that President Johnson may succeed in broadening Southern support for foreign policies, including foreign aid, very similar to those of President Kennedy. In this task an effective Southern President should enjoy marked advantage over his Ivy League-educated, New England-reared predecessor. If the Texan does generate wider Southern popularity for such programs as foreign aid to neutralists, his success will undoubtedly be due in considerable measure to his avoidance of the theoretical, liberal, idealistic abstractions of his predecessor and his emphasis instead on more personal, anecdotal, folksy, pragmatic, and evangelistic appeals familiar to his Southern colleagues.

tive than the rest of the country on most public questions, and their conservative tendencies help to account for some of their international postures. Interregional differences have been considerably reduced when Southerners have been compared with Northerners of similar education, occupation, and rural, urban, or small-town status, but somewhat greater conservatism has been evident in the South on a number of issues even when these factors have been controlled.

Support for More Conservative Political Figures

Thus, white Southerners at both Democratic and Republican National Conventions have in disproportionately large numbers supported nomination of the more conservative candidates. For instance, Southern delegates were more inclined to favor Robert Taft over Wendell Wilkie in 1940 and over Earl Warren or Thomas Dewey in 1948,[55] and Barry Goldwater over Nelson Rockefeller in 1960. Prior to and during the 1964 Republican National Convention, a larger proportion of delegates from the South than from the country as a whole favored Senator Barry Goldwater over Nelson Rockefeller, Henry Cabot Lodge, and (later) William Scranton, the less conservative alternatives. Asked in 1961 and 1962 which of several prominent Republicans they preferred, wished to see take over the leadership of the Republican party, or favored for nomination by the Republican National Convention for the 1964 campaign for the presidency, most Southerners either offered no opinion or chose Richard Nixon. Although Nelson Rockefeller was more favorably considered than Barry Goldwater in the South as in the rest of the country as late as September, 1962, the former was less popular and the latter more popular in the South than in the rest of the country combined—the South was most like the Rocky Mountain region and the Midwest and least like the Northeast in its affinity for Senator Goldwater. The Arizona Republican at that time had relatively few admirers among the Southern rank and file with average or below average incomes, but higher-income Southerners, especially those who voted Republican in the 1960 presidential election, were inclined to favor him over Governor Rockefeller and other "liberal" Republicans.[56]

55 Alexander Heard, *A Two Party South?* (Chapel Hill: University of North Carolina Press, 1952), 125–29.
56 From combining replies to similar questions on AIPO 640, 1/10/61 (2,649); AIPO 643, 4/4/61 (2,974); AIPO 644, 5/21/61 (3,545); AIPO 648, 7/25/61 (3,159); AIPO 653, 12/5/61 (2,990); AIPO 658, 5/1/62 (3,664); AIPO 660, 6/26/62 (3,276); and AIPO 661, 7/24/62 (4,040). See also AIPO Release, 9/5/62. AIPO polls by the fall of 1963 indicated that Goldwater had become more popular than Rockefeller as a possible Presidential candidate, probably because of the latter's divorce and remarriage.

Even against our Southern President Johnson, Senator Goldwater by early August, 1964, had amassed wider support in the South than in any other geographical region. When Americans were asked, "Suppose the presidential election were being held today. If Barry Goldwater, the Republican candidate, runs against Lyndon Johnson, the Democratic candidate, which man would you like to see win?" 51 percent (including Negroes) in the South, 19 percent in the Northeast, 30 percent in the Midwest (including the Plains States), and 33 percent in the West were for Goldwater. Those favoring Johnson were 40, 70, 59, and 62 percent, respectively; 9, 11, 11, and 5 percent, respectively, were undecided.[57] Activists in Southern Republican party life among the interviewees in 1959–62 seemed particularly inclined toward Senator Goldwater and his thinking on public matters. The little support for such "modern" Republicans as Governor Rockefeller, Senator Javits, and Senator Case seemed concentrated, at least in the Deep South, among some Northern-born people who brought their liberal Republicanism with them, some prosperous Jews, and a number of broadly educated professional and managerial men in technologically advanced industries and in the larger, more progressive and sophisticated cities.

Moreover, the Southern Republicans who have either won congressional elections or have been nominated have, with some exceptions, been largely on the right of their party in recent years on most problems in both domestic and foreign affairs. Most Republican Congressmen have in the past (after Reconstruction) represented mountain constituencies; in recent years increasing numbers have been elected from urban districts while congressional Democrats have remained strongest in the plantation sections (sugar areas excepted). It was previously noted (see p. 336) that Republican Congressmen from Southern cities have since 1953 been more inclined to vote against foreign aid and other multilateral commitments in nonmilitary spheres than have Southern Democratic Congressmen taken together; the same observation applied to Southern Republican Congressmen in general.[58] With the exception of the two Senators from Kentucky, particularly John Sherman Cooper, the great majority of these Republicans since the mid-1950's have advanced views and voted in the Congress (if they were elected) more or less in keeping with the thinking of Senator Goldwater and others

57 AIPO Release of August 9, 1964. An interregional comparison of whites alone would, of course, have indicated even more widespread support for Senator Goldwater in the South in contrast to the other regions.
58 Lerche, *The Uncertain South*, 185–86.

on the right of the Republican party. Southern Congressional Republicans were more inclined than their Southern Democratic colleagues to oppose foreign aid and other multilateral proposals of the Eisenhower administration, and this difference widened significantly during the Kennedy administration.[59]

Cross tabulations of support for various Republican figures on surveys and interviews with Southerners permit the making of some tentative generalizations about their international thinking. Southerners favorable to Senator Goldwater in the early 1960's were in the majority also favorable to whatever they knew of his international views—particularly concerning foreign aid, Cuba, and a "firmer" policy toward the Communist powers. The small minority who spoke approvingly of Governor Rockefeller (prior to his divorce and remarriage) were on the whole more favorable to nonmilitary as well as military multilateral cooperation, but a fairly large minority of them also felt our aid expenditures were too large. Very few who would eliminate or curtail very sharply our capital assistance programs, for instance, preferred Rockefeller to Goldwater or even to Nixon.

Southern whites have also favored, more than have Northerners, Democratic political figures who have been conservative on domestic questions, particularly on race but not only on that topic. However, during the prewar and early postwar period, there were no significant differences in most international attitudes, including Lend-Lease and the Marshall Plan, between Southerners who preferred more liberal as compared with those who preferred more conservative Democratic presidential candidates. Those who voted for the Dixiecrats in 1948, being disproportionately poorly educated and from the rural Black Belt, included more than their share of isolationists—those who would withdraw from the U.N. and NATO, reduce or terminate Marshall Plan aid, exclude European refugees from our country, and so on. However, they were no more opposed to increased international trade, conscription, and expensive military programs than Southerners generally.

But by 1962 Southerners who preferred that President Kennedy follow policies "to the right of center" and who had basically favorable views of Senator Goldwater were considerably more apt to feel the U.N. was doing a poor job, that it was not important to try to make the U.N. a success, that we should withdraw from the U.N., or some combination of these than were those who preferred that the President pursue policies to the "left of center" or more or less in the center and who harbored favorable views about President Kennedy, Ambassador Stevenson, Governor Rockefeller, or several of these public figures.

59 *Ibid.*

The former were also considerably more inclined than the latter to believe it would be impossible to reach a peaceful settlement of differences with the U.S.S.R.[60]

Liberalism and Civil Liberties

The word "liberal" has not always had a primarily negative connotation in the South, even the Deep South. During the New Deal, when the federal government exerted little pressure on the region to moderate its racial *status quo* and concentrated on domestic economic assistance (of which the South received considerably more than its share of federal taxes), Southerners were more inclined than other regional groups to think of themselves as "liberals" rather than "conservatives." Thus, in early 1937 when asked, "If there were only two political parties in this country—one for conservatives and one for liberals—which would you join?" 61 percent of Southerners replied "liberals" as compared with 47 percent of New Englanders, 54 percent of inhabitants on the Atlantic seaboard between New England and Maryland, 51 percent of Midwesterners, 50 percent of those in the Plains States, 51 percent of those in the Rocky Mountain region, and 54 percent of Far Westerners. Only 39 percent chose the conservative party versus 53 percent, 46 percent, 49 percent, 50 percent, 49 percent, and 46 percent, respectively.[61] Of the Americans queried in June, 1936, "In matters of political preference, do you consider yourself liberal or conservative?" 51 percent of those in the South willing so to identify themselves replied that they thought they were "liberal" as compared with 44 percent in New England, 40 percent in the area between New England and Maryland, 50 percent in the Midwest, 44 percent in the Plains States, and 53 percent in the West.[62] Somewhat amusingly, replies to these and similar questions in Mississippi during the thirties were on the average more liberal than those in the rest of the country taken together. The primarily economic connotation of these terms "liberal" and "conserva-

60 AIPO 654, 1/9/62 (3,421). On the same survey, 4 percent of Southerners expressed favorable impressions of the John Birch Society, 19 percent unfavorable ones, and 77 percent either had never heard of that organization or manifested no opinions of it. Of the small sample of Southerners who knew of this group and thought well of it (twenty-eight individuals), three out of four felt that the U.N. had done a poor job, one out of two would withdraw from that international body, and almost four out of five believed it would be virtually impossible to reach a peaceful settlement with the U.S.S.R.—all proportions far to the right of the general Southern average and, especially, of the average of those whose views of the John Birch Society were negative.

61 AIPO 69, 2/15/37 (3,013). Southerners were also more inclined than Northerners to choose "liberal" over "conservative" on similarly worded queries on AIPO 94, 8/2/37 (2,955), and AIPO 127, 7/2/38 (3,104).

62 AIPO survey of 6/21/36 (3,051). See also AIPO 161, 6/16/39 (3,054).

tive" in the 1930's was indicated by the concentration of liberal replies in the lower rather than in the upper economic and occupational groups.

The proportion of Southern whites who thought of themselves as conservatives rather than as liberals mounted gradually after World War II as they became more prosperous and as pressures for racial change grew;[63] by the late 1950's "liberal" had become to many white Deep Southerners synonymous with "racial agitator," "mongrelizer," "reformer," "left-winger," "anti-States' Righter," "traitor to the South," and the like. By the fall of 1961 over three fifths of responding white Southerners who had some notion of the difference between liberal and conservative—a significantly larger fraction than in the North—said they would prefer a conservative to a liberal party if the two major American parties were reorganized along ideological lines.[64]

Although Southerners during the Depression and New Deal were more inclined than Northerners to approve of the idea of the federal government taking over or intervening vigorously into the management of banks, railroads, and "big business" (see p. 184), they have been more hostile to the words "socialist" and "socialism" since World War II than any other regional group. Over half the newspapers sampled in 1961 presented negative images of these words, of supposed trends of our federal government toward socialism, of foreign societies supposedly run on socialistic principles, or some combination of these; most of these papers said or implied that socialism was a step toward communism or that it was almost synonymous with it. Thus, although Southerners were on the average the regional group least able to afford private medicine, in 1949 they were more opposed than Northerners to the idea of "socialized medicine."[65] They have invariably been more antagonistic than other regional groups to permitting "socialists," "leftists," "radicals," and especially "Communists" the right of free speech —on the radio, in newspapers and magazines, in public forums, or elsewhere.[66] They have agreed in larger proportions than other Amer-

63 AIPO 387, 12/31/46 (2,933); NORC 163, 1/26/49 (1,261); AIPO 454, 3/24/50 (1,458); AIPO 541, 12/29/54 (1,446); AIPO 547, 5/10/55 (1,503); and AIPO 577, 1/15/57 (1,496).
64 AIPO 649, 8/22/61 (3,165). See also AIPO 654, 1/9/62 (3,421).
65 AIPO 437, 2/9/49 (3,160).
66 NORC 239, November, 1945 (2,540); NORC 157, 4/22/48 (1,280); NORC 141, 3/20/46 (1,293); NORC 340, 5/14/53 (1,291); NORC 349, 11/25/53 (1,300); AIPO Release of 12/5/53; NORC 351, 1/21/54 (1,300); NORC 382, 1/26/56 (1,238); NORC 401, 12/28/56 (1,232); NORC 404, 4/26/57 (1,279); and Samuel A. Stouffer, *Communism, Conformity and Civil Liberties* (Garden City: Doubleday, 1955), 109–30.

icans that socialists and others on the left should not be allowed to teach in schools.[67] Larger fractions of Southerners than of other regional groups have felt that newspapers and other mass media and even individuals should not be allowed to criticize our form of government.[68] Although a majority of Southerners venturing opinions agreed in 1945 and 1953 that people should be allowed to say anything they want to in a public speech or otherwise, the majority has been smaller than in other major regions.[69] The proportion of white Southerners who disapprove of freedom of speech for the left has probably increased since the latter date with the apparently growing foreign Communist threat and the augmented white hostility to criticism of its ways, particularly race relations.

Since Southerners who considered themselves liberals in the 1930's were disproportionately numerous in the lower educational and, especially, economic groups, it is not surprising that they tended to be at least somewhat less informed about international developments of the period and less inclined to voice views on world problems than were those who thought of themselves as conservatives. Insofar as there were isolationists in the South at that time—individuals opposed to expanded support of the enemies of the Axis, for instance—they were apparently more likely to consider themselves liberals than conservatives. But Southerners who said they did not know what these terms meant or that they had no opinion about which of the two they considered themselves, being for the most part among the least educated,

67 Stouffer, *Communism, Conformity and Civil Liberties,* 116–24.

68 NORC 239, November, 1945 (2,540); NORC 157, 4/22/48 (1,280); AIPO 443, 6/9/49 (2,765); and NORC 340, 5/14/53 (1,291). At the time of the 1945 survey, the public was asked, "In peacetime, do you think newspapers should be allowed to criticize our form of government?" In reply, 49 percent of all Southerners (53 percent of white Southerners) as compared with 67 percent of Northeasterners, 72 percent of Midwesterners (including residents of the Plains States), and 72 percent of Westerners replied in the affirmative; 45 percent of all Southerners (42 percent of white Southerners) in contrast to 28, 23, and 25 percent, respectively, answered in the negative; and 6, 5, 5, and 3 percent, respectively, ventured no opinion, were undecided, or said they did not know. When asked in 1949, "Do you believe in freedom of speech for everybody; that is, for example, permitting anyone to say anything at any time about our government or our country?" 39 percent of all Southerners (41 percent of white Southerners) versus 46 percent of Northeasterners, 50 percent of Midwesterners, 47 percent of inhabitants of the Plains States, and 48 percent of Westerners answered in the affirmative; 43 percent of all Southerners (42 percent of white Southerners) in contrast to 41, 39, 39, and 42 percent, respectively, in the negative; and 18 percent of all Southerners (17 percent of white Southerners) in contrast to 13, 11, 15, and 10 percent, respectively, ventured no opinion, said they did not know, or indicated that they were undecided.

69 NORC 239, November, 1945 (2,540), and NORC 340, 5/14/53 (1,291).

were also the least informed and most inclined to volunteer isolationist replies.

By 1949 and increasingly afterwards Southerners who considered themselves liberals were disproportionately numerous among the better educated, the more complex, particularly professional, occupations, and among urban rather than rural people. Shortly after President Truman's inaugural address in which he suggested Point Four technical assistance for underdeveloped countries, Southerners who viewed themselves as liberals were more inclined than those who thought of themselves as conservatives to have heard of Point Four and to approve of the idea, to know who Dean Acheson was, and to know about and approve of the Marshall Plan, the Truman Doctrine, and the Voice of America program. The conservatives were more apt to feel that world war was probable within the next decade, that we should not develop trade with Yugoslavia, to sympathize with the Dutch in the conflict in Indonesia, to oppose further compromises with the U.S.S.R., and to advocate that we be "firmer" with that country. Both liberals and conservatives were about equally favorable to spending more money on our military forces and to sending military equipment at our expense to Western Europe.[70]

During the mid-1950's and especially later, Southerners who viewed themselves as liberals or favored a liberal federal administration as compared with those who considered themselves conservatives or favored more conservative national regimes were more inclined to favor active United States collaboration in the U.N., lower tariffs, defeat of the proposed Bricker Amendment and other isolationist or neo-isolationist proposals, and economic aid to neutralist underdeveloped countries. They were more apt to oppose the McCarran Act, to favor immigration of refugees, and to disagree with the position that there were a considerable number of Communists in the United States and in the State Department and other federal agencies and that they were a major danger.[71]

Support of freedom of speech and assembly for socialists and others on the left and of their right to teach in schools during the postwar period has been particularly concentrated among the upper educational groups, especially the college educated, in the South. High positive correlations with education have been evident in the North as well,

70 NORC 163, 1/26/49 (1,261).
71 AIPO 527, 2/23/54 (1,511); AIPO 541, 12/29/54 (1,446); AIPO 547, 5/10/55 (1,503); AIPO 577, 1/15/57 (1,496); AIPO 649, 8/22/61 (3,165); and AIPO 654, 1/9/62 (3,421).

but they have been even higher in the South—the Southern underprivileged have been much less attached to tolerance of "radicals" than the lower strata in the North, whereas the college educated in the South have more nearly approached their Northern counterparts on these questions.[72] Thus, larger proportions of Southern newspapers—run for the most part by college-educated Southerners—than of the Southern population have supported civil liberties and tolerance of ideological controversy and nonconformity.

Moreover, by the late 1950's tolerance of this sort had become closely associated with relatively moderate, if not liberal, thinking among whites on the race question.[73] It is therefore understandable that these on the whole better-educated and racially moderate [74] Southerners have been for the most part among those more favorable to economic assistance to neutralist underdeveloped countries, expanded admission of selected refugees and other immigrants into this country, and active international collaboration generally in diplomatic, economic, and cultural, as well as military, spheres. Southern neo-isolationists and those emphasizing military and generally "tougher" policies toward those who disagree with us in world affairs have been disproportionately numerous among those who would not let socialists teach in local schools, would not allow newspapers and individuals to criticize our form of government, and so on.[75] However, by 1960 a number of college-educated, more sophisticated conservative interviewees who would reduce aid to anti-Western, leftist, and otherwise "undeserving" neutralists and take a firmer approach toward them were also supporters of freedom of expression and nonconformity for domestic leftists and "radicals."

Laissez-Faire Economics

Southern divergence from the rest of the country toward greater conservatism has been less marked in domestic economic affairs than in race relations, civil liberties, tolerance of controversial liberal expression, and social change generally. A considerable fraction of socially and racially conservative Southerners would like economic "progress"

---

72 For discussion of this finding together with supporting data, see Stouffer, *Communism, Conformity and Civil Liberties*, 109–30.
73 NORC 382, 1/26/56 (1,238).
74 For relationships between racial thinking and international behavior, see Chapter 11.
75 AIPO 443, 6/9/49 (2,765); NORC 340, 5/14/53 (1,291); NORC 351, 1/21/54 (1,300); NORC 382, 1/26/56 (1,275); NORC 401, 12/28/56 (1,232); and NORC 404, 4/26/57 (1,279).

without social change and many of them in the early sixties seemed to feel this to be possible. A significantly larger fraction of Southerners than of other citizens have been in the lower economic groups which have been most likely to profit by welfare programs and other liberal domestic economic policies, and their economic status has moderated considerably manifestation of their basically conservative outlook in their thinking on economics at home. The number of liberals on domestic economics in recent years has therefore exceeded that of Southern liberals on most other issues.

Nevertheless, regardless of their significantly lower per capita incomes, the proportion of Southerners who have said they supported liberal domestic economic programs since World War II has usually been smaller than in other major regions of the country. Probably most poorly educated and economically underprivileged Southerners had thought little about these matters prior to being interviewed; they may have provided replies which they felt to be in keeping with the acceptable ones in their locale, particularly among influential groups, rather than expressing views which they themselves held with much intensity.

In spite of this, the conservative atmosphere of the region has shown through in replies of Southerners to questions about taxes, unions, welfare, and the like. The interviews indicated that many Southerners seemed by 1959 to fear that liberals on economics might also be "radicals" on race. Even underprivileged poor whites and hill people seemed frequently to perceive trade union representatives as racial equalitarians ("niggers competing for our jobs") and "foreign-born agitators." Federal welfare programs have benefited Negroes disproportionately since they have been the most economically deprived group in the region, and the racially conservative informants were often concerned that there would be hidden, if not overt, liberal racial and social reform strings attached to federal money. The untrammeled rights of private property and Jefferson's view that the government that governs least (and taxes least) governs best have been supported by pragmatic agrarian individualism—a belief that everyone is responsible for and to only himself, an emotional identification with rural independence and self-reliance, and a tradition of the individual's being in virtually absolute control of his land without "outside dictation" to fit "grandiose plans" or the "hypothetical welfare of some fabulous creature called society." [76]

Thus, in the Great Depression when the number of wealthy individuals in the South was small indeed, Southerners were most inclined of regional groups to feel that no government should have the right to

76 Twelve Southerners, *I'll Take My Stand*, xviii.

limit private fortunes.[77] Asked in 1954 whether they would favor or oppose a federal law requiring that the federal government never take more than 35 percent of any person's income in taxes, only 27 percent in the South were opposed, compared with 36 percent in the Northeast, 44 percent in the Midwest (Plains States included), and 44 percent in the West; 59 percent in the South favored such a law as compared with 57 percent in the Northeast, 45 percent in the Midwest (Plains States included), and 45 percent in the West.[78] Likewise, larger proportions of Southerners than of other citizens responding have opposed unbalanced federal budgets, increasing national debts,[79] and further trends toward a "welfare state."[80] Although Southerners have been more in need of federal money for their educational institutions than the on the average more affluent Northerners, smaller majorities of the former than of residents in other regions have favored federal assistance even for school buildings and larger minorities in the South than elsewhere have been opposed to federal aid to help build new public schools.[81] Differences between the South and other regions have been markedly greater for aid for teachers' salaries and other nonmaterial aspects of education.[82] Apparently Southern whites in recent years have feared that acceptance of any aid for education would entail further pressures to desegregate schools, for opposition to such aid has been closely connected with more conservative racial views.[83]

The proportion of Southerners, as of other Americans, who have harbored antagonistic attitudes toward trade unions has gradually declined since the 1930's, but at any given time the former have been more inclined to express negative opinions of labor unions and their leaders than have inhabitants of other major regions in the same eco-

---

77 AIPO 60, 12/7/36 (2,672). Forty percent of those replying in the South, 44 percent in the Northeast, 47 percent in the Midwest, 45 percent in the Plains States, 52 percent in the Rocky Mountain region, and 64 percent in the Far West felt that the "government should limit the size of private fortunes."

78 AIPO 541, 12/29/54 (1,446).

79 AIPO 511, 1/29/53 (1,599); AIPO 516, 5/28/53 (1,549); and AIPO Release of 2/22/56.

80 AIPO 448, 9/23/49 (2,919).

81 When asked in late 1955, "Do you favor or oppose federal aid to help build new public schools?" 60 percent in the South in contrast to 69 percent in the Northeast, 69 percent in the Midwest (including the Plains States), and 75 percent in the West were in favor; 29 percent in the South in contrast to 23, 22, and 17 percent, respectively, were opposed; and 11, 8, 9, and 8 percent, respectively, were undecided, did not know, or ventured no opinion. See AIPO 557, 12/6/55 (1,434).

82 AIPO 550, 7/12/55 (1,397); AIPO 577, 1/15/57 (1,496); AIPO 585, 6/25/57 (1,521); AIPO 593, 12/31/57 (1,522); and AIPO 641, 2/8/61 (2,873).

83 AIPO 557, 12/6/55 (1,434).

nomic circumstances. In fact, working-class and other low-income Southerners have often been more likely than the professional and managerial classes in the rest of the country to accord unfavorable stereotypes to labor unions.[84] Antiunion thinking among the less affluent in the Deep South has been almost synonymous with racism, but among the more prosperous and educated Southerners many moderates and a few liberals on race have been very critical of labor organizations and their leaders.[85] Antistrike proposals, right-to-work laws, and other programs designed to limit the activities and influence of unions have been more popular in the South than in any other major geographical region;[86] larger fractions of Southerners than of other Americans have

84 AIPO 73, 3/10/37 (2,959); AIPO 127, 7/2/38 (3,104); AIPO 195, 5/16/40 (3,139); AIPO 225, 1/14/41 (3,026); AIPO 232, 3/7/41 (3,044); AIPO 238, 5/29/41 (3,152); AIPO 249, 10/13/41 (2,949); AIPO 250, 10/7/41 (3,059); AIPO 265, 3/31/42 (3,053); AIPO 268, 5/21/42 (3,000); AIPO Release of 3/20/46; AIPO 365, 2/13/46 (2,946); AIPO 375, 7/24/46 (3,124); AIPO 400, 7/2/47 (3,000); AIPO Release of August 31, 1947; AIPO 418, 5/15/48 (3,000); AIPO 434, 12/8/48 (2,977); AIPO 483, 12/7/51 (1,317); AIPO Release of November 11, 1953; AIPO 521, 10/7/53 (1,488); AIPO 577, 1/15/57 (1,496); AIPO 581, 4/4/57 (1,654); AIPO 588, 8/27/57 (1,528); AIPO 606, 10/13/58 (1,553); AIPO 609, 1/5/59 (1,593); AIPO 617, 8/18/59 (2,982); AIPO 640, 1/10/61 (2,649); AIPO 644, 5/2/61 (3,545); and AIPO 650, 9/19/61 (3,476). Proportions of Southerners and of other Americans advancing unfavorable versus favorable impressions on unions varied with the wording of the question and not whether or not labor-management tension was prominent at the time in the news. Majorities of those offering views in the South said they approved of trade unions even in the immediate prewar period; in October, 1941, for instance, 44 percent of Southerners said they approved of trade unions whereas 42 percent said they disapproved as compared with 64 percent who approved and 29 percent who disapproved in the rest of the country. See AIPO 249, 10/13/41 (2,949). By early 1961, when the same question was posed, 59 percent in the South approved whereas 28 percent disapproved; the Northern figures were 72 percent and 17 percent. See AIPO 640, 1/10/61 (2,649). On the other hand, 78 percent of Southerners in August, 1938, said there should be more federal regulation of labor unions; as did 65 percent of New Englanders, 70 percent of the residents between New England and Maryland along the Atlantic Coast, 70 percent of Midwesterners, 74 percent of those in the Plains States, and 73 percent of Westerners. AIPO 127, 7/2/38 (3,104). By May, 1941, 95 percent of Southerners as compared with 84, 78, 85, 84, and 86 percent, respectively, thought so. See AIPO 238, 5/29/41 (3,152). In May, 1939, only 14 percent of Southerners were in favor of "the union shop, that is, requiring every worker in a factory or mine to join the union"; other regional figures were 42, 40, 28, 22, and 27 percent, respectively. AIPO 158, 5/18/39 (3,043). The Bureau of Applied Social Research study discovered that Southerners who had finished college were about one-third more likely than their Northern counterparts to harbor unfavorable images of Walter Reuther.
85 AIPO 400, 7/12/47 (3,000); AIPO 456, 6/2/50 (1,450); and interviews for this study.
86 AIPO Release of 11/13/38; AIPO Release of 12/10/39; AIPO 158, 5/18/39 (3,043); AIPO 215, 10/9/40 (3,135); AIPO 232, 3/7/41 (3,044); AIPO 237, 5/20/41 (3,089); AIPO 238, 5/29/41 (3,152); AIPO Release of 8/3/47; AIPO 434, 12/8/48 (2,977); AIPO 456, 6/2/50 (1,450); AIPO 492, 5/9/52 (2,097); AIPO 521, 10/7/53 (1,488); and AIPO 644, 5/12/61 (3,545).

sided with management in labor disputes; [87] and a greater proportion of Southerners than of other regional groups have opposed increases in the minimum wages in the United States.[88]

However, one should estimate the extent of conservative economic attitudes from the content of Southern newspapers with caution. For, although a majority of Southern papers in the sample ranged from reactionary to conservative on trade unions, wage-and-hour legislation, right-to-work laws, and domestic welfare programs, significantly more than half of the Southern adult population, and particularly of those who manifested opinions on these matters, disagreed with them. In early 1961, for instance, only 28 percent of Southerners, compared with 17 percent of Northeasterners, 14 percent of Midwesterners (residents of the Plains States included), and 20 percent of Westerners, said they disapproved of labor unions; 59 percent of Southerners versus 70 percent, 75 percent, and 70 percent, respectively, said they approved.[89] Particularly in the lower economic groups, considerable majorities of those expressing opinions have in recent years approved of unionization, of increases in the minimum wage, and even of aid for building schools—provided that the race issue was not injected into the discussion.

The relatively few Southern Congressmen who voted with the Northern isolationists prior to our entry into World War II were with few exceptions either mountain Republicans or among the minority of "liberals" on domestic economic and welfare issues from their region. Often demagogues in the Populist tradition, with the exceptions of Huey Long [90] and "Bob" Reynolds [91] they coupled their proposed expendi-

---

87 AIPO 68, 2/8/37 (2,916); AIPO 88, 6/21/37 (2,970); AIPO 107, 12/28/37 (2,957); AIPO 490, 4/11/52 (1,900); AIPO 507, 10/15/52 (3,114); and AIPO 620, 11/10/59 (2,750).

88 AIPO 58, 11/20/36 (2,717); AIPO 83, 5/17/37 (2,945); AIPO 93, 7/26/37 (2,896); AIPO Release of 1/9/38; AIPO Release of 5/11/39; AIPO 411, 1/21/48 (3,161); AIPO 520, 9/10/53 (1,535); AIPO 541, 2/29/54 (1,446); AIPO 544, 3/1/55 (1,395); and AIPO 641, 2/8/61. (2,873). By the time of the last of these surveys, interregional differences had narrowed considerably; 67 percent in the South favored increasing the minimum wage from the then current $1.00 per hour, compared with 83 percent in the Northeast, 73 percent in the Midwest (Plains States included), and 80 percent in the West. Twenty-two percent in the South versus 12, 19, and 16 percent, respectively, disapproved of this suggestion.

89 AIPO 640, 1/10/61 (2,649).

90 *Congressional Record*, 74th Congress, 1st Session, 565, 568, and 577.

91 Burke Davis, "Senator Bob Reynolds: Retrospective View," *Harper's* CLXXXVIII (1944), 365–68. If Oklahoma were included in the South, blind Senator Thomas Gore might be added to the list of economic liberals who voted with the isolationists but was not a Negrophobe. See Monroe Billington, "Thomas P. Gore and Oklahoma Public Opinion, 1917–1918," *Journal of Southern History*, XXVII, (1961), 344–53.

tures for the benefit of the white underprivileged with overt appeals to Negrophobia prevalent among the economically deprived from whom most of their electoral support came. Thus, Tom Watson (in his later, anti-Negro period),[92] Hoke Smith (from about 1906 on),[93] James K. Vardaman,[94] "Pitchfork Ben" Tillman,[95] Cole Blease,[96] Theodore Bilbo,[97] and John Rankin typically combined racism, support of shifts of political power and wealth from the prosperous to the less fortunate, progressive taxation, public electric power and highways, more stringent control of corporations, attacks on "Wall Street" bankers who were supposedly responsible for both the poverty of most Southern whites and our "needless" involvement in wars to defend their foreign economic interests with Anglophobia, hostility to the assumed Anglophilia of the Northeastern and Southern upper classes, and opposition to United States entry into both world wars, United States membership in the League of Nations and the Permanent Court of International Justice, and the measures such as Lend-Lease suggested by President Roosevelt to aid the enemies of the Axis and otherwise thwart the latter's aggressions. The important exception to their isolationism was international trade—most of these Southern congressional opponents of international commitments voted along with Southern interventionists for freer trade. Most Southern supporters of world involvements other than trade came from,[98] or represented the interests of, the privileged

92   C. Vann Woodward, *Tom Watson, Agrarian Rebel* (New York: MacMillan, 1938), 426, 451, 452, 454–64, 466–67, 480, and 483.

93   Grantham, *Hoke Smith and the Politics of the New South*, 331–43, 345, and 360; and Dewey W. Grantham, Jr., "Hoke Smith and the New Freedom," in J. Carlyle Sitterson (ed.), *Studies in Southern History*, Vol. XXXIX (Chapel Hill: University of North Carolina Press, 1957), 147.

94   Kirwan, *Revolt of the Rednecks*, 279–82; Fleming, *The United States and the World Court*, 60, 128; and Osborn, *John Sharp Williams*, 269.

95   Simkins, *Pitchfork Ben Tillman*, 490.

96   *Ibid.*, 536–37; O. L. Warr, "Mr. Blease of South Carolina," *American Mercury*, XVI (1929), 25, 28, and 31; Fleming, *The United States and the World Court*, 60; and *Congressional Record*, 69th Congress, 2nd Session, 1425, 1969, 2024, 2046–47, 2106–2107, 2298, 2304, 2349, 2572, 2574–75, 2590, 2593, 2657, 2740, 2747, 2753, 2818, 2819, and 3327.

97   Howards, "The Influence of Southern Senators," 96.

98   Most Southern political leaders who were friends of the underdog were also from relatively prosperous, or at least economically comfortable, parentage. Thomas Watson's planter father owned over fifty slaves prior to the Civil war; Tillman's was an even bigger planter with a larger number of slaves; Cole Blease's operated a profitable small business; and Huey Long's was a middle-class farmer whose standard of living was well above average in the Louisiana hills. Some Southern politicians who were originally elected based on economic (and racist) appeals to the underprivileged later voted in the Congress with the economic conservatives ("sold out to the interests"), but most of those who voted with the isolationists expressed the economic aspirations of the poorer hill folk at the time.

classes and favored federal action abroad but circumscribed conservative government at home.

Likewise, in the early postwar years, Senator Bilbo was among the handful of Southern Senators who opposed important international involvements requested by President Truman.[99] Domestic economic liberal and friend of trade unions, Senator Olin Johnston was also among this Southern congressional minority, particularly in his opposition to foreign aid.[100] "Jim" Folsom, champion of the underprivileged, in his successful 1946 gubernatorial campaign in Alabama supported expansion of domestic welfare programs and opposed the proposed loan to Britain, since the money, he proclaimed, was needed for old age pensions, education, roads, and other domestic programs.[101]

Senator Johnston of South Carolina and several other "liberals" on taxation, welfare, trade unions, and other domestic economic issues in the Senate and House voted against foreign aid, the U.N. bond issue of 1962, and other multilateral commitments in the late 1950's and early 1960's. But Southern congressional supporters of foreign aid, international organization, intercultural exchange with Communist and other relatively hostile societies, the U.N. bond issue, and other multilateral programs beyond the military field since the mid-1950's were for the most part relatively liberal on most domestic issues as well, including economics but excluding race relations.[102]

Similar linkages between economic and international attitudes have been apparent among the Southern public, except that correlations between the two have been lower. Since Southerners who favored more progressive taxation, expanded social welfare, minimum wages and hours legislation, and the like in the prewar period were disproportionately numerous among the economically deprived and poorly educated, it is not surprising to discover that Southerners who approved of these as compared with those who opposed them were less informed about world affairs, less interested, and less enthusiastic about international involvement with respect to the issues of the day. The economic "liberals" were typically at least somewhat and sometimes much less inclined to favor expanded world trade, Lend-Lease, peacetime conscription, liberalization of the Johnson and Neutrality acts, the destroyer "swap" for bases with Britain, United States naval convoys carrying supplies to Britain, the arming of United States merchant ships, the

99 Howards, "The Influence of Southern Senators," 96–97.
100 *Ibid.*, 105–106 and 117.
101 W. Bradley Twitty, *Y'all Come* (Nashville: Hermitage Press, 1962), 149.
102 Lerche, *The Uncertain South*, 170–73.

sending of draftees overseas, and helping Britain in general "at the risk of war."[103]

These observations also applied with but relatively minor modification to the early postwar years. The economic "liberals," still disproportionately concentrated among the less educated and underprivileged, included the larger fraction of the remaining isolationists and of those who were poorly informed about and uninterested in foreign relations. Most privileged Southerners who were quite critical of the behavior of trade unions and their leaders, who felt that the taxes in the upper brackets were too high, who believed that "handouts" were ruining individual integrity and "get up and go" in this country, and who were otherwise conservative on domestic economics favored active participation in the U.N., maintenance of expensive armed forces and military commitments with West European allies, continued garrisoning of United States forces abroad, admission of additional displaced persons and other refugees to this country, the Truman Doctrine and the Marshall Plan, and most of the other international programs of President Truman.

However, a considerable fraction of economic conservatives of the middle and upper socioeconomic strata began to feel that the Marshall Plan had gone on too long by early 1951 or so. Moreover, the more widespread aversion of Southerners than other regional groups to high taxation and "big government" showed through in their replies to queries about their willingness to pay higher taxes for rehabilitation of Europe during and immediately after the war, the Marshall Plan and Point Four later, and even military aid for West European allies. Even though Southerners, particularly whites, were as or more favorable to these aid programs in the abstract than other regional groups, Southerners were distinctly less willing than Northerners to support these programs if tax increases would be necessary to carry them out.[104]

103   AIPO 88, 6/21/37 (2,970), and AIPO 97, 8/23/37 (2,955).
104   AIPO 307, 11/23/43 (2,980); AIPO 400, 7/2/47 (3,000); SRC survey of April-May, 1950 (342); and AIPO 477, 7/6/51 (2,013). In the fall of 1948, for instance, 58 percent of white Southerners (54 percent of all Southerners) as compared with 54 percent of both white and all Northerners said they approved of our sending military supplies to West European countries which had recently signed an agreement to defend one another against future attack; 33 percent of white Southerners (36 percent of all Southerners) as compared with 40 percent of white Northerners (39 percent of all Northerners) disapproved. But when those who said they approved were asked whether they would still approve of sending military supplies "if it meant higher taxes next year," only 72 percent of those Southern whites (70 percent of all Southerners) who had originally favored this suggestion continued to do so, whereas 94 percent of Northerners who had approved of this idea before were of like mind. See NORC 161, 10/13/48 (1,300). As in other parts of the country, more prosperous Southerners—who paid the higher taxes—were con-

By the late 1950's and early 1960's the Southern working and lower-middle classes were still considerably more liberal about domestic economics than the more affluent groups, particularly the noncollege-trained among the latter. The large proportion of these lower- and lower-middle-class economic "liberals" who offered no opinions on a variety of queries about foreign policy seemed to indicate that most of them were still rather apathetic about most aspects of world affairs which were not patently related to war and peace, military action, and other spheres which would affect them directly. Among individuals who were liberal on trade unions, progressive taxation, and the like and who held views on such international matters, most continued to reply that the U.N. is a basically desirable international institution in which the United States should participate, few would reduce our armed forces or eliminate military conscription, and most continued to support active participation in NATO and other West European arrangements. But according to small samples on national surveys which cannot be readily subjected to tests of statistical significance, domestic economic liberals of the less prosperous strata were more likely than economic conservatives on these issues to oppose expanded immigration, international exchange of persons, and training of foreigners in this country at our expense. Insofar as they manifested opinions on economic aid to underdeveloped neutralist countries in Africa and Asia, most seemed to agree with Senator Olin Johnston, for whom large majorities of the less privileged of South Carolina usually voted, that much of these funds could be better expended on the less well off in this country.

Domestic economic conservatives among the lower socioeconomic groups—again according to small samples on national surveys—seemed in recent years to have been as, or perhaps even more, apathetic about foreign affairs than their economically liberal peers. When they have ventured opinions, they have apparently been somewhat more opposed to foreign economic assistance to underdeveloped countries, more likely to view world politics and our national security in purely military terms and to advance neo-isolationist if not isolationist views, and more inclined to oppose liberalized immigration. It is questionable, however, that economic conservatism among the underprivileged has had a causal relation except on spending money abroad. Working-class economic conservatives have been in large measure racists, rural dwellers, religious fundamentalists, and culturally isolated—all factors correlated with "Fortress America" proclivities, nativist xenophobia, and ignorance of international phenomena.

---

sistently more willing to pay still higher taxes for foreign aid than were less comfortably off Southerners who paid lower ones.

As was observed previously, strongly conservative domestic economic thinking among the prosperous in the South has very often implied disaffection with foreign economic assistance at the orders of magnitude of these programs in the early 1960's. Those of arch-conservative economic ideology among the interviewees were for the most part critical of our assistance to "socialist" (and neutralist, for the most part) foreign regimes, and they were even more inclined to oppose aid to Yugoslavia and Poland. Although most prosperous arch-free enterprisers have not been particularly well informed in foreign affairs, they have had more information and more defined views than most Southerners of the lower strata. Judging from interviews and small survey samples, it appeared that relatively well-off isolationists and neo-isolationists have been to a large extent strongly conservative on most issues—foreign affairs, trade unions, minimum wages, and social and political change. But most affluent strong economic conservatives would not accept the label "isolationist" or "neo-isolationist" (if they had heard of the latter term). They were willing to pay higher taxes for our military defense and that of our more competent and reliable allies, few would have us withdraw our military help to Vietnam and other societies under Communist threat, and a number of them favored expanded world trade. Even as early as June, 1960, most would probably not have been chagrined by United States military intervention in Cuba and general military enforcement of the Monroe Doctrine.

A small minority within economically comfortable professional and, in fewer cases, business groups have harbored relatively liberal economic and social views. Their proportion of the population has been too small for statistical treatment in surveys, but interviews and other experiences with these rather atypical prosperous Southerners indicate that the vast majority of them have been internationalists or multilateralists on most aspects of foreign policy, and in fact relative liberals on most public questions. These observations are understandable since the thinking which has produced economic liberals among the Southern prosperous—against their apparent short-term interests—has been much akin to that which has produced cosmopolitan supporters of the international orientations of Congressmen and former Congressmen like J. William Fulbright, John Sparkman, Lister Hill, Hale Boggs, Brooks Hays, Estes Kefauver, and Frank E. Smith. They have developed an empathy with and sympathy for people very different from and less privileged than themselves and have absorbed views contrary to those prevalent among their own social group.

CHAPTER II

SOUTHERN WHITES, DESEGREGATION, AND WORLD AFFAIRS

The changing role of the Southern Negro and his demands for equal rights together with the emergence and increasing importance to American foreign policy of independent Africa and, to a lesser extent, other colored nations have had more profound impacts on white Southern thinking about world affairs than any other single development of the period 1954–62. Demographic factors, traditions, personality and value variables, and basic social and political orientations have had their effects, but they have long been present and they have been gradually evolving toward national norms, whereas in some major aspects of international behavior Southerners have been diverging more and more from other Americans. Industrialization and its concomitants have exerted considerable influence on Southerners' world views, but the most marked turning away from support of a number of active international involvements proposed by Presidents Eisenhower and Kennedy has taken place in traditional plantation and other Old South areas least affected by economic development. Of all the individual and social attributes that have come to the author's attention, Southerners' attitudes toward the Negro have been the best single predictor of their international postures in the late fifties and early sixties.

This has not always been so. Insularity and isolationism among Southerners have been evident primarily when Northern and other liberals were pressing the region to change its racial patterns. Thomas

Jefferson was a champion of cosmopolitanism and freedom of thought and expression in all fields of human endeavor, including world affairs, as were George Mason, James Madison, John Taylor, and other Southerners of education and influence in the first quarter of the nineteenth century and before.[1] But the advent of the accelerating abolitionist movement in the North, manifested in William Lloyd Garrison's *Liberator* founded in 1831 and Horace Greeley's New York *Tribune*, and the resulting fear of slave unrest reinforced by Nat Turner's uprising in the same year produced in Southerners a persecution complex, a defensiveness and distrust of outsiders and their ideas, and a stifling of critical discussion initially about race, but gradually about other controversial public questions as well. Educated Southerners shifted their intellectual energies from broad national and international problems to developing apologias for the Southern racial and related social *status quo*.[2] The defeat of 1865 and the following Reconstruction intensified distrust of and internal pressures against "foreign" ideas and analytical discussion which might result in criticism of Southern mores.[3]

The presence of the Negro continued thereafter to influence Southern thinking about social and public questions and to limit critical discussion, particularly of issues which might lead to the race question. But the compromise of 1877 between Northern Republicans and like-minded influential Southern Democrats whereby Rutherford B. Hayes rather than Samuel J. Tilden became President left the fate of the Negro to Southern whites.[4] In 1896 the Supreme Court decision of *Plessy v. Ferguson* accepted the principle of "separate but equal" facilities. Al-

1 Clement Eaton, "The Resistance of the South to Northern Radicalism," *New England Quarterly*, VIII (1935), 215–17. Even George Fitzhugh, future champion par excellence of slavery and the attendant social system of inequality, antiliberalism, and paternalistic feudalism against the North in his *Sociology for the South*, was a Jeffersonian liberal during this earlier period. (Wish, in the Introduction to his *Ante-Bellum: Writings of George Fitzhugh and Hinton Rowan Helper on Slavery*, 5.)

2 Frederick Law Olmsted, *A Journey in the Back Country* (New York: Mason Bros., 1860), pp. 280–82; Williams, *Romance and Realism in Southern Politics*, 10–11; Eaton, *Freedom of Thought in the Old South*, 89 ff.; Osterweis, *Romanticism and Nationalism in the Old South*, 21, 22, 44; Polk, *Southern Accent: From Uncle Remus to Oak Ridge*, 188 and 203–209; William E. Dodd, *The Cotton Kingdom* (New Haven: Yale University Press, 1921), 62 and 70; Eaton, *The Growth of Southern Civilization*, 97 and 289–317; Kendrick and Arnett, *The South Looks at Its Past*, 9–10, 84–85, and 93; Savage, *Seeds of Time*, 52–68, 81–82, and 105–106; and Woodward, *The Burden of Southern History*, 178–82.

3 Nicholls, *Southern Tradition and Regional Progress*, 134–35; Cash, *The Mind of the South*, 19, 99–101, 144–46, and 150; Carter, *The Angry Scar*, 387; and Dykeman and Stokely, *Neither Black Nor White*, 16.

4 Nicholls, *Southern Tradition and Regional Progress*, 80; Woodward, *Reunion and Reaction*, 6, 229–30, 232–33, 265–67; and Smith, *Killers of the Dream*, 194.

though there continued to be unrest among some Southern Negroes, backed by some Negroes and liberal whites in the North, the national executive, the Congress, and the federal courts made little serious attempt until the 1940's to change traditional Southern race relations. During this period Southerners and their political representatives in Washington remained on their guard against attempts to modify Southern racial mores, but they did not feel particularly threatened on the issue about which they were most touchy; Southern Congressmen could devote their energies to other issues, including world affairs.

Combined with this sense of relative security at home was the virtual absence of the Negro question in world affairs. World politics was directed predominantly by white nations; with but three exceptions —Haiti, Ethiopia, and Liberia—black peoples were under white control. Social revolutions against white elites by colored majorities in agrarian societies were seldom a matter of concern. Little foreign criticism of the "peculiar institution" came to the attention of Southerners, and whites were not retreating before demands of colored peoples in Africa and Asia. The League of Nations and the United Nations were controlled by whites; internationalism implied support of Britain and France against the Central Powers in 1914–18 and against the Axis later; and foreign aid went to Western Europe and, in the immediate postwar period, to Japan.

However, whenever the Negro did become a subject of international relations, Southerners' attitudes toward local Negroes did influence their reactions. For instance, Southerners and their Congressmen long opposed recognition of Haiti—independent through a slave insurrection —and only the secession in 1861 permitted the establishment of diplomatic relations with the black republic.[5] In 1926, Senator Coleman L. Blease of South Carolina attacked the proposed United States participation in the Permanent Court of International Justice, observing that "Haiti has a voice in the election of the judges to a court where we are to sit side-by-side with a full-blooded 'nigger,'" which would "throw the destinies of Southern women and Southern men into the lap of a black man." [6] Racially conservative Southern newspapers disapproved of President Franklin D. Roosevelt's entertaining the president of Liberia in the White House, and they also objected to Mrs. Roosevelt's generally liberal behavior toward Negroes, domestic and foreign.

5 Rayford W. Logan, *The Diplomatic Relations of the United States with Haiti, 1776–1891* (Chapel Hill: University of North Carolina Press, 1941), 70–72, 77, 79–81, 154, 195–96, and 200–202; and Ludwell L. Montague, *Haiti and the United States, 1714–1938* (Durham: Duke University Press, 1940), 51–53, 55–57, and 66–90.
6 *Congressional Record*, 69th Congress, 1st Session, 2819.

Before "Black Monday"

The paternalist segregationist of the 1960's probably speaks considerable truth in saying that Southern race relations had been gradually improving and becoming more rational until the North exacerbated the issue by supporting demands of militant Negroes.[7] Although most whites were emotionally tied to segregation and white control, lynchings and other violence against Negroes had sharply declined. Even the more traditionalist newspapers in areas with large Negro populations—papers which would be preoccupied almost daily with race relations after the 1954 Supreme Court school desegregation decision —mentioned the issue only infrequently, and then largely to attack some isolated "outside" effort to change the *status quo*. Most of the Southern urban press condemned lynching, the Ku Klux Klan, and other extralegal actions unjust to the Negro.[8] Many educated whites, even of plantation backgrounds, can recall little discussion about race —as in the case of the author they undoubtedly assumed that the race question was settled, that there was not much of a race problem, and that segregated white supremacy would remain unchanged for at least their lifetimes, and probably longer. Since segregation was assumed, many politicians were able to omit overt reference to this question— the campaign of Frank Graham for the Senate in 1950 was the first in many years in which race was a major open issue in North Carolina, for instance. Here and there a Negro won a case against a white in court, a Negro physician was allowed to practice in a white hospital, a Negro was put on the police force in the Negro part of town, or a Negro was elected to a minor public office. Relatively little issue was made of most of these gradual developments, and, without incurring much antagonism from those who disagreed, white Southerners could express themselves—at least in educated circles—in favor of further gradual change within the segregated system.

The Paternalist Segregationist

Such limited, slow change favorable to the Negro was accepted by a small minority who did not feel much threatened economically or

7 Many Negroes active in the integration movement would disagree with this generalization, but the author tends to agree in this case with these Southern paternalists.

8 There were exceptions, such as the Jackson *Daily News* and the Nashville *Banner*, which managed to condone in one way or another extralegal injustices from time to time.

socially by the black race. These whites in the Deep South came largely from privileged, better-educated parentage—the planter gentry, their urban counterparts, and some, of less elevated origins, who had married into these groups and adopted much of their racial thinking. A few other whites from underprivileged families attended college and adopted benevolent paternalist behavior, but the total number of truly paternalist whites might be liberally estimated at 2 percent of the white population in areas with considerable proportions of Negroes. Perhaps as many as 10 percent had learned some of these attitudes, typically adulterated with inconsistent racial sentiments gleaned from their own social origins. But even many of the newer planter elite, particularly Northerners moved South and self-made Southerners, were known as "tough on niggers."

Many of this small minority had played with Negroes as children and had known servants almost as members of the family. They had learned at an early age disdain for the violence against Negroes (and other habits) of poor whites and had come to understand that a gentleman or lady should not take advantage of Negroes but should be kind and, within limits, helpful to them. Faithful Negroes were kept in the "quarters" and cared for when sick or old. A gentleman saw that "his" Negroes' medical bills were paid and that loyal workers were given rewards and protected from "white trash" and "rednecks." Many paternalists' *noblesse oblige* went so far as to get faithful Negroes out of jail, to appear as character witnesses in court for those unjustly accused by lower-class whites, and even to engage in rather candid conversations with trusted Negroes about the failings of Negrophobe whites. The author recalls some paternalists here and there who felt that gradual change in race relations leading to Negro responsibility and even some desegregation might result in another generation or two, as education increased and the standards of the black race shifted toward those of educated whites.

Yet, benevolent aristocratic paternalism contained seeds of serious difficulties for the future when increasing numbers of Negroes, backed by the federal government and liberal whites, would demand civil equality and desegregation. Most paternalists held many of the same racial views as the white majority—that Negroes were unreliable, hedonistic, shiftless, loose in morals, lacking in "character," childlike, and innately inferior to whites. They would need the guidance and protection of upper-class whites for generations. Only those Negroes with "plenty of white in them" could be expected to absorb white civilization. Although some patricians had favored enfranchisement of

Negroes during the post-Reconstruction period as a means of counter-balancing the votes of the white underprivileged with ballots which the elite could expect to control, most were opposed to independent Negro voting after the defeat of the Populists. Given their prestige and social and economic influence, paternalists could have greatly lessened injustices by their open condemnation of the excesses of other, particularly poor, whites; yet few did so. They were white supremacists and they profited from the crude racism of the masses which prevented the dispossessed of both races from cooperating politically to force liberal economic programs. The benevolence of most aristocrats was a patronizing and condescending one which depended upon the Negro's accepting his "place" and being grateful for the charity and leadership of genteel whites. Moreover, they tended to feel that only Southerners had the experience and wisdom to understand Negroes and to help them evolve. The paternalist and his press were usually quick to attack Northern liberals who rendered advice or tried to hasten this process of evolution. Most of the "trouble" in the South was due to these "meddlers," "Yankee agitators," "bleeding hearts," and "platitudinous theorists and do-gooders" who were jealous of the leisurely Southern way of life and wished to undermine it by racial unrest.

A few of these paternalistic individuals were isolationists, even vociferous ones, during the interwar and early postwar period; one politically and economically influential planter and his sister in Delta County—descended from a Civil War general and antebellum political leaders—were proud that both they and their father had been hostile to Woodrow Wilson, John Sharp Williams, and "their" League of Nations, had opposed United States membership in the Permanent Court of International Justice, had agreed with Senator Gerald P. Nye on the Neutrality Act, and had been unfavorable to Lend-Lease, the Marshall Plan, economic aid to Japan, and so on. But the impression derived from personal experience, analysis of newspapers operated by genteel paternalists, interviews, and examination of international responses of small survey samples who had been to college and who advanced traditional Southern racial attitudes [9] is that racial paternalists with relatively few exceptions were among the minority in America who were willing to see involvement by their federal government in the world affairs of their day.[10]

The genteel segregationist Montgomery (Alabama) *Advertiser* even

9 All college-educated whites who favored continued segregation, believed Negroes were constitutionally inferior, and so forth were not, of course, paternalists. However, this category included most paternalists.
10 With the notable exception of paternalists engaged in sugar production, who tended to be protectionists.

used as favorable adjectives "liberal" and "progressive" to describe the foreign posture of Senator Lister Hill, also an aristocrat (see, e.g., June 20, 1945, issue). The patrician paternalist newspaper par excellence, the Charleston *News and Courier*, supported United States entry into the League in 1919 and most of the major international commitments advocated by Presidents Roosevelt and Truman between 1936 and 1952, as did the popular Southern syndicated columnist, John Temple Graves, paternalist great-grandnephew of John C. Calhoun.

College-educated whites, included in small survey samples in the first postwar decade, who replied that Negroes were innately less intelligent than whites, who opposed President Truman's civil rights and fair employment practices proposals, repeal of poll taxes, and desegregation, who believed that Negroes were treated fairly in the South, and who were critical of Eleanor Roosevelt were favorably inclined to the major international commitments of this country. There was little difference between their views on these matters and those of the few racial equalitarians in the South. To at least as great a degree as Northerners of similar education, they felt that the United States should help to build a stronger U.N.,[11] that Congress should support the Marshall Plan,[12] that local schools should teach "the facts about all forms of government, including fascism, communism, and socialism," [13] that Universal Military Training was a good idea,[14] and that Senator Joseph McCarthy was exerting an undesirable influence at home and/or abroad.[15]

Moreover, although most paternalists of privileged backgrounds were political and economic conservatives, they were for the most part tolerant of others expressing views diverging from their own and those prevailing in their communities. Internationally thoughtful interviewees of this stratum recalled repeatedly the rather wide freedom for discussion—certainly for the South—among even the more conservative paternalists; liberal international, economic, and political ideas and even controversial thinking on race were expressed from time to time without apparent ostracism of those who advanced them.

Poor-White Racism

Significantly different from this condescending benevolence of the true patrician was the insecure, impulsive, even violent dislike for the Negro among economically and educationally deprived whites, especially in sections with many Negroes where these unsophisticated whites feared competition for unskilled and semiskilled jobs in a surplus labor

---

11 AIPO 376, 8/14/46 (3,000).   12 AIPO 439, 3/17/49 (2,193).
13 AIPO 510, 1/9/53 (1,558).   14 *Ibid.*
15 AIPO 532, 6/10/54 (1,435).

economy. The underprivileged white in plantation sections often found that planters preferred the more docile Negroes as tenants and that a number of Negroes were more prosperous than he. The poor white knew the disdain of the white upper and middle classes toward him (Negroes did not think much of him either), and he found a scapegoat, someone to whom he could feel superior, in the Negro. Many overseers, having come from simple backgrounds, likewise manifested these prejudices to a marked degree. Although "rednecks" from the hills were on the average less worried about Negro competition, few of them had much love for the black race, and whites from the mountains showed considerable racial antagonism in the relatively few cases when Negroes were actually in competition with them. Working-class urbanites who came from these deprived rural environments did not shed these prejudices, as has been patently evident in New Southtown, Birmingham, and Jackson.

There have always been some Southern whites of limited education and lowly station who treated Negroes with kindness and even justice; they were, however, concentrated primarily outside the areas with large numbers of Negroes. Thus, only 9 percent of Southern whites who had not completed high school felt in 1946 that Negroes were treated unfairly as compared with 23 percent of better-educated whites who felt so.[16] Whereas 34 percent of better-educated whites said at that time that Negroes were on the average as intelligent as white people and could perform as well if given equal opportunities, only 14 percent of the poorly educated whites agreed.[17] In 1946 one out of three more-privileged whites replied that Negroes should have as good a chance as whites to get any kind of job, but only one out of eight underprivileged whites thought so.[18] Fourteen percent of the former, compared with only 5 percent of the latter, approved in 1953 of the idea of a Fair Employment Practices Act requiring hiring without regard to race, color, or creed.[19] One out of six better-educated white Southerners approved of President Truman's civil rights proposals in 1948, but only one out of twenty little-educated, economically deprived whites did.[20] Approval of the Ku Klux Klan and other violently anti-Negro groups was concentrated among these underprivileged groups and their leaders.[21] Moreover, these samples included mountain whites, upper South whites, southern Floridians, and Louisiana Catholics whose racial views were, on the whole, less extreme. It is apparent that the small degree of

16 NORC 241, May, 1946 (2,589).   17 *Ibid.*
18 *Ibid.*   19 AIPO 510, 1/9/53 (1,558).
20 AIPO 414, 3/3/48 (3,041), and AIPO 433, 11/24/48 (3,061).
21 AIPO 376, 8/14/46 (3,000).

equalitarianism and the few even kindly feelings toward the Negro in the heavily Negro sections were limited with relatively few exceptions to a minority among the better-educated, privileged classes.

It was observed previously (see p. 378) that most of the few Southern Democratic isolationist Congressmen were arch-racists who were liberal on domestic economics. Several others, like Senator "Cotton Ed" Smith of South Carolina, were racists who made deals with the affluent classes and voted in Congress against the economic interests of the poor who had elected them.[22] Their racism and homespun nativism more than counterbalanced their economic conservatism in securing votes from the racist dispossessed. When a political leader of the underprivileged who supported active international collaboration in a wide range of fields in addition to foreign trade emerged, he was likely to come from the mountains, the border states, or at least the hills where there were relatively few Negroes, or from the few cities where racial antagonisms were more moderate. The few thoughtful internationalists who received the enthusiastic support of the economically and culturally deprived whites were relative liberals on economics and moderates or, more typically, silent on race, like Hugo Black, John Sparkman, Hale Boggs, and Claude Pepper.[23]

The Ku Klux Klan was openly hostile to immigration, "hyphenated" Americans, foreigners, the Vatican, "internationalist Jews," United States entry in the World Court, and the League of Nations.[24] Of those poorly educated and economically deprived whites who disapproved of President Truman's civil rights proposals shortly after the Dixiecrats had waged a political campaign against them in 1948, approximately half did not know of the civil war in China which had been going on for several years and was about to result in the retreat of the Nationalists to Formosa.[25] In a sample taken shortly before this poll, one third of Southern whites of low income and less than high-school education who favored the poll tax (which effectively stripped many of them of the vote at the same time it helped disfranchise many Negroes) had never heard of any fighting in Palestine, which had been in the headlines and on radio newscasts month after month.[26] Among a small survey sample of poorly educated whites who voted for the

22   Cash, *The Mind of the South*, 249–56.
23   For a discussion of correlations between racism and isolationism among Southern Congressmen of this period, see Seabury, "The Waning of Southern 'Internationalism,' " 11–13.
24   E.g., Grassmuck, *Sectional Biases in Congress on Foreign Policy*, 75; Fleming, *The Treaty Veto of the American Senate*, 188; and James Graham Cook, *The Segregationists* (New York: Appleton, Century, Crofts, 1962), 123.
25   AIPO 433, 11/24/48 (3,061).   26   AIPO 414, 3/3/48 (3,041).

racist Dixiecrats in 1948—mostly inhabitants of heavily Negro sections —three quarters had never heard by early 1949 of any dispute between the U.S.S.R. and Yugoslavia; [27] similar proportions knew nothing of major meetings among foreign ministers of the Western Big Three and the U.S.S.R.; [28] in mid-1951 two thirds or more could not identify Dean Acheson, Clement Atlee, Warren Austin, Chiang Kai-shek, George C. Marshall, or Tito; and none out of this small sample of twenty-one could identify as many as half of them.[29] Over half of a small sample of Southern voters for Strom Thurmond and Fielding Wright in 1948 who were among the lower educational and economic groups could not name their Congressman, although in most cases he had served for several terms. When they were asked how much interest they took in the coming elections or primaries in the fall of 1954, three fourths replied little or none.[30]

These were small samples, but the rather consistent findings of different polls by independent survey agencies tend to indicate that their results were probably fairly valid. As has been the case among other Americans as poorly informed and as indifferent about foreign policy as these, most Southern underprivileged racists had few real attitudes about most complex issues of international politics, even those which had been in the headlines year after year. Lacking information, concern, and critical facilities, they expressed views which were frequently inconsistent, rather illogical, and based on personal leanings and personalized projections of their local experience to the international sphere. Many of them failed to give answers to interviewers' questions on world affairs or said they had no opinion, did not know, or had not thought about the issue. The more specific or theoretical the attitude requested, the higher the percentage who failed to venture opinions. But one did not need to pose very detailed or abstract queries about foreign affairs to elicit blank replies; questions about Lend-Lease, the Truman Doctrine, the Marshall Plan, the reciprocal Trade Agreements Act, the Berlin Blockade, Point Four, and so on drew many blanks during periods when these issues were current. Most of these citizens probably did not have opinions on these questions, but only rather vague proclivities which, when stimulated by the questioner, produced a simplistic reply of yes or no, agree or disagree, or, more likely, a blank.

It is possible to generalize from those in small samples of November, 1948–November, 1952, who said they had voted for the Dixiecrats

27 NORC 163, 1/26/49 (1,261).
28 NORC 166, 6/1/49 (1,300), and NORC 282, 6/14/50 (1,276).
29 NORC 303, 6/29/51 (1,300).   30 AIPO 537, 9/14/54 (1,465).

or expressed patently racist attitudes and who had not completed high school that poor-white racists were among the most antiforeign citizens of the United States, the most hostile to immigration and international exchanges of persons (when informed of such programs), the most unenthusiastic about capital assistance to neutralists, and the most inclined to view international relations primarily in terms of war and peace, military policy, and violence or the threat of it. They were less apt to oppose peacetime conscription, the shifting of national resources to defense programs, and, to a lesser extent, military alliance with Western Europe. However, even on these latter questions they were very likely to be poorly informed and more inclined than most Americans (other than Southern Negroes) to offer no opinions.

Other Whites

Although the great majority of whites in the South prior to 1954 agreed that Negroes are innately inferior to whites, that they were by and large treated fairly, and that desegregation would be a bad thing, there was in fact a range of intensity of racial feelings, attachments to traditional stereotypes about Negroes, and preoccupations with preserving white supremacy in addition to those already noted. In those areas where there were few Negroes, like the mountains and some border regions, most whites were relatively indifferent to them. An influential group, the growing middle class in cities and larger towns, tended also to be rather indifferent, for they were neither in competition with the Negro nor directly responsible for him. Except for perhaps a household servant or two, they had only rather impersonal contacts with Negroes.

The majority of these whites relatively indifferent to the race question supported the major international programs requested by Presidents Roosevelt and Truman, or at least did not oppose them. Subtraction of poor, little-educated whites, particularly racists, and Negroes from survey samples typically reduced sharply the proportions of Southerners giving isolationist opinions; differences between North and South virtually disappeared on matters of immigration, including Chinese exclusion, and on most other issues of the period toward which Southerners in general appeared less favorable to international cooperation.

Segregationists Under Pressure

Southern segregationists—the great majority of whites—became increasingly concerned about efforts to upset the "Southern way of life" after 1944, about the time of the Supreme Court decision outlawing the white primary. Black-belt whites were particularly upset by this apparent effort to give the vote to Negro majorities in their counties. World War II, in exposing young Negroes and whites to more equalitarian systems, tended to undermine the "peculiar institution." Southerners read increasingly critical comments on Southern race relations in national magazines like *Time, Life,* and *Look.* President Truman's appointment of a commission to examine and report on civil rights, the report of this commission in October, 1947, his request to Congress that the proposals of the report be enacted into law, and the insertion of a civil rights plank into the 1948 platform of the Democratic party stimulated a veritable furor in Southern locales of plantation tradition and reinforced support for the Dixiecrat revolt initiated earlier by Governor Fielding Wright of Mississippi in his inaugural address. Then, during the Korean War, the armed forces were integrated, despite opposing Deep Southern white sentiment. The ruling in the early 1950's of the Interstate Commerce Commission against segregated transportation further upset Southern segregationists. Meanwhile, they became increasingly aware of growing protest, particularly among younger, educated Negroes and supported by white liberals, a number of national organizations, and the federal authorities.

The Shock of 1954 and After

All these developments were widely resented. Large majorities of Southern whites, according to surveys, had opposed each effort to change their racial mores.[31] For instance, only between 18 and 20 percent approved the Interstate Commerce Commission's ruling on segregated transportation, a percentage that had not increased substantially by 1961.[32]

But none of these measures approached the decision of May 17, 1954, outlawing "separate but equal" education, plus the "with all deliberate speed" decision, implementing it the following year, in stirring the most profound Southern fears of social equality, direct competition, mixing of the sexes, sexual intercourse between Negro boys and white girls, and intermarriage. Even when southern Floridians, mountaineers, Southerners in the upper South, and urbanites and other whites who were less adamant about segregation were included, only 15 percent

31 NORC 241, May, 1946 (2,589); AIPO 376, 8/14/46 (3,000); and AIPO 510 1/9/53 (1,558).
32 AIPO 577, 12/6/55 (1,496); AIPO Release of February 27, 1956; and AIPO 646, 5/26/61 (3,522).

approved of this decision, and the percentage remained virtually unchanged into the early 1960's.[33] Only one white out of two hundred approved of interracial marriage,[34] and most of the great majority of Southerners opposed to the decision feared that miscegenation would eventually result.

Irritation at this "intrusion" into what they felt were their private affairs continued to grow after the 1954 decision. Of the fifty-three newspapers sampled, four more or less accepted the decision in the summer of 1954, another seven took no position but noted that the desegregation process, if implemented, would entail traumatic experiences for the South, and the rest openly opposed it. A number of educated Southerners of the author's acquaintance, even in the heavily Negro sections, noted to family and friends that they felt it could be "lived with" or the equivalent. Many others did not believe it would actually be carried out, as most previous federal pronouncements were not. As late as immediately before the Little Rock affair, only 45 percent of all Southerners, including Negroes and mountain and border-state whites, thought "the day would ever come" when whites and Negroes in the region would be going to the same schools, eating in the same restaurants, and generally sharing the same public accommodations.[35]

The hostility of the racially conservative South, as revealed by press content and opinion surveys, continued to grow with each successive step of the federal courts and executive, of white equalitarians generally, and of militant Negroes to implement Negro franchise in rural and small-town sections of the Deep South and to desegregate schools, transportation, restaurants, and other facilities. By 1961 the proportion of the South, including Negroes, who felt these federal decisions would be enforced had risen to 76 percent, although still only 15 percent of Southern whites favored desegregation.[36] In 1959 only 6 percent of whites in the Deep South felt that the decision of 1954 had not been "a lot more trouble than it was worth."[37] Only 4 percent of Deep Southern whites approved of the freedom ("friction") riders,[38] and nine out of ten replying felt that the sit-ins, the freedom rides, and other demonstrations for desegregation had hurt rather than helped the cause of the Negro in the South.[39] Increasing majorities of whites

33 AIPO 532, 6/10/54 (1,435); AIPO Releases of February 27, 1956, December 1, 1957, and August 31, 1958; AIPO 614, 5/27/59 (1,537); and AIPO 646, 5/26/61 (3,522).
34 AIPO 605, 9/22/58 (1,665).   35 AIPO Release of 6/22/57.
36 AIPO 640, 1/10/61 (2,649).   37 AIPO 614, 5/27/59 (1,537).
38 AIPO 646, 5/26/61 (3,522).   39 AIPO 640, 1/10/61 (2,649).

expressed the view that relations between the races were getting worse and would continue to worsen if pressures for integration continued.[40]

The growing realization that the "peculiar institution" probably could not be perpetuated coupled with the continuing belief that desegregation was wrong resulted in increasing hostility to the federal executive and courts and organizations and individuals who were pressing for racial change. An attitude of defiance, fanned by Citizens Councils and other strongly segregationist groups, developed among emotionally committed segregationists in sections with many Negroes. By 1961 many Southern newspapers, including a number of paternalist ones and others which had been relatively benevolent or indifferent before, and many of the interviewees for this study were speaking of the "Second Reconstruction," the "new war of Yankee aggression," the "crusade" of "radical agitators," "outside interference," "leftist mongrelizers," Washington "oppression" or "dictatorship," or the like. States' rights sympathies expanded and feelings of unjust persecution, paranoid suspicion of outsiders and liberals, insularity, and withdrawal from national and international affairs accelerated.

Whereas one could conduct a relatively relaxed conversation on many issues without mentioning race among educated Southerners before the decision, by the early sixties Deep Southern thought, discussion, and action had become preoccupied to a much greater extent with this issue, tending to lessen considerably attention to other problems not directly pertinent to it. Many in the former middle group which had been more moderate on race and favorable to international collaboration pulled back from their relatively exposed positions of tolerance of gradual social change in the South.[41] Silence or neutrality on race was no longer enough in the Deep South—one was expected to declare himself for the "Southern way of life." Only in areas of few Negroes and little plantation tradition, such as Lexington, Kentucky, could newspapers and individuals remain as silent about, or as unconcerned with, race relations as they had managed to be before.

Advent of the Racist Syndrome of International Thought

Whereas in the past there had been only rather small differences in international ideology among white Southerners who thought differ-

40 In January, 1957, 46 percent felt relations between the races would get worse, 33 percent that they would get better. In June, 1961, the respective figures were 65 percent and 21 percent (AIPO Release of June, 1961).

41 For a discussion of the withdrawal after 1954 of many moderates from support of racial change in New Orleans, see Daniel C. Thompson, *The Negro Leadership Class* (Englewood Cliffs, N.J.: Prentice-Hall, 1963), 161.

ently about the Negro—poor-white and "redneck" racists excepted—as early as 1956 more adamant segregationists were adopting a number of interrelated international attitudes, which for purpose of this study will be entitled the racist syndrome. Similarly, racially conservative newspapers which had tended to agree in principle with more racially moderate or liberal ones on international issues of the earlier periods were diverging more and more from them on world affairs, also toward this syndrome.

Thus, when Southern whites who believed in 1956 that Negroes were treated fairly in this country were separated from those who felt they were treated unfairly, differences were apparent concerning even aspects of foreign policies which had traditionally been accorded wide support in the South. Eighty-two percent of those who felt Negroes were treated unfairly would continue aid to our military allies as compared with 74 percent of those who felt they were treated fairly. The former were also approximately a fourth more likely than the latter to feel that close collaboration with England in world affairs was important and that the objectives of the two peoples were similar, even though the British government was then a Tory one.[42]

The differences between the two groups were wider for questions directly related to communism. Sixty percent of those who felt Negroes were fairly treated thought there would be a thermonuclear war with the Reds, but only 41 percent of those who felt they were treated unfairly thought so. Sixty percent of the first group as compared with 74 percent of the second supported the idea of reduction of United States armaments if an agreement with the Soviet bloc on inspection and controls could be negotiated; 31 percent of the former as compared with 45 percent of the latter would have liberalized our embargo on trade with Communist China. By 1956, 59 percent of those agreeing that Negroes were treated unfairly versus 77 percent of those with the opposite view replied that "it is more important to find all domestic Communists" than to protect "innocent" citizens from harassment.[43]

Although none of the new African states had yet achieved its independence, entered the U.N., declared itself neutralist, or requested American aid, the substantial difference between the racial conservatives on the one hand and the white moderates and liberals on the other with respect to the colored (but non-Negroid), newly independent, under-developed neutralist states then on the world scene was a precursor of the future. Thirty-two percent who believed that Negroes were treated fairly in contrast to 46 percent who thought they were treated unfairly

42 NORC 382, 1/26/56 (1,238).   43 *Ibid.*

said we should try harder to win the friendship of "countries like India, Burma, and Egypt" who had declined to ally themselves with the West against the Communists; 43 percent of the former versus 60 percent of the latter said we should send them economic aid; and 19 percent versus 31 percent would put some economic aid to such countries on a long-term rather than a year-to-year basis.[44]

Two other surveys in 1956 indicated similar differences on these and other issues between white school segregationists and the 15 percent who favored desegregation. There were some differences even with respect to military alliances—91 percent of the integrationists as compared with 79 percent of the segregationists favored NATO; 93 percent of the former versus 86 percent of the latter supported aiding allies "who have agreed to stand with us against Communism." Segregationists were already, before the entry in force of the Africans into the U.N., 50 percent more inclined than the integrationists to feel we should terminate our membership in that organization. As with the question about fairness of treatment of Negroes in the South, segregationists were less apt to approve of possible inspection for arms control —56 percent of the segregationists as compared with 77 percent of integrationists approved of President Eisenhower's then current proposal for arms control with mutual aerial inspection. An ominous statistic for the future was the large difference in support for economic aid to neutralist underdeveloped (and largely colored) countries—63 percent of the small sample of white desegregationists favored such assistance, but only 29 percent of segregationists did.[45]

When the ultimate test of racist ideology was posed in 1956, "In general, do you think Negroes are as intelligent as white people—that is, can they learn just as well if they are given the same education," the differences in replies were at least as large on this or comparable questions, and in some cases larger.[46] The pattern was clear: although only a minority of white supremacists could be termed isolationists by 1956, the proportion who were of this orientation was roughly 50 percent larger than among racial equalitarians. The differences in international thinking between the two groups were relatively small for participation in military alliances, particularly with Western Europe, larger for negotiations and possible compromises with the Communists, but still larger for foreign economic aid and other collaboration with unaligned,

44 *Ibid.*
45 NORC 386, 4/20/56 (1,224), and NORC 390, 6/26/56 (1,275).
46 NORC 382, 1/26/56 (1,238); NORC 386, 4/20/56 (1,224); and NORC 390, 6/26/56 (1,275).

underdeveloped, non-Western colored countries recently under colonial control. On the other hand, relatively inexpensive technical assistance to such regimes was still favored by more racists than not.

Since the same questions about world affairs and race have not been posed to comparable samples after 1956,[47] completely comparative figures cannot be presented for later periods in the evolution of racial tension in the South and independence of African states. However, several surveys between 1956 and 1961 tended to indicate increasing divergencies on world affairs in the same directions between the strong segregationists on the one hand and the moderates and, especially, the liberals on the other.[48] For instance, whereas in late 1960, 61 percent of Southern and border-state whites who "disagreed strongly" with the view that "the government in Washington should stay out of the question of whether white and colored children go to the same school" felt that "the United States should give economic help to the poorer countries of the world even if those countries can't pay for it," only 48 percent of whites who "agreed strongly" with the former view were of like opinion about economic aid to underdeveloped lands.[49] Of whites in the Deep South who replied to a poll in early 1961 that the day would never come in the South when whites and Negroes would go to the same schools and use the same buses, restaurants, and other facilities, three out of five venturing replies opposed the idea of summit meetings between President Kennedy and Premier Khrushchev with or without other national leaders, less than half had favorable views of the Peace Corps, and two out of three disagreed with the idea of building a strong enough U.N. emergency force to deal with small wars throughout the world. A majority of Southerners who believed that further desegregation was likely held the opposite opinions on these international matters.[50]

Later in 1961 a national survey determined that Southern whites who replied that federal aid to education should not discriminate between

47 The last NORC surveys of United States opinions on world affairs under contract with the Department of State were completed in the spring of 1957.
48 AIPO 563, 4/17/56 (1,975); AIPO 590, 10/8/57 (1,573); AIPO 604, 9/8/58 (1,522); AIPO 605, 9/22/58 (1,665); AIPO 614, 5/27/59 (1,537); SRC 440, October–November, 1960 (1954); AIPO 640, 1/10/61 (2,649); AIPO 642, 3/8/61 (3,511); and AIPO 646, 5/26/61 (3,522).
49 SRC 440, October–November, 1960 (1,954). This Southern sample included Maryland, Delaware, the District of Columbia, and Kentucky, as well as the former Confederate States. Differences in opinion on economic aid were very probably larger between conservatives and liberals on race relations in the Deep South alone.
50 AIPO 640, 1/10/61 (2,649).

segregated and integrated schools were almost twice as apt to predict another world war in five years and about a third more inclined to oppose admission of Communist China to the U.N. under any probable circumstances as were the small minority who felt that aid should favor schools which had taken some steps toward at least token desegregation.[51] When a survey examined in mid-1961 those Southern whites who opposed the Supreme Court decision of 1954 and the Interstate Commerce Commission ruling which outlawed segregated trains, buses, and waiting rooms, who replied that desegregation should never be brought about, who felt that the situation in the South between the races would become worse, who disapproved of what the sit-ins and freedom riders had done, and who felt that President Kennedy had been wrong in sending United States marshals into Montgomery, it was discovered that three out of five agreeing with all these racially conservative views were willing to make further sacrifices, including even increased individual federal taxes, for stronger armed forces for the United States. But only one out of five was willing to make sacrifices for expanded foreign economic aid.[52]

Thus, even in 1961 a minority of white supremacists continued to favor economic aid and other collaboration with underdeveloped countries which refused to align themselves with the West against the Communists and other international cooperation beyond Western Europe. Large numbers, as in the past—being poorly educated, culturally deprived, and absorbed with race relations and other local concerns—ventured few opinions on world affairs.

Nevertheless, most articulate racists who were influential in or active in Citizens Councils, Defenders of State Sovereignty and Civil Liberties, States' Rights Councils, North Carolina Patriots, State Sovereignty Commissions, and like groups and who ventured views on world problems tended to agree in a general way with one another about what was happening in the world, what was wrong with American foreign policy, and what we should do in foreign affairs. Their thinking was repeated in interviews, in their meetings and publications, and in the eleven most racially conservative papers of the fifty-three sampled.

The syndrome approximated the following: If we continue our recent policies, a major war with the Communists is likely, and it will probably be a nuclear one. Since military power and willingness to use it are all the Reds and their fellow travelers among the so-called neutralists really respect, adequate military preparedness is essential, even if it should cost more money than currently. However, some of the

51 AIPO 642, 3/8/61 (3,511).   52 AIPO 646, 5/26/61 (3,522).

"fat" in the armed forces could be reduced and much of the resources devoted to foreign economic aid could be used for improved defense without raising taxes. Prosperous arch-segregationists also tended to feel that some of the domestic spending in the welfare field could be reduced and used for either national security purposes, lowering the national debt, or cutting taxes.

Strongly "anti-Communist," influential adamant segregationists felt that it was naïve to think that we could accomplish much by negotiation and compromise with the Communists. It seems absurd to combine emphasis on military preparedness and disarmament talk. The probability of our opponents agreeing to reasonable inspection is virtually nil, and continued endless and fruitless negotiations result in delays in our own preparedness and in misleading the public into believing that arms control is likely. Nor should we bow to demands for summit conferences and tolerate rudeness to our leaders when we know our opponents are not really interested in sensible negotiations and are only after propaganda. Although only a minority of Deep Southerners would launch a preventive war since the Communists have large numbers of nuclear weapons, almost all of them who felt such a war was an alternative worthy of serious consideration were very conservative on race. The Communists seemed to be winning under our current policies, and it is time we stood up to them in Asia, Africa, and particularly Cuba and Latin America. Most strong racists were not impressed much by arguments in favor of keeping wars limited—when you get into a fight you fight to win, as General MacArthur had advocated. They believed that faced with such determination the Communists would probably desist from their aggressions and the so-called neutralists would respect us as a nation with the courage of its convictions. If the Reds were to react to more aggressive United States policies with World War III, then it would be better to get it over with rather than letting them choose the moment when we are weakest.

Deep Southern whites who approved of policies amounting to "Fortress America" or isolationism were a minority, but they were primarily white supremacists. They tended to think that our allies, other than the Canadians, probably would capitulate "when the chips are down." A larger number of racists, however, believed more or less in NATO and that West European countries constituted our real allies with whom we have much in common. Many were irritated that the other NATO powers did not devote more of their energies, manpower, and resources to our collective defense—they felt we were bearing an unjust share of the military load. However, only the isolationist minority would withdraw or seriously reduce our forces in Europe. More racists than not would channel more of our major foreign policies through our European allies rather than through the U.N. which had supposedly become controlled by a hostile Communist-socialist-leftist-neutralist-anti-United States coalition.

Racist support of the U.N. had apparently fallen with the pronouncements and activities of the Human Rights Commission, UNESCO, the General Assembly, and other organs in fields related to race and with the entry of so many non-Western new states, particularly those of Africa south of the Sahara. Most Deep Southern whites who would withdraw from the U.N. were very conservative on race, but the majority of strong segregationists would continue our membership. The number who would advocate withdrawal if Communist China were to become a member was considerably larger, depending on the details of her possible entry. The U.N. had no business meddling in internal affairs of its members—as in the Republic of South Africa and Angola—and we were wrong to support these infringements on sovereignty which might one day be practiced against us. There was considerable concern among those who had heard of the International Court of Justice that it would meddle in our domestic affairs as well, particularly if it should acquire an anti-Western majority.

These racists also thought that we should give more support to European governments in their differences with the anticolonial leaders in Africa and Asia, with whom we have few real mutual interests. We were mistaken in encouraging the *métropoles* to capitulate to anticolonialist movements, starting with Ghandi in India. The European powers have shown little courage before native demagogues and naïve criticisms by liberals in standing up for their programs of gradual development and education of these backward societies. Colonialism has brought these peoples into touch with civilization and whatever economic development, education, medical services, and other modern conveniences they have. They would still be savages in Africa but for the British, French, Belgians, and Portuguese. Many of them are not very far removed from cannibalism now, and we can expect chaos, demagoguery, irresponsible leftist nonsense, expropriation of private property, and Communist penetration of these immature, emotional societies with the removal of civilized guidance. In fact, many of the independence movements have been Communist fronts, and when they did not begin that way their leaders soon made deals with our enemies. These states have been at best opportunistically playing both ends against the middle in an effort to extort from the West and Reds alike whatever aid they can secure. Interviewees who sided with the South African govern-ment against the Bantu, with the Portuguese against the Angolans, with *colons* in the Rhodesias against the African majority, with the extremist Europeans in Algeria against the Algerian Moslems, and with Presi-dent Tshombe of Katanga against the Leopoldville government were almost without exception white supremacists.

Strong segregationists tended to feel we should give firmer support to conservative regimes throughout the underdeveloped world—we made mistakes in backing Castro against Batista and the anti-Trujillo elements against the Benefactor, and we should have accorded Chiang Kai-shek more assistance against the Communists in the 1940's. Because of its level-headed government controlled by conservative white men, the Republic of South Africa is our only real friend on that continent. Our policies have been too altruistic and idealistic toward backward societies, and their masses of illiterates are most likely to avoid disorder, rape, and other excesses under balanced conservative leaders. We have paid too much attention to so-called world opinion, that is, the supposed views of these unsophisticated, emotional populations who have not really cared much about anything beyond their immediate environment.

More racists disapproved of capital assistance than less expensive technical assistance, but a large minority felt that neither had been effective. These underdeveloped countries do not count for much in the struggle with communism anyway. As one gentleman remarked, "Let the Russians take over Africa if the Africans are stupid enough to bring them in and sell out to them. Once the Soviets have 150,000,000 'niggers' that will be the end of the U.S.S.R." Most of these regimes are corrupt or otherwise unlikely to use aid intelligently. Even if they did, their countries would have no more in common with us than before; we cannot buy friends. In many cases we are only building up future enemies and allies of the Communists. Charity will make these peoples more shiftless; the more you give them the more they will demand. If they got down to work and organized responsible governments, they could do a great deal for themselves and private capital would become available both from here and from other developed countries. Many of them would shift to our side if we gained their respect by refusing to appease both the Communists and their own demagogues.

Most white supremacists would reduce immigration from its current levels and would accept fewer refugees from Eastern Europe (many are probably spies, or at least leftist agitators). They were unimpressed about the desirability of intercultural exchanges at our expense and were particularly opposed to such programs with Communist countries.

They tended to think that there are too many foreign-born (and other) leftists, "fellow travelers," and Communists here now. They feared that our Department of State, Agency for International Development (A.I.D.), Peace Corps, and other policy-making and implementing agencies in the field of foreign affairs were already too much influenced by leftists, naïve idealists, and the like. They had little faith in most of our diplomatic personnel's "hardheadedness" in dealing with foreign powers. Deep Southern whites who believed that Communists had penetrated in significant numbers the major governmental and private institutions of our country were almost invariably strongly opposed to desegregation, as were active members of arch-conservative groups like the John Birch Society, the Charleston Alert, and the Christian Anti-Communist Crusade which emphasized the danger of domestic communism.

Upper-Class White Supremacists

According to interviews in 1959–62 and impressions from other experiences with this group, a considerable fraction of former paternalists —apparently a majority in some traditionalist settings—have developed more uncompromising opposition to racial change as the quickening tempo of desegregation or the threat of it seemed to menace their secure, traditionally related, genteel, hierarchical system. They, too, have believed that they know the Negro from direct experience, that he does not want these changes and abstractions which the "outside agitators" have put into his head to the detriment of polite relations between white and black.

Some of these Southerners of genteel ancestry, such as Judge Tom Brady of Mississippi, have become leaders in Citizens Councils, State Sovereignty Commissions, and other groups designed to prevent racial change. Others have supported these organizations as pressures for racial equality accelerated. Still others have agreed with the objectives of these groups, but have resisted participating in sections where the leadership and active membership have been made up largely of "uncouth" people from the lower orders.

Most patricians who opposed desegregation to this extent seemed by the early 1960's to have shifted along with other arch-segregationists toward neo-isolationism or unilateralism. Some had even "soured" on collaboration with Western Europe, but more of them than not would have us maintain much of that cooperation while sharply modifying our relations with underdeveloped countries. For example, paternalist columnist John Temple Graves and the Charleston *News and Courier*, both strongly segregationist, had shifted to the racist international syndrome by 1961, as had the Montgomery *Advertiser* to a lesser extent. By 1960 traditionalist "historical" groups like local chapters of the Daughters and Sons of the American Revolution, the Colonial Dames, and the Sons of 1812 were voicing neo-isolationist, if not isolationist, views. Most chapters of the United Daughters of the Confederacy (U.D.C.) and genealogical groups took few public positions on world affairs, but conversations with active members indicated that they usually subscribed to similar neo-isolationist interpretations of foreign questions. Far from all participants in such organizations were of paternalist heritage—the U.D.C. has been primarily a middle-class group—but members who were pro-U.N., pro-foreign aid, and critical of the international interpretations of the racist syndrome seemed to be relatively inactive in these tradition-directed bodies.

As with Southern whites generally, the traditional upper class appeared most inclined in Southern areas of high Negro concentration and antebellum heritage to adopt intransigent racial orientations. And it was in such locales that interviewees among "old families" were most apt in the early sixties to manifest the racist syndrome of international opinions. Thus, perhaps as many as three fourths of the genteel gentry of Charleston who had opinions on these matters agreed with more of these racist international views than not—with interpretations expressed in detail by the two Charleston newspapers which were owned and run by members of old Charleston families. The international attitudes of the Rivertown elite were roughly comparable—it was likewise antebellum traditionalist, economically static, and highly ingrown. A smaller fraction, perhaps three fifths, felt this way among the genteel of Kent, a traditionalist town but one with only a third Negroes and significant piedmont influences nearby. A similar proportion of patricians of Antebellum Town seemed to agree with those views on international affairs—over half its population was Negro and its history had been intimately involved with plantations, but the influx of complex industry with attendant trade unions and "outsiders" had exerted some impact. The proportion of New Orleanians of this background accepting these racial and international postures would be smaller still—probably less than a third—since its multiethnic population, active port, and the Roman Catholic religion of many of its old families had much moderated racial "standpatism."

However, upper-class white supremacists of Charleston, Rivertown, Kent, Antebellum Town, and other old societies were more inclined than most other racists to advance relatively informed international opinions, to ramify, limit, and render more complex the syndrome of views associated with racism. The difference between their thinking on world issues and that of racists of "newer" origins could be observed in the international content of the Charleston *News and Courier*, the Montgomery *Advertiser*, and the Richmond *News Leader* as compared with that of the Jackson *Clarion-Ledger* and the Shreveport *Journal*. The former three, especially the *News and Courier*, contained relatively detailed coverage of international news. The latter two were among the lowest of the fifty-three Southern newspapers sampled with respect to adequacy of coverage of international developments. The *News and Courier* has cited Plato, Burke, and other philosophers of elitism, has frequently commented on views expressed in sophisticated periodicals —including liberal ones such as the *New Republic*, *The Reporter*, *Harper's*, *Atlantic*, the New York *Times*, and even *The Economist*, the Manchester *Guardian*, and *Foreign Affairs*—and published almost daily, sometimes erudite editorials on international developments, most of them sophisticated versions of the racially conservative syndrome. The Jackson and Shreveport papers, on the other hand, contained relatively little interpretation of foreign policy matters, and what did appear was often unsophisticated and even ignorant. The genteel segregationist papers seemed to feel that world affairs were important, that liberal internationalists should be attacked with some erudition, and that intellectual attainment, at least in the classical tradition, was desirable. The nativist papers displayed little respect for intellectuality, aristocratic refinements, and serious debate. Thus, the most sophisticated, dignified racists were from privileged backgrounds, and they were the most likely to manifest rather informed ideas within the racist syndrome about foreign policy.

The Racist Cosmopolitan

From conversations in the communities examined for this study, it was evident that a minority of the paternalist group in the early sixties were also among the small proportion of white supremacists who favored most of the general objectives and policies of our government abroad. They seemed in most cases individuals of atypical intellectual alertness who read critical national and, in some cases, international publications. Some had had extensive experience abroad or had engaged in careers closely related to foreign developments. Seldom did they have major economic interests likely to be adversely affected by more liberal trade. Traditions of internationalism in their families, who had long been engaged in cotton, tobacco, or other enterprises associated with international involvement, were often still strong in their thinking. Some women of traditional racial inclinations had been significantly influenced by the liberal international ideas expressed in church groups in which they were active. Moreover, few of these cosmopolitan paternalists seemed to accept the more extreme white supremacy arguments, although a number of them did feel that Negroes are intellectually and morally inferior and that desegregation would destroy some of the best values of the South.

Thus, one segregationist cosmopolitan Episcopal minister who considered himself a Wilsonian read several sophisticated foreign newspapers in three languages regularly, as well as the New York *Times* (Sunday edition), the *Sewanee Review,* and other serious publications. Another internationally thoughtful Episcopal minister, reader of *Harper's* and *The Economist,* had lived abroad for several years prior to attending seminary. A Tidewater traditionalist gentleman, husband of a European noblewoman, read on a regular basis *Foreign Affairs* and other internationally sophisticated literature and was highly critical of the generally low intellectuality of even his First Family of Virginia social peers. A fourth person who consumed books and several magazines of high quality, plus the New York *Times* (Sunday edition), was the great-great-great-grandnephew of a famous Revolutionary War general and descendant of other prominent antebellum families. An elderly lady of cosmopolitan and elitist segregationist persuasion talked about T. S. Eliot, Arnold Toynbee, William Faulkner, Allen Tate, and "The News of the Week in Review" of the New York *Times.* Two others had retired from careers in the Foreign Service and still another had gone to West Point, attained the rank of general, and retired to his acres in the Black Belt. An upper-class Presbyterian minister, trained in Scotland, fitted this cosmopolitan segregationist description, as did a gentleman closely connected with international trade and an erudite, elderly, strongly segregationist lawyer, both of respected old families in New Orleans.

However, paternalist racial assumptions almost invariably had exerted some influence on the international thinking of even the most sophisticated among those who felt that Negroes are inferior and that desegregation is very unfortunate. Elitist views usually showed through on one international issue or another. Their support of aid to Africa tended to have kindly paternalist overtones of *noblesse oblige* charity to the unfortunate in contradistinction to economic assistance for basic development. There were hardly any optimistic abstractions about the "brotherhood of man," "revolution of rising expectations," desire of the masses for "democracy" and "freedom," though these cosmopolitans had read such expressions in the *Atlantic*, Sunday New York *Times*, or the like. They tended to smile at such concepts, as liberal clichés little related to reality; "those Yankee intellectuals sound like they never took a hard look at the illiterate folk in India or the Congo from the ideas these idealists think they have in their illiterate heads."

But interviewees of this persuasion and social status in most cases supported the traditional free-trade ideology of their ancestors and often tended to think of protectionists as greedy businessmen comparable to the Northern protectionist "money grubbers" of the past. Their knowledge about world events had made substantial modifications in the racist syndrome, and they rejected large parts of it entirely. Several favored repeal of the Connally Amendment and wider powers for the International Court of Justice. A few would bring Communist China into the U.N. and recognize it diplomatically, and more favored expanded trade and other contacts if feasible with Communist China. They tended to agree that some economic assistance to the more efficiently run underdeveloped countries with relatively stable, honest governments (particularly India) should be continued, even expanded, but felt that we should be more discriminating in our choices and not submit to "blackmail." They usually supported technical assistance and international exchanges, even with the Soviets and the Africans, and the training of Africans in America (but not in Southern white colleges) at our expense.

The interviewers also encountered some racists from less privileged backgrounds who supported relatively liberal or multilateralist international programs, including foreign aid to underdeveloped countries at more or less the levels requested by our Presidents in 1959–62. As in the case of cosmopolitan segregationist patricians, potent forces had counterbalanced their racial inclinations, and none of them among the interviewees were really extreme segregationists. One trade-union representative was opposed to racial liberalism at his national headquarters, but advocated aid to Africa, recognition of Communist China, and other policies which he had obviously heard of at meetings of trade-union leaders. Racist whites of limited education employed on the New Orleans docks loading and unloading foreign ships, according to several interviews and reports, had in many cases been favorable to most international programs of the Kennedy administration of which they have known, including foreign aid. Missionary societies and other church groups have influenced some relatively unsophisticated strong segregationists to support economic assistance—even to Africa. However, according to surveys of the last few years,[53] the college educated among those who felt Negroes are constitutionally inferior and who accepted other racist ideas were by far the most likely to disagree with important parts of the racist syndrome of international attitudes.

Racial Liberals and Moderates

However, most of the white Southerners of the early sixties who supported the major international programs of our national executive, including economic assistance to such countries as Nigeria, Tunisia, India, and Brazil, were either liberals or moderates on race. Whereas there were some racist internationalists, there were very few isolationist integrationists—except for Negroes and some mountaineer Republicans.

White Integrationists View the World

There has long been a small liberal minority, even in the Deep South, who have regarded Negroes as biologically (though not culturally) equal to whites and who have worked for improvement of the black man's lot, including even gradual desegregation.[54] Such liberalism on the Negro in the Deep South has been the ultimate in nonconformity, and it has typically carried with it liberalism, by Southern standards, on most other issues as well. Thus, of the 6 percent of Deep Southern whites in 1961 who said they approved of the Supreme Court decision on school integration, of the freedom rides, and of the sit-ins, four out of five venturing opinions on foreign economic aid said they would be willing to make sacrifices, such as paying taxes, for that purpose.[55] Only one out of eleven among Deep Southern whites agreeing that federal assistance to schools should be withheld from those which failed to integrate believed there would be another world war in the next five years, and one out of three, well above the national average, favored acceptance of the credentials of Communist China for admission into the U.N.[56] In 1959, a small sample of fifty-one Southern whites approving of the school desegregation decision was almost twice as likely as the national average to feel that tariffs should be lower—only four out of fifty-one felt they should be higher.[57]

All eleven Southern newspapers in the sample for this study which

53 AIPO 614, 5/27/59 (1,537); AIPO 642, 3/8/61 (3,511); AIPO 646, 5/26/61 (3,522); and AIPO 682, 12/10/63 (1,330).
54 See, for instance, Ezell, *The South Since 1865*, Chapter 20; and Dykeman and Stokely, *Seeds of Southern Change*.
55 AIPO 646, 5/26/61 (3,522).   56 AIPO 642, 3/8/61 (3,511).
57 AIPO 614, 5/27/59 (1,537).

were least conservative on race in 1961—only two openly supported integration—were basically internationalist or multilateralist in their locally written editorials, that is, their editorials were generally similar in orientation (if not in quality) to those of the New York *Times* and *Christian Science Monitor*. Many of the better-educated desegregationists among the interviewees considered the local racial struggle as part of a worldwide conflict—"colonialism is ending everywhere." World developments had exerted some effect on their thinking about American Negroes. Without notable exceptions, active white participants in Urban Leagues, Southern Regional Council affiliates, Save Our Schools in New Orleans, and Help Our Public Education in Atlanta favored, in general, foreign economic and technical assistance at approximately the then current or higher levels, responsible efforts to strengthen international organization and multilateral cooperation, expanded world trade, continued negotiations with Communist powers, and other aspects of an active, multidimensional foreign policy. Conversely, wherever local groups devoted serious attention to world affairs—Committees on Foreign Relations, Leagues of Women Voters, chapters of the American Association of University Women and of the American Association for the United Nations, programs encouraged by the Foreign Policy Association, university extensions, and so on—considerable overlap in sympathy with progressive race relations was apparent.

However, discussions of world problems with white integrationists lead to the conclusion that many, perhaps most, of them have not given much attention to foreign affairs in recent years; whatever international opinions they had in 1959–62 were usually rather liberal ones, but only a minority of this small Deep Southern minority were really well informed about international developments. A number of them did not appear to be particularly intellectual. The relatively few poorly educated liberals and the more numerous rather naïve female humanitarians seemed favorable to the objectives of Negro desegregationists largely because of religious convictions, identification with the underdog, and compassion and a sense of justice rather than on account of analytical habits of mind. The responsible internationalist in the South as elsewhere in America, on the other hand, has almost invariably been well read on foreign affairs and rather systematic (for the South) in his thinking. However, the racial liberal's idealism, sympathy for people different from himself, and indifference to social prestige atypical of much of the Deep South have been associated with internationalist sympathies even among the poorly informed. For instance, one of the relatively rare religious fundamentalists who was a desegregationist among interviewees in the Deep South was a poorly educated minister of a sect composed primarily of simple folk; he knew little of world affairs and did not even read a newsmagazine. In explaining how he became so liberal, he said, "I've been reading the Bible so long 'til I finally came to believe what it said about all races and all nations." However, he agreed that Asians and Africans should be allowed to come to this country if they met the standards of ability and character required of European immigrants, that taxes should be increased if required for adequate (whatever that might imply) aid to underdeveloped countries, that the U.N. was a "hope of the world for peace," and that we ought to help educate promising Africans and Asians in this country at public expense. He said that he did not believe he had ever met a Communist in Mississippi and that the House Un-American Activities Committee ought to investigate "the most un-American of them all, the race baiters and Citizens Councils, including Ross Barnett and Jim Eastland."

Moreover, many better-educated desegregationists who would undoubtedly have devoted more attention to world affairs if they lived in the North appeared to have been so emotionally involved in the issue which they probably rightfully considered the basis of many other Southern problems that they have paid only spasmodic attention to foreign relations. They agreed that foreign questions are equally or even more important to the nation as a whole, but often pointed out that there have been so few capable people working at *the* Southern problem and that the difficulties have been so formidable that their talents must be concentrated there.

It is difficult for the Northerner, or even the Southerner outside the plantation belts and traditional smaller cities, to visualize the emotional strain of being even a relatively inactive racial liberal in these parts of the South. The distaste of the white supremacist in 1959–62 was more intense with regard to the native "scalawag" or "traitor to the South" than to the "Yankee mongrelizer." Social ostracism by their childhood friends, even by their parents and siblings, anonymous threats by the telephone, humiliation of their children by peers who learned from their own parents of the racial nonconformity of the parents of their school chums, and even economic reprisals have been frequent against the few outspoken desegregationists in heavily Negro Deep Southern areas. The emotional tension involved in keeping quiet except when the impact of nonconformity is likely to be worth the personal costs and the lessening of future effectiveness in one's community is not a milieu which stimulates systematic thinking about world affairs and encourages one to express "odd" ideas in that field. As a black-belt liberal in both world affairs and race commented, "People here suspect I am a 'nigger lover,' and I work behind the scenes some to thwart the racists. One of these days I'll probably conclude that it's worth losing whatever little local influence I have to speak out, but if I am run out of town I won't be around to do whatever I can when they try to integrate our school and the fat is really in the fire. You can't expect people like me to sound off for Fulbright's memorandum on 'muzzling the military' and against Thurmond and for aid to 'niggers' in Africa in a place like this. When I open my mouth, it has to be likely to help make something important happen which otherwise wouldn't."

The marked tendency of Deep Southern integrationists among survey samples and interviewees for this study to be liberal internationalists can in large measure be explained by the similarities in their personalities, values, and experience. Although apparently more cautious about rapid social change and somewhat less optimistic about "progress" and the effects of mass democracy than Northern liberals, for they are Southerners, too (see pp. 363–65), both internationalists and white desegregationists have been less authoritarian and less pessimistic about the human race and the possibility of individual, social, and political progress than most Southerners.[58] Both have been more inclined than other Southerners to accept the utility of some theories, abstractions, rational analyses, critical discussions, social science, and so on, although, again, they have tended to be more pragmatic, concrete, and gradualistic than most liberal Northerners.

Both white integrationists and internationalists in 1959–62 were quite likely to have come from rather socially (if not economically) secure families. Both ideologies have tended to develop most frequently in those who have enjoyed a measure of detachment from the sheer daily struggle for a living and from strivings for social acceptance. Southerners who have expressed nonconformist views on either subject have typically not been scared of anybody. Both racial and international liberals have tended to have known nonconformists and well-read adults in their families or among friends while they were youngsters, and both have been highly likely to have received well above average educations, typically including college. Both internationalism and racial nonconformity have been more prevalent among graduates of the more rather than the less stimulating colleges, among liberal arts rather than technical graduates, among those who made good grades in college

58 John McConaughy, "The Politicometrics of International Aggression" (MS in Department of Political Science, University of South Carolina, 1960).

rather than among those who were below average students, and among those who have continued to read serious books and periodicals after leaving school rather than among others who have not.[59]

Heterogeneous Thinking of Racial Moderates

The term "moderate" has been employed to mean different orientations to desegregation, depending on the local racial situation and other factors. Although only some 15 percent of white Southerners, and much smaller proportions of white Deep Southerners—especially in areas of plantation traditions—as late as 1961 approved of the desegregation decision of 1954,[60] the proportion of Southern whites who have responded to surveys to the effect that Negroes are on the whole as intelligent as whites if given the same opportunities rose from 30 percent in 1946[61] to 58 percent in 1956[62] (and undoubtedly higher by 1962). And those who felt that desegregation will come eventually have also expanded from a minority shortly after the decision to three quarters in 1961.[63]

Perhaps the broadest definition of moderates would encompass all those white Southerners in the early sixties who preferred segregation but believed desegregation would proceed regardless of Southern white opposition and who told pollsters they agreed with the view that Negroes, given wider opportunities in the future, could gradually approach white standards of morality, ability, and general sophistication. Survey data indicated that these were about two fifths of the total white population, and perhaps a quarter or so even in Deep Southern states. No one survey asked these three questions, but it is apparent from the results of such questions among rather small samples of such Southerners between 1956 and 1961 that these white Southerners were on the average less inclined to favor foreign economic assistance to underdeveloped, neutralist countries than were integrationist whites, but more apt to do so than those who felt Negroes are constitutionally inferior and that integration would not take place. Likewise, they seemed to be between the integrationists and the confirmed racists on arms control and other aspects of compromise and negotiation with the Soviet bloc.

59 From tabulations of reading habits and public attitudes in the Bureau of Applied Social Research study and interviews for this study with Southern subscribers to several serious magazines.
60 AIPO 646, 5/26/61 (3,522).   61 NORC 241, May, 1946 (2,589).
62 NORC 386, 4/20/56 (1,224).
63 AIPO Release of 6/22/57; AIPO 605, 9/22/58 (1,665); and AIPO 640, 1/10/61 (2,649).

But this definition of moderates seems too broad a one to be meaningful in practical terms. As late as mid-1963, a survey by Louis Harris and Associates determined that 61 percent of Southern whites felt that "Negroes want to live off the handout," 60 percent believed that "Negroes have less native intelligence" than whites, and 51 percent were of the view that "Negroes are inferior to whites." [64] Moreover, the interviewers' experiences with Deep Southern, particularly black-belt and traditionalist, whites causes one to be suspicious of the large fractions reported by surveys as agreeing that Negroes are innately of equal intelligence to whites. Many better-educated whites who comment in this fashion to an interviewer previously unknown to them probably feel subconsciously, at least, that Negroes really are innately on a lower level than whites. And many who really believed in 1959–62 that Negroes are biologically as capable as whites and that desegregation would come still opposed integration at the rate demanded by federal authorities and strongly resented sit-ins, freedom rides, and other efforts to bring about racial change. They felt that cultural differences between the two races, except for a small Negro educated class, were enormous and would not be sufficiently narrowed for a generation or more to permit the sorts of integration envisaged by these pressures. Their practical impacts on their communities and on their Congressmen were frequently similar to those of more extreme segregationists—they voted for racial conservatives who were normally also international conservatives in the sense of the racist international syndrome.

The author's inclination is to reserve the term "moderate" for only those among white Southerners who have felt that Negroes are probably about as able as whites to develop themselves if accorded equal opportunities over several generations; have accepted desegregation, usually with considerable reluctance, as probable in the long run; and have been willing to accept some change rather than witness increased racial strife, economic disruption, and other undesirable developments. They have deviated from one another in the changes they would accept, depending on local conditions and the attitudes of both races in their environs. However, they have all opposed violence and supported due process of law, including implementation of disliked civil rights court decisions. They have wished that these edicts were not the law, and they have felt that the federal courts, Negro militants, and white liberals were trying to push the process too fast. The racial liberalism of G.

64 Cited in William Brink and Louis Harris, *The Negro Revolution in America* (New York: Simon and Schuster, 1964), 141. Comparable nationwide figures, including the South, were 41, 39, and 31 percent, respectively. The white national sample exceeded 1,200.

Mennen Williams, Hubert Humphrey, Jacob Javits, and other "reformers" has struck them as too abstract, unrealistic, and brash. Many would agree with Gavin Stevens in Faulkner's *Intruder in the Dust* that "Sambo" should be defended,

from the North and East and West—the outlanders who will fling him decades back . . . into grief and agony and violence . . . by forcing on us laws based on the idea that man's injustice to man can be abolished overnight by police . . . the injustice is ours, the South's. We must expiate and abolish it ourselves, alone, and without help or even (with thanks) advice.[65]

Such moderates in the Deep South have been much more numerous than the minuscule minority who have welcomed racial change. The forces which have produced them, or influenced them, have been similar to those which have led to the development of integrationists and Southerners who are thoughtful about world affairs. It would appear from interviews for this study of a number of moderates that either these experiences did not impinge upon them as vigorously as on the desegregationists, or the moderates were more conservative or traditional from the beginning, or the local conditions were more unfavorable to change. But like integrationists and Southerners who have favored foreign aid to Africa and multilateral cooperation generally, moderates were likely to have come from relatively secure backgrounds, most of their parents were also apparently relatively well educated, and they have been more prevalent in areas with relatively few Negroes and less tenacious plantation heritages. Few of them seemed to have been irrational authoritarians, many interviewees of racially moderate inclinations could recall contacts as children with atypically thoughtful adults, many (though only a minority) attended esteemed colleges within or outside the South, and most of the rest had been to some college. A considerable fraction of paternalists had evolved to one version or another of the moderate stance toward desegregation; few moderates seemed to have ever really hated Negroes (in contradistinction to regarding them as lazy, immoral, and inferior) and probably most had stood for equal justice before the law much of their lives. Many with whom world affairs were discussed in 1959–62 read one or more national publications of the quality of *Harper's*, and most of the others had more than average Southern contact with ideas from outside their communities. Irritating to many Negro and white liberals, many moderates have nevertheless been rather thoughtful, realistic, and responsible conservatives.

For example, an aristocratic woman in her fifties living in Plantation

65 Faulkner, *Intruder in the Dust,* 131–32.

County, who believed that teachers and other well-educated Negroes should be allowed to vote, was a moderate in terms of that locale. She thought literacy tests should be made more rigorous and applied equally to black and white, and that Negroes who would "pass" such tests would vote for better candidates than the whites who did not. She was regarded as a "radical" by her peers who had not permitted any Negro in Plantation County to vote since Reconstruction. However, this woman was opposed to even token integration in the local schools, feeling that the great gap between Negro and white cultures would destroy the educational system and result in widespread violence by poor whites.

A woman of similar pedigree in Kent, where only a third of the population was Negro and where the better-educated Negroes already voted, was willing to go further. Although still emotionally uncomfortable about the prospect of integration and the drastic changes she feared it would entail for the genteel South she had known, she criticized the Daughters of the American Revolution and other traditionalist groups of which she was a formal (but inactive) member for racial "intransigence." The educated minority should think more responsibly than had been the case locally on this trying issue and take public action to limit the influence of the "peckerwoods" and their leaders. An elderly gentleman descended from Southern Louisiana old families noted that many Jews had been excluded from the better New Orleans hotels several generations ago, but that these restrictions against them had disappeared as they had become educated and refined. He believed the same situation would probably transpire someday with respect to Negroes, but he feared that the federal government and Northern "theorists" and "do-gooders" were pushing the process too fast; human beings and their institutions are complicated, and they do not change overnight.

A hundred moderates, largely of upper- and upper-middle-class backgrounds, published a statement in the New Orleans papers at the time of the violence there upon token integration of two schools in late 1960. The statement said that they preferred segregation but that every legal means to prevent integration had been tried and defeated, that closing of public schools was less preferable than token integration, and that the law should be obeyed. Most of them had been unwilling to speak out in favor of integration of the schools before the violence. A number of Southerners, mostly of inherited wealth, have contributed to Negro colleges so that talented Negroes can be prepared to serve "their own race." A number of them also have opposed rapid desegregation, felt uncomfortable in equal-status relations with Negroes, and have been rather patronizing toward colored people.

International orientations of such moderates among interviewees for this study in the Deep South seemed to run the spectrum from a few neo-islationists to cautious internationalists who supported the major programs of the Kennedy administration in 1961–62. According to interviews, editorial content of papers which pursued moderate lines on desegregation, and the survey evidence cited above, a number of prosperous moderates, such as one regional vice-president of a national textile firm, were staunch economic conservatives. These moderates felt that a great deal of "waste" should be removed from foreign aid, that economic assistance should be put on a more "businesslike" basis through private investment abroad and international loans comparable to those of the International Bank or some of the major private and public banks of the Western world, and that other industrialized countries should be more active along with the United States in financing development. Few seemed opposed to technical assistance, if staffed by able American and foreign technicians. Some opposed purchase of U.N. bonds since the debtor had no secure means of repayment. Among the Deep Southern interviewees none favored rupturing diplomatic relations with the U.S.S.R. or withdrawing from the U.N. But a number felt that the U.N.'s usefulness to our objectives had been considerably reduced by the shift of the voting majority from Western hands. No racial moderate among the Deep Southern interviewees advocated preventive war, or policies amounting to it.

A considerable fraction, probably a majority, of moderates interviewed seemed uncomfortable with some New Frontier optimistic abstractions in foreign affairs, many of which they considered unrealistic. Several agreed in late 1962 that Senator Allen J. Ellender had probably spoken considerable truth in observing that Africans and their leaders were by and large incapable of running their countries responsibly. Many feared that the rate of independence was too fast in Africa, as was the pace of racial change in the South. However, none of the informants of this racial orientation seemed to feel that Portuguese policy in Angola would succeed in preventing its eventual independence. They were, with few exceptions, in agreement that we should assist in training the leaders of newly independent, backward countries. The terror of the O.A.S. in Algeria struck them as stupid and unfortunate. Although almost all of them were willing to pay higher taxes for national defense, if really necessary, they wished inefficiency and waste could be reduced in the armed forces and most tended to see the military as only one of a number of means of carrying out our international objectives. Criticism of the quality of personnel executing our policies abroad was widespread, and most were likewise upset about the publicized corruption and misutilization of our aid by foreign elite groups. They usually agreed that semifeudal landed groups in underdeveloped countries should be pressed to "accept the twentieth century" before economic aid should be advanced.

The international interpretations of the thirty-one newspapers in the sample which were either moderate or indifferent (in areas with few Negroes) on race were likewise heterogeneous. None of them accepted the more extreme postulates of the racist international syndrome, and most patently disagreed with some of the general assumptions and policies advanced by strong segregationists. On the other hand, few were entirely free of elements of the syndrome; few were as optimistic and willing to take risks in foreign policy as were the eleven racially liberal papers. None carried the columns of Ralph McGill, for instance, who was both desegregationist and basically New Frontier on foreign policy. They tended to be at least somewhat more conservative in locally written editorials about major aspects of international affairs than was Walter Lippmann, whose column some of them carried, but none was as monolithically conservative as Barry Goldwater, George Sokolsky, Thurmond Sensing, Westbrook Pegler, W. D. Workman, Holmes Alexander, Paul Harvey, or Edith Kermit Roosevelt, whose columns some of them also published. The papers which were nearer to the "Confederate" ones on race agreed on the whole with more of the tenets of the racist international syndrome than did those which approached the racially liberal papers, but there were exceptions, depending on the particular feature of foreign policy under discussion. The more racially conservative papers were most likely to print editorials approaching the international syndrome of the "Confederate" papers on subjects related to Africa south of the Sahara, but even on this topic their views were not homogeneous. In short, as with other moderate Southerners, local race relations influenced moderate editors' thinking about foreign affairs, but most of their international views were not dominated emotionally by preoccupation with the local Negro.

Many moderate interviewees were not particularly interested in foreign affairs, but a minority of them were. This minority in the cities tended to associate occasionally (in some cases frequently) in organizations where world affairs were discussed. Some racial moderates had been active organizers of groups to promote understanding of foreign relations. Some had been instrumental here and there in Chambers of

Commerce, Rotaries, and other groups only peripherally concerned with foreign policy in inviting responsibly conservative and cautiously internationalist experts in this field—like Eugene Black, Christian Herter, and Hale Boggs—to speak before their organizations. Some lent their names to, and even in a few cases were active on, boards of local and even national groups seriously concerned with promoting a more effective foreign policy through either exerting influence in Washington or communicating to interested publics.

Some Processes of Change

The Issues Have Changed

Southerners of ardently segregationist inclinations would very probably have disagreed with the racial liberals in the South and the North on some important international issues of the early 1960's even had there been little increase in pressure for modification of Southern racial mores. They had disagreed in the past in the relatively few instances when the race issue was engaged in world affairs, and they would undoubtedly have reacted similarly as race became more patent in our international problems.

Black African demands for independence and equality and the overt behavior of some Africans after their countries had become sovereign states tended, particularly, to activate the concerns of racially conservative Southerners about their own social system. Decolonization and the entry into diplomatic discussions of colored leaders, many of them critical of race relations in the South, their criticisms of Western (including United States) policies, and their general anticolonialism have been part of the passing of the hegemony of the "superior" white race. Independence has overthrown white control, resulted in economic losses by many whites, and subjected the remaining white minorities to rule by black majorities and in some cases to rape, murder, and other violence by blacks against whites—all included in the subconscious fears of many whites in heavily Negro areas of the South. Anticolonialism has been seen as antiwhite prejudice. Africans in the U.N. have exerted influences to defeat the objectives of the United States and white Western nations generally, with the result that Southern segregationist confidence in that international organization as a major channel for important American policies has diminished.

Strongly segregationist newspapers and Southerners of like mind who knew something of events in Africa by the early 1960's were identifying to a significant extent with whites in the Congo, Angola, the Rhodesias, and especially the Republic of South Africa. The Society of the Two Souths—the American and African ones—became active. Strongly segregationist papers portrayed the Union of South Africa as a bastion of Western civilization and anticommunism on the continent and devoted considerable attention to atrocities against *colons* by "cannibals," "savages," and "bushmen." Racist papers and the more sophisticated of the interviewees for this study of similar views tended to draw parallels between these African incidents and whites living among large numbers of Negroes in the South.

Moreover, Southern segregationists among the consultants for this study were convinced that Africans and colored foreigners generally had "meddled" in the South. They observed that the Supreme Court decision of 1954 was based not on legal arguments, but rather on "so-called social science," a "socialist Swede's uninformed theories," and supposed opinion in underdeveloped colored lands. "We feed these people and they don't like our ways. We don't like theirs either, and we will let them be if they will reciprocate. But they want to run our private affairs and rewrite our Constitution when they are unable to run their own intelligently." "Where's all the democracy and free speech in Ghana?" "This is our way of life and nobody else's business." Statements by our own leaders and American mass media to the effect that Africans and other underdeveloped nations criticized Southern racial mores and that foreign policy considerations required changes in the South had apparently boomeranged in driving many segregationists toward insularity rather than stimulating change in their racial habits. A number had become hostile to the world in part since it demanded change in their way of life, and they felt that our government's policies toward the South had depended more on criticisms abroad than on the merits of the Southern case. This thinking partly accounted for the rather widespread segregationist sentiment that exaggerated emphasis had been accorded to "world opinion" by our government in its policies abroad as well.

Segregationist Southerners would probably cooperate in world affairs again if that cooperation meant collaboration with Britain and Western Europe. Some segregationist interviewees stated flatly that the Truman Doctrine and Marshall Plan were aid and cooperation with white people of culture and traditions similar to ours (except for Turkey), whereas the current aid programs went to colored peoples of very different cultural mores; other segregationists undoubtedly harbored subjective feelings of this sort. Technical assistance, the Peace Corps, and other aspects of assistance in 1959–62 involved equal-status relationships between Americans and colored, particularly Negroid, peoples which would be emotionally upsetting for many Southerners, especially if they occurred in the South. Aid was somehow, usually vaguely, linked in the minds of segregationists with whom world affairs were discussed with self-assertion and demands for recognition and equality by these formerly dependent colored folks. A number of segregationists noted that the very people demanding aid had been among the most critical of the South.

Moreover, adamant segregationists—such as those who voted for the Dixiecrats in 1948, were favorably inclined toward the Ku Klux Klan, and expressed ardently racist views on surveys in the late 1940's and early 1950's—although on the whole more or less willing to continue economic and other aid to allies, particularly European ones, had been more opposed than Northerners and less segregationist Southern whites to economic and other nonmilitary assistance to unaligned or neutralist countries, at that time largely in Asia, before the intensification of the race issue beginning in the mid-fifties.[66] As American aid shifted from allies to neutrals, they would almost certainly have been more inclined to oppose the shift than Northerners even without racial agitation in the South. Likewise, many of the arguments for aid to underdeveloped countries, particularly during the Kennedy administration, have been rather equalitarian, reformist, idealistic, and abstract, as had been those of abolitionists and their successors; desegregation at home made segregationists much more sensitive to these ideas, but they had long been more inclined to regard them unfavorably than most Northerners and the small racially equalitarian Southern white minority.

Furthermore, strong segregationists, before the school desegregation decision by the Supreme Court in 1954 as afterwards, were more inclined than Northerners and less intensely segregationist and more equalitarian white Southerners to view foreign policy primarily in very nationalistic terms, to favor harsher orientations toward governments which disagreed with us (particularly Communist regimes), to think largely in military terms of restraining aggressors through force or the threat of it, and to feel that we should "go it alone" if our allies did not support us in fighting to win wars into which we might be drawn.[67] With or without pressure on the South, the more intensely segregationist whites would probably have tended more than other Americans to feel we should adopt a harsher, less compromising posture toward the Communist powers as it appeared in 1960–62 that our enemies were

66 AIPO 400, 7/2/47 (3,002); AIPO 439, 3/17/49 (2,193); NORC 167, 6/30/49 (1,284); NORC 168, 8/11/49 (1,232); AIPO 473, 2/24/51 (2,104); and AIPO 546, 4/29/55 (1,539).

67 NORC 241, May, 1946 (2,589); AIPO 376, 8/14/46 (3,000); and AIPO 532, 6/10/54 (1,435).

"winning" the cold war by advancing into Southeast Asia, Latin America (particularly Cuba), and supposedly Africa.

Opposition to the "Outside"

But desegregation in the South had tended to exacerbate these latent tendencies of white supremacists. One result has been a considerable increase in provincialism, in alienation from and defensiveness against apparently hostile extra-Southern forces, both national and international. The "outside" became the enemy, trying to change the "Southern way of life" against the will of most white Southerners. Southern racial conservatives wanted to preserve a static social system in a world where change was the order of the day. Feeling persecuted by foreigners, Northerners, and their own national government, segregationists tried to withdraw from it all and to shield themselves from all external pressures for racial and social change. They wanted to be left alone, to live in contentment with their own ways and views by withdrawing from both national and international criticism and pressure.

Increased antagonism to the federal executive, courts, and racial liberals in the two houses of Congress was particularly apparent within the more racially conservative Southern newspapers and among like-minded interviewees examined. White supremacists interviewed after mid-1959 tended by that time to think of the federal government as almost a hostile foreign regime: "I don't feel any closer to that dictatorship in Washington than to the one in Moscow," commented a college-educated paternalist segregationist about the Eisenhower administration. Segregationists have felt the South has long been the most patriotic part of the country—white Southerners disproportionately officered the armed forces, filled the enlisted ranks, and died valiantly on many battlefields; now they were being stabbed in the back by "liberals" in Washington to appease Africans and gather Negro votes in the North. The South was being shoved around again and held up as an object of scorn around the globe, despite the fact that it was the South that had resisted fascist and communist enemies both within and without.

This alienation from the national society and its central government resulted in increased opposition to some of its foreign policies. Even some racially conservative Southern Congressmen seemed by 1959 to pursue the line of thought that they could not effectively parry the government's pressures for change in the South, but they could frustrate its programs in world affairs, particularly if they themselves were interested primarily in domestic problems and if there was no strong support for active multilateral programs at home—as was often the case.

Opposition to economic aid abroad was one way to get back at their liberal Northern tormentors. Furthermore, generalizing from interviews and examination of newspaper content it appeared that many segregationists had so little faith in the federal government which had been so "impossible" and "lacking in common sense" in dealing with race problems in the South that they felt that its judgment in world affairs should not be trusted either. And even if foreign aid might accomplish desirable ends in the national interest, the "leftists" and intellectuals running it would implement it naïvely, because of all sorts of "silly" idealist notions. Finally, strongly segregationist newspapers and interviewees noted that if the government were expanded and strengthened to carry out the foreign aid programs, it would be that much more able to intrude into the domestic segregation controversy.

White supremacist interviewees and newspapers of like racial sentiments were most inclined to take out their frustrations against the national government in the foreign field if they really were not much interested in and did not accord much importance to foreign affairs themselves. But it was observed above (see pp. 391–93) that white supremacists at the level of the common man in the South have been largely indifferent to, uninformed about, and irresponsible on world affairs all along. Southerners who have known much about foreign relations have been among the educated elements and have also largely been among the racial moderates, liberals, and relatively reasonable segregationists. Increasing insecurity due to pressure for racial change apparently diverted whatever little attention there was among more uncompromising segregationists away from national and international phenomena to the local scene. Adamant segregationists seemed so emotionally involved in and appeared to feel so threatened by the Negro at home that all other ideas had to be amended to preserve segregation; issues which might upset the racial *status quo* were ignored or distorted. Even those racist leaders interviewed who spoke about "giveaways," "money down the rat hole," how "you can't buy friends," "Congolese raping your daughters," and so forth did not appear to be for the most part really much interested in foreign assistance or in Africa, except as means for flailing their supposed enemies, the racial (and international) liberals, and for cutting taxes.

The Shift of Attention to Conservative International Interpretations

Lack of real interest, knowledge, concrete views, and contact with sources of information and interpretation of world affairs from outside the South among most white supremacists, and particularly among the less-educated groups which have provided the majority of the more uncompromising racists, left a vacuum in which the racist international syndrome developed. As the pressure for racial change increased their insecurity, the racist press, politicians, and other segregationist leaders increasingly identified "internationalists," "one-worlders," "international do-gooders," "world reformers," "those who would turn over our sovereignty to the World Court and the U.N.," "zionist Jews," and so on with racial liberals. By 1961 segregationist leaders and the eleven more racially conservative newspapers in the sample for this study were telling their readers that integrationists and "mongrelizers" were also "soft on Communism," had adopted the "Communist line," were "Communist inspired," or were actually "Communists"; that they favored "continued taxation for a U.S. world Santa Claus"; that they would "flood our country with foreign radicals"; that they wanted to "muzzle our patriotic generals" (General Edwin Walker); and so on. By the early 1960's "internationalist" had become a dirty word among perhaps most emotionally committed segregationists.

Leaders of racist groups increasingly provided their audiences with international interpretations in keeping with the racist international syndrome, often in extreme form. Many of the more adamant of these men—the ones most inclined to give their time to segregationist organizations—were very probably neo-isolationists if not isolationists before 1954.[68] Because of changed emphases in our foreign policies, their conservative racial views, and the growing sensitivities of segregationist masses about integration, these spokesmen seemed to have much larger audiences than previously. Furthermore, it appeared that segregationist leaders concluded sometime in the late 1950's that race alone was not a sufficient appeal to attract the required support and that they should broaden their messages to draw in contributors, members, and allies who harbored ultraconservative thoughts on other issues but were only tangentially concerned about integration. White supremacy leaders had long been hostile to trade unions and to "socialism." The addition of ultranationalism (actually ultra-Southernism) and articulate isolationism or neo-isolationism to their utterances took place primarily after 1954.

Thus, by late 1956 and early 1957 many racist groups had proclaimed their opposition to foreign aid. After the Little Rock incident and the

68 See, for example, Sarah M. Lemmon, "The Ideology of the 'Dixiecrat' Movement," *Social Forces*, XXX (1951), 162–71. Some of our interviewees of these inclinations hastened to point out that their international thinking was not new to them; they had long questioned such ideas as the Marshall Plan, Lend-Lease, and even United States entry into the U.N.

emergence of several African states in 1957, segregationist leaders and publications began to speak of "cannibals," "lack of courage" of white colonial governments, and "savages in the U.N." The charge was increasingly made that the NAACP, CORE, the National Council of Churches, trade unions, and other racially liberal groups were duped by Communists, infiltrated by Communists, controlled by Communists, and the like. This trend, together with other reinforcing influences, resulted in growing apprehension of segregationists that Communists were indeed influential in this country. In July, 1961, Reverend Billy James Hargis, a fundamentalist evangelist leader of the Christian Crusade and active "anti-Communist," who was formerly critical of Catholicism, addressed the Citizens Council in New Orleans. His audience, composed of large numbers of pleasure-loving, south Louisiana Catholics, would have avoided such a personality ten years before; now they were attracted because of his racial extremism. Once in the Municipal Auditorium, they heard an emotional address attacking foreign aid and the U.N., "one-worlders," our "no win" policy of appeasing Reds and domestic "Communists," and our continued diplomatic relations with the U.S.S.R. The Reverend Hargis went on to advocate invasion of Cuba and other views of the racist international syndrome. By late 1961 the content of communications of arch-segregationist leaders and organizations on world affairs was very much like those of the John Birch Society, the Christian Anti-Communist Crusade, and other isolationist or neo-isolationist groups. And rank-and-file racists among interviewees for the study seemed inclined to give considerable credence to thinking on world affairs of leaders who were "right" on race.

Moreover, national conservative groups and politicians who wished to attract support in the South—such as Senator Goldwater, the John Birch Society, and Young Americans for Freedom—had increasingly expressed their adherence to "states' rights," their feeling that the Supreme Court had exceeded its authority under the Constitution, and their belief that race relations should be left to the judgment of local authorities. Formerly they apparently devoted themselves to conservative thinking on foreign affairs, taxation, welfare programs, and other issues which had only limited interest to less affluent Southern segregationists. These groups gained the attention of segregationists, established that they were against outside pressure for racial change, and then apparently succeeded in communicating the whole congeries of ultraconservative ideas, on world affairs as well as domestic issues.

Meanwhile, segregationists were gradually shifting their attention from national mass media which had been favorable to relatively liberal, cooperative policies abroad to others whose international views were more conservative. A considerable proportion of better-educated segregationists among those interviewed, for example, had in the past read national publications of internationalist hue. But periodicals which have been relatively internationalist or liberal on foreign policy have in recent years tended to be overtly critical of Southern racial mores, and at the same time segregationists have been becoming more sensitive to criticism of their "peculiar institution" and to "outside" criticism generally. Consequently, many racial conservatives among the interviewees had discontinued reading *Time, Life, Look,* the New York *Times* (Sunday edition), and the like. These periodicals were actually banned from high-school libraries in several Louisiana parishes.[69] Conservative (by Northeastern standards) *Time* came to be viewed as "leftist," "anti-Southern," "nigger loving," and even "Communist" by racially conservative Southerners; those who continued to read it in some black-belt areas with Negro majorities were viewed with some suspicion. Segregationist newspapers even attacked the Chicago *Tribune*, hardly a leftist publication, as having adopted the anti-Southern thinking of the "Yankee bleeding hearts." Meanwhile, racially conservative *U.S. News and World Report,* also more conservative on foreign affairs than the more racially liberal magazines, received the praises of segregationists and their press. As a result, the circulation of *U.S. News and World Report* increased at a more rapid rate in the South than did either of the other major newsmagazines between 1950 and 1960. That of *Time* actually decreased in many counties with heavy Negro populations and Old South traditions, although its national circulation more than doubled during the same period.[70]

Approximately three fourths of the interviewees for this study who had discontinued reading *Time* gave as their reasons that it was "prejudiced against the South," "pro-Negro," or the like, and virtually all of these were much opposed to desegregation. More than half were frequent readers of *U.S. News and World Report* at the time of the interview. Southern whites who continued to read internationally liberal periodicals which were also desegregationist were for the most part themselves liberals, moderates, or less extreme segregationists. Many of the moderate and relatively mild segregationists who still read *Life, Time,* or other racially liberal publications also noted that they were "unfair to the South" and that their Southern coverage was "distorted,"

69 Muse, *Ten Years of Prelude,* 171.
70 From circulation statistics by state, county, and city made available by the publishers.

or made comparable observations. They often ventured the opinion that since these periodicals were so "unbalanced" on the South, about which they themselves knew a good deal, these publications were probably as "irresponsible" on foreign developments as well. Many of these Southerners had also begun to read *U.S. News and World Report* or other racially (and internationally) conservative materials. Because these periodicals were "sensible," gave "both sides," and were "balanced" on the South, segregationist readers gave their international content more credence than that of racially (and internationally) more liberal publications. In effect, the race issue shifted their attention to more conservative, even neo-isolationist, sources of information and interpretations in foreign relations.

Similar processes seemed to have taken place with respect to attention to internationally liberal radio and television content and to sophisticated international forums and other educational and organizational programs. The more ardent segregationists and traditionalists among those interviewed had largely ceased to view television appearances of Dave Garroway, Chet Huntley, David Brinkley (a North Carolinian), and Howard K. Smith (a Louisianian), whom they called "slanderers of the South" or comparable names. Less adamant segregationists continued to pay some attention to such newscasters, but such white Southerners among those interviewed seemed to tend to discount their international thinking primarily because of their liberalism on race. But these television personalities also advanced basically internationalist views.

Organizations of internationalist orientation in the South tended to lose their white supremacist members and to attract few replacements as prevention of integration became these Southerners' increasing preoccupation. In part these withdrawals and failures to involve other segregationists were due to the increasing differences of opinion between the internationalist leadership of these organizations and racially conservative Southerners as the underdeveloped, unaligned world became a growing emphasis in our foreign relations. But some Leagues of Women Voters, for instance, became integrated to one measure or another, and in the process either lost their conservative members entirely or lost their active participation. As one active member of a Committee on Foreign Relations (one of thirty-three affiliates of the Council on Foreign Relations in New York) explained, one could discuss in a searching way international problems facing America in the early 1950's and before without coming face-to-face with the race issue, but it was virtually impossible to analyze the issues of 1961 without running into race both at home and abroad. Alert segregationists observed that internationally oriented groups were "filled with race-mixers," "carpetbagger radicals," "too many leftist Jews," and so on, and they felt apprehensive that participants whom they did not know might likewise be "soft on race." Liberal internationalist speakers before Deep Southern audiences were by 1959 attacked or even "disinvited" due to their known or reputed liberalism on race. Strong segregationists seemed to have become increasingly suspicious that sophisticates on foreign affairs and cosmopolitans generally were "critical of the South," were in favor of "mongrelization," or held similarly unpalatable views on race.

Observant interviewees interested in world affairs noted similar developments were evident in informal interpersonal relations where foreign affairs might be discussed. Similar to the several decades preceding the Civil War when slavery was under attack from the "outside," pressures against expression of unconventional views, especially on race but also to a significant degree on world affairs and other public fields, had become more compelling since 1954. Even during the McCarthy period, educated Southerners often disagreed with one another openly without hard feelings. Senator Joseph McCarthy was somewhat less popular in the South than in the rest of the country taken together,[71] probably in part because of his Northern background, Catholic religion, and Republican connections. But charges of communism in high places in government and private institutions fell on less receptive Southern ears during the Senator's heyday prior to the Supreme Court decision on segregation than would have been the case thereafter.

Prior to "Black Monday" national organizations such as the American Association for the United Nations, the Carnegie Endowment for International Peace, the Foreign Policy Association, the American Heritage Foundation, the Great Books Foundation, and the League of Women Voters sponsored discussions in heavily Negro, plantation, and traditionalist sections, including the Mississippi Delta, Birmingham, and Charleston. Participants in these groups noted in 1959–62 that even the race issue was discussed prior to 1954 with considerable candor and realism among a small, well-read minority.

71 AIPO 454, 3/24/50 (1,458); AIPO 456, 6/2/50 (1,450); AIPO 513, 3/26/53 (1,590); NORC 341-2, 6/30/53 (1,291); AIPO 524, 12/9/53 (1,483); AIPO Releases of 1/15/54 and 3/14/54; AIPO 532, 6/10/54 (1,435); AIPO Releases of 5/2/54 and 6/9/54; AIPO 534, 7/14/54 (1,549); AIPO 537, 9/14/54 (1,465); and AIPO Release of 12/3/54. Senator McCarthy was most favorably viewed in the Northeast, then in the Midwest, and least in the South. Proportions of Catholics in these regions help to account for these differences, since the Wisconsin Senator was more popular among them than among Protestants, Jews, and religiously unaffiliated groups.

Participants in these programs and other thoughtful Southerners observed that it would be considerably more difficult, if not impossible, to assemble the same or comparable people in 1959–62 to discuss similarly controversial questions in Deep Southern communities with Old South traditions and large fractions of Negroes. Their racially conservative colleagues had become so emotionally distraught about integration that they were unable to expand their horizons to world affairs, and they were anything but detached and analytical about public issues which had some connection, even implicit, with the Southern Negro problem. Participants in discussion groups sponsored by the Fund for Adult Education in the pre-1954 period in the Mississippi Delta refused in 1961 to be interviewed by representatives of "Yankee" organizations for fear of local reactions to meetings with assumedly liberal agencies. Well-read cosmopolitans in the South Carolina low country hesitated to express even moderately atypical views to people they had known all their lives. Although the most potent pressures operated in the field of race, cosmopolitans in Charleston, Delta County, Antebellum Town, and Plantation County observed that someone who openly agreed with Prime Minister MacMillan's "Winds of Change" speech in the Union of South Africa, with the U.N. against President Tshombe of Katanga, with critics of the Portuguese in Angola, with those who felt Belgium was considerably to blame for the Congo in failing to train native leaders, and even with the supporters of foreign aid for Yugoslavia would incur considerable local criticism. Indeed, many would feel, in most cases correctly, that the multilateralist or liberal on foreign affairs was probably also a "traitor to the South" on segregation.

Consequently, internationalists had become increasingly hesitant to contradict or disagree with the racist international syndrome in public and had more and more restricted their discussion of foreign policy to the handful of those of like inclinations. In the tensest communities a number of cosmopolitan interviewees feared that even their international discussions with other cosmopolitans might "leak" to the local racist press, Citizens Council, Sovereignty Commission, and the public generally. Disagreement with one or more aspects of the racist international syndrome appearing in the local newspaper marked a man as "controversial" in some black-belt and traditionalist locales and threatened to lead to social ostracism if not worse pressures. As the race issue intensified, segregationists isolated themselves from both local and outside individuals, organizations, and mass media that might place alternative ideas before them, and they exchanged international ideas almost exclusively with other segregationists who also tended to agree with the racist international syndrome. Dialogue between people of divergent views lessened, and international opinions among white supremacists became more homogeneous.

Some Congressional Effects

Although some Congressmen from constituencies with large percentages of Negroes among their inhabitants continued to support foreign economic aid and other multilateral programs on roll calls, the larger the proportion of Negroes in a district, the more apt was the Congressman to vote against these measures between 1953 and 1962. Congressmen from the border states and upper South, where there were relatively few Negroes, were on the average among the more inclined from the region to vote for these international commitments, whereas those from the two states with the largest percentages of Negroes and the most Deep Southern traditions, Mississippi and South Carolina, were the most inclined among state delegations to oppose them.[72]

Racially conservative Congressmen, like other segregationist Southerners, have tended to shift their thinking and votes in Washington toward the racist syndrome of international views. Strongly segregationist Congressmen who voted for the loans to Britain in the early postwar years, the Truman Doctrine, and the Marshall Plan were typically voting against economic assistance to underdeveloped countries and other multilateral proposals outside the defense field in the late 1950's and early 1960's.[73]

72 Lerche, *The Uncertain South*, 151–53, 295–300.
73 For instance, Senator Samuel Ervin of North Carolina, a rather consistent voter against economic assistance bills in the early 1960's, signed a petition favorable to world government in the late 1940's. Representative John Bell Williams of Mississippi, strongly opposed to economic aid and other activist, costly, nonmilitary programs abroad in 1960–62, was making speeches in favor of the Marshall Plan and the Truman Doctrine in the late 1940's. Both Senator Strom Thurmond of South Carolina and Representative William Colmer of Mississippi were significantly less conservative on world affairs in the 1940's. Paternalist segregationist Senator Richard B. Russell of Georgia was somewhat more critical of foreign aid during the first decade following World War II than most Southern Congressmen of that period, but he tended, nevertheless, to vote with the majority of Democrats on the Marshall Plan and the Truman Doctrine. He voted almost without exception with those who would reduce or eliminate foreign aid during the early 1960's. Senator Russell Long of Louisiana, in 1960–62 a milder opponent of large foreign expenditures other than for defense, was more favorable to such spending a decade before. Different from most Southern Congressmen who appealed primarily to poor whites, the Longs had never used racism for political purposes. However, by 1961 Senator Russell Long was requesting publicly that President Kennedy refrain from promoting Judge Skelley Wright of New Orleans, who had rendered decisions forcing token desegregation of two public schools, from the District Court to the Circuit Court of Appeals.

Moreover, Congressmen who had supported such commitments and who were also moderates on segregation have been subjected to increasing electoral pressures by opponents willing to appeal to the insecurities and accompanying racism of underprivileged whites through demogogic white-supremacy appeals. After declining as an overt election appeal for several decades before 1954, race quickly became a major, and in some cases the principal, political issue thereafter in constituencies composed of high percentages of Negroes. The Deep Southern Congressman who could be successfully accused of being "soft on niggers" or the like experienced increasing difficulties in defeating racially extreme opponents. Even in areas where Negroes were not particularly numerous, increased federal or other pressures for racial change before an election tended to exacerbate white sensibilities and permitted neo-isolationist, unilateralist racists to defeat internationalist multilateralists who were moderates on race. An example of this situation was the defeat of Congressman Brooks Hays by arch-segregationist Dale Alford after federal troops had entered Little Rock. Violation of racial taboos—such as failure to sign the Southern Manifesto by internationalist Congressman Charles B. Deane of North Carolina—has likewise contributed to defeat of responsible multilateralists even in areas with few Negroes and under no immediate pressures for desegregation. Relatively minor deviations, or failure to declare one's racial conservatism vigorously, has permitted racists to develop majority support against internationalist incumbents in plantation and traditionalist Old South areas. Senator Walter George's reputation of racial moderation (for Georgia) was one important reason for apparent majority support of Herman Talmadge and the withdrawal of the former from the primary. Talmadge coupled attack on foreign aid and internationalism generally with appeal to the racial insecurity of white Georgians.

The defeat of internationalist Congressman Frank E. Smith of the Mississippi Delta in 1962 illustrates some of the difficulties of internationally responsible Congressmen from heavily Negro areas. Even had Smith been known as a strong segregationist and opponent of foreign aid, he would undoubtedly have experienced considerable difficulty in defeating his opponent Congressman Jamie L. Whitten, since the latter had a considerably larger number of voters in his hillier district where prejudices against the Delta have been traditional. But another major reason for Smith's defeat was his liberal voting record on world affairs, including foreign aid, and his moderation on race (although he had consistently voted against civil rights bills before the House). Whitten had demonstrated his ultraconservative racial views in supporting the

States' Rights Independent Electors against the national Democratic party in 1960, whereas Smith had been one of the few active supporters of presidential candidate John F. Kennedy among Mississippi politicians. Whitten accused his opponent of voting against expansion of the House Rules Committee in 1961 only after it was obvious that the proposal would be defeated anyway. Whitten stressed his own all-out support of states' rights, the "Southern way of life," and segregation: "It is a contest between my conservatism and opposition to internationalism . . . against the liberalism and support of internationalism" of Frank Smith.[74] Whitten boasted that he opposed the U.N., the Peace Corps, and foreign aid, while Smith noted that the choice was between insularity and isolationism versus responsible participation of Mississippi in national and international affairs.[75]

Augmented racial insecurity of white Southerners also played into the hands of the growing prosperous business and manufacturing class. Racism has long been a major weapon used by economic conservatives to pit underprivileged whites against poor Negroes and to bring the former to elect economic conservatives to Congress. Exacerbated racial sensibilities since 1954 permitted continuation of this phenomenon, notwithstanding the growing industrialization of the South and the expanding influence of trade unions and other groups of economically liberal orientations. As long as racial extremism remains a major criterion for support by the mass of white voters, the racist Congressman need not be responsible about international or national affairs and can even vote against the economic interests of the majority at home.[76]

74 Jackson *Clarion-Ledger*, June 5, 1962.
75 For a first-hand description of the roles of racism and isolationism in the unseating of Congressman Frank E. Smith, see his *Congressman from Mississippi* (New York: Pantheon Books, 1964), 278–300. The defeat of former Governor James P. Coleman by Paul Johnson in the second Democratic gubernatorial primary in Mississippi in the summer of 1963 was another indication of the potency of some of these factors. Coleman, like former Congressman Smith a racial moderate by Mississippi standards and a supporter of John F. Kennedy in his presidential campaign in 1960, had previously favored active United States collaboration in the U.N. and broad multilateral cooperation generally. Johnson, then lieutenant governor in the administration of Ross Barnett, attacked Coleman for his former approval of President Kennedy, his "softness" on segregation, and his support of the U.N., foreign aid, and other international cooperation. The realities of voter opinion in the state were such that Coleman apparently felt virtually forced to declare publicly that he had come to agree with the view that the U.N. had been a failure and with other isolationist or unilateralist thinking. Nevertheless, he was defeated by a wide margin.
76 For an insightful discussion by a former Southern Congressman of use of racism by conservative Southern Congressmen as a smoke screen to cover their attacks on liberal economic, social, and international legislation, see Frank E. Smith, "The Southern Politician," *The Nation*, CXCIX (September 21, 1964), 132–34.

A frequent concomitant of strongly laissez-faire economic conservatism among Congressmen has been opposition to spending money abroad on economic aid and other nonmilitary measures,[77] as has been the case among their Southern businessmen supporters (see p. 306).

Furthermore, growing pressure on the Congress and within it for passage of civil rights legislation has driven Southern Congressmen to seek allies wherever they could be found. Northern Congressmen most inclined to support Southerners on civil rights and states' rights have tended to be conservative Republicans from the Midwest, Plains States, Rocky Mountain section, and Southwest, many of whom continued to harbor, in attenuated form, residues of isolationist sentiments formerly centered in these areas. Southerners who have been relatively little interested in foreign affairs have voted with these Northern conservatives in their fields of interest in return for support on states' rights, race relations, and other issues in which Southerners had particular concern.

Thus, a number of segregationists in the Congress have become more conservative about important aspects of foreign policy and some Deep Southern internationalists who were unable or unwilling to compete with racist opponents on the segregation question have been defeated, to be replaced often by racial conservatives, typically also unilateralists or neo-isolationists. As other multilateralists died or retired, candidates who could realistically hope to win their seats were pressed to equal or exceed the racial intransigence of their opponents. Individuals who have been willing to engage in racial demagoguery have tended not to be thoughtful, interested, or responsible in the field of foreign relations. New incumbents have often seemed to follow the ultraconservative international habits of more senior Congressmen from their states. Men most likely to be or to become responsible multilateralists have been unwilling to run in elections in which racism has been a requirement for success. Race tended to drive out whatever little responsible debate on international relations there might otherwise have been in heavily Negro constituencies. Most Southerners have not voted for or against international programs since 1954, but in choosing intransigent segregationists they have put neo-isolationists into office. The likely defeat of more moderate candidates, who have also been inclined to be more responsible about foreign policy, has permitted a number of neo-isolationists to remain in office for successive terms without serious opposition at the polls.[78]

77 *Ibid.;* and Lerche, *The Uncertain South,* 175 and 295–300.
78 The foregoing observations about the impacts of the race problem on behavior of Southern Congressmen toward foreign policy are derived primarily from

These developments, together with the overrepresentation in the Congress of rural and small-town areas where irreconcilable segregationist thinking has been particularly prevalent, have been partly responsible for the more drastic shift in Southern votes against foreign aid and other international cooperation than changes in Southern public opinion on world affairs during the decade prior to 1963 would lead one to expect.

---

interviews with Southern Congressmen and former Congressmen of varied international and racial orientations and from conversations with politically active and perceptive individuals in their districts. For a thoughtful and revealing discussion of these phenomena in greater detail by the liberal Congressman from the Mississippi Delta between 1951 and 1963, see the two publications of Frank E. Smith cited above.

CHAPTER 12

PROTESTANTS,
ROMAN CATHOLICS,
AND THEIR CLERGY

Southern Protestants
and World Affairs

P rotestant churches and organizations affiliated with them have
exerted much greater influence on thought and action in the South
than in other regions. In the mid-1950's church-affiliated Protestants
constituted 79 percent of adult Southerners as compared with 41 percent of the rest of the United States adult population.[1] Moreover, the
concentration of the small Roman Catholic minority, along the coast of
the Gulf of Mexico, in southern Florida, in the river towns along the
Mississippi, and—particularly since World War II—in larger inland
cities, has left much of the Southern interior almost entirely Protestant.[2]
For example, there were no known Catholics, Jews, or other non-
Protestants in Mountain, Hill, or Plantation counties.

But even such statistics fail to indicate the profound impact of
Protestant churches in most of the region. Although Protestant Southerners have been significantly less apt to take part in secular organizations than have Protestant Northerners,[3] they have been more inclined

1 "Churches and Church Membership in the United States" (National Council
of Churches, Series A, Bull. 4 [New York, 1957]), Table 7.
2 See, for instance, Harold F. Kaufman, *Mississippi Churches: A Half Century
of Change* (Mississippi State University, Social Science Research Center, Bull. 12
[Starkville, 1959]), 12–21; and Harold F. Kaufman, *et al., Mississippi Churches:
A Statistical Supplement* (Mississippi State University, Social Science Research
Center, (Bull. 12–S [Starkville, 1949]).
3 NORC 335, January, 1953 (2,809); NORC 367, January, 1955 (2,379); Harold
F. Kaufman, "Concerns of Adult Education in Mississippi," *Adult Education,* VIII
(1957), 23; and Murray Hausknecht, *The Joiners: A Sociological Description of*

to participate in religious organizations.[4] Even when compared with Northern rural people, Southern country folk have been more likely to be active in a church;[5] and instead of decreasing church participation, recent urbanization, increased education, and prosperity in the South have resulted in more widespread religious affiliation than ever.[6] University faculty members and other intellectuals have continued for the most part to attend church in the South, although most of their counterparts of Protestant inclinations up North have seemed to be relatively inactive in organized religion.

When Southerners have been affiliated with only one organization —as most of them still were in the late 1950's—it has in most cases been a Protestant church. In Mississippi, for instance, church membership outnumbered in 1957 all other memberships combined, and in many rural settings memberships in churches have outnumbered affiliations with all other groups taken together by as much as four to one.[7] Particularly in the lower two thirds of the educational and social spectra and in rural and small-town locales, the church has tended to be the center of social life, virtually the only formal organization through which ideas may be communicated on a face-to-face basis,[8] and a major

---

Voluntary Association Membership in the United States (New York: The Bedminster Press, 1962), 16–19, 21, and 23–27. Paucity of active participation in voluntary organizations in the South is partly explained by the correlation of organizational activity throughout the country with education, socio-economic status, income, and urban and, especially, suburban residence—all factors in which Southerners have ranked below the national average. Moreover, trade unions, which have included a large proportion of the Northern working class, have had relatively few members in the South.

4 "Churches and Church Membership in the United States" (National Council of Churches, Series A, Bull. 3 [New York, 1957]), Table 6.

5 Raymond Payne, "Some Comparisons of Participation in Rural Mississippi, Kentucky, Ohio, Illinois, and New York," *Rural Sociology*, XVIII (1953), 171–72.

6 Active affiliation with churches in the South has been positively correlated with education, income, social status, and urban or suburban rather than rural residence. See Earl D. C. Brewer, "Religion and the Churches," in *The Southern Appalachian Region*, 202 ff; and Kaufman, *Mississippi Churches*, 25.

7 Kaufman, *Mississippi Churches*, 2. See also Raymond Payne and Harold F. Kaufman, "Organizational Activities of Rural People in Mississippi" (Mississippi Agricultural Station, Circular 189 [Starkville, 1953]); Alvin L. Bertrand and Harold W. Osborne, "The Impact of Industrialization on a Rural Community," *Journal of Farm Economics*, XLI (1959), 1,133; and Wilfred C. Bailey, "Designing Education Programs for Specific Audiences," (Starkville; Mississippi State College Agricultural Experiment Station, 1957), 8 and 14.

8 Kaufman, *Mississippi Churches*, 25; Alvin Bertrand and Harold W. Osborne, *Rural Industrialization in a Louisiana Community* (Louisiana State University Agricultural Experiment Station, Bull. 524 [Baton Rouge, 1959]), 34; Payne and Kaufman, "Organizational Activities of Rural People in Mississippi," 5; Maitland and Wilbur, *Industrialization in Chickasaw County, Mississippi*, 15; and Bailey, "Designing Education Programs for Specific Audiences," 8 and 14.

force in shaping values and attitudes.[9] Ministers as late as 1955 still had considerably more prestige [10] and influence among Southern Protestants than Northern ones. Southern Protestants have gone to church more frequently and spent more hours per year in their churches and affiliated groups than have Northern Protestants.[11] Many small-town and rural dwellers have habitually attended church several times a week —services on Sunday, prayer meetings on one or more week nights, Bible school, baptisms, and all manner of picnics, church suppers, fish fries, and so on.

The Character and Distribution of Protestant Groups

Episcopalians, Roman Catholics, and to a lesser measure Presbyterians originally populated the coastline of the South and the lower Mississippi Valley. As less privileged and unsophisticated segments of the coastal population migrated into the interior "wilds," they reacted against the restrained religious leaders along the coast and produced from among their own number untrained, part-time preachers whose appeals were for the most part passionately "enthusiastic," otherworldly, and otherwise attuned to the illiterates and semiliterates of the frontier. Widely separated farms and villages were served by Baptist and Methodist circuit riders of little formal education and of revivalist orientations.[12] These rustic preachers differed sharply from the more abstract, intellectual, formal, and restrained clergymen of the educated classes along the seaboard.

Episcopal parishes in the interior came later, with the migration of more elevated strata from the coast and the emergence of a successful indigenous planter class who tended to shift from the emotional religious forms of their childhoods to others more fitting to their prosperity and influence.[13] Antebellum Episcopal churches were built along the Missis-

9 See for instance, Brewer, "Religion and the Churches," in *The Southern Appalachian Region*, 214; Charles P. Loomis (ed.), *Rural Social Systems and Adult Education* (East Lansing: Michigan State College Press, 1953), 196 and 372; Harold F. Kaufman, *Religious Organizations in Kentucky* (Kentucky Agricultural Experiment Station, Bull. No. 524 [Lexington, 1948]); H. Paul Douglass and Edmund DeS. Brunner, *The Protestant Church as a Social Institution* (New York: Harpers, 1935), 40; Payne, *Rural Sociology*, XVIII (1953), 171–72; Morland, *Millways of Kent*, 106 ff; and Rubin, *Plantation County*, Chapter 8.

10 "Attitudes of Adult Civilians toward Military Service as a Career" (Public Opinion Surveys, Inc., 1955).

11 Payne, *Rural Sociology*, XVIII (1953), 171–72.

12 Osterweis, *Romanticism and Nationalism in the Old South*, 188; Savage, *Seeds of Time*, 97–98; H. Richard Niebuhr, *The Social Forces of Denominationalism* (New York: Henry Holt and Co., 1929), 26–76 and 146–47; and Campbell, *The Southern Highlander and His Homeland*, 152–94.

13 Niebuhr, *The Social Forces of Denominationalism*, 168–78 and 184–88; and Eaton, *The Growth of Southern Civilization*, 2, 4–5, 13, 104–105 and 313.

sippi River in such towns as Natchez, Woodville, and Rivertown by these groups; however, only a minority of second and later generation planters and successful commercial people became Anglicans, especially in the interior. More either remained or became Presbyterians. After several generations those who had remained Methodists were likewise demanding formally trained ministers and more sedate religious observances. The Baptists in the newer parts of the South managed to keep the allegiance of some of the influential descendants of hill farmers, mountaineers, and poor whites, but these upper-middle-class Baptists were in churches composed primarily of the better educated and served by clergy fitting their station.[14]

By 1962 Anglicanism was a denomination populated largely by urban, educated classes and their counterparts in older smaller communities of antebellum plantation traditions. However, the Presbyterians had also become primarily an upper- and upper-middle-class denomination. There was no Episcopal church in Plantation County; the Presbyterians and, to a lesser measure, the Methodists, included most of the influential and educated elements. In Kent, a much older community than most of the Black Belt, the prestige of the Presbyterian church was equal to that of the Episcopal one. Presbyterianism in 1962 was an "acceptable" denomination among the upper classes throughout the South, but in communities which were well established in 1861, such as Charleston and much of Tidewater Virginia, Anglicanism has long been the most esteemed branch of Christianity among the gentry. Many successful businessmen in 1962 were Presbyterians, as well as Methodists and, particularly in sections of newer prosperity, Baptists affiliated with the Southern Baptist Convention. The Associate Reformed Presbyterians, most of whose ministers seemed more conservative theologically than those of the Presbyterian Church in the United States (Southern Presbyterian Church), were concentrated in the Piedmont, Black Belt, and nearby areas, and had attracted in recent decades few lower-class people. The few Unitarians were concentrated in larger cities and university communities, where they tended to be former Northerners, intellectuals, university faculty members, psychiatrists, former Jews, and other upper-middle class, largely professional individuals and their families.

Forty-seven percent of the Methodists in the United States lived in the South in the late 1950's—the largest denomination in the region

14 For a discussion of social stratification among Protestant churches in a textile society in the late 1930's, see Pope, *Millhands and Preachers*, especially Chapters 5, 6, and 7.

next to the Baptists.[15] Although originally a religion of the masses, by 1962 their largely college- and seminary-educated ministers were not attracting many Southerners below the middle class. They were stronger in the country and small towns, relatively weaker in the cities.

The Southern Baptists—comprising about ten million in the region in 1962 and the largest religious group in every Southern state except Louisiana and Virginia—were by far the most numerous group.[16] They have been growing faster than other denominations, largely among those who were formerly unchurched or affiliated with fundamentalist sects; a considerable number of them are the first generation in their families to finish high school and make a decent living. Congregational control has developed individual parishes along a spectrum ranging from very fundamentalist inclinations to beliefs close to Presbyterianism. In a typical Southern town of around ten thousand, several white Baptist churches have been usual: one populated by the better-educated, more prosperous and more sophisticated middle class, often with a college- and seminary-trained minister who may have some interest in international and other issues; another supported mostly by lower-middle and more literate working-class people in the local textile mill, paper plant, or other local enterprises; and one or more others—sometimes affiliated with the Southern Baptist Convention, sometimes not—with a little-educated minister, or one who went through Bible school without the benefit of college, whose preaching to economically and educationally deprived members has tended to be emotional and literalist. The Baptists in 1962 were still primarily a rural and small-town people, and in the cities Baptists were mainly of those origins. In general, the more rural the atmosphere (except in southern Louisiana), the greater the proportion of Baptists; Mississippi, the most rural state, had in 1957 a Baptist population of 54 percent of church-affiliated persons, but the proportion was as high as 80 percent in some of the rural hill counties of the northeastern part of the state.[17]

The more emotional fundamentalists in 1962 were strongest among the "holiness" and Pentecostal sects, the unaffiliated Baptists, and to a lesser degree the Southern Baptists in rural and small-town areas. They were strongest among mountain country folk, next in the hills, third in

15 Kaufman, *Mississippi Churches*, 13.
16 New York *Times*, June 5, 1962, and May 10, 1963. This figure did not include white Baptists of congregations unaffiliated with the Southern Baptist Convention (perhaps another million or so) or Negro Baptists. Baptist churches include an even larger proportion of Negroes than of whites affiliated with religious organizations.
17 Kaufman, *Mississippi Churches*, 1.

the newly developed sections of large-scale agriculture, fourth in growing cities composed of many migrants from such rural locales, and
weakest in older cities which had received few recent newcomers from
the country. Relatively few remained fundamentalists (by Southern
standards) after the first generation of higher education and prosperity;
fundamentalists were primarily working and, to a lesser degree, lower-
middle class, plus some relatively well-to-do of such origins.

However, in comparison with Protestants in the North, including
Northern Baptists, most clergymen and active laymen in the Southern
Baptist Convention were relatively fundamentalist in 1962, and the
evangelist, literal tradition had exerted considerable impact throughout
Southern Protestantism.[18] The proportion of individuals with fundamentalist leanings varied with the denomination—higher among Southern Baptists than among Associate Reformed Presbyterians, lower
among members of the Presbyterian Church in the United States
(Southern Presbyterian Church), and lower still among Episcopalians.
The Methodists, who were typically accustomed to emotional revivals
as late as the 1930's, have in recent decades become increasingly oriented toward social action and analysis, interested in well-educated
clergy, and, according to conservative Southerners, "afflicted with
modernism."

But even Southern Presbyterian ministers among the interviewees for
this study seemed more inclined than Northern Presbyterian clergymen
of the author's acquaintance to use biblical expressions in discussing
secular issues, including world affairs, to think in terms of saving individual souls and converting the unchurched (and members of other
denominations, too) to their particular denomination, rather than of
thinking through and explaining to their congregations relationships
between Christianity and complex social and political questions. The
differences between Southern and Northern Baptist ministers in these
respects appeared considerably larger.

The potent residues of literalism, fundamentalism, and emphasis on
individual salvation even among the denominations populated by better-
educated Southerners have been reinforced by other forces in the
region. The great influence on organized religion by economically

18 Thomas R. Ford, "Status, Residence, and Fundamentalist Religious Beliefs in
the Southern Appalachians," *Social Forces*, XXXIX (1960), 41–49, noted some
change from fundamentalist thinking and behavior among mountain folk with education and urbanization, but the process was very slow. Education was more effective in attenuating fundamentalism than was urbanization without much education,
but even the urban middle classes in mountain cities were considerably influenced
by this heritage.

conservative members of the elite fearful of analysis of the local social and economic systems has discouraged ministers who would critically examine controversial issues before their congregations. The race question has been another major reason for the relatively weak impact of the social gospel movement on the South, since critical examination of social and public issues would inevitably lead to problems of Negro-white relations.

Denominational Preferences and International Thought

Thus, fundamentalism in its purer form has been associated with a number of other factors which have themselves been related to relative ignorance about, and indifference to, world affairs and to opposition to foreign economic assistance to underdeveloped, unaligned countries, immigration, subtle relations and possible compromises with the Communist bloc, and other attitudes akin to neo-isolationism (except in national defense). One cannot separate the influence of fundamentalist inclinations on international thought from the effects of low education, rural underprivileged childhoods, low social status, passive resignation to fate, economic *laissez faire*, political conservatism, pessimism about human nature and the possibilities of social and international progress, and so on—phenomena which tend to coexist with fundamentalism. When these factors have been present in the same individuals, as has been frequently the case, they have tended to reinforce one another.

But fundamentalist attitudes themselves have intensified some of the effects of these other variables. Directly related to this phenomenon has been the more widespread feeling in the South than in the North that the clergy should confine themselves to religion in its narrower sense and should not express themselves on such problems as foreign affairs. Southern Protestants have been much less favorable than Northern Protestants to ecumenical movements on the national or international levels [19]—such as interdenominational cooperation through the National and World Council of Churches—on account of fundamentalist inclinations, distrust of collaboration with other Christian groups, suspicion of the "outside" generally, and the liberal pronouncements of these interdenominational groups on public questions, especially race. Southerners have therefore been on the whole less affected by the predominantly liberal or multilateralist international thinking among these ecumenical groups than have Northern Protestants.

Fundamentalism has also encouraged people to think in dogmatic, oversimplified ways, to apply black-and-white moralism to international

19 For instance, AIPO 454, 3/24/50 (1,458), and AIPO 642, 3/8/61 (3,511).

questions, and to press for clear-cut, direct "solutions" or "victories" abroad, whereas world issues in the 1960's are typically complicated and foreign policy choices a problem of selection among complex shades of gray. The enthusiastic overstatement and emotionalism of the evangelist and the fundamentalist, the emphasis of many ministers on rhetoric rather than analysis, and the focus on the next world rather than on social and public action in line with Christian ethics in this one have discouraged, or failed to stimulate, critical interest in foreign policy. It is up to God, not man, to change this world.[20]

Anti-Catholicism has also been intimately related to these proclivities; Southern Protestants have been more apt than Northern Protestants to say that they would prefer not to have an otherwise qualified man for President if he were a Roman Catholic [21] (before the 1960 election) and to oppose the idea of sending a personal representative of the President, particularly an ambassador, to the Vatican.[22] Opposition to immigration in the South also has sprung in part from Southern Protestants' anxieties over entry of predominantly Catholic foreigners—removal of Jews and Catholics from Southern survey samples has typically resulted in increased differences between the North and South in the direction of greater nativism of the latter.[23]

Moreover, the frontier individualism of the sects and of the more theologically conservative congregations in the Southern Baptist Convention and to lesser extent among some Lutherans, Presbyterians, and even Episcopalians has helped to foster similarly individualistic frames of reference of an extreme free enterprise sort in economics, social relations, and political affairs, including international relations. These, as noted previously, have been related to opposition to capital assistance

20 For more detailed analyses of relationships between religious fundamentalism and neo-isolationism and other ultraconservative attitudes, see David Danzig, "The Radical Right and the Rise of the Fundamentalist Minority," *Commentary*, XXXIII (April, 1962); Alan F. Westin, "The John Birch Society: 'Radical Right' and 'Extreme Left' in Political Context of Post World War II—1962," in *The Radical Right*, especially 218 ff; and David Riesman, "The Intellectuals and Discontented Classes: Some Further Reflections," in *ibid.*, 116 and 123–24.
21 AIPO 67, 2/1/37 (2,970); AIPO 188, 3/26/40 (3,266); NORC 365, 11/26/54 (1,201); AIPO 542, 1/18/55 (1,477); AIPO 585, 5/29/56 (1,521); AIPO 604, 9/8/58 (1,522); and AIPO 631, 7/14/60 (2,900).
22 AIPO 457, 6/27/50 (1,363), and AIPO 482, 11/9/51 (2,021). In late 1951 only one Southerner out of ten felt the U.S. Senate should approve the appointment of an ambassador to the Vatican, whereas almost a third of Northerners felt so. When Protestants alone were compared, 81 percent of Southerners venturing opinions in contrast to 68 percent of Northerners opposed this proposal.
23 NORC 243, 8/21/46 (1,286); AIPO 377, 8/28/46 (3,163); AIPO 395, 4/23/47 (3,142); NORC 157, 4/22/48 (1,280); AIPO 444, 6/30/49 (2,826); NORC 323, 4/22/52 (1,250); NORC 327, 6/30/52 (1,285); and NORC 333, 11/17/52 (1,291).

for backward countries, dislike of social welfare and socialist regimes abroad, and apathy or opposition toward coordinated, long-term planning on the international as well as the national level.

With some exceptions literalists and theological conservatives in areas with large numbers of Negroes have been strong racial conservatives. Preachers of the sects and some Southern Baptist ministers have been active in the Ku Klux Klan, and clergymen who have said blessings for or otherwise supported Citizens Councils and related segregationist groups have come disproportionately from among fundamentalists. When a Presbyterian minister among the informants for this study was of strongly segregationist persuasion, he was typically among the more literalist minority of his denomination who emphasized individual conversion and salvation rather than social relevance of the gospel. Only a minuscule minority of fundamentalists outside the mountains and hill areas with few Negroes have been liberal on race—for example, the little-educated preacher who had come "to believe what the Bible said about all races and all nations" (see p. 411) and another who wondered how white racists "could love God whom they have never seen if they hate Negroes whom they see every day." Apparently even when Southerners of similar education have been compared, those of more fundamentalist denominations have been more segregationist; for instance, Baptist undergraduate students at the University of Texas were significantly more opposed to desegregation and generally racist on a variety of questions than were Methodists, Presbyterians, Episcopalians, and other less-fundamentalist Protestants, and, particularly, than Roman Catholics and Jews.[24] As one would surmise, conservative racial thinking among whites in surveys has been correlated with anti-Catholicism, advocacy of legal prohibition of alcoholic drink, antagonism to the National Council of Churches and ecumenical programs generally, hostility to theories of biological evolution, antifeminism, and other views associated with fundamentalism.[25]

It is, therefore, understandable that a number of international attitudes within the syndrome related to racism have been correlated with fundamentalist thinking. Southerners who have opposed the idea of a Catholic as President, women in high elective office, women wearing shorts in public, and their church becoming affiliated with the National

---

24 James G. Kelly, Jean E. Ferson, Wayne H. Holtzman, "The Measurement of Attitudes toward the Negro in the South," *Journal of Social Psychology,* XLVIII (1958), 305–17.
25 AIPO 542, 1/18/55 (1,477); AIPO 565, 5/29/56 (1,975); and AIPO 644, 5/2/61 (3,545).

Council and World Council of Churches or other collaboration with
Christian denominations different from their own, who have favored
legal prohibition of alcohol, who have believed that Christ would
physically return to earth and who have felt that churches and ministers
should remain silent on social and public issues have been more likely
than those replying the opposite to such questions [26] to:

(1) be uninformed and venture no opinions about foreign policy
issues; [27]

(2) say they did not vote in the last presidential or congressional
election or primary; [28]

(3) say they have not written to their Congressman; [29]

(4) oppose economic assistance, particularly capital aid to underdeveloped and neutralist countries; [30]

(5) believe that arms-control negotiations and proposals for limiting weapons by our leaders are not worth the effort and that we
should not accept exchanges of information on our defenses
with Communists and international inspection of our own
country; [31]

(6) feel that another world war is likely; [32]

(7) disapprove of proposals to establish a permanent international
force to implement the decisions of the U.N.; [33]

(8) think we should not go along with any majority decision of the
General Assembly to recognize the credentials of Communist
China for purposes of her admission into the U.N.[34]

---

26 These intercorrelations applied whether or not Negroes were removed from
the Southern samples. Since Negroes have been more apt than whites to harbor
fundamentalist views, their removal reduced the proportion of fundamentalists in
Southern samples considerably.

27 NORC 237, September, 1945 (1,270); AIPO 454, 3/24/50 (1,458); NORC 365,
11/26/54 (1,201); AIPO 580, 3/13/57 (1,624); and AIPO 594, 1/22/58 (1,550).

28 NORC 237, September, 1945 (1,270); AIPO 360, 11/21/45 (3,086); AIPO 454,
3/24/50 (1,458); NORC 365, 11/26/54 (1,201); AIPO 542, 1/18/55 (1,477); AIPO
551, 8/2/55 (1,502); AIPO 558, 1/4/56 (1,385); AIPO 565, 5/29/56 (1,975); AIPO
580, 3/13/57 (1,624); AIPO 594, 1/22/58 (1,550); AIPO 604, 9/8/58 (1,522); AIPO
622, 12/8/59 (2,550); AIPO 631, 7/14/60 (2,800); and AIPO 644, 5/2/61 (3,545).

29 AIPO 580, 3/13/57 (1,624).

30 AIPO 360, 11/21/45 (3,086); AIPO 454, 3/24/50 (1,458); NORC 365, 11/26/
54 (1,201); and AIPO 558, 1/4/56 (1,385).

31 AIPO 551, 8/2/55 (1,502); AIPO 594, 1/22/58 (1,550); and AIPO 622, 12/8/59
(2,550).

32 NORC 365, 11/26/54 (1,201); AIPO 558, 1/4/56 (1,385); AIPO 622, 12/8/59
(2,550); and AIPO 631, 7/14/60 (2,800).

33 AIPO 580, 3/13/57 (1,624).

34 AIPO 551, 8/2/55 (1,502). See also AIPO 594, 1/22/58 (1,550).

On the other hand, fundamentalists venturing opinions have been about as inclined as other Southerners to favor peacetime conscription.[35]

The lower educational and social groups of fundamentalist orientations in surveys and among the interviewees in Mountain and Hill counties and elsewhere were typically poorly informed and little interested in world affairs. Disproportionately large numbers of Southern isolationists—those who felt we should be less active in world affairs in general—have fallen into this group. Their isolationism has been made up largely of feelings that we have enough domestic problems to devote our resources to, that foreign aid should be spent at home (perhaps on people like themselves), that we should mind our own business, and the like. The prosperous Southerners who were still relatively fundamentalist among the informants tended to be Harry Byrd, James Eastland, and Barry Goldwater conservatives both at home and abroad.

There have been, of course, exceptions. Two racially liberal fundamentalist ministers were favorable to foreign aid, intercultural exchanges, and most other programs of our federal government abroad of which they had heard. Interviewers encountered internationalist prohibitionists, Anglo-Catholic Episcopalians of high education who were reserved about collaboration with Protestants, but rather sophisticated and responsible about foreign policy, Protestants of all denominations who feared the influence of the Roman Catholic church but felt our aid programs to Latin America, India, and certain African countries should be increased, and so on. But on the whole, the more attitudes correlated with fundamentalism Southerners have accepted, the more inclined have they been to oppose or be indifferent to active international cooperation beyond Western Europe and outside the military field.

On the other hand, far from all Southerners relatively little affected by fundamentalism have favored international cooperation in the major fields advocated by Presidents Kennedy and Eisenhower. A considerable minority of prosperous Episcopalians, Presbyterians, and Methodists who have rejected thinking of an evangelist, fundamentalist tone were opposed to aid at the levels of the early sixties for neutralist, socialist, underdeveloped countries and felt we should have invaded Cuba as early as the summer of 1960. Local John Birch Societies, Discussions Unlimited (in New Orleans), Charleston Alerts, Christian Anti-Communist Crusade "Schools," Citizens Councils, and other pre-

35 AIPO 360, 11/21/45 (3,086), and AIPO 542, 1/18/55 (1,477).

dominantly neo-isolationist or unilateralist groups included in 1959–62 some such individuals of considerable education, affluence, and social prestige.

However, on the whole, less fundamentalist Southerners have tended more than more fundamentalist ones to go along with the major policies of our Presidents. At the other pole from the fundamentalists, Unitarians have apparently been for the most part liberals or responsible conservatives on world affairs. Most seem to have accepted the general international postures of the internationally oriented wing of the Republican party or of the national Democrats. Although the emphasis on social analysis and action of Methodists in the South has seemed considerably less than in the North, the National Council of Churches, their own national church, and several national groups connected with the Methodist church—such as the Women's Division of Christian Service of the Board of Missions—have been of liberal or multilateralist international persuasion, and they have apparently had significant effects on many Methodists south of the Mason-Dixon Line, especially on active church women. It is risky to generalize from the small sample interviewed for this study and impressions of participant observers, but the proportion of neo-isolationist Methodists seemed somewhat smaller than that of Presbyterians and Episcopalians. The relatively privileged classes which made up the Episcopal, Presbyterian, Methodist, and Unitarian churches included most of the thoughtful non-Jewish cosmopolitans in the region.

Protestant Clergy as Communicators of World Affairs

The international thinking of the ministers of the sects among the interviewees for this study—largely part-time, without the benefit of college or accredited seminary, and with small congregations—was along the same lines as that of most of their fundamentalist laity, insofar as they had opinions. Most tended to feel that foreign policy had little to do with their functions as ministers. Being on the whole more emotionally committed to their fundamentalist beliefs than their followers, these ministers held international views which tended in some respects to be more dogmatic, if not more extreme. They were almost uniformly hostile to the Vatican and any United States relations with it. They tended to feel that the best long-term solution in underdeveloped countries would be conversion of these groups to their brand of Christianity. They were inclined to suggest that foreign aid be channeled into missionary work rather than into intergovernmental economic and cultural programs. The idea that the U.N. is "atheistic" or "godless" seemed to have taken root with many of them. However, these ministers usually supported strong military forces, even if higher taxes were necessary. A considerable number of Southern Baptist clergymen, particularly those with little formal training and of more emotional, fundamentalist persuasion, have also harbored international thinking correlated with fundamentalism, or less extreme forms of these views.

But as early as 1947, college-educated ministers in the South, including Southern Baptists and other denominations, were on the average more cosmopolitan in their reading habits, knowledge, and thinking than Southerners as a whole, and even than most Southern college graduates outside of teaching and perhaps one or two other professions.[36] The impression from interviews and other indications is that Southern ministers who had graduated from college and theological school by the late 1950's were significantly more interested and informed about world affairs and more internationalist or liberal on foreign policy questions than in the late 1940's and that the gap between them and their congregations had widened as the clergymen developed greater sophistication and liberalism in world affairs.

College-educated clergymen in each denomination differed considerably among themselves in 1959–62 about foreign affairs. In general, the more fundamentalist or conservative the theology, the more conservative the international thinking of the seminary-trained minister. Younger seminary-educated men tended to be better informed, more interested, and more favorable to nonmilitary multilateral commitments in world affairs than their elders.[37] Those in larger cities and college towns were on the whole more intellectually alert and more cosmopolitan in their thinking than others in small towns and rural sections. When they were conservative on race, their international views were usually also conservative. For instance, one Northern-raised Episcopal minister, occupying an esteemed pulpit, cited Kipling on the white man's burden as indicative of his thinking on Negroes in the area as well as in Africa, noted that he would probably prefer educated Negroes to "white trash" in his church, voiced domestic political ideas approaching those of former President McKinley, and expressed concern that we had gone too far in "trying to save the world," that foreign aid had done little

36 The Bureau of Applied Social Research study. Ministers throughout the country were more liberal and better read in international affairs than the average of college graduates.
37 This finding corresponded with that of Thomas F. Pettigrew and Ernest Q. Campbell, *Christians in Racial Crisis* (Washington, D.C.: Public Affairs Press, 1959). According to this study of Little Rock clergy, younger seminary-trained ministers were more actively liberal on race than their more influential seniors.

good abroad since the end of the Marshall Plan, and that we had been too "permissive" with Communists at home and abroad. However, some segregationist Episcopal and Presbyterian ministers interviewed remained Wilsonians, free traders, and otherwise traditional Southern genteel internationalists.

But the greater average of cosmopolitanism among educated ministers of all denominations than among their congregations was readily apparent during the early 1960's in the sample communities of this study in their thinking about both world affairs and related public issues. Thus, various degrees of racism affected the thinking of most white Episcopalians, from arch-white supremacists to moderate paternalists favoring minimum desegregation legally feasible. But no more than several dozen Episcopal ministers in 1959–62 were known publicly among their clerical colleagues and active Episcopal laymen as segregationists, and probably less than a hundred privately agreed with them out of a total of some sixteen hundred white clergymen. The proportion among Presbyterians seemed significantly larger, and that among Methodists smaller than among Anglican ministers. Interviewers located no Unitarian minister who believed that whites were innately superior to Negroes and that desegregation should be reversed or stopped, although some had been under pressure from their congregations not to "stir up trouble" in the community on the race question.

Seminary-educated Southern Baptist ministers seemed on the average more conservative about world affairs and related questions than Presbyterian, Episcopalian, and Methodist, and particularly than Unitarian clergymen. A considerable proportion of them were still very much in the evangelist tradition. A number seemed to agree with a Southern Baptist minister in Antebellum Town; a man in his early forties with a doctoral degree, he noted that "an unfortunate number of seminary students from prosperous families turn left," and continued that he had "nothing against a social gospel, but not the one which the liberals want and not the content they put into it." Or they agreed with the international thinking of another, older educated Baptist minister in Hill County who quoted with approval contents of *Human Events, Christianity Today, Christian Economics,* and an editorial by David Lawrence.

However, when the results of studies of public attitudes of Baptist ministers in the 1930's were compared with interviews of Baptist ministers in 1959–62,[38] it was apparent that Southern Baptist seminaries have stimulated considerable interest in social ethics since World War II. The

38 E.g., Pope, *op. cit.*, esp. Chapter 10.

Christian Life Commission of the Southern Baptist Convention and a number of cosmopolitan Southern Baptist lay and clerical leaders have for some years been encouraging concern with the social implications of Christianity.[39] Although only a minority among the interviewees for this study were more than tangentially interested in world affairs, over two thirds of those who had graduated from colleges and seminaries read the foreign news and some editorials in a daily newspaper and approximately half also read a weekly newsmagazine. Their opinions on foreign policy ranged from the two cited above to others who agreed more or less with the thinking of Brooks Hays, recently President of the Southern Baptist Convention and long associated with the application of religion to public questions and with thoughtful internationalism.

Cosmopolitan ministers who would broaden the thinking of their congregations and others on world issues have typically labored under major difficulties. The gap between the internationally thoughtful minister and his congregation has typically been large, especially among Baptists. Although the congregations of the better-educated, more socially and politically sophisticated Baptist clergymen have tended to be among the better educated of that denomination, many laymen still felt in 1962 that ministers should limit themselves to preaching on individual salvation and that discussions of such fields as world affairs had no business in the church. And many educated Baptist ministers have had poorly educated, insular congregations—one cosmopolitan in Mountain County interested in the social implications of the gospel, including world developments, felt it was virtually impossible to communicate such ideas to his congregation of very limited, rural experience. The pressures against such discussions have been, on the whole, less formidable among the Methodists, Presbyterians, and Episcopalians, but a cosmopolitan Northern Presbyterian minister with the most prestigious congregation in Mountain County observed that most of his parishioners—largely of fundamentalist childhoods—felt as well that he should "stick to the Scriptures" and that few could understand the ideas he had cautiously advanced on world issues.

One Baptist minister who read *Harper's* described the situation of a number of his colleagues, saying that "the three most reactionary millionaires in town run this church." The well-to-do of Baptist persuasion, those most apt to influence the hiring and firing of cosmopolitan min-

---

39 For a critical examination of the Christian Life Commission and its predecessors and dissension among Southern Baptists about the individual versus the social gospel and the content of the latter, see John Lee Eighmy, *The Social Conscience of Southern Baptists from 1900 to the Present as Reflected in Their Organized Life*, Unpublished Ph.D. dissertation, University of Missouri, 1959.

isters and the operation of their churches, have frequently been self-made men of limited intellectual cultivation. Methodist, Presbyterian, and Episcopal ministers have been somewhat less dependent on popularity with their parishioners due to less congregational methods of church control, but they too have feared antagonizing influential members. Their vestries, elders, deacons, and other members of influence have likewise been typically quite conservative on public questions, including foreign policy, often more so than much of the rank and file in their congregations. In many textile towns, for instance, manufacturers and their representatives have continued as in the past [40] to subsidize and greatly influence local churches and ministers.

Augmented racial tensions in many Southern settings have tended to drive wedges between internationally thoughtful ministers and their more conservative congregations. The more tense the local feelings on race relations, the more difficult has it been for the clergyman to express cosmopolitan ideas vigorously. As in other walks of life, the more liberal and intellectually alert the minister, the more likely has he been to leave the Deep South. Even with Baptist congregations of broader backgrounds, for example, internationalism in a minister was rather likely to be associated in the minds of conservative members with relative liberalism on other locally controversial issues, such as race and economics.

Thus, in the early 1960's ministers who would maintain effective parishes feared splitting their congregations on public questions. In many Deep Southern settings a minister would generate discord and potent pressures if he became known as being favorable to aid to Poland and Yugoslavia, or even to African neutralists, more flexible policies toward Communist China, a compromise solution of the "two-Chinas" problem, UNESCO, expansion of exchanges with Communist countries, or forceful negotiations with the Portuguese for gradual steps toward independence of their African colonies.

Nevertheless, most fields of world affairs were not as controversial as race or even trade unions and other aspects of domestic economics and most ministers who have been interested in foreign relations have felt freer to deal with this area. Except for those with the more reactionary congregational leaderships, few would experience much difficulty in speaking out in favor of technical assistance, the Peace Corps, broadened hospitality for white international visitors and even—with more exceptions—contributions to UNICEF. If a minister were truly interested in introducing some national program on world affairs of his denomination or even of the National Council of Churches into his

40 See, for instance, Pope, *Millhands and Preachers,* especially Chapter 8.

parish, he could typically guide some of the lay leadership to support the program. He may have been obliged to ally himself to some extent with the more cosmopolitan minority in the parish against the arch-conservatives, but the socially skilled minister could often exert some impact if he were willing to take some risks and be patient. In making such programs available and in expressing internationalist views even cautiously, the clergyman tended to encourage those in his congregation of similar inclinations and to provide his laymen with views different from those they would normally have heard locally. Even though the thoughtful minister who has expressed atypical opinions has often been obliged to change parishes, he has usually encouraged some responsible thought and deviation from local thinking on foreign policy in a minority of his congregation before moving on.

In fact, however, most Southern ministers of cosmopolitan leanings, like Southerners of similar inclinations in other professions, exerted in 1959–62 only rather limited influence on thinking about world affairs. Many in smaller, conservative communities despaired of changing prevailing international attitudes or stimulating intelligent interest where there was little. Ministers, like others, had tended to find local inertia and opposition formidable; they had in many cases gradually curtailed their attention to international developments and lost their intellectual vigor unless encouraged by others of cosmopolitan orientations from within or, at least, without their communities.

Southern Roman Catholics

Roman Catholics comprise such a small proportion of the Southern population that they have been too few in individual surveys to permit comparisons with Southern Protestants, Northern Catholics, or other groups. The generalizations to follow have, therefore, necessarily been derived from combining replies to often differently worded questions on similar issues in a number of surveys and from interviews of approximately a hundred and fifty Catholics, mostly in Bayou Parish, New Orleans, and elsewhere in southern Louisiana. Most of the observations about Catholic as compared with Protestant attitudes in the South should therefore be viewed as tentative pending more systematic study of larger samples.

Less Inclination to Neo-Isolationism

The combined results of surveys indicate that Southern Catholics as a group were on the average somewhat more favorable to foreign economic assistance during the period 1954–62 than Southern Protestants taken together. The small minority of Catholics who would withdraw from the U.N. since the end of the Korean War has been slightly smaller than that of Southern Protestants. Catholics have also been less apt to accept protectionist arguments, undoubtedly because of their concentration around New Orleans and other coastal and Mississippi River communities and on account of their low numbers in protectionist industries other than sugar and seafood rather than because of any religious factors. They have been more inclined to support liberalization of immigration laws, particularly to permit entry of European refugees. They have been, of course, considerably more favorable to establishment of diplomatic relations with the Vatican.

Catholics have also been somewhat more likely to reject isolationist ideas and to feel that we should "take an active part in world affairs." They have likewise been more apt to know something about international issues, to be able to identify international figures and problems, and to venture some opinion rather than replying "don't know," "no opinion," or the like.

On the other hand, differences have been very small or nonexistent between Catholics and Protestants with respect to support of strong military defenses, peacetime conscription, and active participation in NATO and other defense alliances. Differences have disappeared when the Communist issue has been central. Catholics have been as opposed as Protestants to entry of Communist China into the U.N. and, more still, to United States recognition of that government. They have been just as inclined as Protestants to think that negotiations with the Communists for arms control and other relaxations of international tensions will probably fail.

Moreover, as in the case of racial attitudes, Catholic international views, understanding, and interest have been more like those of Southern Protestants than like those of Southern Jews. On virtually every issue other than diplomatic relations with the Papacy, Jews have been considerably better informed, more interested, more exposed to serious coverage in national publications, and more favorable to close international collaboration than either Catholics or Protestants taken together (see Chapter 13).

There have been, of course, major differences in international behavior among Southern Catholics, related to the same factors correlated with thinking about foreign policy among Southern Protestants. The greater proportion of Catholics than Protestants among those demographic, social, and psychological groups most inclined to favor international cooperation beyond the military sphere and to be informed about world affairs probably accounts to a large degree for whatever differences there might have been between the international postures of the two groups.

A much smaller proportion of Catholics than of Protestants are Negroes, the Southern group least inclined to be informed about world issues and to harbor opinions favorable to most international involvements (see Chapter 14). Negro Catholics, who are concentrated in southern Louisiana, have been disproportionately among the better-educated, largely mulatto, middle class—those of their race most inclined to support active international cooperation—and exceedingly few among the most culturally underprivileged, or lower-lower class.[41] White Catholics of racist inclinations have apparently accepted much of the racist syndrome of international thinking prevalent among Protestant white supremacists.[42] But Southern white Catholics as a group have been somewhat less conservative about Negro-white relations than white Protestants taken together. Interreligious differences have not been large, and only a small minority of Catholic whites could be termed "liberals" or "integrationists" on race—if these labels imply acceptance of desegregation as desirable as well as inevitable. Furthermore, much of this interreligious difference has been accounted for by the upper South and border states. In 1959, for instance, 90 percent of

41 Southern Louisiana reportedly contained in the late 1950's approximately a quarter of the estimated 525,000 Negro Catholics in the United States. Liston Pope, *The Kingdom beyond Caste* (New York: Friendship Press, 1957), 138. Thompson in *The Negro Leadership Class*, 31, estimated that a third of Negro churchgoers in New Orleans itself were Roman Catholics in the early 1960's. Many of their ancestors appeared among Baptismal records at St. Louis Cathedral in the early 1800's. Their forebears were frequently free men of color in 1861 rather than slaves; most of these antebellum Negroes were in pursuits which involved education or skill and were better off at that time than free Negroes in Northern cities like New York. See Shugg, *Origins of Class Struggle in Louisiana*, 119. By 1962 their descendants were disproportionately numerous among the educated middle class in the city, most of whom had been urban for several generations. See Thompson, *The Negro Leadership Class*, 32. The relatively few rural Negro Catholics have tended to spring from ancestors who were household servants rather than field hands, the elite of plantation Negroes. Many still in the rural areas in the early sixties were independent farmers, artisans, skilled sugar-mill workers, and other self-employed or skilled individuals.

42 A recent unpublished study of over two thousand priests and a like number of active Catholic laymen by Joseph H. Fichter, S.J., of Loyola University of the South discovered a positive correlation between liberalism on civil rights for Negroes and other minorities and support of foreign aid. Individuals who were relatively liberal on both race relations and foreign aid were highly likely to be liberal on most other public, moral, and social questions as well. Those who were conservative on both these issues were, on the other hand, very apt to be conservative on most other issues of both domestic and international affairs.

white Catholics as compared with 94 percent of white Protestants in the Deep South disapproved of the idea of desegregation of the schools as required by the Supreme Court. However, the respective figures were 37 percent and 75 percent in the border South.[43]

The concentration of Catholics in urban environments, except in country parishes of south Louisiana, has been another explanatory factor in the somewhat higher average support for international collaboration among them than among Protestants. Moreover, differences in international interest, knowledge, and attitudes have been larger between Catholics and those Protestants who have accepted fundamentalist thinking on surveys. It is questionable that Catholics have been any better informed, more thoughtful, and more favorable to multilateral cooperation than Episcopalians, Unitarians, Presbyterians, Methodists, Quakers, and those Southern Baptists and members of other denominations who were among the better-educated strata; samples were too small for such comparisons.

Many Catholic cosmopolitans and internationalists have been among the more devout. A recent study of over two thousand Catholics selected by their pastors as being actively identified with the Church determined that 38.9 percent would have expanded foreign economic assistance, 24.1 percent would have kept it at the then current level, and only 35.2 percent would have reduced it; Southerners were about as inclined to favor aid as Northerners among these practicing Catholics.[44] They were considerably more favorable to foreign economic aid than were Southerners in general, or Southern Catholics taken together, according to national surveys.[45]

43 American Jewish Committee, "The Nationwide Poll of March, 1959" (1959), 5. See also the study of undergraduates at the University of Texas cited above, p. 443. Moreover, the proportion of Negroes registered to vote in 1960 in the South was positively correlated ($r = +.31$) with percent of Catholics in the county or parish. Some positive correlation of Negro registrations and prevalence of Catholics was apparent even when such factors as urban-rural and Negro-white ratios were held constant. See Donald R. Matthews and James W. Prothro, "Social and Economic Factors and Negro Voter Registration in the South," *American Political Science Review*, LVII (1963), 38.

44 An unpublished study by Joseph H. Fichter, S.J. The Catholics were also above average education, another variable helping to account for their relatively widespread support of foreign economic assistance. These data were gathered prior to the publication of *Mater et Magistra*.

45 For example, when asked in December, 1963, "Do you think the U.S. Government's program of foreign economic aid to assist other nations should be kept at the present level, or reduced, or ended altogether?" 29 percent in the South thought it should be "kept at the present level at least," 41 percent felt that it should be reduced, 16 percent preferred that it be "ended altogether," and 14 percent offered no opinion, did not know, or were undecided (AIPO 682, 12/10/63 [1,330]).

The impression from interviews and the observations of local informants is that Catholic fundamentalists who have been inclined to feel that the Church should confine its attention to saving individual souls and that parish priests should limit themselves to saying mass, hearing confessions, and other "religious" and parish functions, and who have been uninterested in, or hostile to, the application of Christian principles to social and public questions—including world affairs—have tended to be among the more conservative about foreign aid and to emphasize military rather than diplomatic, economic, and cultural approaches to foreign policy.

Likewise, Catholics who were antagonistic to organized labor, welfare legislation, progressive taxation, and other liberal domestic economic programs usually opposed foreign aid or recommended its reduction, as their Protestant colleagues of similar inclinations tended to do. The bulk of poorly educated, underprivileged Catholics—concentrated in southern Louisiana—seemed to feel that the money for foreign aid should be spent in this country, whereas most internationally thoughtful Catholics were college-educated.[46] The few Catholics in managerial roles in textile mills and garment plants and Catholic sugar planters were with few exceptions protectionists, whereas those in the International House, the International Trade Mart, and the Cotton Exchange in New Orleans favored expanded trade.

Catholics in Predominantly Protestant Areas

The interviewers' conversations with a few priests and laymen in parts of the South where Catholics have comprised minute fractions of the population and other bits of evidence tend to indicate that they probably have differed in international thought from their coreligionists in areas of long Catholic tradition.

A study in 1958 of members of the Catholic parish in Tallahassee—well north of the tourist, retirement, or "Yankeefied" areas of Florida—is probably applicable with some amendments to many other Southern Catholics outside southern Louisiana, old Gulf and Atlantic coastal areas, and old communities along the Mississippi.[47] Catholics in Tallahassee in 1904 numbered four. By 1958 they had grown to approximately 287 families and 87 unattached individuals out of a total population of nearly 40,000; the preponderant majority had migrated

46 The recent study of active Catholics by the Reverend Fichter discovered correlations between education and international attitudes similar to those evident in other surveys among Southern Protestants and Americans generally.
47 William T. Liu, "A Study of the Social Integration of Catholic Migrants in a Southern Community" (Ph.D. dissertation, Florida State University, 1958).

from the North. Whereas most Southerners were raised in rural areas and small rurally based towns, only 6 percent of Tallahassee Catholics had spent their childhood and adolescence in rural settings. Furthermore, Catholics in Tallahassee were educated and prosperous—far above the Southern Protestant average. Sixty-six percent of the men and 54 percent of the women had been to college, and 20 percent of the former and 14 percent of the latter had been to graduate or professional schools. Only 17 percent of the men and 10 percent of the women had not finished high school. More than seven out of ten Catholic families had earned more than six thousand dollars in the previous year. Thirty-two percent of the husbands were professional and technical people, 31 percent were proprietors and officials, and only 9 percent could be considered foremen or semiskilled and 3 percent domestic, manual, or other lower-class labor. Although the ecclesiastical parish included five counties, only a fractional minority were farmers or otherwise made a living in rural pursuits.

Thus, the minute minority of Catholics in most of the South have diverged fundamentally in many characteristics from most Protestant Southerners: they have lived with minor exceptions in cities; they were raised in Northern cities and have had few rural values; and they have been concentrated in the college-educated, prosperous, professional, technical, and managerial classes. The author is unable to speak in statistical terms about the international and related attitudes of these Catholics in comparison with those of southern Louisiana and the few other areas of historic Catholic habitation since samples on national surveys are too small even when similar questions on successive polls are combined. However, each of these demographic factors has been positively correlated with greater rather than lesser interest and knowledge about world affairs, exposure to newspaper, newsmagazine, and especially relatively sophisticated periodical content on foreign affairs, a dispassionate, thoughtful posture toward alternative lines of foreign policy, and internationally responsible attitudes.

The interviews for this study and limited additional evidence tend to indicate, however, that one should be cautious about estimating the support for multilateral cooperation among these Southern Catholics. Like other Northern migrants to the region, they have been on the average better educated than native Southerners.[48] But many Catholics,

48 In 1956, some 10 percent of whites in the South had immigrated from the North; a third of these new Southerners had attended college, nine out of ten had at least some high-school education, and two out of five were in business and professional occupations. See Campbell, Converse, Miller, and Stokes, *The American Voter*, 449.

as well as other former Northerners, came South to take advantage of
the kind of physical and psychological climate available in the region
—right-to-work laws, cheap, passive labor, comfortable, leisurely living
with Negro servants, and so on. Once in the South a considerable proportion have adopted local thinking or remained silent on issues when
they have disagreed with local attitudes on them. Only a few Northern
idealists, Catholic or otherwise, have gone South with any idea of
changing the thinking there on world affairs or other issues; most who
have migrated for economic purposes seem to have taken on Southern
mores of both mind and action in order to minimize frictions with the
natives and "succeed" in the homogeneous culture. Northerners who
have moved South permanently—in contradistinction to those sent there
for a brief period by the armed forces or national corporations—were
probably less intellectually oriented, more authoritarian and conservative, and in general more like Southern norms than college-educated
Northerners in general even before they left the Midwest or Northeast.

For instance, a Catholic dentist from a large Northeastern city decided to settle in a small Southern community after spending some time
near there during the war and, apparently, observing that his ultra-
conservative, racist, and elitist views were more acceptable there than
around his former home; a Canadian physician of similar opinions did
likewise in a Mississippi town. Catholics in Tallahassee were less conservative about race relations than Southerners in general, according
to national surveys in the late 1950's. But 29 percent agreed to at least
some extent that the Negro is "naturally inferior" to whites, 64 percent
felt that intermarriage should be prohibited "forever" by law, and 72
percent believed Negroes should have "separate but equal" facilities.
The longer these relatively prosperous Catholics had been in the South
and the more they identified themselves with that region, the more
conservative they were about race, trade unions, and probably world
affairs as well. Some former Northerners, Catholic and otherwise, have
become even more racist than most native white Southerners.

Although the Roman Catholic church has repeatedly declared itself
in favor of racial equality, desegregation, and participation in trade
unions, involvement in Southern society has entailed gradual acceptance
of theories of racial inequality and conservative views on economics and
other public questions by many, perhaps most, Catholic arrivals from
the North. The study of Tallahassee Catholics found little relation
between active Catholicism, as indicated by participation in the Sacra-
ments, and attitudes on race and trade unions, and it is questionable that
results would have been different for international affairs. It seems

realistic to assume that many Catholic (or other) migrants to the South will be among the last to change their behavior, even after their Southern-born non-Jewish colleagues have done so.

Some of these well-educated, Northern urban-born Catholics, like Protestant and Jewish Northerners moved South, have retained the international thinking prevalent among their coreligionists of similar background who stayed in the North, and they have exerted increasing influence upon Southern attitudes in this and other fields. However, the views of even the more liberal of them on foreign policy in more cases than not have not been particularly intense, clear-cut, nor relevant to their daily thinking. Few have been so interested that they have taken public positions in this field contrary to the expressed views of the local media, conservative politicians, and associates. Nor have many, according to the informants for this study, contradicted acquaintances in informal conversations when the latter have expressed irresponsible opinions on world issues. In general, with certain exceptions, relatively internationally sophisticated former Northerners, of Catholic or other faiths, have seemed more cautious about expressing ideas different from those about them, or, as "outsiders," they have apparently had less effect on local opinion than Southerners of similar international persuasion who could be identified as "one of us" even though "a bit different."

Roman Catholics of Southern Louisiana

Except for southern Florida, some three quarters of Southern Catholics in 1961 lived in southern Louisiana and on the adjoining Gulf Coast of east Texas and Mississippi.[49] In contrast with most of the rest of the region, Catholics have from the beginning formed a majority of the population of southern Louisiana;[50] the most Catholic diocese in the country, in proportion to the total local population, has been that of Lafayette.[51]

Unlike their coreligionists in the Bible Belt, most of these Catholics were born in the South, as were their ancestors for several and, often, many generations. A considerable number of them in 1962 were rural

49 *The Official Catholic Directory* (New York: P. J. Kennedy and Sons, 1961); and Smith and Hitt, *The People of Louisiana*, 131–32.

50 See, for example, Joseph H. Fichter, S.J., *Dynamics of a City Church* (Chicago: University of Chicago Press, 1951), 17–18 and 26–27; Kammer, *A Socio-Economic Survey of the Marshdwellers;* Parenton, "The Rural French Speaking People," 6–7; Eaton, *The Growth of Southern Civilization*, 128–29; and Shugg, *Origins of Class Struggle in Louisiana*, 62–63.

51 New York *Times*, July 30, 1963.

farmers and fishermen rather than urban people. Most had lost whatever attachments their ancestors might have had a hundred years or more before to the "old country." A small group in 1962 were descendants of Louisiana Creoles of wealth and influence in the eighteenth century. But New Orleans and, to a lesser measure, the rural parishes have received successive waves of Catholic immigration from France, Spain, Holland, Germany, Italy, Croatia, Ireland, Cuba, Switzerland, and elsewhere. Southern Louisiana has been the most ethnically and culturally heterogeneous section of the South for over two centuries.[52]

These Catholics had acculturated the incoming Protestants more than the reverse, as had been the case in most of the rest of the South. They also incorporated in the early 1960's the whole spectrum of Southern demographic characteristics as other Southern Catholics for the most part did not. The rural Catholics in Cajun country had in 1960 a rate of illiteracy (in both French and English) as high as the more isolated mountaineers, and higher than most other Southerners. They had been at least as isolated from "American" influences as the people of Mountain County. Many Catholic old families at the top of the social prestige pyramid in New Orleans and the plantation country have been as elitist and exclusive toward their newly prosperous coreligionists as Episcopalian gentry in the low country of South Carolina or the Tidewater of Virginia toward Protestant "upstarts." [53] One should expect, therefore, considerable heterogeneity of international behavior.

Although large enough samples to speak statistically of the thinking of south Louisiana Catholics are not available, their more relaxed, warm relations with Negroes (and with human beings generally) as compared with whites in north Louisiana and throughout most of the Protestant South have been intuitively apparent. Louisiana Catholics, except for a small minority, have not liked the idea of integration, but only a small fraction, led by a vociferous handful of racists, has been as extreme as the active white supremacists in the rural Protestant-dominated Deep South. White children in the country have played with colored youngsters for generations, as they did in 1962, and adults in the early 1960's were working side by side with Negroes in sugar mills. Negroes were members of integrated trade unions in some of the larger mills. Influential union leaders in Bayou Parish and in several mills nearby were comparatively liberal on race and other social questions, particularly in the light of their predominantly rural Cajun background and limited

52 See, for instance, Shugg, *Origins of Class Struggle in Louisiana*, 39–43.
53 *Ibid.*, 29–30.

education. The Citizens Council in Bayou Parish was feeble indeed as compared with its counterpart in Delta County, and with the exception of one or, perhaps, two parishes [54] racist organizations have been much weaker in southern Louisiana than in predominantly Protestant rural sections with considerable numbers of Negroes. The warm Catholic culture has encouraged a "live and let live" philosophy and discouraged the harsh human relationships—with whites or blacks—which are prevalent in much of the fundamentalist area.

The Roman Catholic church did not seem to have communicated much cosmopolitan thought or intellectual content to the less-educated majority of the faithful, but it has provided an educated clergy and at least some indirect contact with civilization and the outside world. Furthermore, its parishes have usually included a much broader range of social and educational strata—all lacking in the culturally deprived atmosphere of the Protestant poor whites, hill folk, mountaineers, and other poorly educated groups who have attended churches populated almost exclusively by people as uninformed and isolated as themselves and ministered by clergy of similar characteristics. Moreover, the proximity of the largest city in the region for over two centuries has moderated rural nativism and provincialism.

The greater cosmopolitanism of south Louisiana Catholics compared with Protestant Southerners of similar education and social status has been, of course, relative. There seems to be considerable truth in the joke that they have not concerned themselves much with ideologies, abstractions, education, or government, but rather with really fundamental matters, such as slot machines, horse races, good food and alcohol, hunting and fishing, and attractive women.[55]

In absolute terms, few rural and small-town Catholics in the early 1960's were much interested in, informed on, or thoughtful about world affairs. It was observed previously in discussing sugar interests and their

54 Antagonism to racial change has been most apparent in south Louisiana in the author's native parish, Plaquemines. It is his contention that citizens there would be no more hostile to racial evolution than in Bayou Parish or other predominantly Roman Catholic settings in Louisiana but for the influence of one local political leader, Leander Perez.

55 For some of the historical sources of such values in New Orleans and surrounding areas, see Herbert Asbury, *The French Quarter* (New York: Garden City Publishing Co., 1936); Carter, *The Lower Mississippi*; Fossier, *New Orleans: The Glamour Period, 1800–1840*; Shugg, *Origins of Class Struggle in Louisiana*; Joseph G. Tregle, Jr., "Early New Orleans Society: A Reappraisal," *Journal of Southern History*, XVIII, (1952), 20–36; Pellegrin, "A Sociological Analysis of Pointe Coupée Parish"; Vernon J. Parenton and T. Lynn Smith, "Acculturation among the Louisiana French," *American Journal of Sociology*, XLIV (November, 1938), 355–64; and Kammer, *A Socio-Economic Survey of the Marsh Dwellers*.

employees in Bayou Parish that most tended to go along with the international thinking of Senator Allen J. Ellender, insofar as they had views. The same might be said about much of the rest of the population, some 85 precent Roman Catholic. Only a small minority, composed primarily of college-trained Catholics—largely made up of some of the professors (far from all) at the local state college, a weekly-newspaper editor and publisher, most of the local priests, the organizer and leader of the trade-union local in the largest sugar mill, several lawyers, a few social-studies teachers in secondary schools, and a few college-trained wives of professional and managerial-class husbands—supported the arguments of the Kennedy administration against those in the Congress, like Senator Ellender, who would have reduced greatly foreign aid. These Catholics were also relatively well read on world issues and had some general idea of the content of Pope John XXIII's encyclical, *Mater et Magistra*, which had been made public several months before. The majority of Bayou Parish Catholics seemed unable to describe even vaguely any implications of this encyclical for assistance to underdeveloped countries.

Children of rural Catholics who became interested in foreign affairs or other broad questions have in most cases migrated after attending college to New Orleans or, in fewer instances, to other cities or university communities, as has been the case in Protestant rural areas. There these cosmopolitans have joined the ranks of New Orleanians of similar sensitivities and concerns. The city has long been the center for cosmopolitan southern Louisianians.

By comparison with most of the rest of the South, the Catholics in New Orleans—who comprised in 1960 a slight majority of the white church-affiliated population and a considerable minority of the Negroes [56]—together with its Protestants and Jews have been rather cosmopolitan in a number of respects. The city in 1960, as throughout most of its history, was more dependent on world trade than any other important metropolitan community in America. The second port after New York in value of imports and exports combined, New Orleans had the least industry and the smallest proportion of population in manufacturing of the first ten ports in the United States. [57] Moreover, for-

56 According to a survey in the early 1950's, 62 percent of church-affiliated whites and 47 percent of all church-affiliated New Orleanians were Roman Catholics. See Leonard Reissman, K. H. Silvert, and Cliff W. Wing, *The New Orleans Voter* (Tulane Studies in Political Science, [New Orleans, 1955]), 105.

57 According to an estimate by the New Orleans Dock Board, the port in 1961 accounted, directly or indirectly, for roughly 75 cents out of every dollar spent in New Orleans (Paul A. Fabry, "Needed: More Trade Exports," *Times-Picayune,*

eign exports from New Orleans have expanded faster in recent years than those of most other major United States ports. By 1962, annual exports through New Orleans totaled 14,012,453 tons, imports only 4,699,711 tons, a much higher ratio of exports to imports than the average of the first ten ports of the country.[58] Thus, a larger fraction of its total economy—its commission merchants, retailers, professional and service personnel, as well as inhabitants directly employed in the port —has depended on exports than in other American cities. Most of the major industries which had entered the Mississippi Valley by 1962, from the mouth of the river through Baton Rouge, exported, imported raw materials, or were oriented toward intensive capital investment and research (often all three)—for example, Freeport Nickel (dormant for lack of Cuban ore), Kaiser Aluminum (bauxite from Jamaica), Olin Mathieson, a major federal space research and development center, Standard Oil of California and New Jersey, Socony Mobile Oil, other extracting, refining, importing, and petrochemical enterprises, and sugar refineries using Caribbean crude sugars.

Protectionists were among local manufacturers of ties, shirts, cordage, and canned shrimp, a handful of independent oil operators, some owners of oil and sugar land, and a few others. They generated much more vocal protectionist propaganda in the community than their relatively minor economic importance would seem to warrant, but their overall influence was limited. Therefore, the tone of the community generally was one of minimum restrictions on trade. Many members of the community elite who had no direct involvement in trade participated actively in the International House—its president in 1962 was a prominent physician whose patients included many Latin Americans, and a predecessor was a distributor of electrical products manufactured for the most part in the United States. The New Orleans morning and afternoon newspapers were both favorable to expanded trade—even with Communist countries—and one of its Congressmen, Hale Boggs, a champion of freer trade, was chairman of the House Subcommittee on Foreign Trade Policy, and the other, F. Edward Hébert, had voted consistently for liberal trade legislation. Insofar as they had views on

---

December 23, 1962). See also *Times-Picayune*, July 10, 1963. For trade during the mid-nineteenth century, see Shugg, *Origins of Class Struggle in Louisiana*, 112–18.
58 From annual *Reports of the Chief of Engineers of the U.S. Army*. In 1953, for instance, New Orleans exports were 6,025,374 tons versus 4,467,317 tons of imports; in 1946 the respective figures were 4,843,272 tons versus 3,090,682. Exports through the San Francisco Bay area in 1962 were 4,741,233 tons versus 6,976,717 tons of imports. The figures for Baltimore in 1961 (1962 figures not available at this writing) were 4,541,228 tons of exports compared with 15,185,394 tons of imports.

the subject, the vast majority of New Orleanians, Catholic or not, were free traders.

The profound dependence of New Orleans on world trade for over two centuries had exerted some impact on the local residents, including those who did not know what a tariff or a quota is. The constant flow of foreign visitors through the port and airlines in and out of the city, the sight of sailors speaking foreign languages, and the presence of a multiethnic and multireligious population had together led to more interest in foreign relations than among comparable social groups in Shreveport, Jackson, or Birmingham, for instance.

But comparisons with most major Northern ports of even lesser economic importance—San Francisco, Baltimore, Philadelphia, Boston, Cleveland, and Chicago—seemed unfavorable to the Crescent City with respect to serious interest in, thought about, and understanding of world affairs. The proportion of people truly informed and sophisticated in the international sphere in any of these Northern ports has been at least several and in some cases many times that in New Orleans. Circulation of critical publications dealing with world affairs, such as the New York *Times* (Sunday edition), the *Christian Science Monitor, Harper's*, the *Atlantic*, and *The Reporter*, was in 1959 significantly smaller per unit of population in New Orleans than in any of these Northern ports, and even less than in Atlanta with its more dynamic ethic and larger immigration of energetic Northerners. Discussions of world affairs in New Orleans in the early sixties, even among educated groups, tended to be less vigorous, searching, and systematic than in Boston, Philadelphia, Chicago, San Francisco, or Baltimore. Nor had local universities exerted as potent an impact on local thinking among the better educated as seemed the case in these other ports.

The few New Orleanians who were thoughtful in foreign relations had received considerably more encouragement to develop their understanding of international relations from associates and contacts with university faculty, visitors from elsewhere, and others of cosmopolitan inclinations than had been the case in most of the South. Wider opportunities arose for them to use their comprehension and interests in foreign relations informally in interpersonal relations and more formally through urban organizations like the International House, the League of Women Voters, the Foreign Relations Association, and so on than for country Catholics or other rural and small-town groups.

But, in general, practical dependence on international economics and diverse ethnic origins had not generated much thoughtful interest—even among those directly involved in the port—in underlying world phenomena on which the city's prosperity has been based for generations. Even the local International House and other agencies connected with world trade have done relatively little to increase the comprehension of local people regarding more general foreign issues, including problems of economic development abroad. Paucity of concern with systematic, responsible discussion and critical analysis of international phenomena was even more patent in political and other less primarily economic spheres. Intellectually alert cosmopolitans complained of lack of local stimulation, of opportunities to compare ideas on international questions with diversified individuals who really knew a good deal about these matters, and of much of a local market for their own knowledge and interest. Those who could, welcomed opportunities to participate in serious discussions in Washington, New York, and other centers.

Much of the business and professional class, including free traders active in world commerce, seemed to be unconvinced that grants, long-term loans at low rates of interest, and other intergovernmental aid to underdeveloped neutralist countries are necessary or desirable, except perhaps at sharply reduced levels from those of 1959–62. "Trade, not aid" was a popular slogan with many prosperous citizens. Many of even those active in the International House and the port itself felt that our government has been supporting socialistic, leftist, anti-American regimes and "dangerous," or "radical" elements at the expense of our "real friends" abroad in Western Europe and among the conservative elites of the underdeveloped world. The proportion favorable to more vigorous, interventionist military policies, particularly in Cuba and Latin America generally, and to reduced emphasis on more complex, indirect, and subtle diplomatic, political, and economic programs was considerable, perhaps a small majority of the well-to-do and comfortably-off classes who had opinions on such matters. These generalizations applied likewise more or less to the local press, when it infrequently ventured interpretations of international relations other than trade. Even Congressman Boggs had made little mention of foreign aid, although he had long been articulate locally on freer trade. Perhaps he sensed that most of his constituents were more conservative than he on this issue.

The causes of these tendencies are to be found partly in the influence of the general Southern culture on the society, Catholic and Protestant alike: apathy or even hostility to abstractions, theories, and critical thinking, deeply rooted emotional conservatism, disbelief in utopias and "progress," traditionalism, the presence of large numbers of Negroes, and cultural isolation from the intellectual ferment of Northern metropolitan and university centers. But unique features of New Orleans mores, values, and history have also tended to discourage vigorous thought on foreign policy.

The city has been the capital of a cultural island surrounded by hundreds of miles of Bible Belt fundamentalism. In some respects the flavor of Latin religion and the history and traditions of the locale have rendered it more like Latin America than like the Protestant South. The community has been known as a place where work was seldom viewed as a major virtue and where pleasures denied in most of the South were readily available—gambling, good food and drink, prostitutes for a range of prices, the enjoyment of Sunday as a special day for amusement, and a general Catholic unseriousness capped by a carnival ethic. Entertainment and social life seemed to have been more active and time-consuming than perhaps any other place in America, among virtually all segments of society, including Negroes. New Orleans has been a gay city to which many types—planters, river boatmen, country poor whites and Negroes, seamen, and so on—have come to enjoy themselves.[59]

The pleasantness of this unique atmosphere has resulted in a strong provincialism notwithstanding a very active port and a population of heterogeneous ancestry. New Orleanians have resisted departing from their city with a tenacity incomprehensible to most Northern urbanites. Most New Orleanians could not imagine living anywhere else; wives have left husbands who have moved to better career opportunities elsewhere; employees of local branches of national corporations have refused promotions rather than accept transfers; Negro jazz musicians have given up lucrative jobs in New York, Chicago, and other large cities to return to the red beans and rice, orange wine, creole gumbo, crawfish bisque, Mardi Gras, and warm interpersonal relations of their native city; and even internationally oriented natives who have returned for brief visits have quickly become so immersed in traditional relationships with family and friends as to virtually forget that the rest of the world exists.

These attitudes which have tended to discourage critical thought about the world outside have not been limited to Catholic New Orleanians, but Latin Catholics have been the primary source of them. Most New Orleanians who have not been Catholics have been intimately associated

59 See, for instance, Asbury, *The French Quarter;* Carter, *The Lower Mississippi,* 253–62; Eaton, *The Growth of Southern Civilization,* 144–47; and Fossier, *New Orleans: The Glamour Period, 1800–1840,* iii, 296–97 and 387–91.

with and influenced by them. Northerners and Protestants who have moved there permanently have usually been "Creolized" to the relaxed art of enjoying oneself and of being unconcerned with much that transpires beyond south Louisiana. As in Cajun country, newcomers have more often than not been converted to local easygoing ways rather than the reverse.

The examples set by the privileged class of Creoles seldom included serious reading or critical thinking on matters beyond their part of Louisiana.[60] They were noted for flamboyant frivolity, balls and card and crap games far into the night, lavish parties and *soirées*, flowery pageants, the first opera in America, theater, a contempt for *les affaires* (business), and a haughty disdain for much of the rest of society, especially "Americans," whom they regarded as uncultivated types primarily interested in making money. Duelling, sophisticated tastes in cookery, brandy, wine, horses, and women, dancing, races and cock-fights, hunting, fishing, socializing in their clubs and restaurants, and the like were the major spheres of interest and expertise of the men. The ladies devoted themselves largely to *la famille*, fancy embroidery, music, running the servants and household, entertaining, and gossip.

Though greatly attenuated, these values remained influential in the early 1960's. New Orleanians of privileged status who might otherwise devote some attention to international affairs were likely to find their leisure time absorbed in carnivals, rounds of parties, and a congeries of expectations and commitments among their extended families and friends. Those few who wanted to read much serious literature and think critically about world or other questions were to a considerable extent required to withdraw from such incessant demands. It is small wonder that a large fraction of the relatively few New Orleanians who have thought critically about foreign relations seemed to have come to town from elsewhere and somehow to have resisted the forces of acculturation. And apparently a number of these migrants have gradually regressed to the local norms after some years of residence in the "city that care forgot."

60 See, for instance, Shugg, *Origins of Class Struggle in Louisiana*, 28–29; Asbury, *The French Quarter;* Tregle, *Journal of Southern History*, XVIII (1952); George Washington Cable, *The Creoles of Louisiana* (New York: Charles Scribner's Sons, 1910); Eaton, *The Growth of Southern Civilization*, 129–30 and 296; Fossier, *New Orleans, The Glamour Period 1800–1840*, 266–78 and 452–84; Grace King, *Creole Families of New Orleans* (New York: Macmillan, 1921); and Robert Tallant, *The Romantic New Orleanians* (New York: E. P. Dutton and Co., 1950), 62–78.

Consequently, even most of the better educated and privileged have tended to regard world trade as pragmatic business rather than as part of a sensitive, active, foreign policy. Only a very small minority has been really interested in the complexities of foreign policy beyond the level of entertaining foreign dignitaries at social gatherings, visiting abroad, and a rather frothy, superficial identification with cosmopolitan drink, food, and amusements. Serious reading and thinking on world affairs (or other problems) have seemed less evident than among the socially secure in the Anglo-Saxon South. A tradition of attention to international content of the better national and international periodicals, such as the New York *Times*, *Harper's*, and the Manchester *Guardian*, has existed in a few old families, both Catholic and Protestant, but particularly Jewish. In recent years one or two individuals in a considerable number of other families of education and influence have read such material frequently, and most of them have been relatively liberal or responsibly conservative on world affairs. A larger minority among those of inherited social standing have been influenced in the direction of realistic thinking on foreign policy by news magazines, their careers, the Church, or similar sources. As elsewhere, there has been a considerable increase in cosmopolitanism among the college-educated younger generation.

A small minority of middle-class professional people of Catholic (or other) faith—lawyers, teachers, clergy in the religious orders, some diocesan priests, and nuns in the teaching orders—have also been among the readers of analytical literature on foreign affairs and have thought in relatively responsible, cause-and-effect terms. Those Catholic union leaders (most have been Catholics) who have been relatively "open-minded" on race have been emotionally or latently sympathetic to international collaboration, including foreign economic assistance, but very few have devoted much attention to world affairs or have known much about it. Italian-Americans and other second generation citizens who were themselves discriminated against by the privileged classes have seemed especially prone to anti-Negro thinking, and both New Orleans Catholics and Protestants—like other Southerners—of racist inclinations have tended to be strongly conservative on foreign policy, international trade excepted.

Priests and Communication of World Affairs

Virtually no Southern priest has agreed publicly with white supremacist ideology, although only a minority in 1959–61 were active advocates of integration. Confidential interviews by Catholic social scientists

indicate that many priests who have been relatives of racial conservatives in their locales or have known white supremacists as friends for
years have, at least until recently, felt very hesitant about taking positions for racial equality among predominantly segregationist parishioners. Some older parish clergy who were born in the South have been
paternalists toward the Negro and uncomfortable about integration
themselves,[61] although they probably accepted it rationally as inevitable
and morally correct. Younger parish priests have tended on the average
to be more actively desegregationist.

Being among the better educated and less conservative on race in the
region, relatively few priests either among the twenty-six interviewees
for this study or a sample of over two thousand priests throughout the
country (including the South) studied by Father Joseph H. Fichter
in 1960–61 agreed with international attitudes of the racist syndrome.
Thus, priests in the latter study were slightly more favorable to expanded foreign economic assistance and somewhat less inclined to feel
it should be reduced than were active Catholic laymen examined in
the same investigation; 40.4 percent of the priests favored increasing
foreign aid, 23.6 percent thought it should remain at about the current
levels, and only 32.8 percent suggested that it be reduced. Differences
between priests in the South and those elsewhere were insignificant.[62]
According to opinion polls of the period, Southern priests were considerably more favorable to foreign aid than were Southerners in general,
and at least somewhat more favorable than Catholic laymen in general
or even better-educated Protestants (see pp. 211–13, 454).

The interviewers' discussions with twenty-six priests, sixteen of them
in southern Louisiana, indicated that most of them supported active
international collaboration in other nonmilitary fields as well. *Mater et
Magistra* and other public statements by the Pope, American bishops,
and other Church leaders in the last few years have undoubtedly
increased identification of priests with economic and technical assistance
and with decolonization of remaining dependencies in Africa, but the
study cited above and the interviews for this study prior to the release
of this encyclical showed that most priests in the South probably
favored general policies of this sort before.

Priests, like others in the region, have been far from homogeneous
in their international thinking. The study by Father Fichter cited previously discovered that those who were trained at seminaries outside

61 Raymond Bernard, S.J., "Attitudes and Opinions on Race Relations" (MS,
1958).
62 Fichter, unpublished study, see n. 42.

their diocese were on the average more favorable to foreign economic assistance and in general more liberal about world, domestic, and social questions than those who were educated locally, as has been true of Southern college graduates generally.[63] Pastors among the priests in his study tended to be more liberal about foreign policy (and other issues) than older curates (assistants) who had not reached that station. As among other Southerners, younger priests have been more favorable to liberal international programs than older ones. The interviews for this study indicated that some older priests in rural sections and small towns servicing them in southern Louisiana have been identified in the minds of at least some of their working-class parishioners, including union representatives, with big landowners, cane planters, sugar mill owners and managers, and others of major economic influence, most of whom have been conservative on virtually everything, including foreign policy. If participating in joint hunting and fishing trips and being entertained at the homes of influential conservatives have implied agreement with their social and political ideas, then these priests have been considerably to the right of the foreign policies pressed by either President Eisenhower or President Kennedy. The interviews for this study with six priests in such semifeudal settings indicated that a considerable fraction of them were probably conservative on world problems in 1959–62, but perhaps few to the degree of their local lay associates among the rural elite.

However, judging from this small sample and the impressions of participant observers, it appears that a rather large proportion of priests in early middle age and younger, even in rural settings, have been relatively well-informed cosmopolitans. Whereas Protestant ministers of intellectual orientations have migrated for the most part to cities and college communities, Catholic bishops in the South have frequently sent a number of priests of similar inclinations to country and small-town parishes. Typically at least one and often several priests in south Louisiana rural governmental parishes read the New York *Times* (Sunday edition) or equally sophisticated material on world affairs. The few interviews for this study indicated that many approved of the proposed exchange of tractors for prisoners in Cuba in the summer of 1961, at least until Castro increased his demands. None of the fourteen rural and small-town priests in the sample advocated overt United States

63 See above, p. 249. The rather large fraction of priests in the South who were born abroad also helps to account for their relatively cosmopolitan attitudes and sensitivities. One in Bayou Parish was formerly a Mexican and two in Antebellum Town and the one in Deltatown were raised in Ireland. Many of the remainder outside the few traditionally Catholic areas have been Northerners moved South.

military intervention in Cuba in 1960–61, although many of their parishioners did. Twelve of these fourteen felt that foreign aid was a major instrument of United States policy, even though most had reservations about its administration. The Peace Corps was considerably more popular among rural and small-town priests than among their more influential parishioners interviewed in the same locales. Interviewers found no staunch protectionists; however, few felt that we could remove restrictions rapidly without undue damage at home. All fourteen felt that independence of Angola and other African dependencies was virtually inevitable and that we should help the colonial powers prepare the local inhabitants for that development through education, technical assistance, or other means. The idea that Communists were a major domestic menace was so closely associated with strongly segregationist thinking that few priests seemed to believe this.

The actual and potential impacts of the clergy on international thinking of their congregations are difficult questions to examine. As has been true among ministers, priests have varied widely in their own interest and understanding of world affairs. They have also accorded different priorities to efforts to stimulate thought in this field. As in the case of laymen and Protestant ministers, many priests have so strongly emphasized salvation of souls that they have devoted little attention to public questions, including international phenomena.

However, an increasing number of the younger clergy seem to have developed considerable interest in world developments through the postwar seminaries, encouragement by national and international Church leadership, and their generally broader experience in the armed services and elsewhere. Moreover, some older priests have likewise been interested in this field. In Shreveport, for instance, forums and other programs sponsored by the internationally liberal Louisiana-born pastor of a Catholic parish have for a number of years dealt intelligently with world issues and attracted thoughtful non-Catholics as well as Catholics. This activity has been one of the few sources of internationalist ideas in a community where the newspapers, the most prestigious Episcopal rector and his lay associates, much of the Protestant leadership, and even the Jewish community and the most influential rabbi have presented much more conservative thinking on foreign policy.

Cosmopolitan clergy in southern Louisiana seem to have experienced considerable difficulty in communicating the public and social thinking of the Church and of themselves to local Catholics. Although most rural folk of French-Canadian heritage have been rather closely identified with their local church and clergy, many of the men and a significant proportion of the women of other ethnic groups—even in country parishes—have not been active churchgoers.[64] Historically many males of French ancestry in the city were baptized, made their first communion, were married, and received last rites, but only infrequently attended church.[65] Anticlericalism, especially among privileged southern Louisiana Catholics, both rural and urban, has been evident. Pleasure-loving and religiously "relaxed" New Orleans Catholics stood behind their easygoing French priests against efforts of stricter Spanish ecclesiastical superiors to discipline them in the late eighteenth century. Influential laymen elected their own pastors for a brief period, supported a popular and "tolerant" priest, Père Antoine, against their Vicar-General who, they felt, was trying to "reform" them, attempted to introduce congregational control of church property, refused to recognize one unpopular bishop appointed over them, and so obstructed another that he moved his diocesan headquarters to St. Louis for three years in the early 1800's.[66]

A systematic study of residents of a New Orleans parish a decade ago found that at least 30 percent of baptized infants had ceased to function as Catholics and parishioners; that about 40 percent who reported their religion as Catholic said that they "didn't go to church any more," that they were "supposed to be Catholics but didn't bother with it," or that they were connected with no parish, did not know the name of the parish church or the parish clergy, or the like; that 48 percent hardly attended mass at all, another 18 percent attended only irregularly, and only 34 percent attended regularly. Only one Catholic out of eight received weekly communion and one out of twenty was a "nuclear" parishioner, that is, usually attended mass once a week, made his confession at least once a year, participated in Sunday communion, and took some part in parish organizations.[67] Although studies of Catholic parishes outside south Louisiana have not been completely comparable, active identification with the clergy and the Church in those Northern

64   Kammer, *A Socio-economic Survey of the Marsh Dwellers*, 46–52; and Parenton, "The Rural French-Speaking People," 7–8.
65   Fossier, *New Orleans, The Glamour Period 1800–1840*, 299; and Shugg, *Origins of Class Struggle in Louisiana*, 63.
66   *Ibid.*, pp. 306–307 and 310–35; Carter, *The Lower Mississippi*, 67–81; Parenton, "The Rural French-Speaking People," 7, 99, 163, and 171–85; and Roger Baudier, *The Catholic Church in Louisiana* (New Orleans: A. W. Hyatt Co., 1937), especially 97–99, 152–59, 268–80, and 300 ff.
67   Joseph H. Fichter, S.J., *Social Relations in the Urban Parish* (Chicago: University of Chicago Press, 1954), 14, 17, and 23–25; Joseph B. Schuyler, S.J., *Northern Parish: A Sociological and Pastoral Study* (Chicago: Loyola University Press, 1960), 203 ff; and Joseph H. Fichter, S.J., *Dynamics of a City Church*.

parishes which have been examined appeared significantly higher.[68] A recent study of Catholic students at Jesuit colleges tended to support this conclusion—25 percent at Loyola University in New Orleans as compared with 33 percent at Northern institutions considered themselves "very religious." [69]

Support of racial equality and, to a lesser extent, of labor organization by at least the more liberal clergy in recent years seems to have developed further rifts between them and their more conservative laymen. Most diocesan priests, like racially liberal or moderate Protestant ministers, have been obliged to work in parishes populated in the vast majority by segregationists of various hues [70] whose views on foreign affairs in recent years have either been conservative—about like those of Senator Allen J. Ellender—or nonexistent. Segregationist laity wondered in 1959–62 "why these busy-body priests became so convinced all of a sudden that segregation is morally wrong when they never said so before 1954." Many strong conservatives on race, economics, and foreign affairs have viewed liberals among the clergy as "rabble-rousers" and "leftists," and most appeared to feel that the clergy should confine their activities to "religion" narrowly defined rather than "agitation" about social and public questions, about which they supposedly had little practical knowledge and which were "none of their business."

Although many southern Louisianians were active Catholics in 1962, these observations indicate that priests who have been well read in world affairs have typically had only limited opportunities to influence the thinking of Catholics who have opposed foreign aid and other active nonmilitary collaboration abroad and who have accepted neo-isolationist views. Catholic pastors, like ministers, have been obliged to

68 Schuyler, *Northern Parish*, 295. The Reverend Schuyler noted that the Reverend Fichter's findings in New Orleans of 48 percent nonpractice and 40 percent dormancy had no counterpart in the parish he studied in the Bronx, which was composed primarily of immigrants and first and second generation Americans (*Ibid.*, 204). However, Irish-Americans in this Bronx parish, being more active in religious activities than most other Catholics in the parish, were largely responsible for the low proportion of nonpractice. Residents of the parish of Italian-American and Puerto Rican background more nearly approached the religious behavior of the Reverend Fichter's New Orleanians. Another study determined that 93 percent of the parishioners of a rather prosperous Chicago parish normally attended Mass weekly. See Andrew M. Greeley, "Some Information on the Present Situation of American Catholics," *Social Order*, XIII (April, 1963), 19.

69 Unpublished data furnished by the Reverend Joseph H. Fichter, S.J., of Loyola University at New Orleans.

70 Only 12 percent in the Reverend Fichter's New Orleans Catholic sample favored desegregated over segregated religious activities in the late 1940's, compared with 95 percent in the Bronx parish examined by the Reverend Schuyler. See his *Northern Parish*, 267.

finance their parishes, schools, building programs, and other activities, and have wanted to maintain good rapport with their conservative, even reactionary, parishioners. Whereas most cosmopolitan ministers have had smaller churches with relatively homogeneous congregations, with the exception of a handful of upper- and upper-middle-class parishes in New Orleans priests have been obliged to prepare sermons which would appeal to heterogeneous faithful, from illiterates to Ph.D.'s. Cosmopolitan priests have typically communicated best on world problems with more internationally sophisticated, usually college-educated, Catholics (and non-Catholics) whose views have been similar to their own.

Rural priests, and to a lesser extent urban ones, have tended to be most popular and perhaps most effective when regarded locally as *bon vivants* and "good Joes" who fished, handled a shotgun with competence, enjoyed good food, and otherwise manifested the interests of their faithful.[71] Some have attempted to familiarize their parishioners with the implications of Christianity for world affairs. However, cosmopolitan rural priests noted that sermons on social and public issues tended to "lose," if not antagonize, country and small-town folk at most one generation removed from illiteracy; these clergymen were inclined to feel that they were more apt to be effective through indirect approaches, such as education of the children, informal interpersonal contacts with their parishioners, and emphasis on the significance of religion for individual thought and action.

71 See, for instance, Kammer, *A Socio-economic Survey of the Marsh Dwellers*, 33.

CHAPTER 13

SOUTHERN JEWS

J̲ews constituted in 1960 some 200,000 inhabitants of the South, omitting most of Texas, suburbs of the District of Columbia in Virginia, and southern Florida; this number comprises a little over one half of one percent of the population of the region.[1] Nevertheless, their interest and knowledge in world affairs, which are far above the average, their on the whole more cosmopolitan thinking on foreign policy, their economic and community standing, and their potential influence on local thought in foreign relations suggest special consideration.

Jews have made up such a small fraction of the Southern population that their replies to national surveys cannot be compared statistically with those of other Southern and Northern groups. The interviews for this study with slightly less than two hundred Jews in the sample communities and in several other locales were also too few for statistical analysis. Furthermore, the interviewers were unable to contact cross sections of Jews of varied backgrounds and roles in all the major types of Jewish communities in the region. Most of the observations to follow are, therefore, relatively speculative in nature, pending systematic study of a carefully drawn representative sample of Southern Jewry, which would necessarily number several thousand interviewees.

1 Estimate derived from *The American Jewish Yearbook* (Philadelphia: the Jewish Publication Society of America [for the American Jewish Committee], 1961), 62–63.

Jews, Gentiles, and World Affairs

Less Internationally Thoughtful than Northern Jews

Since a comparable sample of Northern Jews was not interviewed, the speculations about differences in international outlook and actions between them and their Southern coreligionists are based on replies by Northern Jews to survey questions dealing with world affairs [2] and the author's impressions from contacts with Northern Jewry over the years.

The Jewish informants differed considerably among themselves in their international thinking. But as a group they seemed less well read, less intellectually alert, less cosmopolitan, and more conservative about international relations than their Northern coreligionists of similar status. Southern traditions about the Negro as well as other subjects seemed to have exerted significant effects on most of the Southern-born Jewish informants. According to national surveys, only a limited minority of Northern Jews have felt as did over half the Jewish interviewees for this study that the process of desegregation was proceeding too fast in the South. A considerable fraction of the Southern-born Jews interviewed made observations to the effect that they were emotionally ill at ease about integration even when they accepted it as inevitable and in the long run desirable. Moreover, the interviewers' confidential discussions of Jews' private attitudes about race relations undoubtedly resulted in considerably more equalitarian replies than their public postures in their communities, a phenomenon which will be examined shortly.

Replies of Northern Jews to national surveys indicated that disparity between Southern and Northern Jewish attitudes toward world affairs appeared most marked on issues related to Negro-white relations—such as sentiments about the Union of South Africa, Sir Roy Welensky and the protection of white interests against the African majority in the Central African Federation, the behavior of anticolonialist, neutralist leaders of newly independent African states in the U.N. and international affairs generally, and the rapid rate at which underdeveloped African societies have been accorded independence from European tutelage.

Interviewers for this study did not encounter Southern counterparts of the small Northern urban Jewish leftist or socialist minority. There were no unilateral disarmers among the interviewees, nor were there

2 Typical surveys of NORC and AIPO until the end of the 1950's included 45 to 65 Jews. However, samples of AIPO starting in 1959 included as many as 3,500 interviewees, of which 110 to 150 have typically been Jews.

individuals who thought we should make much greater concessions to the Soviets in order to achieve agreement on arms control or other issues. Only two former New Yorkers advocated United States acceptance of a disarmament agreement without effective inspection. Moreover, interviewers did not observe the anti-military overtones which have been evident among a number of Northern Jewish liberals. Knowledge that the author had attended Virginia Military Institute, graduated from West Point, and served for eight years in the Regular Army stimulated considerably more favorable comment than among most liberal Northern Jews of the author's acquaintance.

Leading rabbis in Richmond and Savannah and other influential Southern Jews were active during and shortly after World War II in developing local support for the American Council for Judaism and other movements critical of arguments favorable to the establishment of a Jewish state in Palestine.[3] The interviews for this study indicated that a considerable fraction of Southern Jews of established position and inherited wealth and prestige, particularly in older, more traditional Southern communities, have agreed to a significant extent with thinking opposed to Zionism, although only a minority of those of such standing have accepted the more extreme such orientations critical of Israel. Given the strong pressures for acculturation and against being overtly different from Gentiles in much of the South, identification with Israel has probably been weaker there than in the rest of the country taken together.

However, such Jews of several generations of residence and influence in the South were by 1959 a limited minority, and most of the Jewish interviewees seemed relatively favorably inclined toward Israel and appeared to feel that it is useful to have a government which could complain about maltreatment of Jews abroad and that Arab countries have been intransigent and unreasonable and more guilty than the Israelis in the disagreements between them. Most of the interviews for this study were completed before the hanging of Adolph Eichmann, but only about a fifth, largely Southern-born and in small communities or among the highly acculturated in the older cities, were much concerned about his abduction from Argentina and trial before an Israeli court, and some of these seemed more worried about criticism among Gentiles than about the procedure itself. Furthermore, it appears that

3 Harry Simonhoff, *Under Strange Skies* (New York: Philosophical Library, 1953), 250 and 267; and Mrs. David J. Greenberg, *Through the Years: A Study of the Richmond Jewish Community* (Richmond: American Jewish Tercentenary Committee, 1654–1954, 1954), 47.

contributions to philanthropies devoted to a considerable extent to programs in Israel have been approximately as large per individual Jew, in proportion to his income, in the South as elsewhere in the United States.

On the other hand, some of the genteel, upper-class interviewees felt that the methods used to raise money for programs in Israel had been "crass." Only a minuscule handful among the sample favored the view of strong Zionists that Jews should be encouraged to migrate to Israel even though they were not under heavy pressure or discrimination. A considerable minority of the Southern-born consultants apparently believed that the Israelis had not been candid on some of their policies and disagreements with the Arabs and that they had been partly responsible for border and other difficulties.

The Most Cosmopolitan Southern Ethnic Group

However, Jewish traditions of learning and rational analysis, contacts with Jews from outside the South and with liberal Jewish organizations, identifications with coreligionists abroad, and other influences have continued to move many, and probably most, Southern Jews in varying degrees in the direction of cosmopolitans. Moreover, Jews throughout the South have been on the average much better off, better educated, more concentrated in elevated social and occupational groups, and more urban than Gentiles—all factors associated with greater interest, knowledge, and exposure to world affairs and with more cosmopolitan, multilateralist, international attitudes. But even when compared with Gentiles of similar education, occupation, and income in their own communities, Jews in the sample for this study were on the whole more internationally minded.

Approximately one out of seven of this predominantly middle- and upper-class Jewish group often read about world affairs in some critical publication such as the New York *Times* (Sunday edition), *The Atlantic*, or the *Christian Science Monitor*. Three fifths of the remainder read newsmagazines or their equivalents. Approximately three fifths tended to agree that our foreign aid budgets had not been excessive in recent years or that they should have been pared only relatively little. Although some of the Jewish respondents were in garment and textile manufacturing and other import-vulnerable industries, over half believed we should increase imports, another third would maintain them at approximately the then current level, and only one out of eight would decrease them. Less than one out of twenty felt that Portugal would be able to maintain her control of her African dependencies over the long term, although almost half of those venturing replies felt that independence had come to many African countries too rapidly for orderly development and stability. Only five out of almost two hundred wanted us to withdraw from the U.N. and not many more urged reorganizing it without the Soviet Union. No more than 3 percent would have us pull out of NATO or pursue policies likely to weaken that alliance system. Except for a handful of vociferous racists, hardly any Jews proposed reduction of international exchanges, even with the Communists, or opposed the Peace Corps, technical assistance, and sale of agricultural surpluses for local currencies. The proportion of Jews accepting isolationist or neo-isolationist thinking was roughly half that among Gentiles of similar education and occupation in the same communities.

These less conservative attitudes on world affairs were related to the fact that the great majority of the Jewish interviewees, even in smaller communities in the Black Belt, ranged from mild segregationists to integrationists.[4] The informants were more than twice as likely as the Southern Protestant white average in surveys to feel that desegregation is both inevitable and, in general, desirable in the long run, and only about one third as inclined as the latter to believe that Negroes are constitutionally inferior. Few Jews even in Mississippi and Alabama apparently voted for independent electors in 1960. Only a handful of Jews were actively racist beyond the conformity apparently required for maintaining their businesses or professional careers in strongly segregationist communities. The majority of the small number of Jews on the rolls of Citizens Councils and other racist groups were by and large rather inactive and probably joined primarily to appease their segregationist neighbors, clients, and customers, to help keep these organizations "respectable," and to prevent development of anti-Semitism which many feared might be latent in such groups.[5]

Moreover, even when Jews seemed relatively conservative about race relations, their racial attitudes typically had less apparent effect on their international views than was the case among most racist Gentiles. Perhaps a considerable fraction of the relatively cosmopolitan Jewish interviewees exaggerated their attachment to segregation since public liberalism on this issue would in many cases have entailed serious local

4 For comparable findings in three dissimilar Southern cities, see Leonard Reissman, "The New Orleans Jewish Community," *Jewish Journal of Sociology,* IV (1962), 111; Joshua A. Fishman, "Southern City," *Midstream,* VII (1961), 39–50; and Manheim S. Shapiro, "The Southville Survey of Jewish Attitudes," (MS of American Jewish Committee, New York, 1959).

5 Fear of anti-Semitism in these white supremacy groups probably also discouraged some segregationist Jews from joining.

pressures, whereas they could express their true thinking on most issues of foreign policy without energizing as unpleasant local reactions. Their racial attitudes had some influence in the expected directions on their world thinking, especially where Africa was an issue. But the greater interest in world affairs of Jews, their wider exposure to cosmopolitan ideas in mass media and Jewish religious and secular organizations, and the tradition of learning—albeit much attenuated among many Southern Jews—had significantly moderated the impact of their racial traditionalism upon their international opinions.

Furthermore, extended conversations with even the more conservative Jews in the more traditionalist, racist, Deep Southern settings usually uncovered important liberal exceptions to the international syndrome related to racism. Few Jews who still identified themselves as such were as consistently isolationist, unilateralist, military interventionist, and generally reactionary as their ultra-conservative Gentile colleagues. Jewish interviewees in each of the sample communities were asked who were the Jews most conservative on foreign aid, the U.N., trade, and world affairs generally. With some exceptions those named turned out to be less isolationist or reactionary than the most conservative Gentiles of their same social and economic standing. Even the word "reactionary" used by Jews to describe other Jews typically referred to people whose views on world issues were comparable to those of the average self-made, successful Gentile businessman in the area. The spectrum of international and related attitudes among Jews was significantly less conservative than that among local Gentiles of like status.

It was noted earlier that even small Jewish manufacturers of clothing in competition with cheap imports who were not above using racism to prevent unionization of their plants were for the most part apologetic protectionists, noting that they understood that expanded trade is in our national interest, that we should not drive the Japanese into the arms of Peking, and so on. Moreover, whereas most Gentile protectionists in the sample would reduce sharply foreign economic assistance to underdeveloped countries, most Jewish ones would not.

An influential Jewish state politician in the Deep South was profoundly uncomfortable about "turmoil" in his state due to "leftist Northern agitators" sowing unrest among "maladjusted" and "misled" Southern Negroes. He had advised his coreligionists to "keep quiet" on race, since "there is no race problem here except when it is created from the outside." He helped pass the state right-to-work law, was worried about the size of the national debt, the erosion of "states' rights," "big government," "waste" abroad, trying to "buy friends" among the underdeveloped countries, and "kowtowing to opportunists who are making fools out of us" in Africa and Asia. However, he would increase technical assistance, both bilaterally and through the U.N., stress foreign languages more than currently even in grade school in his state, and encourage more Americans to take foreigners, including non-Negroid colored peoples, into their homes to "learn about their countries and how they think." Another prominent Jewish business leader, who was considered on the right on most issues (including world affairs) by the rest of the Jewish community in his city, became the president of a voluntary organization devoted to adult education in world affairs in his community—most of the speakers before this organization had been less conservative than he.

Even the most conservative, extreme free enterprise, anti-foreign spending, pro-military interventionist Jews among planters in the Delta were seldom as solidly so as their Gentile counterparts. Discussion with two brothers and an in-law who had considerably expanded the interests of their prosperous father in cotton plantations, a bank, and retail stores in the Delta indicated that they favored free trade, but as a part of free enterprise in general. Free foreign trade, they seemed to feel, could not operate with minimum wage and hours laws, monopolistic trade unions backed by the President of the United States, federal intervention in agriculture and business, and other domestic "socialism." They opposed intergovernmental aid abroad, especially to countries which refused to declare themselves against Communism; United States refusal to oppose emotional, anti-Western politicians in Africa and Asia; "desertion" of the interests of our "real allies" in Europe; and toleration of seizures of American private property in underdeveloped lands, particularly in Latin America. One launched out against "fuzzy dreamers and impractical idealists" running our foreign policy—at that time the Eisenhower administration. One of these individuals had encouraged Jews in his part of the state to join the Citizens Council and to refrain from criticizing the racial *status quo*. He had also tried to convince at least one national Jewish organization to moderate its publicized liberalism on race. James Eastland, a planter like themselves, was "one of the best men in Washington."

But they also liked their Congressman, one of the most liberal legislators on both international and domestic questions from the Deep South (since defeated by a racist-isolationist). They were supporting Senator Kennedy and were opposed to both Vice-President Nixon and the independent electors in the forthcoming election. They wanted to have our colleges make room for more competent foreign students by admitting fewer "trifling" Americans. They felt that we should assist in educating the Africans, although not by putting them into white Southern colleges. They were viewed by Negroes in the county as "very fine" people, true paternalist humanitarians and fair toward Negroes. They contributed to liberal Jewish organizations, including the B'nai B'rith and the Anti-Defamation League.

Diversity of Jewish World Views

Most of the variables related to international thought among Southern Gentiles apply to Jews as well. Those with the most advanced educations, particularly at the better universities and colleges, have been more favorable to international cooperation in nonmilitary fields than those who did not go to college; the same is true of Jews in the liberal professions as opposed to merchants, of urban rather than small-town and rural Jews, and so on. As among Gentiles, critical attitudes in world affairs have usually been part of a general intellectual alertness and interest in ideas. Although, as observed previously, conservative racial attitudes among Jews were on the whole less closely connected with their international thinking than among Gentiles, the direction of correlation was similar. In general, the more cosmopolitan the Gentile middle and upper classes, the more internationally thoughtful the local Jews in similar roles; in any given community, however, at least a somewhat larger fraction of Jews than non-Jews in the professional, proprietary and managerial classes were relatively well read, thoughtful, and favorable to liberal, or multilateral, foreign policies.

Aspects Particularly Applicable to Jews

The smaller and more homogeneous the backgrounds of the local Jewish community, the more conservative its international attitudes. This variable is, of course, closely associated with the size and complexity of the general community—the small Jewish groups, most members of which were raised in Southern towns and villages, have tended to be in less populous, less dynamic places rather than in growing metropolitan areas where New South influences have been more marked. However, within cities of about the same size, opposition to foreign aid for underdeveloped neutralists, and particularly for Communist Poland and Yugoslavia, and to repeal of the Connally Amendment as well as support of unilateral intervention against leftist, anti-United States regimes in Latin America were more widespread where the great majority of Jews was raised in the South.

Related to this observation is the degree to which Jews have taken on the coloration of and been assimilated into the Gentile majority. Where they have been living for several generations without substantial influx of new Jewish people from the North and Europe, rewards for adjustment to Gentile mores have been considerable and penalties for overt maintenance of divergent Jewish values and attitudes compelling. Growing tensions about race relations in the last decade have accentuated pressures against Jewish nonconformity, as will be discussed later. But most Jews outside the few Southern cities were long isolated from Jewish religion and culture until recent decades. Resident rabbis within easy access of small towns and rural sections are largely a recent phenomenon—since the advent of good highways and urbanization. National Jewish organizations had few members in these isolated locales until the last several decades. In many small communities there were only half a dozen or so Jewish families.[6] Their contacts with other Jews were limited to a few wandering peddlers and alms collectors and infrequent trips to New Orleans, Richmond, Charleston, and a handful of other cities.

Isolated in their local communities and profoundly dependent upon local good will and friendly relations with local white Gentiles, most of these Jews adapted themselves to prevailing values and habits. They played poker with the sheriff, fished with the county judge, hunted with the planters, and became leaders of the local Chamber of Commerce, Rotary, and other service groups. Evangelical ministers and laymen were often persistent, and, since the church was a social as well as a religious organization, a considerable fraction of Jews, or their children, joined the Presbyterian, Methodist, Episcopal, or other church which included influential members of the community. Having few Jewish choices, sons and daughters frequently married Gentiles. Even if they did not change their own religious affiliations, their children generally became Protestants.[7] In some cases a parent of Jewish tradition transferred some of its emphases on intellectual pursuits, identification with the underdog, and contact with cosmopolitan values. However, as the generations succeeded one another, more and more Southerners of Jewish ancestry became virtually indistinguishable in ideology from the rest of the local power structure of planters and merchants.

This assimilation was also apparent in attenuated form in the older cities. Much of the early Sephardic Jewish population of Charleston has disappeared into the genteel Episcopalian group. Some descendants

6 See, for example, Shugg, *Origins of Class Struggle in Louisiana*, 43.
7 In Opelousas, Louisiana, for instance, sixteen out of eighteen marriages of Jews during a thirty year period prior to 1955 were with Gentiles; none of the offspring of these mixed marriages was raised in the Jewish faith. See Benjamin Kaplan, *The Eternal Stranger* (New York: Bookman Associates, 1957), 96–98.

of these early settlers were still affiliated with the Reform Temple in 1960–61, but most of those citizens who identified themselves as Jewish arrived in the late antebellum period or after. And a considerable number of even third generation Jews in the South have also become Episcopalians, Presbyterians, Methodists, Unitarians, or otherwise disassociated from Jewish religious and secular organizations. Similarly, many offspring of Jewish families who have lived in New Orleans for several generations are no longer, for practical purposes, Jews in religion or ethnic identification. Even in much newer cities like Greensboro, third and later generations of families of high social and economic standing have included a significant fraction of individuals married to Gentiles whose children will be affiliated with high-status Christian churches.

Jews who married Gentiles but maintained their Jewish religion and affiliation with such Jewish organizations as the American Jewish Committee, the National Council of Jewish Women, the B'nai B'rith, and the Anti-Defamation League seemed in many more cases than not more liberal in international orientation than the majority of local Gentiles of similar status. Frequently, their Christian spouses were more conservative about Negroes, foreign aid, domestic "Communism," and other public issues. Those who became Unitarians seemed predominantly liberals or responsible conservatives on world affairs—they were often more thoughtful and better informed about foreign policy than most Jews.

However, a disproportionately large number of first-generation Gentiles among the middle and upper strata—Unitarians excepted—appeared strongly conservative on race and world affairs. The dynamics of this rejection of Jewish cosmopolitanism require more systematic research, but it is apparent that many such new converts have been even more careful to adopt the more conservative attitudes prevalent in the Gentile power structure than many who were born into the Episcopal or Presbyterian church. Many of these prosperous Jews married above their own social origins. Insecurity about acceptance among the Gentile elite is probably at work in a number of these cases.

Likewise, Jews who have had little interest in Judaism or Jewish affairs seemed to include a disproportionate number of opponents of foreign aid and Goldwater supporters on both domestic and foreign policy within the Jewish community. Four of the six Jewish ultraconservatives who were also favorable to Citizens Councils were little identified with Jewish thought and activities. Two were newly prosperous businessmen who had not been to college and a third was a planter who had not completed his higher education.

Prosperous, well-educated Jews of several generations of Southern ancestry who were very active in the Gentile community and who maintained only formal affiliations with Judaism included as well a number of quite conservative people on world affairs. Urban Jews who have been accepted socially by upper-class Gentiles, whose contacts outside the Jewish community continued after office hours and beyond business, professional, and formal organizational relationships, who belonged to esteemed Gentile clubs rather than to the Jewish country club, and so on, have been mostly individuals of several generations of inherited wealth and social position in the South. Most of these have been relatively inactive in Jewish organizations, confining any memberships to paying dues and perhaps participation in a large, formal meeting now and then. The Jewish groups were frequented and run largely by "newer," more "Jewish" folk.[8]

Thus, in Charleston the minority of Jews who agreed with much of the foreign policy proposed by the two local newspapers, by the presidents of the two local colleges, by Senator Strom Thurmond and Congressman L. Mendel Rivers, and by the Goldwater wing of the Republican party (at the time of interviews, 1960–61) was composed primarily of those whose social contacts and organizational memberships were more with Gentiles than with Jews and Jewish agencies. They were among those most assimilated into prominent Gentile circles, the majority of whose members were racial paternalists, social standpatters, Old South traditionalists, and strong conservatives on foreign policy.

However, the Jewish aristocracy has also produced a disproportionately large fraction of the most intellectually sophisticated, internationally concerned minority of their communities—a much larger proportion of them than of upper-class Gentiles in the sample communities were well-read cosmopolitans of responsible internationalist persuasion. Nor should one assume that assimilationists among these old Jewish families, largely of Sephardic, German, French, and other West European origins, have necessarily been neo-isolationists or otherwise strongly conservative in world affairs. Among the sample, of the twelve college-educated anti-Zionists (including three affiliated with the American Council for Judaism), seven approved of foreign aid at approximately the then current or higher levels, all favored active collaboration in the U.N. and its specialized agencies, ten felt international trade (including imports) should be expanded, and several were active in internationally oriented organizations like the Foreign Relations As-

8 Fishman, *Midstream*, VII (1961); Leonard Reissman, *Jewish Journal of Sociology*, IV (1962), 117–18; and John C. Rosen, "A Study of Leadership in the New Orleans Jewish Community" (Master's thesis, Tulane University, 1960).

sociation of New Orleans, the AAUW, and the League of Women Voters.

The most sophisticated cosmopolitans among those urban Jews who were active in Jewish secular organizations—typically people of newer prosperity and often more recent Northern or foreign antecedents [9] —were on relatively intimate terms and were in rapport primarily with other Jews of similar background and Jewishness, with a handful of the most intellectually oriented members of the Jewish upper class, and with the comparable small cosmopolitan and liberal Gentile minority. Their relationships with more typical middle- and upper-class non-Jews tended to be confined to business and professional contacts and activities within formal organizations like Rotaries, Chambers of Commerce, United Funds, hospital boards, and school committees.

Only a small fraction of middle-class Jews active in Jewish groups could be considered sophisticated and well read on world affairs by national standards. However, with but few exceptions Jewish organizations and rabbis have been relatively liberal on world matters, and even when rank-and-file members have not been particularly thoughtful or well informed, this internationalism has exerted significant effects on their thinking. Some Jews in agrarian sections who were active members of the B'nai B'rith, the Anti-Defamation League, and a Reform Temple and its affiliated societies were segregationists and otherwise conservative on public questions, including world affairs, because of the atmosphere in which they lived and worked. But, such persons who would greatly reduce foreign aid or intervene militarily in Cuba against the opposition of a majority of Latin American governments seemed a small minority in cities.

Many Northern Jews moved South, like many Southern Gentiles raised in the North, were probably among the less intellectually oriented, socially conscious, cosmopolitan, and more conservative of Northern Jewry before migrating. A number of Jews also undoubtedly moved South to take advantage of cheap labor, right-to-work laws, inexpensive Negro servants, and other Southern "advantages." But a recent study of Memphis Jews, only 28 percent of whom had two American-born parents, determined that 70 percent felt that "members of all races have the same basic capacities for education and training"; 60 percent felt that the destruction of Israel would entail a very deep personal loss for them; and 90 percent commented that it would be a personal loss to some extent.[10] The sample for the author's study was too

9 *Ibid.*
10 Shapiro, "The Southville Survey of Jewish Attitudes."

small for definitive generalizations, but the impression was that Northern Jews who have moved South temporarily with corporations or other
organizations have been more liberal about world affairs than those who
came South to go into business themselves and spend the rest of their
lives in the region. Nevertheless, many in this former category have
been thoughtful internationalists as well. Perhaps crucial are the education and degree of attachment of the former Northerner with Jewish
organizations; college graduates who have been active in Jewish bodies,
as noted above, have tended to identify with active international cooperation in diplomatic, economic, and cultural as well as military affairs.

Urban Jewry

Thus, international thinking among Jews has varied from one city
to the next and within the same community, depending on the relative
prevalence of the characteristics mentioned above. Jews of Birmingham
have appeared considerably less cosmopolitan in their interests and
knowledge and less liberal in their international opinions than those
of Atlanta, Jews in Shreveport and Charleston less than their counterparts in New Orleans. But the same comparative generalizations would
apply to Gentiles of similar social standing, education, and occupation
in these cities.

The Jewish community of Greensboro was among the more internationally liberal. Located in the North Carolina Piedmont where there
has been little plantation experience, high (for the South) industrialization, relatively few Negroes, and relatively little racial tension,
Greensboro has several colleges, one of them among the best in the
South, and an educational tradition. The county in which it is located
is the center of Southern Quaker population, and the only Quaker
college in the region is located there. Although the textile industry was
in 1961 strong and protectionist, the scientifically oriented and forward
looking point of view of the Burlington Industries was influential. Other
major textile industries in the area were divisions of Cone Mills, locally
controlled by a prominent Jewish family. The two Greensboro newspapers were among the most internationally liberal in the region, even on
international trade. Consequently, although the general community
included a number of strongly conservative people, some of them of
considerable influence, countervailing forces were potent.

Approximately half the members of the Reform Temple were raised
outside the South, compared with nine out of ten in the Conservative
Temple. The upper class of Southern origins, as elsewhere in the South,
was concentrated in the former. They, as in the South generally, were
the ones who belonged to the most esteemed country club, were mem-

bers of law firms and other enterprises with Gentiles, and circulated socially with the local Gentile elite. There has been in recent years virtually no Jewish working class in Greensboro, or elsewhere in the South;[11] most of the salesmen, proprietors of smaller stores, and less prestigous professional people were in the Conservative Temple—there was little Conservative Judaism in the South before the Northern "invasion."

Perhaps as many as a third of Jewish adults in Greensboro read some of the international coverage in either the New York *Times* (Sunday edition) or other periodicals of comparable sophistication. There may have been a few Jews in Greensboro in 1961 who would send the Marines into Cuba, drastically reduce aid to India, withdraw from the U.N. if Communist China were admitted as a member, shift most of our foreign policy out of the U.N. on account of the influence of colored neutralists and underdeveloped states, support the arguments of the conservative *colons* in Africa and of the semifeudal white landowners in the underdeveloped world, and terminate negotiations for the reduction of armaments and other sources of tension. But the Jewish interviewees for this study, including the rabbis, did not know of any among those individuals who still considered themselves Jews. No more than three or four out of approximately fifteen hundred were known to have supported the strongly segregationist candidate for governor I. Beverly Lake in the recent election, and only a small minority would assist those who wished to obstruct gradual desegregation. A few wealthy Jews agreed more or less with Senator Goldwater on domestic economic policy, but on world affairs almost all who had views seemed to agree with most of the general international orientations of the "modern" Republicans or the moderate or liberal Democrats. These generalizations applied to the manufacturers of textiles, although they wanted more protection from imports in their fields.

Charleston is a very different society from Greensboro and other New South communities, and its Jewish community differs as well.[12] It includes one of the oldest settlements in America. Sephardic Jews arrived in the late 1600's and by the mid-1700's a number of them were among the leading citizens of Charleston.[13] In 1800 the town had the

11 *Ibid.;* Fishman, *Midstream,* VII (1961); and Reissman, *Jewish Journal of Sociology,* IV (1962), 112.
12 Richmond Jewry seemed to have much in common with its coreligionists in Charleston, except that influences from outside the Old South have exerted considerably more influence in Richmond. See Greenberg, *Through the Years.*
13 Elzas, *The Jews of South Carolina,* 19–22; and Thomas J. Tobias, "Joseph Tobias of Charleston: 'Linguister,' " *Publication of the American Jewish Historical Society,* XLIX (1959), 33–38.

largest, most prosperous, and probably most cultivated and intellectually sophisticated Jewish community in the New World; [14] in 1818 one third of the Jews in the United States resided in the low country.[15] By 1951, 41.5 percent of the Jews in Charleston were born there, 12 percent had been there for three or more generations, and well over half were natives of the South.[16]

Many Charleston Jews, particularly among the old established families, have a keen interest in their historic heritage and genealogies and, as is true of most Gentiles of like backgrounds, they would not live anywhere else.[17] As one cosmopolitan gentleman—whose family had been leaders in both the Jewish and general Charleston communities since the middle of the eighteenth century—explained, he walked over the same protruding bricks in the same sidewalks and listened to the birds in the trees in the same gardens when coming home to lunch as his ancestors had. He had grown up with most of the people with whom he associated, and he knew a great deal about each of them and their forebears. He loved his genteel society of politeness, warm interpersonal relations, and lack of needless rush, although he disagreed with prevailing ideas about many issues, including race relations, foreign aid, the U.N., Africa, and so on.[18]

Thoughtful Charlestonians, Jewish and otherwise, complained that the more vigorous critical minds who had a serious interest in world affairs usually did not return after college, or, if they did, tended not to remain. Charleston Jewry did seem considerably more conservative than the Jews of Greensboro on foreign policy.

Nevertheless, not more than 2 percent of Charleston Jewry were more outspoken segregationists in 1960–61 than their careers would require, and probably only about one out of four agreed privately with local white supremacists. A considerable proportion had been influ-

14 Elzas, *The Jews of South Carolina*, 120–30; Simonhoff, *Under Strange Skies*, 252; Tobias, *Publication of the American Jewish Historical Society*, XLIX (1959), 44–62; Reznikoff and Engelman, *The Jews of Charleston*, 67; and Thomas J. Tobias, *The Hebrew Orphan Society of Charleston, S.C.*, (Charleston: Published by the Society, 1957) v and 1.
15 Elzas, *The Jews of South Carolina*, 132.
16 Uriah Z. Engelman, "The Jewish Population of Charleston," *Jewish Social Studies*, XIII (1951), 202.
17 *Ibid.*, 195–212; Reznikoff and Engelman, *The Jews of Charleston*, 243; and Elzas, *The Jews of South Carolina*, 132 and 289.
18 Louis Rubin, Jr., *The Golden Weather* (New York: Atheneum, 1961), describes the values of the Jewish gentry of Charleston as a youngster growing up within it. He notes that he learned as a child that he was "no kike with thick lips and a hook nose; I was a member of one of the Fine Old Jewish Families." (p. 263.) His Jewish peers thought of themselves more as part of upper-class Charleston than as Jews; they minimized their differences in religion and ethnic traditions from the rest of the aristocracy. (pp. 81 ff.)

enced to some extent by local criticisms of foreign aid—that it had involved much waste, had not prevented drift of underdeveloped countries toward the left and anti-Americanism, had been siphoned off by the corrupt leadership and landed elite groups, and so on—and of other aspects of our foreign policy as well. However, no more than 10–15 percent in 1960–61 seemed to agree with the extreme anti-foreign aid, anti-U.N., colonialist, and otherwise arch-conservative editorials of the local papers and the similar views of Congressman Rivers and Senator Thurmond. Perhaps as many as two thirds of the Gentiles of similar status—professional, managerial, and proprietory—agreed with the general tone of those opinions, if not with the details. Very few Jews were members of neo-isolationist and military interventionist groups like the Charleston Alert and the John Birch Society, and virtually none were active members. Those Jews who did agree with their Gentile peers, as elsewhere in the South, tended to be more "Southern," more "standpat" about local racial and other social change, and to be concentrated among those who associated socially primarily with conservative Gentiles and participated little in Jewish organizations.

New Orleans Jewry, like its general population, incorporates some of the attributes of Charleston and some of Greensboro Jews as well as other characteristics which are unique. Some New Orleanians can trace their forebears to Jews who settled in the city almost 250 years ago;[19] a large proportion of even antebellum Jewish migrants to the community came from well-established Southern communities like Charleston rather than from abroad.[20] Even in 1958, 41 percent of New Orleans Jews had been born in the city, another 24 percent had lived there for thirty or more years, an additional 24 percent had resided locally for at least a decade, and only 11 percent had been present for less than ten years.[21] Relatively few Jews have originated from Eastern Europe until quite recently. Prosperous Jews mixed on relatively intimate terms with Gentiles of like status prior to the Civil War.[22] Charleston-raised and Yale-educated Judah P. Benjamin of New Or-

19 Leo Shpall, *The Jews in Louisiana* (New Orleans: Steeg Publishing Co., 1936), 18 ff.
20 Bertram W. Korn, "Jews and Negro Slavery in the Old South, 1789–1865," *Publication of the American Jewish Historical Society*, L (1961), 157.
21 Reissman, *Jewish Journal of Sociology*, IV (1962), 113. For earlier examinations of New Orleans Jewry, see Julian B. Feibelman, *A Social and Economic Study of the New Orleans Jewish Community* (Philadelphia: The Jewish Publication Society of America, 1941); and Benjamin Goldman, *The Jewish Population of New Orleans, 1953* (New York: Council of Jewish Federations and Welfare Funds, 1953).
22 See, for instance, Leo Shpall, "Early Jewish Philanthropy in New Orleans," *The Jewish Forum*, XXXVIII (1955), 14.

leans and nearby Belle Chasse Plantation married into a Creole old family, was sent to the U.S. Senate by the state legislature, and subsequently became Attorney General, Secretary of War, and Secretary of State in Jefferson Davis' Cabinet.[23] Louis Solomon was the first king of the Mardi Gras, Rex, in 1872.[24]

The New Orleans Jewish community in 1960 was considerably more "Southern" than that of Greensboro or Atlanta, but less so than that of Charleston and Antebellum Town. A recent survey found that over 90 percent agreed that "insofar as possible, Jewish people should try to fit in with the community where they live rather than trying to keep themselves separate in any way." [25] Few have been active Zionists, and those who have been have tended to have lesser social prestige. As in other old Jewish communities, social status was clear-cut and relationships between the aristocracy of inherited money and "newer" people were largely limited to relatively formal situations. The exceptions were primarily cosmopolitans of the upper class who associated with equally sophisticated people of lesser social standing. Likewise, college-educated "successful" Jews who have migrated from elsewhere or have risen from more lowly local origins circulated little with Gentiles after office hours and beyond formal organizations, except for the cosmopolitans of both groups.

But more than in Charleston, dynamic, thoughtful Jews have returned from Harvard, Yale, and other stimulating national colleges to New Orleans, where they could find a considerably larger number of other sophisticated people and where the spheres of action open to them were, by comparison, greater. Although a relatively large number of New Orleanians who identify themselves as Jews have been paternalist segregationists by preference and uncomfortable with changing race relations in their city, virtually none have agreed publicly with the intransigent position of the Citizens Council. Many have been seriously affected by the general local apathy about intellectual matters and the emphasis on warm human relationships, "not rocking the boat," and relaxed enjoyment of life and have, therefore, been relatively indifferent to, poorly informed about, and rather conservative on world affairs. However, neo-isolationist, anti-U.N., anti-aid to India Jews in the early

23 Korn, *Publication of the American Jewish Historical Society*, L (1961), 153; and Harry Simonhoff, *Jewish Participants in the Civil War* (New York: Arco Publishing Co., 1963), 161–71.
24 Tallant, *The Romantic New Orleanians*, 130.
25 Leonard Reissman, "Profile of a Community: A Sociological Study of the New Orleans Jewish Community," (MS at Jewish Federation of New Orleans, 1958), 118.

sixties were a small minority. Discussions Unlimited, the local upper and upper-middle class organization which expressed that international posture, had virtually no active Jewish participation.

Small Towns and Open Country

There were no Jews in many Southern counties in 1960, including some with towns comprising as many as five thousand inhabitants. Jews did not settle where little prosperity and few potential customers for merchants were to be found, and, when the boll weevil or other economic misfortune struck, many of them left. In other counties or towns many of their descendants became Protestants and disappeared as Jews. Unless the community had access over the years to a resident or nearby rabbi, or was in contact with urban Jewish organizations, or attracted "new" Jews from outside within the last two generations, it usually had few or no inhabitants who considered themselves Jewish by 1960.[26]

All the factors mentioned so far applied to Jews in rural market towns and other small communities; those in the Deep South, particularly in heavily Negro areas, were the most conservative about world affairs and the most hesitant about expressing views diverging from local norms; the better educated, particularly at national colleges, were the most informed, interested, and internationalist; those most active in Jewish organizations were least inclined to be neo-isolationists; and so on. But these variables were compounded and reinforced by others in smaller places.

There was one Jewish lawyer and one rabbi in both Deltatown and Antebellum Town—otherwise there were no Jewish professional men in the eight communities of less than thirty thousand population in which interviews were conducted. Young Jews who received sophisticated higher educations and became interested and thoughtful about world issues were even more inclined to migrate to big cities and college communities than were equally cosmopolitan Gentiles. Moreover, sons and daughters of prosperous small-town Jews have been considerably more apt to go to excellent colleges outside the South than have offspring of Gentiles, an experience closely connected with migration out of small Southern cities and towns. In many cases these analytically inclined youngsters have sold the family business or real estate or left it to the supervision of their less intellectual siblings or in-laws. Others returned from college or married into these merchant families, but "couldn't stand it" and left for further graduate education and a city

26 For a description of the disappearance of Jews in small Louisiana towns, see Kaplan, *The Eternal Stranger.*

or university community. Small-town and rural Southern Jewry in 1960 was therefore composed largely of merchants, small manufacturers of soft goods, bankers, a few planters, and other non-professional folk, many of whom did not have college degrees. Most of these were regarded as "dull," "uncultivated," or "bourgeois," by the Jewish professional class in the cities. They were also, of course, highly vulnerable economically and socially to local opinion.

In fact, few well-informed, internationally sophisticated Jews lived outside of cities and university towns in 1959–62. Now and then a thoughtful cosmopolitan returned from college with his subscriptions to serious national periodicals, or a relatively unsophisticated son of a merchant brought in a bride who was considerably more interested in ideas than he, including world affairs. But the inducements toward conformity to parochial thinking were usually compelling for these Jews—there was little stimulation to discuss world affairs in a cause and effect fashion; few local people were interested in talking about this field; business contacts were usually relatively uninterested and uninformed about foreign policy; virtually no sophisticates in international relations came to town; the race issue inhibited discussion of controversial issues; and making a living was time-consuming. The result typically was that the returnee, like his cosmopolitan Gentile counterparts, gradually tapered off in his critical thinking and reading, lost much of his former ability to discuss world issues critically, and conformed more and more in his international concepts to local norms.

It was difficult to assess the private attitudes of small-town Jews. Many were obviously little interested in this field and had only rather vague inclinations. Increased racial tension and related pressures had caused many of them to project a more conservative public image of their international thinking than their true opinions warranted. On the other hand, many of them seemed to offer more internationalist or liberal views to interviewers from universities and research agencies than they were known for locally—and perhaps than their true thinking. The proportion of neo-isolationist Jews, or Jews who accepted many of the international attitudes associated with racism, was considerably greater outside cities and their suburbs. Most of their international thinking seemed to diverge less from that of local Gentile businessmen than was the case in metropolitan areas.

But the small-town Jews interviewed were privately at least somewhat more internationally inclined and less conservative than comparable local Gentiles in the same places. If there were as many as half a dozen Jewish families in a community, at least one Jew read the international content in one or more critical, relatively internationalist, periodicals. The more Jews in towns of comparable size, the larger the circulations of the New York *Times*, *Harper's*, *The Atlantic*, and the like. Causation is difficult to determine—perhaps Jews have gone to or stayed in towns where there were more Gentiles of cosmopolitan bent; existence of a few thoughtful Gentiles may stimulate more Jews to interest themselves in world matters; or the presence of internationally concerned and informed Jews may encourage more of the college educated Gentiles to be so. Probably a combination of these and other factors has operated in most cases. Only a minority of small-town Jews read such material frequently, but Jews were considerably more likely to do so than comparable Gentile elites in the same towns. Most Jews who did not read more analytical publications read *Newsweek*, or even *Time*, although many of them criticized the latter as unfairly biased against the South. *U.S. News and World Report* was more popular with small-town Southern Jews than with their urban coreligionists, but the former tended to be at least somewhat less enamored of its international views than were local Gentile merchants and planters. Moreover, a considerable number of Gentiles subscribed to periodicals like the New York *Times* (Sunday edition) to see what the "enemy" is saying, or to keep up with drama, literature, fashions, or other fields and ignored or read in fundamental disagreement the international coverage. Few Jews seemed to read these for "ammunition," and although these publications were more liberal on world affairs than most of their small-town Jewish readers, Jews typically were less hostile to the international interpretations therein than were a considerable minority of Gentile readers.

Impacts on the General Community

As among Gentiles, the public position of cosmopolitan Jews before less internationally interested, informed, and thoughtful colleagues has depended on their own sense of self-assurance both in the subject matter of international relations and in their communities; their economic, social, and emotional vulnerability to local pressures; the degree of difference between their own thinking on foreign relations and that among their prospective local audiences; the local level of tension over the race question; personality factors; and the encouragement they may receive from persons and organizations of similar persuasion both within and without their locales. But the interviewees indicated that cosmopolitan Jews with relatively liberal or responsibly conservative international views have in recent years been considerably less inclined than Gentiles of similar knowledge and ideology to express themselves before fellow Southerners of markedly more conservative international opinion; Jewish cosmopolitans have been anxious about calling attention to Jewish divergence from local thinking on controversial issues.

Increasing Fear of Anti-Semitism

Concern that expression of liberal opinion may stimulate negative reactions by conservative Gentiles against themselves and Jews in general has been particularly apparent since the Supreme Court decision of May 17, 1954. Growing insecurity has tended to silence many thoughtful Jews, particularly on the race issue and national and international questions with racial overtones, but also indirectly in other controversial fields as well.

For generations Southern Jews and Gentiles have been saying that there is less anti-Semitism in the South than elsewhere in the United States and have taken pride in the rapport between Jews and Gentiles in the region. Virtually no Jews in the South were publicly critical of slavery during the antebellum period; although there were relatively few Jewish planters, concentration of Jews in the commercial class in the towns resulted in a probably larger fraction of Jews than white Gentiles owning some slaves.[27] Florida as well as Louisiana sent a Jew to the U.S. Senate before the war.[28] Most Jews in the region were pro-Dixie and they fought actively against the North in the Civil War.[29] In addition to Benjamin, the Quartermaster General, the Surgeon General, several Congressmen, and other high public and military officers of the Confederacy were Jewish,[30] although Jews were but a minuscule proportion of the Southern population.[31] The number of Jews in 1962 even in Southern cities has been small, and a larger proportion of them than of their Northern coreligionists have been there

27 Korn, *Publication of the American Jewish Historical Society*, L (1961), 153–57.
28 Bertram W. Korn, *American Jewry and the Civil War* (Philadelphia: Jewish Publication Society of America, 1951), 3.
29 Simonhoff, *Jewish Participants in the Civil War*, xiii, xv, xvi, 161–71, 183–285, and 310; Korn, *Publication of the American Jewish Historical Society* L (1961), 191–98; James A. Wax, "The Jews of Memphis, 1860–1865," *Papers of the West Tennessee Historical Society*, No. 3, (1949), 84–88; Louis Ginsberg, *History of the Jews of Petersburg* (Petersburg, Va.: privately published, 1954), 42–43; and Korn, *American Jews and the Civil War*, ix and 49 ff.
30 Simonhoff, *Jewish Participants in the Civil War*, xv, xvi, and 310 ff; and Oscar Cohen, "Public Opinion and Anti-Jewish Prejudice in the South" (MS of the Anti-Defamation League, New York, 1959).
31 Korn, *Publications of the American Jewish Historical Society*, L (1961), 199.

for several generations and have integrated local accents, mores, and thought patterns into their personalities. It has been pointed out that Southern Protestantism emphasized the Old Testament, as does Judaism, that Jews have long socialized with Gentiles in small Southern towns, and that Southern prejudices and aggressions have been focused on the Negro and the "Yankee meddler." Although there have been several unfortunate bombings of synagogues and other anti-Semitic incidents in the region since 1954, the incidence of such acts has been less in the South than in the rest of the country.[32] The smallest number of incidents occurred in states which had by 1960 engaged in no desegregation at all; the largest number of incidents took place in Southern states which had undergone some token integration.[33] These few incidents in the South were concentrated in the handful of larger cities.[34]

The few surveys of attitudes toward Jews have been equivocal on prejudices among Southern as compared with Northern Gentiles, depending on the sphere of relationships examined. Thus, the proportion of Southerners, as of Northerners, who said they had heard any "criticism or talk against Jews in the last six months" declined considerably between 1945 and 1959; in the latter year 8 percent in the South as compared with 13 percent in the North answered in the affirmative.[35] This interregional difference was understandable, considering the few Jews that have existed in many Southern locales. White Southerners were about as apt as white Northerners in the late 1930's and 1940's to feel that we should allow a larger number of Jewish refugees from Nazism to enter this country,[36] contrary to the general tendency of Southerners to be more unfavorable to immigration than Northerners. Immediately after the war, Southern whites were distinctly less likely than Northern ones to think that Jews had "too much influence in the business world"; only in the South did less than half the population feel this way.[37] Questions that asked about the desirability of Jews as neighbors showed little difference between the South and the rest of the nation.[38]

But 35 percent of Southern whites as compared with 29 percent of Northern whites felt in 1959 that Jewish businessmen are "shrewd and

32 David Caplovitz and Candace Rogers, *Swastika 1960: The Epidemic of Anti-Semitic Vandalism in America* (New York: Anti-Defamation League, 1961), 22.
33 *Ibid.,* 27.   34 *Ibid.,* 46–47.
35 Summary of previous surveys in an unpublished study by the American Jewish Committee, "The Nationwide Poll of March, 1959," Appendix D.
36 AIPO 139, 11/22/38 (3,131), and NORC 231, December, 1944 (2,471).
37 NORC 239, November, 1945 (2,540).
38 American Jewish Committee, "The Nationwide Poll of March, 1959," Table D–6.

tricky." [39] When a national survey asked in 1959, "If your party nominated a generally well-qualified person for President and he happened
to be a Jew, would you vote for him?" 33 percent in the South, 11
percent in the Northeast, 22 percent in the West, and 25 percent in
the Midwest said they would not.[40] However, a number of Jews have
been elected to public office in the South; one encounters Southerners
who voted for Mr. Levy down the street but want no part of "Yankee
Jewish radicals."

In fact, most Southern Jews have been so quiet on controversial
issues, including race, in the South that Southern Gentiles have greatly
underestimated their real divergence from Protestant thinking on public
and social questions. In 1959 only one percent of white Gentiles in
the region felt that Jews were the group which had "done the most
to stir up trouble over the (race) issue in those Southern communities
where a serious dispute exists over the Supreme Court decision." When
the public was asked, "In your community, which of the following
groups of people do you feel are in favor of, or opposed to, integrating
the public schools in the South?" only 15 percent said Jews favored
integration, 10 percent said they opposed integration, 8 percent said
they were neutral, and 67 percent said they did not know. Southern
non-Jews tended to believe Catholics to be more liberal on race than
Jews, contrary to the fact.[41]

However, surveys of communities under pressure for desegregation
have found significantly higher incidence of anti-Semitic feelings among
white segregationists than in the region generally; [42] in a period of
mounting local racial tension, anti-Semitism apparently does rise considerably. And even when relatively cosmopolitan Jews in small Deep
Southern communities said there had been little overt anti-Semitism,
they usually admitted that they feared it would develop as racial disputes became central in local thinking, particularly if local Jews disagreed overtly with the attitudes of the white majority. They were
anxious that expression of ideas less conservative than the prevailing
thought on social and public questions, especially but not exclusively
racial ones, would result in many Gentiles turning on them and the
Jewish minority generally. The more intense the race issue in the community, the more insecure the local Jews have felt about expressing
critical views on virtually any controversial issue. Thus, the discomfort

39 *Ibid.*
40 AIPO 622, 12/18/59 (4,077). See also AIPO 604, 9/8/58 (1,522).
41 American Jewish Committee, "The Nationwide Poll of March, 1959," 47–50;
and Cohen, "Public Opinion and Anti-Jewish Prejudice in the South."
42 Cohen, "Public Opinion and Anti-Jewish Prejudice in the South."

among many Southern Jews over support of desegregation and racial equality by national Jewish organizations, like the Anti-Defamation League, the American Jewish Committee, the American Jewish Congress, and the National Council of Jewish Women, is understandable, as is their sensitivity to any Jewish prominence in liberal movements, especially racially oriented ones.[43]

City, Town, and Country

The larger the Jewish community and the less racially conservative the local white Gentiles, the more articulate Jews have been on such issues as independence of colonial territories, foreign aid, the U.N., domestic "anti-Communism," and other issues of foreign affairs.

For instance, the rabbis in Greensboro had not experienced any pressures from their coreligionists to tone down their liberal public positions on public questions, including race and foreign policy. Few Jews there felt much inhibited about expressing their views—more liberal and internationalist than those of the general community for the most part —on international relations, although most were reticent on race. Greensboro Jewry was in 1961 greatly overrepresented among participants in and supporters of such declared internationalist groups as the World Affairs Council, the League of Women Voters, the AAUW, college forums and lectures, and UNESCO-sponsored discussions.

Likewise, in New Orleans cosmopolitan Jews have with few exceptions felt free to express their opinions on foreign policy. If it had not been for their funds and energies in the early sixties, the relatively few agencies and groups offering or encouraging critical thought about foreign relations would either not have existed or would have experienced much greater difficulties than was actually the case. Although Jews have not been particularly numerous among the formal leaders on organizational letterheads, they have typically been major financial contributors and active workers. As elsewhere in the region, many Jews, as well as thoughtful Gentiles, have played down the proportion of Jews in liberal or internationally sophisticated organizations, because they have feared that too "Jewish" an image would seriously limit their effectiveness among the general public.

43 Many Southern Jews seemed to manifest an ambivalence toward these liberal Jewish organizations. While wanting to separate themselves in the local Gentile mind from them and their equalitarian pronouncements and accusing them of generating anti-Semitism among segregationists, they have wanted the support of these agencies in case of anti-Semitic developments in the region. And many who have objected to the public statements favoring interracial justice by these agencies probably privately agreed with them. See also Fishman, *Midstream*, VII (1961), 50.

However, Jews of relatively liberal international bent in traditionalist Charleston have been much more hesitant about criticizing prevailing international thinking among their Gentile peers. Not only the most intellectually alert and cosmopolitan but also the most activist and articulate among the internationally thoughtful have left Charleston in disproportionately large numbers after college. Those who have remained have been primarily those willing to keep their peace when confronted by viewpoints very different from their own on controversial international matters, like aid to Africa and United States policy toward Moise Tshombe in 1961. Many, perhaps most, cosmopolitans who stayed tended to have abandoned much hope of changing the thinking of their arch-conservative associates; there were hardly any "crusaders" or "martyrs" among Jewish readers of *The Reporter, The Atlantic,* and the New York *Times.*

Even strongly conservative regular associates of Jews who favored most of the foreign policy of the Kennedy administration and disagreed with much of the international opinions of the local press, Congressman Rivers, and Senator Thurmond tended to feel the views of these privately liberal Jews were roughly the same as their own on world problems. One prominent Jewish businessman noted that public knowledge of his criticisms of the thinking current in Charleston on such issues as the supposed domestic Communist menace, Katanga versus the U.N. in the Congo (1961), economic assistance to Poland and foreign aid generally, and possible admission of Communist China into the U.N., would not only alienate many of his customers, but would probably also make it difficult for him to borrow money at banks run by "British Empire Loyalist" and "white man's burden" types. Lawyers and physicians believed that they would do damage to their practices by openly expressing their views. Jewish cosmopolitans who wanted to continue to live and prosper in Charleston seemed even more cautious about speaking out in opposition to the thinking of the *News and Courier* than were Gentiles of like mind. Conversations about world affairs were limited largely to a small circle of internationally thoughtful and relatively liberal intimates, but even then one feared "leaks" to the general community and social, if not economic, repercussions. Only individuals who were economically invulnerable to local pressures—a slender fraction of cosmopolitans indeed—felt free to criticize prevailing viewpoints, but even most of them did not wish to isolate themselves from relatives and friends.

The discouraging pressures operating on Deep Southern small-town and rural Gentile cosmopolitans have usually been even more compelling for Jews. A rabbi who had retired because of illness to Antebellum Town and who read widely and was generally cosmopolitan remarked that he had tended to voice disagreement with views expressed in face-to-face conversations when he first returned there. However, the shift to the right on foreign policy had been so acute, the local racial feelings so sensitized and emotionalized, and his previous efforts to advance responsible views so unsuccessful that he had given up trying to change people's thinking. When someone next to him at a Chamber of Commerce or other meeting expressed irresponsible neo-isolationist views, by 1961 he either let him "rave on" or changed the subject.

A Jewish merchant in Deltatown who had majored in political science, obtained a law degree at a major Midwestern university, married a cosmopolitan Northerner, and worked for an internationalist Jewish organization in the North, returned home to take over his sick father's business. A good customer came in to collect Citizens Council dues after the 1954 decision, and, having heard of loss of trade among merchants who did not join, the former lawyer became a member, though an inactive one. He commented that he felt like he was talking to himself much of the time and that his critical reading of serious periodicals had dropped off because of lack of opportunities to do anything with his knowledge. His sensibilities and his ability to express himself, he felt, had become dulled. He still managed to participate in thoughtful discussions with several other Jewish and Gentile cosmopolitans who also read the New York *Times* (Sunday edition), *The Atlantic,* or other thoughtful publications, but he remained "quiet" before most anti-foreign aid, anti-U.N. people. He noted that it was one thing for Judge X, descendant of several esteemed families of the region, leader in the Episcopal church, and relative of the socially prominent in the Deep South, to write critical letters to the arch-conservative papers in the state, chair the discussion groups in the library on public issues, and inform all and sundry of his views on world affairs—people merely said he was getting old and was just another genteel eccentric. A Jew who did likewise needed considerably more courage or less sensitivity to probable public reactions. The whole Jewish community might become a target for antagonism—other Jews would fear that one was risking the status of the entire ethnic group, and many local Jews felt that no one had any right to upset the delicate balance whereby Jews had been treated well and accepted generally as fellow Southerners.

A Jewish businessman in a conservative Deep Southern community of less than thirty thousand people who had an excellent education kept copies of *U.S. News and World Report* and the ultra-conservative daily paper of a nearby city in his office waiting room. His study at home, however, contained perhaps the best private library in town, including the *New Republic*, *The Economist*, and the New York *Times*. His favorite columnists on world affairs were James Reston and Walter Lippmann. He said he read this material as an indirect way of attacking local thinking, "instead of taking action," and as an escape from the ever present realities. Action in conformity with his real views would mean "bankruptcy." If it were not for contact with responsible thinking in such publications and frequent "buying" trips to New York, "I would go nuts." Reading and visiting cosmopolitans in cities seemed to serve this purpose for a number of such undercover "eggheads"—as another thoughtful Jew noted, "If the local bunch thought I was an 'intellectual,' that would be my finish."

Southern Jews have been more inclined than Northern ones to be affiliated with and active in synagogues, as part of the general Southern involvement in organized religion; according to expert estimates by rabbis and Jewish organizations in the South, perhaps as many as 90 percent were members of synagogues in 1960.[44] Moreover, the rabbi has been a more central figure in most Southern Jewish communities than in most Reform groups in the North. At least until recently members of predominantly small congregations probably tended more than in the North to listen carefully to the rabbi's views. Although most Reform rabbis who have held pulpits in smaller Southern communities have not been among the more intellectually vigorous, and such congregations have in a number of cases called relatively conservative spiritual leaders, most rabbis in the region in the early sixties were considerably better informed and more favorable to multilateral commitments in world affairs than their average members. Conservative Jews have wanted rabbis to limit themselves to rituals and ceremonies and to remain silent on social and political questions. Nevertheless, most rabbis seemed to continue to inform their congregations of their views on world affairs as on other public issues, including race.

But Southern Jews tend to judge their rabbis in terms of their popularity in the white Gentile community. Even when many members of a congregation have more or less agreed privately with their rabbi's views, they have felt anxious about his image with non-Jewish segregationists. As one intellectually alert and articulate rabbi in a very conservative Deep Southern community noted, his rapport with mem-

---

44 For example, some 80 percent of New Orleans Jews were synagogue affiliated in the late 1950's; this is above the Northern urban average. See Reissman, *Jewish Journal of Sociology*, IV (1962), 123.

bers of his temple and security as their rabbi were closely related to their fears about Gentiles hearing of his liberal thoughts. They were particularly anxious about the reactions of the local racist press to his behavior. Another rabbi whose liberal ideas did become known to the general community left town for several weeks to find upon returning that the leaders of his temple had been warned by representatives of a potent white supremacist and otherwise ultra-conservative organization that Jews might suffer undescribed reprisals if the rabbi did not depart permanently.[45] Consequently, most rabbis have presented considerably more conservative, or noncommittal, positions to non-Jews than to their own people and have had relatively little direct impact on international attitudes beyond their congregations.

Similar depressants to active cosmopolitanism vis-à-vis the Gentile community have been exerted as well on Jewish laymen by their coreligionists; small-town, Deep Southern Jews have feared especially that someone with a Jewish name would express controversial ideas and thus stimulate unfavorable reactions to Jews in general. There have been subtle pressures to keep quiet on such matters with the result that Jews in some communities have been willing to declare themselves against irresponsible views only when under direct attack themselves—they have been afraid even to criticize overt anti-Semitism by racists.

For instance, a graduate of the University of North Carolina, an institution regarded as ultraliberal in the Black Belt, married into a merchant family in a Deep Southern town. The word was gradually transmitted to him by asides and other subtle means that he should keep his ideas to himself and not "spout off" any "Frank Graham socialism" and the like if he wished to prosper and keep friends. He was informed that the rest of the Jewish community would not appreciate an "eager beaver" Goldberg (pseudonym) antagonizing the local conservatives. Since his father-in-law controlled the money and the family business in which he was employed, he "behaved." Another example was a local Jewish merchant who, when called upon by a regional representative (born and raised in Virginia) of a sophisticated national Jewish agency, grilled him about his background for fear he was "another one of those obnoxious, radical New York Jews." A recent study in a black-belt city of 120,000 determined that liberal Jews who had indicated publicly their disagreement with local conservative

45 This incident was the climax of increasing pressures against this cosmopolitan rabbi. Although it was finally agreed that the rabbi would be more cautious in his public expressions and that he would remain as spiritual leader, further difficulties with the Gentile community developed and he finally departed for a temple outside the Deep South after interviews for this study were completed.

thinking, particularly on race, had been informed that they had become a source of embarrassment to other Jews.[46]

Moreover, in small Deep Southern communities, cosmopolitan Jews seemed even fearful of expressing their true thinking before one another. In one such town the author met with several Jewish couples in a Jewish home for discussion of their international views. The initial half hour was spent in interrogating the interviewer—where was he born and raised, where did he go to college, what was he doing in the North, why did he want to know their opinions, was he not really the representative of some "leftist" or integrationist organization? Opinions expressed on foreign policy ranged from very conservative by national standards to what would be responsibly conservative in Boston. Views were particularly conservative on international questions related to race, and even more so on race in the South. Later questioning of several of them individually indicated that their private opinions were considerably less conservative than those they voiced before their local Jewish colleagues. Each thought that each of the others was more opposed to foreign aid, long-term commitments to economic assistance, entry of Communist China into the U.N., domestic "Communism," and, particularly, school desegregation than was actually the case. One said before his colleagues that he would never send his children to school with Negroes and that he could understand people who would meet Negroes with loaded shotguns should they try to "force themselves" on whites. Later, he commented privately that he could not understand why the local Negroes were so "docile" and that they might achieve some of their "rights" if they were more activist. Another volunteered that he had to live with his Jewish colleagues and that one's criticisms of local thinking would be known to "everybody" in a town like his within a week.

Nevertheless, more than in cities, small-town and the few rural Jews have long circulated with local Gentiles in the proprietory, managerial, and professional classes after as well as during the work day. Some of their divergent thinking on world affairs—on cooperation with colored nations in the U.N. and in economic development, for example—has rubbed off on at least the less extreme opponents of foreign aid and has moderated somewhat the latter's opinions. And one or more internationally thoughtful Jews from even communities with a dozen or less families have usually discussed international matters at least now and then with the handful of local Gentiles of like inclinations. In the few communities where there have been organized groups interested,

46 Fishman, *Midstream*, VII (1961), 51.

inter alia, in world affairs, such as a library or American Heritage discussion group, or in some towns of larger population a small League of Women Voters, several Jews have typically been active therein. The presence of a few Jewish families has helped to limit the natural provincialism and ignorance of ideas from outside of many Southern towns and to make life more tolerable for the few Gentiles of similarly broad horizons.

On the whole, however, Jews in Deltatown, Antebellum Town, and other small Deep Southern communities offer in the short run only very limited vehicles for communicating broader international thinking to the general population. Racial tension and Gentile hostility to gradual desegregation must lessen before cosmopolitan Jews in greatly increased numbers will express their more liberal (or less conservative) international ideas. As one noted, Jews could not be "fooled" by relatively liberal Quakers and Unitarians associated with cosmopolitan activities any more—the publicly declared cosmopolitans must be "big" Episcopalians, Presbyterians, Methodists, and Baptists for Jews to participate and express their support for active international cooperation in the U.N., in Africa, and in other touchy fields. In many Southern settings internationally thoughtful Jews will probably be the last to state their views publicly, after prominent Protestant leaders in considerable numbers have already spoken out in similar vein.

CHAPTER 14

SOUTHERN NEGROES

I n 1962 Negroes in the South were in a number of respects more "Southern" than the whites. As observed previously, many Southern white attitudes in world affairs have resulted from rural poverty, ignorance, isolation from the "outside," and frustration about changing one's human and physical environment and controlling one's own future. But the Southern Negro, even more than the white, has been unlettered, poor, close to the soil, insulated from events and ideas beyond his community, and convinced that only God could change his fate. His thinking and loyalties too have been intimately linked with family and traditions of the past. He more than most whites has been a hedonist who has tried to extract enjoyment from the present rather than to plan for some future bliss which would probably never come through his striving anyway. In a region where otherworldly, individually salvationist, emotional, and fundamentalist religion has influenced whites' international thinking, the Negro's religious experience has been the most escapist, revivalist, and literalist of all; he would find his fulfillment "over Jordan" in the "sweet bye-and-bye," not through efforts to comprehend and take action toward problems of this world.

Therefore, it is not surprising that Negroes as a group have been as or more conservative than Southern whites in a number of spheres related to international attitudes. As one would anticipate, Negroes have been more inclined than whites to reply "don't know," "no opinion," "undecided," or the like to such questions as "in matters of political preference, do you consider yourself a liberal or conservative?" Negroes more than whites have not understood what these terms imply. However, somewhat larger proportions of Negroes than of whites in the South expressing views have classified themselves as liberals [1] or said they would support a liberal rather than a conservative party or candidate if given the opportunity.[2] But it has been readily apparent that liberalism for most Negroes has meant more equalitarian race relations and expanded welfare programs—on these questions Southern Negroes have been more "liberal" than whites.[3] Even on desegregation, however, many Negroes, particularly older ones, have not been as enthusiastic about "reform" as most liberals had hoped: as late as 1959, when interviewed by other Negroes, only 42 percent in the Deep South approved of school desegregation as provided in the Supreme Court decision of May 17, 1954; 39 percent said they were opposed; and 19 percent said they had no opinion, did not care, or that it made little difference to them one way or the other.[4]

But on aspects which have been most correlated with liberal or multilateralist international thinking among Southern Negroes, they have been as or more conservative than Southern whites. Insofar as they have ventured opinions, Southern Negroes have been as or more apt than Southern whites to feel that "socialists," "radicals," and particularly "Communists" should not be allowed to criticize our "form of government" in the mass media or before face-to-face audiences and that they should not be permitted to teach in their schools.[5] They have been as or slightly more inclined than Southern whites to say that

1 AIPO 387, 12/31/46 (2,933); NORC 163, 1/26/49 (1,261); AIPO 454, 3/24/50 (1,458); AIPO 541, 12/29/54 (1,446); AIPO 547, 5/10/55 (1,503); and AIPO 577, 1/15/57 (1,496).

2 AIPO 649, 8/22/61 (3,165), and AIPO 654, 1/9/62 (3,421).

3 For support of social welfare, see AIPO 448, 9/23/49 (2,919), and AIPO 541, 12/29/54 (1,446). For attitudes toward racial change, see AIPO 532, 6/10/54 (1,435); AIPO 614, 5/27/59 (1,537); and AIPO 646, 5/26/61 (3,522).

4 American Jewish Committee, "The Nationwide Survey of March, 1959," and correspondence with Marshall Sklare, Director of Research of the American Jewish Committee. The survey was performed by the American Institute of Public Opinion by Negro interviewers on an enlarged sample to permit statistical comparison of Negroes in the Deep South with those in the Upper South and of major demographic groups among Negroes. Upper South Negroes were distinctly more favorable to desegregation than Deep South ones, and younger Negroes than older ones. The proportion of Negroes favorable to desegregation has undoubtedly increased since 1959.

5 NORC 239, November, 1945 (2,540); NORC 141, 3/20/46 (1,293); NORC 157, 4/22/48 (1,280); NORC 340, 5/14/53 (1,291); NORC 351, 1/21/54 (1,300); NORC 401, 12/28/56 (1,232); and NORC 404, 4/26/57 (1,279).

people should not be allowed to say anything they want in a public speech.[6] Negroes have been significantly more authoritarian than whites in the South. Negroes more than whites have tended to view society as hierarchical, as composed of superiors and inferiors; to see people as strong and weak, leaders and followers; to feel that most people, including most of their own race, cannot be trusted; to see problems in blacks and whites with few grays; and to eschew notions of progress in this world.[7] Most Negroes have had less and poorer education and have lived in more rural settings than whites; these factors have been largely responsible for the former's greater authoritarianism. However, even Negro college students and graduates have been discovered to be more authoritarian than white college students and graduates on the average.[8] Because exceedingly few Southern Negroes have been abstract idealists, the utopias of the North have passed most of them by as much as they have white Southerners.

These patterns of thought correlated with international behavior are changing, as they are among white Southerners. Each succeeding generation is less authoritarian, more integrationist, less generally conservative and traditionalist, more interested in "progress" in the future, better educated, less otherworldly in religion, more knowledgeable about the nation and the world, and less rural than its antecedent. Change away from Old South Negro docility has been especially evident among the educated Negro group, particularly in the larger cities. But the process is slow among the great mass of Negroes, and so is the gradual improvement of their understanding of national and international affairs.

International Interest, Knowledge, and Attention

The observations above and those to follow have been derived primarily from national surveys, usually from combining replies to similar questions on several of them, supplemented by interviews of 178 Southern, mostly middle class, Negroes. The emphasis on survey data entails certain reservations about the interpretations.

The proportions of Negroes among Southern survey samples have

6 NORC 239, November, 1945 (2,540), and NORC 340, 5/14/53 (1,291).

7 John B. McConaughy, "The Politicometrics of International Aggression," *Journal of Social Issues*, XV, No. 4, 1959; NORC 156, 3/25/48 (1,289); NORC 341-2, 5/30/53 (1,291); AIPO 538, 10/13/54 (1,530); NORC 365, 11/26/54 (1,201); and AIPO 593, 12/31/57 (1,522).

8 P. M. Smith and James W. Prothro, "Ethnic Differences in Authoritarian Personality," *Social Forces*, XXXV (1957), 334-38; S. A. Steckter, "Authoritarian Ideology in Negro College Students," *Journal of Abnormal and Social Psychology*, LIV (1957), 396-99; and the Bureau of Applied Social Research study.

been for the most part smaller than their number among the Southern population would suggest—for instance, typically between 50 and 100 Negroes out of between 280 and 420 Southerners on NORC surveys between 1946 and 1957, and between 110 and 200 out of between 650 and 840 Southerners on most AIPO surveys prior to 1950 and after mid-1959. Moreover, Negroes interviewed on any particular survey have usually resided in a smaller number of sample communities than have white interviewees. When interview samples of whites have used twenty areas in the region, for example, Negro samples have employed as few as six in some cases in order to make maximal use of the relatively few competent Negro interviewers available. Thus, those generalizations for this study which are based on only one survey wherein the national sample numbered from 1,200 to 1,400 should be regarded as tentative, pending further research of larger, more representative samples. Observations derived from Roper and AIPO samples of 2,500 or more Americans may be regarded as more secure, as may those based on combined replies to similar questions on several surveys of smaller samples, although most of these are also subject to qualification through further research on more numerous and representative Negro samples.

The comparisons herein of the international thinking of Southern with that of Northern Negroes are for the most part even more tentative in nature. Because most Negroes resided in the South until relatively recently, Northern Negro samples until the last few years have been even smaller than Southern ones. Moreover, survey categories have been white and nonwhite. For practical purposes, nonwhite in the South has meant Negro, but in the North it has included considerable numbers of Asians, most of whom, like the Chinese and Japanese-Americans, have been on the average better informed and more cosmopolitan in world affairs than Northern (or Southern) Negroes.

The race of the interviewer has also introduced problems of interpretation of survey results. Most Southern Negroes interviewed since World War II by NORC have been queried by Negroes,[9] as have most of those questioned by AIPO in recent years.[10] Approximately 80 to 85 percent of Negroes in Roper surveys since the mid-1940's were likewise interviewed by Negroes.[11] However, considerably smaller proportions of Negroes in SRC samples since even as late as 1956 were

9 From a conversation with Paul B. Sheatsley of NORC, who directed the NORC surveys on contract with the U. S. Department of State from 1945 through April, 1957.
10 From a conversation with Louis Vexler of AIPO.
11 From a conservation with Joel I. Brooke, partner at Elmo Roper and Associates.

queried by Negro interviewers.[12] Moreover, many of the earlier interviews of Southern Negroes were conducted by whites, and even in 1962 Negroes who resided in predominantly white neighborhoods in either the North or the South were questioned for the most part by whites.

Several studies have determined that rural Negroes particularly and others economically and otherwise directly dependent on whites have tended to reply differently to white as compared with Negro interviewers; especially on issues related to race relations, they have given more conservative replies to the former than to the latter and they have also appeared less interested and informed about public affairs before white than before Negro interviewers.[13] In general, Negroes have tended to tell interviewers what they thought they wanted to hear—perhaps they have appeared less interested in public questions and more conservative to white interviewers and more interested and liberal to college-educated, middle-class Negro ones than their actual interests and attitudes warranted. In Memphis in 1942, for instance, when residents were asked, "Would Negroes be treated better or worse here if the Japanese conquered the U.S.A.?" almost twice as large a proportion of equivalent samples of Negroes answered "worse" to white interviewers as to Negro interviewers.[14] Thus, surveys employing either white or Negro interviewers have probably both resulted in replies distorted with respect to their real thinking on world affairs. Most of the statistical observations for this study about Negro international behavior since World War II were derived from surveys in which whites interviewed Southern whites and Negroes interviewed Southern Negroes, whereas most of the generalizations about Negro thinking on world affairs before Pearl Harbor spring from samples interviewed in considerable measure by whites. Actual Negro international attitudes for the postwar period were, therefore, perhaps somewhat more conservative and less cosmopolitan than these results tend to indicate.

12 SRC samples have typically included fewer interviewees in each locale sampled than has usually been the case with the other major national surveying agencies. Except in special surveys, SRC has deemed it economically and administratively desirable to hire Negro interviewers primarily for those relatively few settings sampled where Negroes predominated and to leave the small number of Negro interviewees in areas where Negroes are a minority to white interviewers. (From a conversation with Charles Cannell of SRC.)
13 Hadley Cantril, *Gauging Public Opinion* (Princeton: Princeton University Press, 1944), 114–16; Herbert Hyman *et al., Interviewing in Social Research* (Chicago: University of Chicago Press, 1954), 159; and Daniel O. Price and Ruth Searles, "Some Effects of Interviewer-Respondent Interaction on Responses in a Survey Situation," in American Statistical Association, *Proceedings of the Social Statistics Section* (1961), 211–21.
14 Cantril, *Gauging Public Opinion*, 114–16.

Information on World Affairs

Regardless of the race of the survey interviewers, Southern Negroes as a group have been consistently less informed about virtually all international questions than both Southern whites and Northern Negroes. Considerably larger proportions of Southern Negroes than of Southern whites or Northern Negroes have replied "don't know," "no opinion," or equivalent answers to poll and survey questions on foreign policy. On some international matters the percentage of Southern Negroes who have not ventured replies or have answered that they do not know about the issue posed has been so high that it is difficult to interpret the significance of the minority who did offer opinions. For instance, as late as March, 1962, in the midst of public discussion of the proposed Trade Expansion Act before the Congress, almost two thirds of Southern Negroes said they did not know, had no opinion, were uninformed, or otherwise failed to reply whether they favored higher tariffs, lower tariffs, or about the same level of tariffs as were then in effect; [15] throughout the 1950's less than two out of five Southern Negroes interviewed were able or willing to express opinions on general questions about whether tariffs or other barriers to trade should be higher or lower, whether we should expand world commerce, including imports, whether the reciprocal trade agreements program should be continued, and the like.[16] The more specific the aspect of foreign policy, the greater the proportion of those not venturing opinions and the greater the incidence of Negro compared to white "don't know's." Only on the broadest issues, such as, "Do you expect a world war with the Communist powers in the next ten years?" has the fraction of Southern Negroes offering opinions approached the proportion of Southern whites (or Northern nonwhites) doing so.

Exposure to Mass Media

Since interest and knowledge in world affairs has been closely associated with attention to content in this field in printed and, to a lesser extent, electronic media, it is understandable that Negroes have been much less inclined than whites to expose themselves to serious coverage of this field.

The proportion of Southern Negroes among readers of books on

15 AIPO 656, 3/6/62 (3,486).
16 NORC 298, 1/30/51 (1,236); NORC 313, 10/2/51 (1,237); NORC 325, 5/28/52 (1,265); NORC 332, 10/15/52 (1,291); NORC 333, 11/17/52 (1,291); NORC 334, 12/29/52 (1,291); AIPO 512, 2/20/53 (1,548); AIPO 513, 3/26/53 (1,590); AIPO 516, 5/28/53 (1,549); and NORC 371, 4/29/55 (1,226).

world affairs and of such critical publications as the New York *Times*
(Sunday edition), *Harper's*, *The Reporter*, and *The Atlantic* has been
extremely small indeed, roughly one tenth that among Southern whites.
Differences have declined when education has been controlled, but in
the late 1940's Negro college graduates were only approximately one
third as likely as white college graduates to read about national and
international affairs in such publications.[17] Among Negroes frequent
exposure to such material in the early 1960's was typical of only a very
select intellectual elite—the most alert college teachers; a few young,
well-educated, vigorous ministers; a handful of the most cosmopolitan
lawyers, publishers, and editors; a tiny fraction of college-educated
businessmen in the more progressive cities; and a very small minority
of the college-graduated wives of such people. Whereas there have
usually been half a dozen or more readers of one or more of these
publications in rural black-belt counties and at least one or two in hill
counties, they virtually never included Negroes at the time of the
interviews for this study.

Negro readers in the South of a weekly newsmagazine—*Time*, *Newsweek*, *Life*, or *Look*—were in 1957–60 more than ten times as numerous.
Exposure to *U.S. News and World Report*, the most popular newsmagazine among white segregationists, was confined among the interviewees to more conservative, rather prosperous, college-educated Negroes, largely aged fifty and above. These Negroes were typically either
opposed or at least relatively indifferent to militantly integrationist
Negroes. The proportion of Southern Negro college graduates who
read the international coverage even in racially liberal *Time* in 1947 [18]
and again in 1957–60 was significantly smaller than among Southern
white college graduates, and much smaller than among Northern college people. The disparity between the races in the South in the late
1950's among newsmagazine readers was less than among readers of the
more analytical periodicals, but it was still considerable. The Negro
college graduate who read about foreign affairs in *Newsweek* or *Time*
in the early sixties tended to be regarded as an "intellectual" among
most Negro businessmen, and to a lesser extent among many Negro
professional people. Pictorial news magazines, *Life* and *Look*, have
been more popular, but even they were read predominantly by middle-
class Negroes with at least a high school diploma.[19]

Readership of international news and, especially, editorials in local
daily papers has also been much less prevalent statistically among

17 From the Bureau of Applied Social Research of Columbia University study.
18 *Ibid.*   19 Hero, *Mass Media in World Affairs*, 68.

Southern Negroes than among Southern whites.[20] The differences, however, have been less marked as the printed matter became less abstract, analytical, and sophisticated. The majority of middle-class Negroes, even among the few in the country, read a daily paper in 1959–62, although most of them probably skipped over the international editorials. The Negro middle class seemed to pay considerably more attention, however, to the editorial pages of the minority of papers which are relatively liberal on race relations—like the Nashville *Tennesseean*, the *Delta Democrat-Times* of Greenville, Mississippi, the Atlanta *Constitution*, and most of the dailies in North Carolina. The editorials of these papers were virtually without exception favorable to active collaboration abroad, including continuing foreign aid to underdeveloped societies, and they also carried one or more internationalist syndicated columnists, such as Marquis Childs, Walter Lippmann, or William White, or the analysts of the New York *Times*. However, only a fraction of those Negroes who read the editorials which pertained to race relations seemed to read these columnists regularly. Those who did typically also read international coverage in *Time* or *Newsweek*, if not in the more analytical periodicals.

Negro middle-class people who desired desegregation in areas served by racist or paternalistic papers like the Columbia *State* and Columbia *Record*, the Jackson *Clarion-Ledger*, the Richmond *News Leader*, and the Charleston *News and Courier* and *Evening Post*, either did not read their editorial pages or, as one Negro Charlestonian commented, read "to find out how not to interpret the news." In communities where there were no less racially conservative papers, many educated Negroes read international news in these media, but the racism of these papers tended to alienate Negroes from reading editorials on world affairs as well as on race within them.

Nevertheless, some of the conservative international thinking typical of strongly segregationist papers had influenced the attitudes of many middle-class Negroes, even those quite discontented with the local racial *status quo*. Many Negroes had integrated much more of their racially conservative paper's international thinking than of its racial position into their own views. Although there were major exceptions, the international opinions of middle-class Negroes in areas monopolized by racist presses tended to be more conservative than among their counterparts in communities served by more internationalist papers.

20 SRC surveys of June–August, 1946 (1,177) and March–April, 1957 (1,919), and NORC 393, 9/13/56 (1,263).

As was true among more internationally inclined Southern whites, middle-class, usually college-educated Negroes in the South who favored active collaboration in international organizations and other liberal measures in areas where the press was neo-isolationist or hostile to foreign aid derived their views from countervailing sources, typically internationalist national periodicals reinforced by public affairs programs on national television networks or local educational stations. As was the case among those well-educated whites who read international content of newsmagazines or, especially, analytical periodicals, such Negroes utilized TV newscasts as their initial source of information which they later read about in greater detail. They viewed comments on the news and critical public affairs programs on TV as supplements to their reading and as contacts with international figures whereby they might judge them as individuals.

But for rank-and-file Negroes, TV was by the 1950's the principal, often the sole, contact with world affairs. Only in rural sections where TV signals were weak or most Negroes were still very poor did most Negroes not have access to a TV set. Many who did not own a set viewed programs in the homes of relatives or friends, or at a store, pool hall, or other meeting place. Attention to programs like "Meet the Press" and other network presentations of international problems has been most frequent among better-educated Negroes, typically those who also read about world affairs in a newspaper if not in a magazine. However, such TV programs have reached further down the Negro educational and social spectra, as they have among Southerners generally, than have newspaper columnists and editorials, and much further into the common man strata.[21] Network newscasts like the "Huntley-Brinkley Report," although most popular among better-educated Negroes, attracted the attention at least now and then of a considerable minority of the Negro masses. Most Negroes of limited education seemed to use their TV mostly for sports events and entertainment and paid little attention to international content. But an increasing number of them have paid attention, particularly when these newscasters and analysts were apparently liberal on race relations and commented on American racial incidents and on developments in Africa south of the Sahara. The combination of availability of TV, its coverage of Southern Negro-white difficulties, and its concern with African matters has drawn the attention of at least several millions of Southern Negroes who did not complete high school or whose parents prior to World War II had virtually no contact with the world beyond the lower-class Negro groups in the nearest Southern city.

21 Hero, *Mass Media in World Affairs*, Chapter 5.

A considerable proportion of the middle-class Negro interviewees for this study, and a few of the urban working class as well, read a weekly Negro paper, either one published locally or a national one. A number also read such Negro magazines as *Ebony* and *Jet*. Some issues were passed from one Negro family to the next, thus multiplying audiences.

Unfortunately, no systematic examination of international content of the Negro press has come to our attention. The *raison d'être* of most Negro papers and magazines has been protest against racial inequities, presentation of news or views pertinent to Negroes which fill lacunae in the general press, or presentation of alternatives to interpretations which middle-class Negroes feel are distorted in media controlled by whites.[22] Cursory reading of issues of a number of Negro publications popular in the South indicates that coverage of activities among Negroes and criticism of discrimination against Negroes remained their central focus in 1961. Moreover, the owners of most Negro publications were predominantly businessmen, so that much of the editorial content was quite conservative except on race relations.[23] Even in the few cases where the owner or editor read critical publications like the *New Republic*, he tended to feel that world affairs was not the proper emphasis for his paper. The need to sell newspapers to a poorly educated ethnic group, most of which came from farms and were first generation middle class or still working class, did not encourage publication of abstract or analytical discussions of foreign policy.

Habitual readers of the Negro press among the interviewees noted that the independent movements in Africa and developments subsequent to termination of colonial control had in recent years received increasing attention in many Negro popular periodicals. A few of these publications, such as the Norfolk *Journal and Guide*, have dealt relatively responsibly with the underlying problems facing the new African states, as well as world affairs in general. However, most editorials on Africa and other world issues seemed superficial and generally poor, and even the news presented was frequently overly dramatic and sensational, sometimes rather obviously appealing to middle-class status strivings. A considerable proportion of the coverage of Africa seemed to fall into the category of, "Mrs. W, prominent social figure in X city, and her daughter, Cynthia, attended a reception on X date for Ambassador Y of Z African country." Perhaps a number of readers of these

22 Maxwell R. Brooks, *The Negro Press Re-Examined: Political Content of Leading Negro Newspapers* (Boston: The Christopher Publishing House, 1959), especially Chapter 4.
23 *Ibid.*, 75.

Negro papers have learned some bits of disconnected information about world developments therefrom.

Organizations and Informal Groups
Communicating World Affairs

Southern Negroes as a group have been less likely to participate actively in organizations other than churches and fraternal orders than Southern whites, who have been, in turn, less apt to do so than Northerners.[24] Moreover, very few Negro organizations outside a small number of college communities have sponsored discussions of world affairs. When a national survey asked the public in the late forties whether they participated in organizations in which international affairs were discussed, a much smaller proportion of Negroes than of other Southerners replied in the affirmative, even though the latter were less apt to have taken part in such groups than Northerners.[25] The same relationship applied to informal discussion of world affairs with friends and associates—Southern Negroes were less inclined to do so than either Southern whites or Northern Negroes, both of whom were below the norms of Northern whites.[26] As has been true of Americans generally, Negroes who have discussed world affairs in a fairly thoughtful way with others in organizational meetings have tended to do so in informal interpersonal relationships as well, and these same individuals have done most of the reading about world questions and viewing of the better television programs on the subject.[27]

The gap in sophistication between this intellectual elite and the great mass of Southern Negroes in 1962 was still enormous, even wider than that between cosmopolitan whites and the white majority, and it is understandable that most internationally alert Negroes seemed even more inclined than their Southern white counterparts to feel that attempts to communicate their thinking on foreign policy to the Negro rank and file would achieve little success and that their limited time and energy could best be employed in other fields.

Most of the thoughtful, critical examination of world affairs conducted by organizations took place in the early 1960's either in a few desegregated meetings with white cosmopolitans who were liberal on

24 NORC 335, January, 1953 (2,809); NORC 367, January, 1955 (2,379); Hero, *Voluntary Organizations in World Affairs Communication*, 74; and Raymond Payne, "Organizational Activities of Rural Negroes in Mississippi" (Mississippi State College Agricultural Experiment Station, Circular 192 [Starkville, 1953]), 14.
25 SRC surveys of June–August, 1946 (1,177), and NORC 148, 2/20/47 (1,239).
26 *Ibid.*
27 Hero, *Voluntary Organizations in World Affairs Communication*, 15.

race, in a handful of urban luncheon or dinner groups composed of college-educated, "successful" Negroes, in groups sponsored by Negro colleges, or within a small minority of churches with sophisticated, cosmopolitan ministers and lay leaders.

In fact, most organizations sponsoring such discussions in the South have operated only in the white community, have tended to be cautious about conducting interracial discussions of foreign policy, or, in a few cases, have sponsored such sessions in Negro settings, where the participants have been largely Negroes with perhaps one or two liberal whites present. Only the most self-assured, vigorous Negro cosmopolitans of college background have participated in desegregated discussions of foreign relations in groups composed mainly of whites.

There has been little Negro equivalent of the civic groups prevalent among some middle- and, particularly, upper-class whites. Interest in international relations has been natural to only a very few Negro groups. A few service, luncheon, or dinner groups among professional-class Negroes have in recent years devoted some relatively responsible attention to international affairs, particularly to Africa south of the Sahara and other issues related to the Negro and race relations. Among these have been the Hungry Club in Atlanta and the Frontiers Clubs in a number of cities.

Negro institutions of higher learning were the loci in 1959–62 of most of the serious discussions on world issues in the Negro community. At Atlanta University, for example, Town Hall meetings once a month, with biracial audiences of both college and intellectually oriented community people, discussed world affairs in a thoughtful way. The same institution received in the early 1960's a sizeable foundation grant for faculty seminars, new courses, public lectures and other activities on non-Western cultures, particularly China, India, and Africa. The Crossroads Africa program has been active on some campuses, and more and more foreign guests have been visiting with students and faculty of the better Negro colleges. Professors note that student interest in world affairs, particularly Africa, has increased considerably in recent years.

But efforts of this sort require time, resources, talents, and administrative concern which have been apparent in only the strongest Negro colleges. Nonacademic Negroes have observed that most university teachers interested in foreign affairs have mixed little with the local Negro middle-class community and have exerted only indirect effects, largely through their students. In the few cases where faculty members have attempted to work with the local educated adult Negro population, either informally or through open forums, panels, lectures, extension programs, and other means sponsored by their colleges, they tended to feel that there was relatively little interest and participation beyond the faculty, some students, and a few teachers, lawyers, ministers, and college-educated wives of business and professional people who took part repeatedly in most programs of liberal adult education in the Negro community. Businessmen themselves have usually been indifferent or "too busy" to take part, unless the function was a meal or reception for invited members of the elite in honor of a renowned personality.

Churches have been the social and communication centers of Southern Negro life to an even greater degree than among Southern whites. They have had much more contact with the majority of Negroes than most Negro colleges. In many respects the church has been the most natural locale for progressive, cosmopolitan ideas to develop among Negroes since it has not been economically or otherwise controlled by whites. However, its impact on Negro thinking in the field of foreign affairs, with notable exceptions, has been minimal.

In slavery days and for several decades thereafter whites succeeded in discouraging discussion of social and public issues in Negro religious groups. White clergy conducted Negro services, or Negroes sat in separate parts of white churches during the antebellum period. After the withdrawal of Negroes from white religious groups to form their own congregations following the Civil War, Negro ministers were with few exceptions untrained or poorly trained and unsophisticated about public issues. Isolated from white supervision, the church served as an emotional escape from the poverty, hard manual labor, frustrations, and discrimination which were the lot of Negroes. These conditions have been changing, but the otherworldly emphasis has remained strong in the Baptist and, to a lesser degree, Methodist congregations which included the vast majority of church-affiliated Negroes in 1959–62. The proportion of well-educated ministers and lay leaders interested in and thoughtful about world affairs was still a very small minority in 1962 —much smaller than among whites. The minister who wished to stimulate his congregation to think realistically in this field would take on a difficult task indeed, except in a handful of college and urban congregations populated by the best-educated Negroes.[28] Moreover, because very few Southern Negro churches have been financially able or otherwise willing to support foreign missionaries, there have been scarcely any missionaries returning to speak of their experiences abroad as in many white churches.[29]

28 See also Pope, *The Kingdom Beyond Caste,* 121.   29 *Ibid.,* 137.

Nevertheless, in 1959–62 there was usually in even smaller cities at least one Negro minister, typically younger and college and seminary trained, who was himself rather interested in the broad issues facing this country abroad. He sometimes tried to express his thinking in sermons, to sponsor lectures and discussions on foreign affairs, particularly on Africa, or to collaborate with a local college or other group interested in stimulating thought on world issues among the more alert members of the Negro middle class. Virtually all these ministers were active supporters of faster racial integration and were critical of the more conservative attitudes of older "successful" Negro businessmen, "backdoor politicians" who mediated between the interests of Negroes and the white power structure, and many of the Negro leaders who had influenced thinking and action among their people in the past.

Although in most instances this small, alert, Negro ministerial minority's task of broadening interest in world affairs is formidable, in at least one respect it is considerably freer to do so than white ministers of similar international inclinations. The major depressant to analysis of controversial issues, including world affairs, in Southern white churches and in discussion generally is fear of "unsettling" the race issue. Such is not the case in most Negro churches. Rather, the church has been the principal locale for generating support for desegregation, and the middle-class Negroes who form the bulk of the communicants of these well-educated ministers have come to expect their clergy to emphasize the social implications of the gospel. Whereas the white minister must contend with both apathy about foreign policy and opposition to discussion which might lead to controversy, the Negro minister must overcome only the first obstacle, albeit a very difficult one.

Sources of Low Interest and Lack of Knowledge

Demographic and social factors alone go far to explain the phenomena just described. The same variables related to sophistication and concern about world affairs among whites have been associated with international interest and knowledge among Southern Negroes. In fact, they have been compounded among Negroes.

Thus, not only has their average formal education been less than among whites in terms of number of years in school, but the quality of whatever education they have received has been on the whole lower. A given number of years of schooling has typically not actually been equivalent among the two races in the South. The gap between the two parts of the segregated system has gradually narrowed as more resources have been allocated to Negro education than ever before. But Negro

teachers in most public high schools—dependent on conservative white
school boards—have continued to remain rather timid about stimulating
critical discussion of controversial issues. And, even if the physical
plants were equivalent and the teachers as well-trained and intellectually
vigorous, the depressed cultural background of most of the youngsters
virtually forced lower standards of performance. Perceptive college
teachers in international affairs and related fields commented that most
of their Negro students must struggle against limited high-school preparation and, therefore, had difficulties dealing with abstract problems like
those of world affairs. In addition, students from lowly backgrounds
must prepare to make a living in a region where there have been few
attractive jobs for Negroes. Emphasis on practical courses has been
natural. Finally, only three or four Southern Negro colleges have
compared favorably in terms of general intellectual excellence with
even the middle range of American colleges, not to mention the best
national ones or even the most stimulating of Southern white institutions.

Moreover, it was observed previously (see p. 248) that Southern
white college graduates most inclined to have a thoughtful interest in
foreign affairs have been disproportionately numerous among those
whose parents also were well educated and comfortably off. Much of
the lay participation in organized discussions of world affairs among
whites has been by the offspring of the upper or upper-middle classes;
few Negro college graduates came from such social origins. Nor were
there many Negroes in the early sixties in the liberal professions (other
than teaching), the group among Southern whites most apt to participate in such discussions and to think critically on world problems. And,
as already noted, few competent efforts have been expended either on
trying to attract the most intellectually alert and cosmopolitan educated Negroes to desegregated white activities in world affairs or to
generate serious adult programs for them in predominantly Negro
institutions.

On the contrary, the typical atmosphere surrounding the Negro
college graduate—the group likely to think seriously about international
phenomena—has offered little encouragement. The most intellectually
able—particularly those who have attended Northern colleges, completed professional or graduate school, and majored in fields bearing on
international relations—have been highly likely to move out of the
region. Although the same generalization has applied to whites of similar training and intellectual accomplishment, the proportion of migrants
to the North of such Negroes has been much larger. Those who have
remained in the South frequently have spent their lives in jobs out of

keeping with their university educations—such as mail clerks and other lower-middle- and even working-class callings. These occupations have not stimulated much interest in international affairs among whites, and they have done so even less among Negroes.

Even college-educated Negroes in the region who have succeeded in the professions or other high-status occupations have been at a serious disadvantage with respect to learning about international relations. Most of their patients, clients, and other associates have been Negroes of relatively low sophistication in this field. Their average annual incomes have been far below those of most white physicians, lawyers, professors, and other professional men. Furthermore, a variety of civic and other leadership roles unrelated or only tangentially related to their formal callings has demanded much of their leisure time. The number of educated, competent, dynamic Negro leaders has been so small in most communities that these few have been obliged to provide the leadership and vigor for diverse, time-consuming activities which have been divided among many times their number of able individuals in the white community.

Furthermore, the struggle against segregation and discrimination has fallen heaviest on the shoulders of the best-educated, most intellectually alert and able, younger leaders who, if they were not so occupied, would be the most likely to show interest and understanding in world affairs. These Negroes have been the most discontented with the racial *status quo* and under the most pressure from the Negro community to do something about it. Their little available time and emotional energy have tended in recent years to be allocated to this issue, which they have felt to be the most crucial one facing their race and the South. Most of these Negroes in 1959–62 were cosmopolitans on those issues of world affairs on which they had views, but many of them preferred to leave interest in foreign policy to the future, when desegregation would be further advanced. They would ask questions and talk about foreign policy when confronted with someone interested and knowledgeable in that field, but it has been difficult to involve them in organized discussions of international relations. More of them could be induced to participate when the international topic was linked to race relations, but only a few were willing to accord high priority even to analytical programs on Africa.

Finally, since Negroes have not been involved in decision-making on the international level, they have tended not to "waste time" in reading or otherwise seeking information about world affairs. Negroes have been isolated from the political process in the South. In most of the region even college-educated ones could not vote in Democratic pri-

maries, usually tantamount to elections, until the mid-1940's, and many
with college degrees were still prevented from voting in rural and
small-town settings in 1962. Surveys and other studies have repeatedly
found that the major reason given for lack of interest in foreign policy
throughout America has been the feeling that one cannot do much to
influence events. This frustration about changing policy has applied
still more to people who could not even vote. Moreover, foreign relations has been the particular reserve of Southern privileged whites—
even most of the white masses have in the past left that sphere of public
affairs to their "betters" in the elitist Southern society.

Negro Attitudes toward Foreign Policy

Assessing Negro attitudes on world affairs poses several additional
problems. It was noted that significantly larger proportions of Negroes
than whites have failed to reply to survey questions on world affairs;
on some issues those who have ventured opinions have been outnumbered by those who have replied "no opinion," "don't know," or the
equivalent. Given the concentration of isolationist sentiments among
the less informed and little interested, the subconscious leanings of most
Negroes who have ventured no opinions probably have not tended to
support activist foreign policies, particularly those demanding individual sacrifices, such as military service and foreign economic assistance.
Moreover, the intensity of most international opinions offered by Negroes has been low; it is questionable that the answers many have
offered have been seriously enough held to create a preference strong
enough to determine important aspects of their behavior, like their
votes at the polls. As previously observed, the vast majority of Negroes
have not been confronted with world affairs in a sufficiently meaningful way to cause them really to think about such questions and to give
considered answers.

Greater Isolationism on Many World Issues

Leaving aside the problem of intensity, even when one does not
attribute any international opinions to Negroes who failed to offer
any, those who have ventured views were more often than not less in
favor of international commitments and cooperation in most fields of
foreign policy than Southern whites. On most questions related to
internationalism and isolationism, Southern Negroes have been more
isolationist than Southern whites, Northern whites, or even Northern
nonwhites.

Throughout the period since 1946 larger fractions of Southern Negroes offering opinions than of Southern whites venturing views have said it would be "best for the future of this country if we stay out of rather than take an active part in world affairs," or the like. The differences have typically been large: a majority of Negroes replying has often advised that we "stay out," whereas a majority of Southern whites has always recommended that we "take an active part." [30] The percentage of Negroes replying who favored surrenders of sovereignty to international organizations, particularly in the extreme form of transforming the U.N. into a world government,[31] and who approved of the idea of letting the U.N. call United States, along with other national, troops to repel aggression [32] as compared with those opposed in the late forties and early fifties was smaller than among Southern whites.

Larger proportions of Southern Negroes than of whites venturing opinions have advocated reductions of United States military and other commitments abroad; [33] have felt that "entangling alliances" like

30 In the spring of 1954, for instance, 67 percent of Southern whites said we should take an active part, 25 percent that we should stay out, and 8 percent did not know; but only 36 percent of Southern Negroes said we should take an active part, 49 percent that we should stay out, and 15 percent did not know. See NORC 355, 4/22/54 (1,207). In late 1956, 74 percent of Southern whites felt we should "take an active part" as compared with 48 percent of Negroes in the South. Only 22 percent of the former as compared with 42 percent of the latter would have us "stay out." See NORC 399, 11/15/56 (1,286). See also AIPO 366, 2/27/46 (3,122); NORC 143, 6/21/46 (1,307); AIPO 384, 11/14/46 (3,203); NORC 151, 6/24/47 (1,273); NORC 156, 3/25/48 (1,289); NORC 159, 6/29/48 (1,301); NORC 165, 4/19/49 (1,300); NORC 169, 9/16/49 (1,300); NORC 170, 10/12/49 (1,300); NORC 273, 1/18/50 (1,284); AIPO 455, 5/2/50 (2,850); NORC 282, 6/14/50 (1,276); NORC 295, 12/28/50 (1,258); AIPO 469, 12/30/50 (1,389); NORC 332, 10/15/52 (1,291); NORC 337, 2/11/53 (1,291); Roper 737, August 1953 (3,502); NORC 348, 9/24/53 (526); NORC 355, 4/22/54 (1,207); AIPO 534, 7/14/54 (1,549); and NORC 370, 3/11/55 (1,225).

31 AIPO 545, 3/22/55 (1,630), found, for example, that 35 percent of Southern whites as compared with 22 percent of Southern Negroes felt that the U.N. should be strengthened to make it a "world government," whereas 42 percent of whites in contrast to 27 percent of Negroes were opposed. Twenty-two percent of whites and 51 percent of Negroes ventured no opinions. See also: AIPO 373, 6/12/46 (3,071); AIPO 375, 7/24/46 (3,124); NORC 146, 11/15/46 (1,300); NORC 157, 4/22/48 (1,280); NORC 166, 6/1/49 (1,300); NORC 167, 6/30/49 (1,284); NORC 171, 11/11/49 (1,300); AIPO 455, 5/2/50 (2,850); NORC 291, 10/18/50 (1,305); and AIPO 473, 3/24/51 (2,102).

32 In the spring of 1951, for instance, 53 percent of Southern whites as compared with 37 percent of Southern Negroes favored this arrangement, compared with 33 and 34 percent, respectively, opposed. See NORC 307, 5/24/51 (1,282). See also NORC 155, 2/25/48 (1,271); NORC 157, 4/22/48 (1,280); NORC 158, 6/2/48 (1,295); NORC 162, 11/23/48 (1,300); AIPO 462, 9/29/50 (1,500); AIPO 517, 7/2/53 (1,545); and AIPO 574, 11/7/56 (1,505).

33 NORC 137, 12/12/45 (1,300); NORC 142, 5/17/46 (1,292); NORC 169, 9/16/49 (1,300); NORC 298, 1/30/51 (1,236); NORC 349, 11/25/53 (1,300); NORC 363, 9/10/54 (1,198); and NORC 399, 11/15/56 (1,286).

NATO,[34] the Organization of American States,[35] and SEATO [36] are "bad" ideas; and have disapproved of sending military supplies at our expense to our allies in Europe, Latin America, and Asia.[37] A larger minority of Southern Negroes than Southern whites replying agreed in 1956 that "we should stop trying to work with allies if they often fail to do what we want and concentrate on building up our defenses in America." [38] A higher percentage of Southern Negroes than Southern whites offering views felt that we should not have entered the war in Korea in 1950–53 and, once in it, that we should have withdrawn and let the Koreans fight it out.[39] A significant minority apparently agreed with the relatively well-to-do Negro businessman and veteran of Korea, who wondered why "we were so excited about saving such a crummy country and bunch of people." In the summer of 1961, a considerably larger minority of Negroes than Southern whites felt that we should not keep our troops in Berlin if doing so might risk war.[40] Smaller fractions of Negroes than of whites replying in the South have answered "very important" to such questions as, "Do you think that what happens

34 Informed of the agreement between West European countries to defend one another against attack and asked if the United States should promise "to go to war on their side if these Western European countries are attacked by someone else," in November, 1948, 22 percent of southern Negroes replied in the affirmative and 62 percent in the negative; the respective Southern white figures were 49 and 39 percent. NORC 161, 10/13/48 (1,300). For less Negro than white support of NATO in the South, see NORC 165, 4/19/49 (1,300); NORC 166, 6/1/49 (1,300); NORC 169, 9/16/49 (1,300); AIPO 438, 3/4/49 (3,090); AIPO 440, 4/7/49 (2,719); AIPO 443, 6/9/49 (2,765); NORC 167, 6/30/49 (1,284); NORC 276, 3/1/50 (1,300); AIPO 455, 5/2/50 (2,850); NORC 287, 7/24/50 (1,302); NORC 295, 12/28/50 (1,258); NORC 312, 8/27/51 (1,237); NORC 357, 5/18/54 (517); NORC 378, 10/6/55 (527); NORC 379, 11/23/55 (1,276); NORC 386, 4/20/56 (1,224); NORC 399, 11/15/56 (1,286); and AIPO 592, 11/23/57 (1,542).
35 NORC 165, 4/19/49 (1,300); NORC 169, 9/16/49 (1,300); and NORC 386, 4/20/56 (1,224).
36 NORC 359, 6/30/54 (1,217); NORC 363, 9/10/54 (1,198); NORC 365, 11/26/54 (1,201); NORC 370, 3/11/55 (1,225); and NORC 386, 4/20/56 (1,224).
37 In November, 1948, only 37 percent of Southern Negroes as compared with 58 percent of Southern whites favored sending military supplies at our expense to the countries of Western Europe which had recently signed an agreement to defend each other against attack; 50 percent of the former and 33 percent of the latter disapproved. See NORC 161, 10/13/48 (1,300). See also NORC 149, 4/13/47 (1,307); NORC 155, 2/25/48 (1,271); NORC 292, 11/22/50 (1,258); NORC 314, 11/22/51 (1,237); NORC 329, 8/28/52 (1,300); NORC 340, 5/14/53 (1,291); NORC 351, 1/21/54 (1,300); NORC 386, 4/20/56 (1,224); and NORC 399, 11/15/56 (1,286).
38 NORC 399, 11/15/56 (1,286).
39 NORC 298, 1/30/51 (1,236); AIPO 473, 3/24/51 (2,102); NORC 314, 11/22/51 (1,237); NORC 333, 11/17/52 (1,291); and AIPO 516, 5/28/53 (1,549).
40 AIPO 648, 7/25/61 (3,159).

in the Middle East like Egypt and Iran, is very important, only fairly important, or unimportant to the United States?"[41]

Negroes venturing opinions about international trade have been such a small fraction of those questioned that it is hazardous to speculate from these data about Negro thinking in that field. In March, 1962, for example, during the discussion of the proposed Trade Expansion Act, 3 percent of Southern Negroes favored higher tariffs, 10 percent lower ones, 23 percent the then current level of tariffs, and 64 percent offered no views.[42] Few Negroes have held better than the more menial jobs in protectionist industries such as textiles, garment-manufacturing, and seafood-canning. Even better-educated, middle-class Negroes among the interviewees, except for college teachers and a few other intellectually oriented middle-class individuals, had for the most part few ideas and little information on trade.

On most questions about foreign technical and, especially, capital assistance, with the possible exception of aid to Africa south of the Sahara, Southern Negroes venturing opinions have tended more than whites to say that aid should not be extended or that it should be considerably reduced, and that the money could be spent better here or that it should not be spent and taxes reduced instead. For instance, in mid-1946, 43 percent of Southern whites compared with 23 percent of Southern Negroes approved of the proposed loan to Britain; 40 percent of whites and 61 percent of Negroes disapproved.[43] In April, 1947, shortly after announcement of the Truman Doctrine, only 39 percent of Southern Negroes favored such aid to Greece as compared with 52 percent of Southern whites; 38 percent of the former versus 45 percent of the latter favored aid to Turkey.[44] In late 1950, midway in the Marshall Plan, 36 percent of Southern Negroes versus 47 percent of Southern whites felt we should "go on sending Marshall Plan aid," whereas 42 percent of the former as compared with 36 percent of the latter believed we should "stop it whether they need it or not."[45]

41 NORC 329, 8/28/52 (1,300).   42 AIPO 656, 3/6/62 (3,486).
43 NORC 142, 5/17/46 (1,292). See also AIPO 355, 9/6/45 (3,084); NORC 135, 10/17/45 (1,260); NORC 137, 12/12/45 (1,300); NORC 139, 2/2/46 (1,263); AIPO 366, 2/27/46 (3,122); AIPO 367, 2/13/46 (3,249); NORC 141, 3/20/46 (1,293); AIPO 370, 4/24/46 (3,227); and AIPO 372, 5/29/46 (3,118). Southern Negroes were also less inclined than Southern whites to approve of another proposed loan to Britain in 1949. See AIPO 446, 8/12/49 (3,272).
44 AIPO 394, 4/9/47 (3,044). Similar differences between the two races in the South were apparent on a differently worded question about the Truman Doctrine posed two and a half months later. See NORC 151, 6/24/47 (1,273). See also NORC 149, 4/3/47 (1,307), and AIPO 392, 3/12/47 (2,884).
45 NORC 292, 11/22/50 (1,258). See also NORC 155, 2/25/48 (1,271); AIPO

Larger minorities of Negroes than of whites have replied that we should not continue to send economic aid to allies and "countries that have agreed to stand with us against Communist aggression." [46] Asked in the summer of 1951 whether they favored or opposed the United States helping to rebuild South Korean cities destroyed in the fighting there, 31 percent of Southern Negroes versus 42 percent of Southern whites favored this suggestion, whereas 50 percent versus 47 percent opposed it.[47] In the spring of 1957, 29 percent of Southern Negroes felt we should send "economic aid to some countries like India, which have not joined us as allies against the Communists," and 62 percent believed we should not. The corresponding figures for Southern whites were 35 percent and 59 percent.[48] Shortly after the unrest in Poland in late 1956, 37 percent of Southern Negroes approved and 54 percent disapproved of aid to that country in contrast to 43 percent and 50 percent, respectively, of Southern whites.[49] On general questions concerning whether the current level of aid or the figure proposed by the administration for the coming year was too much, too little, or about right, Southern Negroes have been less inclined than Southern whites to reply "too little" or "about right" and somewhat more inclined to reply "too much." [50] In late 1960, only 38 percent of Southern Negroes as compared with 47 percent of Southern whites agreed that the "United States should give economic help to the poorer countries of the world even if those countries can't pay for it." [51] Even when queried about the desirability of "our government spending money on technical assistance to backward countries . . . with American experts helping them solve their farming and health problems," larger minorities of Southern Negroes than of Southern whites offering views have dis-

439, 3/17/48 (2,193); AIPO 452, 1/26/50 (2,899); AIPO 478, 8/1/51 (2,200); and NORC 327, 6/30/52 (1,285).

46 NORC 167, 6/30/49 (1,284); NORC 321, 3/12/52 (521); NORC 323, 4/22/52 (1,250); NORC 329, 8/28/52 (1,300); NORC 340, 5/14/53 (1,291); NORC 351, 1/21/54 (1,300); NORC 355, 4/22/54 (1,207); NORC 366, 1/21/55 (1,209); NORC 378, 10/6/55 (527); NORC 382, 1/26/56 (1,238); NORC 386, 4/20/56 (1,224); NORC 393, 9/3/56 (1,263); NORC 399, 11/15/56 (1,286); and NORC 404, 4/26/57 (1,279). Questions were differently worded, such as sending economic aid to "friends," "our allies," "friendly countries," "countries that have agreed to stand with us against Communist aggression," and so on. Negroes were more often than not more opposed than whites in the region to economic assistance regardless of the wording of the query.

47 AIPO 477, 7/6/51 (2,013).   48 NORC 404, 4/26/57 (1,279).

49 Combined results of NORC 399, 11/15/56 (1,286); NORC 402, 3/18/57 (536); and NORC 404, 4/26/57 (1,279).

50 AIPO 558, 1/4/56 (1,385); AIPO 576, 12/12/56 (539); NORC 402, 3/18/57 (536); NORC 404, 4/26/57 (1,279); and AIPO 682, 12/10/63 (1,330).

51 SRC 440, October–November, 1960 (1,954).

approved.[52] Negroes in the South have also been less favorable than the whites to placing even "a small portion of our economic aid on a long term basis," committing it "to help a few countries build such things as highways and dams that would take five or ten years to complete." [53] Moreover, although Southern Negroes have been less apt to support the idea of sending military aid to allies than have Southern whites, they have been more inclined than whites in the region to say that it is "more important to send . . . military aid, like tanks and guns . . . than economic aid, like machinery and supplies." [54]

Survey results do not support the thesis that Southern Negroes have felt considerably greater affinity for non-Negroid colored peoples abroad and considerably less for white foreigners than have Southern whites. Negroes have been about as inclined as Southern whites to apply negative stereotypes to Indians, Chinese, and other Asians. Southern Negroes have typically preferred the French and even the West Germans (in the mid and late 1950's) over non-Negroid colored peoples and their governments.[55] Negroes apparently have absorbed much of the Anglo-Saxon Southerners' favorable feelings toward the British. Majorities of those Southern Negroes offering opinions have replied that Britain is our most important ally, that they have a favorable impression of the British and their government, and that it is more important that we cooperate closely with the British than with any other nation outside the Western Hemisphere.[56]

Southern Negroes who have volunteered opinions have been as likely as Southern whites to feel that another world war, this time with the Communist powers, is probable [57] and that major compromises with the Communists are unlikely to advance our national interests.[58] Negroes

52 In the spring of 1956, for example, 23 percent of Southern Negroes versus 11 percent of Southern whites disapproved of such technical aid. NORC 386, 4/20/56 (1,224).

53 NORC 382, 1/26/56 (1,238); NORC 386, 4/20/56 (1,224); and NORC 404, 4/26/57 (1,279).

54 NORC 363, 9/10/54 (1,198); NORC 379, 11/23/55 (1,276); NORC 390, 6/26/56 (1,275); and NORC 404, 4/26/57 (1,279).

55 NORC 355, 4/22/54 (1,207); NORC 371, 4/29/55 (1,226); NORC 390, 6/26/56 (1,275); NORC 399, 11/15/56 (1,286); NORC 401, 12/28/56 (1,232); and NORC 404, 4/26/57 (1,279).

56 NORC 139, 2/2/46 (1,263); NORC 149, 4/3/47 (1,307); NORC 169, 9/16/49 (1,300); NORC 382, 1/26/56 (1,238); NORC 399, 11/15/56 (1,286); and NORC 404, 4/26/57 (1,279).

57 AIPO 620, 10/14/59 (2,750); AIPO 631, 7/14/60 (2,800); AIPO 639, 12/6/60 (2,846); AIPO 642, 3/8/61 (3,511); and AIPO 650, 9/16/61 (3,476).

58 AIPO 460, 7/2/47 (1,541); NORC 165, 4/19/49 (1,300); AIPO 472, 3/24/51 (1,500); AIPO 527, 2/23/54 (1,511); AIPO 582, 4/23/57 (1,626); and AIPO 639, 12/6/60 (2,846).

as a group, insofar as they have had opinions, have been as "tough" on the Russians and Chinese as have white Southerners.[59] The proportion of "appeasers," "unilateral disarmers," or "leftists" in world affairs among Southern Negroes has been as small or perhaps even smaller than among Southern whites. Even among the small minority of college students actively involved in sit-ins, freedom rides, and other programs of passive resistance against segregation, only a minor fraction seemed to believe in pacifism vis-à-vis the Communist powers. A few had actually read Gandhi and other advocates of nonviolence and had gradually applied this ideology to world politics. But these few themselves estimated in 1961 that 85 percent or more of their activist colleagues did not agree and that the percentage of their persuasion among the Negro general student population was almost infinitesimal. Southern Negroes have not shared the military tradition of Southern whites, but they too have been raised in an atmosphere and tradition of frontier-like violence, and they likewise have had little interest in abstract idealistic utopias about world affairs (or other issues). Southern Negro conscientious objectors have been few indeed.

In fact, the minority of those replying who have advocated termination of diplomatic relations with the U.S.S.R. has been somewhat larger than among Southern whites—the combined figure for two surveys in 1956–57 was 27 percent of Southern Negroes as compared with 23 percent of Southern whites favoring a diplomatic rupture.[60] In like manner, no larger fraction of Southern Negroes than of Southern whites have approved the idea of diplomatic recognition of Communist China or its entry into the U.N.,[61] nor have they been more opposed to using nuclear weapons against Chinese cities in case of aggression against Formosa.[62] Negroes in the South have been no more favorable than whites to international inspection as part of arms control: 65 percent of them as compared with 55 percent of whites in the region

59 In 1953, for instance, 47 percent of Southern Negroes compared with 58 percent of Southern whites agreed with the view, "While keeping up our military strength, at the same time we should make every reasonable attempt to find a way to live peacefully with Russia in the same world." Since the Southern sample was large—1,007 of which 206 were Negroes—this difference was statistically significant at the 10 percent level. Roper 737, August, 1953.
60 NORC 401, 12/28/56 (1,232), and NORC 404, 4/26/57 (1,279). See also NORC 332, 10/15/52 (1,291); NORC 363, 9/10/54 (1,198); and AIPO 540, 11/30/54 (1,473).
61 AIPO 443, 6/9/49 (2,765); AIPO 449, 10/28/49 (2,904); NORC 273, 1/18/50 (1,284); AIPO 455, 5/15/50 (2,850); AIPO 456, 6/2/50 (1,450); AIPO 519, 8/13/53 (1,613); AIPO 534, 7/14/54 (1,549); NORC 365, 11/26/54 (1,201); AIPO 552, 8/23/55 (1,500); NORC 393, 9/13/56 (1,263); and AIPO 603, 5/18/58 (1,563).
62 NORC 355, 4/22/54 (1,207); AIPO 537, 9/14/54 (1,465); AIPO 544, 3/1/55 (1,395); and AIPO 604, 9/8/58 (1,522).

disapproved in 1955 and early 1956 of President Eisenhower's "open skies" proposal, permitting reciprocal aerial photographing of Soviet and United States military installations; [63] and 31 percent of the former as compared with 38 percent of the latter approved in late 1960 of the United States disarming "under careful inspection by the U.N.," if we had adequate assurances that the Soviets would do likewise.[64] A summation of replies to six surveys since 1946 indicates that about the same percentage of Negroes as whites in the region who have expressed opinions have felt it unsafe to reduce our armed forces, even if "other countries agree to limit the size of theirs." [65]

As in the case of interest, information, and exposure in world affairs, demographic factors alone account for much of these white-Negro attitudinal comparisons. But most of these issues themselves have not been such as to stir much Southern Negro interest or support. Alliance with aid to Western Europe in the first postwar decade was not for Negroes, as for whites, collaboration with and help for British "cousins" and other whites damaged by the war. Why assist Slavs, Hungarians, and other Communists? When they have come to this country they have immediately enjoyed more rights and better jobs than Negroes of many generations of residence. Nor have the Chinese, Japanese, Indians, or Koreans shown much sympathy for or done much to assist Southern Negroes. In this country they have not associated with Negroes— Chinese in the Delta went to white schools (in recent years) and were treated as whites in the eyes of the few middle-class Negroes of Delta-town. Almost no Asian has wanted to be identified as a Negro during his stays in the South, including many of those at Southern Negro colleges; a number of them have been condescending toward Negro fellow students.

Issues on Which Negroes Have Been Less Conservative

Negroes have appeared more "liberal" than whites in the South primarily on those international issues wherein Negroes tended to identify to some extent with equalitarian foreign policies of our federal government or with Negroes in foreign countries, or wherein Southern whites feared developments which might directly or indirectly weaken the separation of the races in the region.

One example of the latter was the larger minority of whites than of

63 Combined replies to AIPO 551, 8/2/55 (1,502); NORC 374, 8/4/56 (1,262); NORC 376, 9/29/55 (1,250); and NORC 382, 1/26/56 (1,238).
64 AIPO 635, 9/7/60 (1,581).
65 NORC 146, 11/15/46 (1,300); NORC 314, 11/22/51 (1,237); NORC 325, 5/28/52 (1,265); NORC 382, 1/26/56 (1,238); AIPO 585, 6/25/57 (1,521); and AIPO 596, 3/4/58 (1,610).

Negroes among the interviewees who felt the domestic Communist menace to be a major threat. Although many Negroes have been conservative on most issues other than race and social welfare and many prosperous ones, according to the interviews, would agree with much of Senator Goldwater's economic ideas, only an "Uncle Tom" here and there expressed the opinion of many white supremacists that communism at home had become a national danger of serious proportions. This view among whites, as already observed, was typically connected with fears that organizations like the NAACP and CORE were either infiltrated by Communists or dupes of them.

Similarly, Negroes have seemed somewhat less opposed to expanded immigration, even when the proposed new Americans have been East and Central Europeans rather than Chinese and other colored peoples.[66] As noted previously, antagonism to liberalized immigration laws has been most widespread among the little educated and the humbler social and occupational strata, categories in which Negroes have been particularly overrepresented in the South. It appears that Negroes have been decidedly less hostile to increased immigration than Southern whites of similarly low average education and working- and lower-middle-class roles. Apparently few Negroes have felt that immigrants would compete for their jobs in the South, and they have not been motivated, of course, by the concern among segregationist whites that newcomers might criticize or otherwise undermine white supremacy. Related to this observation, perhaps, is the finding that Southern Negroes have been slightly less inclined than Southern whites to oppose international exchanges of persons, provided that American taxpayers do not bear all or most of the expense entailed.[67]

Another example has been the greater tendency of white racial conservatives to feel that we have paid too much attention to "world opinion" in determining our foreign policies and that we should adopt a more vigorous, forceful posture and thus attract the "respect" of the "backward" peoples. This assignment of low priority to public images of this country abroad was usually paired with concern that foreign attitudes had influenced the policies of our federal government toward race relations in the South. Although a number of the middle-class Negro informants for this study also thought that we should be less worried about criticisms of our policies toward the Communist powers

66 AIPO 575, 11/20/56 (1,502); NORC 401, 12/28/56 (1,232); and AIPO 589, 9/17/57 (1,530).
67 NORC 313, 10/21/51 (1,237); AIPO 566, 6/13/56 (2,078); and AIPO 630, 6/28/60 (3,248).

by leaders of "backward" nations and that these politicians would respect us more if we stood up to the Reds more, they were normally gratified that foreign criticisms of racial discrimination had exerted pressure on white Americans to modify their behavior toward American Negroes.

Southern Negroes who knew about international developments with overtones of "human rights" were more "liberal" or "internationalist" toward them than Southern segregationist whites. Thus, Negroes who had heard about UNESCO, the Human Rights Commission, and other U.N. activities supposedly devoted in part to lessening discrimination against racial or ethnic groups were on the average more favorably inclined than Southern whites toward them.[68] This has been true regardless of the finding that Negroes have been no more favorable toward the U.N. in general than whites. They have been no more likely, for instance, to believe that the U.N. is useful,[69] that it has done a "good job in trying to solve the problems it has had to face," [70] that it is important for us to try to make the U.N. a success,[71] that the U.N. will succeed in spite of disagreements,[72] or that it is better to have the U.S.S.R. in than out of the U.N.[73]

As one would surmise, surveys indicated that Negroes have accorded less support than whites in the South to colonial powers in their disputes with their dependencies. For instance, whereas 36 percent of Southern whites in the spring of 1947 felt that Britain had recently treated the peoples in its colonies and possessions fairly and 32 percent that it had treated them unfairly, the respective figures among Southern Negroes were 10 percent and 28 percent.[74] When queried similarly in early 1953 about French treatment of dependent peoples, 20 percent of Southern Negroes felt the French had treated them "fairly in the last year or so" and 18 percent felt they had treated them "unfairly"; respective white percentages were 24 per cent and 14 percent.[75] In early 1949, only one Southern Negro out of a sample of seventy-seven

68 NORC 374, 8/4/55 (1,262). The sample was too small for statistical significance.
69 NORC 386, 4/20/56 (1,224); and NORC 399, 11/15/56 (1,286).
70 AIPO 468, 12/1/50 (1,500); AIPO 475, 5/17/51 (2,070); AIPO 519, 8/13/53 (1,613); AIPO 534, 7/11/54 (1,549); and AIPO 554, 10/4/55 (1,500).
71 NORC 164, 3/3/49 (1,300); NORC 314, 11/22/51 (1,237); and AIPO 575, 11/20/56 (1,502).
72 NORC 141, 3/20/46 (1,293); NORC 143, 6/21/46 (1,307); and NORC 370, 3/11/55 (1,225).
73 NORC 288, 9/20/50 (1,254); NORC 314, 11/22/51 (1,237); NORC 334, 12/29/52 (1,291); NORC 363, 9/10/54 (1,198); NORC 370, 3/11/55 (1,225); and NORC 399, 11/15/56 (1,286).
74 NORC 149, 4/3/47 (1,307).   75 NORC 337, 2/11/53 (1,291).

said he sympathized with the Dutch in the Dutch East Indies whereas nineteen sympathized with the Indonesians; 16 percent of Southern whites who knew of this conflict sympathized with the Dutch, 31 percent with the Indonesians, and the rest were undecided or had no views.[76] During the Suez crisis of 1956, only one Southern Negro out of a sample of sixty-four (2 percent) approved of "England and France's action," 29 (45 percent) disapproved, and 34 (53 percent) had no opinions; 17 percent of Southern whites approved, 41 percent disapproved, and 40 percent ventured no views.[77] When a national survey asked in early 1956 whether "our government should try harder to win the friendship of countries like India, Egypt, and Burma, or are we doing all we should now," 48 percent of Southern Negroes as compared with 34 percent of Southern whites felt we should "try harder"; 46 percent and 58 percent, respectively, thought we were "doing all we should now." [78]

The advent of newly independent African states since 1957 has stimulated increased interest in that aspect of world affairs and, perhaps indirectly, in foreign policy generally among Southern Negroes. As noted previously, Negro periodicals read primarily by middle-class Southern Negroes have devoted increasing attention, most of it rather superficial, to African developments during the period since the independence of Ghana in 1957. Negro integrationist leaders have used changing relations between the races in Africa and the end of colonial control by whites to arouse Southern Negroes against local white supremacy. They have argued, for instance, that progressive relations between the races in the South would improve our public image and the effectiveness of our policies toward Africa and other colored areas; that Africans have terminated white supremacy very quickly whereas Southern Negroes have been unable to achieve their constitutional rights even a century after slavery; and that more equalitarian race relations is part of a worldwide movement against colonialism. A number of influential Negro business and professional people have visited Africa and then written articles for Negro newspapers and spoken before Negro organizations upon their return. In larger cities and college communities educated Negroes have exchanged ideas now and then with visitors from Africa.

The primarily middle-class, Negro interviewees for this study also read news about Africa in the local press and viewed content on this topic on television. The advent of television has been a major factor in

76 NORC 163, 1/26/49 (1,261).   77 AIPO 574, 1/7/56 (1,505).
78 NORC 382, 1/26/56 (1,238).

broadening Negro horizons and sensitivities on a mass level as well. Many of the Negro rank and file have learned from TV, and to a lesser extent from other media, that all Negroes in 1959–62 were not in menial, segregated situations and that some were leaders of independent countries who were honored by leading officials of the United States and other powers. The middle-class informants told of hearing comments by typical Negroes in barber shops and not-so-elite clubs on these questions. Contacts with African affairs together with other influences probably lay the groundwork, at least on a subconscious level, for discontent with local white discrimination and for appeals by desegregationist leaders.

The Negro minority which was really interested in developments in Africa to the extent of reading on the subject in books and more critical periodicals was almost invariably among those more restless under the Southern racial *status quo* and was frequently among the more active leaders in the effort to integrate Southern society. Such Negroes among the interviewees were concentrated among the younger, better-educated, progressive minority of the largely urban middle class, most of whom were relatively liberal on world affairs generally; they typically favored foreign aid to India and Latin America as well as to Africa, approved of active collaboration in the U.N. and other international organizations, and so on.

This group, however, seemed a slender minority. Many other Negroes who were active during 1959–62 in the desegregation movement apparently had only vague images of Africa, typically incorporating relatively few facts and often including considerable incorrect "information." Most of their emotional commitment was against discrimination in this country. Moreover, their feelings about Africa often seemed ambivalent. They wanted to disassociate Southern Negroes from violence and lawlessness in the Congo, by the Mau Mau, and elsewhere in Africa, and they were embarrassed by the behavior of some African politicians.

The majority of the Negro middle class which was not active in the desegregation process in 1959–62 paid even less attention to Africa. Many of the less sophisticated seemed still to harbor some of the Southern white images of Africans as half-naked savages carrying spears. Some who had attended meetings with Africans in the larger Southern cities and Negro college communities were apparently surprised that they were so "civilized." Alert African visitors to the South have complained of the rather feeble interest in Africa among typical Southern Negro students and middle-class adults. Negro students have often felt

that many African students and other visitors have been rather pompous, convinced of their superiority to American Negroes, and not
particularly interested in close relationships with their American fellows. Southern Negro college graduates interested in achieving higher
status and security in America have rarely volunteered to participate
in the Peace Corps or other federal or nongovernmental programs in
Africa. Professors at Negro colleges noted that it was typically difficult
to fill requests from governmental and private agencies for competent
students and young graduates to fill vacancies, most of which were
poorly paid and seemed remote from the objectives of the vast majority
of graduating youngsters.

Negro university professors who have spent considerable time in
Africa have complained that only a few intellectuals and particularly
alert students seemed interested in what they had learned. Most Negro
business and even professional men usually limited their participation
to "fashionable" meetings with Africans who had prestigious titles; they
tended to pay little attention to serious scholars of Africa, black or
white, who came to town. Librarians and publishers of books and
periodicals dealing in a thoughtful way with African problems have
noted that readers among even middle-class Southern Negroes, including college students, have been a small minority. Even the Sharpeville
incident stirred only a limited group; some who heard of the shootings
reacted to the effect, "That's no worse than a series of Saturday nights
in some counties in Mississippi." Given the underprivileged, segregated
childhoods of so many middle-class Negroes, it is understandable that
most of them have experienced difficulties projecting their sensibilities
beyond their own communities, not to mention to Nigeria and Tan-
ganyika.

Moreover, the entry of so many Africans into the U.N. has not been
reflected in much apparent increase in Negro as compared with white
support of that organization. The proportions of the two races in the
South which have approved of the U.N. have risen and fallen together
throughout most of the period since 1946; as noted previously (see
p. 224), Negroes have been less interested in and informed about the
U.N. and certainly no more favorable to active American collaboration
there than Southern whites. Even by late 1960 after most of Africa had
become independent and had joined the U.N., 59 percent of Southern
Negroes as compared with 66 percent of Southern whites opposed the
proposal that the U.N. be moved to another country; 66 percent of
Negroes versus 80 percent of whites felt it was "very important" for
the United States to try to make the U.N. a success; 34 percent of
Negroes versus 45 percent of whites thought the U.N. was "doing a

good job in trying to solve the problems it has had to face"; and 17 percent of the former as compared with 13 percent of the latter replied that it was doing a "poor job." [79]

Nor has the entry of Africa into our aid programs eliminated the difference between mass Negro and white support in the South for foreign economic aid. As education among Negroes increased during the postwar period, they gradually approached white norms of thought about international assistance. But when asked in early 1963, "In general, how do you feel about foreign aid, are you for it or against it?" Southern Negroes were still significantly less inclined to express opinions and to manifest support for this general idea than were Americans generally and, to a lesser measure, than were Southern whites.[80]

On Africa itself only one national survey since mid-1957 has been located. When asked in the spring of 1957 how important it was for our government to help African countries improve their standard of living, 44 percent of Southern Negroes interviewed said they had no views on this issue in contrast to only 16 percent of Southern whites. However, those Negroes who did express opinions were more inclined than Southern whites to consider such help to Africa important: 45 percent of Southern Negroes felt it was "very important," 7 percent that it was "fairly important," and only 4 percent that it was not important at all; 43 percent of Southern whites felt such aid to be "very important," 28 percent that it was "fairly important," and 12 percent that it was not important at all.[81] When asked in July, 1963, "Thinking of our own future well-being, with which of these groups of countries do you think our ties are going to be the most important to us?" 18 percent of Southern Negroes chose Africa over Western Europe, South America, and Asia, whereas only one percent of Southern whites did. At that time only 11 percent of Southern Negroes, compared with 36 percent of Southern whites, felt that our ties would be least important with Africa as compared with Western Europe, South America, and Asia. Negroes were sharply less inclined than whites in the South to stress ties with Western Europe and Latin America over those with Africa and, to a much lesser extent, Asia; however, even as late as mid-1963, a large majority of Southern Negroes accorded greater importance to ties with Western Europe, Latin America, or both than to those with Africa.[82]

79 AIPO 637, 10/18/60 (2,993).   80 AIPO 667, January, 1963 (4,383).
81 NORC 404, 4/26/57 (1,279).
82 Roper 148, July, 1963 (3,007). These generalizations with but minor amendment applied to Northern Negroes as compared with Northern whites as well. Thus, whereas among American whites taken together 47 percent stressed ties with Western Europe, 32 percent with South America, 5 percent with Asia and 3 per-

Only one in six of the middle-class Negro interviewees in 1959–62 felt that we should send more aid to Africa in the near future than our government planned, and about half advised that aid be reduced in general, including in Africa. On the other hand, only a minuscule minority (all older Negroes) manifested the colonialist views of many segregationist whites, and none identified themselves as some white racists did with whites in the Republic of South Africa and elsewhere on that continent. Negroes among the informants were also on the whole better informed about Africa than other underdeveloped foreign areas; however, most seemed to know more about Western Europe than Africa.

Diversity of International Thinking

As in the case of knowledge about world affairs, the gap in most attitudes between the tiny internationally thoughtful minority in the cities and college towns, particularly among the professions, and the Negro masses was wide in the early sixties. Except for a few teachers and perhaps one or two ministers and successful farmers, most Negroes in rural areas and small towns either had no opinions on most world issues or advanced those of their white employers, which were typically conservative. Support for expanded aid to underdeveloped lands, including Africa, under the Kennedy administration was feeble indeed among these Negroes, most of whom seemed to accept the paternalist system and their "place" in it. Although a rural or small-town Negro teacher occasionally held surprisingly atypical internationalist views, most teachers and especially high-school principals in these environments ranged from conservative to very conservative about such questions as foreign economic aid, intercultural relations with Communist countries, and negotiation of arms control. Their caution is understandable, considering their dependence on whites for their jobs, but a number seemed more conservative on world affairs than most college-educated whites in the same counties. Perhaps they adopted the views of the more conservative local influential whites to be certain they did not offend.

---

cent with Africa as "most important" for the future, among American Negroes taken together 26 percent stressed Western Europe, 21 percent South America, 6 percent Asia, and 22 percent Africa. Conversely, whereas among whites 34 percent felt ties with Africa would be least important to our future, 18 percent felt ties with Asia fitted this description, 6 percent so labeled ties with Asia, and only 2 percent those with Western Europe, among Negroes 11 percent felt ties with Africa would be "least important," 15 percent felt so about ties with Asia, 5 percent about those with South America, and 7 percent about ties with Western Europe.

Interest and attitudes among the urban working class seemed only somewhat more progressive than in rural settings. Middle-aged and older Negroes in lowly stations generally appeared to have integrated a number of assumptions of segregated society into their own thinking. Few seemed to have many international views, and those who did tended to express whatever they may have heard among their employers. Younger Negroes of the working class appeared somewhat less conservative and more inclined to voice opinions. As in the case of whites, those relatively few in trade unions probably were somewhat more internationalist than the majority who were not, but Negroes in 1962 were concentrated in the less-skilled jobs, and union leadership seemed to feel that labor education must concentrate on bread-and-butter issues and leave such matters as foreign trade, aid, and the U.N., to a later generation which would be more sophisticated.

Thus, most of the consideration of world affairs—except on foreign aid and issues demanding personal sacrifices—was among the urban middle class. In general, middle-class Negroes tended to reflect on most issues much of the thinking prevalent among local whites of similar or higher status. To a considerable degree, they were influenced by the same newspapers and general community atmosphere. When the newspapers and the white leadership were largely opposed to foreign aid at prevailing orders of magnitude, the Negro middle class tended to feel similarly. If the whites were more favorable, then so were the Negroes.

For example, although there was considerable diversity in international opinions, most Negro businessmen and professional people, including educators, in New Orleans seemed to have adopted much of the emphasis on enjoying oneself, good food, and "socializing" prevalent among whites. They too tended to feel that they lived in "paradise," to confine their thinking to the local cultural oasis of relative tolerance compared with the surrounding Bible Belt, and to show little interest in wider problems, national or international. Whatever views they had on such matters as foreign economic assistance tended to be conservative. The Negro middle class in Atlanta, on the other hand, seemed to place more stress on education, ability to deal with ideas, and "improvement" of the *status quo,* and less on warm, smooth, personal relations and having a good time. More of the latter seemed relatively interested and informed in international affairs, and their opinions tended to be less conservative and insular. Negroes in Charleston of higher status were with notable exceptions traditionalists and conservatives on questions other than race relations and social welfare, whereas middle-class Negroes of the North Carolina Piedmont in such cities as Charlotte, Durham, and Greensboro were more liberal on world affairs as on other issues. But the same generalizations seemed to apply to whites of similar status in these places.

E. Franklin Frazier perhaps exaggerated the tendencies of the Negro middle class to separate themselves from "lesser" Negroes and to ape superficial white "cafe society" or "celebrity" values in his *Black Bourgeoisie*.[83] Certainly many of the more talented, achievement-oriented professionals and leading business men and women have not been primarily interested in conspicuous consumption of expensive homes, cars, and swimming pools or the amount of space devoted to their parties and social life in the Negro press.

But much, perhaps most, of the small prosperous Negro minority has been relatively "class-oriented." [84] Since there has been very little old, secure economic comfort among Negroes, most of the Negro businessmen in 1962, even in a large, old city like New Orleans, were in small retail and service enterprises like grocery and clothing stores, taxi companies, undertaking establishments, and insurance companies run by the same individuals who founded them or, at most, their children. The typical "successful" Negro businessman came from economically deprived parentage, did not go to college, and was in the early sixties considerably less secure economically than his white counterparts.[85] Many have been reputed to be exploiters of their race and have not been at all liberal about social and public issues, including world affairs. A large proportion have apparently adopted much of the conservative ideology of the newly prosperous, little-cultivated, socially insecure white commercial classes—concern about high taxes and "too much" money being wasted abroad and distrust of intellectuals in colleges or the government, including those who seemed to be "running" our foreign policy. Senator Goldwater would have been popular among these individuals but for his stand on states' rights; many of them considered themselves conservative Republicans in 1959–62. One self-made Negro businessman who had not completed high school reflected the thinking of a number of his parvenu white counterparts in complaining that he had been obliged to pay over five thousand dollars to "Uncle Sam" in 1960 to "support loafers around the world and put shoes on peasants and savages who never wore any before."

83 Frazier, *Black Bourgeoisie* (Glencoe: The Free Press, 1957).
84 Thompson, *The Negro Leadership Class*, 27 and 43–44. See also Gunnar Myrdal, *An American Dilemma* (New York: Harper and Bros., 1944) 764.
85 Thompson, *The Negro Leadership Class*, 30 and 130.

The role of the Negro leader vis-à-vis the white community and his posture toward racial integration also seemed related to his international thinking. The "old style" Negro leader mediated and negotiated between the white power structure and the urban Negro community. He was contacted by whites to organize political support, to collect for the Red Cross, Community Chest, and other charities, and to transmit white wishes to the Negro rank and file. Negroes with grievances came to these leaders; if the latter felt their complaints deserved attention by the white leadership, they took these matters up with it. They accepted the segregated system and worked within it. In order to develop rapport with the white elite, they either were conservative to begin with or became so as they ascended the ladder of influence with Negroes and confidence among whites.

The influence among other Negroes of these older "back-door politicians" has been eroding, but those who remained in 1962 usually reflected the conservative thinking of the influential whites with whom they dealt; indeed some even held exaggerated versions of white conservatism. Most would welcome better opportunities for Negroes, but they would not "rock the boat" of the system itself. They criticized more militant Negro desegregationists as "radicals" who might be doing more damage than good in upsetting smooth relations with upper-class or moderate whites. They tended to feel that our foreign aid programs had gone on too long and that aid to neutralists was foolish and to accept much of the other international thinking prevalent among the more conservative elements of the white elite. Among the most conservative on world affairs—those hostile to foreign aid, negotiation with the Soviet Union over arms control, and intercultural exchanges with Communist countries—were four "Uncle Toms" who had publicly opposed desegregation, two as newspapermen, one as educator, and another as a member of the segregationist Mutual Association of Colored People of the South.

But even in Old South communities like Charleston and Kent, these expedient intermediaries have been gradually losing their influence on Negro opinion and action, particularly among younger Negroes, to a more vigorous, college-trained, often younger group of ministers, lawyers, social workers, college teachers, and other professionals, plus a few well-educated, idealistic undertakers, businessmen, and other Negroes who, for the most part, have not been economically directly dependent on whites.[86] This group has rejected the segregated system and encouraged other Negroes to take legal action supported by dem-

86 For this process in New Orleans, see *ibid.*, especially Chapter 5 and 166–68.

onstrations and economic pressures if necessary to change it. They had little contact in 1959–62 with conservative whites and were usually distrusted by the latter as "agitators." Their white acquaintances were limited to liberals and a few "moderates." [87]

Some of these leaders in 1959–62 were perhaps self-seeking opportunists, whose views on world affairs depended on their pragmatic local value at the moment. However, the great majority seemed to agree in general with the more liberal white cosmopolitans on world issues.[88] Most of these Negroes were too emotionally involved in the local race problem and in making a decent living to devote much attention to foreign policy, although a considerable minority of them among the interviewees for this study read such national literature as the New York *Times* (Sunday edition) and *The Reporter*. Many were not particularly well informed on foreign developments, but they generally felt we should expand education, medical care, and other domestic programs and carry on active economic assistance abroad. They normally did not limit their support of foreign aid to Africa or accord that continent any special advantages over Brazil, India, or other underdeveloped lands. They would make more scholarships available to poor American students capable of obtaining a college education, but they would also broaden opportunities for promising foreigners to study here.

Most urban middle-class Negroes with opinions on foreign policy in 1959–62 took positions on world affairs which fell between the views of these two minorities among their race—the thoughtful active integrationists and the supporters of the Southern *status quo*. Except for these two poles on the spectrum of Negro thinking about segregation, feelings on race relations among Negroes were not so closely associated with international thought as among whites—Negroes could be "liberals" on race through self-interest, whereas Deep Southern whites who preferred desegregation were adopting postures against their short-run interests and the social pressures about them. Thus, a much larger fraction of Negro than white integrationists were rather provincial

87 E.g., *ibid.*, 119.
88 Pearl M. Gore and J. B. Rotter, "A Personality Correlate of Social-Action," *Journal of Personality*, XXXI (1963), 58–64, found that Southern Negro college students at a Deep Southern state institution who were ready and willing to participate in public desegregation protests differed sharply from their less willing peers in the degree to which they believed that their fate lay in their own control rather than in the hands of chance and that they could change social and public policies and practices through action. It was noted previously that such factors have been correlated with relatively favorable attitudes toward international cooperation in nonmilitary as well as collective security spheres.

neo-isolationists unfavorable to foreign aid at its current level, and so forth. However, in general Negroes who accepted their "place" in the paternalist Southern system and felt uneasy about the freedom riders, the sit-ins, and other militant efforts tended to reflect the views of more conservative whites on international affairs (insofar as they offered any opinions). Older college graduates were on the whole (though far from invariably) more conservative than younger graduates on foreign aid and most other international issues, and seemingly on domestic issues as well. Younger college-trained ministers, lawyers, social workers, and college (and to a lesser measure high-school) teachers were the most liberal of all.

Potential Political Impacts

Even by 1962 only one Southern Negro adult out of four was registered to vote; in half the counties and parishes of the South less than 10 percent of adult Negroes were registered; in many black-belt rural counties virtually none were registered; and the proportions who actually voted in congressional primaries or elections were considerably less than these figures suggest.[89] Most Negro voters were in cities where pressures against registration and voting were weakest. But even in larger, relatively populous cities apathy arising from educational and economic underprivilege, paucity of a tradition of political participation, lack of candidates attractive to Negroes, and other factors have limited Negro votes considerably.[90] Thus, in a Democratic primary for mayor of New Orleans in 1961 where one of the candidates was significantly less conservative on racial issues, public welfare, and other subjects important to Negroes (as well as on world affairs) and where a considerable effort was expended to "turn out" the Negro vote, only 17 percent of the voters were Negroes although they constituted 37.4 percent of the population.

Furthermore, Negroes who have voted so far have been on the whole among those with the more enlightened views and with greater information on world affairs. When Negro voters in the immediately previous national or congressional election or primary were compared with nonvoters on surveys, the former were almost invariably better informed, more in contact with mass media and other communications

89   New York *Times*, April 28, 1963, and May 12, 1963.
90   For an empirical examination of differential Southern Negro registration, see Donald R. Matthews and James W. Prothro, "Social and Economic Factors and Negro Voter Registration in the South," *American Political Science Review*, LVII (1963), 24–44.

on foreign affairs, and more favorable to active international collaboration—even when it might cost more money—than were the nonvoters. The same was true of Southern whites, but the discrepancies between voters and nonvoters in international thinking were greater among Negroes. This is understandable since Negro voters much more than nonvoters tended to be educated, young, urban dwellers, who worked at less menial jobs—all correlated with broader international attitudes.

However, more and more Negroes will vote in the future, with the encouragement of the federal government, their own local leaders, and liberal whites. What will be the probable effects of this expansion of the Negro franchise?

One unfortunate outcome could conceivably be expansion of political support for Congressmen who are isolationists or otherwise irresponsible about international challenges to the United States. If Southern Congressmen came more to reflect the international attitudes of most Negroes who did not vote in 1962, the result could be an increase in congressional opposition to foreign aid and a number of other multilateral programs. An opportunist politician might perhaps appeal to underprivileged Negroes on a platform of increased public welfare, transfer of more wealth from the upper to the lower income groups, accelerated desegregation, termination of "waste" and "money down the rathole" for "ingrates" abroad, and the shifting of these funds to underprivileged people in this country. Thus, James Folsom has attracted much of the Negro vote in Alabama when he has run. He has been silent or moderate on race, even relatively liberal by Deep Southern standards, favorable to expanded social services, and critical of spending abroad. Senator Olin Johnston of South Carolina, a domestic economic liberal and opponent of foreign aid, has attracted much of the Negro vote in his state regardless of his consistent support of segregation.

Still another unfortunate possibility, springing from growing emotional identification with Africans comparable to that of American Zionists with Israel, might be the increasing development of biases in favor of black African states over conflicting United States interests abroad. However, given the relatively low interest in Africa among the Negro masses, such emotional involvements would develop only over a number of years, and are unlikely even then. Even among most better-educated Negroes, attachment to Africa has been much weaker than empathy with Israel among American Jews.

A third potential danger is that rural and small-town Negroes—largely poorly educated, lower-class Southerners who know little of national and international issues—will be unduly influenced by conservative white landowners and other members of the elite. In states where the poll tax is still a prerequisite for voting, the candidate with the best financial backing (often one of the more conservative on foreign affairs) can often add to his support by payment of the poll taxes of unsophisticated, economically deprived citizens, of which Negroes are a disproportionately large number. In one of the sample counties for this study, Negro ministers, like white ones in Mountain County, were reportedly "paid off" to influence the votes of their followers, apparently with considerable success. In another, Negro voters were furnished with sample ballots by their employers or their agents and physically "delivered" to the polls where most of them apparently voted for the more conservative candidates as suggested. Informants in Bayou Parish described parties the night before elections with ample orange wine, hogshead cheese, and other attractions for Negroes, accompanied by talks by supporters of the candidates preferred by planters and other strong conservatives. A recent study in east Texas found that most rural Negro voters were manipulated by landowners and other influential conservatives without much open pressure and inducement. Older Negroes were especially resistant to change, manifested an ingrained sense of inferiority to whites, accepted the caste system, wanted to appease whites, and accepted their advice on public questions. Particularly when they lived on a white's place or depended on him economically did they vote as he did. The majority of these east Texas rural Negroes voted against the liberal candidate and for the more conservative one.[91]

These are threatening possibilities and they should not be brushed aside. However, countervailing influences may in the long run prove more crucial. The political, economic, and social pressures and traditions are such in most heavily Negro rural areas that the Negro masses there—those most likely to be isolationist and influenced by conservative white leaders—are unlikely to vote in large numbers for some time. The better educated, more self-assured, and those more opposed to segregation, who are most inclined to favor active multilateral cooperation beyond military defense, will vote first.

Even should the vote come faster than expected in the rural Black Belt, the likelihood of election of a Negro demagogue favorable to desegregation and domestic welfare programs but opposed to foreign aid and other international commitments seems slim. Whites outnum-

91 Harry Halloway, "The Negro Vote: The Case of Texas," *Journal of Politics,* XXIII (1961), 544–45.

bered Negroes of voting age in all congressional constituencies but one in 1960—that one containing the Mississippi Delta.[92] The Negro percentage of the population will undoubtedly continue to decrease in other plantation-belt constituencies where it is almost half the population. In the foreseeable future whites would close ranks against a Negro congressional candidate and defeat him.

Moreover, as already noted, Southern Negroes are much more interested in congressional candidates' postures on race relations and welfare legislation than on world affairs; the international attitudes of Negroes who dislike capital aid and other commitments abroad tend to be of low saliency among their motivations. As the magnitude of the Negro vote increases, it will gradually defeat the racists and economic arch-conservatives in Congress, thus eliminating the majority of Southern legislators who favor a return to "gun-boat diplomacy," sharp reduction of foreign economic assistance, and so on. Most Negroes will vote for white liberals or moderates on race and domestic economics, most of whom are relatively favorable to active international involvements in economic, diplomatic, and cultural, as well as military, fields. The conservatism of the Negro on foreign policy will not be sufficient to swing the vote of many of them to racist and economically conservative candidates who think similarly on world problems.

Furthermore, urban Negroes are voting more and more as the younger, educated, integrationist ministers, lawyers, college teachers, and other liberal Negroes suggest. Few of the Negro majority know much about, understand, or pay much attention to international issues. But Russell Sugarmon, Harvard-trained Memphis lawyer, the Reverend Kelley Smith of Nashville, the late Medgar W. Evers of Jackson, Mississippi, and most comparable younger militantly desegregationist, Negro leaders elsewhere in areas where the Negro vote is increasing favor active international policies even though they may not be particularly well informed about them, and they are organizing Negroes to vote for whites who are generally liberal, at least by Southern standards, and against strong conservatives. In so doing, they are preparing the defeat of isolationists and opponents of foreign aid, intercultural exchange, the U.N., arms-control agreements, and other multilateral arrangements by more internationally liberal and thoughtful white politicians.

92 In one other, the Second Congressional District of North Carolina, 50.5 percent of the population was Negro at the time of the 1960 census. However, due to the larger proportion of children to adults among Negroes, adult whites slightly outnumbered adult Negroes. Moreover, as in most heavily Negro rural counties, Negroes were migrating out at considerably faster rates than whites, rapidly decreasing the Negro to white ratio.

Finally, in the long run more and more Negroes will become educated and identify themselves with racial integration and its leaders, and the older "handkerchief heads" will lose whatever influence they now have with the Negro masses and will finally pass away. As the "Negro revolution" continues to accelerate, increasing numbers of even lower-middle- and lower-class Negroes will become emotionally involved in the desegregation movement. Given the positive relationship between militancy on integration and approval of liberal foreign programs among Negroes, one should be able realistically to expect not only gradually increasing interest in foreign developments by the growing number of anti-segregationist Negro voters, but also more widespread support for multilateral commitments in most international spheres.

PART III

Where To From Here?

CHAPTER 15

THE PRESENT
AND
THE FUTURE

Southerners have evolved since the mid-1930's from the regional group most enthusiastic about collective security and more active United States participation in the international problems of the period to the geographic minority most hesitant about some of the major spheres of international cooperation advocated by Presidents Eisenhower and Kennedy and the leading foreign policy spokesmen of their administrations. The shift has been more marked in certain fields than in others, and in several areas Southerners in 1962 were still more favorable toward activist policies than were most other Americans. Shifts in Southern international opinion have been due to changes in international issues, in our policies toward them, and in the South itself.

An Overview

Divergence from National Opinion

In general, Southern popular opinion on world affairs has shifted in the same directions as have the votes of Southern Congressmen. In the early 1960's Southerners differed in their international postures from inhabitants of other regions more or less as the roll-call votes of their respective Senators and Representatives differed from those of Northern Congressmen, except that divergencies between Southern and Northern Congressmen were on the whole wider than those between their constituents on the same international issues.

Southern thinking has changed more sharply on international economic matters than it has in most other spheres of world affairs, both
in absolute terms and with respect to attitudes in other parts of the
country. From the regional group most favorable to expanded world
commerce, the South has become on the average somewhat less enthusiastic about broadened trade than the rest of the country taken
together. However, attitudinal differences between the South and the
North in the early 1960's were small, of the order of a few percentage
points, but Southerners were still quite a bit less likely than other
Americans to be informed about trade and to have opinions in that field.
Industrialization of the South by primarily low-technology enterprises
in competition with imports from low-wage countries, expansion of
foreign production during the postwar period, and gradual decline of
the relative influence of cotton production largely account for this trend
toward protectionism.

A gradual shift of Southern opinion from support of foreign economic aid has also been evident. Whereas Southerners were significantly
more inclined than other regional groups to support liberalization of
the Neutrality Act, Lend-Lease, and other assistance to the Allies before
World War II and at least as likely as other Americans to approve of the
Truman Doctrine, the Marshall Plan, and most other aid programs of
the late 1940's, by the early 1960's Southerners were more apt than
other citizens to approve of major reductions of foreign capital assistance to most underdeveloped nations. Rising opposition to continued
foreign economic aid can be accounted for by the shift of assistance
from primarily European allies to little-developed, colored neutralists
of anticolonial and anti-Western hues and even to some Communist
regimes, the increasing racial tension and sensitivity to foreign criticism
in the South, the reported corruption and waste of aid, the opposition
to encouraging the development of competing industries abroad, and
the rising frustration with complicated, indirect, nonmilitary means of
preventing further Communist successes.

Southerners during the interwar period took a more favorable attitude than other Americans toward United States participation in the
League of Nations and the Permanent Court of International Justice
and more active collaboration with those organizations. Those in the
South were about as favorably inclined as those in the country generally toward the U.N. during the initial postwar years. Intensified
racial feelings in the white South simultaneous with the entry of many
African members into the U.N., growing difficulties of securing approval in the General Assembly and other organs of the U.N. for

American-sponsored programs, apparent U.N. assistance to "leftists" and others critical of the United States, fear of future U.N. intervention in Southern race relations, and general frustration with the Sino-Soviet bloc and the neutralists have exerted some influence on Southern thinking about the U.N. Support for active American involvement in the world body was more widespread throughout the country during the early sixties than during the Korean War and much of the previous period, but the growth of approval in the South has been somewhat smaller than in the rest of the country combined. However, differences in thinking about the U.N. between the regions in 1962 were small except where Negro-white disputes were salient. Large majorities in the South felt in 1962 that we should remain in the U.N. and try to make it a success, and a majority of those venturing opinions recommended that we remain in the organization even if Communist China were admitted.

Attitudes toward world affairs in the South in the early sixties were related to most of the same individual and social factors as elsewhere in the country. Thus, correlations of particular international views with education, social and occupational status, rural, urban, or small-town residence, assumptions about human nature and the feasibility of improving it, authoritarianism, and conservatism in the several major domestic spheres were in the same directions in the South as in the North. The disproportionately large number of Southerners in those individual and social categories where understanding of foreign affairs has been least apparent and support of multilateral cooperation feeblest explains most of the differences in international behavior between the South and the North in the early sixties.

Southern white attitudes deviated considerably from Northern ones in 1959–62 on issues related to the Negro and to disputes between Negroes and whites abroad. Southerners also tended to disagree with other Americans on policies which apparently strengthened "socialist," "leftist," anticolonialist, and antiwhite groups and their leaders against more conservative, "anti-Communist" regimes either in European *métropoles* or in the underdeveloped lands themselves. They were, furthermore, apt to diverge from Northern thinking insofar as it was based on optimistic views of human nature, assumptions about the reformability of foreign peoples, and belief in the likelihood of moderating Communist behavior through concessions rather than "firmness." Because residents of the South still had in 1962, on the average, less information about foreign affairs than other regional groups, they were less inclined to have distinct opinions on issues when opinions were closely related to

knowledge. Finally, Southerners were less apt than other citizens to em-
pathize with or feel favorably toward non-Western foreigners, to
approve of increased intercultural contacts with them and, particularly, with Communist countries, at our financial expense, and to
support augmented immigration into this country.

However, Southerners have long differed statistically from Northerners on international phenomena related to race, "socialism," welfare
economics, anticolonialism, optimism about human motives and rationality, social reform, compromise with our enemies, sophistication
in world affairs, intercultural relations, and immigration. Actually,
Southern views in most of these areas in 1962 more nearly approached
those of Northerners than they had in the past. Rising opposition to
some foreign policies supported by Northern liberal internationalists
during the late fifties and early sixties stemmed in considerable measure from the fact that the problems of this recent period and our policies toward them impinged more directly on basic divergences between
Southern and Northern assumptions and values.

Military resistance to the Axis and the Communists, collaboration
with Britain and Western Europe, expanded trade with Western Europe, anti-Communist military and economic aid to highly skilled but
war-ravaged Europeans, and participation in international organizations
usually amenable to the wishes of white nations and their allies prior
to the mid-1950's ran counter to few prevailing Southern attitudes. But
some of the major issues of 1962 engaged these Southern sensibilities
and basic beliefs much more directly:

(1) Military intervention and all-out war against aggressors were
no longer the major policies for which public support was
solicited.

(2) Our national leaders and mass media in 1962 talked in terms
of stalemate, limited war, and restricted objectives vis-à-vis our
enemies.

(3) The world was in considerably greater social and political ferment in 1962 than was the case before the mid-1950's.

(4) The new states were largely alien to Southern culture, ideology,
and economy—their economies often competed with that of
the South.

(5) Black African countries had become independent, critical of
the white South, and important to our foreign objectives.

(6) Little of the materiel purchased for foreign economic assistance
to the underdeveloped world came from the South in 1959–62.

(7) Capital aid went primarily to colored neutralists—many of socialist inclinations—who were critical of our posture toward the Communists.

(8) We were trying to pursue long-range programs to transform mores and whole social structures of backward nations.

(9) Intercultural relations with colored people and Communists expanded greatly and became a major aspect of our policy.

(10) Comprehension of complex challenges and subtle American policies of the sixties required one's having considerable information and analytical ability.

(11) International developments impinged much more directly on exacerbated Southern white racial feelings.

It is, in fact, somewhat surprising that differences in attitudes in the South as compared with the North on these issues were not larger than national surveys indicated in the late 1950's and after. Even when differences in international attitudes between the South and other regions were statistically significant at the 10 percent level of confidence, they were usually relatively small, smaller than during the prewar period when Southerners were considerably more favorable than other regional groups to most international involvements suggested by President Roosevelt and his principal foreign-policy advisors. But correlations between conservatism on domestic social and economic issues and opposition to foreign aid, neutralism, "softness" or "appeasement" toward Communism, and liberal internationalist policies generally increased during the period since 1945. Whereas many economic and racial conservatives favored the Marshall Plan, relatively few in 1959–62 supported economic aid to underdeveloped countries at similar orders of magnitude. Had the current generation of Southern whites remained as conservative about the Negro, trade unions, taxation, the national debt, human nature, social "progress," and welfare programs as that of 1939, or even 1945, Southern opposition to many programs of the sixties outside the defense and trade spheres would have been more prevalent than seemed the case. More widespread and better education; greater exposure to outside peoples and ideas through travel, mass media, organizations, and other sources; and attenuation of Southern traditions by industrialization and urbanization partially accounted for the reduced magnitude of Southern deviations from national thinking on such matters. These developments have also lessened the differences between North and South in knowledge about world affairs, although Southerners still lagged behind Northerners considerably in their average knowledge of the subject in 1962.

Considerable Progress

Southerners, however, were as ready in 1962 as in the past to defend their country, the Western Hemisphere, Western Europe, and any other free countries which were willing to help defend themselves. Southerners were still at least as willing, and in some cases more willing, than Northerners to pay higher taxes, serve in the armed forces, and undergo other sacrifices if necessary for intensified national defense. They were no more opposed to being stationed overseas than were other citizens. Opposition to active United States participation in alliances around the world, provided that our allies fulfilled their just obligations to us, was feeble in the South, and certainly no greater than in the country generally. Nor was there much criticism of training allied military personnel in this country at our expense. Southerners were still somewhat more willing to fight for their rights and those of others of good faith than were Northerners taken together. These attitudes do not constitute isolationism.

While the proportion opposed to foreign capital assistance and other active nonmilitary programs has grown at least somewhat in the South, so has the thoughtful, relatively informed, responsibly internationalist or multilateralist minority. The proportion of Southerners who expressed no attitudes to survey interviewers when queried on international issues has declined gradually since the thirties, although it was still significantly larger than in other regions in 1962 on most foreign problems. Even the isolationists were better informed about the facts of world affairs than were their ideological predecessors a generation or more before. The fraction of Southerners interested sufficiently in foreign policy to have some information and relatively distinct views has expanded considerably since World War II. The small minority who read serious analyses of world affairs in books, critical magazines, and the best national newspapers has multiplied since 1945. The larger minority who kept up with international events in newsmagazines has also increased significantly faster than adult population growth. More Southerners than ever before were reading foreign news and even syndicated columns and editorials in their local press in 1962. Television was acquainting many even on the common-man level with news and had at least personalized and dramatized international phenomena which were unknown to them or their parents in 1945. Although voluntary organizations other than religious ones still reached a smaller fraction of Southerners than of Northerners and fewer such agencies in the South devoted attention to world affairs in a responsible way, international content had gradually crept into the programs of a sizeable minority of Southern groups which scarcely mentioned this field before.

The small, though growing, minority of Southerners who read international coverage and interpretation in the better national publications and devoted some laymen's attention to foreign policy were gradually approaching the thinking and level of sophistication of their Northern, particularly Northeastern, counterparts in 1962. They still differed with Northern liberal internationalists in some respects, for they were Southerners, too, and the forces discussed in this study affected most of them to some extent. As a group they were somewhat more cautious about foreign policy as about most other public and social issues. They were more hesitant to accept the feasibility and desirability of rapid change abroad, particularly in the underdeveloped countries. They tended to be more pragmatic, less unrealistically idealistic, and less theoretical or abstract about the lines of action this country should pursue. They were less optimistic about modifying foreigners' thinking toward our objectives and about the viability of democratic processes in backward nations. They were more inclined to consider military power the major aspect of our national security and a crucial instrumentality in effectuating our objectives abroad. Almost none were socialists, unilateral disarmers, or liberal utopians, and they were more conservative on the average than equally well-informed Northerners. The Southern internationalists who most nearly approached the thought of the Northern liberals had migrated in disproportionate numbers out of the South. Those remaining were inclined to feel that they could be more effective by conforming with most local norms, even many with which they privately tended to disagree, in order to be effective in one or two spheres they considered most important. They tended to feel they would be overwhelmed in multiple-front local "wars." Most Southern cosmopolitans thought in terms of gradual advances bit-by-bit, the cumulative effects of the efforts of many individuals over several generations. They were less optimistic in 1962 than their Northern confreres about accomplishing important desirable changes quickly or through drastic action. But they and their larger number of successors remained a major long-term hope for broader dissemination of knowledge about world affairs in the South.

The Coming Decade?

The prognosis depends on international developments, the policies of our government toward them, changes in the South, and the effectiveness of efforts to stimulate responsible thought on foreign relations in the region.

Some Unfortunate Possibilities

If Communist influence should seem to advance further, Southerners in growing numbers will demand more uncompromising reactions toward our opponents. The sense of frustration in the South about the apparent lack of success of many of our policies and the feeling that we were in a stronger world position in 1945 than we are currently are likely to grow if we should undergo many more setbacks of the type which seemed to many in 1962 to have taken place in Laos and, especially, in Cuba—a Communist take over in Vietnam or, particularly, in some important Latin-American country like Brazil, for instance.

Violent revolts against whites in Angola, Mozambique, Southern Rhodesia, and, particularly, the Republic of South Africa would tend to energize segregationists against the African nationalists and for the whites concerned. A shift of more underdeveloped countries toward the left in the direction of Cambodia, Indonesia, and Ghana; increased anti-Americanism, expropriation, and other maltreatment of whites and their interests in the underdeveloped world, particularly in colored countries; more widespread confusion and disorder in Latin America, Asia, and Africa; more news of corruption, waste, misuse of American foreign aid, and other excesses in aided countries—all would strengthen opposition in the South to capital assistance and generate greater demand for "tougher" policies toward these lands. Intensification of Communist influence in Cuba and further development of its potential elsewhere in Latin America would result in increased Southern demands that we invade, blockade, or employ other drastic action against the Castro regime.

An unlikely revision of the U.N. Charter to provide more votes and influence in the General Assembly for members with large populations and heavy financial contributions than for small, weak, impoverished states would significantly augment Southern approval of the international body. So would less emotional, more mature and responsible behavior on the part of the newly independent members, particularly the underdeveloped, neutralist, colored, formerly colonial countries.

On the other hand, entry of Communist China into the U.N. would reinforce the hostility among the minority already critical of the international organization and would propel a number of other Southerners who currently acquiesce in our active participation in the U.N. into opposition. Much would depend on how our national leaders prepared the Southern (and national) public for Communist Chinese admission.

Even the minority which believed in 1959–62 that we shall very probably have to accept Communist China as a member in the next decade—whether or not she moderates her aggressive behavior and pronouncements—felt with few exceptions that we should delay this development as long as possible without major damage to our world position. Admission of Peking without more intelligent preparation of the voters by the federal government, mass media, and other means of communication than hitherto would probably triple the Southern proportion favoring termination of United States membership and expand greatly the larger number of Southerners who would channel our foreign policies around rather than through the U.N. Careful explanation over the next several years of the probable effects of alternative United States postures toward possible Chinese admission could significantly reduce potentially unfortunate impacts on Southern opinion.

Furthermore, a shift of the policies and public utterances of delegates from the underdeveloped countries toward the left, toward socialistic, anticapitalist slogans and clichés, and toward more militant attacks on the West and on United States security policy without comparable criticism of the Communist powers would likewise entail serious loss of support for the international agency and for active United States collaboration therein. This eventuality would also generate strong demands in the South that we place less emphasis on the U.N. in our foreign policy. Finally, active agitation in the U.N. for desegregation and other racial changes in the United States, comparable to recent demands by colored members of the U.N. concerning the relations of whites and Negroes in South Africa, Southern Rhodesia, and the Portuguese dependencies in Africa, would augment opposition to the U.N. among many more racial conservatives, and even racial "moderates," who thus far have been indifferent to the world body or even favorable to United States cooperation therein.

The reactions of Southerners to trade expansion will depend on specific arrangements with respect to items of interest to the region. Increased trade with Western Europe, as envisaged by the Trade Expansion Act of 1962, would, in general, be relatively popular in the South. However, development of a more inward-looking Common Market, particularly if it should result in heightened barriers against Southern agricultural exports as in the case of poultry in 1963, would stimulate further protectionist sentiment among traditionally liberal-trade farmers. Widespread demand for reprisals through increased United States tariffs and other barriers to Common Market exports would probably develop.

Many Southerners will probably continue for several generations to think at least somewhat differently from the rest of Americans on some of the issues of world affairs. Several probable developments in the South are rather likely to intensify some of the trends in international opinions discussed in this study, at least in the short run. For instance, industrialization will produce more newly prosperous former "country boys" who are typically ultraconservative about foreign affairs as well as domestic fields. Furthermore, as underdeveloped countries build competing textile, food-processing, wood products, and other labor-intensive industries, protectionism among the new manufacturing class in the South may grow along with opposition to foreign aid to these countries. The influence of the leaders of the New South will continue to expand at the expense of that of the more traditional, genteel classes, some of whose members are considerably more thoughtful and well informed in world affairs than the growing newly prosperous business class.

New waves of rural poor whites and indigent independent farmers from the hills and mountains—mostly of fundamentalist religion, limited education, and strongly agrarian individualism—will move to urban employment as industrialization continues. Large numbers of them will probably become, as have their predecessors, rather insecure, confused, and vulnerable to simplistic demagoguery—which usually includes attacks on foreign aid and international collaboration in general. As in the past, most of them will manifest little interest in world issues, but will constitute a potential reservoir for political manipulators of xenophobic, neo-isolationist, and unilateralist inclinations. Unless trade unions can exert more influence on the thinking of these Southerners than currently, they and the newly prosperous of similar backgrounds in a number of fast-growing cities will probably elect an increasing number of right-wing Republicans with Goldwater inclinations on foreign policy, at least until these newly urban populations become more psychologically remote from rustic values, more urban in their thinking, and better educated.

The race issue, moreover, will be with the South for many years, and it will continue to exert unfortunate impacts on behavior toward world problems. Most of the relatively limited school and job desegregation has taken place in the upper South and in cities; where it has transpired, it is usually token in degree. Negro leaders with the backing of white liberals inside and outside the South and the federal government will press for several decades to broaden integration in these communities. Communities where racism and opposition to desegregation are the strongest—rural sections and small towns in plantation belts —have, however, hardly begun to experience forceful pressures to implement the Civil Rights Act of 1964. Racial antagonisms in these areas may worsen before they improve, with the attendant side effects on international thinking. Congressmen from such areas may move even further to the right in foreign affairs, and those few who do not may be replaced by men of more conservative international hue, as was the case of Congressman Frank E. Smith in the Mississippi Delta in 1962. Pressure for desegregation of a school, for registration of large numbers of Negro voters, or for other racial changes in small towns and rural areas with large numbers of Negroes before an election is rather likely to assist in the election of a white supremacist who is also apt to be a neo-isolationist.

Expanded voting among the less-educated and unsophisticated Southerners, who are disproportionately indifferent to world affairs, opposed to active international collaboration and to foreign economic aid, anti-foreign, and generally neo-isolationist, may reinforce the electoral appeals of politicians of like mind. The relative influence of better-educated, informed, and more thoughtful voters may therefore decline vis-à-vis that of simple poor whites and Negroes. As the South comprises a smaller and smaller proportion of the national population, as its legislators constitute a decreasing fraction of the Congress, and as the border states and Florida become more like the rest of the country, Deep Southern white electorates and their elected representatives could, under the impact of these forces, become more extreme and more obstructionist than before.

The Presence of Many Favorable Forces

On the other hand, successes abroad—in Berlin, Vietnam, the Congo, Latin America, or elsewhere—would help to increase the influence of the more internationally liberal (or less conservative) Southerners and broaden the base of support for foreign aid, intercultural exchange, the U.N., arms control, and other nonmilitary collaboration. If relations with the Communist powers and their allies become tenser and our national leaders feel we need more expensive military forces and expanded military conscription, Southerners will support these measures, probably to a greater degree than most other Americans. On the other hand, relaxation of tensions with the Soviet Union and those other members of the Communist bloc who follow the Soviet rather than the Chinese Communist international orientation would tend to encourage more widespread Southern approval of arms-control agreements, intercultural exchanges, and other arrangements with the Communist powers concerned.

The vast majority of Southerners likely to have international opinions would approve of closer collaboration with Western Europe in economic, cultural, and political spheres. Acceptance of more of the burden of foreign aid to underdeveloped countries by those West European powers which have not contributed much in this field so far would result in less opposition among Southerners to economic assistance abroad. As of 1964, it appeared that our federal government may become more demanding and discriminating toward the recipients of foreign aid—that would-be receivers of aid should make serious efforts to put their own financial and political houses in better order, tax their prosperous classes at rates comparable to those in the United States, reduce corruption and waste in assistance, apply aid to economically viable programs, encourage responsible private investment, and adopt responsibly neutralist rather than demagogically antiwhite, anti-Western, and anti-United States positions. Such shifts in our aid policy would lessen considerably Southern opposition to some of our current programs.

Moreover, our national leaders might make more concerted attempts to reach better accommodation with the more responsible Southern criticisms of some of our foreign programs. Far from all Southern disagreement with some of our international behavior is ill informed or destructive, and a number of thoughtful Southerners felt irritated at being unconsulted or "ridden over roughshod" during the interviews for this study from 1959 to 1962. The Kennedy administration, for instance, was able to secure the support of the American Cotton Manufacturers Institute (the organization composed primarily of Southern textile manufacturers which became the American Textile Manufacturers Institute in 1963) for its proposed Trade Expansion Act in 1962. This group adopted and publicized a resolution which expressed appreciation for the President's "unprecedented degree of thoughtful consideration and constructive action" and continued with the words, "We believe that the authority to deal with foreign nations proposed by the President [the Trade Expansion Bill] will be wisely exercised and should be granted by the Congress."[1] Partly as a result, some Congressmen from Southern textile districts voted for this bill. The federal government could gradually build support for its foreign economic assistance programs by presenting to Southerners (and other

1 Mimeographed copies of this resolution are available from the American Textile Manufacturers Institute, The Johnston Building, Charlotte, N.C. For the measures taken by the Kennedy administration to secure support for the proposed Trade Expansion Act in textile districts, see p. 153.

citizens) more balanced, realistic descriptions of what we can truly expect to accomplish on a long-run basis through aid rather than continuing the overly optimistic "sales talks" about transforming semifeudal Latin American societies and economies within ten years, withdrawing military and other forms of assistance from Vietnam by 1965, and so on.

Moreover, if certain long-run forces in the South are intelligently encouraged, aided, and guided by able Southerners with the sensitive assistance of federal agencies, Northern organizations, and individuals of cosmopolitan inclinations, the overall evolution of the region should be toward more cosmopolitan public thinking and behavior of its Congressmen. Termination of the county-unit system in Georgia and forced redistricting of Southern states generally promise to reduce the proportion of rurally oriented arch-conservative legislators from the region. Although some fast-growing cities like Dallas and Jackson and traditional ones like Charleston may elect ultra-conservatives like Bruce Alger, John Bell Williams, and L. Mendel Rivers to Congress, the likelihood of election in the long run of more internationalist and generally less-conservative legislators will be greater in the cities than in most rural sections.

Although racial tensions may get worse before they improve as pressure for desegregation is exerted in heavily Negro sections of the Deep South, eventually most whites will come to terms, however grudgingly, with legalized, formal use of public facilities while preserving as much informal segregation as possible. Patent defeat of the racial intransigents should decrease their influence on Deep Southern thinking in world affairs as in other fields. Gradual extension of the vote to Negroes and the raising of the educational level of the forthcoming Negro generation should ultimately defeat most Southern Congressmen who are racists and, usually, isolationists or unilateralists as well. Although Negroes are on the average less sophisticated, less interested, and more isolationist with respect to most aspects of world affairs than whites, in electing racially liberal or moderate whites they will usually be sending more internationally responsible representatives to Washington. Enfranchisement of Negroes should encourage more of them to pay more attention to public questions since they will be able to have some influence on policy with respect to them. Acceptance of at least slow change toward desegregation among whites should free more of them to think more realistically and critically about other issues, including foreign relations.

Furthermore, Southern states, counties, and municipalities are doing more to raise the general level of education than ever before. Barring unforeseen developments, availability and quality of education should gradually approach national standards. Although the most stimulating and cosmopolitan college teachers may continue to migrate to less frustrating and more rewarding positions in the North, more Southern colleges will undoubtedly narrow the gap between themselves and Northern institutions in respects associated with broader interest and understanding in world affairs among their graduates. Travel outside the South, exposure to national communication media and organizations advancing responsible interpretations of world developments, and other growing contacts with foreign relations should influence the thought of increasing numbers of younger, better-educated Southerners and exert at least some limited impacts even on older inhabitants who are not among the racist, ultra-conservative extreme. Larger fractions of younger, better-educated Southerners than of their elders tend to be relatively knowledgeable and thoughtful about world affairs; they are inclined to be more internationally sophisticated than were their elders when they were of the same age; and the indications are that the forthcoming generations will be still more informed and realistic about foreign developments.

Moreover, the rugged individualism and arch-conservatism often associated with agrarian experience should be attenuated as the distribution of the Southern population continues to shift to cities and, as the years pass, more and more Southerners are raised in urban settings. Unfortunately, Southerners may lose some agrarian values which some of us of rural backgrounds cherish—warm, unhurried interpersonal relationships, close family life, sensitivity to nature, and indifference to the exaggerations and false appeals of the public relations men and urban hucksters in general. Perhaps some of these desirable attributes may be preserved to a greater extent than in Northern cities. At the same time, however, religious fundamentalism, emotionalism, preoccupation with the hereafter rather than with the issues of this world, opposition to social change, ignorance, cultural isolation, and other rural features associated with indifference, paucity of understanding, and ultra-conservatism in world affairs should be dissipated by urbanization and education, at least among the offspring of city dwellers.

Furthermore, quality industry which stresses research and innovation will probably become an increasingly important employer in the South. Marginal, low-wage enterprises will be squeezed out as they become less able to compete with capital-intensive manufacturers for competent manpower. The leadership of the former will probably be, as they now are, more knowledgeable and less irresponsible about foreign policy that the latter. The more progressive and informed views of scientific industries on foreign as well as domestic issues should exert expanding impacts in their communities. Increasing prosperity and declining provincialism should attract more and more Northerners and even foreign-born people of education and talent to the South. At least some of them will probably preserve some cosmopolitan aspects of their Northern urban backgrounds and education. Even first generation prosperous businessmen should be increasingly better educated and informed about the world, and the sons and daughters of the currently arch-conservative parvenus promise to be more broadly educated and more internationally sophisticated on the average than their parents. As education, wealth, and economic security are experienced by successive generations, the proportion of relatively cosmopolitan Southerners will probably increase as in the past. Moreover, the influence of trade unions should grow among workers as racism and paternalism become less effective weapons against them, and their relatively internationalist orientation should make itself felt to some extent among unionized Southerners.

Finally, the advent of a nationally popular Southern President since the completion of this study permits some cautious optimism about possibly broadened Southern support for multilateral international cooperation, including even economic aid to neutralist, underdeveloped countries. Whether President Johnson will be able to generate wider approval among Southerners both in the Congress and at home for his foreign policies comparable with that enjoyed by our last President of Southern heritage—a man of quite different personality, experience, and intellectual interests—in his unsuccessful struggle to bring the United States into the League of Nations and into a generally more active role abroad remains to be seen.

Lyndon B. Johnson's defeat in the five Deep Southern states of Louisiana, Mississippi, Alabama, Georgia, and South Carolina on November 3, 1964, was attributable primarily to his active role in securing passage of the Civil Rights Act shortly before. Surveys during the campaign indicated that more Southerners than not preferred President Johnson over his opponent in most respects other than his equalitarian stand on Negro-white relations. Thus, 49 percent in the South felt that President Johnson and the Democratic party would "do the best job of keeping the country prosperous," compared with only 22 percent who thought Senator Goldwater and the Republican party would do so;[2] 36 percent believed the former would be "more likely to keep the United States out of World War III," compared with 27 percent who

2 AIPO Release of 10/9/64.

chose the latter;[3] and 47 percent would have preferred to go to hear a speech in a nearby community by President Johnson, whereas only 33 percent would rather have attended one by Senator Goldwater in an equally convenient place.[4]

President Johnson's success in the South relative to American foreign policy will depend to a considerable extent on his ability to moderate feelings of persecution and hostility among segregationists and to develop gradually more widespread acceptance of change in relationships between the races. Left to its natural course, racial tension in the region might accelerate as Negroes become more militant in their demands for equality of opportunity and treatment and as the pressures by the federal authorities grow more persistent and compelling in the rural and small-town environments with large proportions of Negroes among their populations. If President Johnson can capitalize on his Southern manners of thought and action to reduce the negative impacts of desegregation and to speed up the evolution of white Southern thinking toward more cosmopolitan and generally responsible behavior toward racial problems, he will have in effect succeeded in bringing the South closer to acceptance of more responsible foreign policies as well.

The President's actions toward other domestic problems of major import in the region may also indirectly result in more widespread acceptance of active international collaboration. Thus, the legislation passed in the spring of 1964 with the President's active support whereby textile manufacturers may purchase cotton at the world price seems to have weakened resentments and protectionist inclinations among Southern mill owners, executives, and workers. Serious attention to Appalachian and other Southern poverty may stimulate greater identification with the federal government among these underprivileged Americans, attenuate the pressures of economic want, and thereby encourage them to devote some attention to problems beyond their own subsistence and weaken their feeling that the energies and resources spent abroad should be expended at home instead.

By early 1965 President Johnson seemed to have moderated the feelings of alienation from the national society and the federal Executive which had developed to an alarming degree in the segregationist South due in significant measure to the style of the Kennedy administration, especially in race relations. Although President Johnson carried the overall Southern popular vote by only a bare majority, his popularity in the region even so shortly after the passage of the Civil Rights Act of 1964 exceeded that of President Kennedy following his nationwide

3 *Ibid.*   4 AIPO Release of 9/30/64.

television plea of June 11, 1963, for acceptance of desegregation.[5] Southerners other than extreme segregationists are unlikely to think of the patently Southern incumbent of the White House and his influential assistants of Southern upbringing and habits as a "foreign" government composed of Yankees ignorant of and indifferent to Southern sensibilities and uninterested in suggestions emanating from the South, as many of them did of the "Ivy League, Yankee do-gooders, one-world theorists, and impractical reformers" who supposedly ran both our domestic and foreign policies under the "Harvard" regime of the seemingly reserved, intellectually detached, and overtly liberal John Fitzgerald Kennedy. The language, sense of humor, and overall style of our new President are so clearly of the rural and small-town South that he may be able to develop Southern rapport—possibly even support—for policies in fact (though not in rhetoric) more liberal, multilateralist, and even, perhaps, more expensive than those of his predecessor. Whereas the appeals of President Kennedy and a number of his senior assistants tended to be lofty, urbane, transcendental, abstract, and, for the South, grandiose and mischievously and impractically idealistic, the emphases and communications of President Johnson to the South are warmly personal, folksy, anecdotal, agrarian, and pragmatic. His jokes are those of the rural South; he speaks of cattle, hogs, dogs, and cotton; he talks about hunting, fishing, horseback riding, his and his wife's traditional connections and family relationships in the Deep South, and his childhood as the son of a poor Southern farmer; and he stresses "reasoning together" for "better deals" and more effective, workable solutions to concrete, nonabstract problems both at home and abroad.

---

5 AIPO Release of 9/9/64. Shortly after President Kennedy's television appeal, Senator Goldwater held a 59–41 percent lead in the South ("no opinion" excluded) over the President in a trial heat whereby they were matched against one another in the forthcoming 1964 election.

CHAPTER 16

WHAT TO DO ABOUT IT?

E ncouragement of the forces favorable to more widespread understanding of foreign affairs as counter influences to those related to indifference, ignorance, and distorted attitudes with respect to world developments will be a complicated, often frustrating, continuing task for a variety of thoughtful Southerners and Northerners and of their local, regional, and national organizations. Most valid generalizations about potentially effective programs in the South are probably also applicable, perhaps with some amendment, to comparable Northern groups as well, and undoubtedly a good deal of the experience with communicating world affairs in the North [1] is also potentially useful in the South.

Both national and local resources spent on serious educational activities in foreign affairs have been much smaller per capita in the South than in most other parts of the country. Southern philanthropy—until recently of relatively small magnitude—has done relatively little to encourage either research, quality teaching, or public understanding in world affairs; with some exceptions it has devoted itself largely to religious organizations and more traditional, less controversial charities. As observed previously, most of the relatively few Southerners who have been readers of serious material on foreign relations have displayed little interest in trying to stimulate thought and to clear up distorted interpretations in this field among other Southerners.

1 See, for instance, Hero, *Voluntary Organizations in World Affairs Communication.*

Moreover, national organizations in world affairs education and communication have done relatively little to encourage experimentation in the South with potentially effective means of informing and stimulating more realistic thinking on foreign policy. Perhaps this lack of thoughtful attention to the region was due earlier to an assumption that Southerners were already more internationalist than other regional groups and therefore that slender funds and small staffs would be better focused in the supposedly isolationist Plains States and Midwest and in the Northeast where such agencies raised most of their money. If this assumption was ever valid, it certainly is no longer; although most of the talent and energy required on a long-term basis for broadening Southern comprehension of world affairs will necessarily come from the region itself, more sensitive, perceptive, and vigorous assistance and support will be required of national foundations, voluntary organizations, and other agencies than thoughtful Southerners have witnessed to date.

Some perceptive Southern cosmopolitans complain, perhaps with some justice, that most of the relatively few programs sponsored by "Yankee" (that is, national) organizations in the region either have built-in biases of which many rather sophisticated Southerners are critical or employ techniques designed primarily for the upper and upper-middle classes in Northern cities or suburbs. They comment that Northern agencies have made relatively little serious effort to locate and assist those few Southerners and Southern groups most apt to exert some desirable effect on the international thinking in the region or to design programs in conjunction with Southerners sensitive to the mores, communication systems, and power structures of the diverse parts of the South. Several observed that the national frontier for many national world affairs groups has seemed to end at the Potomac, or at the farthest with the upper South and a few "oases" like Atlanta.

A number of internationally concerned Southerners even blame "Yankee" liberals and their organizations in part for trends toward neo-isolationism in the South. Had the latter made continuing, serious efforts to maintain contacts with influential Southerners and had they helped intelligently to organize responsible Southerners as countervailing forces to the increasingly active racist-isolationists, some observers feel that the unfortunate shifts of opinion among both leadership groups and the masses could have been minimized and more Southerners would probably be more receptive to realistic thinking on foreign policy today. Some who are more or less familiar with national foundations and educational organizations add that these bodies would probably have better rapport in the South and be more effective there if they included on their governing boards, advisory groups, and senior staffs more "real" Southerners, still resident in and knowledgeable about their native region.

These criticisms seem somewhat exaggerated. Lyceums, forums, adult education projects, and the like in the liberal arts have long been viewed as connected with liberalism, "modernism," and criticism of Southern race relations and, hence, have experienced but limited popularity. Some national groups in world affairs—such as the Council on Foreign Relations, the Foreign Policy Association, the American Association for the United Nations, and the American Foundation for Political (now Continuing) Education—have attempted to generate more interest in the South from time to time. There have been some successes, but more frequently than not active response has been sparse. Those national organizations which have been interested in adding to their governing bodies, consulting groups, and senior staffs Southerners who are at the same time sensitive to the different Souths, sophisticated about foreign policy, and well regarded among diverse inhabitants of their region have experienced considerable difficulty finding such individuals. The guilt for paucity of thoughtful action is therefore both Southern and national.

Some General Observations

This discussion is too brief to deal with the complicated problems of formal and informal education and communication in world affairs in the South in any detail. Each of the major potential instrumentalities, such as foreign visitors or trade unions, is worthy of special empirical study which those concerned with this study have been unable to conduct. Moreover, few principles apply equally to all the diverse groups within the region. Consequently, this chapter attempts to present some general observations about the overall problem, some objectives and priorities for educational programs, and some suggested roles for those Southern and national institutions which seem particularly well placed to perform useful tasks toward the long-run goals.

Diverse Programs

Impersonal mass media, particularly television and radio, can reach with the same content considerably more heterogeneous Southerners than most projects involving face-to-face contact. For example, the President of the United States can engage on television at peak viewing hours in the evening the attention of Southerners ranging from Ph.D.'s in international relations to semiliterate mountaineers, poor whites, and Negroes of little education, although these diverse Southerners may perceive different concepts in his addresses.

Consequently, popular mass media—especially television, local newspapers, and popular magazines—will be vitally important in the gradual process of improving comprehension of world developments among the majority of Southerners. They will also exert considerable impact on the thinking of the leadership groups, and even of the minority of perhaps one third of one percent who are quite interested in foreign policy and who read critical national publications in that field. But they are too impersonal to serve as the sole sources of stimulation, information, and ideas in world affairs in the South.

Interest in world affairs and attention to thoughtful content in media of communication are typically generated in the South, as elsewhere, by more intimate experiences—through formal education and informal interpersonal contact with foreigners, Americans of foreign experience, and people who have some familiarity with world developments. Without these more personal experiences, most Southerners (or other people) do not read the foreign coverage in their papers and magazines and do not tune in international programs on radio and television.

But no one type of program requiring interpersonal contact will energize more than a rather homogeneous audience—much less diverse than that of even readers of newspaper editorials. The complexity, level of abstraction, and required prior knowledge of a given presentation of foreign affairs will select an audience of a relatively limited spectrum of sophistication. If it is serious enough to attract the relatively well-read cosmopolitans, 99 percent of adult Southerners will not understand much of it and will either not participate, withdraw, or derive little benefit if they remain. If it is less demanding, then the more sophisticated will be bored and likewise will fail to take part or will leave. Only a relatively small fraction of Southerners can be attracted to face-to-face systematic examinations of foreign policy under likely circumstances. If others are to be reached, the communication must be more personal, dramatic, concrete, and probably less analytical.

Similarly, although there is some general interest in world affairs in the South as in other regions, particular issues within the foreign field will tend to attract certain Southerners, but not most others. Discussions of world trade will draw one group, those of economic development in underdeveloped countries largely another, those of intercultural exchange still a third, those of military security a fourth, and so on. There will normally be some overlap, particularly among the more intensely interested in world affairs, but it will tend to be of limited magnitude. Likewise, programs wherein given interpretations of international issues or attitudinal orientations toward them are prevalent will draw primarily participants whose own views are similar while those who disagree will not take part.

However, world affairs are so broad in character that it should be possible to get an increasingly numerous and influential minority of Southerners started on some aspect of foreign developments, depending on the approach and the group attempting it. Getting them started is very important. For instance, many educated Southerners have been interested in literature, history, and the other humanities rather than the social sciences. Perhaps one might begin among some of these Southerners with attention to the impacts of major Southern writers, such as William Faulkner, on foreign literature and thought. The interests of some could probably be gradually extended to other fields of foreign relations.

Social and personality factors will also tend to predetermine who pays attention. Some who would expose themselves to the same content in mass media may feel uncomfortable in social situations with people previously unknown to them. They may be socially inarticulate, introverted, or embarrassed about their limited education, lack of attractive clothing, or social position. Most conferences, seminars, and other discussions of world affairs have been upper and upper-middle class in locale and participation. Class consciousness is more intense in much of the Deep South than outside, and even the atypically alert and vigorous woman of less-privileged station does not usually feel at home with college-trained, professional, proprietary, and managerial-class women at a local League of Women Voters meeting in a prosperous home with Negro servants or in the parish house of the local Episcopal church. Except in a very few organizations, largely in cities in the border states, even the most intellectually alert Negroes would not be invited to such sessions, and even in the upper South most of them would not feel very comfortable there. Organizations sponsoring programs on foreign affairs can in many instances do more than they have to attract the few thoughtful, interested, and able Southerners of less-elevated backgrounds—by holding meetings in more socially neutral locales like public libraries, making serious efforts to find the few potential participants whose education has been largely informal but who are interested in broad questions, and by eliminating unnecessary customs which mark the privileged from the majority in the South. However, care should be taken that changes in subject matter, techniques, and customs do not result in actual if not formal withdrawal from participation of a significant proportion of their current members without the addition of an equivalent number of new ones.

Furthermore, the thinking of an individual Southerner will be the product of a diversity of exposures to international stimuli. In order to exert major effects on large numbers of Southerners and differential effects on the same Southerners, a variety of international programs and communications on various levels of abstraction and sophistication, diverse topics, employing different kinds of stimuli, and presented separately when required to stratified groups are needed. Although this utopia of internationalization of Southerners through many different means is, of course, unattainable in the foreseeable future, as diverse a cafeteria of high-quality programs as can be financed and intelligently conducted should be sought.

"Southernizing" the Programs

A number of cosmopolitans and urbanized, New South professional, business, and executive personnel appreciate opportunities to participate in activities in New York, Washington, and elsewhere in the North and more of the especially competent among them should be invited to do so. For programs directed at most other Southerners, however, it is usually advisable to assist Southern-based agencies which are well regarded among the audience in mind to develop and sponsor educational activities rather than to launch them under the sponsorship of agencies with Northern addresses. Segregationist Deep Southerners particularly have long been hesitant about collaborating on ideas and projects emanating from New York, Boston, and other "outside" centers. In general, the more tense the local race issue, or the more racially conservative the individual Southerners in question, the more inclined they are to shy from communications and other projects originating in "Yankeeland."

Thus, most white Deep Southerners are more likely to cooperate with local organizations, mass media, and individuals, particularly if they are acquainted with them, and more inclined to accept the ideas they advance, than they are with respect to the same ideas coming from unfamiliar Northern sources. Joint ventures with local universities, religious groups, libraries, bar associations, economic clubs, and so on by national agencies are more apt to be well received than programs without such local blessing, particularly if the national organization's other programs or its officials have ever been identified as liberal on religion, economics, and, especially, race. Mere acceptance of financial support from the Ford Foundation, the Fund for the Republic, the Fund for Adult Education, and other Northern, supposedly liberal, sources has stirred up controversy in several cases.

Close collaboration with Southern agencies is also imperative from the point of view of designing programs attractive to Southern audiences. With increased exposure to Northern ideas and techniques on television, in print, through military service and travel, in Northern-owned enterprises in the South, and through other means, more Southerners than ever have become accustomed to Northern ways of doing things. The Foreign Policy Association's reading materials for its Great Decisions discussion programs have been successfully used in Macon, New Orleans, Little Rock, and in some other locales in the Deep South among the college-educated, urban people who have made up the bulk of their participants. Similarly, the critical discussion materials of the American Assembly have been employed successfully among the typically even more knowledgeable and internationally sophisticated participants in Southern Assemblies. Materials prepared by or with the financial assistance of the Fund for Adult Education and other Northern groups for national consumption have been favorably received by Southerners taking part in discussions sponsored by libraries, universities, and other educationally oriented institutions. But these participants, too, have been, with but few exceptions, from among the small, more cosmopolitan, better-educated, typically less-conservative minority.

However, programs which would exert favorable influences on more typical Southerners usually must be carefully scrutinized for their likely impacts on Southern sensibilities and their conformity to Southern attitudes and action. Undocumented generalizations to the effect that Southern segregation exerts important negative effects on accomplishment of our major objectives abroad and other content critical of the South and of white behavior toward Negroes either in the United States or abroad are likely to alienate large numbers of actual or would-be audiences. Nevertheless, it is usually easier to conduct relatively dispassionate discussions concerning race relations in Africa than to do so with respect to Southern racial problems. One does not, of course, focus the program on foreign racial questions and expect to conduct a fruitful exercise except among the small, racially liberal, Southern minority. But those who are sufficiently interested in world affairs to participate in analytical discussions of the topic are, with some exceptions, moderates if not liberals on race.

Furthermore, it is usually even more advisable to emphasize concrete facts rather than abstractions in the South than in the North. Idealistic or supposedly grandiose assumptions about the "brotherhood of man," the "basic goodness of the human race," how illiterates abroad are striving for freedom, democracy, equality, progress, or other liberal abstract objectives tend to stimulate derision and alienation toward the source. Even on controversial issues which are packed with emotion, where Southerners will resist abstract argument, they are more likely to listen to facts. For example, Southern audiences might be informed of the relative values of our imports versus our exports to particular countries, such as the value of Japanese textiles brought into this country as compared with that of United States cotton sold in Japan, the needs of our industries for foreign resources, the proportions of our rice, cotton, tobacco, chickens, and so on which are exported and where they go, the real economic problems of protectionists in the textile industry in addition to foreign imports, and so on.

Even more than elsewhere in America, issues should be personalized, dramatized with examples, and tied to the individual Southerner's own experience and interests. Analytical discussions of international politics or economics in impersonal terms are unlikely to engage the attention of more than a very limited minority of well-educated, primarily internationalist Southerners who have long thought in such terms about public issues and many other questions as well.

Articulate foreign students and more senior visiting foreigners with realistic views of their societies could become significantly more effective vehicles than in the past for communicating the thinking of their compatriots to their Southern hosts. Southerners tend to respect obviously practical people who have had personal experience with the phenomena about which they speak and who have the facts at their fingertips. Many Southerners may for the moment disagree with their interpretations, but expansion of funds of information tends to erode gradually unrealistic thinking. There is considerable potential demand for foreigners as speakers in small-town Rotaries, church groups, and other organizations in isolated communities, and a larger number of foreign students seem interested in visiting these places than are actually invited to do so. Although foreign agricultural specialists and other relatively "apolitical" visitors probably would not communicate much about the foreign policies of their governments, hosts would learn something of their societies and ways of thought. Most white Southerners are willing to accept citizens of virtually all the non-Negroid underdeveloped world, including dark Asians "in uniform." Some effort should be applied to strengthening administrative agencies in the few cities and university communities able to expand the contacts of foreign visitors in smaller, more culturally isolated, places.

Cosmopolitans of Southern background should be utilized more than heretofore where their talents and availability permit. Nationally known public figures from Northern and foreign places can gain the attention of many better-educated Southerners in business and professional life, provided that they are not identified with "anti-Southern" activities. But most of the responsible face-to-face communication of foreign affairs in the South will have to be done by Southerners who know something of the subject, who are fond of at least some aspects of Southern life and society, and who are sensitive to the attitudes and customs of the people to whom they address themselves, rather than by Northerners or alienated Southerners. Moreover, although some Northerners and former Northerners can and do adopt the Southern cosmopolitan's seemingly relaxed posture, easy pace, and generally un-hurried, "uneager" behavior, many of them tend to become frustrated in a society where such ways are most likely to accomplish long-run advances. Educating, energizing, assisting, advising, and supporting the small, Southern, cosmopolitan minority should be a major emphasis of national and regional agencies interested in world-affairs education in the South.

Groups with Audiences

It is probably wise to concentrate resources devoted to conferences, seminars, and other serious examinations of foreign policy, wherein participants are drawn from a number of different membership groups, on the small cosmopolitan and semi-cosmopolitan minority and on individuals of significant influence on foreign-policy making, local opinion, and organizations and mass media in the region. The Southern majority should be educated to foreign affairs through formal education of the forthcoming generation, popular mass media, and international programs within organizations and informal groups with which they are already identified.

Like Southern society generally, voluntary organizations in the region seem even more stratified in terms of social class and other background factors than most Northern ones. Even when the formal membership or claimed audience is more heterogeneous, the actual par-ticipants in activities involving interpersonal contacts tend to be of similar status. This observation is correlated with another, that since Southerners of given social standing tend to harbor rather similar views on public questions, including world affairs, participants in programs sponsored by a given organization are likely to reflect a limited range of opinions. In some cases it will be wise to introduce cosmopolitans from outside the group to insure expression of alternative interpretations and policies.

Although a smaller minority of Southerners than of other regional groups are active in organizations other than churches, most who are well enough educated to be potentially interested in foreign-policy discussions, if attractively presented to them, are now affiliated with one or more such associations.[2] Except for the more intellectually alert, emotionally and socially secure few, it is typically much easier to attract Southerners to international programs within groups with which they are already identified or at least familiar and where they know a number of other people, rather than to draw them to similar projects with other individuals they do not know in settings with which they have had little or no experience. It is also usually much less work for educational agencies to help produce effective programs for groups with audiences than to draw Southerners out of their normal habits to programs sponsored by bodies new to them.

Fortunately, forces potentially favorable to the purposes of enhancing understanding of foreign affairs are already operating within a considerable number of Southern groups which have not so far been particularly active in that field. National governing boards and staffs of organizations with which local Rotaries, Chambers of Commerce, Junior Chambers of Commerce, Kiwanis, bar associations, churches, trade unions, and other community groups are affiliated are in most cases much better informed about international problems and considerably more internationalist and less conservative about foreign policy than are the majority of local members. Mere attention by local chapters to the thinking of their national officers and other leaders would expose many Southerners to ideas on foreign relations significantly more responsible and sophisticated than their own. As perhaps in other parts of the country, it is common to discover that members and even leaders of the local Chamber of Commerce, for instance, do not know what the positions of the U.S. Chamber of Commerce are on such issues as world trade, foreign aid, and the like.

It is, of course, not an easy task to communicate the ideas prevalent in the Washington or New York headquarters to local Southern chapters of loosely organized federations. But enunciation of internationally realistic statements, resolutions, or opinions by annual conferences, boards of directors, committees, and so on at the national level can

2 NORC 335, January, 1953 (2,809), and NORC 367, January, 1955 (2,379).

frequently accord some respectability to such points of view among local members who think differently, or think hardly at all about these issues. They can also provide some entree for those who would encourage local attention to these problems.

Leaders, officers, and senior staff members of local chapters are, moreover, more often than not more interested in world affairs and more inclined to agree with responsible international thinking at the national center than are rank-and-file members. Even when most of the local leadership is not much concerned with problems beyond the parochial, one can usually locate at least one or two among them who are less provincial in their thinking and who may, depending on the circumstances, exert some influence in determining which speakers appear and the like. Admittedly in only a few local organizations is it likely that major segments of the membership can be induced to devote really serious, critical attention to foreign affairs. But many small-town chapters of national organizations experience difficulties in locating interesting speakers for their periodical luncheons and dinners, as do women's book clubs, men's discussion groups, and so on. Few would schedule speakers on world affairs more than once or twice a year, but currently most do not even do that; they well might do so if they were advised of the availability of visitors from abroad, foreign service officers on leave nearby, and other articulate and authoritative potential guests. Much more should be done to introduce gradually some responsible attention to world affairs into groups which have built-in audiences, which reach Southerners in the milieu in which they feel comfortable.

Part of a Much Broader Problem

Expanded understanding of the world in which we live will not be accomplished through communications on world affairs alone. Any influence which tends to raise the general level of sophistication of Southerners beyond their immediate surroundings, to augment their critical facilities, and to broaden their horizons to alternative cultures and ways of thought outside and, even, within the South will indirectly advance comprehension of world phenomena as well.

Advances in race relations in the Deep South are particularly likely to provide bases for more dispassionate, less-biased, and more internationally responsible thought on foreign policy, and vice versa. Examination of racial problems abroad are likely to influence thinking about local Negro-white relations as well. Moreover, even discussion of international matters not directly connected with race trends to break down dogmatic thinking and, indirectly, to moderate sentiments about Southern Negroes. Development of more rational thinking on the latter is apt to permit less emotional, more analytical orientations toward world problems. In the long run, careful efforts devoted to improving local race relations may do more to improve Southern thought about international relations than most programs focused on foreign affairs per se.

Some Priorities and Objectives

Any effort which is likely to broaden the horizons and sensitivities of a significant number of voters or future voters or which has similar effects on even a relative handful of Southerners who may exert important influences on Congressmen, the political process, or the thinking of a number of other Southerners is worthy of funds, talent, and energy. In final analysis the impact of any activity will depend on the persons designing and implementing it—their perceptiveness, vigor, and general ability. A program which is in the abstract of considerably lower priority than another may in fact be more worthy because of the quality, realism, and enthusiasm of the individuals involved.

Moreover, categorization of Southerners for discussion of priorities of audiences and programs is necessarily somewhat arbitrary. Influence on foreign-policy making and on voter opinion is a multifaceted, complex phenomenon. For instance, those who influence their Congressman directly on trade legislation may exert little or no impact on his vote on the U.N. bond issue or military appropriations.[3] Southerners who exert considerable influence on their Senators and Congressmen on a given aspect of foreign policy may have little influence on local opinion with respect to the same aspect. Those who influence one local group, say members of the local Chamber of Commerce, may have little effect on others, such as trade-union members. Furthermore, the influence of any individual may vary from time to time with the specific situation at the moment.

The most internationally sophisticated handful in one community or group within it may be considerably less well informed and generally competent in world affairs than those in others. Those who would communicate international facts and ideas into small towns and rural sections will be obliged to work with considerably less knowledgeable cosmopolitan and semi-cosmopolitan minorities than they would in Greensboro or New Orleans, for instance. Objectives and techniques with

3 Bernard C. Cohen, *The Influence of Non-Governmental Groups on Foreign-Policy Making* (Boston: World Peace Foundation, 1959), 12 ff.

the former will of necessity differ from those with the latter. Likewise, approaches and goals with the Negro community may be different from those with the white group in the same area.

Nevertheless, it seems feasible to advance some general thoughts on priorities to be assigned to various Southern groups, on what one might hope to accomplish with them, and on possible techniques for involving them in world affairs. The speculative observations to follow are subject to exceptions and amendments with actual experience of programs in the field.

Difficult Versus Not-So-Difficult Communities

It is, of course, much easier to generate interest and to communicate responsible ideas in world affairs in locales where there is already a considerable number of people of international sensitivity; where racists, strong traditionalists, and neo-isolationists are of relatively little influence; where the average level of education is rather high; and where there are already one or more good colleges, internationally oriented mass media, and voluntary organizations with international interests. College towns, active ports, and more dynamic, future-directed (and yet matured) cities are thus the least frustrating from this frame of reference. Traditional cities with many Negroes, like Charleston, will probably be more difficult for the foreseeable future, as will many communities which have developed into fairly sizeable cities relatively quickly in recent decades. Rural sections with few genteel readers of serious publications will be difficult indeed to penetrate, except through television and perhaps a few churches with relatively educated, non-fundamentalist congregations and clergy.

The progressive, more matured cities of the South will gradually increase their influence over the less dynamic, rural, and backward-looking areas. As their proportion of the population increases and the disproportionate political influence of the country people is reduced, urban ideas will be much more evident in the Congress. Larger cities, along with university communities, are the natural locales for development of vigorous mass media, organizations, and other activities in foreign affairs which may influence directly or indirectly some of the thinking in the rural hinterlands. In these cities, national groups and cosmopolitan Southerners will find most of their more effective allies against the neo-isolationist trends.

But it seems unwise to ignore parts of the South where racism, ultra-conservatism, and neo-isolationism are more prevalent, to adopt completely the operating assumption that thinking there will change with time and that limited resources and talent available should be focused almost exclusively in less difficult places until formal education, economic development, mass communications, urbanization, and mortality have provided better openings for communication of world affairs. In cities like Charleston, Shreveport, and Jackson and throughout much of the Black Belt, there are few channels through which responsibly multilateralist ideas are expressed, prevailing neo-isolationism is vigorously analyzed and criticized, and alternative interpretations of international developments are offered. Most major means of communication—mass media, organizations, and interpersonal contacts—reinforce attitudes on foreign policy typically correlated with racial conservatism. There are few oases where cosmopolitans may express their views openly without ostracism by their associates, and few internationalist bases with which youngsters may identify. As noted previously, cosmopolitans in such environments feel isolated and the less vigorous personalities among them adopt some of the thinking about them. Other citizens, who have previously had no particular interest or knowledge in world affairs, gradually integrate the explanations and interpretations of the neo-isolationists into their own cognitive processes.

In the short run the few cosmopolitans in such environments, even with maximum support from outside, cannot expect to defeat their opponents. They can be assisted, however, in limiting the effects of the onslaught of the neo-isolationists on the thinking of a significant number of their colleagues. They can be aided in establishing some rallying point of internationally responsible comment about foreign policy, some countervailing influence to the preponderant social pressures and media of communication, such that the neo-isolationists do not enjoy a monopoly and, therefore, gain converts by default. The forum should not be left entirely to the racist-isolationists.

The Isolationists

Certainly some of the "anti-Communist," ultra-conservative, neo-isolationists have gradually drifted into these ways due to lack of information and of differing ideas around them. A number of these individuals who thought little about world affairs until the last few years are people of integrity, basic intelligence, and ability who want to understand what has transpired with respect to American international interests and why, and want to support realistic policies toward resolving our international difficulties. Under favorable circumstances a minority of these Southerners are open-minded to facts and explanations different from their own. These are worthy of some attention and effort at education.

But such ideology in perhaps more cases than not is rooted in basic personality make-up, profoundly conservative assumptions about human beings, social institutions, and international relations, and mutually reinforcing social forces about the individual. Relatively few arch-conservative isolationists or neo-isolationists are well informed or really want to become so; they are for the most part not seeking new information and ideas in an empirical way; they are not interested much in comparing their thinking with that of responsible specialists on world affairs. Whatever activities in the international sphere they participate in tend to be uncritically propagandistic—to further or reinforce their own opinions.

Advantage should be taken of opportunities which might spasmodically occur to place balanced treatments of foreign issues before these Southerners at little effort; now and then some of them may pay attention to programs on television or in organizations in which they are active even though the ideas propounded may vary from their own. But much more basic influences than those available to most world affairs and other educational agencies are typically necessary to encourage more critical, balanced international thinking among most of these individuals. Consequently, the philosophy toward these Southerners should probably be to attempt to minimize their influence on policy and on other citizens and to stimulate other, more moderate and reasonable Southerners to counter their arguments and impacts.

The Middle Group

A considerably larger fraction of Southerners who are hesitant about continued aid to underdeveloped, neutralist societies and other policies of our government are more moderate in their thinking. Many have not been particularly interested or knowledgeable in foreign affairs and they have accepted some of the clichés of the neo-isolationists without much thought or emotional identification. A number of them would probably change their thinking if convinced that their current views are unrealistic or unbalanced. Some of these Southerners have considerable actual or potential influence—executives and future executives, lawyers and other professional people, and other active men and women, often of education and ability and typically in early middle age and younger. They are frequently people actively engaged both in their careers and in the civic, philanthropic, religious, and other extracurricular activities demanded of them. Therefore, they devote relatively little effort to trying to understand foreign affairs. They tend to prefer to concentrate their non-vocational energies on local problems which they can readily understand and where they can observe some results rather than on international ones about which they know little and where they feel their efforts are unlikely to have much effect.

Moreover, they may also shy away from a number of programs in world affairs partly because these seem to be populated largely by participants who they feel are impractical, unrealistically idealistic, and otherwise ineffective and pedantic. Most of them probably cannot be attracted to systematic discussions of foreign policy in seminars, conferences, and other intensive sessions—at least not during the more active and creative years of their careers. Many of them can, however, be exposed to facts and ideas in world affairs now and then through speakers and other means within Chambers of Commerce, economic councils, export clubs, bar associations, bankers' associations, and other non-world-affairs organizations in which they do take part. But some of them, particularly the more intellectually alert, can be attracted to serious discussions sponsored by universities and other agencies which they respect—programs organized with the active assistance of leading business and professional people whom they admire and which are populated primarily by "practical" individuals rather than ineffective "do-gooders and women with nothing better to do."

The Cosmopolitans

Two interrelated objectives should apply to the small minority in the South who read critical literature and who are relatively thoughtful about foreign affairs: expanding their sophistication in international phenomena per se and broadening their influence in their communities and, at least indirectly, on the political process.

Most Southern cosmopolitans, particularly outside the larger cities and college communities, need opportunities to compare ideas they learn from mass media with interpretations of specialists on the subject matter in atmospheres in which they may express themselves freely. Educational programs should bring such Southerners together to discuss their thinking with others of like inclinations and with experts who can help clarify distorted interpretations and assist in developing more systematic thought about foreign relations. Face-to-face contact would also tend to motivate these individuals to continue and expand their interests, to read more of the better literature in the field, to sharpen their critical faculties, and, in general, to resist gradual regression toward the indifference and conservatism on world affairs prevailing about them.

Such contacts with other cosmopolitans and with experts on foreign relations might also tend to give thoughtful citizens in isolated towns and rural sections the courage of their convictions vis-à-vis their local peers in indicating that others who know a great deal about these subjects agree with their general opinions at variance with local norms. Bringing these atypical Southerners together could encourage outspokenness at home. For contacts established with other cosmopolitans and experts in neighboring cities could diminish the individual's feeling of aloneness and render him more likely to express himself and to cooperate with individuals of like mind.

Mere indication of interest from the outside in the problems of small-town, rural, and other isolated cosmopolitans and semi-cosmopolitans tends to reinforce their continued attention to foreign policy and energize them toward expressing their thinking locally. Brief visits by individuals, such as the author, seemed welcomed among internationally thoughtful citizens in Deltatown, Kent, Plantation County, and Bayou Parish as opportunities to talk about world affairs and about frustrations with local attitudes on the subject. Invitations to local cosmopolitans to enter into serious discussions of foreign policy and of local opinion on the matter might provide another means of acknowledging their international interests and accomplishments and reinforcing their local influence.

World-affairs agencies should experiment with a variety of techniques to accord thoughtful cosmopolitans and active organizations in world-affairs education better recognition for their knowledge and achievements in this field. For instance, institutions in other states might consider attempting the high-school speaking contests on the U.N. which are sponsored by the Extension Division of the University of North Carolina. Awards might be made to publishers, editors, educators, librarians, and others who have worked at the difficult task of advancing international understanding in the region. The American Freedom Association in North Carolina has been able to call the attention of others to particularly effective individuals and educational programs in foreign affairs. National agencies should exert themselves more to discover and evaluate efforts in world-affairs education, particularly in the more unfavorable settings in the Deep South, such as those at the University of South Carolina and South Georgia College designed and carried out by Professors John B. McConaughy and E. R. Bradley, respectively. Many Southerners active in this field hunger for national recognition of their efforts against frustrating odds, and such encouragement could be achieved for relatively little expense. In the process of examining existing educational programs, national organizations might learn more about the practical problems of conducting such activities in the Deep

South and pinpoint individuals and organizations worthy of advice and, hopefully, some financial assistance.

Some pilot attempts might also be made to attack the problem of communication of world affairs more directly. An interested agency might work with a regional or local group to bring together responsible cosmopolitans from some particularly neo-isolationist settings to discuss the state of local opinion and understanding in world affairs and what might be done about it. Some might be willing under certain circumstances to take joint public positions with other interested citizens of some influence favorable to selected important foreign policies of their country against neo-isolationist local media and organizations. At a minimum they might be informed of techniques employed with some success elsewhere in similar communities which are trying to moderate the influence of the neo-isolationists and relatively ignorant critics of American behavior abroad. They might also be induced to consider potentially practicable ways over the long term of advancing more responsible world views through local media, organizations, and other groups and at least placed in contact with organizations which might be sources of advice on techniques and competent speakers and other expertise on world affairs.

Some Southern Instrumentalities

Internationalization of Formal Education

Successful efforts toward more education for larger numbers of Southerners combined with improved quality of whatever education they receive are more apt to augment public understanding of foreign-policy questions than any other single endeavor. Quality education in international affairs and related fields will tend to develop in schools and colleges where the overall intellectual atmosphere is stimulating, and the competence of future graduates in foreign affairs will be closely associated with the overall excellence of their educational experience as well as with their academic exposure to international relations itself. Moreover, with some exceptions, the higher the general standards of the educational institution and its faculty, the greater the impact normally on thinking in the surrounding nonacademic community.

But the presence of future voters and leaders of the South as captive audiences in educational institutions, where their major task is absorbing information and learning to handle ideas, offers opportunities in communicating about world affairs per se seldom enjoyed by agencies attempting to attract the attention of busy adults pursuing careers not directly related to foreign relations. If educational institutions do not succeed in energizing thought about foreign relations and the historical and current forces influencing them while Southerners are students, the likelihood of engaging their interest for equally serious analysis later is feeble.

Improved salary scales; lower teaching loads and more time for original research; better libraries; and more effective insulation from racists and other enemies of free inquiry and expression in state legislatures, on boards of regents, and among influential citizens would attract more talented Southerners to their native region after completing study in Northern and foreign graduate schools; keep more able products of the best Southern graduate schools in the South; prevent more vigorous, intellectually stimulating teachers from migrating North; and even draw to the South an increased number of Northern professors of intellectual stature. Establishment of a single chair in international relations with tenure and competitive pay and research facilities in a number of smaller, less well-known institutions could improve considerably the probability that forthcoming students will have an opportunity of systematic exposure to this field.

Virtually any effort which raises the quality and status of foreign affairs on more typical college campuses and leads more students to expose themselves to this field is likely to be fruitful—more foreign students and exchange professors from abroad; more visits, lectures, and seminars by scholars and other experts in international relations whose reputations are such as to attract significant numbers of students and nonacademic members of the surrounding community; more scholarships for promising Southern students of limited means; and so on.

Extracurricular programs in world affairs, if intelligently conceived and carried out, can attract students whose major fields are other than international relations or political science. For instance, a meeting on the U.N. at the University of South Carolina in 1961 attracted considerable attention not only among students but also in the local press which had been hostile to the world organization, on television, and in the nonacademic middle- and upper-class community generally. Summer programs on world affairs at East Carolina College—located in the most heavily Negro, plantation-traditionist, conservative part of North Carolina—have succeeded in attracting significant numbers of more internationally concerned students and adults to lectures and discussions with able specialists. Annual Student Conferences on Paramount Events at the University of Southern Mississippi have attracted interested youngsters from both colleges and high schools throughout Mississippi to critical discussions of international and other public questions. International Relations Clubs (I.R.C.'s) or similar groups, weak or non-existent at most Southern colleges, should be better supported and developed into forums for serious discussion of world developments among more alert students, as has been the case in several colleges in the region. Active, interesting student groups such as these have in a number of cases helped to develop the individual's concerns toward world affairs and have resulted in a continuing interest after graduation. And, in at least one Southern university the I.R.C. has extended its influence to local high schools with junior memberships and through other means. Unfortunately, the race issue has intervened here as in so many endeavors of a cosmopolitan nature: pressure from national sponsors for integrated regional meetings of I.R.C.'s has rendered these student bodies controversial among segregationist parents, state politicians, regents, and others who influence higher education and has made participation in regional sessions more difficult.

But the majority of youngsters from average and underprivileged homes are unlikely to go to college in the foreseeable future. Those who do will be more likely to profit from that educational experience if they have undergone cosmopolitan influences at an earlier age, starting with grade school if feasible. The World Affairs Council of New Hampshire and the University of New Hampshire have experimented with considerable success with institutes on world affairs for high-school teachers in that largely rural state. Similar programs for teachers have been conducted at the University of South Carolina, the University of Southern Mississippi, and several other publicly supported institutions of higher learning in the South. In several instances university specialists on foreign affairs have met with social-studies sections of annual state educational association meetings. Such pilot efforts should be used as prototypes or points of departure by many more Southern colleges, universities, and other institutions to do more than heretofore to develop sophistication in the subject matter and teaching of foreign relations among social-studies teachers and generally to strengthen their contacts with the thinking among university scholars and other specialists in the international field.

In this regard, the recent pressures on the public schools in a number of Southern school districts and on statewide levels in some instances for courses on communism could be turned to good use rather than allowed to result in harm to the educational process and the students affected. Much of the agitation for such material in the high-school curriculum has been among very conservative citizen groups and legislators of similar mind, typically people who are not particularly sophisticated about communism, international relations, the social studies, or education generally. They seem to be more interested in emotional presentations of "anti-Communist" clichés and propaganda than in critical analyses of the phenomenon of communism in historical perspective, in theory, and in practice. Apprehensions about possible damage to the educational process energized Governor Terry Sanford of North Carolina and the North Carolina Educational Council on National Purposes, a statewide group appointed by him, to sponsor through state colleges and universities workshops for high-school teachers and others on the nature of communism and on approaches to teaching youngsters about it. A comparable program was conducted at the University of South Carolina with considerable favorable result. The agitation for teaching about communism apparently created a sizeable market for participation in such analytical examinations of this important worldwide phenomenon such that these courses were well attended. It would appear that other institutions could profit by these examples.

Universities and Communication to Adults

But given the paucity of World Affairs Councils, adult-education centers, and other serious educational agencies able to develop public education on foreign policy beyond the formal student body in most of the South and the concentration of expertise in world affairs in institutions of higher learning, colleges and universities should do much more than currently to stimulate critical thought in this field among adults. Southern institutions of higher learning are potentially the most effective means other than television and newspapers for encouraging responsible thinking beyond their campuses.

At a minimum, more colleges not only should schedule speeches and other programs by visiting figures when local citizens can attend but should also do much more than most have in the past to publicize such activities effectively through local television, radio, press, and voluntary organizations. In some cases collaborating committees from the community leadership might be involved in making generally known well ahead of time the forum, panel, or other program and lend their prestige to the activity as devices for attracting members of local business, professional, and other influential circles.

Extension programs should be sharply upgraded throughout the South. With notable exceptions, it is admittedly difficult to imagine the origination and development of sensitive, vigorous, and high-quality programs on foreign relations by most of the extension staffs of 1962. However, in a number of cases extension personnel might help conduct the program and perform administrative duties if a sophisticated outside agency, such as the Foreign Policy Association, were to assist in designing the technique, organizing the resource specialists, and providing assistance in drawing in particularly able or influential participants. Several of the more able extension or comparable university agencies have organized attractive programs for people of some standing in their communities, and foundations and others should be attentive to possible opportunities to encourage other efforts by competent individuals in creating programs tailored to specific audiences.

However, world-affairs organizations and foundations should not limit their attention to extension divisions. It is at times possible to locate considerable interest and ability among individuals within institutions which place no particular emphasis on communicating with nonstudents. Sometimes the president, a senior dean, or other administrator will be interested, depending on the quality of the proposed program, the amount and type of work required, and the availability of funds. They may be sufficiently motivated to assist in organizing chairmen and committees likely to attract influential participants and to use attractive facilities of the institution as the meeting locale. In others a faculty member in political science, economics, history, law, or other field of the social sciences or humanities may be willing to devote time and energy to one or more high-content programs aimed at a particular nonacademic audience. In a few cases he may have entrees into the professional, occupational, or social groups who are to be involved. In others he may require the assistance of the college administration and able nonacademic people in designing the program to fit the prospective audience and in attracting the desired participants to the program. It will often be necessary to provide some funds for honoraria of the faculty members devoting extensive time to the project, for travel, and for administrative expenses, since few Southern colleges are willing or able to devote funds to such activities.

Divinity schools might be enticed into conducting serious programs in fields like ethics and foreign policy for clergymen and active laymen. Law schools might be induced to sponsor comparable programs for some of the more thoughtful lawyers in their environs. The business school at the University of North Carolina has conducted intensive seminars for more thoughtful business, financial, and manufacturing executives in the state, apparently with considerable success, and it would appear that its experience might be useful to business schools in other parts of the South as a possible prototype. Likewise, Emory University's Institute of Citizenship for individuals of some influence in small Georgia communities who were brought to Emory for intensive seminars on foreign affairs and were later visited by a member of the staff to encourage continuation of their interest and action in their local surroundings is probably worthy of examination by other institutions for possible implementation in other rural and small-town sections. Many cosmopolitan newspapermen tend to be critical of schools of journalism, but serious press institutes sponsored perhaps jointly by journalists' professional organizations, departments in the social sciences and humanities, and some schools of journalism could over the years help to improve the quality of editorial coverage of world affairs.

The possible alternatives for thoughtful and attractive programs sponsored by colleges and universities of varying prestige, talents, and roles in their locales are virtually infinite, depending on the assistance and encouragement of the college administration and faculty and the cooperation which can be secured within the nonacademic community nearby. In some instances the educational institution may conceive and direct the program alone, as a number of projects sponsored by the University of North Carolina and its departments or schools have been. In others, funds and some counsel may come from foundations or other outside agencies, whereas most of the organization and insightful energy is provided from within the educational institution, as has been the case with the American Alumni Seminar for Public Responsibility financed by the Fund for Adult Education and implemented by the Department of Political Science at Southwestern at Memphis. In still other instances, such as the Southern Assembly, the cooperating university and faculty members help provide some of the substantive talent and perform the administrative tasks for programs which have been designed by a national agency. Finally, the university or one or more of its departments may be only one of several local sponsors for a program which has been planned primarily on a national level, such as the Committee for Economic Development Associates program in collaboration with Southern Methodist University, the World Affairs Council of Dallas, and several leading personalities in that city.

The lack of other educational organizations seriously interested and competent in foreign affairs suggests still another important function for extension or other agencies of Southern land-grant colleges or state universities—that of service center and coordinator for other groups interested in conducting programs in world affairs.

Various suggestive prototypes might be examined with a view toward adapting one or a combination of them to Southern situations. The World Affairs Councils of Vermont and New Hampshire, both located at, partially supported by, and closely linked to the public universities of these two primarily rural states, might serve as particularly useful examples for largely rural Southern locales. The World Affairs Continuing Education program at Michigan State University and the Institute for World Affairs Education at the University of Wisconsin provide service-center functions in their respective states. One of the apparently most effective such agencies is the World Affairs Center at the University of Minnesota, which conducts programs of its own with the assistance of other branches of the university and in collaboration with outside organizations and also provides a speakers' bureau, counsel on subject matter, and advice on the design and execution of educational activities for public and private, formal and informal, groups interested in sponsoring international activities of their own. It is thus the major point of contact in the state between citizen activities and scholarly and other expertise in foreign affairs.

Development of such centers in the South will, of course, run head on against a number of strong obstacles. Assignment of an able specialist on international relations who is also a competent adult educator sensitive to community groups on even a part-time basis to such functions, plus limited secretarial help, would require funds difficult to obtain from most Southern state legislatures; consequently, some foundation aid would probably be required, at least initially. Such talent is difficult to find—most specialists in foreign affairs are not particularly interested in continuing often frustrating and futile negotiations with a diversity of groups, many of them run by relatively uninformed and trying people. On the other hand, most extension personnel are not very sophisticated in foreign affairs, nor are they experienced in presenting ideas in the field in a stimulating manner. Many connected with extension work tend to think in terms of "university level" programs wherein they control the subject matter and the method of presentation and choose the instructor. Center staffs would suggest subject matter, experts, and techniques to interested organizations, mass media, and other groups, but the independent group—ranging from sophisticated ones like many American Association of University Women chapters through YWCA's to quite naïve ones like many trade-union locals, farm groups, and fraternal and service organizations—would ultimately determine these factors. Certainly many resulting programs would not initially satisfy the standards of university courses.

Yet one is struck with the need in much of the South for such centers to stimulate demand in their environs and coordinate the effective use of talent. Universities do not have the resources to conduct serious programs in foreign affairs for more than a slender minority of the varied potential audiences about them. Most Southerners, particularly those who have not been to college, tend to feel more at home in their own groups than in unfamiliar college surroundings. Most find it more feasible to participate in local organizations than to travel to more distant colleges. Potentially interested groups do not know where to turn for speakers and are for the most part unable to judge the quality of those who might come to their attention. Foreign and other visitors knowledgeable on world affairs often do not know of attractive opportunities to speak before nearby groups and the latter do not learn of their coming. A sensitive, dynamic individual in touch with visiting experts on foreign relations, Foreign Service officers in the area on home leave, foreign students and professors in the locale, the intellectual resources at his own and at nearby universities, and advice and personnel available from national groups could gradually develop markets for his services and help over the years to raise the standards of programs and informal discussions in a wide range of local organizations, most of which are only tangentially interested in foreign policy. The influence of more irresponsible speakers and groups could be slowly reduced. Such a function might also, incidentally, develop a more favorable public throughout the state for the university and its personnel.

Public Libraries

Universities are not, of course, the only Southern institutions able to advance these purposes. Virtually every organization where some of the leaders are themselves interested and relatively open-minded in world affairs and where audiences pay some attention to programs offered by these leaders is a possible vehicle.

Local libraries are often potential bases for serious programs in this field. Their staffs and most of their trustees or directors are usually among the more cosmopolitan, well informed, better read, and more interested in ideas in their communities. Although there have been attacks against some libraries for the liberal literature which they have displayed, supporters of these institutions have usually defeated such assaults and preserved considerable intellectual freedom even in the Black Belt and in traditional cities like Savannah. Because school boards are often much more politically oriented than library leadership, libraries tend to be more likely sponsors for serious discussion of controversial issues than public high schools. Moreover, the clientele of most small-town libraries includes most of the cosmopolitans, some of whom are financially unable to subscribe to serious periodicals, buy books, or attend conferences away from home. In addition, the librarian is also usually in touch with youngsters of cosmopolitan potential.

These small libraries are typically on slender budgets and can afford but very few books—those most likely to be relatively popular —on foreign affairs. Periodicals like the *Christian Science Monitor*, New York *Times* (Sunday edition), and *Foreign Affairs* must usually be donated to these libraries by interested citizens. Many small libraries receive only a few such periodicals, and some program whereby circulation of thoughtful, easily read literature could be made available to interested libraries by a philanthropy might be useful.

In addition, even in the plantation region the small-town libraries have been the location from time to time for serious discussions of world affairs and other critical topics—in meetings of book review clubs, literary societies, Great Book and American Heritage groups, and other nationally, regionally, or locally organized enterprises. They are potentially open to further efforts to organize, energize, and educate the likely opposition to irresponsible local thought on foreign policy.

Women's Organizations

Women of the educated strata are the prime movers and workers in many internationally concerned organizations, even when men are the ostensible leaders, and they could be similarly active in a number of other groups if steered to activities which seemed interesting and constructive to them. Some of these women are actually searching for projects worth their time and energies.

One of the most effective organizations in the communication of responsible thought about world affairs into the South has been the League of Women Voters. It is undoubtedly correct that in some Southern locales league members have included disproportionately large numbers of émigré Northerners, school teachers, and middle-class women viewed by local traditionalists as "ungracious reformers," "eggheads," and the like. Whereas most middle- and, especially, upper-class women influential in their communities in the region were born and raised there or nearby, the median Southern member of the league in the mid-1950's had resided locally for only 14.4 years.[4] However, on the whole, league members have been relatively well regarded in

4 *A Study of the League of Women Voters of the United States*, Report IV, "Organizational Phase, Part I, Factors in League Functioning" (Ann Arbor: Survey Research Center, University of Michigan, 1957), 111. However, members of Southern leagues had, on the average, resided somewhat longer in their communities than league members outside the South.

recent years by their less politically concerned (and typically less intellectually alert) peers in the region.[5] In a number of communities leagues have included active, public-spirited wives of influential local men as well as women of considerable stature themselves. Most members of Southern leagues in the early 1960's were relatively internationalist, at least by Southern standards; in fact the league was the principal rallying point, or "life raft," for the handful of critical cosmopolitans in a number of locales where there were no other internationally thoughtful agencies.

The agenda adopted by the league's biennial national convention—typically after much prior discussion among competent league leaders on both the national and the local levels—normally has included one or more international issues which all local leagues have supposedly been obliged to discuss. The league publication which goes to every member covers foreign policy regularly in a responsible fashion. Whereas some leagues, such as that in St. Bernard Parish outside New Orleans at the time of the interviews for this study, have been so involved in local problems that they have in fact devoted little attention to foreign relations, some members of most local leagues in the South have been quite interested in world affairs. Many members who have been attracted due to their concern about local issues have been, are in the process of being, or at least could gradually be educated about foreign policy. Those leagues which have included a considerable number of strong conservatives opposed to foreign aid, expanded trade, active collaboration in the U.N., continued negotiations with the U.S.S.R. for the relaxation of tensions, and so on (as in Antebellum Town) have brought these women into some contact with facts and alternative thinking on world developments; although few change their opinions dramatically, such information and ideas tend to limit their more immoderate and unrealistic views. Even in some of the more unfavorable settings, such as Jackson, Mississippi, leagues have succeeded through conferences with expert speakers of Southern origins and other means in drawing the attention of neo-isolationist mass media and individuals of similar orientation to information with which they were previously unfamiliar and views with which they had tended to disregard.

The American Association of University Women has exerted considerably less, yet significant, influence toward nationally responsible world attitudes and comprehension. Although international affairs has

5 *A Study of the League of Women Voters of the United States,* Report II, "Community Attitudes toward the League" (Ann Arbor: Survey Research Center, University of Michigan, 1957), 16–23.

been a major concern of the national leadership of the AAUW and of a number of Southern chapters, local AAUW's are not required to devote their attention to particular issues selected nationally. Less focused on political action than local Leagues of Women Voters, AAUW chapters have dealt with a wider range of problems, with particular concern for those of education. Although some AAUW chapters, such as a considerable fraction of those in North Carolina, have been much interested in foreign relations, many others in the South, as in Antebellum Town, have concentrated their energies on education and other problems of particular interest to college-educated local women. During the late 1950's and early 1960's Southern chapters of the AAUW were on the whole less active in international affairs than seemed to be true in other parts of the country—probably another example of the indirect (and often direct) negative influence of the racial controversy.[6]

Nevertheless, active participants in Southern chapters of the AAUW by and large have harbored views on world affairs similar in orientation to those among Southern women who have taken active parts in Leagues of Women Voters, and their other social and attitudinal attributes have been roughly similar.[7] However, both have been populated primarily by the college-educated, middle and upper classes in urban and suburban environments. It would appear that the league, if not the AAUW, should be encouraged to organize local bases of critical dis-

6 This comparison of Southern with Northern AAUW's in world affairs and the comment about North Carolina were supported by the experience of Dr. Dorothy B. Robins, formerly executive associate at the national headquarters of the AAUW charged with conducting programs on world affairs. The fact that the AAUW has been integrated across the country by policy and action has tended to limit its participation in the South to college women who are liberals or, at least, moderates on race.

7 Although the League of Women Voters, different from the AAUW, has not required a college education for membership, in the mid-1950's, 78 percent of members of the league throughout the country had experienced some college education, 46 percent had received a B.A. or B.S. degree, and 18 percent had been to graduate or professional school. Only 3 percent of league members at that time lived in neighborhoods rated "below average," only one percent came from homes where the breadwinner was an unskilled or semiskilled worker, and only 5 percent from ones where he or she was skilled or supervisory in position. Perhaps as many as 6 percent of members of the league could be classified as of the lower-middle, working, and lower classes combined. As one would surmise (see p. 275), Southern members of the league were somewhat more concentrated in the higher strata than were members in the rest of the country. (*A Study of the League of Women Voters of the United States*, Report III, "Some Problems of League Membership: Cross-Sectional Membership and Member Activity" [Ann Arbor: Survey Research Center, University of Michigan, 1957], 3–8; and author's correspondence with the study director Marjorie N. Donald.)

cussion of international and national affairs among comparable women in a larger number of culturally more isolated communities than has so far been the case, including even smaller towns and rural sections.

But we should not limit our attention to middle- and upper-class women's groups as concerned with public questions as these. There are, for instance, various church-connected groups for women which under some circumstances could gradually be attracted to more adequate attention to foreign affairs. Some of the apparent impact of the Women's Division for Christian Service of the Board of Missions of the Methodist Church was mentioned previously. Interdenominational chapters of the United Church Women in some locales have devoted considerable responsible attention to world problems, becoming in several communities a major springboard for cosmopolitan international thinking where there have been no Leagues of Women Voters or AAUW's. They are probably a potential vehicle in many others where they have not allocated much consideration to this field beyond providing clothing and the like for some foreign mission. Given the widespread interest in the South in missionary work abroad and the increasing sophistication about foreign cultures among nonfundamentalist missionaries, missionary societies of more local churches could probably serve as forums for examination of the social and political forces in the underdeveloped countries bearing on the success of missionary education, public health, and so on. National organizations might consider assisting pertinent authorities in the several denominations to produce study and other material for local groups in this field, comparable to that written in 1961–62 for local affiliates of the National Council of Catholic Women in collaboration with the Foreign Policy Association on Latin America.

Churches and Religious Groups

Since religious organizations reach more Southerners on a face-to-face basis than any other organizations, they offer some long-run potential for stimulating attention to world affairs—even considering the fundamentalist attitudes and pressures on cosmopolitan clergy by conservative congregations.

As observed previously, clergymen of nonfundamentalist persuasion are more often than not better informed and generally more cosmopolitan in their thinking than most of their congregations; as with others of like mind, the basic task is to render some of them more sophisticated about foreign relations and more likely to make their views known to others. More able Southern clergymen could be involved outside the

South and in the border city of Washington in analytical sessions dealing with the role of ethics in foreign policy and other subjects of particular interest to ministers and priests. Such meetings should provide them opportunities to compare ideas with Northern churchmen and scholars. But expenses-paid trips North can include only a small fraction of potentially interested ministers. Many intelligent ministers will feel more comfortable where Southern churchmen are the majority; for, as already noted, the language of most Southern Protestant clergymen tends to be more biblical even when their ideas are similar to those of Northern ministers. Also, Southern churchmen often apparently feel that other Southerners understand their problems better and are more sympathetic than Northerners, or that sophisticated Northern clergymen tend to be critical of them or to look down on them.

More Southern churchmen, both clerical and lay, should be exposed to discussions organized in the South, hopefully with the encouragement and assistance of sensitive national organizations. Ministers who are relatively interested in world affairs (usually those oriented toward general social implications of Christianity) are typically among the least ill at ease with churchmen from other religious groups, and a number of them could even be enticed into discussions with Roman Catholic priests. Such ministers are also among the more likely to interpret their religious duties broadly and to participate now and then in organized discussions with no patent religious connections among professors, teachers, lawyers, thoughtful housewives, and others.

But being on the average more denominationally and less ecumenically inclined than Northerners, most ministers and influential laymen are more easily reached through agencies associated with their particular denomination. There are sensitive, capable cosmopolitans interested in stimulating responsible thought about world affairs among the clergy and laity in positions of influence on the staffs and among the governing bodies of the Southern Baptist Convention, the Presbyterian Church in the United States (Southern Presbyterian Church), the Associate Reformed Presbyterian Church, and in the upper echelons of Methodist organizations in the region. They are frequently opposed by powerful conservative elements within their denomination and on the same boards or commissions who feel their churches are not the place for discussions of foreign affairs and who are hostile to foreign aid, intercultural exchanges with the Communists, and other features of our foreign policy. These thoughtful churchmen have few funds for programs designed to stimulate international thought and they are obliged to be cautious about collaborating with national agencies, including the National Council of Churches, or accepting money from "liberal" foundations in the North. But circumspect encouragement from the North could gradually strengthen the cosmopolitans against their conservative opponents and result in effective programs pertinent to world affairs in their denominations.

Agricultural Groups

The agricultural extension with its county (or parish) agents and home demonstration agents has close rapport with more rural people than any other agency except churches. Moreover, its contacts are particularly with the better-educated and more efficient farm families, those most likely to show some interest and comprehension in world affairs. There are, of course, serious obstacles to working through these agencies. Their purposes have been improvement of agricultural practices and pragmatic homemaking and family and community living. Even at the university level, relatively few officials, researchers, or teachers seem themselves particularly interested in foreign affairs, and even fewer seem likely to support use of their apparatus for education in that field. Few county agents and home demonstration agents are interested and informed enough in world matters to lend much assistance to programs devoted to that field. Moreover, interviews with those in the sample counties and parishes for this study indicated that most of them are conservative Democrats or, in the mountains, equally or more conservative Republicans on foreign policy as well as most domestic questions. Southern audiences of agricultural extensions not only are less informed about world developments but also would undoubtedly be more surprised on the average than Northern farmers to find that field among those to which their attention was directed by their county agents. The little experimentation with serious discussions of foreign policy in agricultural extensions has transpired outside the South—some Great Decisions programs of the Foreign Policy Association in the Northwest, Rocky Mountain area, and Midwest; some distribution of reading materials and sponsorship of discussions by agricultural extension of land-grant colleges in the Midwest; and several projects in California.

But the time has come to try at least a few pilot programs through the more public spirited and effective agricultural extensions in those counties where the agents and the clientele are most likely to respond favorably. Perhaps several of the programs mentioned above or adaptations thereof might be attempted. But even if these win only limited success, much more can be done with foreigners of farm background and Americans of foreign experience both before formal groups and through close informal interpersonal relations. For example, farm youngsters from abroad have been placed in homes of more enterprising, educated farmers in the Mississippi hills. A French-speaking foreign home-economics specialist left favorable impressions in several southern Louisiana parishes while working with rural women. An American agricultural expert from Mississippi who had returned from a tour with the Point Four program in Asia discussed his thoughtful observations before a number of farm groups in and around his part of the state. Opportunities for utilization of such individuals are far greater than those actually used.

Labor Organizations

Unions will probably become increasingly influential among the growing number of industrial and other nonfarm workers of the region. Some unions already exert significant influences on the international thinking of many of their members, and particularly of local officers, through their publications and regional and local meetings for representatives of locals. Many members pay relatively little attention to international content in union periodicals, but a minority do and are thus exposed to more internationally liberal views than they find in most Southern newspapers. As the Southern economy matures, members become better educated and less provincial, and unions feel more secure in the region, opportunities for wider communication of foreign affairs by unions to their members and their families should become more frequent, and union political education should gradually extend beyond bread-and-butter issues and those national economic controversies directly related to members' standards of living. As will be the case with all except a small fraction of primarily better-educated and more critically minded Southerners, much of the effective labor education in foreign affairs must necessarily be by indirection, personalization, and emphasis on labor-related international aspects rather than through examination of foreign policy in the abstract.

Mass Media

Causation is difficult to determine, but those newspapers with more adequate international news coverage and more enlightened editorials and columns are typically found in those communities like Greenville (Mississippi), Atlanta, Greensboro, Raleigh, Charlotte, Little Rock, and Nashville where the public is, on the whole, better informed and more internationally liberal. Although Southern opinion is on the whole less conservative on foreign aid and several other international issues than are most papers in the region, thinking on economic assistance and the U.N. tends to be most conservative where papers are of similar views and less so where papers support economic, diplomatic, and other forms of multilateralism. Even when better-educated readers of papers like the Raleigh *News and Observer* and the Atlanta *Constitution* disagree with their liberal internationalist opinions, they do read some of these interpretations differing from their own at least now and then and they develop some understanding of the rationales for views different from theirs. Such familiarity with alternative thinking is much less evident in communities like Jackson, Charleston, and Shreveport, where all the newspapers advance the racist syndrome of international views with various amendments. Furthermore, the more internationally oriented press, being typically also more liberal on race, attracts to its news and editorials much of the educated Negro group, most of whom are irritated by the racism or condescending paternalism of the conservative papers in their areas.

There is great room for improvement in the quality of the Southern press in foreign affairs. Although most papers in the fifty-three sampled for this study increased the space they devoted to foreign news over the period 1936–61, only half a dozen, such as the Richmond *Times-Dispatch*, the Atlanta *Constitution*, the Charleston *News and Courier*, and the Chattanooga *Times*, approached the international news content in the weekly summary on the first two pages of the New York *Times* "News of the Week in Review." The typical Southern paper leads the reader from one dramatic crisis to another with little attention to the forces which have produced the crisis and the developments from one to the next. In only a relatively small minority of the sampled papers, approximately one out of five, could the interested reader find columns or editorials of the quality and responsibility of a Walter Lippmann, Roscoe Drummond, James B. Reston, or Marquis Childs. In over half of the papers, arch-conservative editorials and columns like those of Paul Harvey, Thurmon Sensing, W. D. Workman, Holmes Alexander, Westbrook Pegler, and Barry Goldwater predominated. Multilateralist opinion was either not represented at all or it was limited to a single column by Drew Pearson, Inez Robb, or another relatively "folksy," unanalytical columnist.

It is probably unrealistic to hope for the establishment of new, more internationally realistic papers in communities currently dominated by neo-isolationist ones. Starting such papers in competition with economically successful existing ones has become much more costly and risky than in generations past. More and more Southern settings are served by a single publisher, often of a strongly conservative hue. In some places the publisher also controls the local radio or television outlet, which tends to reflect similar opinions on foreign relations.

But some progressive influences can be encouraged within a number of conservative papers. It was noted previously that a considerable fraction of the journalists with conservative papers tended to be more internationalist than the pages of the papers employing them would lead the reader to assume. As with internationalist Southerners generally, few of them are truly sophisticated about foreign policy or certain enough of their opinions to exert much influence on their associates in the office. Brief press institutes at universities and other short educational programs in world affairs could help somewhat in deepening their understanding and stimulating them to read more widely and to exert whatever influence within their paper is feasible. However, development of competent editorial writers on foreign affairs requires a longer process and is not the result of a few lectures or conferences unless they form part of a pattern of continuing interest. The more able should be accorded wider opportunities to take advantage of fellowships of a summer or one or two semesters at major universities in the South, North, and abroad (such as the Nieman fellowships at Harvard) and at research institutions like the Council on Foreign Relations where they may deepen their understanding of foreign problems.

Most Southerners who were financed for an extended period of study would probably return to Southern papers, although perhaps not to the less sophisticated of them where they would be most frustrated. Although few would succeed quickly in significantly improving the quality of international coverage and editorials of their papers, most would probably gradually exert some influence in that direction and the exposure of more promising journalists to serious analyses of foreign affairs over the years could slowly raise the standards of the Southern press in foreign relations.

Similar generalizations seem to apply to local television staffs. Unfortunately, many of the more thoughtful national programs in foreign affairs are not carried by local stations in a number of communities. More lucrative and, according to some station owners and managers, more popular programs like sporting events, "Southern" music, and sometimes arch-conservative programs on public affairs tend to replace them. Analytical programs of liberal bent, especially when they use some figure who is known for integrationist and "anti-Southern" views, seem the least likely to be transmitted in black-belt locales where the race situation is tense. Perhaps development of better understanding of foreign affairs among influential individuals connected with Southern stations would result in gradual increase in the fraction of the better network programs used.

Recent passage of legislation by Congress to help finance the establishment of noncommercial television stations should also permit some broadening of attitudes. Educational television in much of the South has broadcast relatively little critical analysis of controversial issues of foreign policy. The opening of new stations and their scheduling of serious international affairs programs will help considerably to deepen understanding of foreign affairs among many of the better educated and among the small number of less educated who have sufficient interest to pay attention. If the stations are established, the quality of their international fare is likely to improve over that of much of the international content now on educational stations since the National Educational Television Center now commands expanded funds to prepare more attractive programs in this field in the future.

Media of lesser importance from the point of view of this study, yet of significant potential value, are the magazines and other publications which either originate from religious groups or other organizations with which the individual Southerner is affiliated or focus on farm practices or other occupational or leisure interests of major groups in the South. Popular papers and magazines of religious denominations or groups affiliated with them have in some cases carried material dealing intelligently with foreign affairs, usually from a frame of reference with religious connotations. Some of the descriptions of the problems of missionaries have at least tangentially spread responsible images of the societies in which they have worked. In at least one case foreign aid has been discussed in terms of its ethical and moral significance for Christians. The clergymen and laymen (among the denominations as differentiated from the sects) who edit these publications tend to be themselves interested in social significance of the gospel, including its implications for foreign affairs. Several of them have noted to the author that they would probably print interesting articles on foreign aid and other foreign matters if written so as to appear relevant to the role of their periodicals in the eyes of their readers. If written by a prominent churchman sophisticated about world affairs and attuned to the religious interests of the subscribers, such material would probably attract the attention of a significant minority of laymen and clergymen in the denomination concerned.

A large minority of adults on Southern farms read one or more farm magazines like the *Progressive Farmer*. Most of these people do not read articles on foreign affairs in newsmagazines or critical periodicals, and a considerable number are not sufficiently interested in world affairs in general to pay much attention to editorials and columns on the subject in the better newspapers. But more of them will read in their regular farm publications attractive material which considers international matters associated with farming, livestock, and other pragmatic interests of the reader. Several of these publications, including the *Progressive Farmer*, have carried from time to time rather thoughtful articles on international exchange of agricultural knowledge and talent, the role of agricultural-surplus disposal abroad in our foreign aid program and in our foreign policy generally, and other topics. Expansion of the number and improvement of the quality of such articles are probably difficult to achieve, but the appearance of a few thoughtful articles in recent years indicates that progress is possible.

Broadening Understanding Among Negroes

As more Negroes become better educated, urbanized, and members of the middle class, as they vote in larger numbers, and as civic and educational organizations become desegregated, both the need for educating them to world affairs and the feasibility of doing so will grow. If the impact on the political process of the naturally indifferent and isolationist inclinations of large numbers of Southern Negroes is to be limited, much more effective educational efforts must be made in the future than in the past.

Negro Institutions

Efforts should be concentrated on formal education and face-to-face programs directed at the small educated group of Negroes in the cities and larger towns. Communication to the majority of Negroes no longer in school will necessarily be largely through popular mass media, especially television and Negro and general periodicals, and through the middle-class people in contact with them, such as ministers, newspapermen, and others. Although much more concerted attempts than at present should be made to desegregate white groups seriously discussing foreign affairs and to attract intellectually alert Negroes to them, the number of Negroes who will be drawn to such programs in the next few years will probably be quite limited. Therefore, the development of attractive programs among those predominantly Negro institutions likely to sponsor responsible discussions of foreign policy should be encouraged.

Negro colleges and universities offer the most likely opportunities for stimulating thought on foreign affairs, even more than the colleges and universities do in the white community. With the one major exception of the recent Ford Foundation grant to Atlanta University for programs on India, China, and Africa, efforts by even the better Negro institutions to secure foundation and other funds for research and teaching activities on Africa and other international matters have enjoyed little success. Although there are many problems—quality of the faculty and administration, interest of potential students, and other considerations—it would appear that the creation of centers devoted to international affairs at several other more intellectually able Negro institutions could have significant effects on the next generation of Negro leaders in the South. Meanwhile, efforts should also be made to augment and improve attention to world affairs at the more run-of-the-mill Negro colleges—for instance, making possible the appointment of at least one stimulating faculty member specialized in international relations; channeling a larger number of the more able Africans and other foreign visitors through less well-known places than has been the case in the past; rendering financially feasible the invitation of American and other specialists on Africa and world affairs generally to speak and meet with students there; and so on. International Relations Clubs, either nonexistent or weak at all except two or three Negro colleges, should be given further attention and assistance.

Perhaps the slender resources, internal and external pressures, and rather limited quality of the staffs and faculties at the majority of predominantly Negro colleges render unlikely the possibility that they can be induced to sponsor or collaborate in effective programs for adults in their environs. However, there are probably three or four where able individuals and administrative support for serious projects directed at more culturally and politically alert Negroes are potentially present, depending on the outside assistance forthcoming. The number of Negro colleges which would be capable of assisting an educational organization in foreign affairs to conduct programs in its facilities or nearby is larger. Although the general quality and prestige of the institution are frequently crucial factors, careful inventories of even some junior colleges sometimes lead one to an intellectually alert faculty member and even an administrator capable of intelligent assistance.

In some cases the university, college, or one of its schools or departments may conduct serious discussion programs as the only or major sponsor. In others one or more nonacademic institutions may cosponsor the project. For instance, the directors and some of the board members of at least one of the more sophisticated Urban Leagues are potentially interested in developing programs for more promising of local Negro leaders in collaboration with a local university, provided that administrative costs and expert assistance could be obtained. Programs for social-studies teachers in secondary schools might be conducted by able faculties at several universities in collaboration with professional organizations of these teachers. A few owners and editors of Negro newspapers are relatively well read and cosmopolitan and could probably be induced to participate in serious sessions conducted by a university, perhaps in collaboration with a professional group such as the National Negro Publishers' Association.

Seminars and other educational programs for social-studies teachers might be reinforced with other cosmopolitan influences in the high schools. The more responsible African and other foreign students at nearby colleges and thoughtful visiting Africans and experts on Africa and other foreign areas could be encouraged to address student assemblies, forums, and other high-school groups in areas where pressures by the conservatives in the white community are not prohibitive.

Discussion of Africa and the international implications of race relations which have taken place in some Frontiers Clubs and other locally organized groups composed of better-educated and influential Negroes should be extended to others in the smaller cities. Careful efforts should be made to gradually introduce speakers on other issues of world affairs, with little direct connection to race relations and Africa, into such groups.

Although the race issue has not prevented development of emphasis on the social implications of the gospel as in many white churches, the literalist and emotional tradition, the restricted formal education of the majority of Negro ministers (particularly older ones), and the paucity of pertinent background and interest among most congregations tend to render opportunities for working through most religious organizations limited, at least in the short run. Most Negro churches do not have the available time, energy, personnel, or audience to become effective instruments for developing interests in world relationships. Moreover, advancement of the individual church is often a consuming interest and collaboration among churches is so infrequent that it is typically necessary to deal with each denomination and sometimes each parish in a given community separately.

However, more should be done to develop the international sophistication of the alert, educated minority among the younger clergy who are potentially interested in foreign affairs. Major obstacles spring from expectations among their members that these clergymen devote their extra energies to desegregation, from their own focus of interest on race relations, and from the minimal interest in their congregations that they participate in discussions of foreign affairs. Nevertheless, serious programs on Africa, United States policies toward Africa, religious and ethical connotations of foreign policy, and perhaps other topics might attract a number of them if they were sponsored by several of the better seminaries or divinity schools connected with universities, perhaps in collaboration with the leadership of a few atypically cosmopolitan ministerial associations under favorable conditions and with active personalized individual persuasion. Although older, less well-trained ministers sometimes regard younger, intellectually oriented clergymen with some irritation and perhaps feelings of inferiority, over the years the cosmopolitan ministers involved in such programs might exert some subtle influences on the other clergy and they, in turn, might come to regard such projects as activities worthy of their own participation.

Africa as a Point of Departure

Well-known speakers from Africa and from among American public figures connected with our policies there could engage the attention of a growing number of better-educated Negroes of influence in their communities. Increased effort should be exerted to channel knowledgeable and attractive individuals beyond the relatively few larger cities that have been their stopping points up to now. Thus, the typically rather superficial interest among middle-class Negroes should present opportunities for introducing some of them to important information and critical analyses of African problems and our relation thereto. With time more of them might be educated to the point of participating in discussions with serious scholars and other analysts of African phenomena.

Although African topics are more likely to attract educated Negro audiences than most other international subjects, discussion of Africa need not focus only on that continent per se. It should be possible, for example, to discuss impacts of Africa on international affairs, the U.N., American foreign policy, and other issues besides events in Africa itself. Or African problems, like economic development, might serve as examples of problems of industrialization and modernization of under-developed countries generally. Or, perhaps a program might deal realistically with African perceptions of Americans, Russians, and their respective foreign policies.

However, small minorities of educated Negroes in 1962 were thoughtful or potentially so about world affairs generally. It would be unfortunate if educational agencies assumed that no topics other than Africa could attract these alert individuals. Forums on China sponsored by Atlanta University, for instance, have attracted a hundred or more of this intellectual group beyond the academic community for individual sessions. Roughly forty subscriptions in New Orleans to such publications as the *New Republic*, the New York *Times* (Sunday edition), *Harper's*, and the *Atlantic* in 1959 went to individuals in Negro neighborhoods, and a larger number read international content in such periodicals in libraries and elsewhere. Interviews with some of these individuals indicate that a significant minority of them could probably be attracted to serious discussions of Latin American affairs and other subjects besides those with patent racial connotations. The few Negroes of this level of sophistication tended to resent efforts to involve them in programs which had obviously been "race angled" for their supposed benefit.

Desegregated Meetings

Much more effort should be made on a personalized basis to attract cosmopolitan whites into discussions of world affairs sponsored by organizations and institutions composed in the majority of Negroes. At least those educated Negroes who took part in such sessions would become slowly accustomed to discussing controversial international questions with friendly whites in preparation for participation in discussions with the white community generally in this field as part of the democratic process. Cosmopolitan whites would tend to voice points of view which might be different from those of most Negroes present and would help to moderate international thinking which might be distorted due to limited experience or frustrations in the local struggle for equal opportunities and desegregation. At the same time, thoughtful whites would learn of the thinking among intelligent Negroes on Africa, colonialism, and other international problems. With time the proportion of whites participating in formerly all-Negro groups could be increased and sessions held alternately in the white and Negro communities.

Desegregation of white groups examining world affairs probably constitutes a more difficult problem. Even with passage of the Civil Rights Act of 1964, there will remain, perhaps for the next several years, significant difficulties in most smaller cities in the Deep South, where such meetings would in fact be limited either to primarily Negro colleges, churches, YMCA's, YWCA's, and a few other Negro institutions, or to recently desegregated hotels, motor courts, public facilities, and like settings in which most Negroes will not for some time feel relaxed and graciously accepted. Since the prestige and general atmosphere of the locale are frequently critical factors in attracting many influential whites, many who have until recently taken part in such sessions in segregated private clubs, hotels, and the like probably would not go to sessions of comparable content in settings with Negro connotations or even in formerly all-white places recently desegregated under federal law. Although most white participants are not strong segregationists, a few sophisticated paternalist segregationists and other relatively conservative whites do take part in segregated sessions. Some of these would probably discontinue their participation or behave condescendingly toward the Negroes and elicit unfavorable reactions by them toward the sessions. Some moderates might also leave either because of their private sentiments or because they wished to avoid criticism by the white community. Indiscriminate rapid desegregation of white groups might entail loss of white participants without commensurate additions of Negroes.

Moreover, except for the small, self-assured, largely professional, intellectually awake, urban Negro group, it will probably remain more difficult to attract Negroes to predominantly white groups rather than the reverse for perhaps some years ahead. The Southern tradition is one of segregation and lack of candid communication on controversial issues across racial lines. Attempts to conduct a desegregated program on a controversial subject of relatively low interest in the Negro community in a society where most activities are still segregated would face difficulties. Even educated Negroes are likely to feel anxious about revealing their often limited knowledge and naïveté and their private thoughts on controversial questions among whites unknown to them. Negroes have learned from early childhood to be noncommittal or silent before whites or to tell them what they think the whites want to hear.

However, mere suspicion that a session is "another segregated enterprise" will virtually ensure that a considerable fraction of the better-educated, well-read, cosmopolitan Negro minority in Atlanta, Nashville, and other larger cities will not take part. Pilot efforts should be made to attract some of these Negroes to serious discussions with whites in formerly all-white universities, libraries, divinity schools, and other institutions which have already been desegregated. Although it is difficult to attract large numbers of Negroes to desegregating white groups, large numbers should not be the objective in the early stages; it should be possible to draw in two or three of the more sophisticated ministers, lawyers, teachers, or other professional-class Negroes who would be able to participate effectively with typical white members of such groups. Negroes have taken part in meetings at the University of North Carolina with prominent Africans; similar sessions should be feasible at Tulane and L.S.U. in New Orleans (a city visited by many interesting foreigners), Vanderbilt, and a number of other desegregated colleges. Such efforts should be expanded as more and more hotels and other facilities become open to Negroes and larger numbers of them become accustomed to taking part in groups composed mostly of whites. Even if only a handful of Negroes can be attracted at first, able members of their race should be continuously led to understand that these sessions are not only nominally desegregated, but that the sponsors really want them present.

Militantly Integrationist Groups

Theoretically, perhaps, Negro groups organized to accelerate desegregation should be potential vehicles for communicating world affairs. As observed previously, most of the Negroes who are active in such movements are relatively liberal about foreign affairs. However, in practice these groups are typically so preoccupied with changing the racial *status quo* that they have little time, energy, or inclination for dispassionate analysis of issues not directly related to their primary concern.

Efforts by Quaker groups to involve participants in sit-ins, freedom rides, or other activist movements in a study of Gandhian philosophy and tactics in India met with little success. They were too busy with militant action and too absorbed in the emotions of the crusade; their emotional commitment and dedication tended to limit their interest in rational, systematic analyses even when the topic was as closely related to their nonviolent techniques as Gandhi and Hindu philosophy.

Conclusion

Since Negroes are less inclined than whites to feel that domestic communism is a major menace and discussions are not inhibited by fear of agitating the racial *status quo* as they are among many segregationist whites, it should be easier to invite controversial speakers and express unconventional international ideas in private, though perhaps not in public, Negro institutions than in most white ones. The involvement of more Negroes in the foreign-policy process itself through the recent assigning of able members of that race as ambassadors, in Europe as well as in Africa and, hopefully, elsewhere in the future, should help gradually to increase interest of Negroes in world affairs.

But in most respects, other than those mentioned, general principles applicable to efforts to improve Southern Negro understanding of foreign affairs are similar to those pertinent to educational programs directed at Southern whites, except that the task is more difficult in most respects with Negroes for the historical, traditional, sociological, and other reasons already discussed. But as with whites it is preferable in most cases to work through organizations with which Negro target audiences are already familiar if not actively identified; programs to be effective should be tailored to fit the experiences and motivations of the particular Negroes in question; and content directed below the small minority of intellectually alert Negroes should perhaps be even more factual, personalized, and nonabstract than that aimed at Southern whites. Increased and improved formal education will probably do more in the long run toward broader understanding of foreign policy than communications devoted to international affairs itself. However, education in world problems should form part of the more general educational process.

As among whites, effective efforts toward resolution of the race issue are likely to do as much or more than exposure to international phenomena per se to encourage more adequate attention to world affairs among Negroes. Extension of the vote should slowly generate greater interest in public questions and more widespread exposure to political phenomena in the mass media, organizations, and face-to-face relations. The idealistic, college-educated, dynamic Negroes who are now absorbed in the struggle for equal opportunities for their race and the next generation like them should be more easily drawn to systematic, serious discussions of foreign affairs as progress in race relations becomes more assured. Improved newspapers, television content, and educational institutions in the general community will result in more responsible thought among Negroes as well as whites who pay attention to mass media coverage on foreign affairs and who study in the desegregated, formerly all-white high schools and colleges. In final analysis, improvement in the quality of thought in any major institution or group in the region is likely to contribute eventually to the general advancement of understanding of world affairs—among both Negro and white Southerners.

Those who would continue to encourage the slow change toward better comprehension of the world in which we live must separately and together attempt to work through many different channels of communication to reach diverse Southerners. If they are unable to gain an entree this year in a given community or a specified group an opening may develop in the next, or five years hence, and some able Southerners, hopefully assisted by national organizations, should be ready to make use of these opportunities.

Appendixes
Bibliography
Index

SOUTHERN NEWSPAPERS
EXAMINED

Editorials, syndicated columns, and other interpretations of international developments appearing in the month of September, 1961, were analyzed in the following Southern newspapers. Foreign news coverage and interpretation of those marked with an asterisk (*) were also examined for the period December, 1960–June, 1961.

Alexandria (La.) *Daily Town Talk*
Atlanta (Ga.) *Constitution*
Augusta (Ga.) *Chronicle*
Baton Rouge (La.) *State-Times*
Biloxi-Gulfport (Miss.) *Daily Herald*
Birmingham (Ala.) *News*
Birmingham (Ala.) *Post-Herald*
Charleston (S.C.) *Evening Post*
*Charleston (S.C.) *News and Courier*
Charlotte (N.C.) *Observer*
Chattanooga (Tenn.) *Times*
Columbia (S.C.) *Record*
*Columbia (S.C.) *State*
Columbus (Ga.) *Enquirer*
Columbus (Miss.) *Commercial Dispatch*
Gainesville (Ga.) *Times*

Greensboro (N.C.) *Daily News*
Greensboro (N.C.) *Record*
Greenville (Miss.) *Delta Democrat-Times*
Greenville (S.C.) *News*
Huntsville (Ala.) *Times*
*Jackson (Miss.) *Clarion-Ledger*
Jackson (Miss.) *State Times*
Knoxville (Tenn.) *Journal*
Knoxville (Tenn.) *News-Sentinel*
Laurel (Miss.) *Leader*
Lexington (Ky.) *Herald*
Lexington (Ky.) *Leader*
*Little Rock *Arkansas Democrat*
Little Rock *Arkansas Gazette*
McComb (Miss.) *Enterprise-Journal*
Memphis (Tenn.) *Commercial Appeal*
Memphis (Tenn.) *Press-Scimitar*
Meridian (Miss.) *Star*
Mobile (Ala.) *Press*
*Montgomery (Ala.) *Advertiser*
Nashville (Tenn.) *Banner*
Nashville *Tennessean*
Natchez (Miss.) *Democrat*
*New Orleans (La.) *Times-Picayune*
Norfolk *Virginian Pilot*
Opelousas (La.) *Times*
Opelika (Ala.) *Daily News*
Raleigh (N.C.) *News and Observer*
*Richmond (Va.) *News Leader*
*Richmond (Va.) *Times-Dispatch*
Rock Hill (S.C.) *Herald*
St. Petersburg (Fla.) *Times*
Savannah (Ga.) *Morning News*
*Shreveport (La.) *Journal*
*Shreveport (La.) *Times*
Wilmington (N.C.) *News*
Wilmington (N.C.) *Star*

SAMPLE QUESTIONS
POSED

The following questions represent issues which were probed rather than verbatim queries posed to the sample of readers of serious national publications and other cosmopolitans and individuals in leadership roles in their communities. In some cases the questions were administered practically verbatim, but conversations with the subjects were usually tailored to their particular interests and roles in their communities. The question about Adolph Eichmann was employed only on the 60 percent of the sample interviewed after January, 1961. Some of the areas indicated were not probed with a number of interviewees due to the shortness of time accorded to the interviewer.

Attitudes, Understanding, and Realism
of the Interviewee on World Affairs

1 What do you regard as the most pressing long-range international issues facing this country?
2 In general, should we allocate more, less, or about the same amount of our energies, resources, and attention to foreign issues in the coming decade as in the last?
3 Should we extend more or less capital assistance in the future than in the past to underdeveloped areas like India, Latin America, and black Africa?

4 a. Should this assistance be mainly in the form of grants or loans?
   b. Under what conditions do grants seem desirable?
5 Should we channel a larger or smaller proportion of future than of past assistance through international agencies, like the U.N.?
6 Do you think the general level of American tariffs and other import restrictions is too high, too low, or about right?
7 Should the United States increase or decrease its trade with Communist countries?
8 Should a larger, smaller, or about the same proportion of our military expenditures as in the past be allocated to foreign rather than United States armed forces?
9 Should we spend more, less, or about the same amount of money as in the past to bring foreign college students, technicians, and leaders to this country?
10 a. What should be our long-term policy relative to Formosa and and Communist China?
   b. Under what conditions should we favor Communist China's representation in the U.N.?
   c. Under what conditions would you favor recognition of Communist China by the United States?
11 What do you think the course of events will be in the Union of South Africa?
12 Should the United States place more, less, or about the same emphasis on the U.N. in the future as in recent years?
13 How do you feel about Israel's handling of Adolph Eichmann?
14 Have your views on any of these matters changed considerably since 1945?

Behavior toward Political Leaders

1 Which political leaders in America most closely approach your views on what our foreign policy should be?
2 What do you think of the congressional behavior on international matters of your Congressman and of the two Senators from this state?
3 Have you spoken to or written to any of your political representatives on any foreign matters during the last five years? On what issues?
4 Are you a member of any voluntary organizations which attempt to influence foreign-policy making? Specify.

Sources of Interviewee's Information and Interpretations of World Affairs

1 Have you read any books about world affairs in the last several years? Specify.
2 Did you tend to agree or disagree with the more important conclusions of these books?
3 What magazines or journals dedicated at least in part to international relations do you read more or less frequently?
4 Which of these magazines give the most competent analyses of international relations?
5 Which local or syndicated columnists do you consider the most thoughtful on interpretation of foreign issues?
6 Which newspapers of your acquaintance do the best job of reporting international events?
7 Which papers do you normally read for international coverage?
8 Does television or radio provide you with important information or interpretations on foreign relations?
9 Which programs on television or radio seem most competent in this field?
10 a. Have you participated in recent years in any group that holds meetings devoted to foreign affairs? Specify.
 b. If, yes: What did you think of these organizational programs? How would you improve them to expand your own and others' understanding of foreign issues?
11 Have you ever been invited to take part in international relations programs of churches, women's groups, service clubs, World Affairs Councils, Committees on Foreign Relations, AAUN's, or other groups? What were your criteria for accepting?
12 Are there individuals either in this community or outside with whom you discuss international matters and from whom you get thoughtful interpretations of foreign questions? Who?
13 Are any of these individuals university or other specialists on international relations?
14 Of the following, which play the most crucial roles in shaping your thinking on foreign policy?
——Books
——Magazines or Journals
——Newspapers
——TV

——Radio
——Voluntary Organizations (Specify)——
——Informal conversations
15 a. Have you ever entertained foreign students, or other international visitors?
b. If, yes: Would you like to do so again?
c. If, no: Would you like to?

The Interviewee's Perception of Attitudes on World Affairs in His Community

1 Do most of your acquaintances agree with your views on the majority of international questions? If no, are they more to the left
or to the right?
2 What, in general, is the pattern of attitudes in this locale toward
the issues we mentioned (who are the neo-isolationists, utopian internationalists, etc.)?
3 a. Would you describe your community as well-informed, fairly
well-informed, or poorly informed on world affairs?
b. Are there particular groups which are especially indifferent to
or shielded from exposure to balanced ideas in this field?
4 What international matters are controversial here? Are there any
which are so controversial that knowledgeable citizens hesitate to
speak out?

Role of Interviewee in Communicating World Affairs

1 Does anyone in this community consult you for interpretations of
international matters? Who? (Get names to check for influence,
interrelationship of roles of influencer and individuals influenced,
etc.)
2 In what sorts of situations does most of your communication to
others on world affairs take place? (formal meetings of organizations, chance contacts, etc.)
3 Are there local citizens who are relatively interested and informed
with respect to international relations in addition to those you have
mentioned so far? Specify.
4 How can one find the reflective, knowledgeable, and interested
minority here?
5 How large do you believe the potential audience for analytical ap-

proaches to international relations is in this locale? Is the main problem one of apathy or of emotionally biased attitudes?

6 Given the limited resources of educational agencies in international relations, what might they do over the coming years to enhance the understanding of the interested local minority and to help expand their influence among a larger proportion of the citizenry?

Genesis of Interest in International Relations

1 Were your father, mother, siblings, or other close relatives interested in international relations?
2 When and how did your concern with foreign policy develop?

Other Attitudes and Habits

1 Compared with foreign affairs, are you more, less, or about as interested in local and/or state problems?
2 What local or regional questions strike you as most crucial? (attitudes and actions on race, labor, taxes, local political phenomena, etc.)
3 What fields other than your career and public affairs receive a considerable portion of your attention? (art, literature, economics, race relations, music, etc.)

For Jewish Interviewees Only

1 Are international relations, other than with Israel, discussed in your synagogue or other primarily Jewish organizations in which you participate? Specify.
2 If Israel were omitted from consideration, do Jews here seem more, less, or about as informed about world affairs as Gentiles in similar walks of life?
3 Is there much anti-Semitism here? Among which groups?
4 Is the Jewish community relatively secure here?
5 Are there any foreign-policy issues on which local Jews, more than Gentiles, hesitate to speak out? Specify.

Demographic and Social Background

1 Sex____
2 Age (estimate)____

3 Region and Type of Community in which reared_____
4 Education
    Grammar School_____
    Some High School_____
    Completed High School_____
    Some College_____
    BA or BS_____
    Graduate or Professional Degree_____
5 Name of College_____
6 College Major_____
    Any international relations, political science, etc., in college?_____
7 Foreign experience_____
8 Occupation or occupation of spouse_____
9 Father's occupation_____
10 Estimated role in community social and communications system_____
11 Religious preference_____

OBSERVATIONS

ON SELECTED SOURCES

A major rationale for the allocation of the considerable time, energy, and other resources for the study on which this book is one of two reports was the paucity of published material based on systematic empirical research on Southern reactions to foreign affairs since the late 1940's. What little systematic research there was beyond impressionistic observations and speculations dealt primarily with Southern Congressmen.

Southern Legislators and Foreign Policy

Scholars and other serious analysts have developed a significant body of knowledge about the behavior of Southern Senators and Representatives toward foreign affairs from about the time of the entry of the United States into World War I through the passage of the initial Marshall Plan legislation and ratification of the North Atlantic Pact in the late 1940's. Rather limited, but thoughtful, attention is devoted to the impact of Southern political, social, cultural, and other factors on congressional votes on international legislation during this period by V. O. Key, Jr., in his definitive volume *Southern Politics in State and Nation* (New York: Alfred A. Knopf, 1949). George L. Grassmuck, *Sectional Biases in Congress on Foreign Policy* (Baltimore: Johns Hopkins University Press, 1951), presents comparative data on the votes of Southern versus other legislators of both parties for much of this period. Irving Howards, "The Influence of Southern Senators on American Foreign Policy" (Ph.D. dissertation, University of Wisconsin, 1955), contains useful data about contributions of Senators from the South both in committee and in the Senate as a whole, particularly during the decade preceding the early 1950's. Although focused primarily on developments in the early and middle 1950's, Paul Seabury, "The Waning of Southern 'Internationalism' " (MS in Center of International Studies, Princeton University, 1957), provides interesting insights on the earlier period as well. Also thoughtful examinations of Southern congressional behavior toward international affairs for these decades are articles by Marian D. Irish, "Foreign Policy and the South," *Journal of Politics*, X (1948), 306–26, and Alexander DeConde, "The South and Isolationism," *Journal of Southern History*, XXIV (1958), 332–46.

With respect to particular issues, material on reactions of Southern Senators to the Versailles Treaty and the League of Nations appears in Denna F. Fleming, *The United States and the League of Nations, 1918–1920* (New York: G. P. Putnam's Sons, 1932); Dewey W. Grantham, Jr., "The Southern Senators and the League of Nations, 1918–1920," *North Carolina Historical Review*, XXVI (1949), 187–205; parts of George C. Osborn, *John Sharp Williams* (Baton Rouge: Louisiana State University Press, 1943); and the previously cited articles by DeConde and Irish. Performance by Southern legislators toward the Permanent Court of International Justice is indicated in Denna F. Fleming, *The United States and the World Court* (Garden City: Doubleday, 1945); Denna F. Fleming, *The Treaty Veto of the American Senate* (New York: G. P. Putnam's Sons, 1930); and the Grassmuck volume mentioned earlier. Kenneth W. Colegrove, *The American Senate and World Peace* (New York: The Vanguard Press, 1944), describes the contributions of Southern as compared with other Senators to repeal of the Johnson and Neutrality acts, Lend-Lease, the destroyer deal, and other measures requested by President Roosevelt to support the Allies against Axis aggression in the late 1930's and early 1940's prior to the attack on Pearl Harbor. Data on Southern legislators' behavior toward international trade are available in Howard R. Smith and John Fraser Hart, "Georgia's Representatives and the Tariff," *Georgia Business*, XV, No. 3 (September, 1955), 1–9; Smith and Hart, "The American Tariff Map," *Geographical Review*, XLV (1955), 327–46; Raymond A. Bauer, Ithiel de Sola Pool, and Lewis A. Dexter, *American Business and Public Policy* (New York: Atherton Press, 1963); several passages in Key's book mentioned above; and in Howards' dissertation. Rowland T. Berthoff, "Southern Attitudes Toward Immigration, 1865–1914," *Journal of Southern History*, XVII (1951), 328–60, traces congressional voting and publicly declared postures on admission of foreigners to this country, most of which behavior continued into the interwar and post-World War II eras.

For discussions of the minority of Southern Congressmen and other influential politicians who tended more toward isolationism than the Southern norm during the years ending in the late 1940's and of the tradition and some of the forces which influenced them in this direction, see the following: Francis B. Simkins, *Pitchfork Ben Tillman* (Baton Rouge: Louisiana State University Press, 1944); Albert D. Kirwan, *Revolt of the Rednecks: Mississippi Politics, 1876–1925* (Lexington: University of Kentucky Press, 1951), especially the sections on James Vardaman; Burke Davis, "Senator Bob Reynolds: Retrospective View," *Harper's*, CLXXXVIII (1944), 362–69; Monroe Billington, "Thomas P. Gore and Oklahoma Public Opinion, 1917–1918," *Journal of Southern History*, XXVII (1961), 344–53; C. Vann Woodward, *Tom Watson, Agrarian Rebel* (New York: Macmillan, 1938); Dewey W. Grantham, Jr., *Hoke Smith and the Politics of the New South* (Baton Rouge: Louisiana State University Press, 1958); Dewey W. Grantham, Jr., "Hoke Smith and the New Freedom," in J. Carlyle Sitterson (ed.), *Studies in Southern History*, XXXIX (Chapel Hill: University of North Carolina Press, 1957); O. L. Warr, "Mr. Blease of South Carolina," *American Mercury*, XVI (1929), 25–32; W. Bradley Twitty, *Y'all Come* (Nashville: Hermitage Press, 1962); Howards' dissertation; Seabury, "The Waning of Southern 'Internationalism' "; and Grantham, "The Southern Senators and the League of Nations, 1918–1920."

However, these studies dealt primarily with a period when Southerners in the Congress were more inclined to support most international measures proposed by the President than were Congressmen from other regions, a phenomenon which changed significantly during the 1950's. It is surprising that so little research had been devoted to so significant a development prior to the work done by Charles O. Lerche, Jr., for this study and reported in his *The Uncertain South: Its Changing Patterns of Politics in Foreign Policy* (Chicago: Quadrangle Books, 1964). The brief publications by Seabury and DeConde cited above were the first to deal seriously with this change, at the time of their writings in its relatively early stages. Malcolm E. Jewell, "Evaluating the Decline of Southern Interventionism through Senatorial Roll-Call Votes," *Journal of Politics*, XXI (1959), 624–46, traces this development in the Senate with respect to foreign aid, reciprocal trade, and collective security from 1947 through 1958. Charles O. Lerche, Jr., "Southern Congressmen and the 'New Isolationism,'" *Political Science Quarterly*, LXXV (1960), 321–37, considers the roll-call votes in the House of Representatives on the Mutual Security Program between 1952 and 1960. It is interesting to note that as late as 1964 the editors of the *Journal of Politics*, the periodical of the Southern Political Science Association, devoted a special issue to "The American South: 1950–1970" without including any serious discussion of impacts of Southern politics and other Southern underlying forces on the foreign policy of the United States.

Southern International Thinking Background Factors

Although little systematic empirical research on Southern public opinion concerning world affairs has appeared in published form, there is available a considerable body of serious analyses of historical, economic, cultural, and social phenomena in the region which have influenced Southern thought and action about foreign relations. Since behavior toward international problems has been an integral part and reflection of more fundamental mores, values, attitudes, social structure, and historical experience, some familiarity with literature on these basic features of Southern society is essential in order to interpret the sources and the reasons for reactions to foreign affairs apparent in opinion surveys, mass media data, newspapers, and other indicators of international postures per se. Unfortunately, few of these studies have considered the relevance of their findings for Southern behavior toward foreign developments and American policies abroad. It is indeed difficult to narrow the list of publications on other aspects of Southern society and politics to manageable proportions since many do add something to one's ability to understand aspects of the behavior toward world affairs of one group or another within the region, although few of them deal explicitly with foreign relations.

Historical Material

Historical experience has been a major contributor to the attitudes encountered in the South on international as well as domestic issues, particularly among the more traditionalist inhabitants of this most traditionally oriented section of the United States. Because the author is not a professional historian and cannot pretend to be a competent critical judge of the plethora of books, monographs, and articles published in the highly specialized field of Southern history, mention is made here only of selected publications which seem particularly relevant to phenomena underlying Southern reactions to the world outside the United States.

Psychological and cultural legacies of the antebellum period continue to influence significantly the thought of most Southerners, particularly those in black-belt and plantation sections. Clement Eaton's *Freedom of Thought in the Old South* (Durham: Duke University Press, 1940), traces the accelerating social pressures against freedom of discussion and analysis, initially on race relations but gradually in public affairs in general, as extra-Southern criticism and agitation against slavery mounted in the period following 1830. This phenomenon is comparable in a number of respects with that apparent since the Supreme Court decision on school segregation in 1954, as indicated, for example, in James W. Silver, *Mississippi: The Closed Society* (New York: Harcourt, Brace and World, 1964). Other thoughtful discussions of the cessation of critical thought during the antebellum period due primarily to fears of racial unrest appear in Clement Eaton, "The Resistance of the South to Northern Radicalism," *New England Quarterly*, VIII (1935), 215–31; Charles S. Sydnor, *The Development of Southern Sectionalism, 1819–1848* (Baton Rouge: Louisiana State University Press, 1948); Introduction to Harvey Wish (ed.) *Ante-Bellum: Writings of George Fitzhugh and Hinton Rowan Helper on Slavery* (New York: Capricorn Books, 1960); T. Harry Williams, *Romance and Realism in Southern Politics* (Athens: University of Georgia Press, 1961); Rollin G. Osterweis, *Romanticism and Nationalism in the Old South* (New Haven: Yale University Press, 1949); William E. Dodd, *The Cotton Kingdom* (New Haven: Yale University Press, 1921); Clement Eaton, *The Growth of Southern Civilization* (New York: Harper and Bros., 1961); Benjamin B. Kendrick and Alex M. Arnett, *The South Looks at Its Past* (Chapel Hill: University of North Carolina Press, 1935); Henry Savage, Jr., *Seeds of Time: The Background of Southern Thinking* (New York: Henry Holt and Co., 1959); and C. Vann Woodward, *The Burden of Southern History* (Baton Rouge: Louisiana State University Press, 1960). For contrasts with the earlier, more intellectually free atmosphere in the older parts of the South, see, in addition to most of the above, Thomas P. Abernethy, *The South in the New Nation, 1789–1819* (Baton Rouge: Louisiana State University Press, 1961).

Several of these volumes, particularly Eaton, *The Growth of Southern Civilization;* Kendrick and Arnett, *The South Looks at Its Past;* Savage, *Seeds of Time;* and Woodward, *The Burden of Southern His-*

tory, examine the impacts of Reconstruction and later Southern experience toward reinforcement of anxiety about open discussion of controversial issues. Also in this connection see William H. Nicholls, *Southern Tradition and Regional Progress* (Chapel Hill: University of North Carolina Press, 1960); Hodding Carter, *The Angry Scar* (Garden City: Doubleday, 1959); Wilma Dykeman and James Stokely, *Neither Black Nor White* (New York: Rinehart, 1957); and Wilbur J. Cash, *The Mind of the South* (Garden City: Doubleday, 1956).

The volume by Osterweis cited above examines the content of the antebellum planter-class tradition, the literature they read (and did not read), and their inclinations toward chivalry, gracious manners, romantic feelings, and hedonistic unreality rather than logical analysis and empiricism. Grace Landrum, "Sir Walter Scott and His Literary Rivals in the Old South," *American Literature*, II (1930), 256–76; and R. M. Weaver, "Southern Chivalry and Total War," *Sewanee Review*, LIX (1945), 267–78, likewise provide helpful insights into this subject. Weaver's article also deals with the strength of the martial spirit in Southern tradition. However, John Hope Franklin's *The Militant South* (Cambridge: Harvard University Press, 1956), is the most comprehensive and penetrating study on the development of interest in and enthusiasm for military life and its values.

The thesis that the defeat of 1865, Reconstruction, and the following experience of frustration, immobilism, and paucity of economic development and "progress" in general engendered widespread general pessimism, disbelief in the efficacy of rationality and in the possibility of social and individual improvement, and conservatism about the nature of man and his institutions is developed in C. Vann Woodward, *The Burden of Southern History;* C. Vann Woodward, *Origins of the New South, 1877–1913* (Baton Rouge: Louisiana State University Press, 1951), especially pp. 107–11; T. Harry Williams, *Romance and Realism in Southern Politics;* Robert Penn Warren, *The Legacy of the Civil War* (New York: Random House, 1961); and Louis D. Rubin, Jr., "Southern Literature: The Historical Image," in Louis D. Rubin, Jr., and Robert D. Jacobs (eds.), *South: Modern Southern Literature in Its Cultural Setting* (Garden City: Doubleday, 1961).

Much of the historical research until relatively recently which focused on the antebellum era dealt primarily with the planter and related commercial elites so influential on the economic, political, and social life of the region. Ulrich B. Phillips offers largely favorable descriptions of the attitudes of the antebellum planter class and of their way of life in his *Life and Labor in the Old South* (Boston: Little,

Brown, and Co., 1951), and in his "Plantations with Slave Labor and Free," *American Historical Review*, XXX (1925), 738–53. William E. Dodd's view of this group is less sympathetic and more critical; see, for instance, his "Social Philosophy of the Old South," *American Journal of Sociology*, XXIII (1918), 735–46. Roger W. Shugg, *Origins of Class Struggle in Louisiana* (Baton Rouge: Louisiana State University Press, 1939), deals competently with the agrarian elite and their influential urban counterparts in New Orleans. Joseph G. Treagle, Jr., "Early New Orleans Society: A Reappraisal," *Journal of Southern History*, XVIII (1952), 20–36, presents what is probably a relatively realistic description of the values and actions of the upper and middle classes of the Crescent City prior to the Civil War. Albert A. Fossier, *New Orleans: The Glamour Period, 1800–1840* (New Orleans: Pelican Publishing Co., 1957), offers a more laudatory, romanticized image of the Creole leadership stratum in the first two generations of the nineteenth century. Grace E. King, *Creole Families of New Orleans* (New York: Macmillan, 1921), describes the births, marriages, accomplishments, and other aspects in the lives of successive generations of New Orleans old Creole families, largely from a sympathetic frame of reference. Herbert Asbury's *The French Quarter* (New York: Garden City Publishing Co., 1936), contains a fascinating discussion of the antecedents of current New Orleans society and attitudes and action, covering the spectrum of classes from mighty to low. Hodding Carter's *Lower Mississippi* (New York: Farrar and Rinehart, 1942), also includes interesting sections on the leadership elements of antebellum Louisiana.

The least privileged whites in the pre–Civil War South (as well as in the later period) are competently examined by the Dutch social scientist A. J. N. Den Hollander in his "The Tradition of the 'Poor Whites,' " in W. T. Couch (ed.), *Culture in the South* (Chapel Hill: University of North Carolina Press, 1934). Interesting reading on the Southern "common man" prior to the Civil War, as well as on other segments of Southern society, is the first-hand account of a perceptive visitor to the region, Frederick Law Olmsted, *A Journey in the Back Country* (New York: Mason Bros., 1860).

The amount of serious material on the postbellum South is considerably larger and more diverse. Nicholls' volume cited earlier deals with the evolution of industrialization of the South and the conflicting values and behavior of Southerners identified with the New South vis-à-vis those still attached to the Old South. C. Vann Woodward's *Origins of the New South, 1877–1913*, discusses in detail the evolution of the increasingly influential commercial, manufacturing, and professional class in the growing Southern urban areas and their impacts on Southern social and political thought and action. Also relevant to this and other aspects of the period following the defeat of 1865 is C. Vann Woodward's *Reunion and Reaction* (Garden City: Doubleday, 1956). More general works worthy of attention include Cash, *The Mind of the South;* Kendrick and Arnett, *The South Looks at Its Past;* Savage, *Seeds of Time;* John Samuel Ezell, *The South Since 1865* (New York: Macmillan, 1963); William T. Polk, *Southern Accent: From Uncle Remus to Oak Ridge* (New York: William Morrow and Co., 1953); James McBride Dabbs, *The Southern Heritage* (New York: Alfred A. Knopf, 1958); Virginius Dabney, *Below the Potomac* (New York and London: Appleton-Century Co., 1942); Thomas D. Clark, *The Emerging South* (New York: Oxford University Press, 1961); and Rudolf Heberle, "The Changing of Social Stratification in the South," *Social Forces,* XXXVIII (1959), 42–50.

Southern Fiction and Drama

Perhaps as suggestive of the mores and mental processes of the diverse South as historical studies and social science research on more recent Southern behavior are some of the novels, plays, and poems by the more perceptive literary figures of the region. Whereas systematic empirical social research for the most part has not been well developed in the South, contributions by Southern authors to serious literature, more often than not focused on the Southern milieu, have been considerably, greater than should be expected from the relatively underdeveloped nature of the region in other spheres. Their works do not, of course, provide balanced, logical analyses of personality variables, social organization, and sociopolitical behavior complete with the degree of incidence of particular thought patterns and actions in diverse Southern groups; characterizations are frequently exaggerated over what might be discovered by competent social research devoted to similar individuals and social settings. However, able Southern writers, historians, and social scientists seem to agree on many basic features of Southern society and thought, and in some respects the litterateurs offer more sensitive, penetrating portrayals than do more empirical and systematic researchers.

Many of William Faulkner's characters, for example, seem in their essence to ring true for the Southern environments in which his plots are based. Thomas Sutpen of *Absalom, Absalom!* (New York: Random House, 1936), appears, albeit in overstated form, a prototype of the mentality and social behavior of many of the *nouveaux riches* who emerged from cotton production in the newer plantation districts shortly prior to the Civil War. Their counterparts in the early part of the twentieth century—the ambitious, bright, but culturally unsophisticated and amoral Snopeses who "did well"; the various personalities among the socially more secure, older family Sartorises and Compsons; the second generation of prosperity embodied in Sutpen's son; the morally upright, well-educated, cosmopolitan, but rather ineffectual Gavin Stevens—son of older social position and influence; and the varied characters of lesser social standing in the Yoknapatawpha County series constitute some of the most penetrating characterizations available of inhabitants of the Deep South, manifesting traits which other thoughtful Southerners observe in personalities they have known. *Absalom, Absalom!; The Sound and the Fury* (New York: Jonathan Cape and Harrison Smith, 1931); and *As I Lay Dying* (New York: Jonathan Cape and Harrison Smith, 1930), are the most useful from this frame of reference. However, also worth reading as portrayals of a spectrum of Southern personality types are *Sartoris* (New York: Harcourt, Brace, and Co., 1929); *Sanctuary* (New York: Jonathan Cape and Harrison Smith, 1931); *Light in August* (New York: Harrison Smith and Robert Haas, 1932); *The Hamlet* (New York: Random House, 1940), with its priceless description of the difference between Southerners and Northerners; *Requiem for a Nun* (New York: Random House, 1951); *Intruder in the Dust* (New York: Random House, 1948); *The Town* (New York: Random House, 1957); and *The Mansion* (New York: Random House, 1959).

John Faulkner's *Dollar Cotton* (New York: Harcourt, Brace, and Co., 1942), provides the best single introduction in print to the cultural background of the society of the Delta, back from the Mississippi River in the canebrake, which was developed shortly before the turn of the century through roughly the 1920's. Otis Towne and his family are probably fairly accurate characterizations of a significant proportion of self-made men, their women, and their intellectually unsophisticated, hedonistic offspring who emerged during this period. Several of the plays by Tennessee Williams deal with personalities in or from the Delta of a more recent period, roughly the 1930's and 1940's. The gushing, status-conscious, materialistic, and socially insensitive mother in the Wingfield family, wife of a good-for-nothing hell-of-a-feller who deserted her, seems to incorporate several of the unfortunate features of a number of similar real females of comparable age and social origins from both the Delta and the Deep South generally; *The Glass Menagerie* (New York: Random House, 1945). Big Daddy in

Cat on a Hot Tin Roof (New York: New American Library, 1955), reminds one of some of the new generation (the one following the Snopeses of William Faulkner) of parvenus from cotton culture and other ventures. Suspicion of the "outsider," particularly the foreigner of other than Anglo-Saxon ancestry, is forcefully presented (along with other aspects of life in the heavily Negro rural and small-town South) in *Baby Doll*, a film adaptation of *Twenty-Seven Wagons Full of Cotton* and *The Long Stay Cut Short*, two one-act plays (New York: New Directions, 1956). *Orpheus Descending* (New York: New Directions, 1956), is another Williams' play worth examining for its insights about Delta society (and to a considerable degree other heavily Negro and agrarian settings).

Harper Lee offers in her more or less autobiographical *To Kill a Mockingbird* (New York: J. B. Lippincott Co., 1960), a thoughtful image of life and people in the somewhat older plantation section of the Black Belt, extending from east central Mississippi through central Alabama and Georgia.

Much of the earlier fiction focused on the traditional upper classes of plantation and related ancestry was of the persuasion of Sir Walter Scott, more romantic and chivalric than analytic and realistic, more laudatory and sentimental than critical—such as the novels of Thomas Nelson Page. More penetrating and generally illuminating are the portrayals of Virginia gentry and fallen gentry during the latter part of the nineteenth and the first part of the twentieth centuries by Ellen Glasgow; for example, *Miller of Old Church* (Garden City: Double-day, Page, 1911); *One Man in His Time* (Garden City: Doubleday, Page, 1922); *They Stooped to Folly* (Garden City: Doubleday, Doran, 1929); and *The Sheltered Life* (Garden City: Doubleday, Doran, 1932).

George Washington Cable, though not himself, as was Miss Glasgow, a member of the traditional class about which he wrote, has provided similarly insightful impressions of the life and mentality of the Creole upper and middle classes of French and (to a much lesser extent) Spanish ancestry in New Orleans and environs. Although Cable wrote of the nineteenth-century Creoles, his observations about some of them appear to apply, though in much attenuated form, to a number of current New Orleanians and other southern Louisiana residents of similar ancestry. See, for instance, Cable's *Old Creole Days* (New York: Charles Scribner's Sons, 1879); *The Grandissimes: A Story of Creole Life* (New York: Charles Scribner's Sons, 1880); *The Creoles of Louisiana* (New York: Charles Scribner's Sons, 1884); *Strange True Stories of Louisiana* (New York: Charles Scribner's Sons, 1893); and *Creoles and Cajuns* (Garden City: Doubleday, 1959). William Faulkner's diverse Compsons and Sartorises remain among the most effective portrayals of Anglo-Saxon Deep South gentry in American literature.

Social Research and Other Nonfiction on the Various Recent Souths

Although dated in a number of respects by developments in the last several decades, Howard W. Odum, *Southern Regions of the United States* (Chapel Hill: University of North Carolina Press, 1936); Rupert B. Vance, *Human Geography of the South* (Chapel Hill: University of North Carolina Press, 1932); and Rupert B. Vance, *All These People: The Nation's Resources in the South* (Chapel Hill: University of North Carolina Press, 1945), continue to provide helpful statistical and other background data on diversity within the region. Several of the general volumes mentioned previously, particularly Cash's *The Mind of the South*, Ezell's *The South Since 1865*, Clark's *The Emerging South*, Savage's *Seeds of Time*, and Dabbs's *The Southern Heritage*, include generally valid comparative comments about subcultural underpinnings of differential behavior toward public questions within the former Confederacy. The most valuable and generally informative single volume on comparative political thought and action in the South is Key's *Southern Politics in the State and Nation*. Although his generalizations are based on research completed in the late 1940's, before the Supreme Court decisions on school segregation and other developments particularly important within the South, most of Key's observations apply with but relatively limited amendment to the early 1960's.

Continuing differences in attitudes and actions toward economic, social, and other aspects of public affairs within the South between rural (particularly plantation section) elites and the industrial, mercantile, managerial, and professional classes of the growing cities are discussed in Nicholls' *Southern Tradition and Regional Progress* cited above. Nicholls' comparisons of these two groups are based on his extensive reading of existing literature about the South, on census and other statistics, and his long, intimate experience in the region as a native Southerner, rather than on interviews or other direct indicators of the views of a broad sample of the groups concerned. Moreover, Nicholls devotes no attention to the comparative thinking of these two leadership elements about foreign policy.

Several excellent empirical studies have been conducted on plantation societies. Allison Davis, Burleigh B. Gardner, and Mary R. Gardner, *Deep South* (Chicago: University of Chicago Press, 1940), reports on

an intensive anthropological study in the mid-1930's of an older plantation society near the Mississippi River, including the county seat and
market town and its agrarian environs. Morton Rubin, *Plantation
County* (Chapel Hill: University of North Carolina Press, 1951), presents the findings of an anthropological investigation in 1947–48 in a
section of the Deep Southern Black Belt which was initially developed
during the two generations immediately prior to the Civil War—the
same locale as the Plantation County in the present volume. Rubin's
observations remained generally applicable with some amendment in
1960. Paul A. Miller *et al., Community Health Action* (East Lansing:
Michigan State College Press, 1953), includes the results of research on
a partly plantation and partly piedmont county on the border of the
Black Belt, also settled between 1820 and the secession. John P. Dollard,
Caste and Class in a Southern Town (New Haven: Yale University
Press, 1937), and Hortense Powdermaker, *After Freedom: A Cultural
Study in the Deep South* (New York: Viking Press, 1939), make available the findings by the two authors in their anthropological study
—the former of the white, the latter of the Negro community—during
the mid-1930's in a cotton plantation milieu in the central Mississippi
Delta relatively distant from the Mississippi River and developed since
roughly 1890. Except for introduction of mechanical cotton pickers
and other farm mechanization, the attendant decrease in Negro labor,
and the development of several small industries, this social system appeared very similar to that of Delta County examined in the World
Peace Foundation study for this present volume over twenty-five years
later.

Three scholarly empirical studies, conducted in the late 1940's
and early 1950's, have been published on a community the authors
fictitiously termed "Kent," the same as the town by that name in the
present volume. Part of the local tradition has been one of plantations
established in the late 1700's, another has been the small-farm agriculture
of the Piedmont, and more recently Kent has acquired textile and carpet mills. The unfortunately still unpublished Ph.D. dissertation of
Ralph C. Patrick, Jr., "A Cultural Approach to Social Stratification"
(Harvard University, 1953), is the most competent (and one of the
extremely few) face-to-face studies of Old South upper-class versus
New South middle-class values, attitudes, and overt behavior in existence. Consistent with the present author's impressions, Patrick discovered that traditionalist agrarian mores and thought have continued
to exert a significant influence on the thinking of a considerable fraction
of current descendants of the antebellum agrarian leadership—ideas such

as those expressed in Twelve Southerners (The Nashville Fugitives or Agrarians), *I'll Take My Stand: The South and the Agrarian Tradition* (New York: Harper Bros., 1930); Donald Davidson, *Still Rebels, Still Yankees* (Baton Rouge: Louisiana State University Press, 1957); Edd Winfield Parks, *Segments of Southern Thought* (Athens: University of Georgia Press, 1938); Louis D. Rubin, Jr., and James J. Kilpatrick (eds.), *The Lasting South* (Chicago: Henry Regnery, 1957); the works of Thomas Nelson Page; and, in more moderate tone, William Alexander Percy's autobiographical *Lanterns on the Levee* (New York: Alfred A. Knopf, 1944).

John Kenneth Morland's *Millways of Kent* (Chapel Hill: University of North Carolina Press, 1958), reports on extensive interviews and observations in 1948–49 within the community of mill workers physically and psychologically isolated from the upper and middle classes examined by Patrick. Together with Morland's unpublished report on his interviews a decade later with some of the same mill people and their offspring presented before the American Sociological Association in 1959, *Millways of Kent* comprises the most thorough study of Southern textile workers and of the relative slowness of change in their social milieu and behavior since World War II. Also enlightening with respect to the culture of mill workers are two articles by the former Director of Research of the United Textile Workers Union of America, Solomon Barkin, based on his long and intimate experience with this group, "The Personality Profile of Southern Textile Workers," *Labor Law Journal*, XI, No. 6 (1960), 457–72, and "Southern Views of Unions," *Labor Today* (Fall, 1962).

Hylan Lewis, *Blackways of Kent* (Chapel Hill: University of North Carolina Press, 1955), is a work of similarly high quality on the Negro society of Kent.

There have been some empirical studies of the processes of recent farm mechanization and of post-World War II industrialization of the small-town and rural South and their impacts on social organization and individual attitudes. Excellent work has been performed in this field by the able rural sociologist Harold F. Kaufman and his associates at Mississippi State University, as reported in Sheridan T. Maitland and George L. Wilber, *Industrialization in Chickasaw County, Mississippi: A Study of Plant Workers* (State University Agricultural Experiment Station, Bull. 566 [Starkville, Miss., 1958]), and several unpublished reports available at the Department of Sociology and Rural Life at Mississippi State University. Alvin L. Bertrand and his colleagues at Louisiana State University have performed systematic research on similar phenomena within both southern and northern Louisiana, such as Paul H. Price, *Louisiana's Rural Population at Mid-Century* (Baton Rouge: Agricultural Experiment Station, Louisiana State University, 1959); Alvin L. Bertrand and Harold W. Osborne, "Rural Industrialization: A Situational Analysis," *Rural Sociology*, XXV (1960), 387–93; Bertrand and Osborne, "The Impact of Industrialization on a Rural Community," *Journal of Farm Economics*, XLI (1959), 1127–37; Bertrand and Osborne, *Rural Industrialization in a Louisiana Community* (Louisiana State University Agricultural Experiment Station, Bull. 524 [Baton Rouge, 1959]); and Alvin L. Bertrand, *Older Youth in Rural Louisiana* (Louisiana State University Experiment Station, Bull. 478 [Baton Rouge, 1953]). See also Daniel E. Alleger, *Agricultural Activities of Industrial Workers and Retirees: A Survey of Small Agricultural Holdings in an Industrial Area of Florida* (Florida Agricultural Extension Service, Bull. 582 [Gainesville, 1953]).

John C. Campbell's authoritative *The Southern Highlander and His Homeland* (New York: Russel Sage Foundation, 1921), has recently been brought up to date by a major social study of the Appalachian Mountain section reported in Thomas R. Ford (ed.), *The Southern Appalachian Region* (Lexington: University of Kentucky Press, 1962). Also useful to those who would understand mountain society is Marion Pearsall's *Little Smoky Ridge* (Tuscaloosa: University of Alabama Press, 1959), a report on an anthropological examination of a relatively isolated rural community in this subregion.

A handy summary of continuing differences between northern and southern Louisiana and within the latter is provided in T. Lynn Smith and Homer L. Hitt, *The People of Louisiana* (Baton Rouge: Louisiana State University Press, 1952). For the social structure, culture, and individual inclinations of inhabitants of rural and small-town southern Louisiana and their historical antecedents, see the Reverend Edward J. Kammer, *A Socio-Economic Survey of Marshdwellers of Four Southeastern Louisiana Parishes* (Washington, D.C.: Catholic University of America Press, 1941); T. Lynn Smith, "An Analysis of Rural Social Organization Among the French-Speaking People of Southern Louisiana," *Journal of Farm Economics*, XVI (1934), 680–88; Vernon J. Parenton, "The Rural French-Speaking People of Quebec and South Louisiana: A Comparative Study of Social Structure and Organization with Emphasis on the Role of the Catholic Church" (Ph.D. dissertation, Harvard University, 1948); Parenton, "Notes on the Social Organization of a French Village in South Louisiana," *Social Forces*, XVII (1938), 73–82; Parenton and T. Lynn Smith, "Acculturation Among the Louisiana French," *American Journal of Sociology*, XLIV (1938), 355–64; Roland J. Pellegrin, "A Sociological Analysis of Pointe Coupée Parish" (Master's thesis, Louisiana State University, 1949); Alvin L. Bertrand, *The Many Louisianas*, Louisiana State University Agricultural Experiment Station, Bull. 496 [Baton Rouge, 1955]); Hodding Carter and Anthony Ragusin, *Gulf Coast Country* (New York: Duell, Sloan, Pearce, 1951); and Carter, *Lower Mississippi*.

The roles of the various Protestant denominations and sects in the lives of Mississippians—similar in most respects among Protestant Southerners elsewhere in small communities and rural sections—have been examined by social scientists at Mississippi State University: Harold F. Kaufman, *Mississippi Churches: A Half Century of Change* (Mississippi State University, Social Science Research Center, Bull. 12 [Starkville, 1959]); Harold F. Kaufman et al., *Mississippi Churches: A Statistical Supplement* (Mississippi State University, Social Science Research Center, Bull. 12-S [Starkville, 1959]); Raymond Payne, "Some Comparisons of Participation in Rural Mississippi, Kentucky, Ohio, Illinois, and New York," *Rural Sociology*, XVIII (1953), 171–72; and Raymond Payne and Harold F. Kaufman, "Organization Activities of Rural People in Mississippi" (Mississippi Agricultural Station, Circular 189 [Starkville, 1953]). For research on similar aspects of Protestant religious behavior in rural and small-town Louisiana, see Bertrand and Osborne, "The Impact of Industrialization on a Rural Community," and Bertrand and Osborne, *Rural Industrialization in a Louisiana Community*. Harold F. Kaufman's *Religious Organizations in Kentucky* (Kentucky Agricultural Experiment Station, Bull. 524 [Lexington, 1948]), presents some general material on Kentucky churches. For the church-connected behavior of residents of the Appalachians, see Thomas R. Ford, "Status, Residence, and Fundamentalist Religious Beliefs in the Southern Appalachians," *Social Forces*, XXXIX (1960), 41–49, and Earl D. C. Brewer, "Religion and the Churches," in Ford (ed.), *The Southern Appalachian Region*, cited above. Liston Pope, *Millhands and Preachers* (New Haven: Yale University Press, 1942), as well as the publications of Patrick, Morland, Morton Rubin, and Ford mentioned heretofore discuss stratification by education, social status, ideological orientations, and other variables among different churches.

Most of Pope's observations in Gastonia in the late 1930's about the sociopolitical attitudes of Protestant ministers and their relationships with the local power structure and their own congregations seem to apply with some modifications to many mill towns of the early 1960's. Although Presbyterian, Methodist, and even Southern Baptist clergymen of the current generation have been more socially sophisticated and analytical and less provincial and conservative about public issues than their counterparts of the late 1930's, significant residues of the patterns of thought, influence, and action described by Pope remain.

Unfortunately, no recent face-to-face study of the social and political thinking of Southern Protestant ministers is available. John Lee Eighmy in his Ph.D. dissertation, "The Social Conscience of Southern Baptists from 1900 to the Present as Reflected in Their Organized Life" (University of Missouri, 1959), analyzed the continuing arguments over the years between the still prevailing social and political conservatives—typically also conservative on theology—and those who have advocated greater concern and action for the Southern Baptists in the social and other problems of their communities, the South, the nation, and the world. Eighmy noted slowly broadened influence of the latter vis-à-vis the former but still potent opposition to further development toward more responsible social concern. Thomas F. Pettigrew and Ernest Q. Campbell, *Christians in Crisis* (Washington, D.C.: Public Affairs Press, 1959), reports on the authors' interviews with Protestant and Jewish clergymen in Little Rock during the school desegregation crisis there. Although their study dealt primarily with the attitudes and actions of these ministers and rabbis with respect to local race relations, most of their generalizations about these men apply with some amendment to public affairs generally. David Danzig, "The Radical Right and the Rise of the Fundamentalist Minority," *Commentary*, XXXIII (1962), 291–98; Alan F. Westin, "The John Birch Society: 'Radical Right' and 'Extreme Left' in Political Context of Post-World War II–1962," in Daniel Bell (ed.), *The Radical Right* (Garden City: Doubleday, 1963); and David Riesman, "The Intellectuals and Discontented Classes: Some Further Reflections," in Bell, *The Radical Right*, discuss the relationships between religious fundamentalism and ultraconservative political behavior, with some limited attention to foreign policy aspects.

The standard history of the Roman Catholic Church in the Southern area where it has long been influential is Roger Baudier, *The Catholic Church in Louisiana* (New Orleans: A. W. Hyatt Co., 1937). This volume and Hodding Carter's *Lower Mississippi* describe some of the tone of Catholicism in New Orleans and its environs from the early French period.

Joseph H. Fichter, S.J., in his *Social Relations in the Urban Parish* (Chicago: University of Chicago Press, 1954), and in his *Dynamics of a City Church* (Chicago: University of Chicago Press, 1951), Volume I of *Southern Parish*, reports on one of the most perceptive sociological studies in existence of religious institutions and their interactions with their communicants. The Reverend Fichter examined through extensive interviews the communicants of a New Orleans ecclesiastical parish composed of a heterogeneous sample of ethnic groups comparable with the Catholic population of New Orleans generally. The major focus of these two volumes is the behavior of these New Orleanians toward their church and clergy and the activities conducted thereby, but they also provide insightful observations relevant to the actual and potential impacts of the Church in questions of general public concern. For a more or less comparative empirical study of a Bronx ecclesiastical parish, see Joseph B. Schuyler, S.J., *Northern Parish: A Sociological and Pastoral Study* (Chicago: Loyola University Press, 1960). Comparative data on a primarily middle-class Chicago parish is presented by the Reverend Andrew M. Greeley, "Some Information on the Present Situation of American Catholics," *Social Order*, XIII (April, 1963).

No empirical study of quality comparable with that of the Reverend Fichter's has been conducted on Catholics elsewhere in the South. Some material on the interaction of the Church and its clergy in rural and small-town southern Louisiana with local citizens of varying attachment to the Catholic religion appears in the Reverend Kammer's volume and in Parenton's doctoral dissertation mentioned above. "Attitudes and Opinions on Race Relations," an unpublished manuscript for the no-longer existing Catholic Committee of the South by the Reverend Raymond Bernard, S.J. (1958), reports on interviews by the Reverend Bernard among priests and laymen in small towns and rural sections of southern Louisiana. The Reverend Bernard describes a milieu of prevailing opposition to liberalization of race relations among the laity, some sentiments of similar orientation among a significant segment of the clergy (particularly among older priests of Southern background), and formidable obstacles to racial change by the Church supported by a small, largely quiet, minority of local equalitarians.

The work of William T. Liu, especially his Ph.D. dissertation, "A Study of the Social Integration of Catholic Migrants in a Southern Community" (Florida State University, 1958), comprises virtually all the systematically gathered empirical material available on the increasing Catholic minority in the predominantly Anglo-Saxon South. A forthcoming volume by the Reverend Joseph H. Fichter, S.J., reports on replies to questionnaires about a range of social and public questions, including foreign affairs, completed by a national sample of approximately two thousand parish priests and an equal number of laymen active within their parishes. It contains some comparative replies of Southern clergy and laity versus their counterparts in other regions.

Extremely little of the rather voluminous social research on American Jewry, primarily by Jewish social scientists, has devoted any attention to Southern Jews. Southern Jewry seems to remain terra incognita to sociologists and others interested in Jews in the United States. No empirical study has been conducted of attitudes and overt behavior of Southern Jews, or of Jews in even one Southern community, toward major public issues (other than race relations) of current interest, including foreign affairs. Moreover, the number of Southern Jews in national samples of AIPO, Roper, SRC, and NORC surveys has been so small that replies cannot be treated statistically even when responses by Southern Jewish interviewees to similar queries on several surveys are combined. Published knowledge about Jews in the South consists of a handful of biographies, autobiographies, and historical works (mostly of dubious quality), and the results of interviews in several Southern Jewish communities.

The most competent historical study devoted in considerable part to Southern Jews is Bertram W. Korn, *American Jews and the Civil War* (Philadelphia: The Jewish Publication Society of America, 1951). A more popularly written but less profound and generally thoughtful volume is Harry Simonhoff, *Jewish Participants in the Civil War* (New York: Arco Publishing Co., 1963). Interesting and generally helpful in understanding Southern Jewry in the antebellum South is Bertram W. Korn, "Jews and Negro Slavery in the Old South, 1789–1865," *Publication of the American Jewish Historical Society*, L (1961), 151–201.

The interested reader can ascertain a good deal about the history, composition, and ways of life of the Charleston Jewish community (the oldest and at one time the largest in the South) from published sources. Barnett A. Elzas, influential Charleston rabbi at the turn of the century, has provided a description of the development of the South Carolina Jewish community from the first Jews to arrive in the seventeenth century through the end of the nineteenth century in his *The Jews of South Carolina* (Philadelphia: J. B. Lippincott, 1905). Likewise interesting for impressions of the cultural antecendents which have exerted so much influence on the present generation among Jews in traditionalist Charleston are two brief publications by Thomas J. Tobias, "Joseph Tobias of Charleston: 'Linguister,' " *Publication of the American Jewish Historical Society*, XLIX (1959), 33–38; and *The Hebrew Orphan Society of Charleston, S.C.* (Charleston: published by the Society, 1957). Although not a trained historian, Mr. Tobias is a thoughtful and generally charming gentleman highly sensitive to the local cultural atmosphere, both current and historical, whose ancestors have been influential in both the Jewish and the general Charleston communities for two centuries. Charles L. Reznikoff and Uriah Z. Engelman, *The Jews of Charleston* (Philadelphia: The Jewish Publication Society of America, 1950), and Uriah Z. Engelman, "The Jewish Population of Charleston: What Sustained Its Growth and Prevented Its Decline?" *Jewish Social Studies*, XIII (1951), 195–210, together provide historical insights and offer data on the composition and character of Charleston Jewry through the late 1940's. Louis D. Rubin, Jr., in his *Golden Weather* (New York: Atheneum, 1961), describes life and interrelationships among the various strata of Jews and Gentiles in Charleston during the 1930's through his own childhood experiences as a member of a "Fine Old Jewish Family" of Charleston.

Some historical material has been published on the other major Jewish community in the South of antebellum influence and tradition, that of New Orleans and environs. Leonard Reissman, in his report on an empirical study of New Orleans Jewry in the late 1950's, "The New Orleans Jewish Community," *Jewish Journal of Sociology*, IV (1962), 110–23, extracts some historical information from other sources, including several unpublished ones. Several of the biographies of Judah P. Benjamin consider his relationships as a Sephardic Jew married to a Catholic Creole with the local Gentile leadership element and some of his personal problems as a conservative Jewish Senator from Louisiana and later as a Jewish member of the Confederate cabinet. See especially S. I. Neiman's *Judah Benjamin* (Indianapolis and New York: Bobbs-Merrill, 1963), which devotes considerable attention to Benjamin's personal experiences and anxieties due to his Jewish origins. See also Pierce Butler, *Judah P. Benjamin* (Philadelphia: G. W. Jacobs and Co., 1907); Rollin Osterweis, *Judah P. Benjamin: Statesman of the Lost Cause* (New York: G. P. Putnam's Sons, 1933); Robert D. Meade, *Judah P. Benjamin: Confederate Statesman* (London: Oxford University Press, 1943); and Martin Rywell, *Judah Benjamin* (Ashville: The Stephens Press, 1948). A popular, largely chronological, and rather pedestrian account of the evolution of Jewish groups of Louisiana is Leo Shpall, *The Jews of Louisiana* (New Orleans: Steeg Publishing Co., 1936). See also Shpall's "Early Jewish Philanthropy in New Orleans," *Jewish Forum*, XXXVIII, Nos. 1, 3, and 7 (1955), 14, 52 and 114–15.

Julian B. Feibelman, *A Social and Economic Study of the New Orleans Jewish Community* (Philadelphia: The Jewish Publication Society

of America, 1941), reports on an empirical study completed in the late
1930's by the thoughtful rabbi of the leading Reform temple in the
city. More recent survey data is available in the article by Reissman
cited earlier and in his more detailed presentation in mimeographed
form, "Profile of a Community: A Sociological Study of the New
Orleans Jewish Community" (Jewish Federation of New Orleans,
1958). John Rosen, "A Study of Leadership in the New Orleans Jewish
Community" (Master's thesis, Tulane University, 1960), based on the
author's interviews among influential Jews of diverse social origins,
reports a tendency of Jews of several generations of affluence and social
standing to devote their energies to activities in the general New Orleans community and to leave leadership of primarily Jewish groups
and programs to "newer" elements of more recent prosperity and
influence—an inclination which seems to apply as well to other older
Jewish communities in the South. For a factual description of New
Orleans Jewry of the post-World War II era, see Benjamin Goldman,
The Jewish Population of New Orleans, 1953 (New York: Council of
Jewish Federations and Welfare Funds, 1953).

Primarily factual, historical accounts—of relatively indifferent qual-
ity—of Jewry in other Southern cities include James A. Wax, "The
Jews of Memphis, 1860–1865," *Papers of the West Tennessee Historical
Society*, III (1949), 84–88; Louis Ginsberg, *History of the Jews of
Petersburg* (Petersburg: privately published, 1954); and Mrs. David J.
Greenberg, *Through the Years: A Study of the Richmond Jewish Com-
munity* (Richmond: American Jewish Tercentenary Committee, 1654–
1954, 1954).

Joshua A. Fishman, "Southern City," *Midstream*, VII (1961), 39–63,
reports on the author's visit to a Deep Southern black-belt city (very
probably Montgomery) and his interviews in 1959 with twenty-seven
influential Jews, Negroes, and other minority group members there.
Fishman deals primarily with the impact on these individuals of the
desegregation controversy, but he also offers some observations about
relationships of these Jews with one another and with the general community which seem from the present author's data to apply more
generally in the region. Manheim S. Shapiro, "The Southville Survey
of Jewish Attitudes" (1959), an unpublished report on interviews conducted under the auspices of the American Jewish Committee in the
late 1950's, provides data on the demographic background, racial attitudes, and postures toward the general community of Memphis Jewry.
The only serious empirical study of small-town Southern Jews which
has come to our attention is reported in the Louisiana State University

doctoral dissertation in sociology of Benjamin Kaplan, published in revised form as *The Eternal Stranger* (New York: Bookman Associates, 1957). Based on his research on the Jewish communities of three Louisiana towns, Kaplan describes the formidable pressures for assimilation and the gradual disappearance of small Jewish groups where they have been isolated from Jewish institutions, particularly religious ones.

The demographic distribution of Jews among the Southern states and major Southern cities may be ascertained from a recent edition of *The American Jewish Yearbook* (Philadelphia: The Jewish Publication Society of America [for the American Jewish Committee]). A journalistic travelogue about Southern Jewry written in popular style is Harry Simonhoff, *Under Strange Skies* (New York: Philosophical Library, 1953).

Gunnar Myrdal's *An American Dilemma* (New York: Harper Bros., 1944), still remains the most insightful single volume on the impacts of race relations on the personalities, values, and social and political behavior of Southern whites. A briefer version in inexpensive paperback form is Arnold Rose, *The Negro in America* (Boston: Beacon Press, 1948). Cash advances some thoughtful observations on these phenomena in his *The Mind of the South.* More recent works which provide some insights into this subject include Key, *Southern Politics in State and Nation;* Sarah M. Lemmon, "The Ideology of the 'Dixiecrat' Movement," *Social Forces,* XXX (1951), 162–71; Wilma Dykeman and James Stokely, *Neither Black Nor White;* Lillian Smith, *Killers of the Dream* (New York: W. W. Norton, 1961); and James Graham Cook, *The Segregationists* (New York: Appleton, Century, Crofts, 1962). Frank E. Smith, *Congressman from Mississippi* (New York: Pantheon Books, 1964), the autobiography of the internationalist and generally liberal former Congressman from the Delta who was defeated in 1962, describes the potent impacts of race relations on Mississippi legislators and on the politics of that state generally.

Another important Southern group which deserves much more systematic attention than it has received is the small, atypically cosmopolitan minority. Useful in comprehending the sorts of family and social backgrounds, personal experiences, and personality factors which have been associated with this sort of divergence from Southern norms are some of the autobiographies and biographies of such individuals, such as Katherine Dupré Lumpkin, *The Making of a Southerner* (New York: Alfred A. Knopf, 1947); Viola Goode Liddell, *With a Southern Accent* (Norman: University of Oklahoma Press, 1948); James McBride Dabbs, *The Road Home* (Philadelphia: Christian Education

Press, 1960); Hodding Carter, *Southern Legacy* (Baton Rouge: Louisiana State University Press, 1950), and *Where Main Street Meets the River* (New York: Rinehart, 1952); Lillian Smith, *Killers of the Dream;* Wilma Dykeman and James Stokely, *Seeds of Southern Change* (Chicago: University of Chicago Press, 1962); Ralph McGill, *The South and the Southerner* (Boston: Little, Brown, and Co., 1963); Frank E. Smith, *Congressman from Mississippi;* and the autobiographical novel by Harper Lee, *To Kill a Mockingbird.* For comparable biographical material on paternalistic segregationist cosmopolitans of the first half of the twentieth century, see William Alexander Percy, *Lanterns on the Levee,* and George C. Osborn, *John Sharp Williams.*

There is a significant body of social research on Southern Negroes prior to the last decade of increasing racial tension and concern among social scientists about them. Some of this material is helpful in comprehending the social, cultural, and individual underpinnings of Negro reactions to foreign affairs (or the paucity thereof). Worthy of attention is the work of Charles S. Johnson, namely, *The Negro in American Civilization: A Study of Negro Life and Race Relations in the Light of Social Research* (New York: Henry Holt and Co., 1930); *Shadow of the Plantation* (Chicago: University of Chicago Press, 1934); with Willis D. Weatherford, *Race Relations: Adjustment of Whites and Negroes in the United States* (Boston and New York: D. C. Heath and Co., 1934); *The Negro College Graduate* (Chapel Hill: University of North Carolina Press, 1938); *Growing Up in the Black Belt* (Washington, D.C.: American Council on Education, 1941); *Patterns of Negro Segregation* (New York: Harper Bros., 1943); and *Into the Main Stream* (Chapel Hill: University of North Carolina Press, 1947). Allison Davis and John Dollard report on their prewar anthropological examination of New Orleans Negro society in their *Children of Bondage* (Washington, D.C.: American Council on Education, 1940). See also the above cited studies by Powdermaker and Lewis, the sections in Allison Davis and the two Gardners devoted to Negroes, and E. Franklin Frazier's *The Negro Family in the United States* (Chicago: University of Chicago Press, 1939); and Frazier's *Negro Youth at the Crossways: Their Personality Development in the Middle States* (Washington, D.C.: American Council on Education, 1940).

Frazier fits together the existing body of knowledge about Negro religious behavior and the role of churches in Negro society in *The Negro Church in America* (New York: Schocken Books, 1963).

The findings of social science about the personality structure and other individual characteristics of Negroes are organized by Thomas

F. Pettigrew in *A Profile of the Negro American* (Princeton: Van Nostrand, 1964). Also worthy of note on psychological aspects of public-affairs behavior are James W. Protho and P. M. Smith, "Ethnic Differences in Authoritarian Personality," *Social Forces*, XXXV (1957), 334–38, a study of comparative scores of Negro and white college students on a scale of authoritarian-democratic attitudes; *Negro American Personality*, a special issue of the *Journal of Social Issues*, XX, No. 2 (April, 1964), edited by Thomas F. Pettigrew and Daniel C. Thompson; Pearl M. Gore and Julian B. Rotter, "A Personality Correlate of Social Action," *Journal of Personality*, XXXI (1963), 58–63; and the restudy in 1953–56 of forty-seven of the Negroes examined two decades before by Davis and Dollard, *Children of Bondage*, reported in John H. Rohrer, *et al.*, *The Eighth Generation: Cultures and Personalities of New Orleans Negroes* (New York: Harper Bros., 1960). The Pettigrew book and the special issue of the *Journal of Social Issues* include helpful references to other research on Negro personality.

Studies of the Negro elite include E. Franklin Frazier's controversial *Black Bourgeoisie* (Glencoe: The Free Press, 1957), and Daniel C. Thompson's study of New Orleans Negro influentials reported in his *The Negro Leadership Class* (Engelwood Cliffs, N.J.: Prentice-Hall, 1963).

Harry Halloway, "The Negro Vote: The Case of Texas," *Journal of Politics*, XXIII (1961), 526–56, documents the thesis that a considerable fraction, perhaps a majority, of Deep Southern Negroes outside the urban areas, once permitted the ballot, are likely to vote for the more conservative candidates favored by local white elites whose guidance they may follow even without direct economic or social pressures. The most thorough research on political behavior of Southern Negroes, including interviews of carefully selected samples, has recently been completed by Donald R. Matthews, James W. Protho, Daniel Price, and their associates at the University of North Carolina. Two reports on this study, Donald R. Matthews and James W. Protho, "Social and Economic Factors and Negro Voter Registration in the South," *American Political Science Review*, LVII (1963), 24–44, and, by the same authors, "Political Factors and Negro Voter Registration in the South," *American Political Science Review*, LVII (1963), 355–67, have already appeared. Forthcoming publications will make available the remaining major findings.

However, none of these studies of Negroes devoted more than very tangential attention to behavior of Negroes toward foreign affairs, and most said nothing whatsoever about this matter. Virtually the only study worthy of attention which constitutes an exception to this generalization is Harold R. Isaacs, *The New World of Negro Americans* (New York: John Day Co., 1963), based on Isaacs' interviews with influential Negroes, primarily but not entirely outside the South, and from his other experiences with middle-class and elite Negroes.

Public Opinion on Foreign Affairs Itself

Most of the studies of behavior of Southern Congressmen toward world affairs and several of the more general analyses of Southern society cited earlier advanced thoughtful observations—mostly of a relatively speculative sort based on more or less impressionistic sources rather than on surveys of Southern individuals—about public attitudes on world affairs prevalent in the region. Key's *Southern Politics in State and Nation* is the most useful single volume in this regard for the period ending in the late 1940's. Irish, "Foreign Policy and the South," is also helpful on the same era. Virginius Dabney's *Below the Potomac* makes some thoughtful observations about the period before the attack on Pearl Harbor, citing some pertinent survey data and other indicators. Wayne S. Cole, "America First and the South: 1940–1941," *Journal of Southern History*, XXII (1956), 36–47, documents the paucity of anti-interventionist, isolationist sentiment in the region during this period. Southern thinking about tariffs, quotas, and other aspects of international trade is discussed in Smith and Hart, "Georgia's Representatives and the Tariff" and "The American Tariff Map"; and in some passages of Dabney, *Below the Potomac;* Kendrick and Arnett, *The South Looks at its Past;* Cash, *The Mind of the South;* Simkins, *Pitchfork Ben Tillman;* and Grantham, *Hoke Smith and the Politics of the New South.* Berthoff, "Southern Attitudes Toward Immigration" discusses reactions of the Southern white rank and file toward foreigners and immigration during the period between the Civil War and World War I and some demographic, social, and political factors accounting for them.

Serious analytical efforts to understand Southern popular reactions to world affairs and their causes since the beginning of the 1950's have been much fewer and less extensive. DeConde, "The South and Isolationism," and Seabury, "The Waning of Southern Internationalism," were among the first to describe in print Southern attitudes of the 1950's toward the changing international challenges and American policies toward them and to analyze basic cultural, sociological, economic, and other factors accounting for these reactions. They were also among the first to observe that former Southern support of freer trade and intervention against the Axis was not associated with any real internationalism in the sense of understanding of foreign affairs, sensitivity to foreign peoples and the policies of their governments, or identification with long-term multilateral cooperation beyond that with Britain and, to a lesser extent, Western Europe. Jewell, "Evaluating the Decline of Southern Interventionism," devoted some attention to pressures with respect to world affairs operating on Southern Senators from their constituencies in the period 1947–58. Jewell emphasized economic factors in the industrially developing South for apparent shifts in public opinion on tariffs and foreign aid. Lemmon, "The Ideology of the 'Dixiecrat' Movement," noted in 1951 some of the international attitudes of activists in the Dixiecrat movement, precursors of the racist international syndrome described by the present volume. Cook, *The Segregationists*, mentioned the international views expressed in the early 1960's by leaders of the segregationist opposition to racial change in the South. Former Mississippi Delta Congressman Frank E. Smith, in *Congressman From Mississippi*, describes some of the popular sentiments toward foreign policy among his constituents in the 1950's and early 1960's. The initial volume reporting on the World Peace Foundation study, Charles O. Lerche, Jr., *The Uncertain South*, contains a number of impressions about the impacts of industrialization, urbanization, racial unrest, and related factors on public attitudes in different types of Southern constituencies toward the international issues faced by their Congressmen in the U.S. House of Representatives. The present author is particularly indebted to Professor Lerche for the concept of the unilateralist-multilateralist continuum—a more useful construct than that of isolationism-internationalism which has not alone been sufficient to describe adequately the various postures toward foreign policy in the South since the rejection of isolationism in its purer form by most Americans after the attack on Pearl Harbor. The present volume has incorporated Professor Lerche's continuum into its frame of reference for examining popular Southern international behavior.

Survey Research

Those who would further explore Southern popular behavior toward foreign affairs during the period since 1936 should consult the considerable body of survey research results of the national surveying agencies or should conduct or have conducted new empirical studies of carefully selected samples of Southerners generally or of those groups of Southerners in which they may be interested.

The body of data currently available among the results of national surveys over the past three decades for those interested in examining Southern reactions in greater detail than has been feasible in the current volume is readily accessible. It seems unfortunate that this significant fund of data has been heretofore so little utilized by students of Southern international behavior.

Copies of questionnaires and punched cards for almost all AIPO (Gallup), NORC, and Roper surveys more than a year old; for several other agencies which have surveyed samples in particular states, regions, or communities; and for a number of foreign survey organizations polling in their own countries may be consulted at the Roper Public Opinion Research Center at Williams College in Williamstown, Massachusetts. Each question has been indexed by topic—such as foreign aid, NATO, defense policy, and international trade—so that the investigator may determine quickly the precise questions posed, the date, and the identity of the surveying agency. He may then consult the questionnaire itself to discover the other questions posed to the same individuals should he wish to examine replies by particular demographic or social groups or correlations among replies to international queries and between such replies and those to questions on domestic or other matters. The student of international behavior may then go directly to the original card decks at the Roper Center, or he may borrow duplicate decks of cards for a reasonable period, or he may have the Center's staff make desired tabulations at cost.

For investigators unable to visit Williamstown, the Roper Center has made depository arrangements with a number of major colleges, universities, research institutions, and governmental agencies throughout the United States and abroad whereby they maintain on a continuing basis duplicate copies of the survey-question index file and of a complete index of all factual information obtained about the respondents interviewed in each study, as well as magnetic computer tapes of survey decks at the Center. Depending on local interest, these depositories also may acquire permanently duplicate cards of individual surveys. Interested researchers may contact the Roper Center to determine the nearest such cooperating institution, consult the two index files there, and either request from the Roper Center duplicate copies of IBM cards or contract with the Roper Center to tabulate such cards for them.

The Roper Center also has on file tabulations it has made for social scientists, institutions, and others requesting them. In some cases it also has copies of some of the tabulations originally made by the agency which conducted the survey. AIPO press releases since the beginning of that agency in the mid-1930's which incorporate many additional tabulations are also available at the Center. Likewise on file are releases of NORC until their termination in the late 1940's.

The surveying agencies themselves have in their files much more extensive tabulations, which are available by special individual arrangement to social scientists and others seriously interested who are able to journey to their headquarters or, in the case of NORC, to its headquarters in Chicago or its eastern regional office in New York City. Almost without exception, for every question posed throughout their existence, agency files include tabulations for the country as a whole and for three major educational groups—some or more college, some high school or high school graduate, and grade school or less. In most cases they also provide tabulations by several other demographic and social categories as well, particularly by geographical region, age, sex, occupation, type of community (farm, rural nonfarm, small town, small city, medium-sized city, large metropolitan complex), religion, race, and political persuasion (Republican, Democrat, Independent, or none). Cross tabulations of replies to questions on different international and domestic issues are considerably fewer, but many of these are available in agency files as well, particularly in those of NORC. The investigator may reduce significantly the expense of having new tabulations made at the Roper Center by first examining the tabulations already available.

Another major body of survey data pertinent to American, including Southern, behavior toward foreign policy is developing under the auspices of the Consortium directed by Warren Miller of the Survey Research Center and Political Science Department at the University of Michigan. As of the summer of 1964, data available at SRC consisted primarily of its own surveys, but within several years the Consortium hopes to become a clearinghouse for results of surveys performed under the sponsorship of a number of institutions of higher learning and research institutions. The Consortium expects to put on computer tape for ready tabulation upon request punched cards of surveys connected with this collective enterprise. Meanwhile, interested researchers may consult the file of questionnaires and tabulations already available on SRC surveys at Ann Arbor, and SRC will make new tabulations upon request at cost.

AIPO surveys have been conducted approximately twice per month since the mid-1930's. They have included questions on virtually all the major international issues faced by our country since the Nazi remilitarization of the Rhineland in 1936, as well as queries on important domestic issues of the time. Since a variety of questions about both domestic and foreign questions typically have appeared on most individual AIPO surveys, determination of patterning of opinions is readily feasible. Moreover, the same or similar questions have been posed about particular issues during their period of saliency, permitting examination of trends over a period of time within the United States population as a whole and particular demographic, social, and ideological groups in America. Furthermore, AIPO samples have been with some exceptions relatively large, usually twenty-five hundred or more, rendering possible statistical treatment of smaller groups within United States society than has been the case with most other surveys. The combination of samples of considerable size and the same questions repeated on several surveys also permits combining the data on more than one study and, thus, achieving a large enough sample to determine comparative replies for relatively small groups—such as college-educated Negroes as compared with college-educated white Catholics, Protestants, etc. Tabulations and cross tabulations available at AIPO are more extensive on surveys prior to roughly the late 1940's than on later ones, but tabulations by major demographic and political categories are filed for most later surveys as well.

Roper (formerly Fortune) data on public reactions to world affairs began with early 1939. Since most Roper surveys were conducted under contract upon request for particular clients rather than on a continuing basis on matters of potential interest to readers of over a hundred newspapers (as were AIPO surveys), questions on foreign relations are much less numerous, less inclusive, and less likely to have been posed successively as long as the issue remained important to the national interest. However, in several instances Roper focused an entire survey on one major foreign issue or on a relatively limited range of international issues, thereby providing data for determining more detailed aspects of public attitudes, interests, and actions on that topic than any other survey.

NORC national surveys containing queries on foreign policy began early in World War II and ran through April, 1957. NORC, Roper, and particularly AIPO tabulations would provide an excellent body of data to researchers interested in examining the detailed processes whereby the American public, or specific groups within that public, changed from profound opposition to foreign commitments in the 1930's to acceptance of the broad, intensive international involvements following World War II—a field of public affairs about which relatively little is known.

But it is on public reactions to foreign policy during the postwar period until the spring of 1957 that NORC surveys provide the most complete and impressive empirical material available. On contract with the Department of State, NORC conducted approximately six surveys per annum devoted primarily to foreign policy during this period. No other agency posed such a range of questions on individual surveys about heterogeneous aspects of world affairs, asked the same questions over the years so consistently, and queried Americans about sources of their views, their knowledge about foreign relations, personality factors, political action, and other political behavior so extensively on the same ballots as did NORC. That agency also has on hand extensive tabulations and cross tabulations for each such survey. The major shortcoming of these NORC studies was the relative smallness of the sample, averaging around 1,250. However, the posing of many of the same questions in several surveys permits combining them for the comparison of replies among relatively small American groups. Unfortunately, discovery by conservative Congressmen of financial support of these surveys by the Department of State resulted in their termination in 1957. Survey data on the period since has, therefore, been much less extensive, systematic, and detailed.

Most SRC surveys have likewise been performed on contract for purposes determined by particular clients. Some were conducted under contract with the Department of State during the same period as those of NORC. Particularly useful in the research for this study on comparative Southern opinion were a study of public reactions to the atomic bomb, proposed loans to Britain and the U.S.S.R., United States relations with Britain and the Soviet Union, and other issues salient in 1946; another study of the major international issues facing the country in 1949; the series of studies focused on the role of various public questions, including aspects of foreign policy, in voting in national and congressional elections in 1952, 1956, 1958, and 1960; and a survey of attitudes toward various aspects of relations with the U.S.S.R. in 1961. The 1958 election study included tallies of votes of a national sample of Congressmen on several foreign as well as domestic issues, interviews with these Congressmen on the same subjects, and a survey of views on the same topics among their constituents; this permitted a juxtaposition of congressional votes, congressional attitudes, and voter attitudes on the same issues.

Although more valid than most other indicators of opinion, certain important cautions must, of course, be exercised in interpreting survey results. Sampling methods in earlier questionnaires were improved upon considerably in later ones. Most of the AIPO surveys during the agency's first decade of operations employed area rather than probability sampling—the latter being significantly more likely to result in interviews of a representative group than the former, provided, obviously, that sample sizes were roughly the same. Moreover, modified probability sampling, less expensive than true probability sampling but also less likely to result in representative interviews, has also been employed on some later surveys by one agency or another. Even when a sample is very nearly representative of the total population in question, the surveys are designed by sophisticated survey specialists, and the interviewers are carefully selected and trained, verbalized attitudes are not always identical with private views and, especially, overt political action. This observation has been demonstrated throughout the present volume.

Newspaper Content

Views expressed in the press have been used by a number of researchers as one indicator of effective public opinion on public questions, as has been done to some extent in this volume. Content of newspapers is perhaps the most valid gauge of opinion among those citizens who actually have views on issues with respect to which no surveys have been conducted and of the period prior to the first national surveys in the mid-1930's. Papers do reflect some of the thinking of publishers and editors, individuals whose influence is frequently considerable both on local opinion and on public officials. Editorials, columns, and other interpretations in the press are read regularly or frequently by a minority—typically concentrated among the better-educated and more articulate who, in turn, influence the thinking of other people. They compete with the content of other media, voluntary organizational programs, and interpersonal contacts in the development of the international opinions of this minority. Moreover, influence of the press on local Congressmen is often considerable; few Congressmen understand or consult the results of empirical surveys, but most read virtually every day newspapers published in their constituencies to determine, *inter alia*, what they are saying about foreign-policy legislation on which Congressmen may be obliged to take a stand.

However, newspaper content must be considered with much more reserve than survey data as a possible indicator of rank-and-file opinion. Most Americans, and particularly most Southerners, do not read editorials and other interpretations of international phenomena in the press. On the average, opinions expressed in newspapers in the South as in other regions are better informed, more realistic and responsible, more detailed, and generally more sophisticated than those prevalent among most of the Southern public. Papers express views on many international topics on which many of the local populace have virtually no views and most have only rather vague ones of low intensity and saliency. On domestic welfare and other internal economic matters the Southern press has been on the average more conservative than most local inhabitants. On the other hand, on tolerance of minorities—such as Negroes and foreigners—NATO, immigration and intercultural exchanges, and taxation and other sacrifices for active foreign policies the newspapers of the South have been more favorable than rank-and-file opinion indicated by survey results. As observed in the present volume, world-affairs programs of national television networks have tended more than Southern papers to support basically multilateralist, internationalist, and generally liberal foreign policies. These are statistical generalizations based on the particular sample of papers for this study, to which there are, of course, important exceptions, but it is readily apparent that even the most representative possible sample of papers would not be sufficient as the lone indicator of public opinion.

The composition of the particular sample of newspapers for this study suggests a further note of caution. A true probability sample would have required random selection among papers weighted by number of readers or, at least, circulation, such that those with larger readerships would have had a greater probability of being chosen for the sample than those with smaller ones. However, other considerations precluded employment of this procedure in the present study. Since the author wished to compare comments about foreign issues in the early 1960's with those of the same papers about Lend-Lease, the Truman Doctrine, the Marshall Plan, and other policies since 1936, it was necessary to select among papers available in the files of an accessible library, in this case the Library of Congress. Moreover, those papers read by interviewees in the several sample communities were to be included. Furthermore, enough papers in smaller places were required to permit comparisons among presses of varying population bases. At least one Southern paper of each of the major international, racial, economic, and other orientations toward local, national, and international problems was needed so that patterns of thought about these issues in the press with those among the public could be compared. The author hesitates to estimate the degree to which the selection of papers to fit these multiple criteria was representative of international interpretations read by the total population of Southern newspaper readers.

Readers interested in exposing themselves to the tone of international thinking and associated views on domestic issues among diverse Southern papers might consult several papers in this sample. In general, correlations between views on different public issues in papers were in the same direction as correlations of similar views among Southerners. For example, the Charleston *News and Courier* expresses many of the international attitudes prevalent among the more intransigent, traditionalist, Old South, genteel segregationists in older areas of plantation background. The Richmond *News Leader* advances more or less similar thinking. Corresponding overtones, but in more moderate form, appear in the Montgomery *Advertiser*. The views on foreign affairs, race relations, and other local issues within the Jackson *Clarion-Ledger* and the Shreveport *Journal* seem similar to those among many articulate white Mississippians and residents of northern Louisiana—on the whole less sophisticated and less informed about foreign affairs and less "polished" than their Charleston, Richmond, and even Montgomery counterparts. Conservative international thinking in a locale where race is of relatively minor significance by Southern standards is observable in the Knoxville *News-Sentinel* and the Knoxville *Journal*. Multilateralism prevalent among most urban North Carolina papers (though less so among the populace of that state) can be seen in either the Charlotte *Observer*, the Greensboro *Record* or *Daily News*, or the Raleigh *News and Observer*. Either the New Orleans *Times-Picayune* or the Little Rock *Arkansas Democrat* could provide examples of papers (and individuals) favorable to freer trade but relatively conservative on foreign aid, neutralism, and other phenomena pertinent to United States cooperation with Africa and Asia. Generally multilateralist, internationalist, and liberal (domestically and internationally) papers, as well as the Southern minority of like mind, are exemplified in the Little Rock *Arkansas Gazette*, the Chattanooga *Times*, the Nashville *Tennesseean*, the Saint Petersburg *Times*, and the North Carolina dailies mentioned above.

The author was unable to examine the international content of a significant sample of the Negro press read extensively in the South. For impressions of Negro newspapers and magazines it was necessary to rely on perusal of a few copies of two dozen or so such publications, observations about them by sophisticated Negroes familiar with locally available Negro papers and periodicals, and the pilot analysis of Maxwell R. Brooks, *The Negro Press Re-Examined: Political Content* (Boston: The Christopher Publishing House, 1959). As comments in Chapter 14 indicated, little international coverage appeared in the early 1960's in most of the Southern-published Negro papers, and most of the little that appeared was sentimental, concerned primarily with personalities, and generally devoid of responsibly critical international content. A systematic content analysis of internationally relevant topics in a cross section of the Negro press could provide information valuable to those interested in Negro behavior toward foreign affairs and in potentially effective means of enhancing comprehension of world affairs among Negro Americans. If effectively popularized, it might also become a possible lever to improve coverage of world developments in Negro publications.

INDEX